TRIAL

MIKAL C. WATTS + SAWNIE A. MCENTIRE

TRIAL

A GUIDE FROM START TO FINISH

PERSPECTIVES FROM OPPOSING COUNSEL

ABA
AMERICAN BAR ASSOCIATION
Solo, Small Firm and General Practice Division

Cover design by Kelly Bock/ABA Publishing.

Printed in the United States of America.

24 23 22 21 20 5 4 3 2 1

Library of Congress Cataloging-in-Publication Data

Names: Watts, Mikal C., author. | McEntire, Sawnie A., author. | American Bar Association. Solo, Small Firm and General Practice Division, sponsoring body.
Title: Trial: a guide from start to finish : perspectives from opposing counsel / Mikal C. Watts, Sawnie A. McEntire.
Description: Chicago, Illinois : American Bar Association, [2020] | Includes index. | Summary: "This book is written to take its readers through each stage of a jury trial, starting with the filing of a lawsuit long before a jury trial begins and ending in the motion practice concluding long after the jury's verdict. The concept of this book is to divide the trial process into its fifteen segments, and with each author giving their perspectives, one from the Plaintiff's perspective and one from the Defendant's perspective. The authors hope and trust that young trial lawyers-to-be will find useful the lessons the authors have learned and shared, within the pages of this book"– Provided by publisher.
Identifiers: LCCN 2020014548 (print) | LCCN 2020014549 (ebook) | ISBN 9781641056854 (paperback) | ISBN 9781641056861 (ebook)
Subjects: LCSH: Trial practice–United States. | Civil procedure–United States.
Classification: LCC KF8915.W38 2020 (print) | LCC KF8915 (ebook) | DDC 347.73/7–dc23
LC record available at https://lccn.loc.gov/2020014548
LC ebook record available at https://lccn.loc.gov/2020014549

Discounts are available for books ordered in bulk. Special consideration is given to state bars, CLE programs, and other bar-related organizations. Inquire at Book Publishing, ABA Publishing, American Bar Association, 321 N. Clark Street, Chicago, Illinois 60654-7598.

www.shopABA.org

CONTENTS

About the Authors

Mikal Watts is a founding partner of Watts Guerra LLP, located in San Antonio, Texas, and has decades of experience litigating complex mass tort cases involving defective products and corporate malfeasance. Watts Guerra has more than twenty lawyers and 100 employees in seven offices located in Texas and California that handle catastrophic personal injury, toxic torts, product liability, automotive defects, medical device, pharmaceutical, and commercial litigation.

Mr. Watts graduated from the University of Texas School of Law with honors at the age of twenty-one and became briefing attorney for Hon. Thomas R. Phillips, Chief Justice of the Supreme Court of Texas. He is board certified in personal injury trial law by the Texas Board of Legal Specialization, is an AV rated lawyer by Martindale-Hubbell, has served on the executive committee for the Texas Trial Lawyers Association and the Attorneys Information Exchange Group, and recently enjoyed induction into the prestigious Inner Circle of Advocates, an organization including the top 100 trial lawyers in the United States.

Mr. Watts has been appointed to leadership positions in numerous multidistrict litigations ("MDLs"). He has served on the plaintiffs' steering committee ("PSC") in *In re FEMA Trailer Formaldehyde Products Liability Litigation* (MDL 1873), *In re Oil Spill by the Oil Rig "Deepwater Horizon" in the Gulf of Mexico* (MDL 2179), *In re California North Bay Fires Cases* (JCCP 4955), *In re: Texas Opioids Litigation* (2018-63587), *In re Valsartan N-Nitrosodimethylamine ("NDMA") Contamination Products Liability Litigation* (MDL 2875), *In re 3M Earplug Product Liability Litigation* (MDL 2885) and *In re Juul Labs, Inc. Marketing, Sales Practices & Products Liability Litigation* (MDL 2913). Mr. Watts has also served a member of the Practices and Procedures Team in *In re Zantac Products Liability Litigation* (MDL 2924), and as co-lead counsel *In re Pradaxa (Dabigatran Etexilate) Products Liability Litigation* (MDL 2385) and in *In re Stand 'N Seal* (MDL 1804), and as co-liaison counsel in *In re Silica* (MDL 1553). Members of Watts Guerra serve as co-lead counsel in *In re Incretins Mimetics Products Liability Litigation* (MDL 2452) and *In re Syngenta Litigation* (Minnesota Consolidated MDL).

In addition to prior membership on PSCs, Mr. Watts has personally tried as lead trial counsel the "first in the nation" trial cases for major pharmaceutical and product liability litigations that were consolidated into MDLs, including trial of the first *Ford/Firestone* tire lawsuit (see MDL 1373); the first *Rezulin* plaintiffs' verdict (see MDL 1348); the only plaintiffs' verdict in *Sulzer* hip implants (see MDL 1401); trial of the first *Baycol* case (see MDL 1431); trial of the first welding rods case during MDL 1525; trial of two bellwether cases during *In re Vioxx* (see MDL 1657); and the only plaintiffs' verdict during *In re Levaquin* (see MDL 1943). Collectively, Mr. Watts's firm has achieved verdicts in excess of $1.6 billion (including four nine-figure verdicts and twenty-three verdicts of $10 million or more) and total recoveries for its clients exceeding $4 billion.

MDL courts also consistently appoint Mr. Watts to fashion the settlements of nationwide torts. In 2019, retired bankruptcy judge Randall Newsome, the court-appointed mediator in *In Re: PG&E Corp.*, Bankruptcy Case No. 19-30088, appointed Mr. Watts to the four-person Plaintiffs' Negotiating Team that secured a $13.5 billion settlement with PG&E for more 70,000 wildfire victims. In 2017, Judge John W. Lungstrum, D. Kanas, appointed Mr. Watts to the four-person Plaintiffs' negotiating team in *In Re: Syngenta Corn*, that achieved a $1.5 billion settlement for more than 200,000 farmers across the United States. In 2014, Judge David Herndon of the Southern District of Illinois appointed Mr. Watts to the Plaintiffs' Negotiating Team in *In Re: Pradaxa*, which resulted in a $650 million settlement before the first bellwether trial in just twenty months following the formation of MDL 2385.

Presently, as a member of the PSC of the Texas state court MDL in the opioids litigation, Mr. Watts worked as the state litigants' liaison to the federal MDL Plaintiffs' Steering Committee and court-appointed special master Francis McGovern to fashion nationwide settlement solutions in *In re National Prescription Opioid Litigation* (MDL 2804).

Sawnie A. McEntire is a founding shareholder in the trial firm of Parsons McEntire McCleary PLLC, which has offices in Dallas, Texas, and Houston, Texas. He also serves as a director of the firm and managing partner of the Dallas office.

Sawnie has been practicing trial law since 1980, and he has tried dozens of cases to successful jury verdicts. Historically, he has specialized in product liability defense and business tort litigation, representing both plaintiffs and defendants. In addition to Texas, he served as lead counsel defending product liability and other types of cases throughout the nation, including in California, New Mexico, Arizona, Washington State, Oklahoma, Louisiana, Missouri, Arkansas, Tennessee, Florida, Missouri, Georgia, Delaware, Virginia, West Virginia, New York, Delaware, Massachusetts, and New Jersey. He also served as a national trial counsel for a Japanese automotive manufacturer, and as lead counsel on several statewide trial teams for several clients in pharmaceutical and medical device litigation.

Sawnie has successfully defended and obtained defense verdicts against some of the nation's top-rated plaintiff's lawyers. He was recognized by *Texas Lawyer* magazine for one of these victories. He also has successfully prosecuted several business tort cases as plaintiff's counsel, and has obtained several significant plaintiffs' verdicts or awards in business tort litigation. One of these awards was valued in excess of nine figures. He also has significant appellate experience, including numerous oral arguments in multiple Texas appellate courts, the Supreme Court of Texas, and the U.S. courts of appeals for the Fifth Circuit, the First Circuit, and the Ninth Circuit. He was previously identified as a top product liability defense lawyer in the United States by Law 360 and is a member of the Texas Bar

Foundation, the American Bar Foundation, and the Federation of Defense and Corporate Counsel. Sawnie is also an AV rated lawyer by Martindale-Hubbell.

Sawnie is a frequent author and speaker on topics relating to trial practice and advocacy skills, and he previously authored the book *Mastering the Art of Depositions*, published by the American Bar Association ("ABA"). He also served as editor and contributing author of *From the Trenches: Pretrial Strategies for Success*, also published by the ABA. Sawnie tried a case to a jury verdict against his co-author, Mikal Watts, but lost. He remembers it well.

Acknowledgments

First, I want to thank my colleague and friend Sawnie McEntire for undertaking this Herculean effort with me. Second, I would like to thank my associate Jennifer Neal for providing substantial editing assistance and keeping the project on schedule. Third, Weston Eismann, one of my firm's law clerks, was involved in this process from beginning to end; he examined every word contained in these pages and spent more time than he cares to admit poring over the Bluebook. Last, but not least, I am grateful for the team of Watts Guerra law clerks who laid the final set of eyes on my portion of the book, including Kelsey Abbey, Logan Cook, Grace Holland, Illiana Parker, Oscar Quiroz, Laura Ramirez, and Amanda Reyes.

Mikal Watts

My contributions to this book would not have been possible without the support of my law partners in both of my firm's offices, in Houston and in Dallas. I also want to thank my long-term assistant, Gini Romero, for her incredible typing skills and patience. I also want to thank Kaye Jones for her patience over long weekends and for her matchless word processing and grammar skills. I also owe a great debt of gratitude to Tim Miller, a young associate in our firm's Dallas office, who labored tirelessly doing legal research, assisting in outlining several chapters of this book, and immersing himself selflessly in the editing process. He devoted dozens of hours to making things work. Lastly, I want to thank Mikal Watts, a worthy opponent, for his collaboration and willingness to participate in this project notwithstanding an extraordinarily busy trial schedule, and for bringing much needed structure and organization to the effort.

Sawnie A. McEntire

Preface

Trial: A Guide from Start to Finish – Perspectives from Opposing Counsel, is a collaboration of two trial lawyers who have tried many complex cases in courtrooms across the country, including one trial where they spent four weeks bloodying each other's noses, only to come out the other side with a profound respect for the integrity and trial skills of the other. Given that respect for each other's courtroom acumen, the authors discussed writing down in detail what each has learned about every aspect of the jury trial process.

Trial: A Guide from Start to Finish – Perspectives from Opposing Counsel, takes its readers through each stage of a jury trial, starting with the filing of a lawsuit long before a jury trial begins, and ending in the motion practice that concludes long after the jury's verdict. The concept of this book was to divide the trial process into its fifteen segments and to have each author write a chapter about each segment. Mikal Watts would write from the plaintiff's perspective and Sawnie McEntire would write from the defendant's perspective. Twice a month, the authors exchanged drafts of their respective new chapters, discussed their progress, and pledged to trudge on to the next chapter that would be due two weeks later. From March through November in 2019, Watts and McEntire worked separately so they would produce truly independent perspectives of each portion of the trial process.

Beginning at the end of October, the two authors merged their efforts, collaboratively editing each other's prior writings, offering additions to and writing tips on the other's work, and adding necessary sections in rejoinder to comments made by the other. In doing so, the authors learned that while they expected to have vastly different perspectives given their disparate backgrounds—one as a plaintiff's lawyer suing corporate America and the other a defense lawyer seeking to protect it from such suits—as they read each other's work in an effort to achieve a cohesive final product, they realized that they agreed with each far more often than they disagreed. The authors learned that a trial is a trial, and that a trial lawyer is a trial lawyer, regardless of whom that lawyer represents. Good practices apply equally across the "v." in any case, and as they began reading each other's work, *Trial: A Guide from Start to Finish – Perspectives from Opposing Counsel,* became clear to both of them. Thus, over the course of the final six weeks before the deadline for the manuscript, the authors worked together to merge their disparate writings into this cohesively constructed book.

To be sure, this is not a book written by trial lawyers who boast that they have never lost a trial; each author has lost more trials than he cares to admit. However, each of their numerous victories and occasional losses in the courtroom have brought them something more valuable—experience and the capacity to learn from the good, the bad, and the ugly of the jury trial process. Putting on paper the lessons learned from losing this trial or that trial has meant revisiting challenges that they each have long since left in the past, but in doing so, they have learned that those mistakes and errors, those things they once did poorly, are wrongs that they have attempted to right over the trajectory of many decades in the courtroom. To coin a phrase, the authors are both still *practicing* law. While the adage that *practice makes perfect* may never apply to them, they do believe that their various jury trials have taught them many important things over the decades. This book is their effort to share those lessons with other trial lawyers and trial lawyers-to-be.

In a world of high-dollar discovery, lengthy motion practice, prohibitively expensive experts, pervasive *Daubert* practice, detailed pretrial exchanges, and more formal trial rules, it is more difficult than ever for young lawyers to get the courtroom experience they so desperately need to become real trial lawyers. It is this deficit of courtroom experience that creates a need for this book.

The authors hope and trust that young trial lawyers-to-be will find useful the lessons that the authors have learned and included in the pages of this book.

Introduction

This introduction to *Trial: A Guide from Start to Finish – Perspectives from Opposing Counsel* is intended to briefly introduce the reader to the scope of the topics in this book.

In *chapters 1 and 2*, authors Mikal Watts and Sawnie McEntire discuss the concepts of personal jurisdiction (where a defendant may be sued) and subject matter jurisdiction (whether the defendant may be sued in federal or state court). Jurisdictional options have changed dramatically in light of changes to the law of general personal jurisdiction based on U.S. Supreme Court recent decisions. In addition to the discussion of general personal jurisdiction, the authors include detailed discussions about specific and pendent personal jurisdiction. As for subject matter jurisdiction, the authors have included discussions on the topic generally, on supplemental jurisdiction, and on removal procedures and deadlines. Watts sets forth both the general venue statute and the venue provided for in specific statutes, and the law as it pertains to discretionary venue transfers and transfers for improper venue. In his chapter "Jurisdiction and Venue: Forum Shopping and Forum Swapping," McEntire addresses important venue considerations and factors, including the jury pool, the trial court's reputation, local procedures and remedies, docket speed, and the scope of permitted discovery. McEntire also addresses the factors a defense lawyer should consider in deciding whether to remove a case to federal court. Finally, the authors discuss the world of multidistrict litigations ("MDLs"), with statistics demonstrating an ever-increasing percentage of all federal court litigation being handled by MDL courts. MDLs are sought by parties who argue that different lawsuits around the country should be consolidated for pretrial purposes before one MDL court. The Judicial Panel on Multidistrict Litigation ("JPML") would then decide whether to consolidate such cases into an MDL. Additionally, the JPML decides which judge to appoint to handle the MDL, considering the most geographically central forum, the location of counsel's offices, docket congestion, the convenience of the parties and the witnesses, the location of relevant documents, a transferee court's prior MDL experience, whether a proposed transferee judge has handled prior litigation activity in the particular litigation at issue, the parties' first and second choices, where the early plaintiffs chose to file suit, diversity, and a district court's willingness to serve.

Chapters 3 and 4 address the final pretrial conference. Watts provides detailed advice about how to prepare and argue pretrial motions and motions in limine, prepare trial briefs on significant legal issues, and prepare, prosecute, and defend expert challenges. He also gives brief thoughts about the preadmission of exhibits. McEntire's chapter addresses the importance of local counsel during the pretrial conference, the significance of the timing of the hearing itself, and the duration and scope of the pretrial conference. McEntire also provides advice about expert surprises, exhibits, and depositions; substantive rulings that can be expected; equalizing jury strikes; and the voir dire procedure.

Chapters 5 and 6 focus on *Daubert* challenges—the effort to exclude the testimony of expert witnesses. Watts provides the legal backdrop of *Daubert* and its progeny, and the fact that challenges to a plaintiff's experts have become ubiquitous as defense lawyers prophylactically use *Daubert* to "preserve the record" for appeal. Of course, because the plaintiff has the burden of proof, such an exclusion of a critical plaintiff's expert might mean the end of the case. To prevent this form of judicial Armageddon, Watts discusses techniques to protect the plaintiff's expert from exclusion under *Daubert*, including advice about choosing one's experts, developing the foundation for opinions to be expressed, writing the expert report, the expert's deposition, and responding to a *Daubert* motion. In his chapter from the defense perspective, "*Daubert* Challenges: Closing the Expert Gate," McEntire defines the standards for admissibility, setting forth the key elements of the *Frye* standard and key elements of the *Daubert* standard. Like Watts, he also addresses the prevalence of *Daubert*, and then discusses tactical considerations, including preparing for and taking the expert's deposition, "*Daubert*-proofing" defense experts, using consulting experts to attack opposing experts, searching for the opposing expert's Achilles heel, and how to keep enemy experts at the gate.

Chapters 7 and 8 address pretrial preparations that take place after jurisdiction is established, a proper venue has been chosen, and discovery is completed. Watts's chapter "The Pretrial Warm-Up" first discusses jury studies and focus groups, with three case studies addressed at length, and then gives thoughts about witness selection, witness order, exhibit selection, demonstrative exhibits, trial logistics, and stipulations. McEntire's chapter "Pretrial: In the Batter's Box" provides the defense lawyer's perspective on a litany of topics involving pretrial preparation, including trial protocols, trial themes, developing useful exhibit lists—with thoughts about exhibit numbering, internal exhibit lists, and consulting with experts about exhibits—demonstrative exhibits, exhibit objections and stipulations, keeping the bad staff out through motions in limine, witness lists and witness order, client witnesses called adversely, witness examination outlines, technology in the courtroom, courtroom reconnaissance, dress rehearsals, pocket briefs, the jury charge, and how to wrap up pretrial preparations.

Chapters 9 and 10 address the intangibles of a successful trial. From the plaintiff's perspective, Watts provides advice on controlling the courtroom, with ways to win over the judge and the court's staff, seizing and maintaining momentum while developing jury rapport, and prosecuting a logical, commonsense case that is both appealing and emotional. Watts also provides ways to efficiently present the plaintiff's case by using both technology and stipulations. In his chapter "The Intangibles of Trial," McEntire focuses on interactions with the court, the demeanor of both the lawyer and the client, the importance of preparation and organization, and techniques for making objections and proper communications between counsel in the courtroom. After discussing jury behavior, McEntire gives his thoughts on how the defense lawyer can control the courtroom and the momentum inside it.

Chapters 11 and 12 are lengthy chapters that address jury selection. Having written considerably on the subject, Watts provides detailed thoughts from the plaintiff's perspective on starting the case with momentum by picking a winning jury. He assesses characteristics of favorable and unfavorable jurors, discusses the use of questionnaires and jury consultants, and offers voir dire tactics of demonstrating empathy to the panel, how to begin the voir dire, developing rapport via courtesy and transparency, using business leaders to gain insight on juror values, and hitting the points that jury research has identified as key. The process of attempting to rehabilitate otherwise disqualified jurors and the exercise of strikes for cause and peremptory challenges also are discussed as Watts provides important conclusions about jury selection. In his chapter "Voir Dire: Striking a Winning Jury," McEntire addresses the defense's advantages of going second, after the plaintiff's lawyer. While divergent voir dire practices exist among the different jurisdictions, common best practices apply equally everywhere; these include making good first impressions, effective information management, and focusing questions on specific panel members. McEntire provides his research on the typical venire panel, and how to obtain information about potential jurors before voir dire begins. He discusses how to develop jury rapport; how to assess potential jurors on paper through jury questionnaires and in person, through their behavior and body language; and how to look for and protect leaders for the defense on the panel. Basic examination strategies are shared, including using favorable jurors as teaching assistants, responding to questions from the panel, and preventing one's opponent from asking commitment questions. The use of jury consultants and jury studies is also analyzed.

Chapters 13 and 14 concern the opening statement. From the plaintiff's perspective, Watts sets forth the goals of opening statements and explains their importance, provides practice tips for substantive content and presentation, gives advice about using demonstratives and substantive evidence during opening statements, and warns plaintiff's lawyers to remember that the defense has the option to defer its opening statement until the end of the plaintiff's case-in-chief. In his chapter "Opening Statements: The First Final Argument," McEntire cautions defense lawyers to avoid reactionary responses during the plaintiff's opening statement. With respect to the defense opening, he advises preparation, preparation, and preparation, and to not waste time. McEntire offers guidance on the elements of an effective opening, advice to avoid an inflated argument, teaches how to combat the "reptile" arguments now so prevalent among the plaintiff's bar, and shows how to readjust momentum with simplicity, repetition, and illustration. McEntire then discusses opening statement techniques, including using Microsoft PowerPoint, demonstrative evidence, and deposition excerpts, and offers advice on how to focus on defense leaders, avoid demonstrative overkill, how to make and how not to make objections during opening statements, and how to address bad evidence.

Chapters 15 and 16 involve the plaintiff's case-in-chief. From the plaintiff's perspective, Watts suggests maximizing impact by sequencing witnesses by topic area and maintaining momentum by changing the manner in which witnesses are called and evidence is introduced. Concerning witness order, he advises to "start strong, finish strong" by starting in one of six good ways: with captivation, brilliance, live confrontation, a sure thing, safety, or emotion. Watts provides six critical "do's" concerning the use of depositions during one's case-in-chief, and also provides advice for live witness examinations, including preparing witnesses for direct and cross-examination, conducting direct and cross-examination, and utilizing effective techniques for impeachment. Watts also provides techniques for putting on expert witnesses; special considerations for appealing to the jurors' five senses; and techniques for depriving the defense lawyer of evidence before resting the plaintiff's case-in-chief. In his chapter, McEntire focuses on defining the defendant's goals during the plaintiff's case; how to effectively prepare for effective cross-examinations of both fact and expert witnesses to undercut the plaintiff's case; whether to waive *Daubert* challenges on certain expert witnesses that may be particularly vulnerable to cross-examination; and preparing corporate witnesses or individual defendants if they are called as adverse witnesses by plaintiff's counsel.

In *chapters 17 and 18*, the authors address the directed verdict stage. From the plaintiff's perspective, Watts recommends preparing for the directed verdict response before discovery begins, and continuing preparation throughout the discovery period and plaintiff's case-in-chief. In writing the rough draft of the motion for directed verdict response, Watts suggests that the writer prominently remind the court of the standard applicable to a Rule 50(a) motion for directed verdict, and the efficiency of timing options for bringing, or ruling on, a motion for judgment as a matter of law. In sum, the written response should be submitted while arguing it orally, but every argument should include the suggestion that the court can efficiently continue the progress of the trial by simply deferring the ruling until after the jury's verdict. From the defense perspective, in his chapter "Direct Verdicts: Crossing the Rubicon," McEntire advises lawyers to know the elements of the claims being defended, the directed verdict standards, and the evidentiary standard involved. McEntire advises against shotgun motions—brevity and precision are key, and a party should pursue directed verdicts only in areas where the plaintiff's proof does not match the elements of the pleaded causes of action. Obtaining daily copy of the trial transcript allows counsel to point out the holes in the proof brought by the plaintiff and prepare written motions that carefully put forth legal defenses contained in prior summary judgment motions before the plaintiff rests his case.

In *chapters 19 and 20*, the authors address in detail the defendant's case-in-chief. On behalf of the defense, McEntire sets forth the basic rules for the defense case, including being organized, denying the plaintiff's lawyer an opportunity to score additional points, empowering defense-minded jurors, and doing more with less. The defense case should follow a dual-focus plan of poking holes in the plaintiff's case while putting in evidence to support the affirmative defenses pleaded by the defendant. McEntire advises time management because some cases are tried with court-imposed time limits. To humanize corporate defendants, the client or corporate representative should always attend the trial and be prepared to testify. However, in selecting witnesses to call during the defendant's case-in-chief, McEntire advises that there's no need to call every witness; instead, particular witness types should be selected, and they should be called in an order that makes the defense case exciting. McEntire offers techniques for witness preparations; the direct examination, including leading questions and witness responsiveness; and dealing with aggressive cross-examinations. During these segments of the defense case-in-chief, McEntire offers important advice about dressing well, behaving appropriately, and optimizing witnesses' attitude, demeanor, and posture. In his chapter from the plaintiff's perspective, Watts reminds the reader of the importance of using key witness examinations during depositions in the plaintiff's case-in-chief; however, if this was not done, key admissions should be utilized via a cross-examination that shows video clips of these key admissions. Another strategy is to quietly induce the defense lawyer into calling witnesses that the defense simply does not know are about to be exposed to annihilation on the stand. Cross-examinations should never be winged; they should be prepared. Watts suggests a trial brief for the court on the subject of cross-examination in the form of a general primer on proper cross-examination topics and the limited constrictions on cross-examination. In constructing the cross-examination outlines, he suggests outlining the goals of each cross-examination well in advance of trial. Watts suggests that important goals of cross-examination include achieving the psychological objectives of *recency* and *repetition*, achieving admissions about helpful facts, populating the evidence with published statements that are helpful to the plaintiff, utilizing the defense expert to immunize the plaintiff's own experts from *Daubert* exclusions on appeal, forcing defense witnesses to provide evidence to meet the plaintiff's required elements of proof, and injecting money into the case via the expert cross-examination.

In *chapters 21 and 22*, the authors address the rebuttal case, a rarely employed segment of the trial in which the plaintiff may introduce rebuttal evidence after the defendant's case-in-chief; the defendant may then, in some instances, offer surrebuttal evidence in response to the plaintiff's rebuttal evidence. From the plaintiff's perspective, Watts cautions about the use of rebuttal experts, including rebuttal expert disclosure rules, requirements for rebuttal expert reports, and the consequences of failing to disclose rebuttal experts. With trial courts enjoying considerable discretion to refuse rebuttal witnesses, Watts cautions that there are important strategic considerations for and against saving witnesses for rebuttal. From the defense perspective, McEntire addresses the rebuttal case and focuses on procedures for challenging the rebuttal witness, objecting to the rebuttal witness, effective techniques for handling a rebuttal expert, taking expert rebuttal witnesses on voir dire, taking trial depositions or conducting interviews of rebuttal witnesses, and time management issues.

Chapters 23 and 24 concern multiparty cases. From the plaintiff's perspective, Watts discusses the law concerning consolidation and severance of multi-plaintiff and multi-defendant petitions—first the joinder of multiple plaintiffs in a single complaint, and then the joinder of multiple defendants in a single complaint. Next, Watts discusses the practice—particularly in MDL bellwether cases—of joining the claims of multiple plaintiffs together in a single trial. Strategically, Watts gives advice about choosing the target defendant by attacking the weakest lawyer—the defendant shown to be at highest risk during jury research—and avoiding the defendant who has the strongest expert. Multi-party cases also present opportunity for skullduggery; shifting alliances and informal *Mary Carter* agreements allow for special strategies for plaintiffs in multi-plaintiff cases and for defendants in multi-defendant cases. In his chapter "Managing the Benefits and Perils of a Multi-Defendant Case," McEntire reflects on the perils of a house divided, where different defendants aim their guns at each other. He provides illustrations of red flags he has observed when one defendant is surreptitiously leaving the defense team and joining an alliance with the plaintiff, and offers remedies including the discovery of *Mary Carter* agreements and a subsequent motion to realign the parties for purposes of jury strike allocations. McEntire discusses joint defense agreements, even offering an exemplar of one in his chapter, and recommends taking the lead with experts, both in depositions and at trial, lest a lawyer be victimized by riding coattails that are cut when a codefendant that is leading the defense settles out.

In *chapters 25 and 26*, the authors address the jury charge. From the plaintiff's perspective, Watts counsels that one should prepare the jury charge before discovery even begins, utilize available pattern jury instructions, and keep it simple (K-I-S-S). Watts reminds the reader that the trial court has wide discretion in formulating the jury charge. He recommends making a plea for simplicity while reminding the Court that a refusal to give jury instructions tendered by the defense will be reviewed only for an abuse of discretion, and that the defendant is not entitled to have a jury instruction about every word ever spoken in a prior opinion. Rather, the court should be reminded that such instructions requested by the defendant may also be denied with the comfort of knowing that the court's charge will not be the basis of an appellate reversal unless the alleged error actually influences the jury's verdict. Finally, Watts offers the reminder that charge error must be preserved, first through an objection, and second, if applicable, by obtaining a ruling to overrule a tendered question or instruction. From the defense perspective, McEntire's provides an important overview of jury charge law, agrees with Watts on the wisdom of using pattern jury charges, and discusses defense strategies that differ from plaintiff strategies. McEntire also reminds the reader that meeting and conferring in advance will reduce the number of charge disputes after a healthy dose of trading and swapping of language by good trial lawyers. McEntire describes how a charge conference should be handled by the defense, teaches how to properly make objections to the charge, and recommends ways to avoid compound jury instructions.

Chapters 27 and 28 concern posttrial motions. From the plaintiff's perspective, Watts first reviews the law concerning motions for judgment as a matter of law or for judgment notwithstanding the verdict (judgment n.o.v.), including the need to preserve issues for appeal through a Rule 50(a)(2) motion made before the case is submitted to the jury, and then again after the verdict is received and the judgment entered. He then lists the reasons for granting a motion for judgment n.o.v., and lays out the de novo appellate standard of review. Next, with regard to motions for a new trial, Watts discusses the deadline to file such a motion and sets forth the reasons a new trial may be granted, including failure to produce materials in discovery, error in evidentiary rulings, or jury answers that may give rise to a new trial. Of course, there can be no new trial for matters that are harmless error, and Watts sets forth his research on appellate review of orders on new trials, including cases that set forth the standards for reviewing denials of motions for new trial and orders that grant motions for new trial. Watts then discusses conditional rulings on motions for new trial pursuant to Rule 50(c) or Rule 50(e) and Motions for Relief from Judgment under Rule 60. From the defense perspective, McEntire's chapter "Posttrial Motions" addresses the importance of polling the jury, interviewing the jury, and practice tips for effective briefing. McEntire also addresses the wisdom of retaining separate appellate counsel to review appellate options and briefing requirements during the posttrial motion stage.

The conclusion of *Trial: A Guide from Start to Finish – Perspectives from Opposing Counsel* ends the book with the authors' profound hope that their readers will find the book helpful to their practices, and that they will now feel equipped to better represent their clients in courtrooms across America. They further hope their readers will feel confident enough to stand in the gap between their clients and the jury verdict that many of them so badly need to achieve justice.

I

Jurisdiction, Venue, and MDL Consolidation

The Plaintiff's Perspective

Lawyers have long held that the three most important components of any case are *venue*, *venue*, and *venue*. However, U.S. Supreme Court decisions on personal jurisdiction and the expansion of federal subject matter jurisdiction in the 1990s transformed the litigation world from one where a plaintiff could choose their state court venue to one where the defendant is presumptively entitled to be sued on their own turf, and often specifically in federal court. With almost half of the cases in federal courts consolidated into multidistrict litigation ("MDL") proceedings, the factors that the Judicial Panel on Multidistrict Litigation ("JPML") uses as a basis to decide where to consolidate MDLs are critical to the ultimate venue where many cases in this country are litigated.

Jurisdictional Options

Beginning in the early 2000s, the U.S. Chamber of Commerce began to noticeably increase its focus on financing political candidates. The Chamber has achieved transformational success, in both the legislative and the judicial branches. The Chamber has been involved in preclearing U.S. Supreme Court candidates; it provided active feedback during the selection and nomination processes for both Chief Justice Roberts and Justice Samuel Alito, who has since voted with the chamber in 75 percent of cases analyzed.[1] Moreover, during the 2016 presidential campaign, then-candidate Donald Trump released a list of twenty-one potential Supreme Court nominees, a list that included Justice Neil Gorsuch, and which was vetted by the conservative Heritage Foundation and the U.S. Chamber of Commerce. In 2017, after taking office, President Trump released a new list that included Justice Brett Kavanaugh.

1. Stephanie Mencimer, *Alito: The Chamber of Commerce's Supreme Court Ringer*, Mother Jones (June 9, 2010), https://www.motherjones.com/crime-justice/2010/06/alito-chambers-high-court-ringer/.

The Constitutional Accountability Center wrote that, "since Chief Justice John Roberts and Justice Samuel Alito joined the Supreme Court (October Term 2005), the Court has become increasingly friendly toward Big Business, often elevating the interests of corporations over those of individuals" with "the Court [ruling] for the U.S. Chamber of Commerce's position 70% of the time."[2] It is no surprise that by 2014, the U.S. Chamber of Commerce had hired five former Supreme Court clerks.[3] The Court now has five reliable conservative votes, and thus a constriction of individual rights against corporations is not unexpected.

There is perhaps no bigger sea change toward the interests of big business and away from individual plaintiffs than in the law of personal jurisdiction. Since 2011, the Supreme Court has dramatically reshaped the law of personal jurisdiction, shifting the plaintiff's choice of venue from anywhere a company did business to only where the company is essentially at home. Furthermore, Republican control of both houses of the U.S. Congress in 1995–2001, 2005–2009, and 2015–2019 also has seen the expansion of federal court subject matter jurisdiction.

Personal Jurisdiction

The rules of personal jurisdiction that were taught to law students for decades no longer exist. Since 2011, the Supreme Court has dramatically scaled back many decades of its jurisprudence concerning both *general* and *specific* personal jurisdiction. General jurisdiction, now referred to as "all-purpose" jurisdiction, must be carefully distinguished from specific jurisdiction, now referred to as *case-linked* jurisdiction.[4]

General *Personal Jurisdiction*

General, all-purpose jurisdiction arises from a defendant's activities in a state when the activities are not related to actions causing the injuries alleged by the plaintiff.

Originally, the concept of general jurisdiction arose from the concept of a defendant's presence in a state for purposes of service or notice. The Supreme Court required a defendant's presence within the territorial jurisdiction of a court as a prerequisite to that court's rendition of a judgment personally binding the defendant.[5]

In *International Shoe Co. v. State of Washington*, the Supreme Court held that with "personal service of summons or other form of notice, due process requires only that in order to subject a defendant to a judgment in personam, if he be not present within the territory of the forum, he have certain minimum contacts with it such that the maintenance of the suit does not offend 'traditional notions of fair play and substantial justice.'"[6] When

2. *Corporations and the Supreme Court*, Constitutional Accountability Center, https://www.theusconstitution.org/series/chamber-study/ (last visited Dec. 11, 2019).

3. Joan Biskupic, Janet Roberts & John Shiffman, *The Echo Chamber: A Handful of Lawyers and Its Outsized Influence at the U.S. Supreme Court*, Reuters (Dec. 8, 2014, 10:30 AM), https://www.reuters.com/investigates/special-report/scotus/.

4. *See BNSF Ry. Co. v. Tyrrell*, 137 S. Ct. 1549, 1558 (2017) ("we have distinguished between specific or case-linked jurisdiction and general or all-purpose jurisdiction").

5. *Pennoyer v. Neff*, 95 U.S. 714 (1878).

6. 326 U.S. 310, 316 (1945).

a corporation's activities in a state were neither "irregular nor causal" but rather "systematic and continuous," the maintenance of suit against it in that state would not involve "an unreasonable or undue procedure" according to the Court's "traditional conception of fair play and substantial justice."[7]

Following its decision in *International Shoe*, the Court decided only two *general* jurisdiction cases for the next 66 years; both cases involved foreign corporations. In 1952, the Court held that exercising general jurisdiction over a Philippines corporation in Ohio was appropriate because the corporation's affairs were overseen in Ohio during World War II.[8] In 1984, the Court held that Texas courts could not assert general personal jurisdiction over a Colombian helicopter company that had contacts in the state only through helicopter purchases.[9] For domestic corporations, in-state business contacts worked to sufficiently give rise to *general* personal jurisdiction. As a result, for almost seven decades, large corporations conducting business across the nation faced suits in each of the states where they conducted business.

Between 2011 and 2017, three Supreme Court cases changed the law of general personal jurisdiction forever. First, in *Goodyear Dunlop Tires Operations, S.A. v. Brown*, an injured party sued one of Goodyear's French parent companies in North Carolina for an auto accident that occurred in France. The Supreme Court cited its decision on general personal jurisdiction in *International Shoe* as requiring contacts "so 'continuous and systematic' as to render [the Defendant] essentially at home in the forum state."[10] Of course, the phrase "essentially at home" does not appear in *International Shoe*, and this requirement by the *Goodyear* court was conjured out of nowhere. Nonetheless, as the highest court in the land, this new standard became precedent ready for later citation.

Second, in *Daimler AG v. Bauman*, Argentinian residents sued Daimler AG, a German corporation, in California, alleging that Daimler's Argentinian subsidiary collaborated with Argentinian state security forces to kidnap, detain, torture, and kill the Plaintiffs or their relatives.[11] The Court extended its holding in *Goodyear*, observing that "the inquiry under *Goodyear* is not whether a foreign corporation's in-forum contacts can be said to be in some sense 'continuous and systematic,' it is whether that corporation's 'affiliations with the State are so "continuous and systematic" as to render [it] essentially at home in the forum State.'"[12] Furthermore, the Court observed that "[i]f Daimler's California activities sufficed to allow adjudication of this Argentina-rooted case in California, the same global reach would presumably be available in every other State in which MBUSA's sales are sizable," and that this would not allow a large corporation "to structure their primary conduct with some minimum assurance as to where that conduct will and will not render them liable to suit."[13]

7. *Id.* at 320.

8. *Perkins v. Benguet Consol. Mining Co.*, 342 U.S. 437, 447 (1952).

9. *Helicopteros Nacionales de Colombia, S.A. v. Hall*, 466 U.S. 408, 418 (1984).

10. 564 U.S. 915, 919 (2011).

11. 571 U.S. 117 (2014).

12. *Id.* at 138–39 (noting that neither Daimler nor its American subsidiary were incorporated in or had its principal place of business in California).

13. *Id.* at 139 (citing *Burger King Corp. v. Rudzewicz*, 471 U.S. 462, 472 (1985)); *but see Shuker v. Smith & Nephew, PLC*, 885 F.3d 760, 781 (3d Cir. 2018) ("the alter ego theory finds support in our case law, which instructs that, if a

Third, and most dramatically, in *BNSF Railway Co. v. Tyrrell*, the Court extended its "essentially at home" holdings in *Goodyear* and *Bauman*—two cases involving international corporations and accidents occurring outside the United States—to an accident occurring in the United States and involving a suit against an American corporation.[14] Two plaintiffs injured in neighboring North Dakota and South Dakota filed suit in Montana against BNSF because it had more than two thousand miles of railroad track and employs more than two thousand workers in Montana. The court quoted from its opinion in *Daimler*, reiterating that "the general jurisdiction inquiry does not focus solely on the magnitude of the defendant's in-state contacts."[15] Rather, the inquiry "calls for an appraisal of a corporation's activities in their entirety," and "[a] corporation that operates in many places can scarcely be deemed at home in all of them."[16] In closing, the Court held that the business BNSF did in Montana was sufficient to subject the railroad to specific personal jurisdiction in Montana on claims related to the business in Montana.[17] However, it held that in-state business does not suffice to permit the assertion of general jurisdiction over claims that are unrelated to any activity occurring in that state.[18]

As a consequence of the Supreme Court's jurisprudence, *general* purpose jurisdiction cannot be asserted—absent "an exceptional case"—unless the corporation sued was incorporated in the state of suit or it positioned its principal place of business there.

Specific *Personal Jurisdiction*

In evaluating whether specific or "case-linked" jurisdiction exists, "a court properly focuses on 'the relationship among the defendant, the forum, and the litigation.'"[19]

In *World-Wide Volkswagen Corp. v. Woodson*, the Supreme Court applied the stream of commerce theory of specific personal jurisdiction as follows:

> [I]f the sale of a product of a manufacturer or distributor such as Audi or Volkswagen is not simply an isolated occurrence, but arises from the efforts of the manufacturer or

---

subsidiary is merely the agent of a parent corporation, or if the parent corporation otherwise 'controls' the subsidiary, then personal jurisdiction exists over the parent whenever personal jurisdiction (whether general or specific) exists over the subsidiary"). Furthermore, a defendant that formerly had its headquarters in the forum state can be shown to have engaged in the "continuous and systematic" activities required. *See also Delphix Corp. v. Embarcadero Tech., Inc.*, 749 F. App'x 502, 506 (9th Cir. 2018) ("Embarcadero is a Delaware corporation that maintained its headquarters in California up until at least October 2015. At that time, Embarcadero was purchased by Idera, Inc., a Texas-based company. Embarcadero claims that its headquarters are now in Austin, Texas . . . . For at least two decades Embarcadero's headquarters were located in California and it engaged in 'continuous and systematic' activities within California . . . The purchase of Embarcadero by Idera, Inc. in October 2015 did not instantaneously dissolve the general jurisdictional nexus Embarcadero had established by its continuous and systematic operations in California."). *See generally RJR Nabisco, Inc. v. European Community*, 136 S. Ct. 2090, 2115 (2016) (Ginsburg, J., concurring in part) ("Due process constraints on the exercise of general personal jurisdiction shelter foreign corporations from suit in the United States based on conduct abroad unless the corporation's 'affiliations with the [forum] in which suit is brought are so constant and pervasive 'as to render it essentially at home [there].'").

14. *Tyrrell*, 137 S. Ct. 1549.
15. *Id.* at 1559 (quoting *Daimler*, 571 U.S. at 762 n.20) (internal quotation marks omitted).
16. *Id.*
17. *Id.*
18. *Id.*
19. *Keeton v. Hustler Magazine, Inc.*, 465 U.S. 770, 775 (1984) (citing *Shaffer v. Heitner*, 433 U.S. 186, 204 (1977)).

> distributor to serve directly or indirectly, the market for its product in other States, it is not unreasonable to subject it to suit in one of those States if its allegedly defective merchandise has there been the source of injury to its owner or to others. The forum State does not exceed its powers under the Due Process Clause if it asserts personal jurisdiction over a corporation that delivers its products into the stream of commerce with the expectation that they will be purchased by consumers in the forum State.[20]

However, the sale of a vehicle in the state of New York did not give rise to specific jurisdiction in Oklahoma just because the actions of others caused the vehicle to end up there. In this regard, the Supreme Court rejected the argument about the foreseeability of vehicles sold in one state ending up in another: "It is foreseeable that the purchasers of automobiles sold by World-Wide and Seaway may take them to Oklahoma. But the mere 'unilateral activity of those who claim some relationship with a nonresident defendant cannot satisfy the requirement of contact with the forum State.'"[21]

In *Burger King Corp. v. Rudzewicz*, Burger King, a Florida corporation, sued Rudzewicz, one of its franchisees from Michigan.[22] The Supreme Court held that the Florida court could assert specific personal jurisdiction over Rudzewicz.[23] First, the Court observed that "it is an inescapable fact of modern commercial life that a substantial amount of business is transacted solely by mail and wire communications across state lines, thus obviating the need for physical presence within a State in which business is conducted," and therefore held that "[s]o long as a commercial actor's efforts are 'purposefully directed' toward residents of another State, we have consistently rejected the notion that an absence of physical contacts can defeat personal jurisdiction there."[24] Furthermore, the Court reasoned that although Rudzewicz had no physical contacts with the state of Florida, "he entered into a carefully structured twenty-year relationship that envisioned continuing and wide-reaching contacts with Burger King in Florida," and concluded that "[i]n light of Rudzewicz' voluntary acceptance of the long-term and exacting regulation of his business from Burger King's Miami headquarters, the 'quality and nature' of his relationship to the company in Florida can in no sense be viewed as 'random,' 'fortuitous,' or 'attenuated.'"[25] Finally, the Supreme Court held:

> Because Rudzewicz established a substantial and continuing relationship with Burger King's Miami headquarters, received fair notice from the contract documents and the course of dealing that he might be subject to suit in Florida, and has failed to demonstrate how jurisdiction in that forum would otherwise be fundamentally unfair, we conclude that the District Court's exercise of jurisdiction pursuant to Fla. Stat. § 48.193(1)(g) (Supp. 1984) did not offend due process.[26]

---

20. 444 U.S. 286, 297–98 (1980).
21. *Id.* at 298.
22. *Rudzewicz*, 471 U.S. at 487.
23. *Id.*
24. *Id.* at 476.
25. *Id.* at 480.
26. *Id.* at 487.

By contrast, the mere act of contracting in a state will not alone give rise to specific jurisdiction.[27]

Two years later, the Court held in *Asahi Metal Industry Co., Ltd. v. Superior Court of California, Solano County*, that Cheng Shin Rubber Industrial Co., Ltd., a Taiwanese manufacturer of a tire tube that ended up in a tire that failed in a vehicular accident in Solano County, California, could not sue Asahi Metal Industry Co., Ltd., a Japanese valve manufacturer that sent valves from Japan to Cheng Shin in Taiwan, in the state of California.[28] The Supreme Court held that awareness of a product that might end up in a particular state is insufficient; rather, "[t]he substantial connection between the defendant and the forum State necessary for a finding of minimum contacts must come about by *an action of the defendant purposefully directed toward the forum State.*"[29] The Court held that "[t]he placement of a product into the stream of commerce, without more, is not an act of the defendant purposefully directed toward the forum State" and that "a defendant's awareness that the stream of commerce may or will sweep the product into the forum State does not convert the mere act of placing the product into the stream into an act purposefully directed toward the forum State."[30] However, the Court did note that "[a]dditional conduct of the defendant may indicate an intent or purpose to serve the market in the forum State, for example, designing the product for the market in the forum State, advertising in the forum State, establishing channels for providing regular advice to customers in the forum State, or marketing the product through a distributor who has agreed to serve as the sales agent in the forum State."[31]

Likewise, the Supreme Court's holding in *Bristol-Myers Squibb v. Superior Court of California* further narrowed the exercise of specific jurisdiction to states where the defendant's connections there relate to the plaintiff's claim.[32] While stating that "a defendant's general connections with the forum are not enough,"[33] the true holding of *Bristol-Myers Squibb* is that "there must be 'an affiliation between the forum and the underlying controversy, principally, [an] activity or an occurrence that takes place in the forum State and is therefore subject to the State's regulation,'" and "[f]or this reason, 'specific jurisdiction is confined to adjudication of issues deriving from, or connected with, the very controversy that establishes jurisdiction.'"[34] Thus, *specific* personal jurisdiction is further restricted by *Bristol-Myers Squibb*, which held that the plaintiff's harm must arise out of the defendant's in-state conduct and that out-of-state plaintiffs could not support this harm absent injury occurring in the forum state.

27. *See PTA-FLA, Inc. v. ZTE Corp.*, 715 F. App'x 237, 242 (4th Cir. 2017) ("PTA-FLA alleges that ZTE Corp. breached two agreements (neither of which was negotiated or entered into in South Carolina) by failing to ship complete base stations to Yakima, Washington and failing to ship handsets to an unspecified location. Neither of these allegations suggest any contacts with South Carolina related to these particular breaches.").

28. 480 U.S. 102, 112 (1987).

29. *Id.* (citations omitted).

30. *Id.*

31. *Id.*

32. 137 S. Ct. 1773 (2017).

33. *Id.* at 1781.

34. *Id.* at 1780 (citing *Goodyear*, 564 U.S. at 919).

So, what constitutes contacts with the forum state sufficient for the exercise of specific personal jurisdiction? First, one can look to dicta in *Bristol-Myers Squibb* where Justice Alito writes for the Court that Bristol-Myers Squibb "did not develop Plavix in California, did not create a marketing strategy for Plavix in California, and did not manufacture, label, package, or work on the regulatory approval of the product in California."[35]

For advertisements in a particular state to constitute sufficient contacts, the defendant must have "purposefully directed" the advertisements toward viewers there; passive websites where users are free to upload their own content to a defendant's web-based platforms will be insufficient.[36] The mere act of sending money to a state in payment of contractual obligations alone is not sufficient to confer specific personal jurisdiction.[37] Furthermore, because "the minimum contacts analysis examines 'the defendant's contacts with the forum State itself, not the defendant's contacts with persons who reside there,'" it also reasons that "a defendant's relationship with a plaintiff or third party, standing alone, is an insufficient basis for jurisdiction."[38]

In a products case, does the location of the injury matter in the specific personal jurisdiction analysis? Yes. However, the Court in *Bristol-Myers Squibb* did suggest plaintiffs elsewhere "could probably sue together in their home States."[39] This is true because of the stream of commerce theory of specific jurisdiction set forth in *World-Wide Volkswagen*.[40] However, the defendant's actions causing the injury must have occurred in that state, not in potential future states.[41]

---

35. *Id.* at 1778.

36. *Triple Up Ltd. v. Youku Tudou Inc.*, No. 17-7033, 2018 WL 4440459, at *3 (D.C. Cir. July 17, 2018) (citing *Rudzewicz*, 471 U.S. at 472). *Compare with Estate of Thompson through Thompson v. Phillips*, 741 F. App'x 94, 98 (3d Cir. July 11, 2018) ("Phillips has personally advertised and promoted the Blue Moon's chartering service through the distribution of business cards and by directing potential passengers to the Blue Moon's website . . ."); *Matus v. Premium Nutraceuticals, LLC*, 715 F. App'x 662, 663 (9th Cir. 2018) ("Matus alleges that Premium's 'intentional act' was false advertising. Premium committed that act in the state of Georgia by publishing language on its public, commercial website, for all the world to see, visit, and consider. This was a global, universal publication without any express aiming at the California market . . . . [W]here an alleged intentional tortfeasor employs a 'passive website,' to establish specific personal jurisdiction as to claims relating to that website, there still needs to be 'something more—conduct directly targeting the forum . . . .").

37. *See Gulf Coast Bank & Trust Co. v. Designed Conveyor Systems, LLC*, 717 F. App'x 394, 399–400 (5th Cir. 2017) ("DCS's mere sending of payment to Louisiana does not constitute purposeful availment to establish minimum contacts . . . . Regardless, while the acknowledgment allowed DCS to deliver payment to Louisiana, it did not require it. DCS was permitted by the acknowledgment's terms to deliver payment to Texas with no interaction with Louisiana whatsoever. While DCS has paid invoices to Gulf Coast in Louisiana over the course of DCS and Gulf Coast's dealing, this dispute does not arise out of those invoices.").

38. *Axiom Foods, Inc. v. Acerchem Int'l, Inc.*, 874 F.3d 1064, 1068 (9th Cir. 2017) (quoting *Walden v. Fiore*, 571 U.S. 277, 286 (2014)) (internal quotation marks omitted).

39. *Bristol-Myers Squibb Co.*, 137 S. Ct at 1783.

40. "The forum State does not exceed its powers under the Due Process Clause if it asserts jurisdiction over a corporation, which delivers its products into the stream of commerce with the expectation they will be purchased by consumers in the forum state." *World-Wide Volkswagen*, 444 U.S. at 297–98.

41. *See Waite v. All Acquisition Corp.*, 901 F.3d 1307, 1316 (11th Cir. 2018) ("The Waites also argue that Union Carbide had an ongoing duty to warn Mr. Waite of the threat of harm from asbestos that continued after he moved to Florida. Following Mr. Waite's exposure to Union Carbide's asbestos in Massachusetts, they argue, Union Carbide was obligated to warn him that he should avoid future exposure. Thus, they say, the tortious conduct occurred in Florida as well as in Massachusetts . . . . Accepting the Waites' argument would mean that Union Carbide would have failed to warn Mr. Waite 'in California, Mississippi, or wherever else [he] might have traveled,' like the passengers in

Does Bristol-Myers Squibb foreclose suits by out-of-state plaintiffs in a different forum based on the defendant's contacts with the forum state? No, if the contacts with the forum state play some role in the injuries claimed by the plaintiff. For example, while "[t]he plaintiff's residence is not, of course, completely irrelevant to the jurisdictional inquiry," the Supreme Court held in *Keeton* that "[t]here is no justification for restricting libel actions to the plaintiff's home forum," holding that "[t]he victim of a libel, like the victim of any other tort, may choose to bring suit in any forum with which the defendant has 'certain minimum contacts . . . such that the maintenance of the suit does not offend 'traditional notions of fair play and substantial justice.'"[42] However, actions in a state will not be sufficient unless those actions are alleged to have caused the injury.[43]

Is the stream of commerce theory universally applied to achieve <u>*specific*</u> *personal jurisdiction*? No. While it appears to be the majority view based on *World-Wide Volkswagen*, one circuit does not acknowledge the stream of commerce theory,[44] and federal district courts have applied the theory inconsistently. Some courts have used a stream of commerce theory to hold that *specific* personal jurisdiction exists,[45] while others have restricted its application in finding no such jurisdiction.[46]

Walden . . . . We thus agree with the district court that the exercise of specific jurisdiction over Union Carbide would violate due process.").

42. *Keeton*, "(quoting *Milliken v. Meyer*, 311 U.S. 457, 463 [61 S.Ct. 339, 343, 85 L.Ed. 278]. and *International Shoe Co. v. Washington*, 326 U.S. 310, 316, 66 S.Ct. 154, 158, 90 L.Ed. 95 (1945).")

43. *See SPV Osus Ltd. v. UBS AG*, 882 F.3d 333, 344-45 (2d Cir. 2018) ("Missing from the complaint is any allegation that OSUS relied on UBS's contacts with the feeder funds when OSUS decided to invest directly with BLMIS. Nor are there any allegations that OSUS based its decision to invest with BLMIS on the fact that the UBS defendants helped create and service the feeder funds."); *Heffington v. Puleo*, No. 18-3034, 2018 WL 4944402, at *3 (10th Cir. Oct. 12, 2018) ("The only Kansas-directed activities Heffington identifies are communications between his family and the defendants . . . . And regardless, Heffington does not allege his injuries stemmed from these communications, but from the defendants' conversion of trust assets and failure to perform their duties to him as a trust beneficiary . . . .").

44. *See Shuker*, 885 F.3d at 780 ("We perceive no merit in the Shukers' stream-of-commerce theory of personal jurisdiction . . . . A plurality of Supreme Court Justices has twice rejected the stream of commerce theory . . .").

45. *See, e.g., Diaz Cardona v. Hitachi Koki Co., Ltd.*, No. CV N15C-09-210 SKR, 2019 WL 449698 (Del. Sup. Ct. Feb. 5, 2019)), *appeal refused sub nom., Hitachi Koki Co. v. Cardona*, 207 A.3d 1128 (Del. 2019); *Cessna Aircraft Co. v. Garcia*, No. 13-17-00259-CV, 2018 WL 6627602 (Tex. App.—Corpus Christi, Edinburg, Dec. 19, 2018); *Bandemer v. Ford Motor Co.*, 913 N.W.2d 710 (Minn. Ct. App. July 17, 2018); *Rush v. STIHL, Inc.*, No. 3:17-CV-915-DPJ-FKB, 2018 WL 3421782 (S.D. Miss. July 13, 2018); *Align Corp. Ltd. v. Allister Mark Boustred*, 421 P.3d 163 (Colo. Nov. 13, 2017); *Marin v. Michelin North America, Inc.*, No. SA-16-CA-0497-FB, 2017 WL 5505323 (W.D. Tex. Sept. 26, 2017); *Lindsley v. American Honda Motor Co., Inc.*, No. CV 16-941, 2017 WL 3217140 (E.D. Pa. July 28, 2017); *Hernandez-Denizac v. Kia Motors Corp.*, 257 F. Supp. 3d 216 (D.P.R. 2017).

46. *See, e.g., Keralink Int'l, Inc. v. Stradis Healthcare, LLC*, No. CV CCB-18-2013, 2018 WL 6790305 (D. Md. Dec. 26, 2018); *Tomas v. Bayerische Motoren Werke AG*, No. 5:17-CV-01664-AKK, 2018 WL 6181172 (N.D. Ala. Nov. 27, 2018); *Brown v. Ford Motor Co.*, 347 F. Supp. 3d 1347 (N.D. Ga. 2018); *A.T. through Travis v. Hahn*, 341 F. Supp. 3d 1031 (E.D. Mo. 2018); *Kuhar v. Petzl Co.*, No. CV 16-395 (JBS/JS), 2018 WL 3727368 (D.N.J. Aug. 6, 2018); *Burnside v. Peterbilt Motors Co.*, No. 3:17-CV-2121, 2018 WL 3186957 (M.D. Pa. June 28, 2018); *Folweiler Chiropractic, PS v. Fair Health, Inc.*, No. 75864-1-1, 2018 WL 2684374, at *4 (Wash. Ct. App. June 4, 2018); *Umoe Schat-Harding, Inc. v. PT Schneider Elec. Mfg. Batam*, No. CV 187-0193-WS-N, 2018 WL 1655368 (S.D. Ala. Apr. 5, 2018), *appeal dismissed*, No. 18-11889-B, 2018 WL 5786036 (11th Cir. May 25, 2018); *Montgomery v. Airbus Helicopters, Inc.*, 414 P.3d 824 (Okla. 2018); *Venuti v. Continental Motors, Inc.*, 414 P.3d 943 (Utah. Ct. App. Jan. 5, 2018); *Ruiz v. TRW Vehicle Safety Systems, Inc.*, No. 3:17-CV-03006-RAL, 2017 WL 4236544 (D.S.D. Sept. 22, 2017).

Pendent *Personal Jurisdiction*

Pendent personal jurisdiction "exists when a court possesses personal jurisdiction over a defendant for one claim, lacks an independent basis for personal jurisdiction over the defendant for another claim that arises out of the same nucleus of operative fact, and then, because it possesses personal jurisdiction over the first claim, asserts personal jurisdiction over the second claim."[47] The concept of pendent personal jurisdiction is federal common law doctrine upheld by every circuit court of appeals and by the majority of federal district courts that have addressed the question.[48]

Typically, district courts apply pendent personal jurisdiction in their discretion when state law claims, for which the court may lack personal jurisdiction, exist together with a federal statutory claim where Congress has authorized nationwide service of process.[49] If the draft of a complaint wishes to achieve pendent personal jurisdiction, it should be specifically pleaded, utilizing the guidance from the states referenced above that have adopted the doctrine.

Subject Matter Jurisdiction

Subject matter jurisdiction addresses the issue of which court system has original jurisdiction to hear the claim—federal courts or state courts. Subject matter jurisdiction exists primarily in two statutory sources: (1) diversity jurisdiction, 28 United States Code (U.S.C.) § 1332, and (2) federal question jurisdiction, 28 U.S.C. § 1331. In addition to diversity and federal question jurisdiction, other statutory, common law, and constitutional bases exist for federal court subject matter jurisdiction.

Federal district courts are courts of limited jurisdiction and may hear cases authorized only by a federal statute and the Constitution.[50] Consequently, in a removed case, the burden of demonstrating federal jurisdiction rests upon the defendants, as they are the parties urging that the action is properly brought before the federal tribunal.[51] When a proceeding is improperly removed to a federal district court, the plaintiff may move to

---

47. *United States v. Botefuhr*, 309 F.3d 1263, 1272 (10th Cir. 2002).

48. *Id.* at 1273. *See, e.g.*, *Silent Drive, Inc. v. Strong Industries, Inc.*, 326 F.3d 1194 (Fed. Cir. 2003); *Helmer v. Doletskaya*, 393 F.3d 201 (D.C. Cir. 2004); *Riley v. Harr*, 292 F.3d 282 (1st Cir. 2002); *IUE AFL-CIO Pension Fund v. Herrmann*, 9 F.3d 1049 (2d Cir. 1993); *ESAB Group, Inc. v. Centricut, Inc.*, 126 F.3d 617 (4th Cir. 1997); *Busch v. Buchman, Buchman & O'Brien, Law Firm*, 11 F.3d 1255 (5th Cir. 1994); *SunCoke Energy, Inc. v. MAN Ferrostaal Aktiengesellschaft*, 563 F.3d 211 (6th Cir. 2009); *Robinson Engineering Co. Pension Plan and Trust v. George*, 223 F.3d 445 (7th Cur. 2000); *Action Embroidery Corp. v. Atlantic Embroidery, Inc.*, 368 F.2d 1174 (9th Cir. 2004); *Botefuhr*, 309 F.3d 1263. *But see Rilley v. MoneyMutual, LLC*, No. CV 16-4001 (DWF/LIB), 2018 WL 4778411, at *2 (D. Minn. Oct. 3, 2018) ("The Eighth Circuit has not specifically adopted pendent personal jurisdiction."); *Siegmund v. Bian*, No. 16-62506-CIV, 2017 WL 5644599, at *11 (S.D. Fla. Sept. 29, 2017 (". . . the Eleventh Circuit has not addressed the issue of pendent personal jurisdiction . . .").

49. *Action Embroidery*, 368 F.3d 1180–81 ("Pendent personal jurisdiction is typically found where one or more federal claims for which there is nationwide personal jurisdiction are combined in the same suit with one or more state or federal claims for which there is not nationwide personal jurisdiction").

50. *Kokkonen v. Guardian Life Ins. Co. of Am.*, 511 U.S. 375, 377 (1994); *Howery v. Allstate Ins. Co.*, 243 F.3d 912, 916 (5th Cir. 2001). The federal removal statute is subject to strict construction because a defendant's use of that statute deprives a state court of a case properly before it and thereby implicates important federalism concerns. *Frank v. Bear Stearns & Co.*, 128 F.3d 919, 922 (5th Cir. 1997).

51. *Shirley v. Maxicare Tex., Inc.*, 921 F.2d 565, 567 (5th Cir. 1991).

have the case remanded to state court.[52] The defendant, wishing to stay in federal court, then has the burden to show that there is, in fact, subject matter jurisdiction.[53] If the defendant fails to carry their burden, the court must remand the action to state court. Without subject matter jurisdiction, the court may not enter any order except for an order of dismissal or remand.[54]

A court is required to strictly construe the removal statute in favor of remand.[55] Consequently, any doubt about the propriety of removal should be resolved in favor of remand.[56] In performing remand analysis, the court must "evaluate all of the factual allegations in the Plaintiff's state court pleadings in the light most favorable to the Plaintiff, resolving all contested issues of substantive fact in favor of Plaintiff."[57] Then, the court must "examine relevant state law and resolve all uncertainties in favor of the non-removing party."[58] Again, when there is no subject matter jurisdiction, remand is mandatory under 28 U.S.C. § 1447(c).

Diversity Jurisdiction, 28 U.S.C. § 1332

Federal courts have diversity jurisdiction if two requirements are met: (1) the parties are citizens of different states[59] or citizens of a state and citizens or subjects of a foreign state,[60] and (2) the amount in controversy exceeds $75,000.[61] Diversity under 28 U.S.C. § 1332 requires "that no plaintiff may be from the same state as any defendant. . . ."[62] For diversity purposes, corporations "are citizens both of the state of incorporation and the state in which the corporation has its principal place of business."[63] However, if a defendant is a limited liability company ("LLC"), "[t]he citizenship for diversity purposes . . . is the citizenship of each of its members."[64] If the members of the limited liability company are themselves limited liability companies, citizenship "must be traced through however many layers of . . . members there may be."[65]

When removal is based on diversity of citizenship, the matter in controversy must exceed the sum or value of $75,000, exclusive of interest and costs, and without regard to any setoff or counterclaim.[66] "When the plaintiff's complaint does not state the amount in controversy, the defendant's notice of removal may do so."[67] Among other ways, the amount in

52. 28 U.S.C. § 1447(c).
53. *St. Paul Reinsurance Co. v. Greenberg*, 134 F.3d 1250, 1253 (5th Cir. 1998).
54. 28 U.S.C. § 1447(c).
55. *In re Hot-Hed Inc.*, 477 F.3d 320, 323 (5th Cir. 2007).
56. *Carpenter v. Wichita Falls Indep. Sch. Dist.*, 44 F.3d 362, 365–66 (5th Cir. 1995).
57. *Green v. Amerada Hess Corp.*, 707 F.2d 201, 205 (5th Cir. 1983).
58. *Id.* at 206.
59. 28 U.S.C. § 1332(a)(1).
60. 28 U.S.C. § 1332(a)(2–4).
61. 28 U.S.C. § 1332(b).
62. *Hart v. FedEx Ground Package Sys. Inc.*, 457 F.3d 675, 676 (7th Cir. 2006).
63. *Wise v. Wachovia Sec., LLC*, 450 F.3d 265, 267 (7th Cir. 2006).
64. *Id.*
65. *Hart v. Terminex Int'l*, 336 F.3d 541, 543 (7th Cir. 2003).
66. *Dart Cherokee Basin Oper. Co. v. Owens*, 135 S. Ct. 547, 551 (2014); 28 U.S.C. § 1332(b).
67. *Dart Cherokee*, 135 S. Ct. at 551 (citing 28 U.S.C. § 1446(c)(2)(A)).

controversy requirement can be met where the allegations in the complaint "make it facially apparent that the amount in controversy exceeds $75,000. . . ."[68]

Removing defendants often claim that the in-state defendant sued by the plaintiff was fraudulently joined. As the removing parties, defendants bear the heavy burden of demonstrating improper joinder.[69] "Merely to traverse the allegations upon which the liability of the resident defendant is rested, or to apply the epithet '[improper]' to the joinder, will not suffice: the showing must be such as compels the conclusion that the joinder is without right. . . ."[70] "Fraudulent joinder can be established in one of two ways: (1) actual fraud in the pleading of jurisdictional facts, or (2) inability of the plaintiff to establish a cause of action against the non-diverse party in state court."[71] With respect to the second method, defendants "must demonstrate that 'there is no reasonable basis for the district court to predict that the plaintiff might be able to recover against the in-state defendant.'"[72] The court need not "determine whether plaintiff will actually or even probably prevail on the merits of the claim, but look only for a possibility that the plaintiff might do so."[73]

A removing defendant's complaint about the alleged generic nature of the plaintiff's other causes of action are rendered irrelevant, as only one will do.[74] In a notice pleading state,[75] if "there is a reasonable basis for recovery against the in-state defendant" stated in the pleading alone,[76] the defendant "was properly joined regardless of the effect that joinder has on the removability of plaintiff's case."[77]

Federal Question Jurisdiction, 28 U.S.C. § 1331

A state court lawsuit is removable to federal court if it includes a claim arising under federal law.[78] The "well-pleaded complaint rule" recognizes that a state court plaintiff is entitled to

---

68. *Gebbia v. Wal-Mart Stores, Inc.*, 233 F.3d 880, 883 (5th Cir. 2000) (affirming denial of motion to remand where Court concluded it was "facially apparent" that claims exceeded $75,000).

69. *Travis v. Irby*, 326 F.3d 644, 649 (5th Cir. 2003).

70. *Chesapeake & Ohio Ry. Co. v. Cockrell*, 232 U.S. 146, 152 (1914).

71. *Travis*, 326 F.3d at 647. *See also De La Cruz v. FedEx Ground Package Sys., Inc.*, Civil Action No. H-14-1729, 2014 WL 5325112, *2 (S.D. Tex. Dec. 17, 2014) (same).

72. *De La Cruz*, 2014 WL 5325112 at *2 (citing *McDonal v. Abbott Labs.*, 408 F.3d 177, 183 (5th Cir. 2005)) (internal quotation marks and citation omitted). *See also Salazar v. Allstate Texas Lloyd's, Inc.*, 455 F.3d 571, 574 (5th Cir. 2006) (defendants must prove that there is absolutely no possibility that the plaintiff will be able to establish a cause of action against the nondiverse defendant).

73. *De La Cruz*, 2014 WL 5325112 at *2 (quoting *Guillory v. PPG Indus., Inc.*, 434 F.3d 303, 308–09 (5th Cir. 2005)) (internal quotation marks omitted).

74. *Riverview Management v. Int'l Ins. Co. of Hannover, Ltd.*, No. 80-1871, 2013 WL 4401431, *2 (S.D. Tex. Aug. 13, 2013) ("In the course of this analysis, the court does not focus on the probability that the plaintiff will prevail on the merits against the non-diverse defendant. Rather, the court must find at least a reasonable possibility of recovery against the non-diverse defendant.")

75. *See generally Kopplow Development, Inc. v. City of San Antonio*, 399 S.W.3d 532, 536 (Tex. 2013) ("Texas is a notice pleading jurisdiction . . . ."); *City of Dallas v. VSC, LLC*, 347 S.W.3d 231, 248 (Tex. 2011) ("Under our rules of notice pleading, VSC satisfied the prerequisites the Court musters. It does not deserve to have its claims dismissed.")

76. *Simon v. Wells Fargo Bank, N.A.*, Civil Action No. H-10-5215, 2011 WL 675355, *1 (S.D. Tex. Feb. 16, 2011) ("In order to determine if joinder is improper, the court must decide, based on the facts and the law, whether a state court could reasonably impose liability.") (citing *B, Inc. v. Miller Brewing Co.*, 663 F.2d 545, 549 (5th Cir. Unit A Dec. 1981)).

77. *Riverview Management*, 2013 WL 4401431 at *2.

78. 28 U.S.C. § 1441.

be master of his or her claims. Thus, as a general rule, absent diversity jurisdiction, a case will not be removable if the complaint does not affirmatively allege a federal claim.[79]

Although federal jurisdiction is generally tested by the petition's allegations, there is an exception to the well-pleaded complaint rule "if Congress 'so completely preempt[s] a particular area that any civil complaint raising this select group of claims is necessarily federal in character.'"[80] In order for the complete preemption doctrine to convert "what otherwise appears as merely a state law claim . . . [into] a claim 'arising under' federal law for jurisdictional purposes because 'the federal statute [must] so forcibly and completely displace state law that the plaintiff's cause of action is either wholly federal or nothing at all.'"[81] The Supreme Court has found complete preemption in only three areas: the usury provisions of the National Bank Act; the Employee Retirement Income Security Act of 1974; and the Labor Management Relations Act.[82] Other courts generally also refuse to find complete preemption by unrelated statutes.[83]

There is also a presumption that the "historic police powers of the States [are] not to be superseded by the Federal Act unless that was the clear and manifest purpose of Congress." The presumption is relevant even when there is an express preemption clause. This is because "when the text of a pre-emption clause is susceptible of more than one plausible reading, courts ordinarily 'accept the reading that disfavors pre-emption.'"[84] Thus, the presumption operates both to prevent and to limit preemption,[85] and because complete preemption represents such an "extraordinary pre-emptive power," it should not be "lightly implied."[86] The reason for this is obvious: unless a statute explicitly says that its remedies are the exclusive remedies available, no complete preemption occurs.

Furthermore, conflict preemption will not give rise to federal question jurisdiction[87] because case law clearly establishes that conflict preemption, unlike complete preemption,

---

79. *Beneficial Nat'l Bank v. Anderson*, 539 U.S. 1, 6 (2003).

80. *Arana v. Ochsner Health Plan*, 338 F.3d 433, 437 (5th Cir. 2003) (*en banc*) (quoting *Metropolitan Life Ins. Co. v. Taylor*, 481 U.S. 58, 63–64 (1987)).

81. *New Orleans & Gulf Coast Ry. Co. v. Barrois*, 533 F.3d 321, 330 (5th Cir. 2008) (quoting *Hoskins v. Bekins Van Lines*, 343 F.3d 769, 773 (5th Cir. 2003) (internal quotations omitted)).

82. *Devon Energy Prod. Co. v. Mosaic Potash Carlsbad, Inc.*, 693 F.3d 1195, 1204-05 (10th Cir. 2012).

83. *See, e.g., Northeastern Rural Elec. Membership Corp. v. Wabash Valley Power Ass'n, Inc.*, 707 F.3d 883, 894, 896 (7th Cir. 2013) ("[t]he exclusive jurisdiction provision in the Federal Power Act, 16 U.S.C. § 825p, does not alter our conclusion . . . . Absent a showing of Congressional intent to preempt *all* state law claims in the area of wholesale power regulation, there is no complete preemption."); *Johnson v. MFA Petroleum Co.*, 701 F.3d 243, 252–53 (8th Cir. 2012) (holding claims not completely preempted by the Petroleum Marketing Practices Act (PMPA)); *Proctor v. Vishay Intertechnology, Inc.*, 584 F.3d 1208, 1220 n.9 (9th Cir. 2009) (finding that *Beneficial National Bank* did not apply, noting "[w]hatever the outer bounds of this first category of cases may be, we very much doubt that SLUSA falls within it."); *Opera Plaza Residential Parcel Homeowners Ass'n v. Hoang*, 376 F.3d 831, 836, 839 (9th Cir. 2004) (remanding, finding no complete preemption by the Telecommunications Act of 1996); *Lippitt v. Raymond James Financial Services, Inc.*, 340 F.3d 1033, 1042 (9th Cir. 2003) ("the Exchange Act does not create exclusive jurisdiction for any and all actions that happen to target false advertising and deceptive sales practices in the sale of callable CDs.").

84. *Altria Group, Inc. v. Good*, 555 U.S. 70, 129 S. Ct. 538, 540 (2008) (quoting *Bates v. Dow Agrosciences LLC*, 544 U.S. 431, 449 (2005)).

85. *Franks Inv. Co. LLC v. Union Pacific R.R. Co.*, 593 F.3d 404, 407 (5th Cir. 2010).

86. *Devon Energy*, 693 F.3d at 1202 (quoting *Metropolitan Life*, 481 U.S. at 65 and *Bill Johnson's Rests., Inc. v. NLRB*, 461 U.S. 731, 752 (1983) (Brennan, J., concurring)).

87. *Vega v. Nat'l Life Ins. Servs., Inc.*, 188 F.3d 287, 291 n.3 (5th Cir. 1999).

does not create federal jurisdiction.[88] Moreover, a subsequent failure to regulate by a federal agency will not give rise to conflict preemption because the U.S. Supreme Court[89] and other federal courts have held that an absence of federal regulation does not cause preemption of state activity.[90]

Other Sources of Subject Matter Jurisdiction

Several federal statutes create federal court jurisdiction.

Federal Officer Jurisdiction, 28 U.S.C. § 1442(a)

Federal officer removal under 28 U.S.C. § 1442(a)(1) is proper when the defendant (1) is a person within the meaning of the statute, (2) is acting under the United States, its agencies, or its officers, (3) is acting under color of federal authority, and (4) has a colorable federal defense.[91]

---

88. *Giles v. NYLCare Health Plans, Inc.*, 172 F.3d 332, 337 (5th Cir. 1999).

89. *See, e.g., Sprietsma v. Mercury Marine*, 537 U.S. 51, 65 (2002) (rejecting "reliance on the Coast Guard's decision not to adopt a regulation requiring propeller guards on motorboats," noting that "[i]t is quite wrong to view that decision as the functional equivalent of a regulation prohibiting all States and their political subdivisions from adopting such a regulation . . . ."); *Altria Group*, 555 U.S. at 90, n.14 (finding no preemption of plaintiffs' claims by the FCLAA, noting that it is "inappropriate to read a policy of authorization into the FTC's inaction . . . ."); *Wyeth v. Levine*, 555 U.S. 555, 590 (2009) (citing *Sprietsma*, noting that "[t]he Court has generally articulated a very narrow 'impossibility standard"). *See generally Williamson v. Mazda Motor of America, Inc.*, 562 U.S. 323, n.3 (2011) (citing *Sprietsma* as holding "that it is 'perfectly rational' for Congress to bar state 'administrative and legislative regulations' while allowing 'private damages remedies' to compensate accident victims . . . .").

90. *See Patriotic Veterans, Inc. v. Indiana*, 736 F.3d 1041, 1050 (7th Cir. 2013) (noting that in *Sprietsma*, "the Court found no conflict preemption where a state adopted a regulation requiring propeller guards on all motorboats where the Coast Guard opted not to so regulate . . . ."); *Hunter v. Philip Morris USA*, 582 F.3d 1039, 1048 (9th Cir. 2009) (finding no implied preemption, observing that "[t]he remaining regulatory provisions concern labeling, research, and education and do not provide strong evidence of a federal policy against more stringent state regulation" and that the Court did "decline to find preemption 'in the absence of clear evidence of a conflict . . . .'"); *Holk v. Snapple Beverage Corp.*, 575 F.3d 329, 341 (3d Cir. 2009) (finding no preemption by FDCA, noting that the FDA's decision to not undertake rulemaking at this time "hardly supports preemption"); *Fellner v. Tri-Union Seafoods, LLC*, 539 F.3d 237, 247, n.5 (3d Cir. 2008) (finding no preemption, noting that "[w]e do not interpret *Sprietsma* to have implied that, had the agency adopted a pro-preemption stance in an informal statement or briefings for the Court, those views alone would have imbued the agency's decision not to regulate with preemptive force"); *Emerson v. Kansas City Southern Ry. Co.*, 503 F.3d 1126, 1129 (10th Cir. 2007) (finding no preemption by the ICCTA, noting that "[e]xcept as otherwise provided in this part, the remedies provided under this part with respect to regulation of rail transportation are exclusive and preempt the remedies provided under Federal or State law," 49 U.S.C. § 10501(b), and concluding that "[b]ecause the ICCTA contains an express preemption clause, our 'task of statutory construction must in the first instance focus on the plain wording of the clause, which necessarily contains the best evidence of Congress' pre-emptive intent.'" (quoting *Sprietsma*, 537 U.S. at 62–63, quoting *CSX Transp., Inc. v. Easterwood*, 507 U.S. 658, 664 (1993))); *United States v. Massachusetts*, 493 F.3d 1, 8, n.9 (1st Cir. 2007) (citing *Sprietsma*, noting that "a decision by the Coast Guard not to regulate in a field does not necessarily mean that the Coast Guard intended to preempt state law"); *Morris v. Cessna Aircraft Co.*, 833 F. Supp. 2d 622, 633 (N.D. Tex. 2011) ("Neither the text of the FAA Act, its legislative history, nor its associated regulations demonstrate a clear and manifest congressional intent to supersede the state law standard of care for common law products liability claims . . . ."). *See also Frank v. Delta Airlines, Inc.*, 314 F.3d 195, 199, n.6 (5th Cir. 2002) (finding preemption, distinguishing *Sprietsma*, noting "this case involves the preemptive effect of adopted FAA regulations as opposed to the preemptive effect of the Coast Guard's decision not to regulate propeller guards in *Sprietsma*").

91. *Mesa v. California*, 489 U.S. 121 (1989); *see also Dahl v. R.J. Reynolds Tobacco Co.*, 478 F.3d 965, 967 n.2 (8th Cir. 2007).

Acting Under the Direction of a Federal Officer

In *Watson v. Phillip Morris Companies, Inc.*, the Supreme Court held that "the help or assistance necessary to bring a private person within the scope of the statute does *not* include simply *complying* with the law" because "a highly regulated firm cannot find a statutory basis for removal in the fact of federal regulation alone."[92]

General federal oversight was found to be insufficient in *City of Walker v. Louisiana through Dept. of Transp. & Devel.*,[93] as was the "general auspices of federal authorities."[94] Neither extensive regulation,[95] nor intense regulation,[96] nor "very extensive supervision" by the government,[97] nor government approval of the product itself,[98] are sufficient to meet the "acting under" requirements for the purpose of federal officer jurisdiction. As the District of Minnesota held in *In re Guidant Corporation Implantable Defibrillators Products Liability Litigation*, Section 1442 should not be read to allow for federal jurisdiction over "virtually any participant in a regulated industry" as that "'would lead to an unprecedented expansion of federal jurisdiction.'"[99]

Causal Connection Between Defendant's Actions and the Official Authority

A defendant seeking to remove on the basis of federal officer removal jurisdiction must also demonstrate a causal connection between their actions and the official authority.

A private corporation is not typically in the class of actors intended to be protected from state court activities by Section 1442(a). "The statute's purpose is to protect . . . federal officials [by providing them] with an unbiased federal forum," and this purpose is not implicated when a private defendant "is not implementing any federal policy at the direction of federal officers or agents."[100] Thus, for a private corporation to show it meets the "causation requirement" of Section 1442(a), it must bear a "special burden" to establish its entitlement to federal court protection.[101] As the Court in *Freiberg* observed, this "burden is substantive and is not satisfied by incantations of government contractor status alone."[102] Without proof attached to its removal, a court will generally order remand.[103]

---

92. 551 U.S. 142, 152 (2007); *Jacks v. Meridian Resource Co., LLC*, 701 F.3d 1224, 1231, 1234 (8th Cir. 2012).
93. 877 F.3d 563, 571 (5th Cir. 2017).
94. *Mobley v. Cerro Flow Products, Inc.*, Civil No 09-697-GPM, 2010 WL 55906, at *5 (S.D. Ill. Jan. 5, 2010); *Ryan v. Dow Chemical Co.*, 781 F. Supp. 934, 947 (E.D.N.Y. 1992).
95. *Mills v. Martin & Bayley, Inc.*, Civil No. 05-888-GPM, 2007 WL 2789431, at *6 (S.D. Ill. Sept. 21, 2007).
96. 877 F.3d 563, 569–70 (5th Cir. 2017).
97. *Perakslis v. 3M Co.*, Civil No. 11-1111-GPM, 2012 WL 113755, at *2 (S.D. Ill. Jan. 13, 2012).
98. *Alsup v. 3-Day Blinds, Inc.*, 435 F. Supp. 2d 838, 848 (S.D. Ill. June 8, 2006).
99. 428 F. Supp. 2d 1014, 1018 (D. Minn. 2006) (quoting *Parks v. Guidant Corp.*, 402 F. Supp. 2d 964, 971 (N.D. Ind. 2005).
100. *Brown & Williamson Tobacco Corp. v. Wigand*, 913 F. Supp. 530, 533–34 (W.D. Ky. 1996). *See also Bakalis v. Crossland Sav. Bank*, 781 F. Supp. 140, 145 (E.D.N.Y. 1991) (observing that "[g]overnment employees are the primary protected class of [Section 1442]," not "a corporation regulated by the government").
101. *See Mills v. Martin & Bayley, Inc.*, Civil No. 05-888-GPM, 2007 WL 2789431, at *1 (S.D. Ill. Sept. 21, 2007) (citing *Freiberg v. Swinerton & Walberg Property Services, Inc.*, 245 F. Supp. 2d 1144, 1150 (D. Colo. 2002) ("[P]rivate actors seeking to benefit from [Section 1442] bear a special burden of establishing the official nature of their activities . . . .")).
102. *Freiberg*, 245 F. Supp. 2d at 1152.
103. *See Schnabel v. BorgWarner Morse TEC*, No. CV 08-04714 R (JTLx), 2008 WL 11336462, at *4 (C.D. Cal. Oct. 6, 2008) (remanding because the defendant "has not presented any evidence, whether in the form of affidavits, declarations, documents or otherwise, demonstrating . . . that there is a causal nexus between Plaintiffs' claims, specifically their claims for failure to warn, and its alleged conduct at the direction of a federal officer . . . .").

Moreover, for a private corporation to show a causal nexus between its failure to warn and the direction of a federal officer, it must demonstrate that federal requirements precluded the corporation from complying with a state law duty to warn.[104]

Asserting a Colorable Federal Defense to the Plaintiff's Claims

Finally, federal officer removal jurisdiction requires a defendant to show that it has asserted a colorable federal defense to the plaintiff's claims.

104. *See Perakslis*, 2012 WL 113755 at *2 ("Rockwell must produce evidence that the USN prevented the company from complying with its duty to warn under state law."); *Vickroy v. A.W. Chesterton, Inc.*, Civil No. 11-531-GPM, 2011 WL 4529467, at *1 (S.D. Ill. Sept. 28, 2011) ("GE must show that the USN approved specific warnings that precluded GE from complying with its state-law duty to warn."); *Baker v. Air & Liquid Systems Corp.*, Civil No. 11-8-GPM, 2011 WL 499963, at *3 (S.D. Ill. Feb. 7, 2011) ("Most importantly, even assuming for the sake of argument that it is the case that, as Schroppe and Lehman claim, the USN exercised the final control over the content of the warnings that accompanied the equipment supplied to it by Foster Wheeler, this does not dispose of the possibility that Foster Wheeler had responsibility for designing the warnings, in whole or in part, or that the USN required contractors like Foster Wheeler to provide safety warnings in accordance with state-law duties of care."); *Glein v. Boeing Co.*, Civil No. 10-452-GPM, 2010 WL 2608284, at *2 (S.D. Ill. June 25, 2010) ("the removing defendant must establish that the government's control over warnings directly interfered with the defendant's ability to fulfill its state-law obligation to warn of safety hazards."); *Brown v. Cerro Flow Products, Inc.*, Civil No. 09-582-GPM, 2010 WL 55905, at *5 (S.D. Ill. Jan. 4, 2010) ("Defendants have adduced no evidence, in the form of exemplar contracts or regulations, for example, showing that the military regulated disposal of toxic waste at the plants operated by the removing Defendants pursuant to contracts with the CWS in a manner that prevented the removing Defendants from complying with their duties under state law."); *Freiberg*, 245 F. Supp. 2d at 1155 ("What [removing defendants] must establish for purpose of [Section] 1442(a)(1) is that the government authority under which they worked required them to act as they did," that is, "they must establish the [government's] direction and control of their activities directly interfered with their ability to fulfill their state law obligation[.]"); *Schnabel*, 2008 WL 11336462 at *7 ("For purposes of Plaintiffs' failure to warn claims, for example, they must establish the DOE's direction and control of their activities directly interfered with their ability to fulfill their state law obligation to warn employees of safety hazards."); *Mouton v. Flexitallic, Inc.*, No. CIV.A. 99-0162, 1999 WL 225438, at *3 (E.D. La. Apr. 14, 1999) ("The federal government provided no direction on warnings when using asbestos, and further did not prevent Avondale from taking its own safety precautions above the minimum standards incorporated in the federal contracts. Thus, the Court finds that Avondale has failed to establish a causal connection between the Navy's direction pursuant to the design contracts and plaintiff's failure to warn claims."); *Gauthe v. Asbestos Corp.*, No. Civ. A 96-2454, 1997 WL 3255, at *3 (E.D. La. Jan. 2, 1997) ("There is no evidence that the Government restricted or prohibited Avondale's ability to notify individuals of the presence of asbestos in the work environment. Assuming that Avondale built ships under the direct supervision of the federal government, nothing about that supervision prevented Avondale from warning Mr. Gauthe about the dangers. Thus, there is no causal connection between the injury alleged by Mr. Gauthe with respect to Avondale's failure to warn and Avondale working on behalf of the federal government."); *In re Joint E. & S. Dist. N.Y. Asbestos Litig.*, 897 F.2d 626, 630 (2d Cir. 1990) ("*Boyle*'s requirement of government approval of 'reasonably precise specifications' mandates that the federal duties be imposed upon the contractor. The contractor must show that whatever warnings accompanied a product resulted from a determination of a government official, . . . and thus that the Government itself 'dictated' the content of the warnings meant to accompany the product."); *Nguyen v. AlliedSignal, Inc.*, No. C 98-03616 SI, 1998 WL 690854, at *4 (N.D. Cal. Sept. 29, 1998) ("As defendants have made no showing that their contractual obligations to the government specifically prohibited them from placing warnings on their products, they cannot raise the government contractor defense in this failure to warn case . . . . [T]his evidence does not demonstrate that the federal government directed defendants not to place warnings on their products. Therefore, there is no causal connection between the control exercised by the United States over defendants and plaintiffs' legal theory of failure to warn consumers of the hazards of asbestos."); *Overly v. Raybestos-Manhattan, Inc.*, No. C-96-2853 SI, 1996 WL 532150, at *4 (N.D. Cal. Sept. 9, 1996) ("The government in no way restricted Avondale's ability to notify individuals of the presence of asbestos in the work environment. Thus, there is no causal connection between the control exercised by the United States over Avondale and the legal theory under which plaintiffs seek to hold Avondale liable."); *Cabalic v. Owens-Corning Fiberglas Corp.*, No. C 94-2571 EFL, 1994 WL 564724, at *3 (N.D. Cal. Oct. 6, 1994) ("The 'government contractor' defense is not colorable. No defendant has produced evidence that it presented specially designed products to the government under federal orders or specifications that directly conflicted with the state law duty upon which the defendants are now being sued.").

Subject Matter Jurisdiction Created by Common Law

Federal common law includes "interstate and international disputes implicating the conflicting rights of States or our relations with foreign nations. . . ."[105] For this reason, federal question jurisdiction exists if the resolution of such claims "necessarily require[s] determinations that will directly and significantly affect American foreign relations."[106] Courts have emphasized that the federal common law of foreign relations encompasses disputes that implicate "foreign policy concerns"—thereby supporting federal question jurisdiction, even where a plaintiff attempts to couch its claims in state law terms.[107]

While in limited circumstances, courts have applied the federal common law of foreign relations to find original federal jurisdiction over removed actions pursuant to 28 U.S.C. § 1331 and § 1441(a), several important qualifiers exist.

First, "[t]he presence or absence of federal-question jurisdiction is governed by the 'well-pleaded complaint rule,' which provides that federal jurisdiction exists only when a federal question is presented on the face of the plaintiff's properly pleaded complaint."[108] Because "[a] defense is not part of a plaintiff's properly pleaded statement of his or her claim,"[109] "a case may not be removed to federal court on the basis of a federal defense. . . ."[110] Thus, a defendant's attempt to spread blame to a foreign government is defensive, unless plaintiff has done so inside the four corners of the complaint.[111]

Second, ordinary state law tort claims do not necessarily *require* determination of any issue under the federal common law of foreign relations. Rather, most plaintiffs' tort claims are "traditional types of torts by private entities"[112] whose tortious actions occurred within the United States. As long as a plaintiff does not ask any court to pass on "the propriety of a

---

105. *Tex. Indus., Inc. v. Radcliff Materials, Inc.*, 451 U.S. 630, 641 (1981); *see also Banco Nacional de Cuba v. Sabbatino*, 376 U.S. 398, 425 (1964) (concluding that "our relationships with other members of the international community must be treated exclusively as an aspect of federal law").

106. *Republic of the Philippines v. Marcos*, 806 F.2d 344, 352–54 (2d Cir. 1986).

107. *Torres v. S. Peru Copper Corp.*, 113 F.3d 540, 542–43 (5th Cir. 1997); *accord, e.g., Pacheco de Perez v. AT&T, Co.*, 139 F.3d 1368, 1377 (11th Cir. 1998); *Republic of the Philippines*, 806 F.2d at 353–54 (emphasizing that "there is federal question jurisdiction over actions having important foreign policy implications"). *See Sequihua v. Texaco, Inc.*, 847 F. Supp. 61, 62–63 (S.D. Tex. 1994) (noting that plaintiffs' claims of nuisance "require them as part of their prima facie case to challenge the policies and regulations of Ecuador, as well as the approvals from Ecuador that Defendants received").

108. *Caterpillar, Inc. v. Williams*, 482 U.S. 386, 392 (1987).

109. *Rivet v. Regions Bank of La.*, 522 U.S. 470, 475 (1998).

110. *Franchise Tax Bd. of State of California v. Constr. Laborers Vacation Trust for Southern Cal.*, 463 U.S. 1, 14 (1983).

111. *See, e.g., Provincial Gov't of Marinduque v. Placer Dome, Inc.*, 582 F.3d 1083, 1090–91 (9th Cir. 2009) (reversing the district court's finding of jurisdiction and holding that "the act of state doctrine is implicated here only defensively and the complaint does not 'necessarily raise a stated federal issue, actually disputed and substantial'") (quoting *Grable*, 545 U.S. at 314); *Patrickson v. Dole Food Co.*, 251 F.3d 795, 800 (9th Cir. 2001) (rejecting jurisdiction where alleged common law of foreign relations issue arose as a defense); *Aquafaith Shipping, Ltd. v. Jarillas*, 963 F.2d 806, 808 (5th Cir. 1992) ("Defense counsel's erudite arguments about the federal common law of foreign relations are foreclosed by the familiar well-pleaded complaint rule."); *Alomang v. Freeport-McMoran, Inc.*, Civ. A. No. 96-2139, 1996 WL 601431, at *9 (E.D. La. Oct. 17, 1996) ("Both the act of state doctrine and foreign relations would be raised defensively in this action . . . Neither defense confers federal jurisdiction for removal purposes."); *A.A.Z.A. v. Doe Run Resources Corp.*, No. 4:07CV1874 CDP, 2008 WL 748328, at *3 (E.D. Mo. Mar. 18, 2008) (similar); *Creditanstalt Inv. Bank AG v. Holme Roberts & Owen, LLP*, No. Civ. A 01-M-827, 2001 WL 35981554, at *1–2 (D. Colo. July 2, 2001) (similar).

112. *Republic of Iraq v. ABB AG*, 768 F.3d 145, 172 (2d Cir. 2014).

foreign sovereign's internal government actions" nor allege that a foreign government itself is a tortfeasor, removal is improper.[113]

Third, on three occasions, the Supreme Court has declined to find federal jurisdiction under the common law of foreign relations because the question at issue was not sufficiently substantial to justify federal jurisdiction over the matter. Initially, in *Grable & Sons Metal Products, Inc. v. Darue Engineering & Manufacturing*, the Supreme Court observed that "[b]ecause arising-under jurisdiction to hear a state law claim always raises the possibility of upsetting the state-federal line drawn (or at least assumed) by Congress, the presence of a disputed federal issue and the ostensible importance of a federal forum are never necessarily dispositive; there must always be an assessment of any disruptive portent in exercising federal jurisdiction."[114] Next, in *Empire HealthChoice Assurance, Inc. v. McVeigh*, the Court declined to find the case federal in nature, noting that "those interests, we are persuaded, do not warrant turning into a discrete and costly 'federal case' an insurer's contract-derived claim to be reimbursed from the proceeds of a federal worker's state-court-initiated tort litigation."[115] Lastly, the Court held in *Gunn v. Minton* that "[t]here is no reason to suppose that Congress meant to bar legal malpractice claims from state courts simply because they require resolution of a hypothetical patent issue."[116]

Constitutionally Based Federal Enclave Jurisdiction

Federal enclave removal jurisdiction, arising from U.S. Const. art. I, § 8, cl. 17, requires that before the United States has exclusive jurisdiction over land of a state, (1) the United States must acquire the land "for any of the purposes mentioned in [the Federal Enclave Clause], (2) the state legislature must "consent" to the jurisdiction of the federal government,[117] and (3) the federal government must accept the jurisdiction "by filing a notice of acceptance with the Governor of the State. . . ."[118]

Cases involving injuries occurring on U.S. military bases are often removed by defendants asserting federal enclave jurisdiction. However, careful practitioners can avoid federal enclave jurisdiction in seven circumstances.

First, state-owned National Guard bases do not constitute federal enclaves for the purpose of removal jurisdiction because the constitutional text itself limits the application of federal enclave jurisdiction over lands *purchased from the states*. Consequently, neither state-owned land, nor foreign lands not purchased from the states, constitute federal enclaves.[119]

---

113. *In re Tobacco/Governmental Health Care Costs Litig.*, 100 F. Supp. 2d 31, 36 (D.D.C. 2000), *appeals dismissed & writ of mandamus denied sub nom.*; *Republic of Venezuela v. Philip Morris, Inc.*, 287 F.3d 192 (D.C. Cir. 2002). *See also, e.g.*, *Patrickson*, 251 F.3d at 800 (rejecting removal where plaintiffs "don't claim that any foreign government participated in such [tortious] activities or that the defendants acted under the color of foreign law"), *aff'd in part, dismissed in part on other grounds*, 538 U.S. 468 (2003).

114. 545 U.S. 308, 314 (2005).

115. 547 U.S. 677, 701 (2006).

116. 568 U.S. 251, 264 (2013).

117. *Paul v. United States*, 371 U.S. 245 (1963).

118. 40 U.S.C. § 3112(b).

119. *See Tucker v. Hunt Const. Group, Inc*, Cause No. 1:15-CV-89-WTL-MJD, 2015 WL 1969375, at *3 (S.D. Ind., Apr. 30, 2015) ("It appears, however, that in this specific instance, the Project and the land on which it sits is owned

Second, U.S. military bases abroad are not federal enclaves because the land on which they sit was not purchased from the states.[120] Indeed, no such case exists. Instead, the courts have uniformly held that bases located on foreign soil are not federal enclaves.[121]

Third, injuries occurring on naval vessels do not occur on lands purchased from the states, and thus do not occur on federal enclaves.[122]

Fourth, if the injury claimed is one arising from exposure over time and the majority of damage occurred on foreign bases or on naval vessels rather than on domestic bases, relevant case law suggests federal enclave jurisdiction will not exist. When some of the plaintiff's injury exposure occurred elsewhere, "the defendants' burden of establishing federal enclave jurisdiction [is] heavier"[123] because "[w]hen exposures allegedly occur partially inside and partially outside the boundaries of an enclave an argument would surface that the state's interest increases proportionally, while the federal interest decreases."[124] As such, in *Blahnik v. BASF*, a mere two-year exposure at Ft. Hood in Texas, a federal enclave, part of a decades-long career of worksite exposure to asbestos elsewhere did not give rise to federal enclave jurisdiction.[125] When the majority of one's exposure takes place outside of a federal enclave, a presumption exists in favor of remand.[126]

Fifth, when decisions giving rise to the tort occur outside of a federal enclave, federal court jurisdiction does not exist.[127]

---

by the Military Department of Indiana, also referred to as the Indiana National Guard. Thus, the land in question is not owned by the federal government, and was thus not 'purchased by' the federal government.").

120. *See Nguyen*, No. C 98-03616 SI, 1998 WL 690854, at *1 (burden not met when "Defendants cite no case involving federal enclave jurisdiction where the military base was located overseas").

121. *See Gavrilovic v. Worldwide Language Resources, Inc.*, 441 F. Supp. 2d 163, 177 (D. Maine 2006) (remanding case involving military service in Iraq because "it is doubtful that the defense applies to military bases that are in foreign countries" and because "the defendants do not cite any case holding that the enclave clause applies to bases on foreign soil"); *Goodwin v. Dyncorp Int'l LLC*, Case No. 3:14-CV-116/RV-EMT, 2014 WL 12570917, at *2 (N.D. Fla. May 16, 2014) ("because the inspection problems giving rise to this case took place in (and the Plaintiff worked out of) Iraq," no federal enclave application). *See also Harris v. Kellogg, Brown & Root Services, Inc.*, 796 F. Supp. 2d 642, 673 n.7 (W.D. Pa. 2011) (discounting the suggestion that Iraq is a federal enclave, noting that "[a]lthough the decisions in this area are limited, courts have reasoned that the enclave clause does not apply to a military installation on foreign soil").

122. *See Scott v. Does 1 through 100*, CV 12-06235 SJO, 2012 WL 13013026, at *10 (C.D. Cal. Oct. 25, 2012); *Dennison v. Shell Oil Co.*, Civil No. 07-802-GPM, 2007 WL 4390346, *2 n.2 (S.D. Ill. Dec. 14, 2007); *Anderson v. Crown Cork & Seal*, 93 F. Supp. 2d 697 (E.D. Va. 2000).

123. *Akin v. Big Three Industries, Inc.*, 851 F. Supp. 819, 825 (E.D. Tex. 1994).

124. *Id.* at n.4.

125. C.A. No. C-06-410, 2006 WL 2850113, at *4 (S.D. Tex. Oct. 3, 2006); *see also Dennison*, 2007 WL 4390346, at *2 (exposure for two weeks does "not make an especially convincing case for the existence of federal enclave jurisdiction" because "nothing in the record suggests that the vast majority of exposure . . . alleged in the complaint in this case occurred at a federal enclave.").

126. *See Anderson*, 93 F. Supp. 2d 697, 703 & n.4 (when the majority of time involves exposure elsewhere, "the Court considers these legal determinations 'close calls,'" justifying remand back to state court). *Cf. Klausner v. Lucas Film Entertainment Co., Ltd.*, No. 09-03502 CW, 2010 WL 1038228, at *4 (N.D. Cal. Mar. 19, 2010) (denying remand because "the vast majority of the alleged acts" took place on the Presidio, a federal enclave).

127. *See Polar Ice Cream & Creamery Co. v. Andrews*, 375 U.S. 361, 379–80 (1964) ("because Florida regulates only producer prices applicable to sales made by producers to the distributor, none of which occur on military bases, its law is not vulnerable as an attempt to legislate with regard to transactions occurring within federal enclaves subject to the exclusive jurisdiction of the United States."); *Camargo v. Gino Morena Enterprises, LLC*, No. EP-10-CV-242-KC, 2010 WL 3516186, at *2 (W.D. Tex., Sept. 2, 2010) ("For federal enclave jurisdiction to apply,

Sixth, courts have held that the well-pleaded complaint rule applies, so plaintiffs may artfully plead injury only in locations other than domestic military bases; in some instances, they may also waive such claims, depriving courts of federal enclave jurisdiction. As the Supreme Court has long held, "the plaintiff is the master of the complaint."[128] This basis for federal question jurisdiction must ordinarily appear on the face of the complaint because "[r]emovals under 28 U.S.C. § 1441are subject to the well-pleaded complaint rule," which provides that federal jurisdiction exists only when a federal question is presented "on the face of the plaintiff's properly pleaded complaint."[129] "Because the basis for federal question jurisdiction must ordinarily appear 'on the face of the complaint,' plaintiffs have the ability to 'eschew[ ] claims based on federal law' and 'choose to have the cause heard in state court.'"[130] State law–only claims do not give rise to federal enclave jurisdiction by virtue of a defense pleaded by the defendant.[131]

Finally, by waiving any damage caused on a federal enclave, a plaintiff may avoid federal enclave jurisdiction.[132]

Supplemental Jurisdiction, 28 U.S.C. § 1367(a)

Supplemental jurisdiction applies when state law claims derive from the same nucleus of operative fact as an asserted federal claim.[133] The supplemental jurisdiction statute enacted in 1990[134] provides in relevant part:

> (a) Except as provided in subsections (b) and (c) or as expressly provided otherwise by Federal statute, in any civil action of which the district courts have original jurisdiction, the district courts shall have supplemental jurisdiction over all other claims that are so related to the claims in the action within such original jurisdiction that they form part of the same case or controversy under Article III of the United States Constitution. Such supplemental jurisdiction shall include claims that involve joinder or intervention of additional parties. . . .

---

in employment discrimination cases, the adverse employment decision must have been made on federal territory, because the locus of decision-making is where such a tort arises").

128. *Caterpillar Inc. v. Williams*, 482 U.S. 386, 398–99 (1987).

129. *Olig v. Xanterra Parks & Resorts, Inc.*, No. CV 13-15-BLG-DLC-RKS, 2013 WL 3936904, at *2 (D. Mont. July 30, 2013), *report and recommendation adopted*, No. CV 13-15-BLG-DLC-RKS, 2013 WL 5234866 (D. Mont. Sept. 17, 2013) (citing *California v. United States*, 215 F.3d 1005, 1014 (9th Cir. 2000)).

130. *Segura v. Griffcon, Inc.*, Case No. SACV17-01209 AG (KESx), 2017 WL 4271206, at *3 (C.D. Cal. Sept. 25, 2017) (citing *Williams*, 482 U.S. at 398–99).

131. *Nationstar Mortg., LLC v. Ilori*, No. EDCV 13-2156-DOC (SHx), 2014 WL 197732, at *3 (C.D. Cal. Jan. 14, 2014) ("Here, Plaintiff's complaint asserts a single cause of action wholly grounded in state law, and it is irrelevant whether Defendants raise any federal questions as defenses."); *Olig*, 2013 WL 3936904, at *2 ("Courts consider what appears in the plaintiff's statement of his claim without regard to anything alleged to avoid federal defenses it anticipates a defendant may assert.").

132. *See Dougherty v. A.O. Smith Corp.*, No. 13-1972-SLR-SRF, 2014 WL 3542243, at *3 (D. Dela. July 16, 2014) ("remand is appropriate, pursuant to 28 U.S.C. § 1367(c), based on Plaintiffs' post-removal disclaimer of any claims relative to Mr. Dougherty's alleged exposure to asbestos during his service in the U.S. Navy and on any federal jobsites and vessels (the 'claim disclaimer')."); *Schulz v. Crane Co.*, No. 2:13-CV-02370-KJM-AC, 2014 WL 280361, at *2, (E.D. Cal. Jan. 23, 2014) ("The court agrees with the several district courts that have found similar waivers in asbestos cases sufficient to justify remand.").

133. *See United Mine Workers of Am. v. Gibbs*, 383 U.S. 715, 725 (1966).

134. 28 U.S.C. § 1367.

(c) The district courts may decline to exercise supplemental jurisdiction over a claim under subsection (a) if—
 (1) the claim raises a novel or complex issue of State law,
 (2) the claim substantially predominates over the claim or claims over which the district court has original jurisdiction,
 (3) the district court has dismissed all claims over which it has original jurisdiction, or
 (4) in exceptional circumstances, there are other compelling reasons for declining jurisdiction.

Supplemental jurisdiction codifies the case law doctrines of "pendent" and "ancillary" jurisdiction. In *United Mine Workers v. Gibbs*, the Supreme Court recognized the doctrine of pendent jurisdiction, wherein the federal court is *permitted* to entertain both federal claims and state claims in the federal forum.[135] "It is apparent that, while allowing federal courts to take supplemental jurisdiction over state law claims, Congress intended for federal courts to have the discretion to decline such jurisdiction when circumstances so warrant."[136]

Removal Procedures and Deadlines

The procedure for removing an action to federal court is found in 28 U.S.C. § 1446. Removal generally must occur within thirty days after the summons and complaint are served on the defendant or their registered agent for service of process.[137]

Venue

Venue in federal courts is authorized either by the general venue statute, or by specific statutory venue provisions found in various pieces of federal legislation.

The General Venue Statute, 28 U.S.C. § 1391

The general venue statute is found at 28 U.S.C. § 1391(b).

Subsection 1 provides that "[a] civil action may be brought in . . . (1) a judicial district in which any defendant resides, if all defendants are residents of the State in which the district is located."[138] "Residency" is defined in 28 U.S.C. § 1391(c)(2), which provides that "[f]or all venue purposes," . . . (2) an entity with the capacity to sue and be sued in its common name under applicable law, whether or not incorporated, shall be deemed to reside, if a defendant, in any judicial district in which such defendant is subject to the court's personal jurisdiction with respect to the civil action in question and, if a plaintiff, only in the judicial district in which it maintains its principal place of business. After *Goodyear*, *Daimler*,

---

135. 383 U.S. 715 (1966).

136. *Crocker v. Boren, Inc.*, 852 F. Supp. 1322, 1328 (E.D. La. 1994).

137. *See Murphy Bros., Inc. v. Michetti Pipe Stringing, Inc.*, 526 U.S. 344, 348–49 (1999); *see also Badon v. RJR Nabisco Inc.*, 224 F.3d 382, 390 n.12 (5th Cir. 2000) ("The 30-day period in no event begins to run prior to service of process on the defendant.") (citing *Murphy Bros.*, 526 U.S. at 353–55).

138. 28 U.S.C. § 1391(b)(1).

and *Tyrell*, this means that residency effectively is defined as the judicial district where a defendant is incorporated or has their principal place of business.

Subsection 2 provides that "[a] civil action may be brought in . . . (2) a judicial district in which a substantial part of the events or omissions giving rise to the claim occurred, or a substantial part of the property that is the subject of the action is situated." It is important for the complaint to specifically allege venue facts invoking this provision. Each federal complaint should contain an allegation about which judicial district is the situs where "a substantial part of the events or omissions giving rise to the claim occurred." Given the *causal* relationship necessitated by *Bristol-Myers-Squibb* for *specific* personal jurisdiction purposes, specific factual allegations giving rise to venue under subsection 2 are recommended as well. A defendant will likely file a Rule 12(b)(3) motion to dismiss for improper venue if a plaintiff fails to allege an event or omission that occurred in the venue, and which gives rise to the alleged claim.

Subsection 3 provides that "if there is no district in which [the] action may otherwise be brought" as provided in § 1391, a civil action may be brought in "any judicial district in which any defendant is subject to the court's personal jurisdiction with respect to such action." The language of 27 U.S.C. § 1391(d) regarding states with more than one judicial district is important here because it provides, "if there is no such district" where a corporation's "contacts would be sufficient to subject it to personal jurisdiction if that district were a separate State," then "the corporation shall be deemed to reside in the district within which it has the most significant contacts."

Statutory-Specific Venue Provisions

Federal statutes often include specific venue provisions that set forth where a plaintiff may file suit for alleged violations of the statute. For example, the federal ERISA statute provides that suit may be brought in the district where the plan is administered, where the breach took place, or where a defendant resides or may be found.[139]

Discretionary Venue Transfer, 28 U.S.C. § 1404(a)

"[W]ithin the federal system, when venue is laid in the wrong district, or when the plaintiff chooses an inconvenient forum, transfer rather than dismissal is ordinarily ordered if 'in the interest of justice.'"[140] "For the convenience of parties and witnesses, in the interest of justice, a district court may transfer any civil action to any other district or division where it might have been brought."[141] A defendant for whom venue is proper but inconvenient may move for a change of venue under 28 U.S.C. § 1404(a). The first inquiry in ruling on a motion to transfer under § 1404(a) is to determine whether the case could have originally

139. 29 U.S.C. § 1132(e)(2).

140. *Ritzen Group, Inc. v. Jackson Masonry, LLC*, 140 S. Ct. 582, 590, n. 3 (2020), citing 28 U.S.C. § 1404(a), 1406. *See also Atlantic Marine Const. Co., Inc. v. U.S. Dist. Court for Western Dist. Of Texas*, 571 U.S. 49, 55-56 (2013) (indicating preference for transfer under section 1404(a) rather than dismissal to enforce a forum selection clause).

141. 28 U.S.C. § 1404(a).

been brought in the transferee forum.[142] This distinguishes a transfer pursuant to § 1404(a) from a transfer pursuant to § 1406(a): "under § 1404(a) both the transferor and the transferee court have venue over the action, but it is more efficient to prosecute the action in the latter court."[143] The Eighth Circuit has held that "the statutory language reveals three general categories of factors that courts must consider when deciding a motion to transfer: (1) the convenience of the parties, (2) the convenience of the witnesses, and (3) the interests of justice."[144] This standard is "intended to place discretion in the district court to adjudicate motions for transfer according to an individualized case-by-case consideration of convenience and fairness. A motion to transfer under § 1404(a) thus calls on the district court to weigh in the balance a number of case-specific factors."[145]

Three mandamus decisions from the Fifth Circuit involving Volkswagen changed the law as it relates to a district court's discretion to deny a 1404(a) venue transfer.

First, in *In re Volkswagen* (*Volkswagen I*), the Fifth Circuit granted a petition for writ of mandamus, and compelled the district court to transfer the case from the Marshall Division of the Eastern District of Texas to the San Antonio Division of the Western District of Texas.[146] The Fifth Circuit held that the trial court abused its discretion in considering the convenience of only the parties and witnesses directly involved in the plaintiff's claims against Volkswagen. The convenience of the parties brought in as third-party defendants also should have been considered, and given that most of those witnesses lived in San Antonio, the court held that:

> "[w]hen the distance between an existing venue for trial of a matter and a proposed venue under § 1404(a) is more than 100 miles, the factor of inconvenience to witnesses increases in direct relationship to the additional distance to be traveled. Additional distance means additional travel time; additional travel time increases the probability for meal and lodging expenses; and additional travel time with overnight stays increases the time which these fact witnesses must be away from their regular employment. Furthermore, the task of scheduling fact witnesses so as to minimize the time when they are removed from their regular work or home responsibilities gets increasingly difficult and complicated when the travel time from their home or work site to the court facility is five or six hours one-way as opposed to 30 minutes or an hour."[147]

Additionally, the Fifth Circuit held that the district court reversibly erred in considering the location of counsel for the parties, holding that convenience of counsel is not a factor to be assessed in determining whether to transfer a case under § 1404(a).[148]

---

142. *Biometics, LLC. v. New Womyn, Inc.*, 112 F. Supp. 2d 869, 875 (E.D. Mo. 2000).
143. *Chrysler Credit Corp. v. Country Chrysler, Inc.*, 928 F.2d 1509, 1515 n.3 (10th Cir. 1991).
144. *Terra Int'l, Inc. v. Mississippi Chem. Corp.*, 119 F.3d 688, 691 (8th Cir.1997).
145. *Stewart Organization, Inc. v. Ricoh Corp.*, 487 U.S. 22, 29 (1988).
146. 371 F.3d 201 (5th Cir. 2004).
147. *Id.* at 204–05.
148. *Id.* at 206 (citing *In re Horseshoe Entm't*, 337 F.3d 429, 434 (5th Cir.), *cert. denied.*, 540 U.S. 1049 (2003)) (finding that the "factor of 'location of counsel' is irrelevant and improper for consideration in determining the question of transfer of venue").

Second, in *In re Volkswagen* (*Volkswagen II*), the Fifth Circuit granted en banc a petition for writ of mandamus, and it compelled the district court to transfer the case from the Marshall Division of the Eastern District of Texas to the Dallas Division of the Northern District of Texas.[149] The Fifth Circuit noted that "[w]hen the transferee forum is no more convenient than the chosen forum, the plaintiff's choice should not be disturbed. When the transferee forum is clearly more convenient, a transfer should be ordered."[150] The Court analyzed three private interest factors and one public interest factor. With respect to the private interest factor of the ease of access to sources of proof, the Court held that advances in copying technology and information storage does not render this factor superfluous.[151] The second private interest factor is the availability of compulsory process to secure the attendance of witnesses. Because court trial subpoenas are effective up to 100 miles, the Court favored transfer because the Dallas Division enjoyed "*absolute* subpoena power for both depositions and trial."[152] The third private interest factor is the cost of attendance for willing witnesses. The Court held that this factor also favored transfer, because "Dallas is approximately 155 miles from the Marshall Division."[153] Finally, as to the public interest factor of "having localized interests decided at home," the Court found the factor neutral, noting that merely because a product is available within a given jurisdiction "is insufficient to neutralize the legitimate local interest in adjudicating local disputes."[154]

Third, on rehearing en banc in *In re Volkswagen* (*Volkswagen II–en banc, on rehearing*), the Fifth Circuit held en banc and on rehearing that mandamus was "entirely appropriate to review for an abuse of discretion that clearly exceeds the bounds of judicial discretion."[155] The Court held that "Congress, however, has tempered the effects of this general venue statute by enacting the venue transfer statute, 28 U.S.C. § 1404. The underlying premise of § 1404(a) is that courts should prevent plaintiffs from abusing their privilege under § 1391 by subjecting defendants to venues that are inconvenient under the terms of § 1404(a)."[156] Finally, the Court noted that "when the transferee venue is not clearly more convenient than the venue chosen by the plaintiff, the plaintiff's choice should be respected. When the movant demonstrates that the transferee venue is clearly more convenient, however, it has shown good cause and the district court should therefore grant the transfer."[157]

Improper Venue Transfer, 28 U.S.C. § 1406

Section 1406(a) provides for the cure of defects in venue as follows: "The district court of a district in which is filed a case laying venue in the wrong *division or district* shall dismiss, or if it be in the interest of justice, transfer such case to any *district or division* in which it could

149. 506 F.3d 376 (5th Cir. 2007) (*en banc*).
150. *Id.* at 384.
151. *Id.* at 385.
152. *Id.*
153. *Id.* at 386.
154. *Id.* at 387.
155. 545 F.3d 304, 311 (5th Cir. 2008).
156. *Id.* at 313.
157. *Id.* at 315.

have been brought."[158] Subject to personal jurisdiction, a court should transfer the case to a venue that is proper under 28 U.S.C. § 1406(a) or 28 U.S.C. § 1631. The legal standard is the same under either statute: the court must transfer "if it is in the interest of justice. . . ."[159] Notably, "Section 1406(a) and Rule 12(b)(3) allow dismissal only when venue is 'wrong' or 'improper.' Whether venue is 'wrong' or 'improper' depends exclusively on whether the court in which the case was brought satisfies the requirements of federal venue laws, and those provisions say nothing about a forum-selection clause."[160]

Considerations Expressed by the JPML

The JPML is appointed by the Chief Justice of the U.S. Supreme Court, and its task is to decide whether to consolidate cases filed across the nation into a single MDL proceeding for purposes of pretrial adjudication, and which the U.S. District Court should be assigned to handle such an MDL.[161] Presently in 2020, the JMPL is chaired by Hon. Karen K. Caldwell, and includes Hon. Ellen Segal Huvelle, Hon. Catherine D. Perry, Hon. Matthew F. Kennelly, Hon. R. David Proctor, Hon. Nathaniel M. Gorton, and Hon. David C. Norton.[162] This lively panel has consistently set forth ten factors that guide its jurisprudence as to where to assign an MDL.

The Most Geographically Central Forum

At least six times in the last three years, the JPML has stated that a geographically central forum is an appropriate consideration in deciding where an MDL should be assigned.[163]

Location of Counsel's Offices

On multiple occasions, the JPML has cited the location of the offices of counsel in the litigation as a factor to support assignment of an MDL.[164]

---

158. 28 U.S.C. § 1406(a) (emphasis added); *see Sundell v. Cisco Systems, Inc.*, No. 96-41191, 111 F.3d 892, 1997 WL 156824, at *1 (5th Cir. 1997) (unpublished).

159. 28 U.S.C. § 1406(a); § 1631.

160. *Atlantic Marine Constr'n Co. v. U.S. Dist. Court for W. Dist. of Tex.*, 571 U.S. 49, 55 (2013).

161. 28 U.S.C. § 1407.

162. *Panel Judges*, U.S. Judicial Panel on Multidistrict Litigation, https://www.jpml.uscourts.gov/content/panel-judges (last visited Mar. 14, 2020).

163. *See In re Local TV Advertising Antitrust Litigation*, 338 F. Supp. 3d 1341, 1343 (J.P.M.L. 2018) ("provides a geographically central and convenient location for the parties and witnesses"); *In re Davol, Inc./C.R. Bard, Inc., Polypropylene Hernia Mesh Prods. Liab. Litig.*, 316 F. Supp. 3d 1380, 1381 (J.P.M.L. 2018) ("It is centrally located geographically, making it a convenient forum for this nationwide litigation."); *In re National Prescription Opiate Litigation*, 290 F. Supp. 3d 1375, 1379 (J.P.M.L. 2017) ("presents a geographically central and accessible forum"); *In re Epipen (Epinephrine Injection, USP) Marketing, Sales Practices and Antitrust Litig.*, 268 F. Supp. 3d 1356, 1360 (J.P.M.L. 2017) ("This district presents a geographically central forum for this nationwide litigation."); *In re Dollar General Corp. Motor Oil Marketing and Sales Practices Litig.*, 190 F. Supp. 3d 1361, 1363 (J.P.M.L. 2016) ("provides a geographically central forum for this litigation that is both convenient and accessible to the parties and witnesses."); *In re Genentech Herceptin (Trastuzumab) Marketing and Sales Practices Litig.*, 178 F. Supp. 3d 1374, 1376 (J.P.M.L. 2016) ("provides a geographically central forum.").

164. *See In re Health Management Associates, Inc. v. Qui Tam Litig. (No. II)*, 11 F. Supp. 3d 1346, 1348 (J.P.M.L. 2014) ("Counsel for both the Government and the HMA defendants are located there . . . "); *In re Yarn Processing Patent Validity Litig.*, 341 F. Supp. 376, 389 (J.P.M.L. 1972); *In re Embro Patent Infringement Litig.*, 328 F. Supp. 507, 508 (J.P.M.L. 1971).

Lack of Docket Congestion

When assigning an MDL to a judicial district with no MDL pending, the JPML cites that transferee court as one that "is not burdened by many MDLs and has the capacity and resources to successfully guide this litigation."[165]

Convenience of the Parties and Witnesses

The JPML has twice held that it looks to "the overall convenience of the parties and witnesses, not just those of a single plaintiff or defendant in isolation."[166] However, whether a transferee district is where the defendant is "essentially at home" for personal jurisdiction purposes is irrelevant; the JPML has made clear that "difficulty in establishing personal jurisdiction over a given defendant or defendants generally is not a factor that we consider in our Section 1407 analysis,"[167] because "the power of the Panel and the courts to effectuate a transfer under § 1407 is not vitiated by the transferor court's lack of personal jurisdiction over a defendant."[168] In this regard, the location of the defendant's witnesses is not singularly important because the panel looks to "the overall convenience of the parties and witnesses, not just those of a single plaintiff or defendant in isolation."[169]

Location of Relevant Documents

When documents were stored and housed in paper warehouses, this panel correctly made the location of the documents an important factor to consider.[170] The Panel has held that when there are "relatively few documents and witnesses relevant . . ." to the case, transfer elsewhere is appropriate.[171]

Prior MDL Experience

The JPML continues to err on the side of assignment of MDLs to federal judges with prior MDL experience, having sent more than half of the MDLs assigned over the past four years to judges who have overseen a prior MDL.[172]

---

165. *In re Simply Orange Juice Marketing and Sales Practices Litig.*, 867 F. Supp. 2d 1344, 1345–46 (J.P.M.L. 2012) (permitting "the Panel to assign the litigation to a less-utilized district with an experienced judge who is not presently overseeing a multidistrict litigation"); *In re E.I. Du Pont de Nemours & Co. C-8 Personal Injury Litig.*, 939 F. Supp. 2d 1374 (J.P.M.L. 2013).

166. *In re Domestic Drywall Antitrust Litig.*, MDL No. 2437, 2018 WL 7153387, at *2 (J.P.M.L. 2018); *In re Watson Fentanyl Patch Prods. Liab. Litig.*, 883 F. Supp. 2d 1350, 1351–52 (J.P.M.L. 2012).

167. *In re RAH Color Technologies LLC Patent Litig.*, 347 F. Supp. 3d 1359, 1359 & n.5 (J.P.M.L. 2018) (citing *In re Highway Accident Near Rockville, Conn. on Dec. 30, 1972*, 388 F. Supp. 574, 576 (J.P.M.L. 1975)).

168. *In re Sugar Industry Antitrust Litig.*, 472 F. Supp. 1018, 1027 & n.11 (J.P.M.L. 1977) (citing *In re Library Editions of Children's Books*, 299 F. Supp. 1139, 1142 (J.P.M.L. 1969); *In re Gypsum Wallboard*, 302 F. Supp. 794, 794 (J.P.M.L. 1969) (citing *In re Library Editions*, 299 F. Supp. 1139, 1142).

169. *In re Domestic Drywall*, 2018 WL 7153387, at *2 (citing *In re Watson*, 883 F. Supp. 2d 1350, 1352).

170. *See In re Air Crash Disaster at Stapleton Airport, Denver, Colorado, on November 15, 1987*, 683 F. Supp. 266, 267 (J.P.M.L. 1988) (transferring to location of the air crash because pertinent . . . documents may be found there."); *In re Air Crash Disaster at Las Vegas, Nev. on Oct. 8, 1968*, 336 F. Supp. 414, 414 (J.P.M.L. 1972) (same).

171. *In re Helicopter Crash in Germany on Sept. 26, 1975*, 443 F. Supp. 447, 450 (J.P.M.L. 1978).

172. *In re Valsartan N-Nitrosodimethylamine (NDMA) Contamination Prods. Liab. Litig.*, 363 F. Supp. 3d 1378, 1382 (J.P.M.L. 2019) ("Judge Robert B. Kugler is an experienced transferee judge with the willingness and ability to manage this litigation."); *In re Ranbaxy Generic Drug Application Antitrust Litig.*, 355 F. Supp. 3d 1382, 1383 (J.P.M.L. 2019)

Prior Litigation Activity by Proposed Transferee Judge

The JPML has assigned MDLs to judges already taking steps to consolidate actions before them.[173] In this regard, a judge's familiarity with a piece of litigation "compels the selection of [that Court] as the only practical transferee forum. . . ."[174] Furthermore, a judge with prior experience with the subject matter of the litigation being transferred is met with favor by the JPML.[175]

("By selecting Judge Nathaniel M. Gorton to preside over this litigation, we are choosing a jurist well-versed in the nuances of complex and multidistrict litigation to steer this matter on a prudent course."); *In re RAH Color Technologies*, 347 F. Supp. 3d at 1359 ("Judge Susan Yvonne Illston is an experienced transferee judge with the ability and willingness to manage this litigation efficiently. We are confident she will steer this matter on a prudent course."); *In re Diisocyanates Antitrust Litig.*, 341 F. Supp. 3d 1376 (J.P.M.L. 2018) ("Judge Donetta W. Ambrose is an experienced transferee judge . . . "); *In re Zimmer M/L Taper Hip Prosthesis or M/L Taper Hip Prosthesis with Kinectiv Technology and VerSys Femoral Head Prods. Liab. Litig.*, 340 F. Supp. 3d 1379, 1381 (J.P.M.L. 2018) ("Judge Paul A. Crotty, to whom we assign the litigation, is . . . an experienced transferee judge, having previously handled three other MDLs."); *In re FedLoan Student Loan Servicing Litig.*, 340 F. Supp. 3d 1377, 1378 (J.P.M.L. 2018) ("Judge C. Darnell Jones, II, an experienced transferee judge . . ."); *In re Zostavax (Zoster Vaccine Live) Prods. Liab. Litig.*, 330 F. Supp. 3d 1378 (J.P.M.L. 2018) ("Judge Harvey Bartle III presides over all related actions in this district, and is familiar with the claims and issues. He is an experienced transferee judge . . ."); *In re Ry. Industry Employee No-Poach Antitrust Litig.*, 326 F. Supp. 3d 1381 (J.P.M.L. 2018) ("Judge Joy Flowers Conti is an experienced transferee judge . . ."); *In re Facebook, Inc. v. Consumer Privacy User Profile Litig.*, 325 F. Supp. 3d 1362 (J.P.M.L. 2018) ("Judge Vince Chhabria, who is presiding over almost half the pending actions, is an experienced transferee judge . . ."); *In re Apple Inc. Device Performance Litig.*, 291 F. Supp. 3d 1371 (J.P.M.L. 2018) ("All but one of the related actions pending in this district are assigned to the Honorable Edward J. Davila, a jurist with prior MDL experience . . ."); *In re Restasis (Cyclosporine Ophthalmic Emulsion) Antitrust Litig.*, 289 F. Supp. 2d 1332, 1334 (J.P.M.L. 2018) (MDL assigned "to the Honorable Nina Gershon, an able jurist with prior MDL experience."); *In re National Prescription Opiate*, 290 F. Supp. 3d 1375, 1379 ("Judge Polster's previous MDL experience, particularly MDL No. 1909—In re Gadolinium Contrast Dyes Products Liability Litigation, which involved several hundred cases, has provided him valuable insight into the management of complex, multidistrict litigation."); *In re Yahoo! Inc. Customer Data Security Breach Litigation*, 223 F. Supp. 3d 1353 (J.P.M.L. 2016) ("Judge Lucy H. Koh, to whom we assign this litigation, is an experienced transferee judge . . ."); *In re Mobile Telecommunications Technologies, LLC Patent Litig.*, 222 F. Supp. 3d 1337, 1338 (J.P.M.L. 2016) ("Judge Stark is an experienced transferee judge who is well-versed in complex and multiparty patent litigation."); *In re Bair Hugger Forced Air Warming Devices Prods. Liab. Litig.*, 148 F. Supp. 3d 1383 (J.P.M.L. 2015) ("The Honorable Joan N. Ericksen, to whom we assign this litigation, is a veteran jurist with previous MDL experience."); *In re Power Morcellator Prods. Liab. Litig.*, 140 F. Supp. 3d 1351, 1354 (J.P.M.L. 2015) ("Furthermore, centralization in this district allows us to assign the litigation to a skilled and efficient jurist with a wealth of MDL experience."); *In re Fluoroquinolone Prods. Liab. Litig.*, 122 F. Supp. 3d 1378 (J.P.M.L. 2015) ("Selection of the District of Minnesota also enables us to assign this litigation to the Honorable John R. Tunheim. Judge Tunheim is an experienced transferee judge familiar with the scientific and regulatory background of Levaquin in his capacity as transferee judge for a separate Levaquin MDL concerning tendon rupture injuries. *See* MDL No. 1943, *In re Levaquin Products Liability Litig*. In our view, Judge Tunheim's experience in overseeing MDL No. 1943 will benefit the parties and facilitate the just and efficient conduct of this litigation."); *In re Disposable Contact Lens Antitrust Litig.*, 109 F. Supp. 3d 1369, 1371 (J.P.M.L. 2015) (". . . we have chosen a jurist who is familiar with the contact lens industry by virtue of his experience presiding over a previous MDL involving allegations of anti-competitive conduct in that industry").

173. *See In re Levaquin Prods. Liab. Litig.*, 560 F. Supp. 2d 1384, 1385 (J.P.M.L. 2008) ("We are persuaded that the District of Minnesota is an appropriate transferee forum for this litigation. Eight actions, including the first-filed action, are pending there . . . . [A]ctions pending in that district have been related before Judge John R. Tunheim, who has familiarized himself with the litigation."). *See also In re Apple Inc.*, 291 F. Supp. 3d at 1372 (assigning MDL to a judge "who already has taken steps to coordinate the actions before him . . . .").

174. *In re Yarn Processing*, 341 F. Supp. at 389 (Weinfeld, J., dissenting).

175. *In re Fluoroquinolone*, 122 F. Supp. 3d at 1378, 1381 (J.P.M.L. 2015) ("Judge Tunheim is an experienced transferee judge familiar with the scientific and regulatory background of Levaquin in his capacity as transferee judge for a separate Levaquin MDL concerning tendon rupture injuries."). *See also In re Valsartan*, 363 F. Supp. 3d at 1382–83 (transferring MDL to Judge Kugler, with prior experience handling an MDL concerning the same class of pharmaceutical).

The Parties' First or Second Choice

In numerous JPML orders over the course of the past four years, the JPML has shown deference to the first or second choices of the litigants before it.[176]

Where Early Plaintiffs Filed Suit

The JPML has cited where the plaintiffs have filed suit on a number of occasions.[177] However, in nationwide litigation, the Panel has cautioned that where the plaintiffs filed suit is not significant, twice acknowledging that "[b]ecause potential plaintiffs and putative class members will reside in every corner of the country and defendants are located in several states, the location of the currently filed cases is not a particularly significant factor in our decision."[178]

Diversity and Willingness to Serve

Finally, diversity has arrived on the federal bench, with 428 women, 215 African-American, 125 Hispanic, 41 Asian-American, 3 Pacific Islander, and 3 Native American article III judges presently serving. This has resulted in the federal bench beginning to look like modern America instead of a judicial oligarchy populated only by white men.

In 2014, the Duke Law Center released its *MDL Standards and Best Practices*, which included Best Practice 3C, urging federal judges to appoint lawyers "to leadership positions, . . . keeping in mind the benefits of diversity of experience, skills and backgrounds." Likewise, the JPML has taken steps to appoint more women and minority jurists to lead various MDL litigations. Of course, before formally being appointed by the JPML, individual federal judges are consulted and must state their willingness to serve.[179]

Conclusion

Supreme Court cases in the 1990s dramatically confined the law of personal jurisdiction to states where the defendant is "essentially at home" by virtue of being the state of their principal place of business or state of incorporation, and to states where a defendant

176. *See In re Valsartan*, 363 F. Supp. 3d at 1382 ("Nearly all responding parties support, or do not oppose, the District of New Jersey as their first or second choice."); *In re Aftermarket Filters Antitrust Litig.*, 572 F. Supp. 2d 1373, 1374 (J.P.M.L. 2018) (". . . plaintiffs in numerous actions pending in this district and elsewhere support the [district] as their first or second choice . . ."); *In re Chicago Board Options Exchange Volatility Index Manipulation Antitrust Litig.*, 325 F. Supp. 3d 1374, 1376 (J.P.M.L. 2018) (". . . this district is the first choice of plaintiffs in ten actions and the second choice of plaintiffs in two [other] actions."); *In re Walgreens Herbal Supplements Marketing and Sales Practices Litig.*, 109 F. Supp. 3d 1373 (J.P.M.L. 2015) ("Responding plaintiffs in over 20 actions also support this district as their first or second choice."); *In re Auto Body Shop Antitrust Litig.*, 37 F. Supp. 3d 1388, 1390 (J.P.M.L. 2014) ("The overwhelming majority of responding defendants support this district as their first or second choice.").

177. *In re Marriott Int'l, Inc. Customer Data Security Breach Litig.*, 363 F. Supp. 3d 1372, 1375 (J.P.M.L. 2019) ("Defendants and the vast majority of responding plaintiffs support selection of this district, and far more actions are pending there than in any other district."); *In re E.I. Du Pont de Nemours*, 939 F. Supp. 2d at 1374, 1375 ("Four of the six water districts allegedly contaminated by C-8 are in the Southern District of Ohio, as are the majority of potential plaintiffs."); *In re Air Crash Disaster Near Saigon, South Vietnam, on Apr. 4, 1975*, 404 F. Supp. 478, 480 (J.P.M.L. 1975) ("[T]he claims of 83 of the 155 decedents are presently before the court in the District of Columbia.").

178. *In re Darvocet, Darvon and Propoxyphene Prods. Liab. Litig.*, 780 F. Supp. 2d 1379 (J.P.M.L. 2011); *In re BP PLC Sec. Litig.*, 734 F. Supp. 2d 1376, 1379 (J.P.M.L. 2010).

179. *In re Valsartan*, 363 F. Supp. 3d at 1382 (assigning the MDL to a judge "with the willingness to serve").

purposefully avails themselves of a state via substantial contacts that are causally related to the damages claimed by the plaintiff. Federal appellate courts likewise have restricted the previously unvarnished discretion of district courts to adjudicate venue matters. As a consequence, jurisdiction and venue options have narrowed from plaintiff-based choices to defendant-based locales. Furthermore, the continued statutory enlargement of federal court jurisdiction has resulted in the requirement that more cases be filed in federal court, where almost half of them will be consolidated into MDL proceedings that are usually adjudicated on the defendant's home turf.

2

Jurisdiction and Venue: Forum Shopping and Forum Swapping

The Defense Perspective

There are many variables that go into making a winning case: good facts, a good client, good law, and skilled lawyers. With that said, a favorable jury and good judge are always critical factors. From a defense perspective, that is why evaluating and, if appropriate, challenging a plaintiff's forum selection involves important strategic considerations. This is because jurisdiction and venue ultimately dictate the jury pool, the procedural rules, the judge and, frequently, the applicable law.

The term "forum shopping" carries a negative connotation in many circles—despite the absence of a single consensus "definition."[1] There are, no doubt, situations where forum shopping is abusive, but procedural mechanisms are available to address those instances.[2] On the other hand, it is without doubt that plaintiff's lawyers and defense lawyers should both *always* seek a forum most favorable to their client and their case. This is basic stuff for every zealous advocate.

Although the plaintiff has an advantage by initially selecting the venue of the case, this selection is not etched in stone. Every defense lawyer must first assess whether there are multiple "proper" venues and, if so, evaluate whether to accept or reject the plaintiff's choice. There are many occasions when no challenge is legally justified and the plaintiff's choice stands. In other instances, after weighing relevant factors, the defense lawyer may conclude that the plaintiff's choice is appropriate, if not beneficial to the defense. In others,

1. *See generally* Markus A. Petsche, *What's Wrong with Forum Shopping? An Attempt to Identify and Assess the Real Issues of a Controversial Practice*, 45 Int'l Law. 1005 (2011) (discussing various scholarly opinions and definitions of forum shopping, and analyzing both the adverse effects and the advantages of forum shopping).

2. *See, e.g.*, 28 United States Code Annotated (U.S.C.A.) § 1404 (motion to transfer venue); *Piper Aircraft Co. v. Reyno*, 454 U.S. 235, 102 S.Ct. 252, 70 L.Ed.2d 419 (1981) (discussing standards of motion to dismiss on forum non conveniens).

the defense lawyer may seek an immediate exit or escape. This is certainly the case in potentially hostile venues. In any event, defense lawyers must assume that the plaintiff chose the venue with his own self-interest in mind; thus, it is axiomatic that the defense must undertake due diligence and evaluate *why* the plaintiff selected that venue and whether a challenge is warranted.

If legitimate opportunities arise for defense counsel to switch or transfer a case to more favorable forums, they should do so. Convenience of the parties is important, but other factors—procedure, jury, judge, law—often provide the defining edge in most cases. Once a lawsuit is filed and jurisdiction and venue are initially lodged, the defense lawyer must stop and ask several basic questions: Why is the lawsuit filed in this specific forum? Is the defendant subject to personal jurisdiction in this particular forum? Is the case removable and, if so, should the case be removed? Is the venue proper and, if not, should it be challenged? Should the case be transferred to a centralized MDL proceeding? The answers to these questions lead to better venue decisions and strategies.

There are a variety of procedural devices available to challenge a plaintiff's jurisdiction and venue choice: challenges to personal jurisdiction; removal to federal court; transfers *within* a forum state based on venue statutes within that state; inter-district transfers among federal courts based on forum non conveniens under 28 U.S.C. § 1404(a), and multi-district transfers under 28 U.S.C. § 1407. This chapter explores these and other procedural tools.

The First Question: Jurisdiction

Depending on the nature and type of case, the plaintiff's bar is confronting new difficulties when selecting the jurisdiction where a case is filed. Although courts frequently defer to plaintiffs on venue choices, a litany of U.S. Supreme Court decisions in the last ten years draw a clear line on where corporate defendants can be sued and where plaintiffs can bring suit. It is now more difficult to sue a corporate defendant in any forum other than its state of incorporation or principal place of business.[3] It is also more difficult for plaintiffs to sue in a forum unrelated to where the causes of action arose.[4] The pendulum is clearly swinging in favor of defendants on jurisdictional issues, and all defense lawyers should take note. One of the first questions a defense lawyer must ask is whether his or her client is subject to personal jurisdiction in the forum state where the case is first filed. Failure to make this evaluation may waive important jurisdictional rights.

All states provide procedures for challenging personal jurisdiction as one of the preliminary pleas or motions filed with the court. Pursuant to Fed. R. Civ. P. 12(b)(2), a plea or motion to challenge personal jurisdiction must be filed as a first plea in the due order of pleadings.[5]

3. *See Daimler AG v. Bauman*, 571 U.S. 117, 137, 134 S. Ct. 746, 760 (2014) (holding that the principal place of incorporation and the principal place of business are paradigm bases for general jurisdiction).

4. *See e.g., Bristol-Myers Squibb Co. v. Superior Court of California*, San Francisco City, 137 S. Ct. 1773 (2017).

5. "A motion asserting any of these defenses must be made before pleading if a responsive pleading is allowed." FED. R. CIV. P. 12(b).

Most states have adopted similar procedural rules. In fact, 35 states have adopted the federal rules, including Rule 12(b)(2),[6] which governs jurisdictional challenges.

Whether a defendant is subject to personal jurisdiction is a matter of constitutional importance. No defendant is subject to personal jurisdiction in a state court or federal court unless that defendant engaged in activities supporting specific jurisdiction or general jurisdiction within the state where the court is physically located. Within the last several years, the U.S. Supreme Court has issued several decisions profoundly impacting this jurisdictional analysis—tipping the scales in favor of nonresident corporate defendants. Every plaintiff's lawyer and defense lawyer should be aware of these decisions when either suing or representing a nonresident defendant. Every defense lawyer representing a nonresident defendant must make a preliminary inquiry whether either general or specific jurisdiction exists. Arguably, this represents a minimum standard of care for defense lawyers. Absent specific jurisdiction, where a nonresident's direct activities within a forum state give rise to the cause of action, the exercise of general jurisdiction over nonresident corporations is problematic. Starting in 2011, the U.S. Supreme Court began clarifying the jurisprudence of personal jurisdiction, making it more difficult for a plaintiff to maintain personal jurisdiction in several situations. These clarified principles are summarized, as follows:

- Exercise of personal jurisdiction over a foreign corporate defendant based on "general jurisdiction" is unlikely unless the state of incorporation or principal place of business of the corporate defendant is located in the forum state; the defendant must be "essentially at home" in the forum state.[7]
- Exercise of general jurisdiction based on a "stream of commerce" theory is no longer viable; that is, even if a nonresident corporate defendant targets distribution of their products into a forum state, this targeting may be insufficient to support general jurisdiction.[8]
- To support personal jurisdiction, the foreign defendant's conduct must occur within the forum state itself, and not merely with residents who reside within the forum, meaning that "the plaintiff cannot be the only link between the defendant and the forum."[9]
- There must be a logical connection between the forum state and the specific claims at issue; stated differently, nonresident plaintiffs may not invoke the jurisdiction of a specific forum unless the plaintiff's claims arise within that forum.[10]

---

6. *See Rules of Civil Procedure*, USLegal.com, https://civilprocedure.uslegal.com/rules-of-civil-procedure/ (last visited Nov. 20, 2019).

7. *Daimler AG v. Bauman*, 571 U.S. 117, 134 S. Ct. 746 (2014).

8. *Goodyear*, 564 U.S. 915(211).

9. *Walden*, 571 U.S. 277(2014).

10. *See Walden*, 571 U.S. 277, 284 ("For a State to exercise jurisdiction consistent with due process, the defendant's suit-related conduct must create a substantial connection with the forum State."), *Bristol-Myers Squibb Co. v. Superior Court of California, San Francisco Cty.*, 137 S. Ct. 1773, 1776 (2017) ("What is needed is a connection between the forum and the specific claims at issue.").

Important Venue Considerations and Factors

Assuming personal jurisdiction exists, every defense lawyer must next consider whether to seek a venue transfer or removal to federal court. Here are some key considerations:

- The demographic characteristics of the expected jury pool.
- The reputation of the state court and judge, and whether the judge has published opinions relevant to the case, or whether the appellate courts have handled appeals of similar cases from that judge's court.
- The reputation of the appellate courts of the forum state and whether they have published favorable or unfavorable opinions regarding the issues in the case.
- The frequency of large plaintiff's verdicts in the particular venue, and the types of cases in which any such verdicts have been rendered.
- Local discovery procedures and the reputation of the trial judge in matters related to the scope of discovery.
- Unique procedural rules relating to dispositive motions and motions relating to experts.
- Substantive differences in relevant legal principles and whether choice of law analysis will impact this analysis.
- Docket speed—the speed by which the case will be pushed to trial.

After completing this inquiry, a similar investigation should be conducted to evaluate the potential transferee court or the potential federal court in the event removal is pursued. Then, the pros and cons of the plaintiff's selected forum can be weighed against potential alternatives. This involves a balancing test between competing venues.

The Jury Pool Is Critical

The characteristics of the likely jury pool are *always* important. Some venues are well known as "plaintiffs' havens." These include jurisdictions where jury verdicts are predictably higher than in other venues. Many factors potentially account for these differences—including plaintiff-friendly legislation or courts. But, jury demographics are also significant factors: urbanization, education levels, income levels, cultural differences, and social stratification. At least some jury research is needed to better understand local demographics and how these demographic characteristics might impact the trial and jury verdict. This is true for plaintiff's and defense counsel.

Skilled plaintiff's lawyers know what type of jury they want in their cases. In product liability, catastrophic injury, wrongful death, or toxic tort cases, the prototypical plaintiff juror likely holds negative views of the business, finance, and corporate world. Conversely, the prototypical defense juror is more likely conservative or business-oriented, including individuals who profess belief in principles of self-reliance and personal responsibility. People's attitudes are molded by their personal experiences and backgrounds, including education, access to resources, and job opportunities. A chosen venue, therefore, may have more plaintiff-oriented jurors than defense-oriented jurors or vice versa. This is an important variable that is part of every venue calculus.

Although demographic characteristics of residents in a defined geographic area may change slowly over time, the composition of the local judiciary, including appellate courts, may change more swiftly. This means that certain jurisdictions that were perceived as "plaintiffs' havens" several years ago may have shifted to more defense-oriented venues—primarily due to substantive changes in the law, such as tort reform, or a more conservative judiciary. Many states have enacted tort reform legislation, and this in turn has impacted the frequency of large plaintiff's verdicts.[11]

Nevertheless, there should be no doubt that competent plaintiffs' counsel already know their preferred "havens." These venues are readily identified by simple research on the Internet, and are often found in large urban areas. According to the American Tort Reform Foundation, the "plaintiffs' havens" for 2018–2019, in ranked order, were California; Florida; New York City; St. Louis; Louisiana; Philadelphia; New Jersey; St. Clair and Madison Counties; the Twin Cities, Minnesota; and Oklahoma.[12] Some of these venues have been considered plaintiffs' havens historically, such as California or Louisiana. Other locations, such as New Jersey[13] and the Twin Cities[14] earned this recognition more recently.

Experienced plaintiff's counsel also nurture localized reputations in their backyards. It is not uncommon for successful plaintiff's lawyers to file their cases within particular regions because of preexisting relationships with local courts and what they perceive to be favorable attributes of the local jury pool. Therefore, every defense lawyer should pause and determine whether a particular plaintiff's lawyer is well-known within a particular venue, suggesting either strong relationships with the judiciary, personal name recognition with potential jurors, or both.

Because lawyers and judges interact routinely, particularly in more rural venues, relationships are formed based on familiarity. This is simple human nature. This is certainly a legitimate consideration for any competent plaintiff's lawyer in making a venue choice. It is also a factor that defense lawyers should consider when deciding whether to remove or not remove a case from state to federal court. An old adage captures this truism: "A good lawyer knows the law. A great lawyer knows the judge." In this vein, there are "great" lawyers on both sides of the counsel table.

---

11. One of the most recognizable areas where tort reform has had an impact is medical malpractice. Approximately thirty-three states have enacted various levels of caps on damages in medical malpractice lawsuits. A list of states that have enacted some type of tort reform, and a description of the reforms, can be found at the website for the American Tort Reform Association. *How States Perform*, American Tort Reform Association, https://www.atra.org/ (last visited Nov. 20, 2019).

12. *Judicial Hellholes*, American Tort Reform Foundation, https://www.judicialhellholes.org/ (last visited Nov. 20, 2019).

13. In 2018, New Jersey legislature passed the Diane B. Allen Equal Pay Act, which is considered the most expansive among equal pay laws in the country, even compared to some of the most progressive states, such as California and Massachusetts. *Judicial Hellholes—New Jersey Legislature*, American Tort Reform Foundation, https://www.judicialhellholes.org/2018-2019/new-jersey-legislature/ (last visited Nov. 20, 2019).

14. In 2018, several Minnesota courts handed down large plaintiff's verdicts that were affected by, and arguably the result of plaintiff-friendly pretrial rulings by the judiciary. Notably, in *Kowalewski v. BNSF Ry. Co.*, Court File No. 27-CV-17-145, Fourth Judicial District of Hennepin County, Minnesota, the trial court imposed harsh discovery sanctions and struck the defendant's liability and causation defenses, ultimately leading to a $15 million plaintiff's verdict. *Judicial Hellholes—Twin Cities, Minnesota*, American Tort Reform Foundation, https://www.judicialhellholes.org/2018-2019/twin-cities-minnesota/ (last visited Nov. 20, 2019).

Defining the Trial Court's Reputation

All courts have reputations—some good, and some not so good. Some courts are perceived as plaintiff-friendly; others are seen as defense-friendly. Some judges make important pretrial rulings quickly and decisively; others may procrastinate and delay. Some judges are students of the law; some rule by the seat of their pants. Certainly, all trial lawyers—on both sides of the bar—should research and identify whether a particular judge has a unique reputation one way or the other. This should be done by the plaintiff's lawyer before the case is filed. This should be done by the defense lawyer when making a decision whether to challenge venue or seek removal.[15]

One important variable to consider always is whether the trial court has published favorable or unfavorable opinions relevant to the case; the importance of this information is self-evident. It is an easy task to locate this type of background information with simple computer searches on Westlaw or LexisNexis. Another simple inquiry is whether the trial court is frequently reversed and, if so, how frequently and in what types of cases. Is the particular judge routinely challenged in mandamus actions? Again, simple online searches can uncover published opinions that might reflect tendencies to grant dispositive motions or strike experts. No fully informed decision is possible without making these types of basic inquiries.

Many state court jurisdictions provide for popular elections of trial judges. A 2019 study confirms that twenty-three states conduct either partisan or nonpartisan elections.[16] Other states appoint trial judges for defined terms and, upon expiration of these terms, the trial judge stands for a "retention" election.[17] Other jurisdictions appoint judges through a "merit" process. Thus, a key question is whether the chosen forum uses popular elections, and whether local, partisan politics might impact the case.

A judge who stands for reelection may be more inclined to "split the baby" in difficult cases—they might not want to alienate certain lawyers. A judge who stands for reelection also may be less inclined to grant dispositive motions if the responding party (or lawyer) is active in local politics. On the other hand, an appointed judge—federal or state—may perceive less political risk associated with dispositive decisions and may be more inclined to grant dispositive relief to one side or the other. If a judge stands for popular election, the defense lawyer should research whether that particular judge receives political donations and, if so, from whom.

Some litigants (mostly defense counsel) typically perceive the federal bench as more disciplined than state courts. Although this may be a gross mischaracterization, there is a general tendency among defense counsel to blindly seek removal to federal court whenever possible. However, a word of caution is needed. Defense lawyers should always consider whether removal is *jumping from the frying pan into the fire*. Defense lawyers should always

---

15. Some jurisdictions, like Texas, publish annual bar polls rating trial judges. This is an important information service to access when making venue challenge decisions.

16. *Selection of Judges*, USLegal.com, https://courts.uslegal.com/selection-of-judges (last visited Nov. 20, 2019).

17. *Id.*

conduct background research on the potential federal judge as part of the removal decision. This may not be possible in federal districts with multiple courts that have multiple judges. But, if possible, a minimum inquiry should seek basic information:

- Is the court's calendar congested?
- Can the plaintiff obtain an accelerated trial setting?
- Has the federal judge(s) published opinions relevant to the case which are favorable or unfavorable?
- Are there published circuit court opinions favorable or unfavorable to the case?
- Does the federal court have a reputation of making timely rulings, or are rulings significantly delayed?
- Are there unique procedural rules for particular federal judges?

Local Procedures and Remedies

Procedural rules, some of which may be uniquely important to a case, undoubtedly will differ from jurisdiction to jurisdiction. The same is true for available remedies. By way of example, some states allow for the recovery of punitive damages, while others do not. The burden of proof on punitive damages also may differ from jurisdiction to jurisdiction. Some jurisdictions require only "preponderance of the evidence"; others require "clear and convincing" proof, and others do not allow them at all.[18] Similarly, many states have adopted the so-called *Daubert* standard to determine whether expert testimony is admissible; however, some states still use a different standard, the so-called *Frye* test.[19] By way of even further example, the recovery of attorneys' fees may differ from jurisdiction to jurisdiction. Some states do not allow recovery of fees even for successful plaintiffs.[20]

Thus, there are a variety of procedural and substantive areas of law that may differ from one forum to another. Subject to applicable choice of law principles, the defense lawyer should determine whether these differences are relevant. Any competent plaintiff's lawyer will evaluate these differences before filing the case. Any competent defense

---

18. *E.g., Bud Wolf Chevrolet, Inc. v. Robertson*, 519 N.E.2d 135 (Ind. 1988) (in Indiana, applying clear and convincing standard to punitive damages), *Whitaker v. Taylor*, 99 Conn.App. 719, 735, 916 A.2d 834 (2007) (in Connecticut, applying the preponderance of evidence standard to punitive damages), *Distinctive Printing & Packaging Co. v. Cox*, 443 N.W.2d 566, 574 (Neb. 1989) (in Nebraska, punitive damages are not allowed pursuant to Neb. Const. art. VII, § 5).

19. *See generally Frye v. United States*, 293 F. 1013 (D.C. Cir. 1923). Seven states still apply the *Frye* test; another four states still apply either a modified version of *Frye* or apply it in certain situations: Infra, Chapter 14, p. 221.

20. In New York, generally, a litigant is "not . . . allow[ed] . . . to recover damages for the amounts expended in the successful prosecution or defense of its rights." *Mighty Midgets, Inc. v. Centennial*, 47 N.Y.2d 12, 21-22, 389 N.E.2d 1080, 416 N.Y.S.2d 559 (N.Y. 1979); *see also Alyeska Pipeline Serv. Co. v. Wilderness Soc'y*, 421 U.S. 240, 247 (1975) ("In the United States, the prevailing litigant is ordinarily not entitled to collect a reasonable attorneys' fee from the loser."). Therefore, the right to recover attorneys' fees "must be statutory or contractual." *Greco v. GSL Enters., Inc.*, 137 Misc.2d 714, 715, 521 N.Y.S.2d 994 (N.Y. City Civ. Ct. 1987); *see also Hooper Assocs., Ltd. v. AGS Computers, Inc.*, 74 N.Y.2d 487, 491 (N.Y. 1989) (an award of attorneys' fees to the prevailing party in litigation must be "authorized by agreement between the parties, statute or court rule").

lawyer should do the same when deciding whether to accept or reject the plaintiff's forum choice. The ultimate conclusions also should consider choice of law principles.[21]

Docket Speed

The speed with which a plaintiff can push his or her case to trial is also important. Successful plaintiff's lawyers typically are aggressive and seek early trial settings. This puts settlement pressure on defendants. Thus, a specific venue may be particularly appealing to a plaintiff's lawyer because of its reputation as a fast-moving docket, or "rocket docket."[22] There also are jurisdictions that impose guidelines on the judiciary on how quickly cases should move from filing to verdict. Some jurisdictions require judges to report case closures on a routine basis, and judges are evaluated by using this criterion.[23] Other judges have established reputations for moving cases quickly. One former U.S. District Judge in the Western District of Texas prided himself on scheduling trials within a few months of case inception. Motions for continuances were denied routinely.

Discovery

Another venue consideration focuses on the discovery rules and procedures of a particular forum. Some states allow broad written discovery; others may limit discovery. There also are differences in how experts are designated and disclosed, and whether experts are, in fact, subject to deposition. Some states provide that expert opinions are identified via interrogatories only.[24] Particular judges within a selected forum also may have differing reputations about their philosophical approaches to discovery—open discovery versus restricted discovery. Likewise, federal courts impose specific limitations on the number of depositions and the duration of depositions. Some state jurisdictions impose more lenient restrictions or no such restrictions.[25]

---

21. By way of example, the author was involved in a case in federal court in Boston, Massachusetts, which was sitting in diversity. Initially, it was determined that New York law applied under choice of law principles, but then the court concluded that the New York Court of Civil Appeals had not yet addressed the legal issue and, accordingly, made an "informed" *Erie* guess concerning how the New York high court would rule.

22. For many years, the U.S. District Court for the Eastern District of Texas, Marshall Division, was perceived as a "Mecca" for plaintiff's patent cases. The federal trial court had a reputation of moving its patent cases quickly. This gave plaintiffs an incentive to seek ways to justify venue in Texas, creating an economic litigation boom in this small East Texas town.

23. *C.f.* Jennifer K. Elek, David B. Rottman, Shelley Spacek Miller & Lydia Hamblin, *Elements of Judicial Excellence: A Framework to Support the Professional Development of State Trial Court Judges*, National Center for State Courts (Dec. 2017), https://www.ncsc.org/~/media/Images/Topics/ Judicial%20Administration/Elements-of-Judicial-Excellence-final-report-Publicv15Dec2017.ashx (A national research report that evaluates judiciary around the country on various elements, including docket management).

24. *See, e.g.* Mo. Sup. Ct. R. 56.01(b)(4) ("Discovery of facts known . . . may be obtained only as follows: (a) A party may through interrogatories require any other party to identify each person whom the other party expects to call as an expert witness at trial.").

25. *Compare* Tex. R. Civ. P. 199.5 (limiting length of deposition to six hours), *with*, Nev. R. Civ. P. 30 (limiting length of deposition to seven hours).

The Removal Decision

When evaluating initial options, a defense lawyer should consider whether a case in state court may be properly removed to federal court. The requirements for removal are set forth in 28 U.S.C. § 1441 and the specific timetable for removal of civil actions is set forth in 28 U.S.C. § 1446.[26] The procedures following removal are set forth in FED. R. CIV. P. 81.

All cases filed in state court involving complete diversity of citizenship, and with an appropriate amount in controversy, may be removed to federal court. However, there is an exception to this rule—if any defendant is a citizen of the state in which the state court proceeding was filed.[27]

There are several procedural requirements involving removal that should be addressed and satisfied before any attempted removal. First, is there complete diversity of citizenship? This is not always immediately apparent.[28] Second, is there a sufficient amount in controversy to satisfy the jurisdictional limits of the federal court?[29] Third, has complete diversity been destroyed by a fraudulently joined defendant?[30] Fourth, in multiparty cases, will all defendants consent and join in the removal?[31] Obviously, all these issues must be addressed to determine whether the case is properly removed or not. With that said, there are equally important tactical issues that should be addressed.

As a general rule, there must be complete diversity before removal to federal court is possible under 28 U.S.C. § 1441. However, there is a robust body of law involving situations where defendants remove cases in the absence of complete diversity on the basis that a nondiverse defendant was fraudulently joined. It is not uncommon for skilled plaintiff's lawyers to join nondiverse defendants for the primary purpose of defeating diversity. However, this motivation alone is insufficient to support a fraudulent joinder claim. As stated by the U.S. Supreme Court in 2014:

> Joinder of a party solely for the purpose of blocking jurisdiction based on diversity may be established by showing (1) actual fraud in the pleadings or (2) the "inability of the plaintiff to establish a cause of action against the nondiverse party in state court."[32]

---

26. "The notice of removal of a civil action or proceeding shall be filed within 30 days after the receipt by the defendant." However, a case removed based on diversity of citizenship may not be removed "more than 1 year after commencement of the action, unless the district court finds that the plaintiff has acted in bad faith in order to prevent a defendant from removing the action." 28 U.S.C. § 1446. *See Ingham v. Johnson & Johnson*, No. 4:17-CV-1857 SNLJ, 2017 WL 3034696, at *1 (E.D. Mo. July 18, 2017) (federal court granted plaintiffs' motion to remand to state court based on "plain reading" of Section 1446(c)(1)—despite acknowledging that "plaintiffs surely secured advantageous forums by manipulating groups of plaintiffs in an attempt to prevent federal jurisdiction ... [however] this manipulation was legal within the confines of federal statutes").

27. *See* FED. R. CIV. P. 1441 (b)(2).

28. Whether a limited liability company is diverse is measured by the citizenship of each of its members. Thus, even though the limited liability company "appears" diverse, this may be irrelevant if one or more of its constituent members is not. Likewise, if one of the constituent members is also a limited liability company, the citizenship of each of its members must be separately ascertained.

29. *See* 28 U.S.C. § 1446(c)(2).

30. *See* 28 U.S.C. § 1446(b), *Ritchey v. Upjohn Drug Co.*, 139 F.3d 1313, 1318 (9th Cir. 1998) (citing *Emrich v. Touche Ross & Co.*, 846 F.2d 1190, 1193 & n.1 (9th Cir.1988)) ("It is commonplace that fraudulently joined defendants will not defeat removal on diversity grounds.").

31. 28 U.S.C. § 1446(b)(2).

32. *Miss. ex rel. Hood vs. AU Optronics Corp.*, 571 U.S. 161, 174 (2014).

Although the cases vary when describing "fraudulent joinder" situations, there is a common denominator. It is clear that if a plaintiff's cause of action against a nondiverse defendant can survive a Rule 12(b)(6) challenge, the nondiverse defendant has *not* been fraudulently joined.[33] The Fifth Circuit holds that the test for fraudulent joinder is established by showing either "(1) actual fraud in the pleading or jurisdictional facts, or (2) inability of the plaintiff to establish a cause of action against the nondiverse party in state court."[34]

Assuming a case is removable, the next strategic issue is whether removal is strategically preferable. Although defendants typically prefer federal courts, there are instances when a defendant or defense lawyer should prefer to remain in state court. This could be the result of a positive relationship between the defense lawyer and the state court, the favorable reputation of the state court judge, a potentially unfavorable reputation of the local federal judiciary, or other intangible factors.

There is no doubt that removal of civil cases to federal courts occurs frequently. Also, the statistical data relating to removal has remained consistent over the past several years. In 2019, 34,727 cases were removed from state court to federal court.[35] In 2018, 32,779 cases were removed.[36] In 2017, 32,039 cases were removed. In these years, cases removed were 11–12 percent of the entire federal trial docket.[37]

Of course, no removed case is guaranteed to remain in federal court. Unless a federal question is involved, it is not uncommon for plaintiffs to challenge removal. Historically, court-ordered remand occurs approximately 20 percent of the time.[38] Because diversity jurisdiction provides the federal court with subject matter jurisdiction, and because a lack of diversity deprives the federal court of subject matter jurisdiction, a remand can occur at any time. Although a motion to remand should be filed within 30 days following removal, a federal district judge can remand the case sua sponte regardless of the passage of time.[39]

Federal Court Venue

The requirements for proper venue in federal court are set forth in 28 U.S.C. § 1390, et seq. Sections 1404 and 1406 provide district courts discretion to dismiss or transfer a matter where there is either an alternate proper forum, or where the forum is wrong:

---

33. *See GranCare, LLC v. Thrower by and through Mills*, 889 F.3d 543, 549-50 (9th Cir. 2018) ("test for fraudulent joinder is roughly equivalent to the test under Rule 12(b)(6)").

34. *Cumpian v. Alcoa World Alumina, LLC*, 910 F.3d 216, 219 (5th Cir. 2018).

35. *Table C-8—U.S. District Courts–Civil Judicial Business (September 30, 2019)*, United States Courts (Sept. 30, 2019), https://www.uscourts.gov/statistics/table/c-8/judicial-business/2019/09/30.

36. *Id.*

37. *See id.*

38. Federal Judicial Center, *Federal Court Cases: Integrated Data Base, 2014 (ICPSR 36110)*, NACJD (Aug. 19, 2015), https://www.icpsr.umich.edu/icpsrweb/NACJD/studies/36110; *see also* Theodore Eisenberg & Trevor W. Morrison, *Overlooked in the Tort Reform Debate: The Growth of Erroneous Removal*, 2 J. Empirical Legal Stud. 551, 556 (Nov. 2005), https://scholarship.law.cornell.edu/facpub/473/.

39. *See Ellenburg v. Spartan Motors Chassis, Inc.*, 519 F.3d 192, 196 (4th Cir. 2008) ("[B]ecause the lack of subject matter jurisdiction may be noticed by the district court sua sponte or by any party, the court may enter a remanded order sua sponte."). The author was involved in a matter in Mississippi where the federal court remanded the case to state court *sua sponte* after substantial discovery had been completed. The court determined that there was a lack of diversity because of the citizenship of upstream members in a limited liability company.

> For the convenience of parties and witnesses, in the interest of justice, a district court may transfer any civil action to any other district or division where it might have been brought or to any district or division to which all parties have consented.[40]
>
> . . . .
>
> The district court of a district in which is filed a case laying venue in the wrong division or district shall dismiss, or if it be in the interest of justice, transfer such case to any district or division in which it could have been brought.[41]
>
> . . . .
>
> Section 1404(a) is merely a codification of the doctrine of forum non conveniens for the subset of cases in which the transferee forum is within the federal court system; in such cases, Congress has replaced the traditional remedy of outright dismissal with transfer.[42]

The general test for applying forum non conveniens (either transfer or dismissal) was explained in *Gulf Oil Corp. v. Gilbert*, in which the Supreme Court stated that the "plaintiff's choice of forum should rarely be disturbed" unless the balance of interests is "strongly in favor of the defendant."[43] The Court then listed the non-exhaustive list of private interest factors, including:

> [1] the relative ease of access to sources of proof; [2] availability of compulsory process for attendance of unwilling, and the cost of obtaining attendance of willing, witnesses; [3] possibility of view of premises, if view would be appropriate to the action; and [4] all other practical problems that make trial of a case easy, expeditious and inexpensive. There may also be questions as to [5] the enforceability of a judgment if one is obtained.[44]

On the federal level, each circuit may have its own application of the same basic test:

> Under the common law doctrine of forum *non conveniens*, "a federal trial court may decline to exercise its jurisdiction, even though the court has jurisdiction and venue, when it appears that the convenience of the parties and the court and the interests of justice indicate that the action should be tried in another forum." Given the "virtually unflagging obligation of the federal courts to exercise the jurisdiction given them," forum *non conveniens* should be invoked only in "rather rare cases." This court applies a three-step test to determine whether dismissal is appropriate: "After [1] the court determines the degree of deference owed the plaintiff's forum choice, the defendant carries the burden of [2] establishing an adequate alternative forum and [3] showing

40. 28 U.S.C.A. § 1404(a).
41. 28 U.S.C.A. § 1406.
42. *Atlantic Marine*, 571 U.S. 49 60 (2013).
43. 330 U.S. 501, 508 (1947).
44. *Id.*

that the plaintiff's chosen forum is unnecessarily burdensome based on public and private interests."[45]

Furthermore, *Gilbert* made clear that "forum non conveniens can never apply if there is absence of jurisdiction" and that "[i]n all cases in which . . . forum *non conveniens* comes into play, it presupposes at least two forums in which the defendant is amenable to process."[46] When this occurs, a balancing test must be undertaken:

> In the typical case not involving a forum-selection clause, a district court considering a § 1404(a) motion (or a *forum non conveniens* motion) must evaluate both the convenience of the parties and various public-interest considerations. Ordinarily, the district court would weigh the relevant factors and decide whether, on balance, a transfer would serve "the convenience of parties and witnesses" and otherwise promote "the interest of justice."[47]

If venue is "wrong" or "improper," then the case *may* be transferred or dismissed. However, if the plaintiff's chosen venue is merely inconvenient, then the case should be transferred to a more convenient venue. Section 1406(a) provides that "[t]he district court of a district in which is filed a case laying venue in the wrong division or district shall dismiss, or if it be in the interest of justice, transfer such case to any district or division in which it could have been brought."[48] Further, Rule 12(b)(3) states that a party may move to dismiss a case for "improper venue."[49] These provisions, therefore, authorize dismissal only when venue is "wrong" or "improper" in the forum in which it was brought.[50]

Current Supreme Court precedent makes clear that dismissal is appropriate only when the case cannot be transferred to another venue within the court's jurisdiction. "[T]he common-law doctrine of forum *non conveniens* 'has continuing application [in federal courts] only in cases where the alternative forum is abroad,' and perhaps in rare instances where a state or territorial court serves litigational convenience best."[51]

Finally, the determination of the district court regarding proper venue may be overturned only by an abuse of discretion standard:

> The forum *non conveniens* determination is committed to the sound discretion of the trial court. It may be reversed only when there has been a clear abuse of discretion; where the court has considered all relevant public and private interest factors, and where its balancing of these factors is reasonable, its decision deserves substantial deference.[52]

---

45. *Associacao Brasileira de Medicina de Grupo v. Stryker Corp.*, 891 F.3d 615, 618-19 (6th Cir. 2018) (internal citations omitted). *See* 28 U.S.C.A. § 1404(a).

46. *Sinochem Int'l Co. v. Malaysia Int'l Shipping Corp.*, 549 U.S. 422, 424 (2007) (quoting *Gilbert* at 506–07).

47. *Atlantic Marine*, 571 U.S. at 62–63.

48. 28 U.S.C.A. § 1406(a).

49. Fed. R. Civ. P. 12(b)(3).

50. *See Atlantic Marine*, 571 U.S. at 55-56 (proper venue is determined by Section 1391, and so long as venue is proper under Section 1391, the case "may not be dismissed under § 1406(a) or Rule 12(b)(3).")

51. *Sinochem Int'l Co. v. Malaysia Int'l Shipping Corp.*, 549 U.S. 422, 430, 127 S. Ct. 1184, 1190, 167 L. Ed. 2d 15 (2007) (quoting *American Dredging Co. v. Miller*, 510 U.S. 443, 449, n.2 (1994)).

52. *Piper Aircraft Co. v. Reyno*, 454 U.S. 235, 257 (1981).

Multidistrict Litigation—The Statistics Tell a Story

The provisions relating to MDLs are set forth under the venue provisions of Chapter 87 of Title 28 of the United States Code ("U.S.C.").[53] Any party—plaintiff or defendant—may initiate proceedings under 28 U.S.C. § 1407 seeking creation of an MDL proceeding that "centralizes" similar cases pending in multiple districts. The procedure requires a motion before the JPML, which will then determine whether the case should be centralized for pretrial purposes only. If the motion is granted, and two or more cases are centralized, then a U.S. District Judge will be appointed to preside over the consolidated MDL matter, having authority over all centralized cases until remand of a case for trial to the court from which it was transferred. The statute provides:

> When civil actions involving one or more common questions of fact are pending in different districts, such actions may be transferred to any district for coordinated or consolidated pre-trial proceedings.[54]

A defendant's right to challenge the exercise of personal jurisdiction by an MDL court is effectively nonexistent. This is because personal jurisdiction is determined by whether the original district court had personal jurisdiction.[55] Assuming the initial district court seeking the MDL—the transferor court—has personal jurisdiction over a defendant, then the MDL court (or the transferee court) also will have personal jurisdiction over that defendant.[56] This means that an MDL judge has exclusive authority over the pretrial development of a case, including dismissal and dispositive motion practice, even though a defendant might not be subject to personal jurisdiction in that court otherwise.

In theory, the MDL procedure provides advantages to both plaintiffs and defendants. The JPML appoints senior or experienced district judges to handle MDL proceedings, and defendants are benefited by having experienced judges who will be responsible for rulings relating to discovery and other pretrial matters. This authority includes "the powers to modify, expand or vacate earlier discovery orders."[57] Although an MDL judge cannot conduct a trial, the MDL judge can make rulings on dispositive motions under Rule 56 of the Federal Rules of Civil Procedure and rulings to dismiss under Rule 12(b)(6).[58] Thus, defendants who have been sued in numerous cases, in multiple venues—may perceive centralization in an

53. 28 U.S.C.A. § 1407. Several states have similar MDL statutes that allow consolidation of cases within a state for pretrial purposes. Examples include California, Colorado, Illinois, New Jersey, New York, Pennsylvania, Texas, and West Virginia. In New Jersey and California, the appointed MDL judges also are encouraged to retain centralized matters for trial.

54. 28 U.S.C.A. § 1407.

55. *In re TelexFree Sec. Litig.*, 357 F. Supp. 3d 78, 79 (D. Mass. 2019) ("While courts have held that the MDL statute, 28 U.S.C.A. § 1407, 'authoriz[es] the federal courts to exercise nationwide personal jurisdiction,' it is also well established that '[i]n an MDL case, personal jurisdiction *is derived from the transferor court*.'") (citation omitted) (original emphasis).

56. *Id.*, see also Andrew D. Bradt, *The Long Arm of Multidistrict Litigation*, 59 Wm. & Mary L. Rev. 1165, 1172 (2017) ("[T]he JPML essentially disclaims that the transferee court is exercising personal jurisdiction at all. In its view, the power of the transferee court is derivative of the power of the transferor court.").

57. *In re Plumbing Fixture Cases*, 298 F. Supp. 484, 489 (J.P.M.L. 1968).

58. *See, e.g., In re Donald J. Trump Casino Sec. Litig.*, 793 F. Supp. 543, 568 (D.M.J. 1992) *aff'd* 7 F.3d 357 (3rd Cir. 1993).

MDL proceeding as a potentially efficient vehicle to narrow the issues and the scope of discovery. MDL proceedings also avoid the chaos of potentially inconsistent discovery rulings in multiple district courts around the country. Furthermore, instead of dealing with multiple lawyers representing plaintiffs in numerous cases, an MDL allows defense counsel to interact with fewer plaintiffs' lawyers who serve as representatives. Ostensibly, all of this reduces the costs of litigation.

From a plaintiff's perspective, MDL proceedings provide a significant marketing tool for well-funded lawyers who can attract new cases with new clients. It also allows plaintiffs an opportunity to consolidate proceedings as an alternative to a class action practice. The chair of the JPML remarked in 2010:

> Plaintiffs' attorneys value some of these same benefits from their own perspective. Additionally, they benefit because the MDL process is an avenue to aggregate claims without the difficulty of meeting increasingly strict class action requirements. This generates greater risk for their adversaries, particularly with relatively weaker cases.[59]

The statistics relating to MDLs tell a compelling story. As of March 15, 2019, of the 25 largest pending MDL matters, 24 were created by motions filed by plaintiffs' lawyers—only one was initiated by a defendant.[60] There were 205 pending MDL cases as of March 15, 2019;[61] more than 147,000 individual cases were centralized within these 205 MDL matters.[62] Of these 205 MDL matters, the ten largest MDL matters include more than 50 percent of the total individual centralized cases, and each of the ten largest proceedings was initiated by the plaintiff. In turn, each of these cases involved product liability claims either for pharmaceuticals or for medical devices.

Of the currently pending 205 MDL matters, more than 68 involve product liability litigation; 49 involve antitrust matters; 23 involve sales practices; and 8 involve securities litigation. Product liability litigation occupies the lead position of all MDL proceedings.[63] Here are the details:

---

59. John G. Heyburn II, *Remarks, ACI Complex Litigation Conference, "Reflections on the Panel's Work,"* Judicial Panel on Multidistrict Litigation (Dec. 2010), https://www.jpml.uscourts.gov/sites/jpml/files/2010-ACI%20Complex%20Litigation%20Conference-Judge%20Heyburn%20Remarks.pdf.

60. *MDL Statistics Report—Distribution of Pending MDL Dockets by Actions Pending*, Judicial Panel on Multidistrict Litigation (Mar. 15, 2019), https://www.jpml.uscourts.gov/sites/jpml/files/Pending_MDL_Dockets_By_Actions_Pending-March-15-2019.pdf; *see, e.g.*, *In re Xarelto (Rivaroxaban) Prod. Liab. Litig.*, 65 F. Supp. 3d 1402, 1404 (J.P.M.L. 2014) (Transfer Order transferring MDL proceedings initiated by plaintiffs to Eastern District of Louisiana), *In re Ford Motor Co. DPS6 PowerShift Transmission Prod. Liab. Litig.*, 289 F. Supp. 3d 1350, 1351 (J.P.M.L. 2018) (Transfer Order transferring MDL proceedings initiated by Defendant to Central District of California).

61. *MDL Statistics Report*, *supra*.

62. *Id.*

63. *MDL Statistics Report*, *supra*.

2019 MDL Statistics[64]				
Ranking	**Year MDL Created**	**Active Cases**	**Initiated By**	**Case Type**
1	2014	23,534	Plaintiff	Product Liability
2	2012	14,229	Plaintiff	Product Liability
3	2016	11,429	Plaintiff	Product Liability
4	2016	11,343	Plaintiff	Product Liability
5	2011	9,889	Plaintiff	Product Liability
6	2012	9,375	Plaintiff	Product Liability
7	2017	8,452	Plaintiff	Product Liability
8	2015	6,753	Plaintiff	Product Liability
9	2014	5,572	Plaintiff	Product Liability
10	2015	5,417	Plaintiff	Product Liability

There also are other significant data points that reflect how MDL proceedings are venued. More than 50 percent of all pending MDL matters are venued in *only* six states. As of March 15, 2019, the federal courts in California are home to 34 MDL proceedings; New York is the venue for 28 proceedings; New Jersey is the venue for 15 proceedings; Illinois is the venue for 16 proceedings; and Pennsylvania is the venue for 15 proceedings.[65] On the other hand, eighteen states have no pending MDL matters, largely the states in the Midwest.[66] This means that corporations headquartered in the Midwest may find themselves doing battle in strange jurisdictions either on the West Coast or on the East Coast.

The use of MDL proceedings was initially very popular, and motions were frequently granted by the JPML. In 2010, 85 motions for centralization were filed with the JPML for MDL status; 35 motions were granted.[67] However, the trend is changing. From a ten-year high of 109 motions in 2011, the number of motions filed have been on a downward slope. In 2019, only 48 motions were filed—a decrease of 43 percent from 2010. Of these, 35 motions were granted.[68]

Thus, statistically, MDLs are currently favored by plaintiffs, especially in large mass tort litigation involving product liability claims. However, that does not mean that defense lawyers should not do due diligence on the potential benefits of MDL litigation, including obtaining consistent discovery rulings and cost consolidation.

64. *See id.*
65. *See id.*
66. *See id.*
67. *Calendar Year Statistics—January through December 2019*, Judicial Panel on Multidistrict Litigation, https://www.jpml.uscourts.gov/sites/jpml/files/JPML_Calendar_Year_Statistics-2019_1.pdf (last visited Nov. 20, 2019).
68. *See id.*

Conclusion

Both plaintiff's and defense counsel should maximize their chances of success by seeking the forum most favorable to their respective cases. Obviously, there are multiple factors to consider as part of this selection process, and no two cases will include the same considerations. Every defense lawyer should assume that the venue selected by a plaintiff was lodged to gain a tactical or strategic advantage. Thus, every defense lawyer should then consider whether the venue is properly challenged to gain a more favorable battleground for when the trial starts.

3
THE INTANGIBLES OF A SUCCESSFUL TRIAL
The Plaintiff's Perspective

Winning at trial involves an equation comprised of about 20 percent evidence, 20 percent trial talent, and 60 percent solid preparation in the form of work that is completed before trial begins. This chapter addresses that intangible component of winning, often referred to as the "it" factor—how to use raw talent to gain the upper hand during trial. How does one best control the courtroom, seize and maintain momentum, develop a rapport with the jury, and use that rapport to prosecute a logical, commonsense case by presenting an appealing, emotional, and credible case, while also communicating in a way that clearly synthesizes the evidence by using technology and stipulations?

Controlling the Courtroom

A dispute between two parties inevitably involves a contest of credibility between the lead plaintiff's lawyer and the lead defense lawyer. Jurors tend to side with whichever lawyer they like, respect, *and* trust. As such, the lawyer who can seize control of the courtroom has a major advantage over her opponent. Initially, the best way to win control of the courtroom is to win over the person who ultimately controls it—the judge.

Winning Over the Judge

Most judges are overworked with docket congestion that would make a factory worker flush with exhaustion. Trial lawyers have convinced themselves that what we do is the highlight in any judge's year. This egocentric view of the court's calendar is most surely in error. While most judges enjoy a good trial, all of them enjoy seeing their docket move, above all else. Consequently, winning over judges begins with respecting their time, which involves bypassing discovery disputes, streamlining the pretrial process, and safeguarding a judge's time during trial.

Avoiding discovery disputes when possible prevents judges from becoming mired in petulant pretrial battles that they often see as a waste of their time. In an Internet world, large swaths of information are available to the lawyer that will dig for it instead of merely rely on written discovery crafted for the other side. Written discovery alone is ripe for a litany of prewritten, formulaic objections by the other side. By contrast, corporate deposition notices with subpoenas duces tecum tend to yield information without a laundry list of objections that are designed only to hide the ball. Likewise, follow-up discovery specifically tailored to focus on information previously learned in initial Rule 30(b)(6) depositions is much more likely to yield meaningful results than just pre-scripted stock objections. Furthermore, well-designed and specifically drafted discovery that follows up on prior discovery responses served will be received well by a judge when they are asked to overrule generic and spurious objections. Moreover, complex cases are built for discovery special masters. If a complex case seeks millions or tens of millions or hundreds of millions of dollars, it can support the plaintiffs collectively bearing one-half of the cost of a discovery master. Rather than hauling a defendant before a judge on numerous occasions to resolve discovery fights, one might consider during the first discovery dispute hearing offering to fund one-half of the cost of a discovery master to resolve future disputes without court intervention. This allows the judge to appoint someone he trusts to handle discovery disputes that otherwise would clog the court's pretrial docket, while also achieving a source of income for a local lawyer who is trusted by the court.

Another way to "win the judge" is to streamline the pretrial process. Federal courts require this through pretrial orders that require the submission of case summaries, position statements, and trial exhibit lists well before trial begins, and then meet-and-confer sessions before submitting objections to exhibits and deposition page and line designations, and motions in limine. While state courts generally do not require this level of pretrial submission, the process is effective in that it requires the parties to work together before submitting matters to the court for pretrial adjudication. As a result, the first way to streamline the pretrial process is to write into the scheduling order this level of pretrial exchange of documentation and required consultation between the parties before the court is brought into the pretrial adjudication process.

The most important way to win over the judge before the trial starts is to convince the judge that you will respect the court's time. Lawyers who "litigate" for years before a trial begins often mistakenly convince themselves that every scrap of documentation, and every line of deposition testimony achieved during the discovery process, must somehow be needed at trial. Lawyers who are asked by the court, "how long will this trial take," often respond with "six weeks" or "two to three months." This invites a judicial eye roll and the immediate contempt of the bench. I learned at the foot of a great trial lawyer who believed that large verdicts required a lengthy process of getting the jury pissed off at the defense. According to my mentor, this process required days for voir dire, multi-hour opening statements, daylong direct examinations of experts, and sometimes even longer cross-examinations of company witnesses. As a young lawyer, I watched judges look at their watches and juries seethe at their perception of this waste of their time.

While my mentor's success caused me to wonder if my concerns about the length of his trials were wrong, I then tried a case in federal court in East Texas for the first time. With a well-known "rocket docket," the Eastern District of Texas became the hub for the nation's patent disputes because of the speed offered by the venue. A corollary of the speed offered there was the notion that no dispute was so complex that it merited more than a week of the court's time to try a case. Armed with a seemingly complex automotive products liability case, I responded "ten days a side" when asked by the federal judge how long it would take to try my case. My suggestion was met with an Article III smirk and the response that "the court will give each side ten hours to complete opening statements, all direct and cross-examinations, and closing arguments." I only then began to acknowledge the reality of the old joke, "What's the difference between God and a federal judge? God doesn't think he's a federal judge."

I left that pretrial hearing knowing that there was no way to put on a complex automotive products case in one week, and then I proceeded to chop back my evidence to do just that. My opening statement outline saw gristle removed in favor of only steak; tertiary portions of my direct examination fell to the editing room floor, leaving only the evidence addressing the elements of proof; rabbit trails in my cross-examination outlines were no longer chased, and time-consuming stories and jokes found no place in my closing argument. As I settled the case while the jury deliberated after the close of both sides' evidence on Friday of the first and only week of trial, I realized for the first time that "less is more," and that the economics of a short trial favor the plaintiff's side. After four days instead of four weeks, the defense faced the same jury verdict they would have faced after paying their lawyers hourly for more than a month to waste my time while I worked possibly for free on a contingency basis. Since that day, there has not been a case I have tried where I did not try to rest at the end of the first week, or shortly into the second. Monthlong trials are the exception rather than the rule, and they are caused by a slow defense rather than a lack of efficiency in my case-in-chief. Now, when trying to curry pretrial favor with the court, I am the one to suggest a quick trial, and the defense lawyer is asking for more of the court's time; inevitably, this puts me on the right track with the only person who controls the courtroom—the person wearing the robe. Safeguarding the court's time is the best way to win over the judge.

Winning Over the Court's Staff

Other than the judge and the jury, the four most important persons in any trial are the bailiff or court security officer, the court reporter, the court coordinator or deputy clerk, and the court's staff attorney or law clerk. The judge selected these four individuals, she is their boss, she often is their direct report in relation to hire and fire authority, she is inevitably their friend, and they are always the persons with whom the judge spends the most time. As a result, winning over the court's staff is almost as important as winning over the judge herself.

Small courtesies early in the case during scheduling conferences, discovery hearings, or pretrial proceedings can be the difference between a warm reception and a cold shoulder. Friendly introductions with a respectful handshake for the bailiff, staff attorney, and court coordinator, and the same with a helpful business card for the court reporter, constitute a small but important step in winning over the court's staff. Asking for permission rather than forgiveness when moving court equipment or sitting in particular seats are small signs of respect not lost on court staff. Cleaning up desks and throwing away papers and cups when hearings conclude are courtesies not lost on courtroom personnel that otherwise would have to clean up after discourteous lawyers. Furthermore, polling court staff about the judge's "do's" and "don'ts," their likes and dislikes, is an empowering inquiry not lost on those spending the most time with the judge. Ordering daily copy from the court reporter supplements his otherwise inadequate pay, and is not only helpful in presenting a case, but also appreciated by the court itself. Finally, a departing handshake, thanking the members of the court's staff, is an act not lost on those working hard in the courtroom.

Seizing and Maintaining Momentum

Momentum is the most important commodity in any jury trial. It begins in pretrial before the jury ever arrives in court. Motions without a sound basis in case law should be discarded, as should responses not likely to be won under existing precedent. Well-crafted yet succinct motions and briefs, accompanied by copies of highly significant cases, with key holdings highlighted and flagged for the court's attention, are a key tool to achieve the confidence of the court. To ensure that the court understands that the plaintiff's lawyer respects the court's time, I believe providing a trial script to the court is the best tool available. Before trial begins, I provide the court (and the court reporter) with a script entitled "Order of Trial Presentation," which is a one-page list of what is to occur, complete with the date, the name of the witness or activity, a brief description of who each witness is, the mode of the presentation of their testimony (live or by video), the anticipated length of the examination, and the name of the person on the plaintiff's trial team who will be conducting the examination of each respective witness. Critically, this "Order of Trial Presentation" contains the date when the plaintiff expects to rest. There is no better tool to assure the court that its schedule will be honored than this script; indeed, I have eliminated witnesses and cut down the plaintiff's case-in-chief to ensure that this schedule provided to the court before the trial began was, in fact, met. A written "Order of Trial Presentation" is visible proof to the court that the plaintiff's lawyer is well-prepared and ready to seize and maintain the momentum of the trial.

Developing Jury Rapport

A pretrial script also enables the plaintiff's lawyer to develop a rapport with the jury. Oftentimes, the first time a plaintiff's lawyer and potential members of the jury meet each other is during the voir dire process. The plaintiff's lawyer needs to remember that every citizen in the room is there involuntarily, having received a jury summons under the threat of contempt of court if they don't interrupt their daily schedule and show up for court. Many have had to travel to a courthouse they have never been in before, have seen their work and childcare schedules interrupted, are worried about seeing their income streams interrupted if they are selected to serve, and already have been forced to wait around in a central jury room before being sent up to the courtroom just before the trial begins. In short, a plaintiff's lawyer begins the jury voir dire process before a hostile group of potential jurors who each understand that it is the fault of one person that they are involuntarily in court—the plaintiff's lawyer.

When cases are won or lost via the credibility battle between the lead plaintiff's lawyer and the lead defense lawyer, the guardian of the jurors' time is most likely to win this battle. As referenced later in chapter 9, voir dire is the start of developing jury rapport. Furthermore, a tight, concise opening statement introducing evidence that surely will be admitted continues that rapport before the evidence allows one to prosecute a logical, commonsense case.

Prosecuting a Logical, Commonsense Case

Prosecuting a logical, commonsense case requires a lawyer to know the forest from the trees. What are the causes of action? What are elements of proof that must be met to win each cause of action? Why is the defendant responsible? Why did this happen? What can we do about it? Inevitably, this requires a trial lawyer to wear two hats: one of a legal scholar marshalling the proof, and one of a journalist telling a story.

By "legal scholar," I mean that one must understand what must be admitted in order to win—not merely in the trial courts, but also in the appellate courts that may eventually review the evidence supporting the jury's verdict and the lower court's judgment. This work must begin at the beginning of the case, long before the case is filed. Prewriting the jury instructions and verdict form before filing the petition is an exercise in organization that will identify potential holes in the proof that must be filled during the discovery process. Deposition summaries are far less helpful to trial lawyers than document and deposition excerpts that fit into particular buckets of proof needed to fill the trial outline. In every case, I use an outline program known as OmniOutliner, an outline software in which I pull deposition and document excerpts and put them into particularized topical components of the elements of proof. The jury instructions and verdict form are the skeleton, and the evidence is the meat on those bones. Until the body of evidence is completely constructed, the plaintiff cannot win. Once trial starts, the good trial lawyer knows exactly what proof must come in, and is in a position to reliably outline what that proof will look like for the jury.

By "journalist," I mean one must remember to tell a story, and to explain what happened as a newspaper writer would, delivering revealing information about *who, what, when, where, why*, and *how*.

Who is critical, and perhaps the most important component of the case. Each good story has a protagonist and an antagonist. In trying the case for the plaintiff, the protagonist has already been chosen; that person hired you as his lawyer. It is the antagonist that must be carefully identified, and in most good stories, there should only be one. If the case involves a lawsuit against a truck driver who caused a wreck and his trucking company who may have failed to train that driver or failed to keep that driver off the road after prior incidents, the plaintiff's lawyer must decide who is the primary villain. Is the villain a rogue truck driver, or is it the massive trucking company who enabled that driver to stay on the road, leading to the plaintiff's injuries? In a products liability case, is it the low-level engineer who designed the defective part, or is it the upper-level manager who compelled that design choice with cost-saving directives? For example, in the post-collision fuel-fed fire cases against Ford involving the Pintos of the 1970s, was the villain the low-level engineer who originally put the fuel tank behind the rear axle in his design drawings, or was it the management committee who evaluated the "let 'em burn" memo in which the decision was made to not relocate that fuel tank after several failed crash tests because the memo's analysis showed it would be cheaper to pay wrongful death claims than it would be to redo the car's design? In a pharmaceutical case, is the antagonist the young physician who missed signals and adverse events during clinical trials, or is it the high-level committee that refused to pull the then-billion dollar-a-year drug off the market, despite clear pharmacovigilance data demonstrating that the drug was killing people? In sum, the plaintiff's lawyer should pick a single villain and shoot at him or her throughout the entire trial.

What is that most important tortious decision executed by the villain. The key here is to leave the realm of legalism and talk like a person. A good lawyer must pretend he or she never went to law school, ignore all the high-powered legalistic thinking learned there, and show the jury what happened, like a normal person having a conversation with a friend on the street. This requires both precision and simplicity. The defendant did not "commit a tort"; he did not "violate a duty owed" to the plaintiff; she did not "breach a warranty"; and she did not "cause the Plaintiff's damages." Instead, the villain "destroyed *Paul Plaintiff*'s life"; he selfishly "put himself first" at the expense of everyone else; she didn't "follow her promise" made to *Paul Plaintiff*; and she "destroyed *Paul Plaintiff*'s life." Use vivid, simple words, spoken as they would be spoken in a bar or on the street. More important than the simplicity of real words is the unitary focus on just *one thing*. While a defendant may have done many things wrong, the best lawsuits are simplified by a plaintiff's lawyer identifying that *one thing* a defendant did wrong. Much like Billy Crystal's "Mitch" being schooled on the secret of life by Jack Palance's "Curly" in *City Slickers*—"Do you know what the secret of life is?" Curly asks, holding up one finger. "One thing. Just one thing. You stick to that and the rest 'don't mean shit.'" When Mitch responds, "But, what is the one thing?," Curly responds, "That's what *you* have to find out."[1] The great plaintiff's lawyer can find out what that *one thing* is that a defendant did wrong. This may occur through informal jury focus groups, through formal and expensive mock trials, through experience trying many cases, or just through good old-fashioned common sense. But, identifying that *one thing* that the defendant did wrong is critical to designing a good trial; some call it the *theme* of the case.

When is important for several reasons. First, for liability purposes, "when" is not the time and date of the accident when your plaintiff was hurt; rather, it is the time and place when the villain did that one thing the plaintiff's lawyer is complaining of that *eventually* caused his or her plaintiff's injury. Again, this is not to say that a good plaintiff's lawyer cannot build a long timeline of malfeasance in showing the defendant deserves to be hit with punitive damages; but inevitably, there will be one act or one decision that rises above

1. *City Slickers*, IMDB, https://www.imdb.com/title/tt0101587/characters/nm0000345 (last visited Mar. 14, 2020).

all others and is more odious than the rest. That one decision, once identified, needs to be carefully illustrated and spotlighted in time. It may be the day Merck decided to keep selling Vioxx after it knew the drug was causing heart attacks, merely because a particular committee document reveals that doing so will result in $250 million in additional sales. It may be the day when Ford stripped its fuel tanks of a key safety part known as a tether at a High Cost Product Review Committee meeting so it could achieve a savings of $0.60 per car. It may be the day when Syngenta's Chief Executive Officer ordered the commercialization of a genetically modified corn trait when he knew it would lock up the export market and harm American farmers financially. Whatever "what" is in a given case must be identified, and then highlighted with a specific time and place. What particular time and date did it occur?

Where is key to visualizing that one thing. This is usually in a corporate boardroom rather than on the shop floor; it is in those high-level corporate management committee meetings held in large conference rooms with wood-paneled walls and gold-plated decorations, rather than down where the low-level engineer works. In the products case about the drug Levaquin, Ortho-McNeil-Janssen Pharmaceuticals doctored a clinical study performed by Ingenix to hide the tendon toxicity of its drug. Because the meeting minutes of the committee that authorized this fraud identified both when and *where* the committee met on the day of its fateful decision—in a high-dollar hotel conference room—part of the plaintiff's evidence was photographs of the very hotel conference room that Ortho-McNeil-Janssen rented for the very day when that *what* occurred, leading to the plaintiff's injuries.

In almost every case, *why* the defendant did what it did leading to the plaintiff's harm always comes down to money. Civil litigation is an exercise in justice in the form of the pursuit of money damages. As such, any wrong perpetrated by the defendant needs to be framed as *what* occurred by reason of the defendant's illicit pursuit of the almighty dollar. Greed. Avarice. Cupidity. Rapacity. As Matthew 6:24 cautions that "no one can serve two masters . . . . You cannot serve both God and money," the plaintiff's lawyer needs to contrast good and evil and explain the defendant's evil act to be the consequence of their chase of money. As Proverbs 11:4 teaches that "wealth is worthless in the day of wrath, but righteousness delivers from death," the plaintiff's lawyer needs to explain that the defendant's pursuit of wealth is exactly *why* the plaintiff died. In other words, the cause-and-effect relationship between the greed of the defendant and the damages caused to the plaintiff is always the *why* we are here in court. *Why* = money. Always.

How is almost always couched in secrecy or in deception. If the evidence demonstrates fraud, that is *how* the defendant did *what* he did to cause the plaintiff's injury. If there are not documents from the defendant's files proving fraud, the defendant's actions speak louder than their words, and the defendant's acts of deception or secrecy become *how* they did *what* they did. Choose *how* the defendant performed the dirty deed, crystalize it, and stick with it consistently throughout the trial.

Prosecuting a logical, commonsense case requires a plaintiff's lawyer to cast themselves both as an appellate specialist, that legal scholar setting forth for the ultimate arbiter of the law—the appeals courts—all the evidence filling each element of the proof required for each cause of action, and at the same time, as a storyteller, providing the ultimate arbiter of the facts—the jury—with the *who, what, when, where, why*, and *how* needed to deliver a rich yet focused story of the plaintiff's case.

Presenting an Appealing, Emotional, and Credible Case

Presenting an appealing, emotional, and credible case requires a good deal of thought and preparation before the trial ever begins, and not merely about what the evidence will be—also how it will be presented.

Presenting an Appealing Case

As discussed in chapter 15, a good trial lawyer, in presenting an appealing case, must recognize that different people learn in different ways, gathering information through each of their five senses.

Presenting an Emotional Case

In presenting an emotional case, the effective trial lawyer must not merely amplify the moment of loss, but also must take the time to tell the full damages story itself.

Most good trial lawyers know that the moment when the plaintiff is injured or dies is a critical moment of focus in any trial, worthy of due care and great attention achieved by detailed evidence. That moment is a story within the story that must be richly told. Appealing to each of the jurors' five senses is a necessity, and telling the story from multiple perspectives and from several witnesses other than the plaintiff are necessary. Persons who did not witness the accident can provide texture to the story. A man's wife and children can set the scene with their breakfast together at home before the plaintiff left in his vehicle the day of the accident. The previously anonymous person who happened to be driving behind the plaintiff's vehicle before stopping to render aid after the collision can serve as a critical mouthpiece of evidence as to why the plaintiff was not contributorily negligent. Obviously, all observers of the accident itself are key witnesses. Likewise, those who rendered aid to the plaintiff—onlookers at the scene, EMTs who arrived soon after, emergency room doctors and nurses, and medical professionals that provided post-acute care—each provide color to what the plaintiff endured as a result of the defendant's actions. Of course, friends and loved ones of the plaintiff tearfully describing what they observed when they first walked into the hospital room are key damage witnesses, as well. Presenting an emotionally powerful case of what happened requires that the plaintiff's lawyer take the time to secure evidence from multiple witnesses to create a powerful artistic rendition of the story, much like a patchwork quilt being assembled one witness at a time.

In both wrongful death and in catastrophic injury cases, spending the time necessary to tell the plaintiff's love story with derivative claimants is critical. Whether it be a loss of a spouse, parent, or child in a wrongful death case or the devastation of their relationship by severe injury, telling the story of the plaintiff's emotional connection with his family members must be done with care. With more than 2 billion smartphones presently in service, accessing family photographs is easier than it has ever been. Likewise, videos documenting a family's love story are omnipresent. Using early-childhood videos and photos, videos of parents bouncing with young children in the blow-up bouncers rented for their early birthday parties, iPhone videos of mothers bellowing out high-pitched yet hilariously off-note renditions of "Happy Birthday," and professional videos of dads walking daughters down the aisle then stepping on their toes during wedding reception dances—each are powerful pieces of evidence available to prove up the love between them before a jury in the courtroom. Moreover, with almost 1.7 billion Facebook users, 2 billion YouTube users, and 330 million Twitter users, many plaintiffs have self-documented their lives and their relationships on social media. Social media posts by your clients' decedent or by your injured client constitute wonderful evidence of his love for his family, and they should be utilized in full via direct examinations of social media friends.

Telling your clients' love story by utilizing words in the court's jury instruction about mental anguish and loss of consortium is a smart way to design a direct examination of the plaintiff and his loved ones. In his book *His Needs, Her Needs—Building an Affair-Proof Marriage* (2011), William F. Harley identified key love needs expressed by a statistically significant sample of more than 27,000 males and females who filled out questionnaires before marital counseling. This means that the emotional needs expressed by females to Harley are statistically likely to be the same as those held by females on any civil jury, and that those expressed by males to Harley are statistically likely to be the same as those held by males on any civil jury. Harley's research identified that the following emotional needs were expressed to him by females: "affection"—the first thing she can't do without; "conversation"—she needs him to talk to her; "honesty and openness"—she needs to trust him totally; "financial support"—she needs enough money to feel secure; and "family commitment"—she needs him to be a good father. His research identified that the following emotional needs were expressed by males: "sexual fulfillment"—the first thing he can't do without; "recreational companionship"—he needs her to be his playmate; "an attractive spouse"—he needs a good-looking wife; "domestic support"—he needs peace and quiet; and "admiration"—he needs her to be proud of him. However outmoded and even sexist these responses seem to a reader in 2020, statisticians would tell an inquisitive trial lawyer that evidence about these emotional needs is most likely to appeal to those persons seated on a jury. As it happens, these very same emotional needs expressed by females in Harley's research appear in the definitions of mental anguish and loss of consortium appearing in the jury instructions of judges across the land: "emotional pain," "grief," "positive benefits flowing," "comfort," "affection," "the relationship between," "sexual relations," "their living arrangements," "companionship," "solace," "assistance," "society," "common interests and activities," "emotional support," "harmony of family relations," "despair," "felicity," "disappointment," "common benefits and activities," "embarrassment," "shame," and "public humiliation." As such, any good trial lawyer will seek to use those words to present an emotional case that is consistent with the wording in the court's jury instruction in order to achieve a verdict that reflects emotion transformed into reason, and the consequent verdict result.

Presenting a Credible Case

Credibility in a jury trial is all about achieving addition by subtraction. Collaring the applicable burden of proof is a battle worth winning—so the plaintiff's lawyer needs to promise only facts that he or she knows can be delivered. The steak of any case involves witness admissions and documentary evidence already adjudicated to be admissible by the court; the gristle of any opening statement are other tertiary matters where the advocate is left guessing about the admissibility of other matters. A trial lawyer should promise only that which she is sure to deliver into evidence; if there is even a sliver of doubt, save it for closing argument, one made long after dubiously admissible evidence has been introduced over objections by opposing counsel. The renown American writer Rebecca Solnit noted, "Credibility is a basic survival tool."[2] She is correct. In trial, the lawyer who sacrifices her credibility before a jury will most surely be punished for it. Never make a promise to a jury that cannot be delivered—delivering the presentation of a credible case is the harbinger of victory in a courtroom.

Using Technology

Technology in the courtroom must be used as the means to an end, not as the end itself. The Venezuelan-American storyteller Jason Silva once correctly observed, "Technology is, of course, a double-edged sword. Fire can cook our food but also burn us."[3] Again, Silva's teaching means that a good trial lawyer needs to treat technology not as the end, but as a means to the end. Without the underlying story of a client's case, technology is merely a gimmick masking the inability of an advocate to do his job. Bill Gates, one of the richest men in the world, and who earned his fortune by pioneering software technology, notes, "Technology is just a tool. In terms of getting the kids working together and motivating them, the teacher is the most important."[4] Gates's classroom truism applies equally in the courtroom—technology sharpens the sword of truth, but it can never replace it. Microsoft PowerPoint is the twenty-first century's version of yellow-pad notes. When well done, it illustrates preparation, organization, and competence. However, no PowerPoint devoid of substance can replace the necessity of solid proof. Whether a PowerPoint, an animation, a high-definition display of visual evidence, or any other new technique of evidence presentation, technology is merely the pen, not the story being written. Technology augments a well-constructed trial presentation, but it can never replace the work it takes to build the evidentiary structure needed to win the case. Technology is only the icing on the necessary cake of solid evidence.

---

2. Goodreads, https://www.goodreads.com/quotes/7336136-credibility-is-a-basic-survival-tool (last visited Mar. 14, 2020).

3. Alex Knapp, *Jason Silva Muses on Humans Turning Into Gods*, Forbes (Aug. 5, 2011, 7:42 AM), https://www.forbes.com/sites/alexknapp/2011/08/05/jason-silva-muses-on-humans-turning-into-gods/#6ba40394301a.

4. Goodreads, https://www.goodreads.com/quotes/1432743-technology-is-just-a-tool-in-terms-of-getting-the (last visited Mar. 14, 2020).

Stipulations

Trial lawyers can never ask opposing counsel to stipulate to evidence in front of a jury; however, experienced lawyers trying a case against each other often can shorten the exercise by hours, if not days, by meeting and conferring, and taking command of their case by accurately predicting what is likely to be admitted and what is likely to be excluded. No judge has ever objected to parties consenting via stipulation of what the admissible evidence should be. Whether state or federal, I have never met a judge who objected to agreements reached by the parties that minimize the number of disputes requiring adjudication by the court. Stipulations are an excellent tool that good trial lawyers use to spare the court from meaningless argument, and to spare twelve jurors from a needless waste of their time. Stipulations assist courts to focus on pure questions of statutory construction,[5] are the friend of efficiency, of the court, and of fine trial lawyers.

5. *See Bolivarian Republic of Venezuela v. Helmerich & Payne Intern. Drilling Co.*, 137 S. Ct. 1312, 1318 (2017), quoting *Republic of Austria v. Altmann*, 541 U.S. 677, 701 (2004) ("Given the parties' stipulations as to all relevant facts, our inquiry poses a 'pure question of statutory construction.'").

4

The Intangibles of Trial

The Defense Perspective

Albert Einstein is credited with the remark "Behind all of the discernable laws and connections, there remains something subtle, intangible and inexplicable."[1] Roger Dawson, a contemporary music composer, also offered the following comment: "Charisma is the intangible that makes people want to follow you, to be around you, to be influenced by you."[2] These two quotes define the essential challenge facing defense lawyers, as well as the solution to that challenge. As defense lawyers, we must define the "subtle and intangible" forces that influence a jury's verdict and, through our example, professionalism, and "charisma," present an appealing case that inspires the jury to follow our lead.

The facts of any case are tangible. That is, facts are either provable or disprovable, logical or illogical. Jury demographics are similar; they are fact-based and testable—turning on geographic venue, education levels, job experiences, socioeconomic classifications, etc. Likewise, a court's historical rulings on specific issues are reflected in prior published opinions or orders. Prior decisions, if published, are accessible and reviewable to discern the court's historical leanings on significant legal and procedural issues.

However, there should be little doubt that so-called "intangibles" always enter the equation of what makes a successful—*or unsuccessful*—trial. How does the judge perceive and react to the facts of the case and to the lawyer's arguments? How does the jury perceive the lawyers' personalities and credibility, the clients' personalities and credibility, and that of the witnesses? Our goal, as defense lawyers, is to appreciate and seek control over these intangibles to better assure a winning verdict.

---

1. Rebecca J. Rosen, *Einstein Letter on Religion and God to Be Auctioned on eBay* (Oct. 7, 2012), The Atlantic, https://www.theatlantic.com/technology/archive/2012/10/einstein-letter-on-religion-and-god-to-be-auctioned-on-ebay/263334/.
2. Roger Dawson, Secrets of Power Persuasion for Salespeople 219 (2008).

The three cornerstones of advocacy are Aristotle's *logos*, *pathos*, and *ethos*. The *logos* of any case consists of the logic, data, testimony, documents, and other provable facts. These facts are either maximized, minimized, bolstered, or undercut during pretrial discovery to advance our clients' cases. Every deposition is a trial deposition and is used for these purposes. However, even then, how facts are ultimately distilled, presented, and received by a jury becomes one of the intangibles. That is where the *ethos* and *pathos* of advocacy become critically important.

The *ethos* of a case is the credibility and likability of the lawyers, the clients, the witnesses, and the factual defense itself. The *pathos* of a case is the appeal and allure, the story line that attracts and motivates a jury to adopt one side or the other. Once this occurs, jurors naturally develop filters for how they view and interpret evidence. These filters either magnify or minimize the significance of evidence depending on a juror's preexisting belief system. Defense lawyers should try to gain control over the *pathos* and the *ethos* in every case, and this is done in several ways.

Interactions with the Court

Jurors are sensitive to tension in the courtroom, and they undoubtedly perceive animosity between a judge and a trial lawyer. As defense lawyers, we should avoid any behavior suggesting hostility. We should make every effort to be courteous and polite when addressing the court, even if the court is openly antagonistic. We should never argue with the court in the jury's presence. Our objections to evidence should be clear and simple, and we should not openly challenge the judge on evidentiary rulings. This is so even if the judge is flat wrong. If the trial judge demonstrates hostility toward us as lawyers, we should not mirror this hostility. Rather, we should continue to be respectful. Most importantly, we should always appear confident, and never lose our temper or display frustration or concern.

The Lawyer's Demeanor and the Client's Demeanor

Lawyers should dress for success. This means appropriate attire should be worn that is consistent with a serious, professional appearance. Most jurors expect lawyers to dress up for trial. Loud clothing or flashy jewelry should be avoided, and this is true for both men and women trial lawyers. These same recommendations apply equally to clients and to client representatives.

Clients should be attired appropriately and consistent with their professional or business position. They should avoid flashy or gaudy jewelry. As defense witnesses, this is particularly important because plaintiffs are frequently presented (and also frequently perceived) as underdogs against corporate Goliaths. Examples of bad choices occur when corporate officers or senior executives wear flashy rings, clothing with visible designer labels, or expensive watches. They will lose empathic appeal with the jury almost immediately. Any empathy between the witness and jury is broken before it is ever formed because the witness is displaying self-importance and arrogance.

Preparation and Organization Are Important

Lawyers should be fully prepared—*always*. As Will Rogers noted, "You only have one chance to make a good first impression."[3]

It is important that every opportunity for oral advocacy is fully exploited with pre-planned, effective presentations. This starts with voir dire, then opening statements, and continues through witness examinations and cross-examinations.

As lawyers, we should anticipate surprise. We should assume a member of the voir dire panel will ask a difficult question in open court. We should be ready if a witness provides unexpected testimony on the witness stand—particularly in response to one of our questions. Of course, we should avoid questions that may risk generating damaging answers, and we should plan our witness examinations accordingly. But it does happen. Thus, it is important for defense lawyers to never display concern or disappointment as a reaction to these types of negative surprises. We also should assume one or more jurors have their eyes focused on us, and they are taking mental notes of our conduct and behavior. Any expressions of concern or anxiety can telegraph negative, destructive messages.

The counsel table should be orderly and organized, and examinations and cross-examinations should be crisp, organized, and focused. Sloppy examinations or sloppy presentations reflect poorly on the lawyer and, ultimately, on the defense case. Excessive talk at counsel table also is ill-advised. It becomes a distraction and could be interpreted as chaotic or a reflection that the defense of the case is not going well.

Lawyers should avoid smirks, laughter, and exaggerated facial expressions in response to a witnesses' testimony, the actions of opposing counsel, or rulings of the court. Once again, these types of behaviors may be misinterpreted and could reinforce negative perceptions or send negative messages. Again, you should assume one or more jurors are watching the lawyers, and that they are looking for nonverbal signs and expressions.

Making Objections

Excessive objections are damaging and create negative impressions for most jurors, particularly those who have no experience in the courtroom. In fact, defense lawyers should object only when necessary. Otherwise, the jury may sense the objecting lawyer has something to hide or is excessively concerned about the evidence. This, in turn, reinforces the significance of "bad" evidence. The jury may also perceive the objecting lawyer as an obstructionist. Nothing good comes out of excessive objections.

When making objections, the objections should be crisp, straightforward, and with minimal drama. Histrionics can antagonize the court, create a hostile courtroom environment or, worst of all, accentuate bad or damaging evidence.

---

3. Forbes, https://www.forbes.com/quotes/9717/ (last visited Mar. 14, 2020).

Communications Between Counsel in the Courtroom

Some lawyers refuse to communicate with opposing lawyers except when doing so before the bench. This is probably the best practice. Engaging in colloquial conversations with opposing counsel in the presence of the jury detracts from the seriousness of the case. If the lawyers are openly friendly or "chummy," the jury may be left with unanswered questions about the importance or seriousness of the case. Communications between lawyers also can be misinterpreted, particularly if the communications involve a dispute or disagreement. Such communications should be directed to the court for resolution.

Jury Behavior

Defense lawyers should make it a routine practice to observe jurors, to monitor their reactions to testimony and evidence. But it is important to not stare at any particular juror. That juror may sense this staring and become uncomfortable.

Defense lawyers should monitor juror behavior during breaks, as well as before trial in the morning, and after trial in the afternoon. Of particular importance are groupings of jurors that logically occur over time. These groupings suggest several possible scenarios. The most obvious explanation is that jurors are becoming friendly with each other and are forming cliques. In turn, these cliques could become voting blocs during jury deliberation. Groupings also may suggest that specific jurors are being excluded by others. We particularly should note if juror groupings change over time. This could indicate that relationships within the jury are changing.

Observing juror conduct during breaks and during jury deliberations is important. We should watch jurors come and go from the jury room because it could signal divisions or voting blocs. Sometimes these subtleties are missed, and these subtleties sometimes provide clear indications of how the jury will vote.

This actually happened in a significant damage exposure case in South Texas. The jury deliberated for approximately three days. The first day of deliberations demonstrated a discrete grouping, with apparent defense jurors leading the pack. By the end of the second day of deliberations, there was a fundamental sea change. The jurors who we had classified as "defense jurors" were suddenly by themselves in a much smaller group. This suggested a shift in the deliberations against the defense and for the plaintiff. These subtleties can become extremely important when making final settlement decisions.

Controlling the Courtroom

One of the most important intangibles is the need to control the courtroom. This is the essence of leadership and advocacy. At a minimum, defense lawyers should at least appear as if they are in control of the witnesses and the flow of evidence.

A jury is less inclined to follow and adopt a lawyer's arguments if the lawyer is retiring or displays discomfort in the courtroom. Defense lawyers, therefore, should maintain an air of confidence in how they treat the court, opposing counsel, and all witnesses. This air of confidence is important to make jurors feel comfortable in adopting your side of the case. A demonstration of a lack of confidence in what you are doing or saying can be fatal.

Charisma comes in many forms. Not all successful trial lawyers need "star power" or a dramatic persona. Effective leadership can be fostered through calm, confident preparations and respectful advocacy. With that said, it is important that defense lawyers not let the plaintiff's lawyer dominate the courtroom with bigger-than-life personalities. Again, this can be achieved by not adversely reacting to personal jabs, quips, or challenges, and by manifesting strength in the facts and witnesses of the case. Never rise to the occasion and lose your temper if prompted to do so by opposing counsel. You should counsel your witnesses to do the same.

Controlling Momentum

Positive momentum is critical. Equally critical is impeding or slowing down the plaintiff's momentum during the plaintiff's voir dire, opening statement, and case-in-chief. If the plaintiff's attorney gets too far ahead, it will be difficult to catch up. Again, that is why effective advocacy is important in each of the initial stages of trial. The defense lawyer should consider how to simplify trial themes to make them more effective, believable, logical, commonsensical, fact-based, and inviting. We want the jury to emotionally invest in our cases. That is why we mold our cases with proper focus on the *ethos*, *pathos*, and *logos* of advocacy.

5
The Pretrial Warm-Up
The Plaintiff's Perspective

The ancient military strategist Sun Tzu wrote in *The Art of War*, "Every battle is won or lost before it's ever fought."[1] The same holds true for jury trials. The pretrial warm-up is every bit as important as the courtroom exercise itself. Pretrial preparation is a harbinger for success at trial. Much like a fine movie, every scene must be written, edited, and rehearsed if one expects an Oscar-worthy performance when the trial film is rolling at the courthouse. Jury studies and focus groups help steer one's path toward trial success, and thoughtful decisions about witness selection, witness order, exhibit selection, demonstrative exhibits, trial logistics, and stipulations must all be made well before the trial begins.

Jury Studies and Focus Groups

Although writing out the court's jury instructions and verdict form before beginning discovery in any case is the best way to avoid holes in one's proof, conducting jury studies and focus groups is the most important way to discern the thematic direction the evidentiary proof needs to take. Succinctly put, focus groups and mock trials are the best mechanism available to prevent a plaintiff's lawyer from incorrectly guessing at trial.

When to do jury research is critical. I often hear lawyers bragging about eleventh-hour focus groups as a predictor of their imminent success at trial, but believe that their words are merely evidence of their foolish decision to delay that which should have been done far earlier in the process. Focus groups are most effective when conducted before the first deposition is taken in the case. This is true for two reasons. First, focus groups or mock trials require lawyers who might otherwise procrastinate to prepare in the first instance. When two lawyers agree to square off as opponents in a focus group or mock trial, their competitive instincts yield preparation. Preparation for the lawyer presenting the plaintiff's

1. Goodreads, https://www.goodreads.com/quotes/720920-every-battle-is-won-before-it-s-ever-fought (last visited Mar. 14, 2020).

case yields an in-depth analysis of the case itself and the evidence and potential themes to be used; this process forces a lawyer to lay out early the pathway to succeed. Conversely, the lawyer presenting the defense (typically number two in the pecking order) seeks to beat his boss, who is playing the plaintiff's lawyer. In this competitive environment, each lawyer will dig deep, scouring the case facts for any argument, any theme, any way to defeat his opponent, and perhaps thereby win a more significant role in the eventual trial of the case. This early jousting between those two attorneys likely to prosecute the actual case as plaintiff's lawyers yields amazing early results. The team "prepares for trial" before discovery begins, thereby providing the client with early effort and work that forever will benefit the case. The team practices the arguments, hopefully on multiple occasions, thereby fine-tuning presentations before the real exercise takes place when it counts. Most importantly, the team listens to strangers who provide feedback on preferred arguments and themes. This feedback is the critical input needed to learn whether the lawyers' preconceived ideas about what will work are, in fact, correct. In my experience, those preconceived ideas about the strength of a case or how it should be presented sometimes could not be further from the truth. Let me discuss three examples.

A Nursing Home Decubitus Ulcer Case

Twenty years ago, a friend referred me a nursing home case. Our clients were three siblings in their fifties, each seemingly successful, with full-time employment where they lived in Dallas, Texas, and each with apparently happy marriages. They hired my friend to sue a local nursing home for the wrongful death of their eighty-year-old mother, who had died from sepsis secondary to decubitus ulcers resulting from an alleged failure by the staff to systematically move her in bed.

My friend and I agreed that I would focus on the liability case, and he would handle damages and client communication. I began liability discovery, which yielded a bonanza of notice evidence, prior instances of decubitus ulcers resulting from deficient care at this very same nursing home, corporate memos about the need to modify treatment protocols to drive down an unacceptable rate of such ulcers seen in its patient population across the corporation's facilities, and two whistleblowers—former employees we located to testify that their complaints about substandard care resulting in decubitus ulcers and unnecessary deaths had been presented to management and had been ignored in the name of saving money. The defense lawyer took the plaintiffs' depositions, with me hearing nothing consequential. By all accounts, my friend and I had built into discovery the foundation of a case that would yield a massive verdict, with both actual and punitive damages.

For some reason, however, the Big Law attorney with vast experience defending such cases did not appear to be concerned, as evidenced by our settlement demands being largely ignored. As we approached trial, my inquiries about settling the case were met with shoulder shrugs and comments to the effect of "we're just not in the same universe when it comes to value." My belief was that the defense lawyer was "tapping the file," and that she didn't want to settle because it would stop her gravy train of high-dollar hourly billing. Consequently, my large settlement demands were met only with comparatively minuscule offers. Surely, the case was not settling because she was withholding from her client the powerful evidence we had uncovered in discovery. With the strong evidence we had amassed, my friend and I stood puzzled—why weren't they seeing the same case we were looking at?

Eventually, one of my communications suggesting settlement was met with a proposal from the experienced nursing home defense lawyer—why don't we just do a mock trial against each other in the morning, watch the 'jury' deliberate for an hour, and then mediate in the afternoon? My evidence was overwhelming. I felt that seeing my evidence would finally and surely put the corporation's general counsel on notice of the freight train about to run him over at trial, and at long last, yield the large settlement figure to which my client was entitled. Therefore, I eagerly accepted defense counsel's invitation. Having agreed that each side would have 30 minutes to present their case, I worked diligently to cull from a large swath of evidence only the strongest and most persuasive kernels of proof. I built a PowerPoint presentation, refined it, rewrote it, and practiced it over and over again until no word was wasted, until it sang like an opera, until Clarence Darrow himself was ready to blush at the sheer force of my persuasive genius. Finally prepared, I walked into the mock trial—less than two weeks before trial—ready to win my case in the morning mock trial, and even better, get handsomely and immediately paid in settlement later that afternoon.

My 30-minute presentation was brilliant—the strongest of deposition admissions; the most powerful of smoking-gun documents; the slickest of graphics; and the most persuasive of arguments. When I sat down, my friend and co-counsel gave me a fist bump; we surely were in the money. Our opponent stood up, and following an opening PowerPoint slide with the word "liability" on it, she meekly explained the science of skin breakdown, the truism that our skin becomes more vulnerable with age, and her view that decubitus ulcers were a fact of life, even with the best of care. After twenty minutes of unpersuasive dribble, I leaned over and whispered to my friend, "They're toast." Next up was a slide that said the word "damages," followed by a map of the city of Dallas, showing the location of each of the three sibling's homes, the location of the nursing home at issue, and the close proximity of those four structures. Her next slide ended the case—it was a graphic synthesizing the nursing home's visitors log. After mom had been deposited in the nursing home twelve years ago by her three kids, who each lived less than ten miles away, the visitors log revealed that our three wrongful death survivors had visited their mother only seven, four, and two times, respectively. In twelve years. Case over.

In the state of Texas, punitive damages are capped at twice the economic damages, plus a maximum of $750,000 in noneconomic damages. In a case involving an eighty-year-old woman's death, there are no economic damages outside of around $10,000 in funeral bills, so any recovery of "mad damages" must come from driving up the actual damages awarded to each plaintiff. When a son visits his mother two times in twelve years, this is difficult to do. The jury began deliberating. I knew we were in trouble when the mock jurors all wrote down "$0" when asked what they would award each of our three "grieving" adult children. Next, several of them asked if they could award punitive damages to someone other than these three surviving children.

The point of this story is that by waiting until two weeks before trial to conduct jury research, we had failed to do our job. We lost the forest from the trees. We had failed to see the big picture. An early focus group would have involved the three plaintiffs describing their relationship with their now-deceased mother, and almost certainly would have yielded the obvious two questions that we missed: first, "why did they put their mother in a nursing home when there were three homes available within ten miles of where she was deposited by her kids?"; second, "if they loved her so much, why didn't they visit her more often?" The obviousness of those flaws in our case are now so apparent to me it is almost embarrassing to put down in writing. However, as I focus-group more and more cases, the lesson I have learned is that putting twenty-four eyes on any fact pattern is the best instrument ever devised to find truth and to discover nonsense. From an economic standpoint, as well, it would have saved me a year of work and several hundred thousand dollars in discovery and expert costs. Do your jury research earlier rather than later.

A Pharmaceutical Products Liability Case

Ten years ago, I found myself in a federal courtroom in New Orleans trying a bellwether case in an MDL involving almost 70,000 individual claims. After a successful beginning, an opening statement that went well, and a fruitful cross-examination of the defendant's corporate representative, who unwittingly was surprised to serve as my first witness, I walked from the courthouse to the hotel to begin work on Day Two in the plaintiffs' war room. Before I walked in, a lawyer I knew asked me if I would be willing to talk to some lawyers handling another MDL involving allegations that a fluoroquinolone marketed by Ortho-McNeil Pharmaceuticals under the name Levaquin caused Achilles tendon ruptures without warning of that side effect. I agreed to do so after I completed the bellwether case that I had just begun trying.

A month later, those lawyers on the Levaquin PSC hired me to try the first Levaquin case in the country, an MDL bellwether case scheduled for trial in Minneapolis in November 2010. Because of my busy 2010 trial schedule (which caused me to try eleven cases that year), we agreed that they would finish out the Levaquin discovery without me, and that my sole obligation was to show up to try the case with their work product. We did agree to a weekly hour-long conference call, where they would teach me the case, and I would direct the troops in how I wanted their evidence synthesized in graphics. Week after week, one hour at a time, we designed the liability case by building graphical slides that illustrated themes that they wanted to address.

As I read their liability depositions and the exhibits used in them, I learned that doctors prescribed Levaquin to treat difficult pneumonia that other drugs could not stop. In its class of drugs, Levaquin was far more powerful than its competitors, marketed as being effective when other drugs were not. That efficacy came with a cost, however; it resulted in more frequent side effects than others, including causing Achilles tendon ruptures at an alarming rate. Enjoying a highly profitable drug, Ortho-McNeil dragged its feet for years and did not warn Americans of this risk, even while foreign regulators forced robust warnings about the drug in Europe and Asia. During this time, when European doctors and consumers were warned of the risk of Achilles tendon ruptures but American doctors and patients were not, a Minnesota gentleman named John Schedin filled his doctor's prescription for Levaquin and promptly suffered bilateral Achilles tendon ruptures. As plaintiffs go, John Schedin provided me with the perfect Exhibit A, a plaintiff that any jury would enjoy far more than my three nursing home plaintiffs.

On our weekly graphics calls, the lawyers who hired me and who knew the facts far better than me convinced me that the U.S. Food and Drug Administration (FDA) should never have approved Levaquin because it was far too dangerous a drug. We prepared for trial advancing their chosen theme that the FDA had denigrated itself into a mere lackey for the powerful pharmaceutical industry, had willfully conspired to allow a bad drug onto the market when it should have known that innocents like John Schedin would be harmed, and had blinded itself to obvious post-marketing side effects data showing the dangers of Levaquin.

Again, violating what I knew to be true—that jury research should be done earlier rather than later—I belatedly suggested to my new colleagues that we should focus-group the case in the venue where it would be tried. Busy lawyers, vacation schedules, and my clogged trial docket prevented us from getting together in Minneapolis to focus-group the case until we were less than thirty days before trial. With 3,500 Levaquin victims behind John Schedin and his case scheduled for trial in less than a month, this delay was bordering on malpractice. Nonetheless, at least we did schedule two focus groups on consecutive days before guessing on our theory before a real jury.

As is typically my practice, I played the defense lawyer, while allowing a colleague to stand in my eventual shoes as the plaintiff's lawyer. After all our plaintiff's points were made as to why Levaquin should never have been approved by the FDA, I stood up to argue Ortho-McNeil's points. I argued that pneumonia was a major killer of older Americans, that only Levaquin stood in the gap to protect those folks from otherwise certain death, and that while it predictably had side effects like Achilles tendon ruptures, such ruptures were a small price to pay when the alternative was a funeral. John Schedin should not sue Ortho-McNeil; he should thank it. Like professional athletes, he would recover from his ruptures with rehab lasting mere months, while thereafter enjoying his life for years or decades to come thanks to Levaquin. The focus group jurors resoundingly did not buy our plaintiff's theory. Their deliberations mimicked the defense talking points, and a roomful of plaintiff's lawyers could feel their wallets being emptied and their credit lines being tapped—they were years into this case, had invested hundreds of thousands of dollars, and had thousands of clients who would never be paid because our theory of the case—frankly pulled out of thin air with no real jury research to justify it—simply did not work. The real trial, where now we would face most certain doom, was merely three weeks away. Our jury consultant suggested that we try a new strategy during the second focus group scheduled for the next day. Instead of advancing the theory that Levaquin was a bad drug, the plaintiffs would describe it as a super-drug. It was too strong; too effective. Ortho-McNeil should have reserved it only for those on their deathbeds due to end-stage pneumonia, and not make it available to doctors who prescribed it to everyone who had just contracted ordinary pneumonia, thereby sparing otherwise healthy individuals like John Schedin from the most certain destruction of their Achilles tendons. Ortho-McNeil wanted the profits that came from its super-drug, but it refused to confine those profits by servicing only those persons who really needed this powerful weapon—people unlike John Schedin. As we delivered this much more confined but medically accurate view of the case, we learned that it did not require jurors to remove Levaquin from the market as an option for doctors who were convinced that it was a last resort for their otherwise end-stage patients. Schedin's doctor agreed, testifying that because he was not warned of the Achilles tendon rupture risk, he did not prescribe other drugs available that likely would have stopped the pneumonia without causing Schedin's side effects. The mock jurors in focus group number two responded favorably. They liked the drug Levaquin, but favored making it an option only of last resort; one should face a risk of Achilles tendon rupture only if their life depended on it. Schedin's life did not, so he unnecessarily suffered Achilles tendon ruptures only because of the greed of Ortho-McNeil wanting to oversell its drug; only because his doctor was never warned about the consequences known only to the greedy pharmaceutical company. The results of focus group number two told me we had a chance.

On the flight home from Minneapolis, I redrafted every graphic in the case to fit our new jury research–tested argument. Three weeks later, I picked a federal court jury, set forth the same argument in a wholly revised opening statement, put on a case-in-chief, and cross-examined defense witnesses while repeatedly pressing the same points vocalized by our second mock jury. After a monthlong trial, a unanimous jury returned a verdict in favor of John Schedin, awarding him both actual and punitive damages. As I returned home victorious and moved on to a new adventure—the BP oil spill case—I watched from afar with dismay as other lawyers lost every subsequent Levaquin trial. As each defense verdict came over the news wires, I wondered if my colleagues had strayed from the answers provided by the second focus group, instead reverting back to the original "pull Levaquin from the market" theme conjured by well-meaning plaintiffs' lawyers who never tested that theme with jury research.

United States v. Mikal Watts

The BP oil spill case was among the most intoxicating cases I ever litigated. Immediately after returning from Minneapolis from the Schedin trial victory, I jumped into the BP case with every ounce of energy I had. For two years, I averaged more than fifty hours a week working on that single case. With sixteen other fine lawyers appointed to the PSC by the Honorable Karl Barbier, U.S. District Judge for the Eastern District of Louisiana, we collectively reviewed over 86 million pages of document production, took approximately 350 depositions in both the United States and England, and prepared for the trial of the century. As I took deposition after deposition from key BP personnel, including from its president, its former CFO, and a worldwide engineering leader, I received favor from my colleagues, who named me a member of the trial team, one of two lawyers assigned the singular focus of taking down BP, while others would focus their efforts on other defendants in the case. After the trial court found BP liable for the oil spill and guilty of gross negligence,

BP eventually paid more than $50 billion to clean up the mess of both the spills and the liabilities created thereby.

However, I never got to try the case. Seventeen days before the trial was to begin, 100 agents from the US. Secret Service raided my offices in San Antonio at the direction of an Assistant U.S. Attorney from the Southern District of Mississippi. Unhappy that his raid went unnoticed by the press and by the other lawyers and the judge in the BP case as the trial began without incident on February 25, 2013, the existence of the raid was leaked to the press. News stories published during the first week of trial trumpeted the breaking news that one of the main lawyers bringing the case against BP was now under federal criminal investigation, and his offices had been raided by the Secret Service. The negative press spread like a wildfire, and the trial court took notice; thereafter, Judge Barbier sent me a private message stating that I was now a distraction to the main case against BP and requested my resignation from the case. Regretfully, I complied.

The spring of 2013 was a lonely time, watching from afar as my colleagues tried the case against BP. With no criminal experience, I hired a well-respected lawyer from Jackson, Mississippi, to advise me. His news was not good—his friends in the U.S. Attorney's office told him that they would be handing down indictments in my case by June. My response was, "Indict me for what? I didn't do anything." June came and went; so did June 2014 and June 2015. Those early rumors of impending indictment later became a comforting belief that the feds had simply moved on. My reaction was, "Of course; they read my files and saw that we acted appropriately." I spent 2013 through 2015 working on other large mass torts, both as a co-lead on a PSC, alleging that another major drug company had needlessly injured thousands of Americans by failing to warn them of Pradaxa's risk of causing internal bleeding, and with my firm, serving as lead counsel for 57,000 American corn farmers filing suit in Minnesota against Swiss agricultural giant Syngenta, alleging that they were financially damaged when Syngenta recklessly commercialized a genetically modified corn trait which caused China to ban all corn exports from America. I also raised money for the upcoming Hillary Clinton presidential campaign. Just as it seemed that my professional life had returned to normal, I read an article from a conservative political website in Washington, D.C., which reported that Senator Ron Johnson, the Republican Chairman of the Senate Homeland Security Committee, was demanding my indictment in a letter to the U.S. Attorney General, Loretta Lynch. Mystified, I realized that larger, darker political forces were at work against me as part of some Machiavellian scheme to tie a greedy trial lawyer from Texas to Hillary Clinton, just as her campaign for president began.

Sure enough, two months later, that same Assistant U.S. Attorney obtained a 95-count felony indictment against me, alleging the crimes of conspiracy, mail fraud, wire fraud, identity theft, and aggravated identity theft. Unknown to me, I apparently had conjured and led a conspiracy to commit fraud by making up BP clients so I could get on the BP PSC and make hundreds of millions of dollars in common benefit fees. While the reasons this prosecutorial fantasy are pure fiction are too numerous for this book, the indictment read like a John Grisham novel and made me look like a scumbag criminal who been caught with his hand in the cookie jar. The potential sentence for my alleged crimes? Life in prison. Watching the indictment of a prominent plaintiff's lawyer is like watching a bomb go off. Suddenly, my "crimes" were detailed in every newspaper in America, with sordid tales of how a major Democratic bundler now faced life in prison, courtesy of the fine gumshoes at the Secret Service. The press was alerted, and hordes of cameras somehow knew where and when to be present to document my capture as I turned myself in a public spectacle known as "the perp walk." Again, my picture and my tale of woe appeared in every major newspaper in America. Having been publicly emasculated, I returned home a broken man—one who had no idea of the peril he faced.

Early research revealed that 99.7 percent of people indicted in the federal criminal justice system in 2015 had their cases end in conviction. I learned that the vast majority of those cases involved plea deals, with defendants either guilty or simply lacking the resources to fight the charges. My wife and I discussed these odds, prayed over it, and decided to fight on anyway. Why would I ever plead guilty to crimes I knew I had not committed, regardless of the risk being the end of my life as I knew it?

The next morning, I received a call from my good friend Lisa Blue and her colleague Robert Hirschhorn. They professed their faith in me and shared their desire to help. With my vast breadth of experience in criminal law—having successfully defended myself in precisely one traffic ticket trial, leaving victorious when the cop failed to show—I meekly asked, "What do you suggest?" Blue and Hirschhorn sprang into action and designed a schedule of multiple focus groups. My partner Frank Guerra prepared to be the prosecutor, building a federal government PowerPoint that outlined the charges listed in the indictment. Our partner Ed Allred agreed to play the case agent, testifying like Sergeant Friday in *Dragnet*, setting forth "just the facts, ma'am" with stunning alacrity. My lawyer from Jackson argued in my defense, and then I testified to what was true: "I was not part of any fraud; any problems with my BP client base were the result of some reason and some person unknown to me." This defense held up as well as that of Bernie Ebbers, the founder and former Chief Executive of WorldCom, whose defense at trial against allegations of massive corporate accounting fraud was "I was the CEO, but I didn't know; the fraud occurred by others far beneath me in the corporate hierarchy." Ebbers was sentenced to 25 years in a federal penitentiary. Focus group number one told me that I was soon to join him there if my defense was merely "I didn't know."

As a result, I unleashed the hounds of federal criminal subpoenas, spending millions of dollars and thousands of hours of work and trying to learn exactly what happened. A federal criminal defense case morphed into a prosecution where my team, rather than that of the government, which already had prejudged the case to be all about me, would do the hard work it would take to uncover exactly what had occurred. We subpoenaed computer records from all others involved; we hired forensic experts to analyze how client records had been altered by others in Mississippi and Louisiana before those modified records were delivered to my office. We subpoenaed the bank records of my codefendants, unmasking how they had stolen millions of dollars from me by diverting dollars invested in the BP project to finance exorbitant personal expenditures having nothing to do with the case. We learned that I had been stolen from, and others who we believed to have been working with us via a referral firm in Mississippi, had in fact committed a massive identity theft to mask their crime of theft. We learned how these individuals had gained access to a Social Security database and lifted Social Security numbers from real people, and provided them to us as belonging to persons whose names they had extracted from phone books. They did so by superimposing data to convert phantom clients into real people by using others' valid identifying information. Stunned at the brazenness of this crime against me, we continued to dig in and prepared to reveal the fraud at trial: "The government is correct that there was a fraud, but it wasn't me that did it; I'm going to show you who did it and how they did it."

Having spent so much time developing my defense, I began to think about another crazy idea. If the government's theory was that I committed a fraud to get onto a PSC to which I otherwise wouldn't have been named, what better way to debunk that theory than to demonstrate before the jury every day at trial that Mikal Watts was a real trial lawyer? Instead of quietly sitting at the defendants' table looking guilty, as my government castigated me, why not spend every day of trial personally advocating my innocence? Wouldn't it be better if I represented myself? Of course, Abraham Lincoln's adage "A man who is his own lawyer has a fool for a client"[2] dominated my thoughts, but when I shared the idea with Lisa Blue and Robert Hirschhorn, they didn't reject it outright; they said, "let's focus-group it." So, we did. The results were stunningly in my favor in focus group number two. Mock jurors who previously assumed my guilt because I was the captain of the ship that was leaking profusely now listened intently as I personally demonstrated how I had been defrauded by others, and argued strenuously that I was innocent. Deliberations shifted the focus of jurors' ire away from me and toward those who truly had committed the crime. It was a revelation.

A third day of focus groups continued to reveal a paradox seen on the first two days of jury research—political party mattered. For decades, I have been one of the most prolific donors to the Democratic party in Texas. Unknown to me, while I had raised money for Barack Obama's reelection campaign by hosting a fundraiser at my home in July 2012, the U.S. Attorney for the Southern District of Mississippi was at that very time in the midst of a massive investigation of me that cost our government more than $10 million. The indictment of me was returned in September 2015 by a grand jury in Jackson, Mississippi—a Democratic party stronghold within the otherwise red state of Mississippi. Knowing I was "a big Democrat," the U.S. Attorney there decided instead that my trial should occur in Gulfport, down on the coast where Republicans outnumbered Democrats three to one. Surely a jury of all Republicans would convict a fraudster who committed the unpardonable sin of supporting candidates from the Democratic party. Our focus groups, however, revealed that Republican jurors had a deep distrust of the federal government, and that they viewed it through a lens that saw the government as overreaching, and often incompetent. We conducted three days of double focus groups, giving us data from six groups of mock jurors along the Gulf Coast in Mississippi and Louisiana. The data leaped off the page: regardless of case theme, Republicans voted to exonerate me far more often than Democrats. While puzzling to a lifelong Democrat, I could not ignore it. It was a revelation.

---

2. Quote Investigator, https://quoteinvestigator.com/2019/07/30/lawyer/ (last visited Mar. 14, 2020).

My life now depended on my willingness to cast aside my initial instincts in favor of what our jury research had revealed—to almost universal incredulity. I read news articles castigating me for replacing my hired counsel in favor of defending myself at trial. I heard the quotes from numerous legal commentators: "Not only is he screwed; he's now gone crazy—nobody represents themselves and walks out of that courtroom." "Watts has a fool for a client." Armed with my jury research, I ignored the naysayers. After my trial began, with me conducting my own voir dire, I permitted others to pick my jury for the first and only time in my life. I watched with great discomfort as Robert Hirschhorn and Lisa Blue blew up a quarter century of my jury-picking orthodoxy and struck Democrats while cheerfully keeping only Republicans on the jury to decide the fate of their Democratic friend Mikal Watts. After a monthlong jury trial, that Republican jury exonerated me on every count, and I tearfully walked out of a federal courtroom located in a bastion of Mississippi Republican political power as an innocent man freed from false allegations. I am a free man today not merely because I was innocent; I am a free man today because I believed in pretrial jury research, and I trusted what we learned. I owe Robert Hirschhorn and Lisa Blue my life, and trial lawyers owe their clients this level of learned counsel gained through jury studies and focus groups.

Witness Selection

Witness selection depends on need and opportunity. With respect to need, appellate case law may require expert testimony on causation in a products liability or a medical malpractice case. However, if the plaintiff's accident reconstructionist concludes that the speed at impact is the exact same as the conclusion reached by the defense expert on the same subject, good trial lawyers can agree to take them both out of the case, saving jury time with a stipulation.

Opportunity exists by virtue of a careful pretrial examination of the strengths and weaknesses of the discovery taken of each witness. A defense lawyer taking a deposition but failing to ask the right questions may cause one to select that witness as a lead trial witness in an effort to achieve the element of surprise. A town leader, a priest, or a veteran—each comes with stature in credibility that justify selecting that person as a witness. If Type A females make it onto the jury, calling an impressive female expert witness might prove wise; likewise, having witnesses of different color may prove advantageous depending on the demographic makeup of one's jury. Because a lawyer does not know the makeup of the jury when witnesses have to be designated, much thought must be given months before trial about who the best witnesses might be.

Long before my criminal trial, which I describe earlier in the chapter, I gave witness selection much thought. Knowing I would be tried in Gulfport, Mississippi, far away from my home in Texas, I researched, found, interviewed, and then selected outstanding experts along the Gulf Coast in the southeastern portion of the United States: a former postmaster from the U.S. Postal Service who now lived in Mississippi; the Chair of Epidemiology at the University of Alabama-Birmingham to perform the statistical analyses in the case; a female expert in databases and data analysis from New Orleans to perform the forensic reconstruction of the subpoenaed records; an older lion of the plaintiff's bar with an impressive military background who practiced along the Gulf Coast to serve as my expert in this case, because the trial would be held in an area known for its heavy military presence. With my law firm being cast as a criminal enterprise much like Bendini, Lambert & Locke—the Memphis firm joined by Tom Cruise's Mitch McDeere in *The Firm*—I also had to select present and former employees of mine to come stand in the gap and reveal the integrity and competence of my law firm. I selected male and female employees, white and Hispanic employees, and young and old employees. We deselected from a larger list only after we learned the composition of the jury.

While some on our trial team favored calling no witnesses and resting at the close of the government's case because we had destroyed the government's case-in-chief with cross-examination, I insisted on calling these experts and firm employees anyway. Our defense case-in-chief consisted of a four-day barrage of twenty-five witnesses. I selected and called these witnesses because the jury focus groups taught me that I could not merely say that I didn't know of the fraud; as CEO of my law firm, I needed to show the jury how it occurred and how we were victimized by our codefendants' actions. The amalgam of experts we had hired accomplished that feat. Moreover, I needed to show the jury that my law firm was not a criminal enterprise as was suggested by misguided prosecutors; rather, it was an excellent law firm made up of good people. When the prosecutors yelled "gotcha" with testimony that we shredded documents, we responded by calling a sixty-year-old female Army veteran who explained to the jury our decade-long migration from being a paper-based law firm with huge document storage costs into a twenty-first-century, digitally based law firm, and that all paper documents were scanned into a database before our papers were shredded to save room. With two prominent female professionals who would clearly be the leaders of our jury seated in the front row, the prosecutors called a disgruntled female employee to suggest something was amiss in our firm. In response, we called a highly competent young female staff member who disarmed this notion. For good measure, we called a very professional, classy, and well-spoken female lawyer at our firm to establish its credibility and bona fides before those same two jurors. Knowing Gulfport to be heavily evangelical, we called the son of my church's pastor, who had worked on the case for the firm as a summer clerk at the very same time the prosecutors alleged the crime was occurring. Not only did the son of my pastor vouch for the work he and the firm did on the case, he did so with his father sitting next to his co-pastor, a nationally well-known author and pastor of my large church sitting in the front row—a subliminal but powerful character attestation that one does not earn if they have committed a crime. This kind of thought about the selection of potential witnesses is critical, but not merely when your liberty is on the line—it is important work that each trial lawyer owes to each and every one of his clients before taking their case before a jury.

Witness Order

Many jury psychologists opine that most trials are decided by the end of voir dire and opening statements. While I certainly believe a winning case can be lost thereafter, I do subscribe to the theory that the early witnesses are the most important ones.

The first witness is the most important witness, and this is true for at least three reasons. First, the law of primacy can be described as "people remember the items at the beginning of a list." Who is the first witness? This is an important question to answer, because most psychologists teach that this witness is most likely to be remembered by the jury. Second, trials are about momentum. Because the plaintiff gets to go first, she should take advantage of the law of primacy and already enjoy a clear lead in a trial where the plaintiff's opening statement occurred before the defendant's. This lead should be extended by the first witness. The first witness should be merely a "set the stage" witness only if the risk of a protracted cross-examination is completely eliminated. Against the teachings of most legal scholars, I often start my case-in-chief with a video-recorded deposition of one of the defendant's employees. I can dictate the length of the witness's testimony with careful editing. I can choose who that witness will be by looking for depositions only where the junior associate assigned to defend the witness commits the rookie mistake of saying, "We'll reserve our questions until the time of trial." When that occurs, I then have a deposition I can use to begin my case, where my excerpts cannot be watered down by questioning that advances the defense's case. Third, the selection of the first witness needs to be made while keeping in mind the chosen theme of the case. Different witnesses provide different pieces of the proof needed. Learn from jury research which element of the proof most effectively conveys the theme chosen, and then identify the singular witness that most hits that critical mark. That witness should be your first witness.

While I entirely script my case-in-chief, and I always intend to have a written and specific order of proof for all my witnesses during the case-in-chief, the reality of trial is such that live witnesses (particularly experts) have schedules to keep. Witnesses are substituted in and out of trial schedules like busboys in a busy restaurant—you never know precisely when you'll see a particular one. This need for flexibility in schedule has caused me to always take a large number of depositions when cases are in state court jurisdictions that allow deposition testimony to be admitted regardless of the "availability" of the witness to be called live. With trial judges sternly admonishing the lawyers to have their witnesses available outside the courtroom so that the trial may always proceed without any interruption caused by witnesses not present at the right time, there is no better buffer to meet that scheduling challenge than to have a litany of video deposition excerpts pre-edited and ready to play, thereby filling gaps in the schedule.

A consistent barrage of different modalities of testimony also is important. Too many videos in a row will most certainly bore a jury. However, a case sequence with live witnesses interspersed between edited video testimony, and the occasional deposition transcript read into the evidence as old-school trial lawyers used to do it, is important to maintain the interest and attention of the jury.

While the law of recency says that people tend to remember items that come at the end of the list, I do not believe that this rule dictates that the last witness of a plaintiff's case-in-chief is the most important. This is true for three reasons. First, if the plaintiff concludes his or her evidence on a Tuesday morning, the judge will likely hear a motion for directed verdict and begin the defense's case in-chief minutes after that motion is denied.

In that case, the end of the plaintiff's list of witnesses will be quickly subsumed by the beginning of the defendant's list of witnesses. Second, during the plaintiff's case-in-chief, the law of recency is achieved more significantly if the plaintiff's attorney can plan who the last witness of each trial day is, and most importantly, if the plaintiff's attorney can ensure that the last witness of each week is the most impactful. If the testimony of the last witness of a trial week is as impactful as a bomb blowing the defendant's case to smithereens, those jurors take that powerful message home with them for the entire weekend. While the court will instruct jurors not to discuss the evidence with anyone, real-world experience teaches that this instruction is oftentimes not followed. Consequently, when a juror's spouse asks on a Friday night dinner date what happened this week down at the courthouse, the first and last witnesses of the week are most likely to be remembered by the jurors over the weekend break. Third, trial weeks are consumed by 18-hour workdays. Saturdays and Sundays, therefore, are the best times for reflection and consideration of whether the case can be settled mid-trial. A witness that goes off like a bomb on the defendant on a Friday afternoon is most likely to spawn settlement discussions over the weekend.

A plaintiff's lawyer typically has no input into the order of witnesses during the defendant's case-in-chief. However, the length of cross-examinations can convey subliminal messages to the jury that are critical. Not every cross-examination needs to be long; not every cross-examination needs to be substantive. My friend Darrell Barger, a defense lawyer in Houston, has tried hundreds of dangerous, catastrophic personal injury and wrongful death cases to verdict. Frankly, he and his mentor Guy Allison, a legendary trial lawyer savant, taught me ninety percent of what I know about trying lawsuits in front of a jury. Barger's best cross-examinations include rising with a friendly wave and saying "no questions" when the direct examination of a grieving widow concludes. When a powerful expert hits him right in the gut with testimony that is undoubtedly true, Barger will rise, ask the expert "Dr. So-And-So, you and I have seen each other in hundreds of cases, haven't we?" After my expert answers in the affirmative, Barger will cheerfully offer, "It's good to see you again" and advise the court, "I've got no questions for him," while sitting down. By doing so, he conveys the message to the jury that nothing that this witness just said really matters. Perhaps most importantly, Barger is the best I've ever seen at distinguishing between what really matters and what doesn't; between what really has hurt him and what won't be dispositive in the jury room. The plaintiff's lawyer should do the same. While one defense witness may merit days of preparation and hours of piercing cross examination, others should be cross-examined in five minutes, hitting only the one or two critical points that matter.

When the defendant concludes her case-in-chief, the court then asks whether there will be rebuttal witnesses. In my view, the court is not really asking for a "yes." Deciding to withhold witnesses for rebuttal is very dangerous for several reasons, as explained in chapter 11. Many judges are ready to conclude the trial and are openly hostile to the idea of calling rebuttal witnesses. Second, defense lawyers inevitably will argue that the witness is not rebuttal at all, and that it should have been called earlier, during the plaintiff's case-in-chief. Third, in the rare instance when the trial judge permits a rebuttal witness, the scope of the testimony permitted will be so narrow that it may detrimentally diminish the power of what the rebuttal witness has to say. In more than 100 jury trials, I have called a rebuttal witness only twice. Only when the defense has foreshadowed a particular defense that is demonstrably disprovable should a rebuttal witness be reserved. If a defense lawyer hits hard on an issue during deposition—so hard that the plaintiff's lawyer can predict it will be a focus of the defense case at trial—a witness destroying that defense issue might be appropriate to serve as a rebuttal witness. However, that witness should be directly and powerfully responsive to the erroneous theory raised only during the defense case-in-chief, and it should be a central issue rather than a tertiary one. Furthermore, any rebuttal testimony should be dramatically short and to the point. The law of recency says that what the rebuttal witness says is likely to be remembered by the jury, so make it good or don't do it at all.

Exhibit Selection

I believe in introducing a lot of exhibits, but I believe it must be done strategically and for a specific purpose.

The most important objective in exhibit selection is deciding what should be the first exhibit. First, the jury must receive a signal from the plaintiff's lawyer indicating what they believe is the most important piece of evidence. That signal is delivered by marking that piece of evidence as plaintiff's Exhibit No. 1. The choice of plaintiff's Exhibit No. 1 is made knowing unequivocally that this piece of evidence is admissible. While pretrial orders requiring pre-marking of exhibits means that plaintiff's Exhibit No. 1 does not need to be introduced first, the law of primacy suggests that it should be. When law school advocacy professors suggest that your case should be able to be described in twenty-five words or less, they are really teaching the K-I-S-S principle—"**K**eep **I**t **S**imple, **S**tupid." What is your case about? Now, say it. Quickly. Simplistically. With Purpose. With Power. Strategically choosing to mark a particular piece of evidence as plaintiff's Exhibit No. 1 is a message to the jury—"this one is most important; remember that." If the message sent by marking a particular photograph of the plaintiff's decedent as plaintiff's Exhibit No. 1 is that this case is all about "Bob," and that his life that was needlessly taken by the tortious actions of the defendant, then plaintiff's Exhibit No. 1 has been earmarked as the most important exhibit about damages. If that is so, plaintiff's Exhibit No. 2 needs to be the most damning exhibit against the defendant with respect to their liability—the most powerful exhibit available demonstrating why Bob died at the hands of this defendant.

The second most important objective in the selection of exhibits is to use exhibits that appeal to all five senses through which jurors learn. As discussed in chapter 8, which is about the plaintiff's case-in-chief, selecting exhibits that appeal to visual learners, audio learners, *and* tactile learners, while also communicating to the senses of taste and smell, is an important exercise for any plaintiff's lawyer to successfully run the table of sensory perception.

The third most significant goal of exhibit selection is preassigning particular exhibits to particular witnesses. If the plaintiff's lawyer wants the jury to remember her witnesses rather than the defendant's, she must pre-plan the specific goal for each witness. Why am I calling Dr. "X"? What is my purpose for calling "Wendy Witness"? Two weeks later, in the jury deliberation room, what is the one thing I want the jury to recall about the testimony of "Ernie Expert"? The allocation of the admission of particular exhibits by witness is a great way to ensure that all the proof will get into evidence, and it ensures that each witness achieves a singular and identifiable, meaningful purpose in the eyes of the jury.

Demonstrative Exhibits

Just as a consistent barrage of different modalities of testimony is important, so is a barrage of different modalities of exhibit evidence. A stack of 8½" × 11" documents may be necessary to have some evidence of each required element of proof in the appellate record, but what is in those documents can easily be lost in the shuffle during jury deliberations. A demonstrative exhibit that calls out through enlargement and yellow highlighting the important paragraph in a fifty-page document is far more likely to be remembered by a jury after a several weeklong trial. Key testimonial admissions can be lost over time unless effort is taken to secure a transcript of the admission, blow up the critical excerpt, and put it up on the screen or up on a hardback board blow up for use again during cross-examination of other witnesses, and again during closing argument. A verbal description of how an accident occurred is interesting, but it is far more likely to be retained by a jury if that same witness signs off on a computer animation as being a fair and accurate description of what she saw. In sum, demonstrative exhibits are just as important as the underlying evidence emphasized therein—they synthesize; they emphasize; they clarify; they teach.

Different modes of demonstratives should be utilized. The three best pieces of evidence should be blown up on hardback boards. Accidents should be illustrated via three-dimensional scale models or via computerized animations. Major concepts should be handwritten on an old-school flip chart. Family photos should be used frequently as a tool to describe relationships lost by virtue of a tortious event. This variance in the mode of presentation allows counsel to make evidentiary points in a manner that teaches jurors accustomed to learning in different ways by utilizing different modes of communication.

Trial Logistics

The pretrial warm-up should be planned like a military invasion, communicated to the generals, the sergeants, and the field infantry alike, and then executed, with each person's roles and responsibilities delegated both in writing and followed-up through systematic trial team meetings. There are at least five elements of trial logistics that are paramount.

The first element of trial logistics is identifying exactly what needs to be accomplished during the six months before trial in terms of securing required proof. Case management or scheduling orders often lay out with alarming detail a wide array of pretrial deadlines. These must be calendared far in advance, and must be discussed before discovery ends. How can one assure their client that all the evidence will be in at trial unless one has written the court's charge and jury instructions, outlined the applicable elements of proof, and planned what evidence will be introduced to fill in the blanks on this required proof outline? Who are the experts that are required by the law in this type of case? Who will explain what happened to lead to the injury or death? Which witnesses and proof have been identified to meet the burden of proof that the defendant's actions caused that injury or death? How will each element of damages be proven, and with what witnesses and exhibits? All these questions must be asked and answered at least six months prior to trial. This exercise—performed that early—inevitably locates gaps in the proof that must be filled prior to the discovery deadline in order to avoid the inevitable motion for summary judgment or motion for directed verdict.

The second element of trial logistics begins when the discovery period ends. We have collected our proof in discovery. Now, we must decide how, when, and through which witness each component of that proof will get into evidence at trial. In complex cases, more than a handful of experts may serve as a witness in the plaintiff's case-in-chief. Often, those experts are chosen because they are known to be excellent; those experts' excellence consequently comes with a busy schedule. It is not sufficient that the order scheduling the trial was long ago sent to each expert. One must know the length of the court's trial day schedule—how many hours of face time before the jury will be available? One must know the court's reputation for time limits on voir dire and opening schedule, and consequently, when during the first week is the evidence likely to commence? By ninety days before trial, a preliminary decision about the order of proof—at least with respect to scheduling the plaintiff's experts—must have been made so that calls can be made to each expert explaining when during the case-in-chief each is likely to be called. Early in the first week? Late in the first week? Early in the second week? Late in the second week? These calls inevitably result in disappointment. The expert you intended to bring early in your case-in-chief is not available until the second week of trial. Your damages expert, with whom you intended to end your case-in-chief late in the second week of trial, has a vacation planned that week and must be off the stand by Wednesday of the first week. Unless these calls are made at least ninety days before trial, a trial lawyer cannot know what their case-in-chief schedule will realistically look like.

The third element of trial logistics involves the allocation and communication of roles both before and during the trial. First, who will be putting on or cross-examining each of the witnesses? With large trial teams, who will prepare the first draft of the direct examination witness outlines, detailing what exhibits will be introduced and what subjects will be covered? My firm has a specific protocol for researching the other side's expert witnesses. Our protocol involves collecting all written articles and past deposition transcripts; doing Google, Bing, and Dunn & Bradstreet research; and collecting publicly available documents via simple gumshoe research or formal Freedom of Information Act requests when applicable. Who is doing this work? When is it due? Do the court's orders exempt materials to be used on cross from being listed in the exhibit list? In either event, what are the exhibits that will be referenced during the cross-examination of each such expert? In complex cases, these kinds of assignments must be made early, and they must be followed up on in order to prevent critical elements of the trial proof from slipping through the cracks until after court deadlines have passed.

The fourth element of trial logistics involves the synthesis of the proof collected via the preparation of graphics. Beginning ninety days before trial, my firm conducts weekly trial team meetings to discuss not merely proof outlines and witness assignments, but also to work on the creation of graphics to help synthesize the proof obtained. In MDL bellwether trials, those meetings involve high-dollar graphics consultants. In smaller, individual personal injury cases, they involve our in-house employees who have experience with presentation software programs such as PowerPoint, CustomShow, Prezi, SlideShark, Keynote, GoAnimate, Windows Movie Maker, SlideShare, iMovie, and others. Single-slide graphics each require thought, purpose, execution, and simplicity. The three most important, or well-designed, graphics should be blown up into large, 4′ × 6′ hardback boards, available for constant use before the jury during opening and closing argument, and in every direct and cross-examination between. Use of these weekly graphics team meetings causes the opening statement to write itself and identifies the strengths of the case, as well as holes in the proof that need to be filled during the case-in-chief at trial.

The fifth element of trial logistics involves personnel, accommodations, and equipment. Who is going to trial? How are they getting there? Who is bringing their vehicle or do rental cars need to be obtained? Who is hauling the stuff back and forth to court each day? Have the hotel rooms been secured for the trial team? Have extra rooms been secured for the parade of witnesses that will be arriving from out of town during the case-in-chief? How many rooms do the clients require? Who is organizing the rental of an extra conference room that will house the trial team's war room, where the trial team works between the end of court each day and the start of court the next day? Have we ensured that the equipment we will need has been secured? Do we have printers and copiers for the war room? Does the conference room have Internet access and the bandwidth necessary to allow multiple trial team members to be on Wi-Fi at once, with sufficient data speed to not slow down the freight train of late-night work coming everyone's way? Is there a refrigerator there to keep drinks cold and food or snacks from spoiling? Does the courtroom have the audiovisual presentation equipment needed to display documents before the jury, the sound system sufficient to play video depositions and computer animations in a way that the jury can both easily see and hear the evidence being offered, and the extra space of a side room where trial documents, large exhibits, and presentation equipment can be stored or where witnesses subject to the rule of exclusion during the testimony of others can wait their turn to testify? Experience during trial over the years or decades teaches that putting on a case in complex litigation requires precision, planning, and execution—each of which must be thought about long before the trial actually begins.

Stipulations

When it comes to the pretrial warm-up, the concept of stipulations should not be confined merely to the admission of evidence. Trials are officiated by judges, but they are conducted by lawyers. Judges rarely, if ever, mind being told that the professionals before them have reached agreements in writing about how *their* case should be tried. Agreements between opposing trial lawyers can be reached on any number of subjects, and most will be enforced by trial judges if they are presented for approval by a time perceived by the court to be an adequate interval before trial. At their core, stipulations are helpful because they are *binding*.[3]

First, the *schedule* of trial can be stipulated to by the lawyers involved. Federal courts have been imposing time limits on trial lawyers for decades. In jurisdictions known for imposing time limits, the lawyers are more likely to achieve a judge's acquiescence to an agreement about time if they are well thought out in advance, reduced to writing via stipulation, and presented in writing to the court in advance of the pretrial conference via an agreed motion for time limits per side, which sets out the desired result of ending the trial by a specific date. Motions about agreed time limits also should offer for the parties to monitor the time themselves. In courts used to imposing such limits, the court staff typically already have time monitoring procedures; when the court does not have an established procedure, I favor an agreed-upon procedure in which one staffer from each side keeps time while sitting next to a counterpart from their opponent's trial team, and twice a day—at the end of the morning trial session and again at the end of the afternoon trial session—they collectively report the amount of time used by each side to the court reporter, who then enters their time report into the transcript of the trial proceedings, and also provides it to the court and to the parties in writing.

Second, the admissibility of witnesses can be stipulated in advance. For example, experienced plaintiff's lawyers know that defense lawyers filing *Daubert* motions on every plaintiff's expert often do so prophylactically to cover their backsides. Plaintiff's lawyers must recognize that defense lawyers who get whacked at trial for an eight-figure or nine-figure verdict are immediately called to answer for it by their clients, and they are then rebuked in writing by appellate lawyers trolling for work by assuring clients that despite their trial lawyer's screwup, they'll get the client the justice they deserve on appeal. In this climate, informal conferences with good defense lawyers often result in a prioritization of items. Experienced trial lawyers recognize that filing *Daubert* motions on every witness dilutes the impact of the one they care about. This recognition often can lead to "off the record" conversations between good lawyers, and then casual chats by both agreeing counsel with the judge in chambers, discussing which matters "I really care about." Informal horse-trading is prevalent: "I'll let this in if you'll give me that" and "If you'll agree to 'X', I'll agree to 'Y'." These side agreements are well known to experienced trial judges, who often will agree to play along because these side deals save massive amounts of court time both before and during trial. An agreement with the plaintiff's lawyer about which witnesses ought to come in and which perhaps should not, and therefore may still be the subject of an honest dispute may be casually expressed to the court as follows: "Judge, we'll rest on our papers on witness *A*, *B*, and *D*, but we really need a live hearing in court as to witnesses *C* and *E*." This kind of backroom work has allowed the defense lawyer to preserve his or her record about all five witnesses—as he or she has been ordered by the client to do—but saved the court sixty

3. *See Standard Fire Ins. Co. v. Knowles*, 568 U.S. 588, 592-93 (2013) ("Stipulations must be binding"); *See also Christian Legal Soc. Chapter of Univ. of Cal., Hastings College of Law v. Martinez*, 130 S. C.t. 2971, 2983 (2010) (describing a stipulation as "binding and conclusive" and "not subject to subsequent variation").

percent of the time that otherwise would have been required to resolve them. This type of deal also may save the plaintiff's lawyer the expense of bringing three additional witnesses to trial early in order to fend off three prophylactic *Daubert* motions.

Third, the admissibility of documentary evidence should be discussed between the parties and negotiated. After all, "evidentiary stipulations are a valuable and integral party of everyday trial practice."[4] In MDL bellwether trials, a corporate defendant faces the first of thousands or tens of thousands of claims, with the jury's verdict perhaps being the difference between potentially billions of dollars of liabilities or a financially acceptable tens of millions paid in eventual settlement. These trials paradoxically result in the defendants spending millions of dollars per bellwether trial, even when the individual damages claimed may be only in the range of five or six figures. I have seen defense war rooms occupying an entire floor of large hotels, with more than a hundred individuals working there at once. These Big Law defense teams, of course, are trying to win, but many are assigned the task of merely objecting to everything so that all is preserved for that appellate savior waiting in the wings should something go wrong at trial. This often leads to junior associates who have never seen the inside of a courtroom being assigned the task of objecting to a huge percentage of the exhibits on the plaintiff's exhibit list. I have approached trial with literally thousands of objections lodged by the defense side. Nothing can blow up the cost of a bellwether trial faster than failing to meet and confer with the other side and instead submitting these thousands of silly objections for ruling by the court. Admissibility fights in open court take time, and when it occurs thousands of times over, it adds weeks—and the resultant costs to those weeks—to any trial. Building a meet-and-confer requirement into the pretrial orders results in meetings between lawyers who understand what is admissible and what is not, rather than wasting time litigating objections lodged by young lawyers who don't have a clue what should be admitted at trial.

Fourth, the admissibility of deposition testimony likewise should be discussed between the parties and negotiated. The same young Big Law first-year, second-year, and third-year lawyers assigned the task of preserving error about the admissibility of exhibits will also be those tasked with lodging a long list of objections to most meaningful deposition testimony designated by the plaintiff's side. Horse-trading here is even more critical. Young defense lawyers will lodge objections to anything that hurts. Only experienced trial lawyers should meet and confer to reduce these long lists of manufactured disputes; they are better equipped to understand what a trial judge is likely to admit and exclude from evidence. Trade-offs should be plentiful, with the goal being to present only the most significant remaining disputes to the court for resolution.

Finally, jury instructions and the court's verdict form should involve extensive work between the parties before the court is engaged. Very few cases involve legal issues not previously addressed by appellate court decisions. Consequently, the overwhelming majority of legal instructions to be given by the court should be agreed to by the parties without requiring the involvement of the court.

4. *United States v. Mezzanatto*, 513 U.S. 196, 203 (1995).

6
Pretrial: In the Batter's Box
The Defense Perspective

Trial preparations should start when the case starts. Every written discovery request and deposition are steps on a pathway to trial. Like preparing for a battle, trial lawyers must pull together the many data points collected during discovery to create simple, cogent, credible, and factual presentations of their client's case. Every trial *is* a battle requiring focused preparations.

The thirty-to-sixty-day period immediately prior to trial is a critical time for final preparations. Scheduling orders issued by the court typically govern trial-related deadlines, including exhibit exchange, exhibit objections, witness lists, etc. In federal district courts, joint pretrial orders typically require the exchange of exhibit lists, witness lists, objections to exhibit lists, proposed jury charges, and more. In state court, even if no such requirements exist, it is a good practice to negotiate such deadlines with opposing counsel or otherwise set internal deadlines to force readiness. Deadlines for the exchange of pretrial materials also are important because they provide defense lawyers with a preview of the plaintiff's case. Any final battle plans must consider the opponent's expected plans. A review of the pretrial submissions of opposing counsel will yield valuable information about the plaintiff's strategy.

Trial Protocols

It is a good idea to establish protocols for the management of the trial on a daily basis. Many courts issue guidelines for the day-to-day conduct of a trial; but even in the absence of court-ordered procedures, defense lawyers should seek stipulations from opposing counsel regarding basic protocols—procedures for previewing demonstrative exhibits before use, prior notice of who will be called as witnesses, agreements regarding the use of technology in the courtroom, stipulations regarding admissibility of exhibits, etc. The goal is to avoid surprises, and both sides of the case will benefit from predictability.

Trial Themes

There is substantial truth to the adage that a lawyer wins or loses a case in the first days of trial. It is therefore imperative to foster good first impressions with the jury. This starts with voir dire and is followed immediately by the opening statement. Bad first impressions linger and can snowball into a losing case. Once a juror has a negative impression of a lawyer or the lawyer's client, the burden of reversing this negativity is difficult. Thus, as trial lawyers, we always should strive to arrive at the courthouse fully prepared and ready. Good first impressions are achieved by presenting cogent, simple, appealing, believable trial themes as you introduce your case and client to the jury. You want the jury to like you, your client, and your case.

Trial themes are not crafted overnight from sudden epiphanies. Rather, they are developed from the start of the case and undergo refinement and evolution as the case progresses. They are modified, enhanced, and simplified during the course of and as a result of discovery. Every trial lawyer should reexamine their trial themes during the period immediately prior to trial to assure simplicity and the common sense of key messages intended for the jury. These thematic messages dictate the substance of opening statements, exhibit selection, and witness testimony.

Good advocacy starts with fundamentals, and, again, the Greek philosopher Aristotle described these basic principles most effectively over 2,000 years ago. They consist of three cornerstones for effective persuasion: *ethos*, *pathos*, and *logos*:

- *Pathos* represents the emotional hook included in the storyteller's message to the intended audience—*the jury*. It is the emotional magnet pulling the jury into the story; it is the story's appeal that inspires interest, empathy, or sympathy.
- *Logos* is the common sense or logical underpinnings of the story—that is, the facts, data, figures, and empirical observations from the witnesses or other evidence.
- *Ethos* is the credibility and trustworthiness of the speaker. Initially, this is the trial lawyer during jury selection and opening statement. The lawyer's witnesses then continue to present the story in what is, hopefully, a trustworthy manner.

Every seasoned trial lawyer knows these three advocacy principles on an instinctive, gut level, even if they are unfamiliar with Aristotle's teachings. Aristotle simply gave these concepts names with timeless explanation. By any other name, every skilled trial lawyer knows he or she must reduce their case to simple messages that are concurrently appealing, logical, and believable. If not, they will lose.

As trial approaches, trial lawyers should reexamine their key trial messages and sharpen these messages to make it easier for the jury to favorably answer special issues or jury questions. To do this, defense lawyers must have a clear understanding of the expected jury charge and the questions the jury will answer. "Buzzwords" from these jury instructions should be lifted and incorporated into the lawyer's trial themes and, accordingly, opening statement and witness examinations. These buzzwords, when repeated, are intended to resonate with the jury and increase the chances of a favorable verdict.

Trial themes should be simple and easily grasped, so there is maximum impact through repetition, repetition, and repetition. The attention span of the average juror ranges from short to shorter. The average juror's ability to focus on a single fact is even lower—substantially lower, and measured in seconds. This reality requires immediate focus for any trial lawyer as they put the final touches on the voir dire examination and opening statement. The successful trial lawyer will:

- Avoid complicated messages.
- Avoid unnecessary messages.
- Craft short, concise messages.
- Craft easily understood messages to be repeated, repeated, and repeated.
- Stand back, evaluate, and ensure that each message is logical, appealing, and believable.

Simplicity is good. Simple themes are easily repeated, and repeated themes are better remembered. When lawyers repeat simple messages frequently, much like marketing sound bites or advertisements, the information is more likely to reside and remain with the target audience. Complicated messages alienate the listener, and the listener's focus is invariably lost or distracted. Unnecessary messages also cloud or dilute what is important. There is no doubt a jury more readily comprehends and remembers simple, logical, and believable messages.

Developing Useful Exhibit Lists

Defense lawyers frequently overload their exhibit lists with unnecessary exhibits. There is an unfortunate tendency among defense lawyers to include everything potentially relevant to the case, as well as the kitchen sink. Thus, a typical defense exhibit list frequently resembles a chaotic mishmash of documents that will never be used. Because defense lawyers often are more risk-averse than their counterparts, there seems to be a paranoid fear of inadvertent omission; thus, everything is included on the exhibit list as a precaution. This often results in an unwieldly exhibit list that may irk the trial judge. A better practice is to identify key exhibits in a disciplined, orderly, topical manner.

A useful technique involves the creation of topic categories based on the type of case. For instance, in a contract case, the lawyer should create categories for key transactional documents, contract negotiations, and damages. In a product liability case, there should be topical categories for engineering, design, and testing documents. In a personal injury case, there should be a category for key medical documents and accident investigation. The list goes on and on, and will depend on the specific type of case.

Exhibit categories are easily developed by using generic topic categories. Regardless of the nature of the case, the topic categories likely will include:

- Key transactional or event documents.
- Key photographs.
- Key documents that explain the defendant's involvement in the events leading up to the plaintiff's claim.

- Key documents that exonerate a defendant from allegations asserted against it.
- Materials identified and relied on by retained defense experts.
- Key materials to be used with opposing experts.
- Critical documents that should come into evidence under any circumstances.

As a practice tip, every deposition exhibit should be reviewed as a potential exhibit. Obviously, someone thought the exhibit was important at some point during discovery.

By organizing an exhibit list by topic category, the trial lawyer is using discipline in determining what is or what is not important. This will not only help ensure that all key exhibits are properly identified and disclosed—this method also helps eliminate unnecessary documents from the list.

Many lawyers opt to not list critical impeachment evidence on exhibit lists. However, to avoid risk, a better practice is to identify such exhibits, particularly if they are well known to plaintiff's counsel. If the existence of an "impeachment exhibit" is known to all parties, it is a close call whether the exhibit is properly labelled as "impeachment only." A safer practice is to disclose the exhibit.

Exhibit Numbering

It is a good practice to identify the most important exhibits at the top of the exhibit list. Some lawyers prefer to arrange exhibits chronologically. However, it is more effective to arrange exhibits in terms of importance or by topic. Critical exhibits should receive low exhibit numbers, e.g. Ex. 1, Ex. 2, Ex. 3, etc. This helps reinforce the importance of these exhibits in the eyes of the jury. The lower the number, the more important the exhibit. Simply put, important exhibits should not be buried in the middle or at the end of the list. This is because the jury will infer that Exhibit No. 1 is more important than Exhibit No. 101. Lower exhibit numbers also are more easily remembered when the jury retires to the jury room for deliberations. If the jury is searching for an exhibit, it is easier to remember and locate Defense Exhibit No. 1 than Defense Exhibit No. 88.

Internal Exhibit Lists

Depending on the number of exhibits, it is useful to prepare internal exhibit lists on a Microsoft Excel spreadsheet, which is subject to electronic manipulation to reorder exhibits chronologically, by topic, or by witness. This provides an excellent mechanism to search for exhibits in an extensive database. An Excel spreadsheet also is valuable because it provides a system for keyword or topic searches. By way of example, the spreadsheet can include a comments field where search terms are inserted for easy computer retrieval, such as *hot document, key document, harmful document, key impeachment, witness name, background information, expert material*, etc. This is particularly useful if there are numerous exhibits or multiple witnesses in a complicated case. This procedure allows rapid-fire searches and exhibit retrieval. An example follows:

Ex. No.	Description	Date	Topic	Comment
Ex. 1	Contract between ABC Company and XYZ Corp.	04/23/1987	Transactional Doc.	> Key Document
Ex. 2	First Amendment to Contract	09/02/1995	Transactional Doc.	> Key Document
Ex. 3	Letter from Smith to Jones informing of intent to terminate Agreement	06/08/2005	Event Document	> Hot Document > Jones Direct
Ex. 4	Plaintiff's Expert Report	10/10/2015	Opposing Expert	> Harmful Document
Ex. 5	Defendant's Expert Report	12/10/2015	Def. Expert	> Key Document

Consulting with Experts

In a case involving multiple expert witnesses, it is a good practice to contact your retained experts and seek their advice about what they consider the most significant documents or other tangible evidence supporting their opinions. Although defense lawyers already know what is important, additional feedback from consulting or testifying experts never hurts. Retained experts also can provide guidance when identifying key exhibits for impeaching opposing experts. A disciplined exhibit list should have a separate category for expert materials, including documents perceived as critical by the experts.

Demonstrative Exhibits

Exhibit numbers should be placed on important demonstrative exhibits. Although these exhibits are not admitted into evidence, demonstratives are more easily referenced during trial if they carry an exhibit number reference. This also imbues the exhibit with added importance in the eyes of the jury.

Exhibit Objections and Stipulations

Few cases are won based on objections to document authenticity. It also is clear that most trial judges frown upon authenticity objections unless there is a legitimate dispute over the origin of a critical document. Thus, to facilitate the admissibility of exhibits, reasonable efforts should be made to reach stipulations about both authenticity and stipulations on business record exceptions to the hearsay rule. This removes substantial uncertainty about the admissibility of exhibits for both sides.

Many courts require the parties to confer after exchanging objections to exhibits. The goal is to reduce the number of substantive objections and facilitate the admissibility of exhibits. Although many defense lawyers feel a compulsive urge to object to all exhibits that may hurt their case, this is not a good practice. Excessive objections likely will irk the trial court, the jury, or both. Thus, we should be encouraged to confer with opposing counsel to reduce the number of objections. Horse-trading is encouraged because substantial benefit can be obtained by swapping concessions on admissibility. There is truth in the saying "What is good for the goose is good for the gander." Reasonable flexibility toward the opponent's exhibits should inspire reciprocal flexibility. The converse also is true.

If exhibit objections are not resolved through conference or pretrial proceedings, many courts will require objections to be made at the time the exhibit is offered. This places the objecting party at a significant disadvantage if there are numerous exhibits that require objection. Multiple objections in the presence of the jury may alienate the jury, causing jurors to perceive the objecting party as obstructionist. Recurring objections create a negative impression with the jury that is not easily overcome. Isolated objections will not have this effect. This is yet another reason why exhibit objections should be minimized to the extent possible.

Keeping the Bad Stuff Out—Motions in Limine

Careful scrutiny of the plaintiff's expected evidence is important. All defense lawyers should study the plaintiff's exhibit list, deposition excerpts, and expected witness testimony to identify the evidence calculated to do the most harm. Obviously, all skilled plaintiff's lawyers intend to inflict as much harm as possible, and their strategies frequently can be gleaned from a review of their exhibit lists. This analysis will lead to more carefully crafted motions in limine.

Many defense lawyers go overboard in their motions in limine. Like a paranoia-inspired exhibit list, a typical defendant's motion in limine tends to be overinclusive, if not excessive. The better practice is to identify particularly harmful evidence that *must* be excluded to get a fair trial. By focusing on fewer issues, the court is more likely to grant a hotly contested motion in limine. Otherwise, the court will view a boilerplate motion in limine as an obstructionist effort to seek exclusion of all potentially harmful evidence. Presenting fewer motions in limine has the benefit of focusing the court's attention on the importance of the issues specially selected for argument.

Many courts refuse to grant motions in limine based on relevance alone. This is because most courts are unwilling to make relevancy determinations before trial. Relevancy decisions require context, and this context is missing until the court hears testimony. Therefore, it is a better practice to identify matters in limine that are properly excluded for reasons other than mere relevance, such as hearsay or matters that inject severe prejudice into the case far outweighing any relevance.

By way of example, gruesome photographs should be excluded under Rule 403 of the Federal Rules of Evidence (or comparable state evidentiary rules). Even though relevant, the probative value of gory, graphic images is frequently outweighed by tremendous risks of prejudice. No one needs to see an amputated limb; no one needs to see multiple images of a bloody, lifeless body at an accident scene. The plaintiff's lawyer wants these types of inflammatory photographs admitted. The defense needs to exclude this evidence, if possible.

Evidence of immoral character or unethical conduct is another example. Whether a defense witness has been indicted is likely irrelevant. Whether a defense witness is promiscuous also may be irrelevant. If such conduct has no remote nexus to the case, it is properly excluded because the risk of jury confusion and undue prejudice is great. Evidence of a witness's bad habits or behavior should be excluded if the sole purpose is to inflame the jury and cause the jury to dislike the defendant or witness. There must be a reasonable nexus to the liability or damage issues in the case.

Likewise, in product liability cases, evidence of other "similar" accidents or incidents should be excluded until a predicate is first established about reasonable or substantial similarity. The prejudicial impact of other accidents—particularly those that cause significant injury or death—is highly prejudicial. Product liability cases are frequently lost on this basis alone. The jury naturally thinks, "Where there's smoke, there's fire."

These are just a few examples. The bottom line is to focus on significant pieces of evidence the defendant needs to exclude to better assure a fair trial. The goal is to maintain an even playing field. Clearly, there are certain types of evidence that are not easily overcome. The plaintiff should not be allowed to get a head start by inflaming the jury. Thus, the defendant's motion in limine should not be used to exclude all potentially negative evidence, but should focus on the stuff that really hurts *even if* it is relevant.

Witness Lists and Witness Order

The identity of important trial witnesses *should* certainly be known well in advance of trial. However, there is an art to sequencing when witnesses are presented in the defense case-in-chief. As a general observation, the defense case should start with a strong witness and end with a strong witness. The jury is expecting an immediate, dramatic start to the defense case. If the defense case starts with a whimper, important momentum is lost. At the same time, the last witness in the defense case-in-chief should be strong because he or she is "batting cleanup"—the last witness is the "closer."

Some witnesses are charismatic, but most are not. Some witnesses may be visibly nervous at the prospect of taking the witness stand. These witnesses should be called in the middle of the defense case, supported by stronger witnesses both before and after their testimony. This helps bolster any weak or tepid performance. This practice tip also applies to witnesses who are more vulnerable on cross-examination. They should be called in the middle of the case and bolstered by stronger witnesses who both precede and follow their testimony. Again, this insulates their testimony and provides the defense lawyer with an opportunity to rebound, if necessary. The lesson is clear: *start strong, end strong.*

When considering "weak" witnesses, you also should consider whether their testimony is necessary at all. Not all witnesses should be called to the stand. Testimony that is purely cumulative should be avoided, if possible. Witnesses who simply reaffirm another witness's testimony may become tiresome to both the court and the jury, and also may confuse the jury. This is particularly so if the trial is expected to last a long time. Juries frequently become impatient with defense lawyers if they perceive the case as being needlessly protracted. Therefore, efforts should be made to hone and sharpen witness presentations for a crisp, efficient case. Both the court and the jury will react favorably.

Client Witnesses Called Adversely

It is always wise to assume that your client or corporate representative may be called to the stand as an adverse witness during the plaintiff's case-in-chief. This is a strategy frequently used by skilled plaintiff's lawyers to throw the defense off balance and potentially catch the defense unprepared. An unprepared defense witness called in the plaintiff's case, when the plaintiff's lawyer has the first shot with an aggressive cross-examination, can severely damage the defense and gives the plaintiff rocket fuel to start his or her case. Defense lawyers therefore are well-advised to devote meaningful time to preparing his or her client for this possibility. It may be too late to start these preparations after opening statements because the defense witness may be the first witness called to the witness stand. Surprises at trial should be avoided. So, as defense lawyers, we should prepare our clients both psychologically and substantively for this possibility.

Witness Examination Outlines

Delaying preparation of witness examination outlines until after trial starts is unwise. Every defense lawyer already should know the key defense themes far in advance of trial. As such, every defense lawyer should know the key examination goals for each witness well before the witness takes the stand. This applies equally to both direct and cross-examinations. Witness outlines should be prepared before trial. Exhibits that will be used in each examination should be identified. Critical impeachment evidence (prior deposition testimony or documents) should be identified and readied for cross-examination.

A good practice tip is to create a witness box for each witness who is expected to testify. At a minimum, this witness box should include:

- At least two copies of the witness's prior deposition testimony (one for the witness and a working copy for the defense lawyer).
- Any prior witness statements.
- A copy of the subpoena, if any.
- Critical exhibits that may be used with the witness.
- Multiple copies of key impeachment exhibits (they should be anticipated and ready for use if the witness is adverse or hostile).

A witness outline that defines key objectives also is recommended. The bottom line is that every examination must be planned, and this planning requires quiet time to consider strategic approaches for each witness and how the defense trial themes can be advanced with each witness. It is difficult to find this quiet time during the middle of trial with long days and even longer nights.

Technology in the Courtroom

Decisions about technology should be made before trial. Many courts provide technology in the courtroom; unfortunately, not all do. As such, trial lawyers frequently must bring their own technology, including projection screens, video monitors, document enlargement devices, and similar equipment, with them to the courthouse. This requires a physical inspection of the courtroom to determine where equipment should be located for the best possible effect. Coordinating these efforts with opposing counsel and the court's staff is advisable. Large pieces of audiovisual equipment should never be ushered into the courtroom without the court's permission.

Similar decisions should be made about the types of computer software used to present documents and deposition clips. There are many software programs available, and these decisions should be made early, with steps taken to ensure that legal assistants or support staff are proficient with these programs. Support staff should practice with these programs to make sure they can handle directions in the courtroom quickly and effectively under pressure. No one wants a sloppy presentation.

Finally, while technology is ubiquitous today, you should always have a backup plan. You never want to be unable to present evidence or argument because a USB flash drive is broken or the court's Internet is down.

Courtroom Reconnaissance

If the trial team is unfamiliar with the courtroom, a visit with court personnel is necessary to understand how voir dire will be conducted and how the voir dire panel will be ushered into the courtroom and seated. Voir dire jury maps are created based on the physical layout of the courtroom and how the voir dire panel is seated. An incorrect voir dire map can cause potential errors during jury selection.

A courtroom visit also is important so defense lawyers can be introduced to court personnel. It is important to have good relationships with all members of the court staff, including the court reporter, the clerk, and the bailiff. Obviously, a good relationship with the judge is *always* a good thing to foster.[1]

Yet another reason for a pretrial visit to the courtroom is to visually define where files may be stored. Coordination on this point with the court staff is necessary. It is a good idea to ask permission and not assume you can place equipment or boxes without the consent and agreement of the court's staff.

Lastly, a trip to the courthouse with your client or client representative is a good idea. This allows the client to see the courtroom and the witness stand. By gaining familiarity with the courtroom surroundings, the client or client representative will be less anxious and fearful because the "unknown" is now known.

Demonstratives

Decisions about demonstrative exhibits should be finalized before trial. Some demonstratives require substantial preparatory work, such as to-scale models, video animations, topographical models, or sophisticated charts. Exhibit preparation experts, model builders, and computer programmers also are sometimes needed. Therefore, substantial lead time may be required to achieve best results. The point here is that delay may prejudice preparation of effective demonstratives.

Many lawyers confer with jury consultants to maximize the effectiveness of demonstrative exhibits. Again, this requires substantial lead time. Depending on the defense budget and the client's financial resources, it is frequently advisable to test the efficacy of

---

1. Always remember the adage: "*A good lawyer knows the law; a great lawyer knows the judge.*"

demonstrative exhibits with focus groups. Again, this cannot be done overnight. Advance planning is necessary.

Jury Studies

Whether to use focus groups or jury studies is a significant issue. Conducting a jury study too early in the life of a case may generate unreliable information because there are insufficient facts presented to the focus groups. The defense lawyer also may have an incomplete understanding of the case. On the other hand, if the trial lawyer postpones jury studies until the last days or weeks before trial, it may be too late to respond or react to negative lessons derived from the study. The discovery period is likely closed, and the opportunity to fix an emerging problem may be lost. Thus, typically, a jury study should be conducted before the close of discovery so discovery options remain available if additional evidence or depositions are needed. As a general rule, conducting a jury study during the last days before trial is not a beneficial use of time. There are some exceptions.

A jury study or focus group often is used to test juror reactions to particular witnesses who invariably will be called to the stand. By obtaining feedback from the focus group, the trial lawyer or jury consultant can better prepare the witness for his or her testimony. Focus group studies during the closing weeks before trial are also valuable to verify the effectiveness of demonstrative evidence. A focus group is shown a variety of demonstrative evidence and then asked to provide feedback. This data is used to enhance or improve the demonstratives before trial.

Dress Rehearsals

Practice, practice, and more practice is a key to success. Sufficient time should be set aside to practice voir dire, the opening statement, and critical witness examinations. The voir dire presentation and opening statement should be rehearsed in the presence of both staff members or attorneys who are familiar with the facts, as well as those who are not. By rehearsing with live audiences, the presentations are better honed. Again, an important benefit derived from live rehearsals is to achieve a smooth delivery. By practicing both voir dire and the opening statement, weak points also are eliminated. The presentations are strengthened from feedback from live audiences.

Mock witness examinations of the client or other important defense witnesses also is helpful. Again, this is important for both the witness and the lawyer. Witness examination outlines are initially prepared and then modified to create a fluid dance between the examining lawyer and the client witness. Covering all significant trial themes within the witness's personal knowledge is an equally important objective. Again, Aristotle's three points of advocacy should be considered in planning every witness outline, making the testimony logical, interesting, inviting, and believable.

Equal time should be invested when preparing client witnesses for cross-examination. Multiple variables should be addressed: demeanor, responding to difficult questions, conceding logical and commonsense points to avoid losing credibility, articulating important trial themes in response to challenging questions. Through practice and rehearsal, the performance of a poor witness can be improved; the performance of a good witness can be made excellent. By doing rehearsals, the client witnesses also become more comfortable and confident in their testimony, and this confidence will pay dividends in the courtroom. Again, such preparations should be undertaken before trial. Waiting until the last minute creates stress for both the lawyer and the witness.

Pocket Briefs

It is a good practice to develop "pocket briefs" on important legal or evidentiary issues. If the defense anticipates significant legal or evidentiary issues during the course of trial, concise briefs should be prepared and submitted to the court when the issues arise. The best practice is to have these briefs fully prepared and ready before trial.

Jury Charge

Most federal courts require the submission of a jury charge as part of the joint pretrial order that is filed before the trial commences. Many state jurisdictions require similar filings. By submitting a jury charge before trial, the parties are forced to identify the key legal issues that will be submitted to the jury, and this forces the parties to better understand their respective cases.

A best practice is to begin preparing a jury charge during the early stages of the case. This is because it is difficult to develop trial themes and discovery strategies unless there is an appreciation for the basic legal principles that will govern the lawsuit. Some lawyers preach that a jury charge should be drafted during the first weeks of a case. Although this is an aggressive, if not impractical, recommendation, the underlying principle is laudable. The sooner the trial lawyer understands and appreciates the operative legal principles, the more effective the lawyer will be in discovery, preparing witnesses, and examining witnesses in depositions.

Thus, during the last weeks before trial, defense lawyers should already have a well-grounded understanding of how the jury will be charged and instructed. By refining the jury charge and instructions during this final preparation period, the defense lawyer is better postured to refine trial themes, witness outlines, and key exhibit selections.

The Wrap-Up

The last weeks before trial are used to refine and sharpen what is already in the lawyer's trial arsenal. Discipline should be used in exhibit selections, witness selections and witness order, and focused motions in limine. Once these decisions are made, it is equally important to hone nonlegal aspects of trial, such as courtroom reconnaissance and familiarizing your witnesses with the court environment and structure of trial.

7

The Pretrial Conference

The Plaintiff's Perspective

For the plaintiff's lawyer, the pretrial conference is the single event in the trial process that brings the most risk and the most opportunity. At this stage, critical evidence can be lost forever in the trash bin of inadmissibility, or it can be preordained as appropriate for the jury, as "[m]ost pretrial orders of district judges are ultimately affirmed by appellate courts,"[1] and with minor exceptions,[2] pretrial rulings are not appealable. "Factual assertions in pleadings and pretrial orders, unless amended, are considered judicial admissions conclusively binding on the party who made them."[3] For this reason, effective and careful planning for the pretrial conference is a precursor to a successful trial; it should include succinct pretrial motions and motions in limine; more-extensive briefs about significant legal issues; strategic presentation of challenges to the other side's experts and careful defenses of one's own experts; and the meticulous effort to pre-admit exhibits.

Preparing and Arguing Pretrial Motions and Motions In Limine

The most important aspect of pretrial motions and motions in limine is to remember that less is more. Judges enjoy only one part of the pretrial conference—the end. Pretrial motions and motions in limine should not be a recycling exercise in which a law firm's form files are pulled out of deep storage, dusted off, and copied with little to no thought about why they are being utilized again. Courts want no part in being asked to rule on motions to enforce the rules of evidence, and neither pretrial motions nor motions in limine should be the vehicle to require an opponent to follow the rules. Instead, a good trial lawyer sits down

1. *Mohawk Industries, Inc. v. Carpenter*, 558 U.S. 100, 110 (2009) (quoting *Richardson-Merrell*, 472 U.S. 424, 434 (1985)).

2. *See Plumhoff v. Rickard*, 572 U.S. 765, 772-73 (2014) (denial of qualified immunity falls within collateral order doctrine, permitting immediate appeal).

3. *Amgen, Inc. v. Connecticut Retirement Plans and Trust Funds*, 568 U.S. 455, 470, n. 6 (2013) (quoting *American Title Ins. Co. v. Lacelaw Corp.*, 861 F.2d 224, 226 (9th Cir. 1988)).

with his or her trial team to decide what absolutely cannot come into evidence because its mere mention will inexorably ruin the upcoming trial. In any case worth trying, there will not be more than a handful of these stink bombs that absolutely must be kept out of the courtroom. I tried my first case almost thirty years ago, before a longtime judge in East Texas. In the pretrial hearing, the judge held up my inch-thick group of motions in limine that came from the firm's "Motions in Limine" forms file and said, "Mr. Watts, it's been my experience that there is never more than five issues that need to be decided by motion in limine; pick your best five." I did, he ruled only five times, and we started trial thirty minutes later. Ever since, I have encouraged lawyers in my law firm to present only five motions in limine to the court. At a pretrial hearing, the lawyer who presents far fewer motions in limine than his or her opponent likely will be ahead of the game in the fight to win the judge's favor. As a plaintiff's lawyer, I try to pare down the number of motions I file against the defendant's evidence. The reason for this is to draw a contrast with the defendant during the pretrial conference. If I argue only three motions in limine, I have a better chance of the judge not splitting the baby by overruling some and granting some. Conversely, if I put forth twenty-five motions in limine, the odds of the judge granting some and overruling some is dramatically increased, introducing risk that evidence that's critical to my case falls to the cutting room floor while the court is trying to make its way through the gauntlet of a long list of motions. It is not necessary to present myriad motions in limine in an effort to require the other side to follow the rules of evidence; that is for objections *during* trial.

In preparing a particular motion in limine or a pretrial motion to exclude evidence, one should again remember that less is more. All that is required is a short, one-page motion that specifically cites an evidentiary rule and a case on point that holds the evidence at issue inadmissible. The Federal Rules of Evidence and their state corollaries have been in effect for decades now; as a consequence, most judges have referenced these rules for their entire judicial careers. Judges understand that under Rule 402, "relevant evidence is admissible," unless the constitution, a statute, or other rules provide otherwise, and that under Rule 401, evidence is relevant if "it has any tendency to make a fact more or less probable than it would be without the evidence" and "the fact is of consequence in determining the action." Consequently, any motion seeking to exclude evidence as irrelevant needs to specifically and succinctly argue why such evidence has no tendency to make a fact of consequence in determining the action more or less probable, and should also specifically cite Rule 402 for the proposition that "irrelevant evidence is not admissible." Motions to exclude evidence for the alleged undesirable baggage of (1) "unfair prejudice," (2) "confuse[ion of] the issues," (3) distortion ("misleading the jury"), (4) "undue delay," or (5) being "needlessly . . . cumulative" should argue with particularity which of these five negative consequences referenced in Rule 403 will occur if the evidence is admitted. Moreover, a cogent argument should be offered about why this otherwise relevant evidence is so harmful that its probative value is substantially outweighed by a danger of one or more of the five undesirable consequences listed in Rule 403. Rule 403 is not a rule of exclusion of evidence that merely hurts; indeed, all evidence admitted helps one side and hurts the other. When Rule 403 is invoked, it should be specifically quoted with a purpose and an appellate court decision applying that rule to exclude the same kind of evidence at issue. Likewise, a motion to exclude character evidence; other crimes, wrongs, or other acts; subsequent remedial measures; settlement offers; offers to pay medical expenses; criminal pleas; liability insurance; previous sexual conduct; or privileged information, should cite the particular rule of evidence calling for exclusion of the evidence, and cite a reported opinion from the highest appellate court excluding similar evidence. With respect to any motion in limine, this can be done in one page or less. Again, less is more.

Arguing motions in limine requires even more brevity. In less than a minute, one should cite the applicable rule of exclusion, offer a case on point that holds that such evidence is inadmissible, and argue why the evidence in the case at bar is similar to the evidence in the cited opinion. *After* the defendant responds, *then* a reply should be offered. The reply should succinctly point out the specific reason that case law offered by the defendant is inapplicable or distinguishable. Likewise, contrasting the distinguishing factors that render the defendant's supposed precedent inapplicable with the reason the case you offered is more on point also is a legitimate exercise for the reply.

Always have the critical cases at issue on hand, pre-flagged and pre-highlighted. If a case is important enough to cite, it is important enough to have copies of it on hand—one for opposing counsel and one for the court, with the particular page at issue pre-flagged and the specific holding at issue pre-highlighted. Pre-flagging and pre-highlighting cases also shows preparation and gives the judge confidence that you, as the lawyer providing the case, are organized enough to protect the court from being reversed. Furthermore, it achieves speed. In mere seconds, the judge should be able to take the case being handed to him or her, find the page at issue because it has been flagged, and find the holding at issue because it has been highlighted. When arguing motions in limine, get to the point, get in, and get out.

Preparing Trial Briefs for Significant Legal Issues

Sources of privilege or statutory exclusion often involve significant legal issues that may require more extensive briefing. Likewise, when issues of evidentiary exclusion lack a case on point from the appellate court immediately above the trial court hearing the motion, more extensive briefing is often appropriate. If the jurisdiction at issue does not have a case on point, holdings from other intermediate appellate courts from the same state can be persuasive. However, if the cases supporting the motion come only from other jurisdictions, necessity requires that those cases be utilized. When citing cases from other jurisdictions, trial briefs explaining why that holding from another jurisdiction is the majority rule can be helpful. Likewise, if cases from jurisdictions reach opposite holdings, trial briefs should specifically argue why the reasoning of one is more persuasive than another.

The Rules of Professional Conduct and most local rules of court require that adverse authority be provided to the court.[4] Consequently, when a case exists with a holding that

4. Model Rule of Professional Conduct 3.3(a)(3) ("A Lawyer shall not knowingly fail to disclose to the tribunal legal authority in the controlling jurisdiction known to the lawyer to be directly adverse to the position of the client and not disclosed by opposing counsel").

supports your opponent's position, you should reference it, but then distinguish it. Never ignore an adverse case because the judge will find your credibility compromised by such a silent intent to mislead the court. Instead, citing a case that supports your position, and then arguing why that case is more appropriately followed than the adverse case honestly and appropriately disclosed to the court as needing to be distinguished, is the best way to win the day. Credibility is the singular weapon a lawyer arguing a motion has in his arsenal. Once credibility is lost, so is the motion at issue, and oftentimes, the motions to come thereafter, as well. By contrast, citing and then distinguishing adverse authority makes it more likely that one's credibility is preserved, yielding dividends on both the present motion and future motions.

Preparing, Prosecuting, and Defending Expert Challenges

While the Supreme Court's ruling in *Daubert v. Merrell Dow Pharmaceuticals, Inc.*, 509 U.S. 579 (1993) was actually a victory for the plaintiff in that case, the dicta contained in that opinion has led to a generation-long cottage industry of "paper litigators" filing roomfuls of motions to exclude experts under *Daubert* in an effort to keep trial lawyers from arguing their cases before a jury. Appellate rules requiring that appellate issues be preserved by first presenting the argument to the trial judge below have caused defense lawyers in high-dollar cases to file *Daubert* motions indiscriminately. These motions require rulings by the trial court, meaning that great care must be exercised in preparing, prosecuting, and defending expert challenges.

For the plaintiff's lawyer, the decision about how many *Daubert* motions to file is critical. Because the plaintiff has the burden to prove the elements of the case, a plaintiff's lawyer often cannot get to the jury if one of his or her experts is struck. In this scenario, why would a plaintiff's lawyer ever move to challenge all the defense experts? As discussed in the chapter "The Pretrial Warm-Up," the defense lawyer may feel compelled to prophylactically challenge every one of a plaintiff's experts, but the plaintiff's lawyer is under no similar obligation to "preserve error."

In thirty years of trying cases, I have never moved to exclude the testimony of more than one defense expert in a trial. There are at least three reasons for this. First, I feel no duty to "preserve error" so that I can appeal an adverse jury verdict. Having won many cases and lost others, I typically have no desire to retry a case I have already lost once. Thus, my tactical choices about what to object to often do not have an appellate record in mind; rather, I object only to those matters that have a practical consequence of making victory at trial more or less likely. Objecting to all the defendant's experts does not appreciably move the ball down the field toward trial court victory; instead, it just irritates the trial judge. Second, as referenced earlier, moving to exclude a defendant's expert makes it more likely that the court might just accidentally exclude a plaintiff's expert, as well. If the plaintiff's expert excluded in this tit-for-tat *Daubert* adjudication game is required to get to the jury, then the unwise decision to try to strike all the defense experts may just be the reason the plaintiff's case is lost before it ever gets to the jury. Third, most flaws in testimony that might render such expert testimony inadmissible under *Daubert*, or otherwise excludable under the rules of evidence, are flaws that could be devastating before a jury on cross-examination. Every juror I have ever interviewed post-verdict has referenced some seminal event during cross-examination that won the day in their eyes. If an expert has a fatal flaw in his or her analysis, why forgo the *mano-y-mano* destruction of that expert before the jury in live combat? There is no greater moment in a jury trial than a devastating cross-examination of a paid expert. For this reason, I would much rather have a flawed expert testify and then be destroyed before the jury than have that expert never appear before the jury at all.

Defending expert challenges must be done meticulously because it is a process fraught with peril. After all, in many product liability cases, or those requiring expert testimony, if you lose your expert, you lose your case. For this reason, every defense of a *Daubert* challenge must be couched in terms of what it is—a motion for summary judgment masked as a *Daubert* motion. Tell the judge, "If you grant this motion to strike *Ed the Expert*, you are telling *Quincy Quadriplegic* he has no redress because that ruling effectively guts his case." The court must be specifically informed about what required element of proof *Ed the Expert* will testify, and it must be educated that without *Ed the Expert*, *Quincy the Quadriplegic* cannot meet his burden of proof under the law of the applicable jurisdiction. Most trial judges avoid granting summary judgment, subliminally understanding that they cannot get reversed for denying a summary judgment, but they can be reversed for granting one. Framing the *Daubert* motion at issue as effectively a motion for summary judgment is another way to suggest to the court that permitting the testimony is perhaps the safer way to go.

In addition to the stakes involved, the court must be educated on the precedents at issue. A national Westlaw search of "*Daubert*" yields more than 10,000 case results since 1993. Appellate review of trial court *Daubert* rulings is perhaps more extensive than any other legal issue reviewed on appeal over the past quarter century. Different jurisdictions have holdings that differ starkly from others. Frankly, there is something in the nation's *Daubert* jurisprudence for everyone. As such, careful research of this *Daubert* case law is a must for four reasons. First, many experts worth calling are hired precisely because they are skilled and experienced at testifying before juries. In the same way that any prior opinion striking an expert is sure to be cited to the court when a motion to strike him or her is presently filed, appellate or federal district court decisions permitting the expert to testify over prior *Daubert* motions should be collected and provided to the court. Likewise, affidavit proof from the expert setting forth their Rule 26 trial and deposition testimony list, together with an affidavit averring that they have never before been struck, is a very persuasive component of a response to a motion to strike that expert. Second, many jurisdictions have dramatically confined the applicability of the *Daubert* decision to novel areas of testimony instead of expert opinions one is qualified to give under Rule 702(a) by virtue of their "knowledge, skill, experience, training or education."[5] The "relevance and reliability" jurisprudence is far more encompassing than jurisprudence that limits all expert testimony to only scenarios where the four *Daubert* factors are met. Third, the appellate case law of any

5. Fed. R. Evid. 702(a).

jurisdiction includes cases where a trial court's decision to exclude an expert has been overturned, requiring a reversal, and a retrial of the case. Utilizing those cases to remind the trial court that erroneously excluding an expert will require a retrial is the most effective way of checking their desire to save themselves an additional trial by granting a *Daubert* motion. Fourth, this *Daubert* case law is replete with examples of appellate court's ruling that expert testimony in given fields and circumstances was, in fact, admissible. Any response to a motion to exclude an expert should be full of such case citations.

In arguing *Daubert* motions, counsel should appeal to the court's sense of *fairness* and its desire for *efficiency*. How is it fair to require a quadriplegic plaintiff to pay for all six of his experts to travel to town to give live testimony at a pretrial *Daubert* hearing—and then have to do it again during trial—merely because a defense lawyer is firing off *Daubert* bullets like a silly child playing cowboy in a video arcade. It is not. *Fairness* and *efficiency* argue for the trial judge using the court's discretion to choose to decide the *Daubert* issue during trial. There is absolutely no rule that prohibits a trial judge from allowing the expert to testify before the judge and jury as to her qualifications and methodology, and then allowing the parties to approach the bench to argue and obtain a ruling on the *Daubert* motion before counsel elicits the first Rule 702 opinion. *Fairness* is a principle that should be argued for by invoking the nobility of our founding fathers choosing to put the right to a civil trial by jury into the Bill of Rights in the form of the Seventh Amendment. How is it fair in light of that constitutional protection to prevent a jury from deciding the case under the guise of a wolf-like motion for summary judgment masquerading as a *Daubert* motion masked in sheep's clothing? *Efficiency* is a principle that should be argued for by setting forth the schedule in advance to the court. The expert at issue is necessary for the plaintiff to meet his burden of proof with respect to element "B" of cause of action "X"; "Judge, we've got to have him to get to the jury, and he won't testify more than 45 minutes." Likewise, *efficiency* can be argued for by agreeing to confine the scope of what an expert will do before the jury. After an expert pops off in deposition, giving an additional opinion or side observation that was not part of their core designated responsibility in the case, responding to a *Daubert* motion seeking to prevent that pop-off from being repeated before the jury is oftentimes best responded to with a simple, "Judge, we're not going to bring that out before this jury." Allowing the court to so modestly trim the sails of the expert's evidence can permit the plaintiff's boat to move briskly toward the port of justice without risking a judicial shipwreck in the form of an order excluding an expert who is needed to meet the burden of proof.

Preadmission of Exhibits

Complex jury trials typically involve deposition testimony of out-of-state corporate and third-party witnesses over whom the trial judge may lack subpoena power. The pretrial adjudication of what pages and lines of deposition testimony are admissible must be accomplished before the trial begins to avoid delays in the presentation of evidence to the jury. Likewise, the admissibility of most deposition exhibits and other forms of documentary evidence must be adjudicated before trial to avoid the same delays. While state court litigants may complain that this detailed pretrial process is making their state court trials like federal court, such pretrial adjudication of contested issues has several benefits. First, it dramatically reduces the time citizens are being asked to spend at the courthouse. Nothing ticks jurors off more than sitting around in the jury room for hours upon hours while lawyers hear themselves talk by making lengthy legal arguments before the court. As a courtesy to the jurors, this should be done before they are compelled to appear for court and give up their time in jury service. Second, with the admissibility of all contested matters adjudicated before trial, the ability to outline what "the evidence will show" during opening statements is amplified considerably. The risk of promising something in the opening statement only to later learn that the court has excluded it from evidence is entirely mitigated when such evidentiary rulings are completed during the pretrial process. Third, the quality of the edited deposition excerpts is much higher when these edits aren't being done on the fly with a jury waiting. If all the contested evidentiary issues are resolved at the pretrial conference, the plaintiff's lawyer who goes first can have the deposition editing process completed well before trial begins. The edited depositions can be carefully watched in advance, providing an opportunity to edit out long gaps between questions. The videos can be flyspecked during a quality control process that ensures that the final product presented to the jury is correctly edited. Finally, in important depositions played to the jury, trial presentation consultants can create an interactive presentation in which close-ups of the document being reviewed by the witness are shown on the screen, excerpts being read aloud during the testimony are highlighted on the screen as the witness reads from the document, and in which both the witness and the document can be seen by the jury at the same time. None of this high-tech visual presentation is possible if rulings on evidence are not obtained before trial.

The preadmission of exhibits allows for prewriting the appellate briefs, to determine whether there is a hole remaining in the proof outline before the trial begins. Gaps in the proof can be filled during testimony elicited during trial. Knowing what is coming into evidence before the trial begins is the best way to ensure that all the evidence needed will end up before the jury in the deliberation room. A meaningful pretrial conference accomplishes all of these objectives.

8

The Final Pretrial Conference

The Defense Perspective

Federal courts conduct final pretrial conferences pursuant to Rule 16(e) of the Federal Rules of Civil Procedure. The stated purpose of a Rule 16(e) conference is to "formulate a trial plan, including plans to facilitate the admission of evidence."[1] At least one attorney for each party that will be involved in the trial must attend. The local rules for specific federal courts frequently add to or provide more details about matters addressed at the Rule 16(e) conference. Federal trial judges typically publish specific pretrial conference requirements for their individual courts.

Most state courts hold pretrial conferences. However, the timing and substantive content varies. Some pretrial conferences are conducted on the morning of trial, leaving little time to adapt to the court's rulings before jury selection. It is, therefore, wise to always contact the court's staff to confirm the scope of the conference, as well as the timing.

As in federal court, state trial courts typically address motions in limine, evidence objections, and trial procedures at these conferences. Basically, the final pretrial hearing is the lawyer's best opportunity to make sure he or she knows the rules of the game before the game starts. Short of summary judgment motions, the pretrial conference is the defense lawyer's best opportunity to narrow the case and exclude particularly harmful evidence.

From the judge's perspective, the final pretrial conference provides an opportunity to evaluate trial readiness and render decisions on pending motions, including dispositive motions, expert challenges, etc. Both federal trial courts and state trial courts also typically dictate the number of jury strikes per side, the length of voir dire, procedures for voir dire, and the length of opening statements.

Depending on the case, there may be unique issues that require resolution at the final pretrial hearing. This includes issues relating to witness availability, taking witnesses out of order, realignment of parties, and equalization of jury strikes in multiparty cases. Some of

1. *See* Fed. R. Civ. P. 16(e).

these issues may be exceptionally important to the parties, and they may require additional briefing for the court. Thus, if there are special issues that must be addressed, the final pretrial conference is the best opportunity to do so, and you should be ready with appropriate legal briefing to support your positions.

Local Counsel

Decisions about whether local counsel is needed typically are made in the early stages of a case, particularly if significant motion practice is expected and the lead defense lawyers are unfamiliar with the venue or trial court. However, when in doubt, it is always a good idea to have local counsel attend the final pretrial conference. An effective local counsel usually can provide valuable insights into local rules and provide important background about the trial judge. Clearly, if the lead defense lawyer is unfamiliar with the venue and the stakes are high, local counsel should be involved.

Many things that have lasting, dramatic impact can happen at a pretrial conference. The court can exclude experts or severely limit their testimony. Evidence can be effectively excluded through motion in limine practice. Local counsel can help you travel safely in these uncharted, potentially dangerous waters. This is even more true if the plaintiff is represented by lawyers who are known to the court. No one wants to get "hometowned."

An example of being "hometowned" involved a wrongful death case in a small, rural Texas town. The case involved an SUV rollover; the wife had been driving while the husband slept on the rear seat. She lost control of the SUV, the SUV tripped and rolled, and the husband was ejected. The husband, who was both well-known and respected in his hometown community, was tragically killed. A key liability issue was whether the husband was wearing his seatbelt or whether the seatbelt failed.

Arriving at the courthouse for our final pretrial conference, we were introduced to a virtual committee of lawyers, who made last-minute appearances on behalf of the plaintiff. The plaintiff had effectively drafted a small army, including a former district attorney from the local area, a well-known state legislator, and a retired county judge. This was maximum firepower for the pretrial conference and the first day of trial. Our forces were comparatively anemic. Although our local counsel was well-known in legal circles, we now confronted popular, powerful personalities on the other side. The plaintiff's obvious goal was to impress both the judge and the jury.

It is important to anticipate the need for local counsel at the earliest stages of a case so you are prepared for any eventuality. If you wait, as we did, local candidates may be picked and plucked by the other side. In this case, there was no doubt the judge was personally familiar with, if not close friends with, several of the newly added members of the plaintiff's trial team. In fact, one of the local lawyers had weekly barbecues at his nearby ranch, and the judge was a frequent guest. Although we ultimately fared well in the case, the journey to a defense verdict was rocky and an uphill battle.

The Timing of the Final Pretrial Conference

The timing of the final pretrial conference will vary depending on the jurisdiction and the court's temperament. Traditionally, federal courts conduct formal pretrial conferences "reasonably" in advance of trial.[2] This may mean any time from several months to several days before trial. Many state jurisdictions, however, conduct pretrial conferences immediately before trial. Some courts even conduct the final pretrial on the first day of trial, moments before the venire panel walks into the courtroom. Of course, this presents potentially significant issues for both the defense and the plaintiff trial teams.

The court may enter orders that significantly impact the defense case, including the exclusion of evidence or the admission of harmful evidence. Having considered expert challenges filed by both sides, the court may issue orders that impact the scope of expert testimony. Some of these rulings may severely limit the permitted scope of voir dire. Defense lawyers, therefore, should be ready for significant rulings from the bench. All trial lawyers need to be ready to rebound and adapt quickly because the horizons of the case are subject to significant and rapid change.

Duration and Scope

Some judges use the pretrial conferences to focus on basic procedures for trial. Other courts conduct substantive hearings on evidentiary issues, objections to exhibits, and objections to deposition testimony. It is wise to contact the court's staff in advance to confirm whether the court has unique procedures or requirements.

An example of a detailed pretrial conference involved a drug liability case relating to a prescription medicine subject to an FDA-mandated product recall. The trial court conducted an extended pretrial conference lasting several days. Every exhibit objection was addressed and a ruling issued. Every motion in limine was considered and decided, but only after significant argument (and reargument) from both sides. Every disputed deposition excerpt was addressed and objections resolved. The court allowed both sides of the case ample time to argue all points. Clearly, the court intended to avoid any delays during trial and, accordingly, the court was determined to resolve all evidence issues before jury selection.

In yet another example of an extended pretrial hearing, a Texas trial court convened the pretrial conference one week before trial in a commercial tort case. Although we represented the nominal plaintiff in a declaratory judgment action, we were confronted with a "bet your company" counterclaim, with nine lawyers appearing on the other side. We previously filed multiple *Daubert* challenges to the opposing experts—one of which was a business valuation expert and the other a forensic accountant, and we came prepared for battle. We brought our own experts and called them to the witness stand to provide live testimony about the deficiencies and lack of reliability of the opposing experts' opinions. After two days of evidentiary hearings, we won—both experts were excluded, a rarity in this venue.

The lesson here is simple. Be prepared to address all aspects of the case. The case can be significantly strengthened or weakened before jury selection begins.

2. *See* Fed. R. Civ. P. 16(e).

Expect Surprises

What happens during the final pretrial conference is not always logical or reasonably anticipated. Therefore, it is important to be nimble, quick, and prepared.

In yet another drug liability case involving a different venue, a different trial judge, and different lawyers on the plaintiff's side, the pretrial conference was scheduled for a Friday morning before a Monday trial date. We expected (and planned for) substantive argument on multiple significant issues. We arrived at the courthouse with dozens of boxes and copies of case law opinions and briefing. But, nothing substantive occurred—except, of course, our defense of the case was severely damaged.

The plaintiff was alleging that her significant health conditions were side effects of her medication. We represented the pharmaceutical manufacturer. This was one of several hundred similar cases filed around the country, and it was one of the first such cases to proceed to trial. As such, the plaintiff was represented by a consortium of lawyers from across the country, including Florida, California, Mississippi, and Texas.

The plaintiff had approximately 100 exhibits to which dozens of substantive, written objections were lodged. Many of these exhibits were inflammatory, some *highly* inflammatory. Even more were rank hearsay. On the other hand, the defense exhibit list contained more than 500 exhibits, most of which were boring, scientific, and not jury-friendly.

Without prior notice, the lead plaintiff's lawyer offered to withdraw all objections to our defense exhibits on condition all plaintiff's exhibits would be pre-admitted. Although we protested loudly and urged the court to consider our written objections, our arguments were largely unsuccessful. The court decided that all exhibits would be pre-admitted, but defense counsel would be provided "another" opportunity to lodge specific objections to specific exhibits once the exhibit was identified on the record with witnesses. Of course, this procedure was calculated to force the defense team to make countless objections in the presence of the jury—which was, of course, the precise result plaintiff's counsel intended.

Thus, the entire pretrial discussion about hundreds of exhibits lasted less than ten minutes. Several harmful plaintiff's exhibits were pre-admitted, and several pre-admitted exhibits were subsequently used in the opening statement over our objections. The rationale was that the opening statement was not evidence. The plaintiff actually presented the jury with highly inflammatory newspaper headlines—hearsay, at best; devastating hearsay, at worst.

In this case, the handling of motions in limine was not substantially different. Our defense team filed detailed motions in limine, together with supporting legal memoranda, addressing more than thirty separate evidentiary points. The plaintiff filed none and boasted that the plaintiff's trial team was not concerned about the defense case. The trial court then expressed reluctance to address each of our motions in limine in detail and, in lieu of allowing argument on each limine issue, directed the defense team to "*pick your best five.*" We scrambled. The judge gave us limited time to argue what we believed to be our most important motions in limine—three minutes per issue. He then denied them sequentially. The entire argument took less than fifteen minutes. We received a written order later that day denying most of the remaining points in our motions in limine.

In sum, our defense team appeared for a pretrial conference in a significant exposure case expecting it to last several hours. It was over in less than thirty minutes. All significant motions in limine were denied. All of plaintiff's exhibits were effectively preadmitted. Following a few minutes of discussion about procedures for jury selection, the pretrial conference adjourned. Our trial team was severely bruised. Although we had engaged local counsel, we were unable to stem the tide. This was not a good start to the case.

The lesson here: be ready for surprises, and be prepared to adapt. Our only effective strategic decision for the day: we had a court reporter and a record.

Exhibits and Depositions

It is good practice to contact the court's staff before the pretrial conference to confirm what materials the court prefers to receive and review. Many trial courts require exhibit binders, with exhibits sequentially marked. The court also may have unique rules relating to how exhibits are marked, with specific rules relating to alpha-numeric labeling and bulk exhibits. The court also may have unique procedures for addressing deposition excerpts, objections to those excerpts, and how these objections are presented to the court. As a practice tip, it is a good idea to determine how much time the court has set aside for the pretrial conference. This is usually a telltale sign of how much time will be devoted to the details of the case.

Expect Substantive Rulings

Courts frequently issue rulings during the pretrial conference for all pending motions, including dispositive rulings and ruling on expert challenges. Obviously, this can have a dramatic impact on the case.

A product liability case in a Texas federal court is illustrative. Just days before trial, the court struck several of the defendant's affirmative defenses and denied the defendant's motion for partial summary judgment on the issue of punitive damages. In a published opinion, the court determined there was sufficient evidence for the jury to conclude the defendant had acted in conscious disregard of the rights of the victim, a two-year-old toddler who suffered permanent, serious injuries in a high-velocity car crash. The court issued the rulings just days before jury selection providing the defendant with little time to respond or react.

If your opponent has filed motions in limine against you, or is seeking to otherwise significantly limit your evidence, you should take care to review the motions and exhibit objections carefully. Short pocket briefs for the court frequently are effective for major issues and will enhance your arguments. Too many lawyers show up at pretrial conferences empty-handed and flat-footed. Again, the simple lesson is, *be prepared.*

Equalizing Jury Strikes

One of the issues that should be addressed during the final pretrial conference involves the equalization of strikes. Ordinarily, the trial court will advise the parties how many strikes each "side" will have, and courts in most jurisdictions are given wide discretion in allotting strikes. But, in some cases, the concept of "side" is blurred.

In multiparty cases, defendants may find themselves adverse to each other on at least some issues. If cross-actions for contribution or indemnity have been filed, additional jury strikes likely are justified on the defense side. If this occurs, the plaintiff will demand additional strikes to offset additional strikes to the defendants. The court also may impose additional requirements that the defendants (theoretically, adverse) cannot collaborate in striking the jury.

In the absence of cross-actions between the defendants, however, it is unlikely that additional strikes will be awarded. The existence of cross-actions is frequently the litmus test for determining conflict or antagonism between defendants. Absent such antagonism, additional strikes are not readily justifiable.

Third-party defendants also are entitled to strikes. Third parties may have been joined for purposes of contribution and indemnity. This posture presents yet another situation where additional strikes are justified. All of these issues should be addressed at the final pretrial conference.

Defining the Voir Dire Procedure

The final pretrial hearing may be the last opportunity for the parties to define any unique rules for voir dire. Both sides should identify the allotted time limits because most courts impose time restrictions on jury selection.

Some courts approach voir dire on a sequenced basis. The first stage involves general voir dire examination of the entire panel. The second stage involves voir dire examination of individual jurors in the presence of the entire panel. The third stage involves an examination of selected jurors before the bench. This typically is when jurors are examined to determine whether they should be struck for cause.

On the other hand, some courts impose no sequencing. When voir dire begins, the lawyers for both sides are expected to conduct both general examinations and specific examinations as they wish. Thus, it is important to define the court's unique preferences before trial. Trial lawyers cannot adequately prepare unless they understand the processes and procedures.

Conclusion

The bottom line is that defense lawyers should prepare for surprises. The more the lawyer prepares, the less likely any surprise will be lasting or irreversible.

9

Jury Selection

The Plaintiff's Perspective

Jury selection is a critically important skill for a successful trial lawyer. It is not taught well in an academic setting, but is instead learned later, only through the repetition of trying case after case while talking with fellow citizens during voir dire. Voir dire precedes jury selection. It is the question-and-answer time that enables a good trial lawyer to start his or her case with momentum, to pick a winning jury by first learning through jury research before trial the characteristics of favorable and unfavorable potential jurors, and then identify such actual favorable and unfavorable jurors through advice from jury consultants after reviewing jury questionnaires. Voir dire tactics often separate great trial lawyers from their weaker opponents. Following general voir dire where answers are received from the entire venire panel, specific voir dire provides a lawyer with the opportunity to achieve or to foreclose rehabilitation of jurors whose answers may originally have disqualified them from service before strikes for cause are presented to the judge. Finally, the parties exercise peremptory challenges, allowing strikes of potential jurors to be made for any legitimate reason, excluding race, religion, and gender. In sum, an effective voir dire and jury selection process is often the difference between victory and defeat at trial.

Starting the Case with Momentum

Conducting a voir dire most effectively requires deciding on its primary purpose, and that purpose is largely a function of where the voir dire is conducted. Most federal courts impose restrictive time limits for voir dire, utilize higher standards for granting strikes for cause, and make fewer peremptory challenges available to each side. By contrast, state court trials often do not impose time limits on voir dire, have case law calling for the automatic striking of venire panel members for cause if they utter answers establishing bias or prejudice, and provide a larger number of peremptory challenges to each side. The court where a case is tried—in a restrictive federal court environment or in a far more permissive state court environment—strongly influences the strategy choice of how to start a case with momentum during the jury selection process.

Federal Court

Before trying a civil case in federal court, it is essential that lead trial counsel personally sit in open court and watch a voir dire in another case in the very same courtroom where his federal judge will preside over the trial to come. Why?

First, each federal court has its own local rules and idiosyncratic procedures which must be carefully studied before incurring the wrath of a perturbed Article III judge in front of the jury deciding the facts of the case. There is an old joke that's important here: "What's the difference between God and a federal judge? God doesn't think he's a federal judge." The lesson of this joke is that federal trial judges enjoy almost unlimited discretion to conduct trials as they see fit. In order to start a federal court case with momentum, an attorney must learn the rules of the road in the particular court where the case will be tried. The procedures employed by a Bush appointee in Texas are not the same as those used by an Obama or Clinton appointee in New Jersey, and certainly will not be the same as a new Trump appointee in Tennessee. The best way to learn what the rules for a particular trial will be is to personally attend a previous civil case pretrial conference and jury selection process before the judge who will preside over the upcoming case.

Second, federal judges have unusually close working relationships with their court staff. The law clerk, court reporter, deputy clerk, and court security officer have close daily access to the judge, and therefore have unique access to the particular preferences and dislikes of the judge. They often appear in the courtroom well before the judge, and remain long after the judge leaves the courtroom. Communicating with them often before and after preliminary hearings is vital to learning the court's preferences. Many federal courts post judge preferences on the court website, including which staff member should be consulted for various issues throughout a case. Consult the court's website to initially obtain the court's preferences. One member of the court personnel team usually is specifically designated by the court to handle inquiries from litigants. If the court's written preferences do not address a topic or are unclear, consult the individual designated as the appropriate contact. That person should be asked repetitively about the judge's rules and preferences before the trial begins. This can begin while you observe previous pretrial hearings and jury selections.

Third, watching the jury selection process of an earlier case allows a trial lawyer to see, in real time, the boundaries likely to be employed by the judge in a later case. Most federal judges have a standard limit on attorney-conducted voir dire, if it is allowed at all.[1] Rare is the day that a court will grant an oral request for more time than what is typically allowed. If a court typically allows attorneys thirty minutes for voir dire, a written motion for a specific amount of additional time, with particularized reasons for the request, stands a much

1. *See Skilling v. U.S.*, 561 U.S. 358, 389 (2010) (affirming conviction though district court "denied Skilling's request for attorney-led voir dire on the ground that potential jurors were more forthcoming with judges than with lawyers.").

greater chance of being granted, especially if the jury can still be empaneled on the very day they are brought to court for jury selection.

In this regard, the primary way to achieve momentum during voir dire in federal court is to learn the judge, and to prevent the judge from killing your momentum just as it begins.

State Court

Different states have many distinct protocols and procedures for jury selection. Some states utilize only general voir dire, where attorneys pose questions to the entire panel together before privately exercising their strikes. Others allow both general voir dire, and a subsequent specific voir dire, where follow up questions are posed to individual jurors in an effort to probe any potential biases or prejudices exhibited during the general voir dire process. Others allow questioning and exercising strikes only on the first twelve panel members, before additional jurors are called up. Most states begin with the plaintiff attorney's voir dire, while Minnesota calls for the defendant to go first. As a trial lawyer trying cases across the United States, I have never felt comfortable picking a jury outside my home state unless I had taken the time well in advance to watch my judge-to-be conduct a civil case voir dire.

Likewise, different state court judges in a single state will have different preferences on how to conduct voir dire in their courts. Some want voir dire to be conducted from location "X," while others command that it takes place from location "Y." Some are generous with the time allotted for jury selection, while others have restrictive limits. Some regularly grant strikes for cause on certain issues, while others hesitate to do so and permit rehabilitation of jurors to avoid striking jurors for cause.

There is simply no way to conduct an effective voir dire and start your case with momentum unless you take the time to learn how to do it before the specific judge who is set to try your case.

Picking a Winning Jury

Juries in various forms have existed for thousands of years. They first appeared in ancient Egypt, Mycenae, Druid England, Greece, Rome, Viking Scandinavia, the Holy Roman Empire, and Saracen Jerusalem before the Crusades.[2] Jury selection dates back over 900 years, since the dawn of the jury trial in England.[3] Peremptory challenges—objections to potential jurors, with no reason given—have been around since the Magna Carta of 1215. Historically, peremptory challenges have been "seen as a way to give defendants confidence in the people who were judging them."[4] Blackstone himself detailed the eighteenth-century

---

2. Morris B. Hoffman, *Peremptory Challenges Should Be Abolished: A Trial Judge's Perspective*, 64 U. Chi. L. Rev. 809, 813 (1997).

3. Jon M. Van Dyke, *Jury Selection Procedures: Our Uncertain Commitment to Representative Panels*, 1–9 (1977); Roger D. Moore, *Voir Dire Examination of Jurors: I. The English Practice*, 16 Geo. L.J. 438 (1928).

4. Sean Fine, *Jury Trials at Risk as Judge Strikes down Federal Ban on Peremptory Challenges Enacted after Boushie Case*, The Globe and Mail (Nov. 6, 2019), https://www.theglobeandmail.com/canada/article-ontario-judge-strikes-down-federal-ban-on-peremptory-jury-selection/.

English practice, and gave several justifications for the practice. The art, or science, of jury selection has achieved almost mystical heights among its practitioners; unfortunately, research demonstrates that voir dire and peremptory challenges often are poorly utilized. Broeder concluded as early as 1965 that voir dire "was grossly ineffective not only in weeding out 'unfavorable' jurors, but even in eliciting the data which would have shown particular jurors as very likely to prove 'unfavorable.'"[5] Other researchers have concluded that peremptory challenges are used so poorly that their use provides little utility toward the deselection of potentially adverse jurors. For example, in 1997, Michael O. Finkelstein and Bruce Levin studied sixteen federal criminal trials in New York in which prosecutors and defense attorneys submitted their peremptory challenges at the same time. They studied the frequency of double strikes—how often potential jurors were challenged by both sides, which should rarely happen if attorneys are indeed effectively employing their peremptory challenges. The authors were able to construct two models dividing the population of potential jurors into those who were "clear choices" to challenge—jurors most attorneys would agree are likely to be biased against a specific side—and those who were mere "guesses"—jurors about whom attorneys would disagree. The authors concluded that almost all challenges were "guesses," and that attorneys often have very little sense of who is actually worth challenging.[6]

Answering the question *why* requires only a look into what lawyers have done and what they failed to do. The science of jury selection is one that must be taken seriously. The biggest mistake lawyers make is operating on hunches after brazenly convincing themselves that because of their unique intellects and trial skills, they alone know what to do and how to pick a winning jury. While facts and evidence often drive favorable jury verdicts, lawyers guessing during jury selection is the fastest way to quickly grab defeat out of the jaws of victory.

Clarence Darrow wrote in his 1936 *Esquire* magazine article "Attorney for the Defense: How to Pick a Jury" that "[c]hoosing jurors is always a delicate task . . . in this undertaking, everything pertaining to the prospective juror needs to be questioned and weighed: his nationality; his business, religion, politics, social standing, family ties, friends, habits of life and thought; the books and newspapers he likes and reads, and many more matters that combine to make a man; all of these qualities and experiences have left their effect on ideas, beliefs and fancies that inhabit his mind."[7] Darrow was (and he almost always was, when he appeared in a courtroom) correct; however, his call for a close probing of all qualities and experiences of potential jurors rings only half the bell of success. Winning requires knowing beforehand the favorable and unfavorable characteristics of jurors for each case.

5. Dale W. Broeder, *Voir Dire Examinations: An Empirical Study*, 38 S. Cal. L. Rev. 503–28 (1965).

6. Michael O. Finkelstein & Bruce Levin, *Clear Choices and Guesswork in Peremptory Challenges in Federal Criminal Trials*, 160 J. Royal Stat. Soc'y, Series A 275, 277–79 (1997).

7. Charles Darrow, *Attorney for the Defense: How to Pick a Jury*, Esquire, May, 1936, at 36.

Characteristics of Favorable and Unfavorable Jurors

To learn the characteristics of favorable and unfavorable jurors for a specific case, trial lawyers must step away from their own prejudices and ignore time-honored premonitions about the beliefs of different demographic groups. Instead, they should move toward case-specific jury research obtained via focus groups, polling, and/or analytics. This data is necessary to scientifically ascertain which potential jurors are best suited for the case.

Many methods exist for evaluating the attitudes of potential jurors. This process was dramatized by the 2003 Hollywood movie *Runaway Jury*, starring Gene Hackman and Dustin Hoffman. The movie is set in New Orleans during a seminal firearm marketing defect trial. Popular folklore there had a massively wealthy corporate defendant lavishly hiring private investigators to individually investigate the predilections of individual members of the voir dire panel in order to secure a "sure thing" jury.[8] In reality, much of the research into potential jurors is conducted projectively—well before the juror lists are provided to the parties and their lawyers. Various methods for juror evaluation exist.[9] As already mentioned, polling in the applicable venue is the earliest method available for potential juror attitude evaluation.

Sequentially and the next least costly is so-called "online juror research." There are numerous online mock juror websites: JuryTalk.com, eJury.com, JuryTest.net, OnlineVerdict.com, ResolutionResearch.com, Signupdirect.com, and VirtualJury.com, among others. JuryTalk.com is conducted by the Wilmington Institute Network and allows jurors to register and submit their evaluations of specific case facts online.[10] JuryTest.net does the same thing; it requires potential jurors to attest that they "are not a lawyer or insurance company representative."[11] OnlineVerdict.com advertises its services by stating that "[i]t is now possible to conduct jury research on almost every case."[12] VirtualJury.com advertises its online jury research as an advantage because it is "effective, affordable and quick."[13]

Live focus groups are more expensive than online services, but the methodology used in a live focus group is more tightly controlled, and thus, results are more likely to yield accurate and useful results. Numerous services offer focus groups to litigants.[14] Google searches of "mock jury" yields hundreds of online solicitations for potential mock juror participants.

Mock trials have a different purpose than focus groups. Although mock trials are significantly more expensive than focus groups, they serve two purposes that are not available to mere focus groups: first, from high schools to law schools, scholastic mock trials prepare and teach future lawyers. Actual mock trials also prepare licensed trial lawyers to

---

8. *Runaway Jury*, IMDb, https://www.imdb.com/title/tt0313542/ (last visited Mar. 14, 2020).

9. *See generally* James L. Mitchell, *Focus Groups, Mock Trials, and Shadow Juries: Evaluating Your Approach*, U. Hous. L. Found. (Aug.–Sept. 2006), https://paynemitchell.com/wp-content/uploads/28-22Shadow-Juries-Focus-Groups-and-Other-Methods-for-Evaluatin.pdf.

10. *See* Jury Talk, http://www.jurytalk.com (last visited Dec. 9, 2019).

11. Jury Test, http://www.jurytest.net (last visited Dec. 9, 2019).

12. Online Verdict, https://www.onlineverdict.com (last visited Dec. 9, 2019).

13. Virtual Jury, http://www.virtualjury.com (last visited Dec. 9, 2019).

14. *See* http://www.amsetcen.com; http://www.resolutionresearch.com/recruitment-mock-jury.html; and http://www.signupdirect.com (last visited Dec. 9, 2019).

get ready for the real thing. Putting aside the huge egos of great trial lawyers, nothing is more effective in preparing for trial than requiring lawyers to prepare several weeks or months ahead. Mock trials accomplish this. Second, juror responses to mock trial presentations are far more acute than the generically presented issue presentations often utilized in focus groups. Properly conducted mock trials are highly intuitive toward eventual results, so much so that some trial firms brag about their early utilization of mock trials,[15] and to play video recordings from the mock trials in settlement brochures presented to the defense.[16]

Regardless of the modality of jury research before trial, the key is the information gleaned therefrom, and the ability to organize that information before actual jury selection occurs. Jury research performed over the decades has led to the conclusion that demographics are not a reliable predictor of juror attitudes. While in some cases, age generally and ethnicity inside large cities may provide some guidance, jurors' experiences and attitudes about their workplace and the civil justice system itself—often arising from political party and media messaging against the civil justice system—are more helpful in predicting eventual jury verdicts. Finally, and perhaps most importantly, jurors' entitlement attitudes and whether jurors' reason via legal authoritarianism provide the strongest correlation with jury verdict results.

Demographics Are Not a Reliable Predictor of Juror Attitudes

Today in American society, now a demographic melting pot stirred together with many different races, nationalities, religious backgrounds, ethnic histories, and disparate value systems, a trial lawyer's use of demographic stereotypes is almost a complete waste during jury selection. Both voir dire and the subsequent use of peremptory challenges often are wasted by trial lawyers' almost instinctive need to apply demographic stereotypes when striking jurors. Olczak found in 1991, and it likely is still true, that lawyers rely on two or three stereotypical characteristics when they exercise peremptory challenges.[17] However, jury research repetitively demonstrates that demographics are not an accurate predictor of juror attitudes:

1. *Stuhan:* "There is, however, mounting evidence that demographics are *not* a reliable predictor of verdict-orientation."[18]
2. *Broda-Bahm:* "[T]here is simply no social science case to be made for the reliability of demographics as a predictor of juror bias. On this point, the consensus of litigation consultants is clear, and the research backs it up."[19]

---

15. *See* https://gmhatlaw.com/mock-trial. ("Gauthier Murphy & Houghtaling firm was one of the first law firms in the world to use mock trials.") (last visited Dec. 9, 2019).

16. *Id.*

17. Paul V. Olczak, Martin F. Kaplan & Steven Penrod, *Attorneys' Lay Psychology and Its Effectiveness in Selecting Jurors: Three Empirical Studies*, 6 J. Soc. Behav. & Person. 431, 440 (1991).

18. Richard G. Stuhan, *Written Juror Questionnaires in Civil Cases*, Drug & Device Law (Jan. 28, 2008), https://www.druganddevicelawblog.com/2008/01/written-juror-questionnaires-in-civi.html.

19. Ken Broda-Bahm, PhD, *Don't Select Your Jury Based on Demographics: A Skeptical Look at JuryQuest*, Persuasive Litigator (Apr. 12, 2012), https://www.persuasivelitigator.com/2012/04/dont-select-your-jury-based-on-demographics.html.

3. *Crocker:* "A direct link between juror demographic characteristics or personality variables and juror verdicts has proven difficult to establish; research in this area has failed to uncover many reliable relationships between demographic or personality variables and verdict."[20]
4. *Fulero:* "[T]he nature and strength of the evidence in a given case is the critical variable in predicting verdict, rather than simple demographics."[21]
5. *Goodman*: "[D]emographic variables were not significantly correlated with the magnitude of damage awards, juror attitudes and suppositions about monetary damages were."[22]
6. *Hastel:* "Individual differences in the jurors' backgrounds were not strongly related to their verdicts; income and ethnicity were weakly related to judgments."[23]
7. *Herde:* "Voir dire focused only on juror demographics offers very little insight into potential jurors' inherent biases, deeply-held prejudices, and overall world views."[24]
8. *Kagehiro:* "Attorneys, often because of the restrictions on voir dire, will use demographic cues and socio-economic assessments that fit their stereotypes of good or bad jurors. These cues may have limited reliability."[25]
9. *Lisko:* "[M]any attorneys believe demographics should be their highest priority in selecting or de-selecting jurors. Certainly, with the increasing limitations on oral voir dire in federal court, there is often little else to go on. However, demographics live on the bottom rung of the predictiveness ladder."[26]
10. *Penrod:* "Up to 27 types of demographic information were tested, including gender, occupational status, and marital status. Demographics accounted for 3.2% to 16% of the variance in jurors' verdicts, meaning that the vast majority (84% to 96.8%) of reasons for jurors' verdict preferences fall *outside* their demographic characteristics."[27]

---

20. Caroline B. Crocker & Margaret Bull Kovera, "Systematic Jury Selection," *in* Richard L. Weiner & Brian H. Bornstein eds., Handbook of Trial Consulting, 17 (Mar. 24, 2011), https://link.springer.com/chapter/10.1007/978-1-4419-7569-0_2.

21. Solomon Fulero, *The Myths and Realities of Attorney Jury Selection Folklore and Scientific Jury Selection: What Works?* 17 Ohio N.U. L. Rev. 229–53 (1990).

22. J. Goodman, E. F. Loftus & E. Greene, *Matters of Money: Voir Dire in Civil Cases*, 3 Forensic Reports 303–29 (1990).

23. Reid Hastel, *A Study of Juror and Jury Judgments in Civil Cases: Deciding Liability for Punitive Damages*, 22 L. & Human Behav. 3 (1998).

24. Gayle Herde, *Take Me to Your Leader: An Examination of Authoritarianism as an Indicator of Juror Bias*, The Jury Expert (Jan. 1, 2009), https://www.thejuryexpert.com/2009/01/take-me-to-your-leader-an-examination-of-authoritarianism-as-an-indicator-of-juror-bias/.

25. Dorothy K. Kagehiro, PhD & Robert D. Minick, PhD, "How Juries Determine Damages Awards," *in* 504: A Quantitative Basis for Litigation Settlement, ACCA's 2002 Annual Meeting, 11, https://www.acc.com/sites/default/files/resources/vl/public/ProgramMaterial/20586_1.pdf (last visited Dec. 9, 2019).

26. Karen Lisko, *What Juries Find Persuasive: There Are Few Dumb Jurors, but Much Poor Teaching*, Attorney Education Center, https://www.jameseducationcenter.com/articles/what-juries-find-persuasive/ (last visited Dec. 9, 2019).

27. S.D. Penrod, "Study of Attorney and 'Scientific' Jury Selection Models," (unpublished PhD diss., Harvard University, 1979). *See also* S.D. Penrod, *Predictors of Jury Decision Making in Criminal and Civil Cases: A Field Experiment*, 3 Forensic Reports 261–77 (1990).

11. *Raif*: "The results indicate that none of the independent variables—urbanicity, income, or major geographic locations—were significantly correlated with final award amounts."[28]
12. *Seidman*: "[T]here is little evidence that winning a liability verdict or obtaining a big damage award predictably results from selecting a jury with particular characteristics," rather, "[r]esearch on decision-making about damages indicates that the strongest predictors or jury damage awards are characteristics of the case rather than attributes of the jurors."[29]
13. *Underwood*: "Saks (2002) posits that demographics has little to do with the outcome of civil trials, and is skeptical of whether they were addressing whether a particular *community* has an idiosyncratic predisposition toward generous awards to plaintiffs, or the question of whether particular *demographic groups* have a like predisposition. If the question is the latter, he argues research offers little support, despite attorney belief to the contrary. . . . Hastie *et al* (1998) for example, found individual differences in jurors' gender, age, education, income and ethnicity were only weakly related to their verdicts. Citing Diamond *et al* (1998) and Wissler *et al* (1999), Saks suggests that the effects of demographics on damage awards were likely minimal. . . ."[30]
14. *Vinson*: "Demographic variables predicted verdict and punitive damage awards only modestly and in different ways in the three cases."[31]

Lawyers in voir dire "traditionally have picked juries on the basis of demographic characteristics—age, gender, marital status, occupation, income, education, etc."[32] However, the data in the research referenced above overwhelmingly demonstrates that this blind utilization of juror demographics will yield disappointing results.

Pretrial Jury Research Is More Likely to Identify Favorable and Unfavorable Jurors

Pretrial focus groups, polling, and analytics are tools trial lawyers can use to identify favorable and unfavorable jurors.

Focus Groups

As described in chapter 2, jury studies and focus groups are the correct way to identify favorable and unfavorable juror attitudes. Whether in a nursing home decubitus ulcer case, a pharmaceutical products liability case, or a case defending an attack on my own liberty, experience has taught me that pretrial jury research is far more helpful than gut intuition in picking a good jury.

---

28. Donna Raef & John David Rausch, Jr., *Urbanicity, Income and Jury Verdict Amounts in Civil Litigation*, PB&J, 1, 14–19 (2010), https://pdfs.semanticscholar.org/dc93/7a9c2082d6a8e9df0416fa085a8a1ec4105f.pdf.

29. Shari Seidman Diamond, Michael J. Saks & Stephan Landsman, *Juror Judgments about Liability and Damages: Sources of Variability and Ways to Increase Consistency*, 48 DePaul L. Rev. 301–25 (1998).

30. James H. Underwood, *Demographics in Civil Trials: Biases and Implications*, 7 J. Bus. & Econ. Res., No. 2, (2009).

31. K.V. Vinson, M.A. Costanzo & D.E. Berger, *Predictors of Verdict and Punitive Damages in High-Stakes Civil Litigation*, 26(2) Behav. Sci. Law 167–86 (2008).

32. Stuhan, *supra*.

Again, early focus groups should take place before discovery begins. Most MDL PSCs now conduct focus groups from the outset of a complicated tort to help them identify problem areas, the strongest causes of action available, and the themes that are likely to resonate with eventual jurors. Stories of weeklong pilgrimages to the wine country to conduct jury research with Rodney Jew are legion amongst the complex tort plaintiff's bar. Robert Hirschhorn and Lisa Blue are omnipresent in jury research conducted by prominent Texas trial lawyers like Mark Lanier, Kurt Arnold, and me. Corporations that are defending themselves often spend more than $100,000 for two days of focus groups, including multiple presentations at once and up to six different juries providing instantaneous feedback with real-time, handheld clickers. Plaintiff's firms, on the other hand, are known for conducting similar jury research on the cheap, with invaluable thematic research conducted for less than $10,000 in bargain-basement focus groups called on the fly. Regardless of how they are done and how much they cost, the only thing a good trial lawyer cannot afford is failing to conduct focus groups at all.

Polling

Pretrial polling in the venue where the trial is to occur can yield invaluable data that correlates polling answers to specific questions to real jurors' eventual attitudes about the facts of a case. Conservative pundits often panned President Bill Clinton's daily polling of the electorate as a failure to lead; however, he never guessed and often succeeded. Clinton always knew the attitude of the electorate, and he shaped his decisions accordingly. Likewise, the upstart publicity gimmick of a renegade business tycoon on an ego trip became a credible and ultimately successful presidential campaign only after tens of millions of dollars in social media interaction with base and swing voters yielded statistically significant data to the Trump campaign. This research molded now-President Donald Trump's campaign message, and portended an electoral college victory by converting Midwest states from the Democratic column to the Republican column, all while political pundits insisted Trump was wasting his time and resources there. The point is that first through political polling by Clinton and then through social media attitude sampling by Trump, each learned the attitudes of those they had to convince before attempting to make their political case. Trial lawyers should do the same.

News and political organizations spend huge amounts of resources each year to conduct polls in advance of political elections. Early polls in 2000 accurately reflected Al Gore's consistent early lead, while late polls showed George Bush's late-October surge. Polls in 2004, 2008, and 2012 predicted what actually occurred on those respective election nights. While most polls in 2012 predicted President Obama's reelection, each consistently underpredicted his margin of victory. Most postelection analyses of the 2012 election attribute this difference in predicted versus actual election performance to an underestimation of Obama's turnout operation.[33] Likewise, criticism that 2016 election-night political polling

33. Harry J. Enten, *How the 2012 Election Polling Really Was Skewed—for Mitt Romney*, The Guardian, Nov. 12, 2012, 3:18 PM, http://www.theguardian.com/commentisfree/2012/nov/21/2012-election-polling-skewed-for-mitt-romney.

missed President Trump's win over Hillary Clinton later disappeared, as their collective prediction that Hillary Clinton would slightly win nationally accurately predicted her popular vote win over Trump by almost three million votes. At the same time, statewide polling in the three Midwest states that put Trump over 270 electoral votes—Pennsylvania, Michigan, and Wisconsin—accurately reflected his surge there. Trump won the presidency because he saw that Midwest surge while Clinton's campaign missed it. In fact, she failed to campaign in the state of Wisconsin even once.

Because of this accuracy of political polling, the use of polling as a component of pretrial jury research has become standard. Potential litigants repeatedly conduct polling in an effort to predict juror attitudes among potential members of the venire panel. The Defense Research Institute ("DRI") conducts annual polling of attitudes about the civil justice system. Instructively, the DRI survey notes significant disparity in sex, age, political affiliation, and political ideology as to whether a person favors an individual versus a corporation in a civil suit: 47 percent of men compared to 59 percent of women; 68 percent of voters under the age of thirty compared to 49 percent of voters over the age of thirty; 64 percent of Democrats compared to 42 percent of Republicans; and 66 percent of liberals compared to 47 percent of conservatives. Likewise, polling respondents favored individuals over corporations depending upon the type of corporation being sued: insurance (59 percent to 20 percent), oil and gas (58 percent to 20 percent); financial (57 percent to 21 percent); pharma (56 percent to 19 percent); auto (52 percent to 22 percent); tech (46 percent to 22 percent); and large corporations (54 percent to 23 percent) versus small business (32 percent to 24 percent).

Jury research organizations also market this polling phenomena. For example, the National Legal Research Group, Inc., markets this as "taking a 'snapshot' of how jurors view your case":

> Just such an approach is available through our "quick poll" method—a small-scale poll conducted in the trial jurisdiction. These polls involve an average of 100 respondents who answer 5 to 15 questions which focus on limited issues at a cost of $5,000 to $7,000. This approach provides a quick and focused look at how jurors view a case. This can be very important when faced with evolving litigation such as products liability or highly publicized cases that are in the public eye for months at a time. Using the quick poll method, you can look at your case at any time (the "snapshot" approach) and even monitor shifting opinion patterns of jurors over the course of the litigation (the "tracking" approach).[34]

Likewise, in Florida, Magnus Research Consultants, Inc., "regularly polls mock jurors on a variety of issues":[35]

---

34. *Taking a "Snapshot" of How Jurors View Your Case*, National Legal Research Group, http://www.nlrg.com/our-services/jury-research-division/jury-research-publications/-taking-a-snapshot-of-how-jurors-view-your-case (last visited Dec. 9, 2019).

35. *The Importance of Venue Specific Jury Research*, Magnus Research Consultants & Graphics, https://magnusweb.com/litigation-tip/the-importance-of-venue-specific-jury-research-3/ (last visited Dec. 9, 2019).

> We are always interested to learn the similarities and differences among the jurors in the venues where we work within Florida. We have asked 697 mock jurors in Palm Beach County and 468 mock jurors in Duval County their political philosophy and their view of caps on damages. Although mock jurors' opinions regarding damages caps were similar in the two counties (with 40% of those surveyed in favor of caps), their political philosophies differed considerably. In Palm Beach County, 27% of mock jurors described themselves as conservative, compared to 39% in Duval County. In Palm Beach County, 16% of mock jurors described themselves as liberal, compared to 10% in Duval County. Political views were strongly related to jurors' opinions on caps on damages: the more conservative jurors were far more likely to favor damages caps than liberal or middle-of-the-road jurors. The differences in these patterns of response are substantial in various parts of Florida, lending strong support for the need to conduct jury research in the trial venue.[36]

In sum, a properly constructed poll in the county of suit will provide data to enable a trial lawyer to construct a meaningful questionnaire that can offer insight into what potential jurors may think. This data is far more instructive than an old trial lawyer's gut instincts. Instead, using polling inside a specific trial venue will yield statistically significant correlations between answers to certain questions and attitudes for or against a particular case. Likewise, data collected from social media interactions with potential jurors long before a trial begins will provide reliable data about what categories of potential jurors will be inclined to believe about a case.

Analytics and Technology-Assisted Research

Much adulation has been conferred upon the analytics brainiacs working for President Barack Obama's 2012 reelection campaign. To put it bluntly, Obama faced a daunting reelection challenge: a down economy, no signature domestic achievement other than the wildly unpopular Affordable Care Act, and no foreign policy achievement other than Osama Bin Laden's assassination in central Asia. A year out, most prognosticators predicted a Republican victory in 2012. However, Obama's campaign manager, Jim Messina, deployed an unprecedented amount of financial resources to analytically predict the issues that matter to a very small number of likely voters in selected counties that would tip the results in a limited number of ten electoral swing states—Ohio, Florida, Virginia, Pennsylvania, New Mexico, Colorado, Nevada, Iowa, Wisconsin, and New Hampshire. Obama won all ten swing states by utilizing an incredibly well-placed allocation of resources in specific counties in the swing states, which the campaign knew would lead to statewide wins. This strategy followed highly specific research into voter preferences on specific issues through a process known as *analytics*.

Some political scientists credit Donald Trump's surprising 2016 victory to the Trump campaign's digital campaign on social media.[37] Trump spent far more on social media

36. Magnus Research, *The Importance of Venue Specific Jury Research*.

37. *Facebook ad campaign helped Donald Trump win election, claims executive*, BBC News, January 8, 2020. https://www.bbc.com/news/technology-51034641.

communications and research than any other campaign before him.[38] Trump's belief that this analytics investment resulted in his election is demonstrated by two facts: first, his digital media director in 2016, Brad Parscale, is now the manager of his entire 2020 reelection campaign;[39] and second, the unprecedented level of early reelection fundraising achieved by President Trump in 2017, 2018, and 2019 has overwhelmingly been spent on the campaign's social media analytics research.[40]

Litigation technology has advanced to include powerful discovery platforms that enable litigators to efficiently search massive quantities of digital discovery to locate only information predicted to be relevant by computer coding. Called *technology-assisted review*, the researches uses artificial intelligence to make predictions about what matters. The same technology is being used in pretrial jury research.

Analytics is science, not voodoo, and its principles may be applied in advance of voir dire to enable a trial lawyer to identify potential jurors who are likely to be more inclined than others to return a verdict in his favor. The task, simply put, is to know the reliable predictors for jury verdicts, and to find them by identifying how and where potential jurors get their information.

Reliable Predictors for Jury Verdicts

Research indicates that jury verdict outcomes can be anticipated by using some reliable predictors. However, conclusions about juror predictions must be scrubbed carefully for the reasons behind them—that is, why potential jurors are predicted to have certain beliefs.

Limited Data That Correlates Demographics with Verdict Outcome

First, there is limited data that suggests that demographic factors, including age in certain cases and education levels among minorities, may positively correlate with verdict outcomes.

Age—In Certain Cases

The age of jurors continues to be hypothesized as a potential indicator of verdict outcome. However, research demonstrates that age rarely provides predictive assistance in this regard. Stephen Meinhold hypothesized in 2001 that age would "be positively related to views about the litigation explosion," assuming that "as adults mature they are more likely to come into contact with the legal system, and, as the axiom goes, 'familiarity breeds contempt.'"[41] He theorized that because "[i]t is also the case that the legal system is viewed

38. Lois Beckett, *Trump digital director says Facebook helped win the White House*, The Guardian, October 8, 2017. https://www.theguardian.com/technology/2017/oct/08/trump-digital-director-brad-parscale-facebook-advertising.

39. David Smith, *Meet the social media master who could win Trump a second term*, The Guardian, January 30, 2020. https://www.theguardian.com/us-news/2020/jan/30/brad-parscale-trump-social-media-rasputin-campaign-manager.

40. David Wright, *Trump and allies dominate digital spending, prompting Democratic jitters*, November 7, 2019. https://www.cnn.com/2019/11/07/politics/trump-digital-advertising-spending/index.html.

41. Stephen Meinhold, *Exploring Attitudes about the Litigation Explosion*, 22 Just. Sys. J. 107, 111 (2001).

by many in our society as a means of leveling the playing field, a place where despite your resources you can win if you have the law on your side," that "[b]ecause older individuals have the most to lose in such a system, it would not be surprising to find that they are critical of those who resort to the courts."[42] His research proved the opposite, revealing that "[a]mong whites, age continues to be unrelated to views about the litigation explosion."[43] Meinhold also found that "young African-American voters were significantly less likely than older voters to be critical of the litigation explosion in both the diffuse and specific form."[44] In pharmaceutical cases, however, older jurors are somewhat more likely to find for the plaintiffs.[45] More recently in 2020, the research of Brian Bornstein and others also concluded that age was "also related to attitudes toward the jury system."[46]

Lower Education Levels/Certain Minority Groups

Several researchers have concluded that minorities who have lower levels of education are more likely to favor the plaintiff than the defendant in certain scenarios. For example, Bornstein concludes that demographic factors that are correlated with student status did affect subjects' liability judgments; Bornstein concludes that "minority and relatively poorly educated subjects were more likely to find for the plaintiff."[47] Likewise, Rose wrote in 2002 that "different demographic compositions and local cultures in the counties could be reflected in the attitudes of juries deciding civil cases, with the poor and minorities tending to favor plaintiffs on liability,"[48] while Gifford and Jones wrote in 2016 that "business leaders, defense counsel, and even some judges and legislators have sometimes been quite transparent in identifying their concerns that urban juries with African-American and low-income jurors are likely to be unfairly generous to plaintiffs."[49] Meinhold found that African Americans are less concerned about the litigation explosion than whites, with young African Americans being the least critical of the civil justice system. He concludes, however, that juror demographics—in and of themselves—are not reliable predictors of verdict outcomes.[50] Even more recent data that suggests the opposite may exist solely because a specific demographic group may collectively exhibit experiences and attitudes that are in fact a reliable predictor of verdict outcome.[51]

42. *Id.*
43. *Id.*
44. *Id.*
45. Vinson, *supra*.
46. Brian H. Bornstein, et al., *JUST: A Measure of Jury System Trustworthiness*, J. Psychology, Crime & Law, March 16, 2020.
47. Brian H. Bornstein & Michelle Rajki, *Extra-Legal Factors and Product Liability: The Influence of Mock Jurors' Demographic Characteristics and Intuitions about the Cause of an Injury*, 12 Behav. Sci. Law 127–47 (1994).
48. Mary R. Rose, *The Bronx 'Bronx Jury': A Profile in Civil Jury Awards in New York Counties*, 80 Tex. L. Rev. 1889 (2002).
49. Donald G. Gifford and Brian Jones, *Keeping Cases from Black Juries: An Empirical Analysis of How Race, Income Inequality, and Regional History Affect Tort Law*, Washington and Lee Law Review, Vol. 73, Issue 2, Article 3 (Spring – April 1, 2016), p. 627.
50. Meinhold, *supra*.
51. *See generally* Bornstein, et al., *supra* (finding "race/ethnicity ... also related to attitudes toward the jury system.").

Juror Experiences and Attitudes Are a More Reliable Predictor of Verdict Outcome

Research demonstrates that above all else, juror experiences and attitudes are most closely correlated with juror attitudes about the civil justice system, political messaging, media that is hostile to the political system, and verdict outcomes. Most important as predictors to verdict outcomes, however, are juror entitlement attitudes and those who reason via legal authoritarianism.

Juror Experiences and Attitudes about the Workplace

Data demonstrates that jurors' experiences are a reliable predictor of verdict outcomes.[52] For example, plaintiff-oriented jurors have been exposed to chemicals in the workplace,[53] while defense-oriented jurors are less fearful of chemicals. Plaintiff-oriented jurors are active in their union and believe corporations put profits over safety, while defense-oriented jurors are not as strongly predisposed against large corporations.[54] Plaintiff-oriented jurors believe the government is responsible for ensuring consumer safety, while defense-oriented jurors believe that individuals alone control their own safety.[55] Plaintiff-oriented jurors are more likely than defense-oriented jurors to have suffered recent life traumas, such as serious financial hardship; therefore, defense-oriented jurors are more financially optimistic about their own lives than are plaintiff-oriented jurors.[56]

Attitudes about the Civil Justice System Are Reliable Verdict Predictors

Research data consistently demonstrates that a venire panel member's attitude about the civil justice system and tort reform is a reliable verdict predictor. Long-held beliefs of the existence of a litigation crisis predicted verdicts, using hierarchical regression analyses, in research involving tobacco and pharmaceutical cases,[57] and has predicted the size of jury awards generally.[58] Jurors in favor of *more* tort reform are less likely to find for the plaintiff, and they tend to award less in damages.[59] Jurors in favor of "damages caps tended to be no- or low-damages jurors while those opposed to caps rendered higher amounts for damages."[60]

---

52. *See generally* J. R. Boyle, *Psychological, Cognitive, Personality and Interpersonal Factors in Jury Verdicts*, 15 L. & Psych. R. 163–84 (1991).
53. Stuhan, *supra*.
54. *See id.*
55. *Id.*
56. *Id.*
57. Vinson, *supra*.
58. Duane Brandon, Jennifer Mueller & Richard Tabor, *Factors Affecting Juror Perceptions in Liability Cases*, The CPA J., May 2005 (citing Edith Greene, Jane Goodman & Elizabeth F. Loftus, *Jurors' Attitudes about Civil Litigation and the Size of Damage Awards*, 40 Amer. Univ. L. Rev. 805–20 (1991)).
59. Brandon, *supra* (citing G. Moran, B.L. Cutler & A. De Lisa, *Attitudes Toward Tort Reform, Scientific Jury Selection, and Juror Bias: Verdict Inclination in Criminal and Civil Trials*, 18 L. & Psych. Rev. 309–28 (1994)).
60. Alan M. Tuerkheimer, *Politics in Civil Jury Selection*, Wisconsin Lawyer, 1–5 (Dec. 4, 2008), https://www.wisbar.org/newspublications/wisconsinlawyer/pages/article.aspx/2005/article.aspx?Volume=81&Issue=12&ArticleID=1573.

Political Party and Media Messaging Against the Civil Justice System

It is important to distinguish between the public's widespread perception that there are too many frivolous lawsuits from the belief of individual venire panel members that more tort reform is needed. In other words, $600 million in politically driven advertising against the civil justice system in the 1990s and 2000s caused many venire panel members to then and now still indicate that they believe there are too many frivolous lawsuits, but this is a *soft* indicator. Only when that panel member also expresses the fixed view that more tort reform is needed does this view become a *hard* indicator.

Moran concluded in 1994 that jurors' attitudes about tort reform are the best predictor of civil case results.[61] However, reliance on this research must be tempered by the fact that Moran's study largely predated $600 million in subsequent tort reform ads.

Indeed, attitudes are formed by information received. A juror in favor of tort reform in 1992 was an unfavorable plaintiff juror because this attitude predated the Republican Party presidential nominee's initial national pronouncement that as the Republican leader, "I am fighting to reform our legal system, to put an end to crazy lawsuits. . . . If that means climbing into the ring with the trial lawyers, well, let me just say, round one starts tonight," and that the Democratic campaign was "backed by practically every trial lawyer who ever wore a tasselled loafer";[62] it was before Karl Rove's subsequent 20-year war against the civil justice system. A consequence of the politicization of civil trials is that party affiliation provides some guidance to a person's views about tort reform and civil jury damages. Tuerkheimer found that "[w]hile political leaning tends to correlate with what jurors say about damages in civil cases, it does not predict how much they actually award," and cautioned that "[t]he actual question, regardless of political party, is what is significant and useful during jury selection." Tuerkheimer further wrote:

> Jurors also were asked if they agree or disagree with the idea of awarding punitive damages. The questionnaire explained that punitive damages are meant to punish a company for its mistakes or to send a message to similar companies. More than 92 percent of Democrats agreed with the idea of awarding punitive damages while 80 percent of Republicans agreed with this concept. This is a significant difference, but because four-fifths of Republicans agree with punitive damages awards, a defense attorney should not feel overly confident simply because she has many Republicans on her jury. This is another example of how political party is predictive of a certain attitude (toward punitives) but is not predictive of the actual rendering of damages. This question alone is a good one to ask because, regardless of political party, jurors who tend to be in favor of punitive damages award higher amounts and jurors who tend to be against punitives are from the low- and no-damages categories.[63]

61. Moran, *supra*.

62. George H.W. Bush, Republican Nominee, Acceptance Speech at the Republican National Convention (Aug. 20, 1992), *in Remarks Accepting the Presidential Nomination at the Republican National Convention in Houston*, The American Presidency Project, https://www.presidency.ucsb.edu/node/266944.

63. Tuerkheimer, *supra*.

Likewise, Valerie Hans found a similar phenomenon:

> Like the public, jurors endorsed a number of statements suggesting that there is a litigation crisis. Factor analysis identified two independent components: general concern over excessive litigation, and criticism of the civil jury. Litigation crisis views were found in all demographic and attitudinal subgroups. However, attitudes about the civil justice system were related to the respondent's political efficacy, claims consciousness, belief in a just world, age, religion, and race.[64]

The pivotal issue is not a matter of affiliation with apolitical party; it is *why* one is affiliated with that party. A plaintiff's lawyer striking Republicans for their party affiliation alone is missing the point. The key inquiry is, why does that juror vote Republican, and does it relate to issues with the civil justice system? Throughout the south, the Democratic Party lost voters to the Republican Party in the late 1960s because of the Voting Rights Act; in the early 1970s, it lost voters because of anti-war views and perceptions that suggested a lack of patriotism; in the late 1970s and 1980s, the Democratic Party lost voters because of support for abortion and gay rights in contract to religion and the purported "family values" issues supported by the Republican Party; and in the 1990s, the Democratic Party lost voters over a litany of other issues that were remote from an individual's economic station in life. Nonetheless, can anyone objectively argue that family-values Republicans will not make good plaintiff's jurors? No. In truth, to strike jurors based solely on political party is foolish.

However, with party platforms now "for"[65] and "against"[66] tort reform, it is important to understand from jurors whether they have been indoctrinated on this particular issue by virtue of their exposure to the partisan political process. Again, jurors in favor of tort reform statistically vote for the defense more often, and for smaller civil jury verdicts, than those who do not share that view. As such, jury research indicates that "Democrats were significantly more likely to consider awarding money for emotional distress: 79 percent of Democrats compared to 65 percent of Republicans said they would consider awarding money for emotional distress."[67] But this data is only valid if one understands why a particular juror is voting Republican as opposed to Democratic.

Entitlement Attitudes

Psychological entitlement "is a personality trait that is instrumental to a wide variety of issues in society, ranging from the mundane, such as access to good seats at a sporting

---

64. Valerie Hans, *Perceptions of Civil Justice: The Litigation Crisis Attitudes of Civil Jurors*, 12 BEHAV. SCI. L., 181–96 (1994).

65. 2016 Republican Party Platform, https://www.presidency.ucsb.edu/documents/2016-republican-party-platform ("We support state and federal legislation to cap non-economic damages in medical malpractice lawsuits, thereby relieving conscientious providers of burdens that are not rightly theirs and addressing a serious cause of higher medical bills.").

66. 2016 Democratic Party Platform, https://democrats.org/wpcontent/uploads/2018/10/2016_DNC_Platform.pdf (we "must not undermine democratic decision-making through special privileges and private courts for corporations…").

67. Tuerkheimer, *supra*.

event, to more important issues, like the distribution of resources including tax breaks and social welfare."[68] Gary Giewat studied the correlation between this trait and damage awards, finding that entitlement items included juror statements such as:

> "I honestly feel I'm more deserving than others."
> "I deserve more things in my life."
> "People like me deserve an extra break now and then."

Giewat concluded that "[e]xamination of these data revealed a clear relationship between entitlement grouping and damage awards. Participants classified as low in entitlement provided the lowest average damage awards, followed by those in the moderate in entitlement group. Participants who were classified as high in entitlement provided the largest average damage awards."[69] Similarly, Tuerkheimer found that "[w]hen political party is disregarded and this question is viewed by itself, the result shows that people who favor mandating that companies provide free health care tend to fall into the higher damages categories."[70] This research has been replicated more recently as well,[71] and may be especially relevant now when many perceive so-called Millennials to be "entitled."[72]

Legal Authoritarianism—How Jurors Reason

Traditional authoritarianism is "characterized by support for governance by a strong authoritative leader and preference for order and discipline. People who are high in traditional authoritarianism advocate adherence to rules and laws and disapprove of those who do not follow societal norms and rules."[73] Legal authoritarianism has been found by many studies to "be a more reliable predictor of juror bias and verdicts than any other *demographic* indicator."[74] Gayle Herde best explains the traits exhibited by persons high in authoritarianism:

> Persons high in authoritarianism are likely to:
>
> > condemn persons who question and/or deviate from societal norms; view the world as black and white; engage in stereotyping of in-group and out-group members; hold conventional or traditional values; wish to be part of an orderly and

---

68. Gary Giewat, PhD, *Damage Awards: Jurors' Sense of Entitlement as a Predictor*, The Jury Expert (May 30, 2011), https://www.thejuryexpert.com/ 2011/05/damages-and-entitlement/.

69. *Id.*

70. Tuerkheimer, *supra*.

71. *What Are the Critical Juror Attitudes to Know before Jury Selection in Medical Malpractice Litigation?*, Litigation Insights, June 19, 2015. https://www.litigationinsights.com/juror-attitudes-medical-malpractice -litigation/ ("Distinguishers that have been shown to be consistently problematic for many medical malpractice defendants include people who … Hold entitlement attitudes or have extremely high expectations for the extent to which corporations and the government are obligated to take care of others (e.g., believe the government should provide free healthcare to all citizens).").

72. *See generally* Peter Hess, *Psychologists Reveal Why It's Harmful to Keep Calling Millennials "Entitled,"* Inverse, May 15, 2019. https://www.inverse.com/article/55854-are-millennials-any-worse-than-anyone-else.

73. Crocker, *supra* (1993) (citing Brian L. Cutler, Gary Moran & Douglas J. Narby, *Jury Selection in Insanity Defense Cases*, 26 J. Res. Pers. 165–82 (1992)).

74. Gayle Herde, *Take Me to Your Leader: An Examination of Authoritarianism as an Indicator of Juror Bias*, www.documents.jdsupra.com—039e16e8-9f90-4381-b535-3aa2e1a105b9.pdf (last visited Dec. 9, 2019).

> powerful society; submit to established authority; and ostracize or otherwise act aggressively against out-group members.
>
> . . .
>
> Authoritarians identify with the majority. If your client belongs to an "out-group" (e.g., racial or ethnic minority; sexual orientation; "adult" industry or other questionable employment), especially if it is relevant to the trial, you want to locate and eliminate the high authoritarians. On the other hand, if your client is an unequivocal member of "mainstream society," you will want to emphasize those characteristics for your high- authoritarian jurors.
>
> Additional questions that might be useful for locating high authoritarianism in jurors include:
>
> > How would you feel if a family member wanted to marry someone who is [African-American, Muslim, an exotic dancer, etc.]?
> >
> > Have you ever been invited to the home of someone who is [homosexual, Hispanic, Jehovah's Witness, etc.]?
> >
> > Is it justifiable to suspend a person's civil rights in the interests of national security?
> >
> > How do you feel about the government using wiretaps and other types of electronic surveillance in investigating potential criminal activity?[75]

Ironically, persons of high authoritarianism in civil cases with strong liability and minimal contributory negligence can be the best jurors for a plaintiff. As Herde explains,

> In civil trials, persons high in legal authoritarianism care as much or more about the *character* of the defendant and witnesses as they care about the evidence. They will resonate with *voir dire* questions about traditional or family values, personal accomplishment, family and national security, and conservative religious organizations. Interact with them about what groups they belong to and the nature of their involvement.[76]

In pharmaceutical case research, for example, "[o]f jurors awarding punitive damages to the plaintiff, those with professional or managerial positions made larger awards."[77]

Amassing Enough Statistically Significant Data to Make Real-Time Predictions

At its core, pretrial jury work is designed to enable a trial lawyer to accurately predict what themes generally will work at trial, and what types of jurors to deselect after voir dire in the hope that the remaining jurors match the research profile of a favorable juror for the specific case. In this regard, early focus groups must have enough participants to achieve sufficient statistical power to yield real data, and not results driven by chance. To capture

75. Herde, *supra*.
76. *Id.*
77. Vinson, *supra*.

pure correlations between demographic and attitudinal questions and eventual juror attitudes about the case, questionnaires must be utilized before the lawyers in a focus group say a word. Presentations of both sides must be carefully designed to avoid stacking the deck. After all, the goal is not to win the fictional focus group exercise; the goal is to collect enough reliable data about what does and does not work to maximize the likelihood of winning the real case at trial. Post-focus group questionnaires must be designed and utilized to get individual jurors' initial attitudinal responses, before they are diluted or swayed by their deliberations with others. With questionnaires being filled out by individuals before any presentation, after each presentation, and both before and after focus group deliberations, a large amount of data is being collected. This data can appropriately be utilized to predict the behavior of the eventual real jurors. Like any other form of science, replication is key—replication reaffirms initial data, if correct, and will dispute initial data if an outlier has occurred. More importantly, as focus groups are repeated, the power of the data collected grows, and the chances that the results are due to chance or some other illegitimate factor drops precipitously.

Using Jury Questionnaires

Jury questionnaires are the most valuable tool available to someone picking a jury. However, many judges initially are reluctant to permit their use and must be educated about why questionnaires are necessary and helpful.

Motion to Use a Jury Questionnaire

Careful motions must be prepared to encourage the judge—in this specific and suggestively isolated instance—to just once permit a jury questionnaire. There are two primary reasons for jury questionnaires: first, to obtain truthful answers, and second, to save the court's time.

Jury questionnaires are necessary to secure truthful and independent answers from potential jurors before the jury selection process begins. Initially, court-conducted voir dire fails to yield truthful responses from venire panel members. An important study by Jones in 1987 demonstrated that jurors are more candid in their responses when questioned by attorneys, rather than by judges, and that jurors tend to defer more to the authority of the bench, often giving the socially desirable response instead of their candid response.[78] Moreover, group dynamics lead to inaccurate responses from members of the venire panel. Research demonstrates that group dynamics cause a room full of diverse jurors to repeat the seemingly "correct" response given by preceding jurors' responses to voir dire questions. Similarly, Schkade determined that the views of a nondiverse group, whose members largely share the same outlook, tend to become more extreme than they were initially.[79]

---

78. S. E. Jones, *Judge- Versus Attorney-Conducted Voir Dire: An Empirical Investigation of Juror Candor*, 11 Law & Hum. Behav. 131–46 (1987).

79. David Schkade, Cass R. Sunstein & Daniel Kahneman, *Deliberating about Dollars: The Severity Shift*, 100 Colum. L. Rev. 1139, 1172–73 (2000).

Fineman's research in 1996 demonstrated that a jury questionnaire might result in answers that were more honest because each juror responds *individually.*[80]

Second, jury questionnaires save time. A motion for a jury questionnaire should be paired with an offer to limit the length of voir dire examinations. Frankly, data obtained from individuals filling out properly designed questionnaires in isolation from each other is far more valid than information obtained in the formal voir dire group setting.

Moreover, motions to use a questionnaire should include provisions that address the other concerns of most courts. First, questionnaires can be made available on Monday mornings when the judge qualifies potential jurors and excuses those who are ineligible to serve because of a felony criminal history and those not required to serve due to advanced age, full-time education schedules, or caretaking obligations to small children or elderly relatives. The court can conduct its own standard voir dire at that time, effectively utilizing a good portion of the first trial day before it sends the panel home as remaining pretrial motions are resolved. The court can order the panel to return for attorney voir dire and the jury selection process the next morning.

Sending the panel home for the night also allows the parties to study the questionnaires and pare down attorney voir dire to only matters not covered by the questionnaire and specific follow-up questions for individual members of the panel based on questionnaire responses. Most importantly, though, this evening of study gives the trial lawyer an opportunity to harness the power of pretrial jury research by correlating the real jurors' questionnaire answers to data gleaned. This time allows the lawyer to accurately predict which of the jurors to strike as likely unfavorable to the case and which jurors to keep as likely favorable to the case.

Contents of a Good Questionnaire—The Data Necessary to Apply Analytics in the Jury Selection Process

As discussed earlier, court-conducted voir dire often is useless because potential jurors are reluctant to speak frankly when it's a federal or state court judge asking them questions in a group setting. Instead of frank answers, potential jurors subconsciously give answers they believe to be acceptable in a group setting. Likewise, attorney voir dire of a panel of fifty potential jurors likely will yield one true response, followed by a cascade of "me too" answers. Venire members two through fifty simply subconsciously parrot the first answer because they believe it is the acceptable one. Consequently, the best vehicle available for obtaining truthful answers from the entire panel of jurors is the juror questionnaire.

Like well-conducted political polling, a well-constructed questionnaire provides survey data that can successfully predict verdicts before the case begins.[81] One obvious caveat is

80. Martin Fineman & Ronald F. Beaton, *The Use of Juror Questionnaires in Civil Cases*, INT'L SOC'Y OF BARRISTERS Q., 343, 344 (1996).

81. Jeffrey T. Frederick, *Social Science Involvement in Voir Dire: Preliminary Data on the Effectiveness of "Scientific Jury Selection,"* 2 BEHAV. SCI. & LAW, 375–94 (1984) ("Data from the civil case indicated that the survey approach could successfully predict verdicts of mock jurors.").

that "the arrangement of trial facts, as set by the organizing principles or themes of the case," is, together with the strength of the evidence presented, "the most determinative feature of trial outcome by virtue of its role in bringing the group to consensus across its lines of social division."[82] The juror questionnaire should elicit information about the juror's life experiences and attitudes, which are the best indicators of verdict outcome. Fineman proposes a questionnaire that seeks information through five types of questions—demographic, experiential, attitudinal, hardship, and cause:

- *Demographic:* These questions are meant to explore a juror's fundamental characteristics—age, place of birth, place of residence, education, occupation, marital status, job status, occupation of the juror's significant other, occupation of the juror's parents, age and occupation of the juror's children, etc.
- *Experiential:* These questions are meant to explore a juror's past experiences. Most courts will allow a broad range of questions in this area, from the seemingly irrelevant (i.e., military experience, in a contract dispute case) to the painfully relevant (i.e., sexual harassment experiences, in a sexual harassment case). Jury research has found these types of questions moderately predictive.
- *Attitudinal:* These questions are meant to explore jurors' attitudes, values, and beliefs. The questions elicit jurors' opinions on case-relevant issues. Jury research unequivocally shows that these types of questions are consistently the best predictors of a juror's biases or predispositions.
- *Hardship:* These questions are meant to give the jurors an opportunity to describe any physical or financial reasons that would make jury service an undue hardship.
- *Cause:* These questions are meant to give the jurors an opportunity to describe any attitudes, values, or beliefs that would make it difficult for them to serve as fair and impartial jurors in this particular case.[83]

Cynthia Cohen proposes the following questionnaire in her paper about effective defense voir dire:

1. ***Media Habits***
   How often do you read a newspaper? How much television do you watch? What are your favorite shows? What have you learned from the media? How often do you watch TV law shows? Have you ever watched newsmagazine shows about airbags, antilock brakes, safety belts, rollovers or tires? Do you read *Consumer Reports*?
2. ***Family and Community Orientation***
   How long have you lived in your community? Do you have children? What child safety practices are you familiar with?

82. Harvey A. Moore & Edward F. Gerecke, *Qualitative Research, Thematic Development and Jury Selection in Mass Tort Litigation*, Defense Research Institute Seminar on Medical Device Claims (May 9–10, 1996), https://www.harveymooreassociates.com/uploads/1/3/0/7/13073311/qualitativeresearch.pdf.

83. Fineman, *supra*.

3. ***Knowledge Questions***
   Are you familiar with quality control procedures? Are you knowledgeable about health and medicine? Are you knowledgeable about how machines work?
4. ***Experience Questions***
   Have you ever worked for a large corporation? Have you ever filed for unemployment or disability? What do you look for most when buying a new car? Do you look for safety features or cost? What kind of car do you own? Have you ever owned a Japanese car? German car? Italian car? Do you listen to traffic reports on the car radio? Have you ever worked on an assembly line? Do you try to repair machines yourself? Do you work with mechanical engines? Do you tinker with machines in your spare time? Are you technologically oriented? Do you tune up your car or change the oil yourself? Do you read operating instructions when using a new machine? Have you ever kept maintenance records on office equipment? Do you read warnings on labels? Do you take vitamin supplements? Have you ever taken diet pills? Has anyone in your family ever worked for a hospital? Have you ever been involved in a lawsuit? Were you being sued or suing someone? Were you satisfied with the outcome?
5. ***Attitude Questions***
   Are you satisfied with your current job or occupation? What are your views about safety consciousness? Do you think that passengers should wear seatbelts? Do you think that an automobile manufacturer should be required to build a fail-safe automobile? Do you think that a car owner is responsible for maintaining a safe car? When a brake pedal only goes halfway to the floor, do you think that is a signal for a driver to stop? Are some people careless? Do you think that there is quackery in the vitamin world? Do manufacturers adequately label products? How do you feel about the FDA's practices? Do you like doctors? Are you concerned with environmental wastes? Do you favor regulation of pesticides, herbicides, and other chemicals? Do you prefer glass bottles to cans? Do some people misrepresent a pre-existing condition or illness? Do you believe that wealthy defendants are common targets for lawsuits?[84]

Finding the Most Reliable Predictors—Where Do Jurors Get Information?

There are well-known statements about a person's values that suggest that where a person spends their time and money tells you all you need to know about what is important to them. The saying "You are what you eat" is a truism that applies equally to where people get their information. Cambridge Professor of Divinity William Ralph Inge accurately observed that "the aim of education is knowledge not of facts, but of values."[85] In the age of news

84. Cynthia R. Cohen, *Effective Defense Voir Dire: Making Sense of Jurors' Experiences*, Verdict Success, http://verdictsuccess.com/pdf/EffectiveDefense_Voir.pdf (last visited Dec. 9, 2019).
85. Quote Investigator, https://quoteinvestigator.com/2018/09/15/values/ (last visited Mar. 14, 2020).

entertainment, where a person chooses to get their news and information provides valuable clues about their worldview. Marshall McLuhan, the Canadian Philosopher of Communication Theory, observed, "All media exist to invest our lives with artificial perceptions and arbitrary values."[86] Thus, in seeking to glean the values of potential jurors, one must determine where they get their media. This inquiry into jurors' values provides a valuable view into their likely decisions. As Roy Disney observed, "It's not hard to make decisions when you know what your values are."[87]

Thus, to find the reliable predictors of jury verdict outcomes, we must determine how potential jurors' values were formulated. We must learn: "Where do jurors get their information?" In order to learn where jurors get their information, we must perform a rank prioritization of how we as Americans spend our time. If someone spends five hours getting information from Source A and only five minutes from Source B, then analyzing Source A is much more important than analyzing Source B. Accordingly, the ability to rank and prioritize potential information sources by the amount of time potential jurors spend on those sources is a key tool for a trial lawyer to understand jurors' values.

Rank Prioritization—How Do We Spend Our Time?

The Bureau of Labor Statistics has long analyzed how Americans spend the twenty-four hours of their day. These statistics are of high value to a trial lawyer who is attempting to identify where potential jurors get their information.

Sleeping—8.5 Hours a Day

Americans spend slightly more than one-third of their day sleeping, with women averaging an additional eleven minutes of sleep per night than men. Asking jurors how much sleep they average per night, however, is unlikely to yield helpful information about their values, with the possible exception of shedding potential light on jurors who work multiple jobs.

Working—4-5 Hours a Day

On average, American men spend approximately five hours a day and women spend just under four hours a day working in an employment setting. This number obviously is depressed by the unemployed and the underemployed, and by population sectors that are not yet in, or that are no longer in, the workforce. Most important, however, is that work is the single block of time where Americans are awake and conscious and can obtain information. Questions should be asked about jurors' experience at work, as well as their perception of corporate America in general.

Perception of the Workplace

A juror's experience at work is critical to determining her potential values and attitudes, which in turn provide clues about probable verdict outcome. As mentioned earlier, research

86. *Marshall McLuhan*, Wikiquote, https://wikiquote.org/wiki/Marshall_McLuhan (last visited Mar. 14, 2020).
87. BrainyQuote, https://www.brainyquote.com/quotes/roy_e_disney_170949 (last visited Mar. 14, 2020).

demonstrates that workers who are exposed to chemicals in the workplace tend to be more inclined to consider a workplace injury case favorably than workers who either are not exposed or who are less fearful of chemicals. Workers who are active in their union or who believe that corporations put profits over safety are more likely to favor plaintiffs over defendants. These are questions that must be posed to each member of the venire panel; research demonstrates a link between these answers and civil verdict outcomes.

Attitudes about Corporate America

A juror's views toward corporations in general are just as important as a juror's views of her own employment experience. One way to elicit information about a potential juror's attitudes toward corporations is a series of questions about which companies they respect least. Four scenarios, involving automobile companies, oil companies, insurance companies, and Wall Street banking companies provide an instructive opportunity to gather critical information about a juror's attitudes about corporate conduct and entitlement perceptions.

In a 2009 questionnaire, a choice of Chrysler, Ford, or GM as the company the juror least respected necessarily involved a choice of two companies that had to be bailed out by the federal government—GM and Chrysler—and another that did not accept government bailout assistance—Ford. A juror who selects GM or Chrysler to answer the question "Which company do you respect the least?" yields important information about her attitude toward government assistance.

In 2010, a massive explosion on the Transocean *Deepwater Horizon* drilling rig in the Gulf of Mexico led to the deaths of eleven men and the largest oil spill in American history. The civil trial to allocate fault for the disaster occurred in early 2013. In 2013, jurors could be given a choice of whether they respect BP, Shell, or ExxonMobil the least. These options include BP, with its safety record in tatters; Shell, which is universally regarded as having the best safety record in the industry; and ExxonMobil, widely known as the largest oil company. A choice of Shell or ExxonMobil as the company "respected the least" yields information either about a juror's lack of information or his or her disregard of the importance of safety.

Jurors have short memories. In 2008, and then again in 2009, during the government's Troubled Asset Relief Program, the AIG corporation accepted the largest sum of "bailout" money from the federal government—more than $130 billion. The question, "Which company do you respect the least?" with the choices Liberty Mutual, AIG, and Zurich, pitted two companies that have generally positive approval ratings—Liberty Mutual and Zurich—against AIG, which was widely panned as the poster child of government bailouts. A juror who selected either Liberty Mutual or Zurich is either guessing, uninformed about government bailouts, or is nonplussed and entirely unaffected by the concept of government intervention. Similar reactions to corporations accepting coronavirus bailouts are already emerging—airlines now pleading COVID-19 poverty who recently spent $50 billion to buy back their own stock,[88]

88. Phillip van Doorn, *Opinion: Airlines and Boeing want a bailout – but look how much they've spent on stock buybacks*, Market Watch, March 18, 2020. https://www.marketwatch.com/story/airlines-and-boeing-want-a-bailout-but-look-how-much-theyve-spent-on-stock-buybacks-2020-03-18.

cruise lines flagged abroad seeking U.S. taxpayer help,[89] and colleges with large endowments accepting aid[90] from the 2020 CARES Act are just three examples among many available.

Likewise, the question, "Which bank do you respect the most?" with a series of two-choice options that include Merrill Lynch or Bank of America, Lehman Brothers or Barclays, Bear Stearns or J.P. Morgan, provide choices that test jurors' knowledge of the government bailout, and whether such bailouts have affected their view of corporate conduct, bailouts, or government assistance. Of course, Merrill Lynch, Lehman Brothers, and Bear Stearns "lost" and saw their assets either put into bankruptcy or bought up by entities that "won" by acquiring those assets, banks like Bank of America, Barclays, and J.P. Morgan. These three choices provide insights into a juror's understanding of government bailouts, and whether it affects their view of such companies. Likewise, Goldman Sachs, largely known to be the richest, most powerful investment bank on Wall Street, a company with unlimited influence and political reach, employed to represent only the very rich, provides a telling contrast with Citibank, a company perceived to be much more accessible to average Americans, but one that required huge sums of government bailout funds to keep afloat during the financial crisis of 2008. A juror's answer to "Which company do you respect the least?" between Goldman Sachs and Citibank provided then telling information about a juror's attitudes toward corporate conduct and government assistance.

Finally, if you ask a juror "Which tire company do you respect the least?" and provide only four options—Cooper, Firestone, Michelin, and Goodyear—you have an opportunity to gather information about a juror's knowledge and attitudes about product safety. Michelin is far and away considered to provide a superior quality tire. In safety reputation, Goodyear is behind Michelin but far ahead of Cooper and Firestone. Moreover, in the early 2000s, Firestone suffered the largest product liability recall ever; 17 million Firestone tires were recalled due to poor quality in the name of corporate profits. A juror who chooses Firestone as the tire company he or she respects the least likely has a recollection of this safety recall. One who chooses Firestone or Cooper has some information about the safety of tires. A choice of Michelin or Goodyear suggests a juror who probably is uninformed on matters of product safety. Automotive scandals that involved Takata airbag failures, GM ignition switch deceptions, and Volkswagen's emissions fraud provide similar fodder for questions that help give insight into juror attitudes about suspect corporate conduct. Likewise, jurors in California might be quizzed about their views of Monsanto, which has been hit with multiple adverse jury verdicts over its weed killer Roundup Ready, or of Pacific Gas and Electric ("PG&E"), whose chronically poor safety record led to it being criminally convicted of felony behavior, and who later caused massive wildfires in Northern California in 2015, 2017, 2018, and 2019.

89. Irene S. Levine, *Why Cruise Lines Should Be At The End Of The Bailout Line*, Forbes, (Mar. 24, 2020). https://www.forbes.com/sites/irenelevine/2020/03/24/why-cruise-lines-should-be-at-the-end-of-the-bailout-line/#1f1572b61f65 ("most cruise ships, although headquartered in the U.S., are registered abroad and don't pay U.S. taxes.").

90. Ellen M. Burstein & Camilla G. Caldera, *Trump Says Harvard Will Have to 'Pay Back' CARES Funds*, The Harvard Crimson, (April 21, 2020). https://www.thecrimson.com/article/2020/4/22/trump-harvard-return-cares-money/.

In conclusion, a trial lawyer should plan in advance a series of timely and topical questions that will allow her to learn from jurors their understanding and attitudes about corporate conduct that can be applied to the case at hand.

Watching Television—3-4 Hours a Day

After sleeping and working, Americans spend the next biggest portion of their day watching television.[91] On average, men spend well over three hours a day and women slightly under three hours a day "glued to the tube."[92] On weekends, American men average 3.71 hours a day watching television, while women average 3.12 hours a day.[93] According to Nielson, Americans spend five hours and 46 minutes a day consuming video content from TV's, computers, and mobile devices.[94] Streaming video has boomed, and now constitutes 19 percent of the time spent watching TV by consumers.[95] In sum, a majority of free time available to Americans is spent gathering information by watching television. Thus, the question of what kind of television jurors watch is the key question to learn how their values are being formulated.

Entertainment Television

The ten most popular television shows of all time are *The Honeymooners*, *I Love Lucy*, *The Andy Griffith Show*, *All in the Family*, *Saturday Night Live*, *David Letterman*, *Seinfeld*, *The Simpsons*, *60 Minutes*, and *The Sopranos*. A question that asks jurors which of these is their favorite provides valuable information only if the answer is *The Sopranos* or *60 Minutes*. Eight of these top ten are comedies. A choice of *60 Minutes* over *The Sopranos* and the eight comedies on this list provides insight that this juror is a news junkie, is inquisitive into matters of right and wrong, and is likely to be a leader in the jury room. A choice of *The Sopranos* may suggest something else, while a choice of one of the eight comedies suggests only that the juror appreciates being entertained with humor.

Nielson ranked the ten most popular television shows of 2019 as follows: *NBC Sunday Night Football*, *The Big Bang Theory*, *NCIS*, *Game of Thrones*, *Fox+NFLN Thursday Night Football*, *Sunday Night NFL Pre-Kick*, *Young Sheldon*, *NFL Regular Season*, *This Is Us*, and *FBI*.[96] Obtaining a juror's answer about their favorite TV show can reveal a sports enthusiast, a person who prefers to be entertained by comedy, an inquisitive mind that enjoys investigating mysteries, or someone who relishes getting lost in the other worlds of history or fantasy.

---

91. *American Time Use Survey Summary*, U.S. Bureau of Labor Statistics, (June 19, 2019). https://www.bls.gov/news.release/atus.nr0.htm.

92. *Id.*, Table 11A.

93. *Id.*, Table 11B.

94. Tom Butts, *Nielsen: U.S. Adults Spend Majority of Waking Hours Interacting With Media*, TV Technology, July 1, 2019. https://www.tvtechnology.com/news/nielsen-u-s-adults-spend-majority-of-waking-hours-interacting-with-media.

95. Todd Spangler, *Streaming Accounts for 19% of Total TV Viewing with Netflix Leading the Pack, Nielson Says*, Variety, (February 11, 2020). https://variety.com/2020/digital/news/streaming-video-netflix-total-tv-viewing-nielsen-1203500634/.

96. *Tops of 2019: Television*, Nielsen (Dec. 18, 2019), https://www.nielsen.com/us/en/insights/article/2019/tops-of-2019-television-2/.

Getting News from Television

The data one can gather from potential jurors about the source of their news on television is far more important than preferences for entertainment television. Women are much more likely than men to favor network TV, as they make up about six-in-ten or more of those who cite network news as their main source for political news.[97]

The Fox News versus CNN/MSNBC Divide The Fox News vs. CNN/MSNBC divide is important in three ways. First, the history of cable news delivery in this country has purposely created a very real political divide among viewers. Second, data reveals that a real divide exists in the values of those who watch Fox News compared to those who watch CNN or MSNBC. Third, a juror's preference for cable television news personalities provides meaningful clues about the juror's values.

CNN began as the innovative brainchild of Ted Turner. Turner used cable technology to expand his local Atlanta television station into a fledgling national cable news channel that attempted to compete with the traditional national network news offerings from ABC, NBC, and CBS. All that changed with the fall of the Iron Curtain in the late 1980s and the first Persian Gulf War in 1991. Bernard Shaw had America hooked with his dramatic coverage of bombs dropping on Baghdad during the start of the first American war effort against Saddam Hussein. In the late 1980s and early 1990s, CNN's market share compared to national network news continued to climb. By 1992, 30 percent of Americans regularly watched CNN for their news.[98] That number grew to a peak of 33 percent in 1994.

Media mogul Rupert Murdoch, having started a fledgling television network he called Fox Broadcasting Company in 1986, made a massive financial commitment in the early 1990s to buy broadcast rights to National Football Conference games from the National Football League (NFL). The network had for several years been broadcasting original programming, including *The Simpsons*, which the audience at first tolerated but then grew to love. The NFL deal, however, immediately expanded Fox's audience by millions of football fans. At the same time, more and more Americans began relying on Fox to provide them with their news. With an edgy but conspicuously conservative bent on the news, the cable outlet Fox News, which began in 1996, gained market share by appealing to Republicans and conservatives while railing against the alleged "liberal media bias" of traditional network news and CNN cable news. It worked. By 1999, Fox News reached 39 million homes.[99]

Microsoft and NBC established a joint venture and created a new cable network called MSNBC. Seeking a countervailing option to Fox News, MSNBC conspicuously tilted to the left and attempted to appeal to Democrats and liberals to drive market share. By 1999, MSNBC reached the homes of 48 million Americans.[100]

---

97. Elizabeth Grieco, *Americans' main sources for political news vary by party and age,* Fact Tank, (April 1, 2020). https://www.pewresearch.org/fact-tank/2020/04/01/americans-main-sources-for-political-news-vary-by-party-and-age/.

98. *Id.*, Question 28dF2-jF2, Q28l-n, Q31a-c; Q36.

99. Lawrie Mifflin, *MEDIA; In This War, CNN has Real Competition*, The New York Times, (April 5, 1999). https://www.nytimes.com/1999/04/05/business/media-in-this-war-cnn-has-real-competition.html.

100. *Id.*

Framed by Fox News as a "liberal media outlet," CNN swung further to the left in an attempt to capture market share—progressive viewers—from MSNBC. Critically, these shows have framed their content and marketed themselves as the news outlets for specific segments of the population. We have transformed our news sources from objective, respected voices like Walter Cronkite and Tom Brokaw, into news entertainment personalities who consider it their job to push a particular political agenda in order to drive market share for the companies that own the network, rather than to merely deliver the news. As such, television news is now an arena where Republicans and conservatives reliably obtain their news from Fox News, while progressives and Democrats reliably obtain their news from either MSNBC or CNN. By 2020, survey data showed that "CNN is trusted by 70 percent of self-described liberal Democrats, but only 16 percent of conservative Republicans—a gap of 54 percentage points. Conversely, Fox News is trusted by 75 percent of conservative Republicans but only 12 percent of liberal Democrats—a 63-point gap."[101]

This divide between Fox News on one hand and MSNBC and CNN on the other provides a trial lawyer who is trying to glean the values of venire panel members with valuable information.

The Pew Research Center has published detailed polling information about the age, gender, income, education history, party (Democrat or Republican), ideology (conservative, moderate, or liberal), and political labels (i.e., "environmentalist," "progressive," "gay rights supporter," "Tea Party activist," "Christian conservative," "NRA supporter") of responders. Although this polling is now dated—taking place from June 8–28, 2010—it is highly instructive to the political divide that began after the passage of Obama's seminal piece of legislation, the Affordable Care Act.

Pew Research Center polling data shows that those who receive their news from *The Daily Show*, *Hardball*, *Countdown with Keith Olbermann*, *The Rachel Maddow Show*, news magazines, the *New York Times*, National Public Radio (NPR), and CNN tend to self-identify as Democrats, progressives, environmentalists, and gay rights supporters. By contrast, people who receive their news from Fox News, *The O'Reilly Factor*, Glenn Beck, Rush Limbaugh, Sean Hannity, news blogs, and the *Wall Street Journal* tend to self-identify as Tea Party supporters, Christian conservatives, NRA supporters, Republicans, and conservatives.[102] Data shows that the vast majority of Democrats obtain their news from CNN and MSNBC, while a major percentage of Republicans receive theirs from Fox News.[103] Importantly, between 31 percent and 40 percent of Democrats believe "all or most" of what is reported by CNN (40 percent), NPR (37 percent), MSNBC (34 percent), and the *New York Times* (31 percent)—up to three times the number of Republicans who believe those same sources. By contrast, 41 percent of Republicans believe "all or most" of what

---

101. John Gramlich, Q&A: *How Pew Research Center evaluated Americans' trust in 30 news sources*, Fact Tank – News in The Numbers, (Jan. 30, 2020). https://www.pewresearch.org/fact-tank/2020/01/24/qa-how-pew-research-center-evaluated-americans-trust-in-30-news-sources/.

102. *Id.*, Question 98c, f, h.

103. *Id.*, Question 98a-h.

Fox News reports, while only 21 percent of Democrats and 22 percent of Independents hold that view.[104]

President Obama is most singularly identified with the Affordable Care Act (nicknamed *Obamacare*),[105] a major piece of entitlement legislation, while his successor Donald Trump is identified with trying to dismantle it.[106] Of course, verdict outcome research cited herein indicates that jurors who place a high value on entitlements are statistically more likely to lean toward the plaintiff. As such, what were Obama's job approval ratings by viewers of different cable television news shows? A large majority of viewers of *Countdown with Nick Olbermann* (84 percent), *The Rachel Maddow Show* (80 percent), *The Daily Show* (69 percent), *Hardball* (68 percent), CNN (67 percent), and MSNBC (65 percent), and readers of the *New York Times* (79 percent) and listeners of NPR (65 percent) approved of President Obama's job performance at the time that legislation was enacted. By contrast, only a small minority of viewers of Fox News (30 percent) and *The O'Reilly Factor* (13 percent), readers of the *Wall Street Journal* (39 percent), and listeners of Rush Limbaugh (9 percent), Glenn Beck (11 percent), and Sean Hannity (7 percent) approved of President Obama's job performance.[107]

More recently, Stephen Colbert, Rachel Maddow, Jake Tapper, Bill Maher, Tucker Carlson, Trevor Noah, and Samantha Bee have seen their ratings soar due to Donald Trump during his presidency.[108] President Trump's persistent demonization of "liberal" media outlets like CNN and MSNBC, and his embrace of more "conservative" media outlets like Fox News make it much more likely that more recent polling would continue to demonstrate this stark reality that where jurors get their news says much about what their attitudes are likely to be.

Jury research cited herein also indicates that venire panel members who believe the government should ensure our safety are more likely to return a verdict for the plaintiff, and in higher amounts than those who believe the government does too much and individuals should ensure their own safety. The Pew Research Center also asked consumers of various news outlets whether they believed the "government does too much" or whether the "government should do more to solve problems." Not surprisingly, the vast majority of consumers of conservative news outlets like Sean Hannity (84 percent), Rush Limbaugh (81 percent), Glenn Beck (79 percent), *The O'Reilly Factor* (77 percent), the *Wall Street Journal* (70 percent), and Fox News (61 percent) answered that they believe the "government does too much." By contrast, consumers of progressive news outlets like the *New York Times* (61 percent), NPR (57 percent), CNN (56 percent), MSNBC (53 percent), *Countdown with*

104. *Id.*, Question 11a-l, n-o.

105. *10 Remarkable Achievements of Barack Obama's Presidency*, TDJakes.com, https://www.tdjakes.com/posts/10-remarkable-achievements-of-barack-obama-s-presidency (last visited Mar. 14, 2020); Steve Anderson, *Obamacare: The Affordable Care Act*, HealthInsurance.org (Nov. 22, 2019), https://www.healthinsurance.org/obamacare/.

106. *Trump tells town hall he plans to cut entitlements, hopes to replace ObamaCare with 'something great'*, The Week (Mar. 6, 2020), https://theweek.com/speedreads/900356/trump-tells-town-hall-plans-cut-entitlements-hopes-replace-obamacare-something-great.

107. Gramlich, *supra*, Question 1.

108. Josef Adalian, *8 TV Stars Who Have Seen Their Ratings Soar Due to Donald Trump*, Vulture (Mar. 3, 2017), https://www.vulture.com/2017/03/trump-bump-stephen-colbert-rachel-maddow-tucker-carlson.html.

Keith Olbermann (61 percent), and *The Rachel Maddow Show* (69 percent) believe that the "government should do more to solve problems."[109]

The American Tort Reform Association is an offshoot of the U.S. Chamber of Commerce. This self-proclaimed lobbying arm of the American business community has endorsed "more tort reform" as a cure to what ails American businesses. Jurors who believe that "more tort reform" is needed are associated with verdict outcomes that favor the defense, and with smaller verdicts than those who do not hold that view. How do viewers of various media outlets self-identify as "pro-business"? Not unexpectedly, the vast majority of consumers of conservative media outlets identify themselves as pro-business: Hannity (86 percent), Limbaugh (86 percent), the *Wall Street Journal* (83 percent), *The O'Reilly Factor* (80 percent), Glenn Beck (79 percent), and Fox News (70 percent).[110]

Testing Cable News Personalities to Identify Which Side of the Fence a Potential Juror Is On

Asking a potential juror which cable news personality they respect the most is a clean and quick way to determine which side of the political fence that juror is on. What do Anderson Cooper, Wolf Blitzer, Erin Burnett, John Berman, Chris Cuomo, John King, Don Lemon, Jake Tapper, and Fareed Zakaria all have in common? Each are CNN news personalities.[111] What do Brian Williams, Rachel Maddow, Steve Kornacki, Chuck Todd, Nicolle Wallace, Eugene Robinson, Steve Schmidt, Lawrence O'Donnell, Mika Brzezinski, and Joe Scarborough have in common? Each are MSNBC news personalities.[112] What do Bret Baier, Maria Bartiromo, Tucker Carlson, Steve Doocy, Ainsley Earhardt, and Juan Williams have in common? Each are Fox News personalities.[113] Through quick, easy questions about a potential juror's favorite or least favorite cable television news personalities, one can glean valuable information about the juror's values, and thereby, his or her potential for a specific verdict outcome.

A Word on Television Advertisements

Television advertising is a multibillion-dollar-a-year industry. Early in the fight for and against tort reform, television ads permeated the airways and played a substantial role in forming and shaping public opinion. In Texas and elsewhere, however, the advertisements about tort reform seem to be specifically related to particular political campaigns. It used to be that television viewers were forced to absorb the messages contained in these advertisements, so the tort reform message was pervasive and had to be dealt with during voir dire.

Recently, however, TiVo and DVR technology has given viewers the ability to prerecord their favorite television shows and watch them later at greater speed by fast-forwarding through advertisements littered through the progression of the show. According to Nielson ratings, the amount of time the average American spends viewing a DVR or TiVo

109. Gramlich, *supra*, Question 100.
110. *Id.*, Question 98d-e.
111. *List of CNN personnel*, Wikipedia, https://wikipedia.org/wiki/List_of_CNN_personnel.
112. *MSNBC Live*, Wikipedia, https://wikipedia.org/wiki/MSNBC_Live#Special_event_anchors_and_contributors.
113. *Fox News personalities*, Wikipedia, https://wikipedia.org/wiki/Template:Fox_News_personalities.

playback has doubled from 2008 to the present. The Pew Research Center reports that only 3 percent of American households had a TiVo or DVR device in 2002; by 2010, that number had climbed to 45 percent.[114] Today, 74 percent of Americans utilize streaming services.[115] As such, unless viewers want to watch advertisements, such as during the Super Bowl, trial practitioners should no longer assume that venire panel members are being barraged with the messaging that's build into advertising during their favorite television shows.

Reading

People who read frequently and who can express what they read reveal a lot about their background and values. This is valuable information to the jury selection process.

Book Readers

A smaller and smaller percentage of Americans spend their time reading books. However, those who do read books read a great deal. When poll participants in 2010 were asked if they read a book the day before responding to polling questions, 45 percent of college graduates answered in the affirmative versus 27 percent of those with a high school education or less.[116] More recently, audiobook sales increased by nearly 25 percent between 2017 and 2018 and total sales approached nearly $1 billion.[117] The top-selling books can provide critical information about a potential juror's source of information, and thus, his or her values. The *New York Times* published its list of top-selling nonfiction book offerings as of March 14, 2020:

1. *The Splendid and the Vile*, by Erik Larson
2. *The Mamba Mentality*, by Kobe Bryant
3. *Unknown Valor*, by Martha MacCallum
4. *The Hope of Glory*, by Jon Meacham
5. *Open Book*, by Jessica Simpson
6. *Educated*, by Tara Westover
7. *A Very Stable Genius*, by Philip Rucker & Carol Leonnig
8. *Talking to Strangers*, by Malcolm Gladwell
9. *Becoming*, by Michelle Obama
10. *Until the End of Time*, by Brian Greene.[118]

Asking a potential juror who responds that he or she is a voracious reader what his or her favorite top-selling nonfiction book is can yield very important information. A reader of

114. Gramlich, *supra*, Questions 75, 76.

115. *Share of Consumers Who Have a Subscription On-Demand (SVOD) Service in the United States from 2015 to 2019*, Statista, https://www.statista.com/statistics/318778/subscription-based-video-streaming-services-usage-usa/ (last visited Mar. 14, 2020).

116. Pew Research Center, *supra*, Questions 24 & 26.

117. *29 Book Sales Statistics Based on Real Numbers and Studies*, Markinblog, (December 6, 2019). https://www.markinblog.com/book-sales-statistics/.

118. *Hardcover Nonfiction*, The New York Times (Mar. 14, 2020), https://www.nytimes.com/books/best-sellers/hardcover-nonfiction/.

The Hope of Glory is likely to be a viewer of *Morning Joe* on MSNBC because the author, Jon Meacham, appears regularly on that show. A reader of *Unknown Valor* is likely to be a viewer of Fox News, because the author, Martha MacCallum, is an anchor there. Consequently, the nonfiction books a juror purports to read can give you an important clue about whether the potential juror's values align in a manner likely to be pro-plaintiff or pro-defendant in litigation.

Fiction offerings provide less insight into political leanings, but they may provide hints as to other aspects of a juror's views. A reader of *Alex Cross* by James Patterson, *The Forgotten* by David Baldacci, or *The Black Box* by Michael Connelly might suggest a consumer of violent thrillers, whereas a reader of *Threat Vector* by Tom Clancy might suggest one interested in the military, and thus high authoritarianism. A reader of *The Racketeer* by John Grisham suggests a reader who has a fascination with the legal system, whereas readers of *Gone Girl* by Gillian Flynn, *Life of Pi* by Yann Martel, and *Fifty Shades of Grey* by E.L. James might suggest one who prefers romance, art, and culture.

Newspaper Readers

The choice of national newspapers can offer important information about personal values. While the choice of the *Houston Chronicle*, the *Dallas Morning News*, the *Austin American-Statesman*, or the *San Antonio Express-News* will provide virtually no meaningful information, the choice of the *New York Times* versus the *Wall Street Journal* provides highly important information about a potential juror's values. In the Pew Research Poll, 62 percent of readers of the *New York Times* self-identified as "Progressive," while only 35 percent of the readers of the *Wall Street Journal* responded similarly.[119] Readers of the *New York Times* and the *Wall Street Journal* respectively, self-identified in far different ways:

"Democrat" (49 percent to 22 percent)
"Republican" (9 percent to 36 percent)
"Conservative" (11 percent to 45 percent)
"Liberal" (38 percent to 12 percent)
"Progressive" (62 percent to 35 percent)[120]
"Environmentalist" (71 percent to 57 percent)[121]
"Gay Rights Supporter" (78 percent to 44 percent)[122]
"Tea Party Supporter" (8 percent to 35 percent)[123]
"Christian Conservative" (12 percent to 29 percent)[124]
"NRA Supporter" (13 percent to 45 percent)[125]

---

119. Pew Research Center, June 8–28, 2010.
120. *Id.*, Question 98f.
121. *Id.*, Question 98c.
122. *Id.*, Question 98h.
123. *Id.*, Question 98a.
124. *Id.*, Question 98b.
125. *Id.*, Question 98g.

"Democrats believing all or most of what is said" by the newspaper (31 percent to 33 percent)[126]
"Republicans believing all or most of what is said" by the newspaper (13 percent to 28 percent)[127]
"Obama Job Approval" (79 percent to 39 percent)[128]
"Government Does Too Much" (34 percent to 70 percent)[129]
"Government Should do More to solve Problems" (61 percent to 29 percent)[130]
"Pro-Business" (61 percent to 83 percent).[131]

This data remains today, with about nine-in-ten of those who name *The New York Times* (91%) and NPR (87%) as their main political news source identify as Democrats, with CNN at about eight-in-ten (79%).[132]

Magazine Readers

Magazine readership has steadily declined with the advent of the Internet. Revenue enjoyed by U.S.-based periodical publishers has fallen from $46 billion in 2007 to around $28 billion in 2017.[133] Likewise, by 2010, only 19 percent of Americans polled said they spent any time reading magazines yesterday, and more than 80 percent said they spent no time reading magazines.[134] "Magazines have sputtered for years, their monopoly on readers and advertising erased by Facebook, Google, and more nimble online competitors."[135] Obviously, however, readers of the *National Review*, *Taki's Magazine*, the *American Spectator*, the *American Conservative*, the *New American*, *FrontPage Magazine*, and the *Christian Science Monitor* are likely to subscribe to conservative viewpoints, whereas readers of *The Progressive*, *Mother Jones*, *Harper's Magazine*, and *The Nation* may subscribe to more progressive viewpoints.

Drive Time

Americans spend almost twice as much time in their vehicles than Europeans. Europeans average 274 hours per person a year in their smart cars; Americans average 541 hours per person a year in their big cars.[136] One key question for a trial lawyer preparing for voir dire is what the venire panel members listen to as they drive around. The answer can be categorized in one of three ways: sports, music, or talk radio news.

---

126. *Id.*, Question 11a-l.
127. *Id.*, Question 11n-o.
128. *Id.*, Question 1.
129. *Id.*, Question 100.
130. *Id.*
131. *Id.*, Question 98d-e.
132. Grieco, *supra*.
133. Amy Watson, *U.S. Magazine Industry - Statistics & Facts*, Statista (Aug. 27, 2019), https://www.statista.com/topics/1265/magazines/.
134. Pew Research Center, *supra*, Question 23.
135. Sydney Ember & Michael M. Grynbaum, *The Not-So-Glossy Future of Magazines*, New York Times (Sept. 23, 2017), https://www.nytimes.com/2017/09/23/business/media/the-not-so-glossy-future-of-magazines.html.
136. Financial Times, www.ft.com (Dec. 22, 2012).

Sports Radio

There is no data correlating sports lovers with verdict outcomes. However, knowing that a potential juror spends his or her drive time listening to SportsRadio 610 or SportsTalk 790 AM is important because it suggests a trial lawyer may want to communicate with more sports examples than they otherwise might. Most important is that it eliminates the other two broad categories of radio time that may prove more illuminating: music and talk radio news.

Music Stations

People who spend their drive time listening to music over-the-air—regardless of AM or FM—are Country, News/Talk, Religion, Contemporary Christian, and Spanish.[137] Knowing which of the four groups of music the members of the jury listen to could end up being significant in terms of the references lawyers should use while talking to jurors or while questioning witnesses. More importantly, it may provide information that is useful in selecting jurors in the first place. Jurors who answer that they spend their drive time listening to KHCB ("Keeping Him Close By"), KKHT ("The Word"), or KSBJ ("God Listens") are much more likely to be members of the Christian Conservative movement and more likely to share its particular ideologies. Depending on the facts of one's case, this could be important information to know in selecting a jury, although certainly not nearly as illuminating as a preference for talk radio news.

Talk Radio News

A venire panel member in Harris County, Texas (or in any large city in America) who answers in a questionnaire that she spends her drive time listening to talk radio news possesses information vital to a trial lawyer who is performing voir dire. With respect to local talk radio, a listener of Michael Berry or Steve Johnson is likely to have far more conservative views of civil litigation and jury trials than those who listen to Liberal Talk Radio on KPFT. With respect to national talk radio, a listener of Glenn Beck or Rush Limbaugh is likely to have far more conservative views than those who listen to NPR or the Public Broadcasting System.

Purchasing Goods and Services—Where?

Research data demonstrates that a demographic factor like income does not relate to verdict outcomes. A decade ago, readers of the *Wall Street Journal* with a median annual income of $135,740 were viewed as conservative, and readers of the *Washington Post* with a median annual income of $120,400 and of *The New York Times* with a median annual income of $155,816 were deemed more progressive.[138] However, the earning power of all such readers is well over the national average.

---

137. *Format Counts: The Most Dominant Radio Genres On AM Vs FM Are…*, Inside Radio, (Oct. 4, 2019). http://www.insideradio.com/format-counts-the-most-dominant-radio-genres-on-am-vs-fm-are/article_f0c9c3f2-e671-11e9-91ce-e347f85b68f5.html.

138. Sean Callahan, *'Wall Street Journal' Readers Have Highest Houshold Income, According to MRI*, AdAge, (Nov. 18, 2009). https://adage.com/article/btob/8216-wall-street-journal-readers-highest-household-income-mri/277474.

Nonetheless, lawyers inevitably place undue importance on the income bracket of potential jurors as some mystical predictor of verdict outcome. In the event that income level is a topic that must be covered, the astute trial lawyer will obtain income-related information by asking questions on where shopping occurs, rather than questions that specifically ask about income levels. While online purchases continue to climb each year, most shopping dollars spent in 2019 before the COVID-19 pandemic were still spent during physical trips to store locations.[139] Asking where a potential juror shops provides some information about disposable income. The question "What department store do you prefer?" may yield a high-end store answer like Saks Fifth Avenue or Neiman Marcus, a moderately priced answer like Macy's or Dillard's, or a low-priced option like JCPenney or Bealls. Likewise, the question "At what store do you like to shop for shoes?" may yield a high-end store answer like Jimmy Choo, a moderately priced answer like Cole Haan, or a low-priced option like the now-defunct Payless ShoeSource. The question "Where do you shop for groceries?" may yield a high-priced store answer like Whole Foods Market, a moderately priced answer like H-E-B, or a low-priced option like Walmart, Target, or Fiesta. Finally, asking for the jewelry store you buy at the most may result in a high-priced response like Tiffany & Co., a moderately priced one like Zales, or a low-priced one like Claire's. Because of the potential for embarrassment, this question should be asked only in questionnaire format, to elicit a private response. Keep in mind that the recent dramatic growth of e-commerce hampers the utility of this question, as home delivery service companies like Amazon have become ubiquitous.

Socializing and Communicating

Americans spend approximately one hour a day socializing or communicating. This is done primarily in one of three ways: eating, going to movies, or communicating by phone or online.

Eating with Friends

As with the shopping questions, asking a potential juror about their favorite place to eat with friends can shed light on their economic situation. An answer in Houston, Texas, of Tony's, the Annie Cafe, Brennan's, La Griglia, or Eddie V's might suggest a comfortable salary, with plenty of disposable income. Pappadeaux, Ninfa's on Navigation, or Houston's might suggest a moderate income. James Coney Island, Golden Corral, IHOP, Waffle House, or Panda Express might suggest either a low income or a frugal outlook.

Going to Movies

Favorite movies are insightful because Americans go to the movies almost 1.4 billion times a year. The ten highest grossing movies in 2019 were *Avengers: Endgame, The Lion King, Star Wars: The Rise of Skywalker, Frozen II, Toy Story 4, Captain Marvel, Spider-Man: Far From Home,*

---

139. Fareeka Ali, *A decade in review: Ecommerce sales vs. retail sales 2007-2019*, Digital Commerce 360, (Mar. 3, 2020). https://www.digitalcommerce360.com/article/e-commerce-sales-retail-sales-ten-year-review/.

Aladdin, *Joker*, and *Jumanji: The Next Level*. The 2020 Oscar nominees included the war epic *1917*, the historical assay *Ford and Ferrari* and *Once Upon a Time in Hollywood*, dark dramas like *The Irishman* and *Joker*, and the artistic foreign-language entry *Parasite*. 2018 brought the Oscar-winning *Bohemian Rhapsody*, the musical biopic of Queen's song "Bohemian Rhapsody," and the Bradley Cooper/Lada Gaga remake of *A Star is Born*, while also serving up highly successful adventure/fantasy films like *Black Panther* and *Avengers: Infinity War*. The question of one's favorite movie last year allows the questioner to learn the preference of the person responding for either thrillers, dramas, or comedies. In 2018, Oscars were awarded to niche artistic films like *The Shape of Water* and *Three Billboards Outside of Ebbing, Missouri*, as well as to historical and political dramas like *Darkest Hour*, *The Post*, and *Vice*. Providing significant variety in a question means that a choice inevitably will yield information about the answering juror.

Communicating by Phone or Online

Learning how jurors communicate is important to enable the trial lawyer to fashion his or her questions to include this modality of communication. Current corporate marketing and communications are centered on device notifications, online marketing, and viral campaigns.[140] This is important discovery information, particularly to younger jurors.

Social Networking

Americans spend an increasing amount of their day relaxing and thinking in the form of the online communication known as social networking. As of January 2018, 43 percent of American adults report that they use the Internet "several times a day," while 26 percent report that they use the Internet "almost constantly."[141] With 292 million Internet users in the United States,[142] approximately 69 percent of those use Facebook.[143] With the age of the Internet, people over age thirty-five now represents more than 30 percent of the entire Facebook user base.

The college demographic grew 74 percent in the past few years; importantly, their mode of social networking has overwhelmingly moved from laptops to mobile devices. Nearly half of people between the ages of eighteen and thirty-four check Facebook right when they wake up; more than one-quarter check Facebook on their cell phones before even getting out of bed.

140. Kurt Wagner, *Digital advertising in the US is finally bigger than print and television*, Vox, (Feb. 20, 2019). https://www.vox.com/2019/2/20/18232433/digital-advertising-facebook-google-growth-tv-print-emarketer-2019.

141. J. Clement, *Internet Usage Frequency of Adults in the United States as of January 2018*, Statista (May 29, 2018), https://www.statista.com/statistics/495078/us-adult-internet-usage-frequency/.

142. J. Clement, *Number of Internet Users in the United States from 2000 to 2019*, Statista (Jan. 7, 2020), https://www.statista.com/statistics/276445/number-of-internet-users-in-the-united-states/.

143. John Gramlich, *10 Facts about Americans and Facebook*, Pew Research Center (May 16, 2019), https://www.pewresearch.org/fact-tank/2019/05/16/facts-about-americans-and-facebook/.

Ninety percent of American adults now use the Internet.[144] Persons who described themselves as "online almost constantly" were more likely to be college graduates (34 percent) than high school graduates or those not graduating (20 percent).[145]

A decade ago, more than one-third of all Americans and more than 46 percent of Americans between the ages of thirty and thirty-nine get their news online.[146] The percentage of those online for news at least three times per week has risen from 2 percent in 1995 to 46 percent in 2010.[147] By September 2019, 89 percent of Americans got their news online.[148]

Given the influence of news on the attitudes of potential jurors, one must ask the question "Where do you get your news online?" With respect to young Americans, more got their news online than through any other source;[149] 48 percent said they found out about news through Facebook, with Facebook-related searches jumping 207 percent between 2009 and 2010. Paradoxically, political blogs are read with greater frequency as Internet users get older.[150]

It is important to learn in voir dire which social media platform potential jurors are utilizing on a frequent basis. Young people do not typically avail themselves of privacy blocks made available on these platforms, which provides access to valuable publicly available information about young potential jurors. Each juror should be asked if they regularly use Google, Facebook, Twitter, Flickr, Reddit, Tumblr, Instamatic, LinkedIn, YouTube, Instagram, Snapchat, TikTok, or Pinterest. This information should be obtained in a jury questionnaire so that these social networking sites can be searched before voir dire for valuable insights into the experiences and attitudes of potential jurors.

Video Games

A few years ago, Americans traveled to arcades to play games. Since the advent of Atari in the early 1980s, electronic games have improved dramatically as technology has advanced. An entire generation of children is being raised with access at home to high-quality, high-resolution, high-interactivity games, and they are spending increasing amounts of time on those games. Approximately 75 percent of Americans have at least one gamer in their household.[151] In 2018, Americans spent $43.4 billion on the video game industry.[152]

---

144. J. Clement, *Share of adults in the United States who use the internet from 2000 to 2019*, Statista, (June 18, 2019). https://www.statista.com/statistics/185700/percentage-of-adult-internet-users-in-the-united-states-since-2000/.

145. Luke Pensworth, 2019 Internet Statistics, Trends & Dats, Daily Wireless, (Mar. 7, 2020). https://www.dailywireless.org/internet/usage-statistics/#Internet_Usage_in_the_United_States.

146. *Id.*, Questions 9, 11, 17, 18, 18a, 52a, 57a, 61a & 71.

147. *Id.*, Questions 41 & 43.

148. Faisal Kalim, *89% of Americans Get News Online, and Other Key Findings from Pew Research*, What's New in Publishing (Sept. 18, 2019), https://whatsnewinpublishing.com/89-of-americans-get-their-news-online-and-other-key-findings-from-pew-research/.

149. *Id.*, Questions 28-31, 41, 49, 51, 55, 57, & 61.

150. *Id.*, Question 46.

151. *2019 Essential Facts about the Computer and Video Game Industry*, Entertainment Software Association, https://www.theesa.com/esa-research/2019-essential-facts-about-the-computer-and-video-game-industry/ (last visited Dec. 10, 2019).

152. *U.S. Video Game Sales Reach Record-Breaking $43.4 Billion in 2018*, Entertainment Software Association, (Jan. 22, 2019), https://www.theesa.com/press-releases/u-s-video-game-sales-reach-record-breaking-43-4-billion-in-2018/.

Moreover, adults now in their twenties and thirties continue to religiously spend free time playing video games. Thus, whether a potential juror prefers military "shoot 'em up" combat games like *Minecraft*, *Fortnite*, *Tom Clancy's Rainbow Six Siege*, *Red Dead Redemption 2*, and *League of Legends*; driving games like *Grand Theft Auto V* and *Rocket League*; and cartoon games like Nintendo's *Super Smash Bros. Ultimate*, *Overwatch 2*, and *Roblox* provide some insight into how the person spends their free time.

Furthermore, with members of Generation Z now eligible for jury service, any trial lawyer wishing to communicate with that generation better be familiar with the most popular games in the world in 2019, such as *Fortnite*, *Counter-Strike: Global Offensive* (CS:Go), and *PlayerUnknown's Battlegrounds* (PUBG). The lexicon of communication with younger jurors now includes these games, together with their story lines, characters, and success mechanisms.

Exercise—How and How Often

Asking a juror *how often they get their exercise* will provide information about both their subconscious view of protecting one's own health (if they exercise regularly), and predict leadership attributes (in the team sports context). Among most adults who have retired from high school team sports like football, basketball, baseball, and track, the question of *how they exercise* also will provide a window of information into the amount of money they spend in pursuit of physical fitness. Exercise choices like walking and running require no expense; cycling can cost some money, but usually without the membership fees required for exercise facilities; aerobics, weightlifting, and swimming are options that can come with considerable facility or group exercise class fees. While group exercise memberships at Orange Theory or Soul Cycle cost some money, golf, tennis, and polo probably require spending substantial discretionary resources.

Sports Franchises and Heroes

Asking questions about favorite sports personalities often can yield insightful information about jurors' preferences. A question about whether the Astros or Rockets, Yankees or Rangers, Lakers or Spurs are the best-run franchise may yield opinions that reflect the importance of thrift.

Similarly, asking a local venire panel who their favorite player is on the local sports team may yield interesting answers that reflect the value systems of particular potential jurors. For example, asking for one's favorite Houston Rocket may lead to sentimental picks Hakeem Olajuwon and Clyde Drexler, both of whom won a championship for the Rockets; Yao Ming, who would be preferred because of his power and size; or on today's team, James Hardin or Russell Westbrook, flamboyant players who demanded top pay, and who took all the steps necessary to get it. Among the choices is the coach, Mike D'Antoni. A juror who chooses the coach over superstar players provides a dead giveaway of his preference for high authoritarianism. Likewise, if a juror chooses Houston Texans' coach Bill O'Brien over his quarterback, star receiver, star running back, star defensive tackle, or star linebacker, signals of high authoritarianism are shown. A New England Patriots choice of Bill Belichick over

Tom Brady suggests the same. Finally, if any member of the venire panel was able to name any starting pitcher for the 2013 Houston Astros, strike that panel member because they are thinking in dollars and cents that are too low to qualify as an acceptable juror to any plaintiff. By contrast, an answer to the same question about the 2017–2019 Astros reflects an adherence to excellence, regardless of cost.

Finally, asking a juror how frequently they attend sporting events in person provides valuable insight into disposable income. Someone with season tickets to the games of an NFL, NBA, or MLB franchise self-evidently has access to a level of disposable income perhaps unavailable to potential jurors who solely follow their pro sports teams on television for free.

Other Miscellaneous Time Spent

Generally, remaining available time is spent in miscellaneous favored free time activities, and in the car travelling to and from work. Americans have very little time remaining to occupy that is not already consumed by the activities described here. However, an open-ended inquiry of "How do you spend your free time?" is a good way to learn about a potential jurors' priorities. As it's been said, "You can learn a lot about a man's priorities by learning how he spends his time." In response to such an open-ended inquiry, a response of "going to church" or "doing chores around the house" provides a different picture of an individual's priorities than a response of "shopping" or "getting a pedicure." The question is valuable, however, because it allows a potential juror to state on his or her own terms how they spend their time, and therefore, what is a priority in their life.

Using Jury Consultants

A good jury consultant is a tool trial lawyers can utilize to capture scientific jury selection ("SJS") research. SJS allows a trial lawyer to correlate juror experiences and attitudes with their views toward a specific case. They also can use SJS to identify potential jurors on the venire panel who have similar experiences and attitudes. Jury consultants should be familiar with the science of SJS, analytics, and the data they produce, and have the expertise to formulate jury questionnaires and voir dire questions that are sufficient to draw from the members of the venire panel their own similar experiences and attitudes so that strikes for cause and peremptory challenges may be exercised intelligently.

Methods of Identifying Juror Experiences and Attitudes

Juror experiences and attitudes predict verdict outcomes far more reliably than demographics. This conclusion results from almost forty years of trial lawyers employing knowledgeable jury selection experts to conduct SJS. This was reaffirmed through the presidential election process with the Obama reelection campaign's use of "analytics," a technique more recently used by Cambridge Analytica for the 2016 Trump campaign,[153] a process long-employed by corporate America to most efficiently market its products.

---

153. Bethania Palma, *Did the Obama Campaign Employ the Sam Tactics as Cambridge Analytica*, Snopes, (Mar. 22, 2018). https://www.snopes.com/fact-check/obama-campaign-use-tactics-cambridge-analytica/.

Scientific Jury Selection

The art of SJS had its genesis in the trial of the Harrisburg Seven. As it often does, Wikipedia most succinctly summarizes the events:

> The Harrisburg Seven were a group of religious anti-war activists led by Philip Berrigan. The "Seven" were Berrigan, Sister Elizabeth McAlister, Rev. Neil McLaughlin, Rev. Joseph Wenderoth, Eqbal Ahmed, Anthony Scoblick, and Mary Cain Scoblick. The group became famous when they were unsuccessfully prosecuted for alleged criminal plots during the Vietnam War era. Six of the seven were Roman Catholic nuns or priests. The seventh was Eqbal Ahmad, a Pakistani journalist, American-trained political scientist and self-described "odd man out" of the group. In 1970, the group attracted government attention when Berrigan, then imprisoned, and Sister Elizabeth McAlister were caught trading letters that alluded to kidnapping National Security Advisor Henry Kissinger and blowing up steam tunnels. . . . U.S. Attorneys charged the Harrisburg Seven with conspiracy to kidnap Kissinger and bomb heating tunnels. They filed the case in the city of Harrisburg, Pennsylvania. Activist attorney and former Attorney General Ramsey Clark led the defense team for their trial during the spring months of 1972. Unconventionally, he didn't call any witnesses in his clients' defense, including the defendants themselves. He reasoned that the jury was sympathetic to his Catholic clients and that that sympathy would be ruined by their testimony that they'd burned their draft cards. After an extraordinarily long deliberation, the jury remained hung and the defendants were freed.[154]

How did Ramsey Clark know to not call even a single witness? He employed the services of academic researchers who were concerned about the government having a disproportionate degree of power and control over the outcome of citizens' lives. They provided him with research on the correlation of certain potential jurors' attitudes regarding the government. This gave Clark educated clues about which potential jurors were most likely to favor the defense position. After the government's failure to obtain a conviction, Clark's use of "jury consultants" was applauded in the press, and a new industry was born. I recommend the work of Joel Lieberman and Bruce Sales for a fine discussion of the evolution of jury selection consulting, and of surveys and related trial consulting services as a professional industry.[155]

Analytics

Most Americans might know of analytics from the postelection explanations of President Obama's 2012 reelection campaign. Obama's campaign manager, Jim Messina, had deployed unprecedented manpower and financial resources to the campaign's analytics department. On election night, almost mystically, Obama's deployment of resources turned

154. *Harrisburg Seven*, Wikipedia, http://wikipedia.org/wiki/Harrisburg_Seven (last visited Dec. 9, 2019).
155. Joel D. Lieberman & Bruce D. Sales, Scientific Jury Selection (2007).

out his voters more effectively than Mitt Romney's. Postelection stories each concluded that it was his campaign's use of analytics that made all the difference.[156]

Four years later, Brad Parscale's use of Facebook to mine data for analytics to support the Trump presidential campaign wildly trumped what Messina had achieved for Obama.[157] Parscale employed hundreds of young writers, who polluted social media with all sorts of provocative spin via posts on issues designed to identify Trump supporters. Whether or not Russian bots exploded the number of social media impressions achieved by these posts is not relevant here (although someone did). The important question is, why? Provocative spin was not used to persuade; it was used to identify. Whenever a post that contained some crazy conspiracy theory was shared or liked, Trump's team secured valuable data about individuals who were likely to be potential Trump voters. In this manner, Trump identified huge numbers of potential voters who should be targeted by the campaign's digital and social media persuasion techniques.[158] Since becoming President, Donald Trump has held political rallies persistently. The primary purpose? To gather cell phone numbers and social media data from hundreds of thousands of hard-core Trump supporters, which Trump can use to identify his likely supporters during the 2020 reelection campaign.[159]

Targeting potential voters this way in the political realm can be utilized in the legal arena to identify probable favorable and unfavorable jurors via the social media footprint left by members of the venire panel before voir dire concludes. The attorney or their staff should completely research the social media history of each member of the jury pool. With this information, data analytics provides invaluable clues about which jurors to try to keep and which to try to get off your jury.

So, what is analytics? That great resource in the cloud, Wikipedia, describes it as follows:

> Analytics is the discovery and communication of meaningful patterns in data . . . . Especially valuable in areas rich with recorded information, analytics relies on the

156. For examples, *see* Christi Parsons & Kathleen Hennessey, *Obama Campaign's Investment in Data Crunching Paid Off*, Los Angeles Times (Nov. 13, 2012), http://articles.latimes.com/2012/nov/13/nation/la-na-obama-analytics-20121113; Eric Siegel, *The Real Story Behind Obama's Election Victory*, Fiscal Times (Jan. 21, 2013), http://www.thefiscaltimes.com/Articles/2013/01/21/The-Real-Story-Behind-Obamas-Election-Victory.aspx; Eric Siegel, *Team Obama Mastered the Science of Mass Persuasion—And Won*, Truth Out (Jan. 22, 2013), http://truth-out.org/news/item/14026-team-obama-mastered-the-science-of-mass-persuasion-and-won; Michael Scherer, *How Obama's Data Crunchers Helped Him Win*, CNN (Nov. 8, 2012), http://www.cnn.com/2012/11/07/tech/web/obama-campaign-tech-team; Josh Peterson, *Report: Internal Analytics Gave Obama Campaign Edge Over Romney Campaign*, Daily Caller (Jan. 3, 2013), http://dailycaller.com/2013/01/03/report-internal-analytics-gave-obama-campaign-edge-over-romney-campaign/; Tim Murphy, *Meet Obama's Digital Gurus*, Mother Jones (Oct. 2012), http://www.motherjones.com/politics/2012/10/obama-campaign-tech-staff.

157. Jacob Pramuk, *Trump's Digital Director Explains How He Used Facebook to Help Win the White House*, CNBC (Oct. 9, 2017, 7:49 PM), https://www.cnbc.com/2017/10/09/brad-parscale-says-trump-campaign-used-facebook-to-beat-clinton.html.

158. Ian Bogost & Alexis C. Madrigal, *How Facebook Works for Trump*, The Atlantic, (April 17, 2020). https://www.theatlantic.com/technology/archive/2020/04/how-facebooks-ad-technology-helps-trump-win/606403/.

159. Rob Crilly, *'We are a data-centric campaign': How Trump 2020 is weaponizing 'MAGA' rallies*, Washington Examiner, (May 20, 2019). https://www.washingtonexaminer.com/news/we-are-a-data-centric-campaign-how-trump-2020-is-weaponizing-maga-rallies.

> simultaneous application of statistics, computer programming and operations research to quantify performance.[160]

Jeffrey Strickland, PhD, statistician and specialist in predictive analytics, writes:

> Firms may commonly apply analytics to business data, to describe, predict, and improve business performance. Specifically, arenas within analytics include enterprise decision management, retail analytics, store assortment and SKU optimization, marketing optimization and marketing mix analytics, web analytics, sales force sizing and optimization, price and promotion modeling, predictive science, credit risk analysis, and fraud analytics. Since analytics can require extensive computation, . . . the algorithms and software used for analytics harness the most current methods in computer science, statistics, and mathematics.[161]

Wikipedia provides three good examples of how to apply "analytics"—through marketing optimization:

> Marketing has evolved from a creative process into a highly data-driven process. Marketing organizations use analytics to determine the outcomes of campaigns or efforts and to guide decisions for investment and consumer targeting. Demographic studies, customer segmentation, conjoint analysis and other techniques allow marketers to use large amounts of consumer purchase, survey and panel data to understand and communicate marketing strategy.
>
> Web analytics allows marketers to collect session-level information about interactions on a website. Those interactions provide the web analytics information systems with the information to track the referrer, search keywords, IP address, and activities of the visitor. With this information, a marketer can improve the marketing campaigns, site creative content, and information architecture.
>
> Analysis techniques frequently used in marketing include marketing mix modeling, pricing and promotion analyses, sales force optimization, customer analytics e.g.: segmentation. Web analytics and optimization of web sites and online campaigns now frequently works hand in hand with the more traditional marketing analysis techniques. A focus on digital media has slightly changed the vocabulary so that marketing mix modeling is commonly referred to as attribution modeling in the digital or mixed-media context.
>
> These tools and techniques support both strategic marketing decisions (such as how much overall to spend on marketing and how to allocate budgets across a portfolio of brands and the marketing mix) and more tactical campaign support in terms of targeting the best potential customer with the optimal message in the most cost effective medium at the ideal time.[162]

---

160. *Analytics*, Wikipedia, http://wikipedia.org/wiki/Analytics (last visited Dec. 13, 2019).
161. Jeffrey Strickland, Data Science and Analytics for Ordinary People, 105 (2015).
162. *Web analytics*, Wikipedia, https://wikipedia.org/wiki/Web_analytics (last visited Dec. 9, 2019).

Portfolio Analysis

Banks typically analyze the risk profile of potential loans through a process known as "portfolio analysis." A common application of business analytics is portfolio analysis. In this, a bank or lending agency has a collection of accounts of varying value and risk. The accounts may differ by the social status (wealthy, middle-class, poor, etc.) of the holder, the geographical location, its net value, and many other factors. The lender must balance the return on the loan with the risk of default for each loan. The question is then how to evaluate the portfolio as a whole.

The least risky loan may be to the very wealthy, but there are a very limited number of wealthy people. On the other hand, there are many poor that can be lent to, but at greater risk. Some balance must be struck that maximizes return and minimizes risk. The analytics solution may combine time series analysis, with many other issues in order to make decisions on when to lend money to these different borrower segments, or decisions on the interest rate charged to members of a portfolio segment to cover any losses among members in that segment."[163]

Risk Analytics

"Predictive models in the banking industry are developed to bring certainty across the risk scores for individual customers. Credit scores are built to predict individual's delinquency behavior and widely used to evaluate the credit worthiness of each applicant."[164]

Analytics can also be used to select juries. But one must be careful. A commercially available computer software known as Jury Quest involves little more than demographic factors, which research shows to be unrelated to verdict performance.[165] The appropriate model for use of analytics can be found in the wide swath of consumer research performed and utilized by corporate America in the marketing of its products. Analytics requires data. Today, that data is available to us. As Rousseau writes,

> [i]n today's world, people are required to produce significant quantities of personal information in order to acquire credit cards, obtain mortgages, receive medical services, and participate in a wide variety of necessary transactions. For the most part, that information is stored in computer databases that are not necessarily secure. Today's technology facilitates the compilation and exchange of information, making it virtually impossible to restrict access to personal data or to even know who has access to the information.[166]

---

163. *Analytics*, Wikipedia, *supra*.

164. *Id.*

165. For a discussion of JuryQuest, *see* Jeff Horwitz, *Jury-Rigging: Can a Computer Pick a Better Jury Than a High-Priced Consultant?* Slate (Aug. 10, 2006), https://slate.com/news-and-politics/2006/08/jury-rigging.html.

166. Lauren A. Rousseau, *Privacy and Jury Selection: Does the Constitution Protect Prospective Jurors from Personally Intrusive Voir Dire Questions?* 3 Rutgers J.L. & Urb. Pol'y 287–320 (2006), https://rutgerspolicyjournal.org/sites/jlpp/files/Rousseau_Jury_Selection.pdf.

As a result, marketers have long relied upon consumer data to identify targets,[167] and now, politicians use it to identify likely supporters."[168]

A Few Warnings about Jury Consultants

The preceding three paragraphs about marketing optimization, portfolio analysis, and risk analytics come straight from Wikipedia (on purpose) because it is important that when you hire a jury consultant, the consultant should bring more to the table than the mere ability to quote the work of others on the subject of jury science. A warning truly is necessary here. In the same way that *Daubert* is meant to keep junk science out of the courtroom, the trial lawyer must remain on guard against marketing gurus masquerading as jury scientists. Our industry is replete with so-called psychologists and jury consultants that make a living off trial lawyers, but who know nothing about the true science behind SJS.

SJS practitioners are not regulated by any national or state body, and due to the nature of their work there are no specified licensure or training requirements for employment in the field. The lawyer who blindly abdicates to a consultant his or her primary role in selecting the jury is a fool. Many jury consultants guess no less than lawyers do. Many subscribe to demographics as the be-all and end-all of jury selection—often with disastrous results. A lawyer should critique the reasoning behind each suggestion a jury consultant makes, and apply only those that make sense and that are shown to be valid by solid research. Instead of "separating the wheat from the chaff," the lawyer must separate the SJS consultants' hunches from the real research data.

Moreover, how a jury consultant is best utilized is key to the success the consultant will achieve. While a lawyer may feel like she has done the job for her client merely by paying a jury consultant to show up on the day of the trial and assist in the jury selection process, this achieves little without hiring the consultant early and with ample time and resources to conduct the jury research during the preseason. Without early research, the consultant lacks the information needed to intelligently pick a jury on game day.

Voir Dire Tactics

Developing a rapport with the members of the venire panel immediately is critical. Long civics lessons about why it is potential jurors' responsibility to be there often fall flat when condescendingly presented by the plaintiff's lawyer; such speeches should be left to the court. Instead, it is the job of the plaintiff's lawyer to immediately secure the empathy of your client's fellow citizens.

---

167. John D. McKinnon, *Political Device Goes Corporate,* Wall Street Journal, 6 (May 21, 2007).

168. Douglas B. Sosnick, Matthew J. Dowd & Ron Fournier, Applebee's America: How Successful Political, Business and Religious Leaders Connect With the New American Community, 33–51 (2006); Michael D. Shear, *Va. Gubernatorial Hopefuls Use Data to Zero In on Voters,* Washington Post, C1 (Aug. 28, 2005); David Von Drehle, *No Stone Is Left Unturned for Turnout; Tight Contest Fires Up Faithful in Record Push for Votes,* Washington Post, A1 (Nov. 7, 2000).

Demonstrating Empathy to the Panel

Demonstrating empathy for the inconvenient plight of the members of the venire panel is an important first step in any voir dire process. Each and every one of us could be in the same position they are in now, and securing justice via the jury service sacrifice of their peers is the reason we're here. While I have served on a jury and was excited to do so, your average citizen does not share the same enthusiasm for the process—at least initially. Recall the feelings of trepidation, if not disgust, at receiving your own jury summons. Share your memory of difficulty in finding a parking spot near the courthouse. Communicate your own past irritation with the delays involved in the process. These shared recollections are an important way of putting yourself in the shoes of the individuals you are about to begin questioning in the voir dire process.

The Beginning of Voir Dire—Its Most Important Part

The most important part of voir dire is its beginning, because if done correctly, the beginning can politely and effectively communicate to impatient members of the venire panel exactly when voir dire will end. Every voir dire I conduct begins with:

- *Introduction*—The panel should learn your name and your client's name before one question is asked.
- *Thanks*—Voice appreciation to the panel from your client and you as the lawyer for responding to the jury summons and performing their civic duty.
- *Empathy*—I mention that I too responded to a jury summons, was picked to serve on a jury, and sat through a weeklong trial—"I know what you're going through."
- *Acknowledgment*—Acknowledge the sacrifice and inconvenience this has caused them.
- *Promise*—Tell them that the bad news is that you'll be asking them questions, but the good news is that you'll do it quickly in an effort to respect their time. I point to the clock in the courtroom, and I promise I will stop in less than one hour, when the big hand hits "X" o'clock. If the court lacks a clock, I pull out an iPhone and, in front of jury panel, set my alarm and promise, "Before that thing rings, I will be done—I promise. Because it's essential that we get all of you back to your kids and your spouses and your jobs by the end of the day."

This routine is critical. The *introduction* is just good manners—politely informing the panel about yourself and your client before intrusively (to them) digging into their lives and opinions. Saying "thanks" also is just good manners, but it quickly makes jurors pleased that they did the right thing by showing up. Sharing your own experience as a juror is a way to put yourself into their position, to demonstrate *empathy*; it makes strangers feel like the lawyer questioning them has some concept of the burden the process is causing them. An *acknowledgment* of the inconvenient burden to them is an important prelude to transferring that burden away from the plaintiff for bringing a lawsuit and onto the defendant for groundlessly making the plaintiff go through this trial with them. The *promise*, however, is the most important mechanism to immediately achieve a rapport with the jurors. The most important commodity in the courtroom to the members of the jury is *their* time. A good lawyer must respect their time. Starting and stopping a voir dire in time is critical. Make a promise on time, and keep it. Whether or not you joke that "as a plaintiff's lawyer, I'm not being paid by the hour like Mr. [Defense Lawyer] over here," you have set the time trap that you intend to honor their time, which may nonetheless be wasted by your opponent. If opposing counsel drags the length of the voir dire process on interminably, the jurors will notice the contrast.

Developing Rapport via Courtesy and Transparency

Rapport also is built during voir dire by being perfectly polite. Very few lawyers have the photographic memory that it takes to look at fifty juror information cards and immediately know each and every panel member's name and information. Instead of calling a live human being *Juror #6*, apologize to the entire panel—"We just got these juror information cards that you filled out. I'm not one of those people who can memorize fifty names on the spot, and I don't want to waste your time by looking down at my notes every time someone raises a hand. If you would hold up your card when I ask a question, I'm going to call out your number instead of your name. I'm not trying to be rude, Mrs. Anderson; I know your real name is not Juror #6, but this will save a bunch of your time if I just call out your numbers. Is everyone okay with that?" By apologizing, you make yourself human. By explaining, you are causing the panel to understand your predicament. By asking for their permission, you are placing them in charge of their time.

Rapport also must be maintained. One way to maintain rapport is to explain the trial process to the venire panel. Explain that *voir dire* is a French term for "jury selection," but it really is a deselection process. Warn them that after strikes, the first twelve jurors left will be on the jury. Explain that what follows will be opening statements, and then you will begin putting on the plaintiff's evidence by calling witnesses. Instead of calling out a long list of names of potential witnesses and asking who knows them, use the witness list strategically. Explain to the panel who your witnesses are and generally what they will testify to during this trial. Do it in the order that you intend to call the witnesses.

After you have determined which members of the panel know which of the witnesses, make your second promise. "I know that's a long list of witnesses, but we're going to do two things to keep it from dragging on and wasting your time." First, many of these witnesses have already given their testimony and can be presented through heavily edited video-recorded depositions. Explain to the panel that if you call the witnesses live, you and your opponent will take a lot longer going tit-for-tat through the list than if you play the recorded testimony that was already given under oath. Explain that although the deposition may have lasted six hours, there are only twenty-two minutes of testimony that have the really important stuff. "Does anyone on the panel have a problem with me saving you five hours and thirty-eight minutes by playing only the important stuff, instead of every ridiculous question that a lawyer billing by the hour could think of that day?" Again, you have obtained the permission of the panel to play video-recorded depositions, you have explained why you are doing it, and you are the one saving the jury panel's time.

Second, by listing the names of all your potential witnesses and pre-editing your video-recorded depositions, you should know how long the case will take. Consequently, I always try to tell the jury when I plan to rest—"by Thursday afternoon at five o'clock, the plaintiff will rest, and then they can put on the defense case." With this promise, you have framed the length of the jurors' time obligation in a way that any time after Thursday at five o'clock is on the defense. Regardless of what happens during the trial, you must rest by Thursday at five o'clock once this promise is made. I have cut both fact and expert witnesses out of my case-in-chief in many trials, because keeping one's word with the jury is far more important than making every last point or playing every last deposition.

Using Favored Political and Business Leaders to Gain Insight into Juror Values

How we spend our time defines who we get our information from *presently*, and it reflects value systems that were passed down to us *in the past*. Retrospective preferences may yield insights into those views from the past. Insights can be reaffirmed with inquiries into present views.

Which President Do You Admire the Most?

Asking a potential juror "Which U.S. president over the past fifty years do you admire the most?" may yield interesting insights into that juror's value system. Data suggests the following conclusions or insight:

- President Kennedy, a Democrat who held office 1961–1963, is known by his admirers for *intelligence* and strength (the Cuban Missile crisis), while having a cavalier attitude toward his marital vows (affair with Marilyn Monroe, etc.). A juror who picks Kennedy may value intellect, but may be willing to exclude aberrant behavior and *excuse contributory negligence*.
- President Johnson, a Democrat who held office 1963–1969, is known by his admirers for *strength* (escalation of the war in Vietnam) and for the Great Society, which dramatically expanded *entitlements* in this country.
- President Nixon, a Republican who held office 1969–1974, is known by his admirers for *strength*. However, surely given the other choices over the past fifty years, a choice of Nixon as a juror's most admired president suggests that they might believe *a defendant can do no wrong*. Paradoxically, the same juror might be willing to *excuse contributory negligence*.
- President Ford, a Republican who held office 1974–1977, is known by his admirers for *compassion* in pardoning Nixon, but most hold the same views of Ford as they do of Nixon. It is, therefore, unlikely that Ford will be chosen.
- President Carter, a Democrat who held office 1977–1981, is known by his admirers for his *compassion* and for his unwavering convictions of *right and wrong*. Considered by many to have a failed presidency, someone who chooses Carter likely has deep convictions of the rights of the dispossessed and the need for social justice.

- President Reagan, a Republican who held office 1981–1989, is known by his admirers for *strength* in confronting the Soviet empire and for causing the eventual end of the Cold War, and is almost deified by being characterized by *high authoritarianism.*
- The first President Bush, a Republican who held office 1989–1993, is known by his admirers for *strength* in confronting Saddam Hussein, yet also for *compassion* by virtue of signing the Americans with Disabilities Act.
- President Clinton, a Democrat who held office 1993–2001, is known by his admirers for his *intelligence*, but he also is known as having a cavalier attitude toward his marital vows (affair with Monica Lewinski, etc.). Thus, one of his admirers may be more apt to excuse aberrant behavior or *excuse contributory negligence.*
- The second President Bush, a Republican who held office 2001–2009, is known by his admirers for *strength* in confronting Saddam Hussein. He is favored by those characterized who value *high authoritarianism* for his use of the Patriot Act to pursue terrorists, although at the expense of civil liberties of U.S. citizens and others.
- President Obama, a Democrat who held office 2009–2017, is known by his admirers for his *intelligence*, but also as one who passed the largest new *entitlement* in more than forty years via the Affordable Care Act, or "Obamacare."
- President Trump, a Republican in office since 2017, is known by his admirers for his *strength* in taking action regardless of the consequences. Far greater than even President Reagan and the second President Bush, his supporters are marked by valuing *high authoritarianism.*

Which of Today's Politicians Do You Respect the Most?

Moreover, asking a potential juror, "Which of today's politicians do you respect the most?" reaffirms the values expressed in the questions about their most and least admired presidents. A roster of ten politicians presented in alphabetical order—Joe Biden, Pete Buttigieg, Lindsey Graham, Amy Klobuchar, Mitch McConnell, Nancy Pelosi, Mitt Romney, Bernie Sanders, Donald Trump, and Elizabeth Warren—provides a long list of possible choices across a wide political spectrum, from left-leaning socialist liberals like Sanders and Warren to moderate Democrats like Biden, Buttigieg, and Klobuchar, to more conservative Republicans like McConnell and Trump. Ironically, our politics are so extreme right now that the safe and conciliatory choices of Joe Biden and Mitt Romney really don't provide key information. However, a choice of Biden from the left suggests a juror who has openly progressive views, while a choice of McConnell from the far right suggests a juror with severely conservative views.

Which of Today's Business Leaders Do You Admire the Most?

Provide potential jurors with a list of six billionaire business leaders, in alphabetical order—Jeff Bezos, Warren Buffett, Larry Ellison, Bill Gates, Donald Trump, and Mark Zuckerberg—and ask them, "Which businessman do you admire the most?" This question provides an opportunity to learn a potential juror's value system about the purpose of business. All six are very successful businessmen. Bezos is the world's richest man, having built the largest corporation ever in under twenty-five years. Buffett is an iconic investor; respect for his business acumen is unparalleled in history. Ellison quickly built Oracle into a high-tech behemoth, only to then use his resources in an openly excessive and public manner. Gates cornered the PC software market in his thirties and forties, and has softened his image since. Trump earned billions through slick business deals, via relentlessly successful self-marketing and by taking tough positions in litigation. Zuckerberg built a social media giant while still in his twenties, and is presently facing calls for his company to be split up in an effort to reduce its power. Yet, there is one factor that separates the first three from the last three—philanthropy. Gates has given away tens of billions of dollars to invest in education and eradicating disease throughout the Third World, and now he is well-known as the most prolific philanthropist ever. Buffett found Gates so successful at philanthropy, he gave away $40 billion to the Bill & Melinda Gates Foundation on the condition that Gates himself must give it away. A choice of Buffett or Gates over Bezos, Ellison, Trump, or Zuckerberg may provide valuable insight into a potential juror's attitude about business.

In sum, by learning where we spend our time, one can gain insights into the sources of our information. By quickly learning how jurors get their information, one can gain important insights into their value systems. Also, by asking basic information about juror views with respect to politics and business, a trial lawyer can efficiently catch a glimpse of those value systems.

Hitting the Points Jury Research Identifies Are Key

Too often, books and articles that discuss voir dire and jury selection consist of specific examples of effective questions from a specific case. Rather than spend hundreds of pages regaling the reader with example after example of clever questions asked in the past, it suffices to say here that each voir dire outline should include questions that are carefully organized by topic to achieve an inquiry of all significant issues identified by the pretrial jury research that was conducted.

Rehabilitation of Jurors

Case law in federal courts, and in many state courts has expanded the ability of good defense lawyers to rehabilitate jurors who have already given a disqualifying answer. The practical consequence of this trend is to require the plaintiff's attorney to expend their limited number of peremptory challenges on jurors who perhaps should already have been excused. There are several techniques to limit this rehabilitation trend.

First, before the defense lawyer ever gets to attempt rehabilitation, the plaintiff's lawyer must first conclude his voir dire examination. Prior to the start of the defense voir dire examination, the plaintiff's lawyer should advise the court of which jurors he believes are disqualified. There are three reasons this should occur before the defense begins. Initially, the court will write down the reasons for the individual motions to strike for cause before the disqualification attempt can begin. Moreover, providing the judge with the plaintiff's list of proposed strikes for cause will subliminally tell the judge that there will be a sufficient number of remaining jurors, even if all the proposed strikes for cause are granted.

Finally, knowing which jurors are alleged to have already disqualified themselves enables the judge to focus on rehabilitation efforts before they begin. Again, knowing that a ruling that denies rehabilitation will not bust the panel inexorably pushes the court toward the original disqualification.

Second, whenever a defense lawyer seeks to rehabilitate a juror who has already disqualified herself, lodge an objection immediately to interrupt the effort. A court being asked to shut down rehabilitation efforts is more likely to do so after he knows that doing so poses no risk to the panel.

Third, if and when rehabilitation occurs, the plaintiff's lawyer should ask that it occur at the bench instead of in open court where all other venire members can hear. The primary reason is that you don't want to give other venire members the script on how to escape jury duty. In addition, rehabilitation efforts at the bench are more susceptible to objections being sustained, or at the very least, to a subsequent rejoinder by the plaintiff's attorney *after* the rehabilitation effort has been completed but *before* the motion to strike for cause is lodged and argued.

Strikes for Cause

In pursuing strikes for cause, there are legal and practical considerations to keep in mind.

In the legal context, before any trial, a pretrial memorandum should be prepared that sets forth each reported case in that jurisdiction where a state appellate court has affirmed a trial court's strike for cause or ruled that a trial court's failure to grant one was an error. Likewise, in federal court, the plaintiff's attorney should file before trial a memorandum that sets forth all federal district court rulings that grant a motion to strike for cause, and all federal courts of appeals rulings that hold that a strike for cause was appropriate. These memoranda should provide pre-flagged and pre-highlighted copies of the specific cases, each at the ready for the court to utilize in deciding on motions to strike.

As a practical matter, courts should be reminded that if the requested strike for cause is granted, plenty of other jurors are available. Foremost in any judge's mind is the risk that too many granted strikes for cause will bust the panel and require another jury panel and another voir dire process—with all the inherent wasted cost and lost time. Short of the risk of a busted panel, there is absolutely no justification for a court not to err on the side of excusing for cause potential jurors that arguably have disqualified themselves. At the same time, a plaintiff's lawyer should not use the strike process as a vehicle to try to excuse every juror he or she simply does not like. Generally, a motion to strike a juror for cause should be based on a specific statement made by the potential juror on their questionnaire or in open court that fits within a published case ruling.

Peremptory Challenges

Peremptory challenges should be exercised based on jury research, not on mere gut instinct or intuition. The issues identified as problematic in jury research should be rank-ordered, so jurors who answer questions to a specific issue adversely also can be rank-ordered for challenges by severity of consequence. Furthermore, when limited strikes are being allocated among too many problematic jurors, leaders should be struck before followers because the consequence of being wrong is more acute.

Finally, as a matter of ethics and the law, race, religion, and gender should never be the reason a strike for cause is exercised. It is no secret that our country generally has a difficult and notorious history with race, and with its exclusion of minorities from jury service in its courtrooms. Historically, attorneys in the nineteenth century "used peremptory strikes to eliminate jurors based on stereotypes regarding race, national origin, religion, and class."[169] Because research indicates that gender may affect how a juror votes, gender is salient in all parts of the voir dire process.[170]

Some legal scholars have argued that "[a]llowing parties to unilaterally strike prospective jurors without explanation has been attacked as undemocratic, prone to manipulation, a potential First Amendment violation, and—most often of all—racist."[171] England discarded peremptory challenges in 1988.[172] Canada's parliament eliminated them in 2019 after a high-profile conviction of an indigenous defendant when prosecutors had used such strikes to remove all indigenous jurors.[173]

In 1986, in *Batson v. Kentucky*, the U.S. Supreme Court prohibited the systematic exclusion of minorities from jury service. The Court created a process that was designed to ensure that race-neutral reasons existed for excluding minority jurors.[174] The Court later extended *Batson* to prohibit the use of peremptory challenges based on gender.[175] Unfortunately, skilled lawyers could meet the *Batson* mandate by "conjuring up" and "parroting out" race-neutral reasons and still achieve the systematic exclusion of minorities within the blessing of the law. In its second decision in *Miller-El v. Dretke*, the U.S. Supreme Court in 2005 analyzed five non-exhaustive yet illustrative factors to demonstrate when a lawyer's stated reasons for exercising peremptory challenges against minorities would not hold muster under the equal protection clause of the U.S. Constitution and *Batson*.[176] First, the Supreme Court performed a statistical analysis of the jurors struck, noting that prosecutors used peremptory strikes to exclude 91 percent of the eligible African-American venire members—a percentage too great to attribute merely to happenstance.[177] Second, the Supreme Court

169. April J. Anderson, *Peremptory Challenges at the Turn of the Nineteenth Century: Development of Modern Jury Selection Strategies as Seen in Practitioners' Trial Manuals*, 16 Stan. J. C.R. & C.L. 1 (2020), https://www-cdn.law.stanford.edu/wp-content/uploads/2020/02/Anderson_Final.pdf.

170. Tasha Ann Lane, "Gender and the Voir Dire Process" (unpublished master's thesis, Portland State U., 2019), 43, 45, https://pdxscholar.library.pdx.edu/open_access_etds/5068/.

171. Joshua Revesz, *Ideological Imbalance and the Peremptory Challenge*, 125 Yale L.J. 2535 (2016), https://digitalcommons.law.yale.edu/cgi/viewcontent.cgi?article=5772&context=ylj.

172. See Criminal Justice Act, 1988, c. 33, § 118(1) (Eng.) http://www.legislation.gov.uk/ukpga/1988/33/section/118 (last visited Mar. 14, 2020) (abolishing the right to challenge jurors without cause in criminal trials).

173. The removal of peremptory challenges was later struck down by an Ontario judge. Fine, *supra* (quoting the judge's ruling: "In order to provide for a measure of protection against the discrimination of jurors, Parliament has abolished [Mr. King's] ability to prevent discrimination against himself").

174. 476 U.S. 79 (1986).

175. *J.E.B. v. Alabama*, 511 U.S. 127 (1994). *See also SmithKline Beecham Corp. v. Abbott Lab.*, 740 F.3d 471, 476 (9th Cir. 2014) (applying *Batson* to peremptory challenges based on sexual orientation).

176. 545 U.S. 231 (2005) (*Miller-El II).*

177. *Id.*, 545 U.S. at 241.

conducted "a comparative juror analysis," noting that "[m]ore powerful than these based statistics, however, are side-by-side comparisons of some black venire panelists who were struck and white panelists who were allowed to serve."[178] The Court noted that the State's proffered reason for striking one particular venire member—that his voir dire answers were inconsistent—seemed plausible, but "its plausibility [was] severely undercut by the prosecution's failure to object to other panel members who expressed views much like [his]."[179] Third, the Supreme Court noted that "the prosecution's decision to seek a jury shuffle when a predominant number of African Americans were seated in the front of the panel raised a suspicion that the State sought to exclude African-Americans from the jury."[180] Fourth, the Supreme Court relied on the "contrasting voir dire questions posed respectively to black and nonblack panel members," observing that black panel members received a grizzly account of the death penalty before asking for their views on the subject, whereas white panel members received a "bland description."[181] Fifth, the Supreme Court also considered the district attorney's formal policy of excluding minorities from jury service, summarized in a manual titled *Jury Selection in a Criminal Case* that was distributed to prosecutors.[182]

In 2016, the conservative Supreme Court showed leadership on this issue in *Foster v. Chatman*. A 7-1 decision written by Chief Justice Roberts held that the Georgia Supreme Court erred by holding that Foster failed to show purposeful discrimination when the state used its challenges to strike all four prospective black jurors that were qualified to serve on a capital murder jury.[183]

In 2019, the Supreme Court held in *Flowers v. Mississippi* that "a State may not discriminate on the basis of race when exercising peremptory challenges against prospective jurors in a criminal trial."[184] Curtis Flowers was tried and convicted for the same crime six times. In the first four trials, District Attorney Doug Evans used all thirty-six of his peremptory challenges to remove African Americans from the jury. The fifth trial ended in a hung jury, and during Flowers's sixth trial, he was convicted by a jury of eleven white jurors and one African-American juror after five African-American potential jurors were struck by the prosecution. The Supreme Court agreed to hear the case to decide whether the history of racially discriminatory jury strikes across Flowers's trials should be a factor in assessing the credibility of Evans's race-neutral explanations for his peremptory strikes in the sixth trial. On June 21, 2019, the Court held that the trial court at Flowers's sixth trial committed clear error in concluding that the State's peremptory strike of one particular black juror was not motivated in substantial part by discriminatory intent. Writing for the Court, Justice Brett Kavanaugh noted that the "extraordinary facts of this case" required the Court's intervention, even as the ruling broke "no new legal ground," because "[e]qual justice under law

---

178. *Id.*
179. *Id.* at 248.
180. *Id.* at 254.
181. *Id.* at 255–63.
182. *Id.* at 266.
183. 136 S. Ct. 1731 (2016).
184. 139 S. Ct. 2228, 2234 (2019).

requires a criminal trial free of racial discrimination in the jury selection process. . . ." Justice Clarence Thomas dissented, arguing that the *Batson* precedent was a mistake: "The 'entire line of cases following *Batson*' is 'a misguided effort to remedy a general societal wrong by using the Constitution to regulate the traditionally discretionary exercise of peremptory challenges.'"[185]

Some legal scholars have urged curtailing the use of peremptory challenges altogether.[186] Others have argued that "[a]wareness of bias is critical for mental decontamination success,"[187] and that "[c]alling attention to race can help minimize racial bias by encouraging jurors to consciously think about the impropriety of racial stereotyping."[188]

Conclusion

Jury selection is the least taught but the most pivotal component of the trial process. An excellent trial lawyer spends considerable time preparing for voir dire and jury selection, realizing that the exercise brings with it constitutional considerations and is, perhaps, the most significant predictor of victory. Remember the famous quip about the difference between trials in England, which abolished peremptory challenges in the 1980s, and trials in the United States: "[I]n England, the trial starts when jury selection is over; in the United States, the trial is already over."[189]

---

185. *See generally* Jess Bravin, *Supreme Court Reaffirms Rule Against Racial Bias in Jury Selection*, Wall Street Journal (June 21, 2019, 6:16 PM), https://www.wsj.com/articles/supreme-court-reaffirms-rule-against-racial-bias-in-jury-selection-11561129358.

186. Caren Myers Morrison, *Negotiating Peremptory Challenges*, 104 J. Crim. L. & Criminology 1 (2014) ("I therefore propose that we jettison the inherently unstable framework of *Batson* and allow peremptory challenges only on consent of both parties with the challenges waived if no agreement is reached.").

187. Carol Izumi, *Implicit Bias and the Illusion of Mediator Neutrality*, 34 Wash. U. J.L. & Pol'y 71, 141 (2010) (citing Laurie Rudman, Richard Ashmore & Melvin Gary, *"Unlearning" Automatic Biases: The Malleability of Implicit Prejudice and Stereotypes*, 81 J. Pers. & Soc. Psychol. 856 (2001)).

188. Cynthia Lee, *A New Approach to Voir Dire on Racial Bias*, 5 UC Irvine L. Rev. 866, 872, n. 204 (2015).

189. Jeffrey Abramson, We, the Jury: The Jury System and the Ideal of Democracy 143 (1994).

10

Voir Dire: Striking a Winning Jury

A Defense Perspective

Voir dire—French for *to see, to speak*—is the first of three occasions when trial lawyers talk directly to jurors. This means it should be used for what it is—a valuable opportunity to kick start your case by making lasting, favorable impressions with individuals who will serve on your jury. The goal is to open strongly, seize momentum, and begin advocating your case from the outset. This requires planning and preparation, with specific voir dire goals defined. It is important for all defense lawyers to know their jury selection and deselection criteria before jury selection begins.

Striking a Jury

Voir dire is a process of "informed" elimination; many trial lawyers describe the process as "striking" a jury. That is, jurors typically are not *selected* because of positive attributes or characteristics, but, more frequently, they are *deselected* through exclusion—using peremptory strikes and challenges for cause to exclude undesirable jurors from the jury box. Some argue the result is a jury of *least common denominators*, and there is some truth to this description. Every party has a right to explore and identify hostile or biased jurors. Every party has a right to exclude jurors who are partial against their case. Deselection is, therefore, an acceptable by-product of voir dire.

The Defense Advantage

Defense lawyers have a distinct advantage in voir dire because they go second. This gives them more time to observe the voir dire panel and how panel members respond to the plaintiff's questioning before the defense voir dire begins. This provides a preview of jury attitudes, which helps guide the focus of the defendant's examination—which panel members to examine in detail and, perhaps, which panel members to avoid completely.

Undoubtedly, the panel will consist of plaintiff-oriented *and* defense-oriented individuals. Some panel members will broadcast positive attitudes in response to plaintiff's counsel.

This dictates immediate tactical choices for the defense: either conduct further questioning to establish a basis to strike for cause or avoid these panel members altogether because of obvious hostility toward the defense case. On the other hand, some panel members will evince positive attitudes toward the defense, thereby providing opportunities to exploit these jurors as "teachers" for the rest of the panel. By directing questions to these panel members and eliciting positive responses, the defense lawyer can use these individuals as advocates to espouse defense-friendly themes. Defense lawyers also should rehabilitate pro-defense panel members to preclude the opposition's efforts to challenge for cause. The bottom line is that the plaintiff's voir dire provides important information that can help guide defense strategy.

Divergent Practices among Jurisdictions

An effective voir dire requires planning. Clearly, a first step is to identify unique jury selection procedures for the specific trial venue—what is allowed, what is disallowed, and what might be tolerated, depending on the preference of the trial court. In federal court, district judges frequently conduct voir dire from the bench based on questions submitted by the parties' counsel. Some federal judges vary this approach and conduct a limited voir dire from the bench; then, they relinquish control to trial counsel for follow-up questions to individual panel members. In most state courts, trial lawyers participate directly in voir dire examinations.

A 2007 national survey of state trial judges and practitioners revealed significant lawyer participation in voir dire in a majority of surveyed jurisdictions.[1] In most of these jurisdictions, trial lawyers had primary responsibility for conducting voir dire with little or no judicial involvement.[2] Jury selection is conducted by the court with little or no lawyer involvement in just a few states.[3]

Some jurisdictions require written jury questions to be submitted to the court for approval in advance of voir dire. However, voir dire in most jurisdictions is open-ended, largely conducted by lawyers, and questions are not previewed by the trial judge. In jurisdictions that allow significant attorney involvement, the average duration of voir dire is approximately two hours.[4] This is more than sufficient time to get to know the jury, and for the jury to get to know you, your client, and your case.

Voir dire procedures also may vary from court to court within a specific jurisdiction. Some state trial judges prefer bifurcated examination of the panel: the first phase involves general questions by all counsel to the entire venire panel; the second phase involves follow-up questions only to individual members. Other courts combine the two in an open-ended voir dire with general and specific questions presented concurrently.

---

1. *See* Gregory E. Mize, Paula Hannaford-Agor & Nicole L Waters, *The State-of-the-States Survey of Jury Improvement Efforts: A Compendium Report*, National Center for State Courts (Apr. 2007), 27-28, https://cdm16501.contentdm.oclc.org/digital/collection/juries/id/112.
2. *See id.* at 28.
3. *See id.*
4. *See id.* at 29.

Every trial lawyer should be familiar with the number of allotted strikes, the legal standards to establish challenges for cause, and the legal standards for rehabilitating a favorable panel member from falling victim to a challenge for cause. Your opposition will undoubtedly seek to challenge any jurors who display favoritism or leanings toward your case. They will do so to preserve their peremptory strikes. It is therefore important to know how to rehabilitate favorable jurors to force plaintiff's counsel to exhaust allotted peremptory strikes. This increases the likelihood of getting favorable jurors into the jury box.

It is important to understand how panel members will be seated during voir dire so appropriate charts for collecting and sorting information can be prepared. Another important variable is when strikes for cause will be exercised—whether at the end of voir dire or during examination of the entire panel. The timing of these challenges will directly impact strategy during questioning. For example, most trial lawyers avoid questioning potentially volatile, hostile jurors who are likely to be struck for cause at the end.

In sum, it is important to know what your specific venue allows and disallows. Otherwise, you will be caught flat-footed and unprepared. What follows is a summary checklist for information you should try to obtain before starting any trial in any jurisdiction:

- When jury information lists become available and what information is on these lists.
- Whether written jury questionnaires are permitted.
- Time limits, if any, on voir dire for each side.
- The size of the seated jury and whether alternates will be selected.
- The number of peremptory jury strikes allotted to each side.
- When automatic juror disqualifications and excuses will be considered by the court.
- When strikes for cause will be considered by the court—after voir dire or during voir dire?[5]
- Whether individual jurors are examined outside the hearing of the venire panel or in the presence of the panel.
- Whether jury alternates will be selected, and if so, how many.
- How many panel members will be seated in the courtroom and how they will be seated.

Making Good First Impressions

Effective trial advocates know the importance of making good first impressions. As trial lawyers, this means we must be prepared to present our case—and our client—in a positive light that is interesting, appealing, and logical. As noted earlier, you only get one chance to make a first impression, and you want to make it count. It is equally true that it's hard to bounce back if poor impressions *are* created first. Many lawyers even say that cases are either won or lost in voir dire.

5. The bases for automatic disqualification vary from state to state, but it may include such things as a relationship to one of the parties, a pecuniary interest in the outcome of the case, a felony conviction, and other statutory bases. Typically, a juror can be struck for cause if the juror is incapable of following the court's instructions or if the juror's feelings or attitudes are so strong that the juror's verdict will not be based on the evidence.

An important initial goal is to make the venire panel comfortable with the voir dire process. Many panel members are newcomers to the courtroom, and they will be anxious or suspicious about their surroundings and the lawyers. Therefore, it is helpful to begin by disarming and reassuring them. This usually involves a brief explanation of the purpose of voir dire and assurances from the lawyers that they are not seeking to invade personal privacy. The panel needs to understand that the lawyer's job is to pick a fair and impartial jury,[6] and that the lawyer's questions are crafted to identify beliefs or attitudes that make individual panel members inappropriate for a particular case. Some personal questions are necessary; the panel will appreciate this candid disclosure.

Lawyers should always appear self-assured. Displaying confidence is critical because voir dire is when our advocacy begins. Any expression of anxiety or concern will be telegraphed to observant panel members.

The examination should be inviting. The lawyer should be courteous and never antagonistic. If hostility from a panel member is encountered, the lawyer should redirect the focus of the examination to other panel members. One basic principle is to never engage in a dispute with a juror in the presence of the panel. Another basic principle is to always be respectful to opposing counsel and the court.

If possible, you should develop a technique to remember jurors' names. The ability to personalize questions to panel members—by using last names—disarms panel members and makes them more comfortable. Take precautionary steps to ensure that a juror's name is not mispronounced. Using first names when talking with jurors may be risky because it suggests *too* much familiarity *too* soon. Thus, prudence dictates that the examining lawyer maintain a courteous formality when speaking with each juror.

Information Management

There are many ways to gather and process information from the panel's answers. During the voir dire, it is helpful to have a second or even a third set of eyes and ears in the courtroom. This is where jury consultants are helpful; they can record juror responses while also observing body language. Another lawyer or trusted legal assistant also can do the job.

An effective system for information management is using a *jury map* that's based on the panel's assigned seating positions. Each panel member usually is assigned a seat. A map of these assigned positions is then created by using the jurors' last names and key information about each juror. Because defense lawyers go second, they have more time to insert the jurors' names into the chart.

A system of coding is applied to identify favorable jurors, unfavorable jurors, and jurors from whom additional information is needed. This system can include simple color coding, numerical coding, or a combination of both. By undertaking this type of juror mapping, you can create a ranking tool for every juror before voir dire is concluded. An illustration for a panel of thirty-two members is provided below. It can be modified

6. *See Pena-Rodriquez v. Colorado*, 137 S. Ct. 855, 858 (2017) ("members of the venire can be examined for impartiality during *voir dire*").

according to the physical layout of the courtroom and how jurors are seated—left to right or right to left.

1 2 3 4 5 Name # 25	1 2 3 4 5 Name # 26	1 2 3 4 5 Name # 27 **X**	1 2 3 4 5 Name # 28	1 2 3 4 5 Name # 29	1 2 3 4 5 Name # 30 **X**	1 2 3 4 5 Name # 31	1 2 3 4 5 Name # 32 **X**
1 2 3 4 5 Name # 17	1 2 3 4 5 Name # 18 **?**	1 2 3 4 5 Name # 19	1 2 3 4 5 Name # 20 **X**	1 2 3 4 5 Name # 21 **?**	1 2 3 4 5 Name # 22	1 2 3 4 5 Name # 23	1 2 3 4 5 Name # 24 **?**
1 2 3 4 5 Name # 9 ✔	1 2 3 4 5 Name # 10	1 2 3 4 5 Name # 11 **?**	1 2 3 4 5 Name # 12	1 2 3 4 5 Name # 13	1 2 3 4 5 Name # 14 **X**	1 2 3 4 5 Name # 15	1 2 3 4 5 Name # 16
1 2 3 4 5 Name # 1 **?**	1 2 3 4 5 Name # 2 **?**	1 2 3 4 5 Name # 3	1 2 3 4 5 Name # 4 **X**	1 2 3 4 5 Name # 5	1 2 3 4 5 Name # 6 ✔	1 2 3 4 5 Name # 7 **X**	1 2 3 4 5 Name # 8 ✔

Coding the jurors is simple. Three colors are usually used: red, yellow, and green (like a traffic light), to signify unfavorable or hostile, questionable, and favorable jurors, respectively. Any alternate coding system can be used, as in the example given, where favorable is denoted by a check mark ("✓"), questionable by a question mark ("?"), and unfavorable by an "X". In the example, a strong defense juror can be coded as "1" (circle "1") or a check mark ("✓"). A strong plaintiff's juror can be coded as "5" or marked with an "X". The numbers in between (the boxes that are marked with a question mark ["?"]) represent the lawyer's conclusion that follow-up questions are needed. Boxes on the map that have no coding indicate that little or no information is known, and follow-up questions are needed. This type of chart is further annotated with responses from jury questionnaires or with specific juror answers during voir dire. The grid therefore becomes an evolving road map leading eventually to informed and educated selection or deselection choices.

By inserting the jurors' last names into the map, you can create an easy system of locating jurors by their number and then referring to them by their name. This will increase each juror's comfort and helps build rapport. The bottom line is that this jury map facilitates the voir dire examination by aggregating important jury information. It will be your primary reference tool when exercising jury strikes.

Focusing Questions on Specific Panel Members

Many lawyers mistakenly believe they should talk to every panel member in detail. As a practical matter, this goal is rarely achieved; as a strategic matter, it is unwise to do so.

Courts frequently impose time limits on the length of voir dire. Trying to question every panel member in detail within strict time restraints may result in a superficial examination. It is more important to focus substantive questions on panel members who are more likely to be selected. These individuals are easily identified as a matter of arithmetic by using a simple formula.

When combined, the size of the seated jury, the number of alternates, and the total number of peremptory strikes for all sides dictate the number of panel members that, at a minimum, should be examined during voir dire. This number is increased as necessary to offset panel members who are disqualified, excused, or struck (or who may be struck) for cause. The formula is as follows:

(# Seated Jurors) + (# Seated Alternates) + (# Total Peremptory Strikes) + (# of Strikes for Cause) + (# Jurors Excused) = # of Panel Members Examined in Detail

By focusing on jurors identified by this formula, lawyers can better use their allotted time. They can and should focus more intensely on panel members who are, numerically speaking, more likely to make it into the jury box. Less time should be devoted to other panel members because they will never be reached under this numerical approach. Here is how the formula works:

- If the court intends to seat a twelve-person jury with two alternates, each of the first fourteen jurors is a candidate for being selected to sit on the jury, and each should be thoroughly examined.
- If each side in a two-party case has six peremptory strikes, a total of twelve jurors may be struck for reasons other than cause. Now, the first twenty-six jurors are candidates for being selected as part of the jury, and each of these twenty-six jurors should be thoroughly examined.
- If one or more of these first twenty-six jurors are struck for cause or otherwise excused, the candidate pool must be increased by a corresponding number. So, if three of these initial jurors are struck for cause, then the candidate pool is increased to twenty-nine jurors, and each new potential juror should be examined thoroughly.

The Typical Venire Panel

The venire panel may be large or small depending on the number of parties, pretrial publicity, and issues in the case. Regardless of size, however, a majority of panel members likely are stepping into a courtroom for the first time. It will be a new experience for most, and some panel members will be uncomfortable and anxious about the process because of their dread of the unknown. Efforts should be made to make these newcomers more comfortable. They will appreciate the effort.

Every panel member will have personality traits and quirks that are different from others—at least in some respects. An essential purpose of voir dire is to identify and explore these differences, and then to determine whether any special traits may adversely or positively impact your case. This is done by watching, observing, asking, and listening.

Every panel member brings with them to the courtroom unique attitudes that spring from divergent backgrounds and experiences. This includes extroverts and introverts; liberals and conservatives; leaders, followers, and loners; the highly educated and the less educated; affluent and those of more modest or less than modest means. Ultimately, a jury will consist of a combination of individuals of varying social and economic backgrounds and personalities. The goal is to empanel a jury that has backgrounds and experiences that will be most favorable to your case. Thus, it is important to identify the attributes of a "favorable" juror and those of an "unfavorable" juror before voir dire begins. You should avoid ad hoc decisions as voir dire unfolds.

Every panel typically includes some eager "talkers" or "volunteers"—individuals who raise their hands at every opportunity. They always stand out, and, predictably, they frequently are struck because they share *too much* information. Invariably, one side of the case or the other will perceive these juror types as either favorable or unfavorable to their case. Thus, an effective strategy is to identify a favorable "talker" and ask him or her a number of questions to generate favorable answers that expose the entire panel to positive messages that benefit the defense. This helps educate the entire panel, and it may force the opponent to use peremptory strikes.

Every panel will include some "quiet" jurors. Quiet jurors appear reticent when responding to questions, and they may avoid eye contact. A warning is needed here: some "quiet" panel members may be disguised time bombs. It is important to know what lies beneath the surface and whether these seemingly quiet jurors are potentially hostile. As trial lawyers, this means we should "leave no stone left unturned." Every potential juror should be questioned to some degree to eliminate surprises. Again, the essential goal is to fully unveil prejudice or bias before jurors are selected.

Obtaining Juror Information before Voir Dire

There are differences in how and when jurisdictions provide basic juror information before jury selection begins. Thus, another step in good planning is to determine what the venue provides and when the information is first available.

Most jurisdictions provide jury information sheets to trial attorneys. The information sheets include basic information relating to a juror's address, marital status, employment status, education, age, and prior jury service. Other jurisdictions provide more detailed information, such as prior accident history and involvements in lawsuits. Juror information sheets sometimes are provided just moments before the venire panel arrives in the courtroom and there is little time to evaluate the information. Some jurisdictions, however, make jury information sheets available before voir dire.

Depending on the complexity of your case, the court may allow a joint questionnaire to the panel *before* voir dire.[7] Clearly, a more detailed understanding of each panel member's background and experience is valuable as part of the selection process. Decision-making is better informed with good, relevant information. Armed with detailed questionnaire responses, you can better focus your questions to individual jurors.

Developing Jury Rapport

Every voir dire begins by educating potential panel members about positive aspects of your case. Your client should always be introduced. If the client is a business entity, some brief

7. Some jurisdictions define the commencement of voir dire with the submission (and not the completion) of the jury questionnaires. This could be procedurally important for determining rights to shuffle a jury. Many jurisdictions allow one shuffle of the panel before voir dire begins. The decision to shuffle is based on the visual observation of the venire panel as it is seated in the courtroom *before* the voir dire begins.

background about the company's business and community involvement is helpful. Every client, including corporate clients, should be personalized.

If possible, you should avoid using the term *client*; instead use first and last names. If representing a corporation or other business entity, make sure to have a real person in the courtroom to serve as the company's representative. The panel will relate more positively to a real person. If your individual client or client representative is missing from the courtroom, the panel may form negative impressions. Members of the panel are being asked to sacrifice time away from their homes and jobs. Intuitively, the parties to a lawsuit are expected to do the same.

You should use voir dire to present key facts of your case in a positive, credible, and empathetic manner. A presentation of key facts is needed to provide context in which more detailed questions are framed—it provides relevance for the questions asked of individual jurors. To the extent the court allows, this factual presentation should be presented as an advocate. After all, a trial is nothing but a staged process of persuasion, and voir dire is the opening curtain to the drama.

It is important for panel members to like your client, your client's case, and you. Thus, as trial lawyers, our objective is to present our case and client with confidence, sincerity, and credibility. This requires a mastery of the facts, and a straightforward presentation of the facts with confidence.

Jury Behavior and Body Language

Simple observations of how jurors act and how they react to questions yields valuable information. Every lawyer should watch jurors as they enter and exit the courtroom, and as they are seated both before and during voir dire. They may be carrying magazines, books, or iPads that telegraph their interests and personalities. A juror may be reading the *Wall Street Journal*; another may be holding a romance novel. Yet another may be playing games on an iPad. Simple observations lead to data points about sophistication, education, and political leanings.

Another important signal is grooming and dress. Is the juror wearing sandals and dirty jeans, or is the person more appropriately dressed? Does the juror appear unkempt? Personal grooming often reflects attitudes and discipline (or a lack thereof) that may impact how a juror will perceive the facts of the case. From a defense perspective, a disciplined, well-dressed juror typically is a good juror. Such individuals tend to be more careful as they sift through the facts, and they are less likely to react on the basis of emotion or anger.

Another valuable observation is whether panel members group together in the hallway before or after court sessions. Some experienced lawyers even visit the jury assembly room before voir dire to get a first look at prospective jurors and how they socialize with each other. As jurors become more familiar with each other, alliances and friendships form; some jurors may hold sway over others. This may become critically important in the jury room. Groupings can be helpful or dangerous depending on the orientation of the group and its leaders.

Some panel members will be loners, standing to the side and not interacting with others. They may be either mavericks or shy. Again, every potential juror should be examined to identify personality traits that may impact deliberations. Are they leaders and potential forepersons? Are they followers? Are they extroverted or withdrawn? Thus, simple observations can generate valuable information.

Body language is important.[8] Does the juror avoid eye contact when you speak but then make eye contact when your opposing counsel speaks or vice versa? Does the juror have his or her arms crossed when you talk, but is more open or inviting when your adversary speaks or vice versa? Does a juror appear comfortable or uncomfortable when answering questions? Each of these observations leads to conclusions about the juror and how he or she perceives the lawyers, the facts, and the clients.

Jury Questionnaires

Jury questionnaires provide valuable information to all trial lawyers. You should use questionnaire responses to craft specific, targeted questions to individual panel members. Typically, jury questionnaires are prepared jointly by all parties with court approval. Therefore, both the plaintiff and defendant will have the opportunity to design their own questions, but every effort should be made to keep the questions neutral. Ultimately, the questions should be tailored to determine whether jurors have backgrounds or experiences that might influence how they perceive the witnesses and the expected evidence.

Jury questionnaires can be either short or long, simple or detailed—it depends on the nature and complexity of the case. Direct questions and open-ended questions are both used for different purposes. Open-ended questions seeking narrative responses tend to generate honest, candid answers that reflect the subtleties of a juror's biases or attitudes. When used in a jury questionnaire, there is no risk of embarrassment, which can occur if the juror is questioned in front of the entire panel. As such, a panel member may feel more at ease when disclosing personal information in response to a more "private" questionnaire.

Jury questionnaires can be designed to elicit information for a more robust understanding of a panel member's background, likes, and dislikes. Here are some examples:

- What is the last book you read?
- When did you last read a book?
- What is your favorite magazine?
- What do you do to have fun?
- How much TV do you watch each week?
- What is your favorite TV show? Do you watch the news?
- Do you read the newspaper? If so, which one?
- Who are the three people in history you admire most, and why?
- Who are the three people in history you admire least, and why?

---

8. There is scientific debate concerning the significance of body language as a means of detecting the differences between truthful and false answers. *See. e.g.*, John Tierney, *At Airports, A Misplaced Faith in Body Language*, New York Times (Mar. 23, 2004), https://www.nytimes.com/2014/03/25/science/in-airport-screening-body-language-is-faulted-as-behavior-sleuth.html.

Again, there are likely differences between individuals who read romance novels and those who watch reality shows, in comparison to those who watch Fox News or read *The Economist*. Likewise, dramatic differences may be gleaned by whether they watch Fox News or MSNBC. All of this information is basic but important.

Looking for and Protecting Leaders

An important objective in jury selection is identifying potential leaders. These are the people who are "influencers," and may be elected to serve as the foreperson. They may be either favorable or unfavorable to your case, and identifying each is equally important. Experienced defense lawyers never want highly vocal plaintiff's jurors in the jury room. The converse also is true. Plaintiff's counsel will be seeking to strike any strong defense jurors who may be leaders.

On the one hand, you should identify and seek to strike any panel member who has strong personality traits and who is potentially adverse to your client or your case. On the other hand, you want to protect favorable leaders from being struck. That is why it is important to fully understand the legal basis and burdens for exercising a challenge for cause and the basis for rehabilitating a juror to prevent a successful challenge for cause. Armed with this knowledge, defense lawyers should strive to rehabilitate strong defense jurors to deprive plaintiff's counsel of the opportunity to strike for cause. Again, this forces your opponent to use peremptory strikes, which increases the chances of getting good defense jurors into the jury box.

Defense leaders are identified in a variety of ways. A successful businessman or businesswoman, who usually are more conservative, are easily identified through a series of simple questions. Their job experience is another clue. Less educated individuals may be more deferential to more highly educated individuals in the jury room. Jury information sheets and questionnaire responses also facilitate identification of these individuals.

Most jurisdictions will provide information that indicates whether a juror has prior jury experience. In that instance, the juror should be asked whether he or she served as a foreperson and whether a verdict was reached during any prior jury service. Prior service as a foreperson is a quick indicator of leadership.

Basic Examination Strategies

Different types of examination strategies can be used, depending on whether large groups or small groups are examined at the same time. Thus, it is important to know what procedures apply. For example, an attorney can be more aggressive when examining a juror to establish cause if this examination is not overheard by the rest of the panel.

There also are different reasons for questions directed to the entire panel. Foremost among these is that general questions provide an efficient way to categorize jurors into specific subgroups that are based on whether individuals raise their hands in response to general questions. This is especially important if the court imposes time limits on the length of voir dire. The identity of jurors who are responding to general questions can be recorded quickly and individual follow-up questions can be pursued, if necessary and as time allows. Here are a few examples of general questions:

- Categorize jurors who are familiar with the parties, with counsel, or with the underlying events, transactions, or incidents at issue in the case.
- Categorize jurors who have been parties or witnesses in prior lawsuits.
- Categorize jurors who served on prior juries or as a foreperson on a prior jury.
- Categorize jurors who previously filed personal injury claims, or who were involved in accidents requiring hospitalization or medical attention.
- Categorize jurors based on occupation, personal background, and past experience that potentially is relevant to the case.

Another important reason for open-ended questions to the entire panel is that it allows the trial lawyer to ferret out volunteers and extroverts from quiet jurors. The extrovert tends to raise his or her hand more frequently in response to general questions. They want to speak and to be heard. They may become the foreperson, try to dominate jury deliberations, or even bully others into a verdict.

On the other hand, a juror may seek to deselect himself or herself by never raising his or her hand. This may be intentional or the result of an introverted personality. In either case, these individuals do not want to be engaged or addressed by the lawyers. Thus, lawyers should pose follow-up questions to these jurors to gain insight into who they are and how they may act in the jury room. Failure to do so creates an unacceptable risk of selecting a ticking time bomb that goes off in final deliberations.

Questions directed to individual panel members are important and have different strategic goals. The ultimate goal is to probe more deeply into a juror's pretrial biases that may adversely impact your case. You should use the responses to this individual examination as a basis for a challenge for cause.

Using Favorable Jurors as Teaching Assistants

An often-used strategy involves identifying a favorable panel member who is then cultivated as an "assistant" to teach the entire panel. A panel member may have a unique job or other experience that is particularly relevant to your case. Once you determine that a juror is favorably inclined to your position, the juror should be asked a series of questions to elicit responses that are favorable to your side, thereby preconditioning other panel members. Here are some examples:

- A panel member with a medical background (doctor, nurse, physician assistant, etc.) can help explain the purpose and importance of warnings in a drug liability case.
- A CPA or bookkeeper can be used to describe the importance of accounting standards and principles in a financial fraud case that involves balance sheets and other financial statements.
- An engineer can be used to explain a failure-tree analysis and why certain products fail under stress.

- A lawyer on the panel can be examined about the differences in the burden of proof in a civil case and how it differs from a criminal case; a plaintiff in a civil case may want to exploit the opportunity to discuss the relaxed burden of proof in a civil case; the criminal defense lawyer may do the same and discuss the presumption of innocence and a heightened burden of proof in a criminal case.

Panel members who are elevated to the role of "teachers" are invariably struck by the opposing side. Your opponent will recognize the favoritism shown to your case, and will be forced to exclude that panel member from the jury box. Thus, two objectives are achieved—the entire panel is favorably educated by another panel member, and the other side is forced to use a peremptory strike.

Responding to Questions from the Panel

Some jurors will raise their hands and ask for permission to ask questions; this is always a dangerous exercise. If indulged, the panel member may ask a difficult question that goes to the heart of your case. There also is a risk that the answer could backfire and hurt your case in front of the entire panel. Clearly, incorrect or incomplete answers may come back to haunt you during the trial. One example comes to mind: a juror once asked if he could ask a plaintiff's lawyer a question. Once given permission, the juror asked the lawyer when he was going to sit down because his presentation was boring. This hurt, and the lesson is to move into such dialogues carefully.

On the other hand, a question from a panel member may be benign. An obvious attempt to ignore or avoid the question may alienate the specific juror or others on the panel. Here, the best advice is, "Wade into the water slowly". A few qualifying questions typically are used in these instances: the panel member can be asked if the question is about procedure or about facts. If the question is procedural, the risks typically are low. If the question is substantive, the panel member should be invited to the bench to ask his or her question, depending on the procedural rules of the court.

Using Jury Consultants and Jury Studies

Depending on the complexity and financial stakes involved in a case, the use of jury consultants may be a prudent investment. Jury consultants are used to conduct focus groups and jury studies for several purposes, but a primary goal is to identify preferred juror types and unfavorable juror types for a specific case. Armed with this information, the trial lawyer is in a better position to hone his or her questions based on previously defined juror profiles. Voir dire becomes more efficient because questions are targeted to specific panel members. The trial advocate also is better able to identify panel members who are more likely to provide favorable answers. Once this is confirmed, use these panel members as teachers for the entire panel. The trial lawyer also is better able to avoid questions with certain jurors who may be primed to provide inflammatory or harmful answers in the presence of the entire panel.

Jury consultants also provide an extra set of eyes and ears during voir dire. They are in an excellent position to observe juror behavior and reactions during the voir dire examination by all the lawyers. They can observe body language, juror groupings, and assist in interpreting specific responses to targeted questions. The net result is a better informed decision when striking the jury.

Commitment Questions

Unveiling a panel member's bias or predisposition requires a reasonable introduction and discussion of the key facts, claims, and defenses in the case. Questions to the panel require relevance, and factual background is needed to provide this context. Because bias and predisposition sometimes are not readily apparent, many jurisdictions recognize that a trial advocate should be provided reasonably broad discretion in how the factual presentation is made and used as a foundation for specific voir dire questions. However, some lawyers take advantage of this opportunity and seek unqualified commitments from jurors in favor of their client based on a set of highly selective, distorted facts. Many jurisdictions discourage th s practice and will sustain objections to this tactic.

In one case, a court noted that an examining lawyer should have "the right to ascertain from the jury panel any bias or prejudice . . . which would render it impossible or difficult for them to render a fair and impartial verdict based upon the evidence and the instructions of the court," but counsel does not have the right to "commit or pledge the jury to a certain verdict or amount thereof in advance of hearing all of the evidence."[9]

The lesson here is simple: listen carefully, and make sure these types of improper questions are not presented by the opposition without objection. No attorney wants a jury that is already committed to vote against his or her client before the first piece evidence is introduced.

9. *Wright v. Chicago, Burlington & Quincy R.R. Co.*, 392 S.W.2d 401, 408 (Mo. 1965).

11
Opening Statements
The Plaintiff's Perspective

"People tend to hold on to their first impressions," noted American filmmaker Miranda July. Especially in the world of court-conducted or vastly constricted rights to attorney voir dire, opening statements often are the key to making a solid first impression. To deliver an effective opening statement, the plaintiff's lawyer must first design the goals for the opening statement, while fully understanding the importance of the exercise itself. Then, he must design the substantive content to be delivered, together with a plan for the presentation of that content via a structural outline, strategic use of demonstrative exhibits, and persistent references to substantive evidence in detailing the case-in-chief. Importantly, in designing the case-in-chief, the plaintiff's lawyer must keep in mind the defendant's option to defer its opening statement until before its case-in-chief.

Goals of Opening Statements

As with any message, script, or story, one should not begin writing an opening statement until its goals are clearly understood. An excellent opening statement is achieved by meeting eight key goals: (1) start strong; (2) appeal to the jurors' minds; (3) appeal to the jurors' hearts; (4) use powerful metaphors as a tool for the case to be synthesized as just "one thing"; (5) appeal to the jurors' collective sense of justice rather than compensation; (6) appeal to the jurors' inclination toward empathy rather than sympathy; (7) transform the undesirable duty of jury service into a desirable, one-time opportunity to do something great in the justice system; and (8) make the trial process empowering in the eyes of the jurors.

Start Strong

The American diplomat Elliott Abrams noted that in matters of diplomacy, "first impressions matter," and that "experts say we size up new people in somewhere between 30 seconds and two minutes."[1] Thus, the first minute or two of any opening statement is paramount to winning. A trial lawyer should remember the law school advice that any good trial lawyer should be able to argue his case in twenty-five words or less. Synthesizing an entire lawsuit into two or three paragraphs requires precision of thought, prioritization of theme, and clarity of delivery. Simply put, what is the most important aspect of your lawsuit? What is the most powerful way to argue it inside of thirty seconds? What are the twenty-five words that express what the case is about better than any others?

These opening twenty-five words should identify the villain as well as their victim; they should include a motive for the crime (whether an actual crime or a tort cast as a crime), which in civil litigation should always be greed, avarice, and money; the mechanism of the criminal's actions or inaction; the consequence of the crime; and the need to do something about it through the process we call justice.

Every opening statement I deliver begins with those twenty-five words. They are written very carefully during the discovery process to capture the essence of the entire case. The humorous advice falsely attributed to Ernest Hemingway, "Write drunk and edit sober," is useful here. A trial lawyer can win through exuberance any case at the time of intake, because we are all drunk with optimism at that time. Editing that exuberance into a powerful initial paragraph of an opening statement is the most important job in any trial.

Appeal to the Mind

Whether an excited trial lawyer already knows it or is about to learn through the stern admonition of a trial judge, opening statements are not the time to argue a case with a shouting fervor. Rather, an opening statement is less likely to draw interruption through objections if it clinically appeals to the jurors' heads, to their minds, and to their empowering desire to study the evidence, carefully adjudicate the claims and the defense, and render a just verdict.

Despite all the clinical data extolled as SJS, my experience has been that jurors from both sides of the political and ideological spectrum—from liberal Democrats to conservative Republicans—take their oath, and then try to do the right thing by following the law as instructed by the court. Because most state court judges and their court staff are extremely professional and courteous to the voters (that is, jurors), and because the formality of most federal courts is intimidatingly structured, jurors are inclined to accept the idea that their service is important business, and that the court's instructions generally should be followed. When a trial judge instructs jurors that she is the judge of the law but the jurors are the judges of the facts, they believe it. When trial judges tell them that they are to evaluate only the evidence in a system where lady justice is blind, jurors accept it. When trial judges instruct jurors on the law and ask for a verdict based on the facts they have heard under the law as instructed, jurors generally follow those instructions as gospel. As such, opening statements should clinically set out the case to be delivered, setting forth by topic or by witness what the evidence will be, and fitting such evidence into the elements of the law

1. BrainyQuote, https://www.brainyquote.com/quotes/elliott_abrams_641360 (last visited Mar. 14, 2020).

that are likely to be provided by the court. In doing so, a good opening statement appeals to the head.

A large graphic containing a list of the witnesses likely to be called is important to bookmark the jurors' experience to come. If some witnesses are to be offered via video-recorded depositions, warn the jurors of that reality, and tell them that these edited testimonies are being offered in that format to save them time. If a deposition is to be read, apologize that it was not video-recorded, but again offer that the heavily edited transcript is being read in a question-and-answer format to save them time. As to the key witnesses to be called live, a good lawyer should physically be at the witness stand, clinically explaining what the witnesses will say from "right here, on this witness stand," thereby previewing the crucial evidence that supports the case. The point of this exercise is to appeal to the head by giving the jurors both a schedule and an outline of the expected witnesses, and the key testimony they will bring with them.

Who the witnesses will be is an important component of appealing to the jurors' heads, but *what* those witnesses will say is just as important. In appealing to the head, I present not merely a list of the likely eyewitnesses, with a predictor of the mode of their testimony—live, video, or transcript—but also an outline of the key evidentiary themes of the case. *These* witnesses will testify as to what the defendant did wrong; these witnesses will testify how that harmed the plaintiff; and these witnesses will testify to the damages caused thereby, how the defendant's wrongful conduct—which harmed the plaintiff—forever changed the plaintiff's life, requiring this lawsuit as an effort to correct the injustice, to right the wrong.

In appealing to the jurors' heads, the presentation should be both logical and methodical. The opening statement should provide both a roadmap of what is to come and the signage that tells jurors how you will complete the journey with them. It should be professional; it should be clinical; and it should be well-designed, preplanned, and efficiently communicated.

Appeal to the Heart

The appeal to the head, however, should never be at the expense of a simultaneous appeal to the heart. An outline about liability should never ignore the consequence of that liability— the damage that was caused. While much of the opening statement should involve a clinical appeal to the head, real trial lawyers know how to also tug at the heartstrings in each of us. The American poet Maya Angelou instructed us to "Write so that people can hear as it slides through the brain and goes straight to the heart."[2] When making an opening statement, the oral communications process can achieve this migration from the head to the heart at the necessary point in time merely by a well-placed slowing of speech, an emphatic lowering of voice tone, a pronounced physical approach toward the jury box, or an intentional focus on the jurors via intensive eye contact at key points in the delivery. Judges tell us that opening statement is not the time for argument. They are wrong. In truth,

2. Goodreads, https://www.goodreads.com/quotes/153402-the-idea-is-to-write-it-so-that-people-hear (last visited Mar. 14, 2020).

effective advocates get away with arguing by using legitimate content that appeals to the head while using persuasive mannerisms that appeal to the heart. No court reporter can capture a difference in voice tone, a contrast in the rate of speech, or the intensity of a lawyer's stare into the eyes of the jury when the time is just right. Because no court reporter can capture these critical maneuvers that appeal to the heart, no judge can stop them, either. While most judges want to maintain control of their courtrooms, they seldom interrupt excellent advocacy during opening statements when the content of what is said appeals to the head, while the way in which it is said appeals to the heart.

Find Powerful Metaphors and Decide on That "One Thing"

Max Lucado has been nicknamed "America's pastor" for his soft-spoken, earnest, yet compelling simple sermons that get right to the point by using a communication technique that appeals to first-graders as well as to people who have post-graduate degrees: the metaphor. Lucado has been preaching at Oak Hills Church in San Antonio, Texas, since his thirties. Lucado, my very good friend, is now in his sixties. I have marveled at how every Christian in America knows of him, how he has sold more than 100 million books and preached to congregations and at gatherings around the globe. But he is selfless, kind, and real. His authenticity arises from his ability to synthesize concepts by communicating them with everyday events in his life, a singular moment that reminds him of "X," "Y," or "Z" in the Bible, or a made-up event recounted with the sly smile of a gifted storyteller. Whether Max is telling a true story or making one up—marked by his honest, wry smile that this one is going to be a doozy—I have realized that I leave church every Sunday remembering not only his message, but also the singular word, joke, analogy, metaphor, or moment that is the connective tissue to the entirety of his sermon. It is the single thing that causes those who are listening to remember everything. It is Curly's "one thing" in *City Slickers*.

I write this chapter while on a cruise ship to Alaska with Max and one thousand vacationers who came to hear him for a week. Predictably, at the introductory opening session, Max announced that the Lord had given him one word for his one thousand new friends to focus on with him during their week of respite—*inhale*. The word singularly captured Max's chosen theme of receiving the Holy Spirit, and of using the gratitude for the same as a tonic against anxiety. One week; one word. That simple. Why not, then, use merely one word to describe an entire lawsuit or case?

Each opening statement should also invoke some example from contemporaneous world events, some event well-known in popular culture, some specific story told by painting a picture of an event worth remembering. Each plaintiff's story has such an event. Any strong opening statement must locate that event, and tell of it as if Mark Twain himself were communicating the message. The opening statement must hold the truth of the entire case in a single story, quip, anecdote, or quote. When that "one thing" is identified, it should be utilized in the opening statement, and then repetitively used again during witness examinations, the closing argument, and during the rebuttal. It is the "one thing" that the jurors will remember. Those who side with your client will use that "one thing" to argue your case in the jury room.

The American novelist Orson Scott Card observed that "metaphors have a way of holding the most truth in the least space."[3] In addition to the "one thing," Max nimbly utilized metaphors and other vocal techniques to paint vivid pictures for those listening to his sermon on *anxiety*. People trapped by anxiety were "wrapped tighter than Egyptian mummies," reacted by "spewing anger like Mt. Vesuvius," and needed to "learn to talk themselves back off the ledge." His message described individuals who overcome anxiety as "a walking Rolex watch, with everything working smoothly when they are in charge." He encouraged people to attack the problem first by themselves—after all, "you are the air traffic controller of your mental airport; you get to decide what lands there and what must leave there." He softly encouraged his listeners by emphasizing that it is perfectly honorable to seek professional counseling or medicinal assistance, reminding them that "we don't feel less Christian if we put a cast on a broken bone." In less than half an hour, Max incorporated six separate metaphors to communicate a cohesive message.[4] One does not need to have sold millions of books to employ metaphors; one needs to think about the message before it is delivered, and invoke everyday examples that are known to the jurors and that will cause them to receive the message.

Appeal to Sense of Justice, Not Compensation

At their core, civil lawsuits are about money damages, and nothing more. However, money damages must be communicated as the means to achieve the end—justice. *Compensation* is a bad word to the good trial lawyer; *justice* is the word to be used. As the famed digital marketing expert Lee Odden instructed us, "Content should ask people to do something and reward them for it."[5] Our society's norms suggest that charity is something done at church, not at the courthouse. Rather, money damages are merely the vehicle to be used to achieve something greater, and that something greater is *justice*. The Supreme Commander of the Allied Expeditionary Forces in Europe, General Dwight D. Eisenhower, described motivation as "the art of getting people to do what you want them to do because they want to do it."[6] As such, any discussion of damages in an opening statement must be couched in terms of the jurors' ability to right a wrong, to set things right. Jurors do not want to view themselves as tools for charity; they want their verdict to be used as a tool to do right in the pursuit of justice.

Appeal to Empathy, Not Sympathy

Jurors are consistently admonished that they must not allow *sympathy* to play any role in their deliberations. In jury instructions across the land, the concept of *sympathy* is a bad

3. Goodreads, https://www.goodreads.com/quotes/67872-metaphors-have-a-way-of-holding-the-most-truth-in (last visited Mar. 14, 2020).

4. *See generally* MAX LUCADO, *ANXIOUS FOR NOTHING: FINDING CALM IN A CHAOTIC WORLD* (2017).

5. Tricia Edgar, *Content Marketing Advice from Lee Odden*, Media Shower (June 29, 2016), https://mediashower.com/blog/content-marketing-advice-from-lee-odden/.

6. Bret Baier, *Seven Business Leadership Lessons from Dwight Eisenhower*, Forbes (Jan. 31, 2017), https://www.forbes.com/sites/forbesleadershipforum/2017/01/31/seven-business-leadership-lessons-from-dwight-eisenhower/#a953e1d43b18.

action. It is one to be shamed and avoided. However, courts never tell jurors that they may not attempt to understand what a plaintiff has gone through. No jury instruction bars the use of *empathy* when a juror is evaluating the evidence.

Jurors love plaintiffs who fight the good fight and who try to overcome insurmountable odds. In injury cases, the plaintiff should never be characterized as a victim who will never recover; rather, they should be pictured as one wrongfully aggrieved and catastrophically injured, but nevertheless, one who continued to fight and who is trying to beat the deep odds hoisted upon them by the tortious conduct of the defendant. The English writer H. G. Wells instructed "If you fell down yesterday, stand up today,"[7] and Babe Ruth observed that "you just can't beat the person who never gives up."[8] In sum, Americans love a fighter. One of this country's founding fathers, Thomas Paine, wrote that "the harder the conflict, the more glorious the triumph."[9] My experience is that jurors heavily compensate those who are injured, but who attempt to come back; they compensate less fully those who are characterized as weak, feeble victims asking for help from the jury.

Lawyers cannot invoke the golden rule, but they can place jurors in that hospital bed where their client fought their pain and tried to get better. The bottom line is that few jurors are unwilling to place themselves in that hospital bed in an effort to try to understand exactly what it is a plaintiff went through. A good lawyer puts the jurors in that very hospital bed by skillfully painting a vivid picture of what it was like to be there, and by carefully appealing to the each of their senses—sight, hearing, touch, smell, and taste—to make the jurors' empathetic experience all the more real. Jurors who possess both a head and a heart will take it from there, utilizing empathy to transform that rich picture into a just verdict.

Transform the Juror's Duty of Jury Service into a Singular Opportunity for Justice

Nothing is more important in your opening statement than transforming the burden of one's jury service into a unique opportunity to do the right thing. This transformation can take place in three different ways.

First, the contrast must be immediately drawn between the inconvenience to a juror caused by serving for just a week or two from the lifetime result the jury's verdict will mean to the plaintiff. This is not a guilt trip to be delivered to the jurors. They don't need it. My experience is that most citizens arrive at the courthouse pissed off about having to be there, but they transform themselves into serious and willing participants in the administration of justice upon taking their juror's oath. Rather than begging them to take a particular case seriously, a good trial lawyer allows the solemn facts of the case at hand to deliver this request subliminally. In a wrongful death case, one might recite the words

7. Goodreads, https://www.goodreads.com/quotes/24163-if-you-fell-down-yesterday-stand-up-today (last visited Mar. 14, 2020).

8. Quote Investigator, https://quoteinvestigator.com/2014/03/07/ruth-give/ (last visited Mar. 14, 2020).

9. Forbes, https://www.forbes.com/quotes/9319/ (last visited Mar. 14, 2020).

of the American novelist Lois McMaster Bujold, who wrote, "The dead cannot cry out for justice; it is a duty of the living to do so for them."[10] In a serious injury case, the service of citizen jurors must be explained to them as the difference between defeat and victory, as the contrast between a life that is effectively over versus one that, with help, will just be starting anew.

Second, the jurors must be taught that their participation in the trial will be unique, and that they will see things that no one before them has ever seen. They will hear a story that was kept from all others before them, and the light of justice will reveal to them alone what has been kept dark until that moment. The University of Southern California law professor Susan Estrich said, "One of the risks of a public trial is a public verdict."[11] Most complex civil cases involve the introduction of company documents stamped *Highly Confidential, Pursuant to Protective Order*, or *Attorneys' Eyes Only*. Subtle suggestions to a jury in opening statements that they alone are about to see these sensitive documents will serve as the motivational precursor to jurors who will recall this prediction when salacious company documents with embedded lawyer stamps are introduced into evidence. This raises both the intensity of the trial to come and the jurors' appreciation of their opportunity to uncover matters previously kept from the public through secrecy.

Third, jurors must be taught that they will become light bearers. Their jury verdict will result in the illumination of matters previously kept from the public through darkness. Their jury service will bring the light of what is good, perform the public service of uncovering what previously had been unknowable, and communicate to others what has occurred through their verdict alone. No one but the twelve citizens lucky enough to be chosen to serve will be able to deliver the message of justice made necessary by the nefarious actions of this defendant. If twelve fellow citizens will sacrifice themselves via jury service in this trial, they will enjoy the unique opportunity to be the messenger of what justice means given the facts to be shared with them. As the famous American trial lawyer Clarence Darrow said, "Justice has nothing to do with what goes on in a courtroom; justice is what comes out of a courtroom."[12] A good trial lawyer in opening statements will couch his or her trial as a singular opportunity for each juror to participate together to form *a jury*, an instrument so monumental that it was fought for in our Revolutionary War and included in the Bill of Rights. He should remind each person serving on the jury that their verdict is the only important part of justice. It is what Darrow reminded us—the only important thing that "comes out of a courtroom." In this way, the good trial lawyer elevates citizen jurors to a status more important than the elevated judge wearing a robe; it doesn't matter what some judge says, it matters what *their* verdict says. This shrewd empowerment of twelve citizens by a lawyer they do not yet know is the lawyer's most important goal of any opening statement.

---

10. Goodreads, https://www.goodreads.com/quotes/94686-the-dead-cannot-cry-out-for-justice-it-is-a (last visited Mar. 14, 2020).

11. BrainyQuote, https://www.brainyquote.com/quotes/susan_estrich_686452 (last visited Mar. 14, 2020).

12. BrainyQuote, https://www.brainyquote.com/quotes/clarence_darrow_386865 (last visited Mar. 14, 2020).

Make the Trial Process Empowering

Justice is achieved in a civil trial not merely through actual damages that compensate the plaintiff, but also through punitive damages meant to punish the defendant and deter others like the defendant from committing future wrongs. Transforming a juror's duty away from mere compensation *for one* and toward punishment and deterrence *for all* is a harbinger of an excellent, just verdict.

First, doing justice itself is the most important role of the entire courtroom process and the jury system exercise. As the father of our nation George Washington noted, "The due administration of justice is the firmest pillar of government."[13] Remind jurors that Washington refused to vote to ratify our nation's constitution until the right to a civil trial by jury was included in the Bill of Rights. Jurors are not in your courtroom against their will because they were mailed a jury summons; they are down at the courthouse because men like George Washington and Thomas Jefferson insisted that they enjoy this very right to be there.

Second, the desire to do good and punish evil is nonpartisan. Simply put, it is much easier to motivate a Republican who is indoctrinated by the message of tort reform into a large civil jury verdict with the message of *punishment*. As Republican President and man among men Theodore Roosevelt said, "Justice consists not in being neutral between right and wrong, but in finding out the right and upholding it, wherever found, against the wrong."[14] Simply said, justice is about upholding right against wrong. Conversely, liberal hero and civil rights leader Martin Luther King, Jr. taught us that "the ultimate tragedy is not the oppression and cruelty by the *bad* people but the silence over that by the *good* people."[15] The jurors' very willingness to adjudicate the conduct of this defendant is the difference between good and evil, between right and wrong, between victory and tragedy. This willingness has nothing to do with party or with ideology; instead, it is embedded in each of us. As the lawyer bringing this case, *you* should feel comfort knowing it is within each of *them*. As Benjamin Franklin taught us, "Justice will not be served until those who are unaffected are as outraged as those who are."[16] A good lawyer in opening statements converts herself into the mere vessel, delivering information to that much more important group, that body, that jury, who now are empowered to transform outrage at the defendant's conduct into a message for others about the consequence of that conduct. "I expect the evidence will show" is merely the lead-in to the purpose of this whole exercise—for the jurors to show the world what the evidence convinced them is the true message of this case. *The verdict!*

When a good trial lawyer ends the opening statement, the jury should be ready, willing, and able to undertake the solemn task at hand. They should be ready to willingly serve as an important vehicle in the search for justice. This is the goal, and it is an important one.

---

13. *From George Washington to Edmund Randolph, 28 September 1789*, Founders Online, https://founders.archives.gov/documents/Washington/05-04-02-0073 (last visited Mar. 14, 2020).

14. Goodreads, https://www.goodreads.com/quotes/423147-justice-consists-not-in-being-neutral-between-right-and-wrong (last visited Mar. 14, 2020).

15. Goodreads, https://www.goodreads.com/quotes/18870-the-ultimate-tragedy-is-not-the-oppression-and-cruelty-by (last visited Mar. 14, 2020).

16. Goodreads, https://www.goodreads.com/quotes/49575-justice-will-not-be-served-until-those-who-are-unaffected (last visited Mar. 14, 2020).

Importance of Opening Statements

Most jury psychologists posit that the vast majority of jury trials are over after voir dire and opening statements. I subscribe to this theory—I believe that most cases are won by the end of opening statements, with only the intensity of actual and punitive damages left to be decided. During the evidentiary phase, a plaintiff's lawyer can lose a case already won in opening, but such an event is rare. In sum, the opening statement is the most critical of trial exercises.

The opening statement is the most important of the trial because of the credibility war between the lawyers who represent the two sides. The plaintiff's lawyer should make no promise that he cannot keep, should make no statement that's not fully backed by admissible evidence, and should carefully share as the trial's script only the portions of the evidence he is absolutely convinced will be admitted into evidence during the trial.

At its core, opening statements are merely the first act of a three-part play. Act One is the introduction to the story, and the advanced script or predictive picture of what the story's painting will look like in the end. Act Two is the evidence itself, a portion of the drama mostly known only to the lawyers, and which will be previewed to jurors, but only the sections of the screenplay that absolutely will be seen by the audience during the actual play. Finally, Act Three does not merely recap the play's events through closing arguments; more importantly, it includes the jury's deliberations and its verdict, which will leave the theatre of the courthouse and appear in the public's eye as the play's review.

The importance of the opening statement is best demonstrated by the experience of watching movies. When movies begin badly or have a weak start, people might walk out of the movie early. Once hooked, however, viewers very rarely leave the movie theatre before the closing credits conclude. Like a Grisham novel hooking its reader early, a good opening statement serves to capture the jury for good; a poor one is likely to lose the listener forever.

Practice Tips for Substantive Content and Presentation

The opening statement should, above all else, provide an outline of what is to come—a road map of the journey to be shared together. In describing the journey, a good lawyer describes what is to occur when the destination is reached and the trip is over. To do so with credibility, the process must be divided up into discrete portions that are easily grasped and understood.

Every opening statement should describe the witnesses to be used to direct our journey, and the direction to be followed by the evidence itself. The road trip must be compartmentalized in order to be understood. As the famed American industrialist Henry Ford said, "Nothing is particularly hard if you divide it into small jobs."[17] Thus, the plaintiff's case-in-chief must be illuminated in detail, both by witness and by topic. Witness lists explained during opening statements should not be provided in alphabetical order, but rather in

17. Goodreads, https://www.goodreads.com/quotes/31505-nothing-is-particularly-hard-if-you-divide-it-into-small (last visited Mar. 14, 2020).

sequential order, and by mode of presentation. Evidence to be introduced should not be outlined sequentially or by exhibit number, but topically, as each major piece of the evidence fits the court's eventual jury instructions and verdict form.

The opening statement should be substantial rather than merely theatrical. Once over, the jury should fully and logically understand most of the evidence to come, and its purpose. Most importantly, the good trial lawyer will repeatedly reference the specific markers laid down in the opening statement as the presentation of substantive content occurs during the plaintiff's case-in-chief.

Using Demonstratives

As the Old English proverb goes, "First impressions are the most lasting." Demonstrative exhibits used early in an opening statement should synthesize the most important theme, setting forth the evidence behind it and the witnesses who will deliver it. Powerful demonstratives capture powerful arguments, but to deliver lasting impact, they should be utilized in both the opening statement and throughout the trial.

Any good trial lawyer should diversify his or her proof—segregate substantive, documentary evidence meant to appeal to the right side of the brain from demonstrative evidence meant to be seen, felt, touched, and received by the left side of the brain. Demonstrative evidence should be carefully selected and planned. Aside from a PowerPoint presentation meant to keep the lawyer on task during the opening statement, only three pieces of demonstrative evidence should be used during opening statements to avoid sensory overload: either one graphic PowerPoint slide that *visually* carefully encapsulates the most important issue in the case, or one enlarged document that in a single space sets forth the most damning piece of evidence against the defendant; one audible piece of evidence in the form of a 911 recording or an admissible audio excerpt that addresses the sense of *hearing*; and one singularly relevant three-dimensional widget that can both be seen by the eyes and tactilely *touched* by the hands of every single juror. Great thought should be invested in deciding what three pieces of demonstrative evidence best encapsulate the case.

Each tort case has a single best document or a document that has an unbelievably powerful admission. Much pretrial study in the form of jury focus groups, mock trials, or merely polling colleagues or neighbors will yield a consensus on the most persuasive excerpt of the most important document in the case. A large hardboard enlargement with a callout of that excerpt is Demonstrative Evidence Exhibit #1.

Likewise, there is a deposition admission, a 911 recording, or a computer animation with sound that best appeals to the sense of hearing. Nothing condemned the presidency of Richard Nixon more than the sound of his own voice committing impeachable high crimes and misdemeanors on the White House tapes. Again, research about what leads to the most powerful reaction of potential jurors will make evident the identity of that piece of *audible* evidence. This does not have to be a deposition excerpt; it can be powerful music that guided the plaintiff through a loss, the sound of a mallet banging down on bone while replacing a hip during surgery, the sound of vehicular braking embedded in a car crash animation. These can be proven up by a testifying witness. Sound works. Noise is remembered. Juries recall in the verdict room what they have learned from audible evidence. The most pivotal audible piece of evidence is Demonstrative Evidence Exhibit #2.

Finally, the impact of evidence that can be held, felt, and touched cannot be overstated. Exercise great care in selecting the single piece of tactile evidence that best communicates the message of the case in the opening statement. A tire tread torn apart by shoddy workmanship; a cutaway of a vehicle cross section wheeled into the courtroom that allows the jury to physically touch the cheap and defectively designed roof; a three-dimensional model with toy car-shaped vehicles one can push across the accident scene; a wax model of a human being showing the level and uneven shape of the leg amputation suffered as a result of the defendant's tortious actions. A good trial lawyer must decide what single piece of three-dimensional evidence can be both demonstrative and admissible. It needs to be publishable to the jury and passed around to each of them during testimony. You want the jurors clutching that piece of tactile evidence with curiosity back in the jury room during the all-important deliberations. The most powerful piece of evidence that can be touched is Demonstrative Evidence Exhibit #3.

Using Substantive Evidence

The Greek philosopher Plato wrote, "We can easily forgive a child who is afraid of the dark; the real tragedy of life is when men are afraid of the light."[18] The most important section of a meaningful opening statement is when documentary evidence or deposition excerpts are expertly annotated for the jury's benefit. Some appellate courts in Texas have held it to be reversible error to play deposition testimony during an opening statement. While it is most certainly error if the court has pre-ruled that testimony as inadmissible, no case stops a lawyer in opening statements from paraphrasing or even directly quoting from evidence known by that lawyer, or believed by that lawyer in good faith, to be admissible at trial. Every document and every deposition excerpt should be utilized to populate a topical proof outline before opening statements. A good opening statement separates the wheat from the chaff, the interesting from the critical, and it details the most powerful evidence that was collected during the discovery process.

In complex litigation, most document reviewers are asked to tag document excerpts with designations of *Relevant*, *Hot*, and *Super hot*. Only matters deemed *Super hot* are worthy of being used in the opening statement. The admission of evidence during trial often can take weeks, whereas the outline of the same evidence during opening statements must be completed in mere minutes or within an hour. Recitations to substantive evidence during the opening statement must be limited to the best of the best or its impact most surely will be lost.

Some lawyers refrain from referencing particular documents for fear of not being able to get the document into evidence later. I respectfully disagree. Nothing short of violating

18. Goodreads, https://www.goodreads.com/quotes/19198-we-can-easily-forgive-a-child-who-is-afraid:of (last visited Mar. 14, 2020).

a pretrial evidentiary ruling or a granted motion in limine prevents a lawyer from referencing every helpful document in their arsenal. Even if a document is not ultimately admitted, an opening statement that refers to the document not previously foreclosed by an adverse court ruling is more powerful than one failing to reference the document. The old adage "Sometimes, it's better to ask for forgiveness rather than to ask for permission" applies here. It is your opponent's job to preclude the mention of questionable plaintiff's evidence via a defense motion in limine; if they fail to do so, every item in the plaintiff's evidentiary toolbox is fair game for use during opening statements.

In this regard, I suggest pre-marking plaintiff's exhibits, and using the dramatic flair of invoking important exhibit numbers during the plaintiff's opening statement. Pre-marking the most important exhibit in the case as plaintiff's Exhibit No. 1 allows a fine trial lawyer to dramatically extoll the law of primacy via the first numbered piece of evidence as the supposed case killer against the defendant. While seemingly trite, never forget that prior to deliberations, jury exhibits are always placed in the jury room in the numerical order in which they are marked. Plaintiff's Exhibit No. 1 will be the first exhibit seen by the jury in the deliberation room. As such, the designation of plaintiff's Exhibit No. 1 should be used to mark the most important piece of evidence in the entire case, and it should be trumpeted as such in the opening statement.

Defense Options—Defer Opening Statements

In constructing the opening statement that describes the plaintiff's case-in-chief, the good plaintiff's lawyer must keep in mind the role of other lawyers in the courtroom. This includes what subsequent plaintiff opening statements will say, or even that the defense lawyer maintains the option to defer the defense opening statement until just before its case-in-chief.

Many complex cases involve multiple plaintiffs' lawyers trying their cases together against a singular defense lawyer. Likewise, many complex cases involve lawsuits filed against many defendants at once. This multiparty trial scenario leads to complexities that must be planned out well before the first lawyer rises to give her opening statement.

If multiple plaintiffs' lawyers are to litigate a case, all lawyers other than the first plaintiff's lawyer have the right, but not the obligation, to defer their respective opening statements until the beginning of their case-in-chief. This is a powerful option. There is no greater waste of jury time than to watch a wonderfully constructed opening statement by plaintiff's Lawyer No. 1 followed by an additional opening statement merely repeating the first. The repetition minimizes the impact. What is to be said by plaintiff's Lawyer No. 1, as opposed to matters reserved for plaintiff's Lawyer No. 2, must be allocated, decided, and prepared before the first lawyer rises to speak. Likewise, if plaintiff's Lawyer No. 1 is carrying the laboring oar of putting forth the liability case because that lawyer's respective plaintiff has greater damages, perhaps plaintiff's Lawyer No. 2 should consider deferring his or her opening statement until days or weeks into the trial, when the first plaintiff's case has been completed. Two, three, or four plaintiff's opening statements at once will see the subsequent statements lost in the shuffle. An opening statement by plaintiff's Lawyer No. 2, reserved until just before evidence specific to plaintiff No. 2 is to be presented, is far more likely to stand out and be remembered. The same is true for lawyers representing the third and fourth plaintiffs.

Likewise, a wise plaintiff's lawyer must understand that some defense lawyers have the foresight to delay their opening statement until after the plaintiff's case-in-chief has been completed. If the plaintiff's lawyer promises the jury who the plaintiff's first witness will be, and if they promise to call that witness live, a good defense lawyer may decide that all points that could be made during a defense opening statement could be achieved by an effective cross of the plaintiff's first witness on the first day. Not many civil defense lawyers have the courage or the foresight to delay their opening statement gratification in this regard, but from personal experience, I can tell you that it is an effective technique.

As referenced previously, I found myself embroiled in a misguided federal criminal indictment in Mississippi that included ninety-five felony counts alleged against myself and six other codefendants, including my brother, my paralegal, and four other defendants outside my firm. Pretrial subpoenas and forensic research revealed to me that I had been swindled by at least two of my codefendants. The prosecution, however, focused its case primarily on me, blindly ignoring what the facts made obvious: I had been ripped off by several codefendants who had stolen identities to hide their crime. The federal government's focus was on harpooning only the whale it wanted to hit—Mikal Watts. To put pressure on me, the United States indicted my brother and my paralegal. Fortunately, both were outraged by the tactic and agreed to stand tall with me at trial to defend the baseless charges. Nonetheless, the exercise required me to hire outstanding criminal defense lawyers for my brother and paralegal—Michael McCrum from San Antonio and Casey Hightower from Gulfport, Mississippi. Four terabytes of information reviewed before trial convinced me that misguided prosecutors indicted me with blinders on. They ignored what the facts plainly revealed in an effort to tar and feather a prominent trial lawyer, the only defendant who would bring them national headlines. The defense was so obvious to anyone who cared to review the large production, but I learned that the individuals in my firm were the only parties—including even the other defendants and the prosecution itself—that had the resources to do the work to review all the evidence. When the trial started, I knew that two longtime and earnest prosecutors—cast into their roles late in the pretrial process, when their cowardly former boss and lead prosecutor, unable to cajole plea bargains in favor of lies against me, had quit just six weeks before trial—had no clue what was actually in the pretrial production. Tradition dictated that shortly after these prosecutors set forth their erroneous allegations, I should give my opening statement and explain fully why they were in error. But I had McCrum and Hightower—defense Lawyer No. 2 and Lawyer No. 3—who knew the case as well as I did. They provided me with a singular opportunity to defer my opening statement.

Against all advice, after federal prosecutors gave an opening statement that suggested I was guilty of ninety-five felonies, I deferred my opening statement until my case-in-chief began, which allowed two very credentialed and experienced criminal trial attorneys, McCrum and Hightower, to give their opening statements first. This strategy was wise for three reasons.

First, my criminal defense experience was not vast. While I was undefeated in criminal matters, having vanquished municipal prosecutors in the parking ticket case against me after the officer failed to show, this was my first felony case. Discretion was the better part of valor, and Mike McCrum's decades of experience, first as a federal prosecutor, then as a white-collar criminal defense lawyer, seemed to me to be a superior calling card to that found in my resume. Moreover, Casey Hightower had valiantly defended criminal defendants in Gulfport, Mississippi, before this very judge, so he instantly enjoyed the credibility of Chief Judge Louis Guirola, who presided over our trial. Starting the trial of my life with opening statements by two fabulous lawyers who knew exactly what they were doing, as opposed to myself pretending to, struck me as smart.

Second, in any opening statement sequence involving multiple lawyers on the same side of the "v.", speaking one right after the other, much can be lost in translation. Frankly, the excellence of an initial opening statement is only as strong as the weakest one that follows it. While I was convinced that nothing McCrum or Hightower would say would diminish the message of my opening statement, I was concerned that the words of court-appointed counsel for my four other codefendants, several of whom I now knew to be guilty, would dilute the message I wanted to deliver with my own words. So, deferring my opening statement until the beginning of my case-in-chief, when I would speak to the jury alone, made a great deal of sense to me.

Third, jury trials often are won not by the excellence of the victor, but by virtue of the mistakes of those who are vanquished. The federal prosecutors from the Southern District of Mississippi clearly did not have a clue about the facts that existed with respect to the indictment they had secured. Telling them in opening statements why they were in error before they ever called Witness No. 1 would allow them to correct course much more proficiently than if they had first called seventy-eight witnesses during their case-in-chief and were proven via cross-examination to be grossly in error. So, I deferred my opening statement until four weeks into the trial. McCrum, arguing for my brother, argued his innocence, the burden of proof, and the general reputational bona fides of my law firm, all without educating the misguided prosecutors about the errors of their allegations. Likewise, Hightower argued the innocence of my paralegal, but in a strategically effective way that did not educate the prosecution about how to refashion its case away from the disaster coming their way. Thus, before the prosecutors' first witness was called, my deferral of opening statements deprived the prosecution of vital information known only to the defense that would have prevented them from eventually convincing the jury by virtue of their hapless case-in-chief. As a result, four weeks into the trial, before I even gave my opening statement, the case against me had been fatally pilloried by the simple truth of the matter shown via cross-examinations.

However, the ability to give a defense opening statement weeks into a trial—and by oneself—was a powerful tool. In one hour during the beginning of week four of the trial against me, I was able to demonstrate the fallacy in the prosecution's theory—made evident by repeated cross-examinations attacking their witnesses, but also by the affirmative evidence to be offered by the defense, which would overwhelmingly demonstrate my innocence. A unanimous jury exonerated me on every felony count. I firmly believe that the deferral of my opening statement was one of the most critical strategy choices made during that trial for my life and liberty.

In every trial since then, I worry that some clever lawyer for a civil defendant will wisely choose to make the same choice.

In conclusion, cases often are won during opening statements. While they may be lost by poor lawyering or improper statements,[19] as warned against in future chapters, the art of the opening statement is the best exercise available during trial to pull ahead of one's opponent in the race toward victory.

19. *See Arizona v. Washington*, 434 U.S. 824, 512 (1978) ("An improper opening statement unquestionably tends to frustrate the public interest in having a just judgment reached by an impartial tribunal" and "such statements create a risk, often not present in the individual juror bias situation, that the entire panel may be tainted" and could require a mistrial).

12
Opening Statements: *The First Final Argument*

The Defense Perspective

The opening statement is the second of only three opportunities when lawyers may talk directly to jurors. Defense lawyers should never squander the valuable opportunity of the opening statement with dull, anemic presentations of the evidence. Rather, the opening is an opportunity to advocate, to enthuse, and to excite the seated jury with your case and your client. Although some courts may discourage *argument* in the opening statement, experienced trial lawyers know that the opening statement is the *first final argument*. Your adversaries know this. So should all defense lawyers. You should use this opportunity for what it is—an opportunity to advocate for and advance your case consistent with the rules of the court.

Lawyers frequently win or lose cases in the first few days of trial. Jurors frequently adopt a viewpoint during the early stages of trial, and then filter the evidence to support that viewpoint. Indeed, as discussed in earlier chapters, many lawyers on both sides of the trial bar believe cases are won or lost during jury selection. Clearly, a strong voir dire, a good jury, and an effective opening statement are critical to trial success. Defense lawyers who fall flat in the opening will fail to achieve a basic strategic goal—slowing the plaintiff's momentum and accelerating defense momentum.

The opening statement also represents the culmination of your hard work paving the way to this moment—the synthesis of important facts developed during discovery which, in turn, are the foundations of your trial themes. These trial themes—the building blocks of your case—are not ad hoc, but instead are crafted and refined over many months or years during pretrial discovery that lead to this point.

Avoid Reactionary Responses

After the plaintiff has delivered its opening statement, defense lawyers may feel an urge to dive into the weeds and react to the details of the plaintiff's presentation. The best advice, though, is to avoid this temptation. Reactionary responses give too much weight and credibility to the plaintiff's remarks and reinforce the plaintiff's themes. A better strategy is to stay on-script and present solid, logical themes that define *your* case—not the plaintiff's case. Again, the defense should not be on the defensive, but should be offensive, with an aggressive, thoughtful, thematic presentation.

Preparation, Preparation, and Preparation

An opening statement should be prepared and rehearsed well before trial. Even though voir dire is over, the seated jury is still getting to know you, your client, and your case. Thus, a polished, prepared, and thoughtful opening is critical. The presentation should be relaxed, confident, and fluid.

Preparation is a key to success. A rule of thumb is that at least one hour of preparation should be devoted to every minute of argument. In simple terms, this means at least thirty hours should be devoted to preparing a thirty-minute opening statement. This includes selection of demonstratives, organization, and practice.

Rehearsals are important. Although any practice is encouraged, dress rehearsals in front of colleagues or staff are more important than practicing alone. As lawyers, we should always welcome feedback, both on substantive content and on presentation style. In this context, a minimum of six practice sessions is a best practice. At least two dress rehearsals is even better.

Depending on budget sensitivity and related expense, opening statements can be rehearsed before a focus group. Jury consultants can provide important assistance by recruiting a focus group, and then honing an opening statement through feedback from the participants. Thematic presentations can be tweaked, reordered, or even overhauled based on this feedback. Particular themes can be reshaped, emphasized, or deemphasized. Jury consultants also are helpful in finalizing the selection of demonstrative exhibits and presentation style. The goal is to maximize the persuasive impact of your opening; the advice of third-party consultants is wisely solicited if the budget allows.

Do Not Waste Time

An opening statement only should be as long as necessary. There is persuasive power in brevity. Any oral presentation—whether an opening statement, a lecture, or a speech—should avoid excessive, unnecessary length. You should avoid unnecessary redundancy. The intended audience will grow weary, and you will lose their focus and attention—or even worse, their support. Brevity becomes more valuable in response to a plaintiff's presentation that is boring or tedious. The jury will draw favorable contrasts.

Elements of an Effective Opening

Again, an effective opening largely rests on three elements of advocacy: *ethos*, *pathos*, and *logos*. These are Aristotle's ancient words, but their meaning still embodies practical common sense. Many trial layers know these basic elements instinctively.

The *ethos* of an argument rests in its *credibility* and *trustworthiness*. In the context of an opening statement, this is achieved by the lawyer's tone, presentation style, and substantive remarks. The opening should include an ethical, principled argument that humanizes the client as a good citizen, with good character and a social conscience. Your goal is to convince the jury to believe you so the jury will like and believe your client. Again, good "first" impressions during voir dire are important. Good "second" impressions during opening statements are equally important.

The *logos* of the case is the logic of the evidence and argument. The opening statement should be reasoned, commonsensical, and easily understood. You should provide an understandable road map to a winning verdict; explain what the evidence will show and how it makes sense. That is, you should explain why the defense case is logical and why the plaintiff's case is illogical. To be sure, the best defense is an offense; but all explanations must be factually supported. An illogical case that is based on distorted or inflated facts will quickly sink.

The *pathos* of a case rests in its emotional allure. This is achieved by telling a story that is interesting, appealing, and easily understood. Your goal is to inspire jury interest and empathy. As Aristotle also is thought to have said, "Every action must be due to one or the other of seven causes: chance, nature, compulsion, habit, reasoning, anger, or appetite." Defense lawyers should take heed of the wisdom in these words when they prepare their opening statements. The defense case is not arbitrary or by chance, but based on reason and nature—that is, the natural and logical sequence of explicable events. On the other hand, the plaintiff's lawyer may seek to inspire anger, fear, or compulsion. The defense lawyer should be candid with the jury and explain why fearmongering or incitements to anger can lead to unjust results. Here, the defense lawyer should remind the jury of its commitment to not let bias, prejudice, or sympathy affect their deliberations.

Defense lawyers should seek to persuade jurors to invest themselves emotionally and intellectually in the defense case. The logic, credibility, and emotion of the defense case, when presented effectively, will push you toward a better start to a favorable verdict.

Avoid Inflated Arguments

You should always avoid exaggerated arguments. Hyperbole in your opening statement will haunt you as the case develops, particularly if the jury discovers you cannot deliver on your promises. Your opposition will certainly remind the jury of your exaggerations when your evidence comes up lacking. You should fully expect to hear pointed criticism in final arguments. The lesson here is, never exaggerate; be truthful and plainspoken, and deliver what you promise. This comes back to *ethos*. You want the jury to feel like they can trust you—and sometimes, even the smallest exaggeration may cost you the jury's trust.

On the flip side, you should make note of the *plaintiff's* exaggerated arguments. If the budget permits, you should order a daily transcript of the plaintiff's opening, and then study this transcript, because it represents a road map of the plaintiff's case. This transcript may become valuable in final argument when the plaintiff comes up short on its evidence. You should use the transcript as a powerful reminder of the plaintiff's empty promises.

Combatting Reptiles

Skilled plaintiff's lawyers use a tactic known as the "reptilian" strategy. This is often the case in trials that involve personal injury or wrongful death claims, and it is frequently used in punitive damage claims.

The tactic is simply defined—the plaintiff's counsel will craft arguments to appeal to human nature, and to subconscious needs for personal safety and security. The concept is that these arguments appeal to the lower brain stem, which houses our survival mechanisms, such as fight or flight. In doing so, the plaintiff's lawyer seeks to inspire anxiety, dread, fear, or anger toward a defendant. This is accomplished, in part, by making the case more important than just the individuals or immediate facts involved. Using this technique, the plaintiff's lawyers present their opening statements to negatively condition the jury against the defendants by making them feel uncomfortable with the defendants or with what the defendants allegedly have done. In personal injury cases, this is achieved by portraying the defendant as an enemy of personal safety, one who does not care about the safety of others, and whose conduct threatens the safety of the community. In a business case, this may include portraying a corporate defendant as having no trustworthiness, ethics, or business morals. Again, the goal is to characterize the defendant as repugnant and to inspire fear by suggesting that the defendant's conduct threatens the economic or financial welfare of a larger community. To be sure, these types of arguments are the bedrock of successful punitive damage claims. As defense lawyers, we must aggressively combat these tactics through a logical, credible, emotional, and *personalized* presentation of the facts.

You should personalize your client—*always*. If defending a corporation, the corporation should be personified by a corporate representative. If not, at least one or more jurors will wonder why there is a corporation with no face, and this absence reinforces erroneous notions that corporations are not "persons." The company also should be "humanized." This is achieved by discussing the important things the company does, referring to its good deeds, reputation, community involvements, and the important products or services it provides. This helps offset any fear, dread, or anxiety inspired in the plaintiff's opening remarks.

The jury should be reminded about the sequence of argument and the jury's obligation to listen to *all* the evidence impartially and without bias. That is, defense counsel should educate the jury on burdens of proof and the order of argument—the plaintiff goes first—and the importance of keeping an open mind. Skilled defense lawyers should appeal to the jurors' individual and collective sense of fairness. Again, the jury should be reminded not to let bias, prejudice, or sympathy influence their decisions.

Readjusting Momentum

Jury studies demonstrate that jurors typically fall into one of four categories based on predisposition and natural bias. Every jury likely will include at least one of the following juror types: (1) strong plaintiff juror, (2) weak plaintiff juror, (3) weak defense juror, and (4) strong defense juror. Again, jurors fall into these categories because of their unique life experiences and socioeconomic backgrounds. Of course, a basic purpose of voir dire is to identify these characteristics and strike a jury that is defense-oriented. From the defense perspective, the goal of jury selection is to have few or no jurors in the "strong plaintiff juror" box.

After the plaintiff delivers its opening statement, it is expected that there will be movement—perhaps significant movement—among the four juror categories. Some strong defense jurors, having just heard a forceful plaintiff's presentation, will be less certain in their defense orientation, and they may soften in their attitudes. Weak defense jurors soften even more and may begin to lean toward the plaintiff's side of the case. Concurrently, weak plaintiff jurors become more galvanized in their attitudes and shift even more strongly toward the plaintiff's position. The chart below demonstrates this shifting:

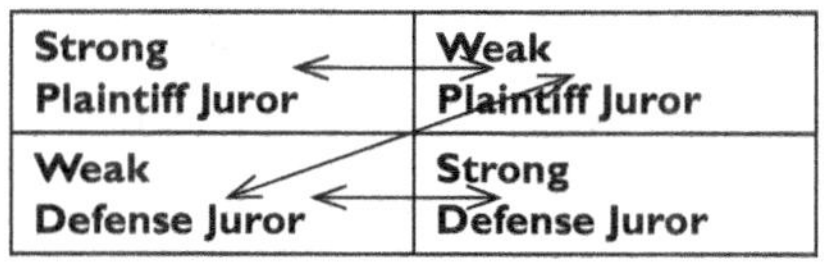

Defense lawyers should use opening statements to reverse this movement. Similar to a game of marbles, the goal is to recapture strong defense jurors and cause weak plaintiff jurors to reverse field and transition back toward the defense. By causing this momentum shift, the defense begins to win the case.

Simplicity, Repetition, and Illustration

An opening statement should present logical, coherent trial themes. Again, these themes are the building blocks for a defense verdict, and they should be simple, readily grasped, and understandable. Complicated themes will be lost in the fog of disputed facts and argument. Simple themes, when repeated, are more easily remembered. Accordingly, the goal is to simplify, simplify, and simplify, and then repeat, repeat, and repeat.

Presentation Techniques: PowerPoint

Microsoft PowerPoint is now a common advocacy tool. Many lawyers view PowerPoint presentations as a necessity, and not just a luxury. Most courtrooms are hardwired with technology to support the effective use and presentation of PowerPoint slides. You should consider using PowerPoint to organize your trial themes and key evidence in a manner that captures jurors' attention, and then holds their attention. An effective PowerPoint presentation should encapsulate the elements of a successful opening statement: it should be short and simple, and it should repeat your themes.

One of the valuable features of PowerPoint is how quickly computer slides can be modified in real time to respond to what is transpiring inside the courtroom. Indeed, a skilled practitioner can create or modify slides while listening to the plaintiff's opening statement, thereby having the ability to immediately refine the defense response. Thematic messages can be reordered or tweaked to respond more effectively to what the plaintiff is stating.

PowerPoint slides frequently include thematic pictures that communicate themes in a more entertaining way. In a case that involved counterclaims of fraud and breach of contract, our client first sued, seeking to vacate security interests and liens that the adverse party held in the corporate assets of our client. Out client sought to vacate these security interests because they stunted the company's ability to borrow money and grow. The defense's focus, therefore, was on the plaintiff's use of these security interests as a chokehold, strangling the company, its future, and the financial security of its employees. With the help of a jury consultant, multiple slides in the PowerPoint presentation included images of a chain with one link colored bright red to impress upon the jury the importance of removing the chokehold. The last slide showed the red link shattered and broken to dramatize the importance of the jury's verdict—releasing and breaking the chokehold.

In another case that involved a lost real estate deal, the defense focused on the economic crash that swept the country in 2008 and 2009. The case involved a real estate broker who was accused of breaching fiduciary duties and his alleged negligence for failing to market and sell commercial property at the highest dollar. The 2008 economic crash was readily understood as an explanation for why all market values dropped, for all types of commercial property in the relevant area—not just the property in question. Several PowerPoint slides used a small cartoon that depicted the 2008 crash, with a graph showing diminution of property values. This helped impress upon the jury the importance of this defense theme, and this defense was repeated frequently. The defense won.

In another case involving a fatal rollover of a sports utility vehicle, an emblem of a seatbelt was incorporated into multiple PowerPoint slides. This was used by the defense to impress upon the jury the importance of wearing a seat belt; plaintiff's failure to do so resulted in his ejection from the SUV and ultimate death. The defense rested on the plaintiff's failure to use his seatbelt when he was riding in the back of the SUV, lying prone and sleeping.

In yet another case, a well-known Texas developer owned a fee-simple interest in the land under a private airstrip. Adjacent homeowners each owned an easement to use the landing strip for their private airplanes; adjacent residences had large garages that served as small aircraft hangers. The subdivision was created so each homeowner could taxi his or her private aircraft to the airstrip. The developer, however, had plans to develop the land commercially, which would destroy the essence of the community. The homeowners countered by describing the easement as their "driveway." The homeowners' trial counsel effectively argued that the developer was attempting to destroy the homeowners' driveways, thereby destroying their ability to use their preferred means of transportation. This was an effective, logical, and winning argument.

Using Demonstrative Evidence

In addition to using PowerPoint presentations, you should consider other types of demonstratives to present trial themes and key evidence. However, prudence dictates that you seek the court's permission before doing so to avoid surprise objections in the presence of the jury. If you invest the time and energy to develop the demonstratives, you want to make sure you get the benefits of using them before the jury.

Depending on the nature of your case, demonstratives can provide the glue that holds the logic of the defense argument together. Charts frequently are used; product hardware can be displayed and explained; photographs are always helpful; and the list goes on and on.

There is an old adage that says, "Seeing is believing." Thus, the use of photographs, if permitted, is always forceful. Exemplar products can be used. In yet another example during the silicone breast implant litigation, defense counsel used a show-and-tell display box that contained multiple medical implants manufactured from silicone. This included knee replacements, hip replacements, other joint replacements, and heart stents. The goal was to show through examples that silicone was not inherently dangerous, but could be used safely in the human body. Again, this show-and-tell box helped communicate the defendant's primary theme—silicone is not unsafe.

Using Deposition Excerpts

Using excerpts from depositions is a standard and powerful technique. Again, however, you should make sure the court approves. You also should consider pursuing an agreement with opposing counsel that either side can use deposition clips, subject to review and resolving any objections. In some instances, the court may have ruled on objections to deposition designations and pre-admitted testimony. This paves the way to use depositions in the opening statement.

If you elect to use deposition clips, you should do so with disciplined care. First, never overdo it. Too many clips can distract the jury and diminish the effectiveness of your opening. Second, the excerpts should be carefully selected for maximum impact. Only the most powerful excerpts should be used. Third, you should limit the use of such excerpts to sound bites, recognizing that the attention span of any jury is short. No excerpt should be longer than two or three minutes. Otherwise, the jury may be confused and distracted, and may lose focus. Jury studies reveal that the attention span of the average juror is quite short. Accordingly, any deposition excerpt should be short so the jury's attention is immediately captured and retained. Video deposition excerpts, which can be incorporated into PowerPoint presentations, are the most effective device for capturing the jury's attention.

Showing video excerpts that reflect admissions from a party opponent or concessions made by an adverse expert is a powerful way to start a case. This is one way to achieve a primary objective in your opening statement—slowing, if not stalling, the plaintiff's momentum. There is nothing more effective than a video record of an admission by a party opponent or adverse witness.

Focus on Defense Leaders

By the time you deliver your opening, you will have obtained significant information about each seated juror. In opening statements, as in voir dire, you should expect sitting jurors will fall into one of four juror boxes: strong plaintiff juror, weak plaintiff juror, weak defense juror, or strong defense juror. You should focus significant attention on jurors you perceive to be defense-oriented. This means you should have substantial eye contact with these individuals and craft your presentation in a way that is appealing to them. If you believe one of these defense-oriented jurors is also a leader, with a strong personality, additional attention should be focused on that individual. Such a juror may end up serving as the foreperson. At a minimum, he or she will be a vocal advocate for your case in the jury room.

You should never ignore any juror, because your impressions about juror types may be flawed; that is, you never want to alienate any juror by suggesting that he or she is not important. Again, defining juror types is more art than science, and initial impressions can be incorrect. Accordingly, you should try to make eye contact with all jurors in the jury box during your opening. No one should be excluded.

Avoid Demonstrative Overkill

Many people are visual learners. That is why using demonstratives, including PowerPoint presentations, is an effective strategy. However, you should be mindful that overuse of demonstratives can be distracting. The opening statement is an opportunity to foster personal rapport with the seated jury. You should use this opportunity to stimulate a positive connection between yourself and individual jurors, recognizing that the jury wants to hear you talk. They want a window into your personality. Your opening is an opportunity to enhance your credibility, which will benefit your client's case. Too many demonstratives, or simply reading a long PowerPoint presentation verbatim will detract from this opportunity.

Objections during Opening Statements

The purpose of opening statements is to present an overview of expected evidence. Again, this overview should be presented as an advocate, and not as an anemic presentation devoid of emotion or drama. You also should expect a dramatic, forceful opening from your opposition, and you should be prepared to respond in kind.

You should understand the risks and dangers of making objections during your opponent's opening statement. You should lodge objections only when it is critical to preserve error; this usually occurs when your opponent says or does something that rises to the level of a mistrial. Some examples include references to settlement negotiations, insurance coverage, inadmissible criminal conduct or evidence excluded in limine. Setting aside these types of extreme instances, you should not object to arguments that are nothing more than good, strong advocacy. This holds true even if it hurts. If you object, you may be perceived as an obstructionist. By objecting, you also accentuate the plaintiff's themes and telegraph concern for what is being said.

Remember, it is still early in the trial, and the jury is still forming impressions about the case, the clients, and you. You do not want to use the opening bell in a way that makes the jury perceive you negatively. Making objections during an opening statement is particularly risky because you also are forcing the court to make a ruling in the presence of the jury. If the court overrules your objection, the plaintiff's statements are highlighted and reinforced.

If you need to make an objection during opening statements, you should ask for permission to approach the bench. Again, typically, no objection should be made unless you are confronted with egregious behavior. If you need to move for a mistrial or otherwise discuss the details of your objection, you should do so outside the hearing of the jury. If your grievance is aired in front of the jury, the jury may be exposed to information it should not hear. Then, if the court overrules your objection, the jury's negative perceptions are reinforced further and the bad evidence accentuated.

Handling Bad Evidence

Opening statements provide an opportunity to address challenging or inflammatory evidence that you expect will be introduced. If you expect inflammatory evidence, you should consider strategies to mitigate its impact before it comes into evidence. One tactic is to acknowledge the evidence in the opening statement, and then explain why it either does not make sense or why it is not relevant.

As an example, in a case tried against my co-author, Mikal Watts, there was an email authored by one of my client's employees. Unfortunately, this email contained inflammatory, disparaging comments. Although a motion in limine had been filed to exclude this email, it was denied. Accordingly, we made the tactical decision to address the issue head-on in our opening statement. We advised the jury that our corporate client did not support or endorse the inflammatory remarks and, in fact, it prohibited this type of conduct as a matter of corporate policy. We also advised the jury that the sole purpose of this evidence was to inflame or anger the jury against us and our client. The jury also was reminded not to let bias or prejudice affect their views of the evidence. Because this was particularly damaging evidence, our goal was to take some sting out of the evidence before it was actually heard and considered.

13
DAUBERT CHALLENGES
The Plaintiff's Perspective

In twenty-first century courtrooms, no trial may begin without the obligatory round of expert challenges under *Daubert v. Merrell Dow Pharmaceuticals, Inc.* This chapter addresses the legal backdrop of *Daubert* and its progeny, which led to an entire generation of defense lawyers systematically challenging every expert proffered by the plaintiff as a prophylactic tool to preserve the record for a possible appeal. In light of the same, a good plaintiff's lawyer must condition the trial judge as to how he can appropriately meet the court's limited procedural obligations under *Daubert* in a manner that is efficient and fair to both sides. However, long before trial, the plaintiff's lawyer must first use care in selecting experts, in assisting them in fully developing their opinions and expressing them in detail in reports and depositions, and in formally fending off the challenges to the admissibility of their testimony in a formal response to the *Daubert* motion that inevitably will come their way.

The Legal Backdrop of Daubert *and Its Progeny*

Rule 702 in the Federal Rules of Evidence sets forth the standard for admissibility of expert testimony. Four opinions provide an important backdrop for the text of Rule 702: *Frye*, *Daubert*, *Joiner*, and *Kumho*.

In *Frye v. United States*, the U.S. Court of Appeals for the District of Columbia held that expert testimony must be based on scientific methods that are sufficiently established and accepted:

> [W]hile courts will go a long way in admitting experimental testimony deduced from a well-recognized scientific principle or discovery, the thing from which the deduction is made *must be sufficiently established to have gained general acceptance* in the particular field in which it belongs.[1]

1. 293 F. 1013, 1014 (D.C. Cir. 1923) (emphasis added).

In 1975, more than half a century after *Frye*, the U.S. Supreme Court adopted the Federal Rules of Evidence for subsequent litigation in federal courts, including rules on expert testimony. The Court's alternative to the *Frye* standard came to be used more broadly because Rule 702 did not strictly require general acceptance of a scientific principal or discovery and was seen to be more flexible. The first version of Fed. R. Evid. 702 provided that "[i]f scientific, technical, or other specialized knowledge will assist the trier of fact to understand the evidence or to determine a fact in issue, a witness qualified as an expert by knowledge, skill, experience, training, or education, may testify thereto in the form of an opinion or otherwise."[2]

Eighteen years after adoption of Rule 702, the Supreme Court held in *Daubert v. Merrell Dow Pharmaceuticals, Inc.*, that Rule 702 did not incorporate the *Frye* "general acceptance" test about scientific expert testimony, and therefore, should no longer be used:

> Given the Rules' permissive backdrop and their inclusion of a specific rule on expert testimony that does not mention "general acceptance," the assertion that the Rules somehow assimilated *Frye* is unconvincing. *Frye* made "general acceptance" the exclusive test for admitting expert scientific testimony. That austere standard, absent from, and incompatible with, the Federal Rules of Evidence, should not be applied in federal trials.[3]

However, the Court held that under Rule 702, "the trial judge must ensure that any and all scientific testimony or evidence admitted is not only relevant, but reliable."[4] Justice Blackmun, writing for the unanimous court, then offered some general observations. First, "a key question to be answered in determining whether a theory or technique is scientific knowledge that will assist the trier of fact will be whether it can be (and has been) tested."[5] Second, a "pertinent consideration is whether the theory or technique has been subjected to peer review and publication."[6] Third, "in the case of a particular scientific technique, the court ordinarily should consider the known or potential rate of error."[7] Fourth, "'general acceptance' can yet have a bearing on the inquiry" because "[w]idespread acceptance can be an important factor in ruling particular evidence admissible, and 'a known technique which has been able to attract only minimal support within the community,' may properly be viewed with skepticism."[8] Finally, the Court noted that "[t]he focus, of course, must be solely on principles and methodology, not on the conclusions that they generate."[9]

Just four years later, the Supreme Court in *General Electric Co. v. Joiner* blurred the *Daubert* distinction between "methodology" and "conclusions" by stating that "conclusions and methodology are not entirely distinct from one another."[10] Furthermore, the *Joiner*

---

2. Fed. R. Evid. 702 (1975).
3. 509 U.S. 579, 589 (1993).
4. *Id.*
5. *Id.* at 593.
6. *Id.*
7. *Id.* at 594.
8. *Id.* (citation omitted).
9. *Id.* at 595.
10. 522 U.S. 136, 146 (1997).

Court empowered trial judges when it held that the proper standard of appellate review of *Daubert* rulings was "abuse of discretion" as opposed to a stricter standard of review that had been used by certain circuits.[11] The Court's decision in *Joiner* empowered federal district judges to make essentially outcome-determinative decisions under the abuse of discretion standard of review rather than the de novo review standard for summary judgment determinations because the exclusion of experts often is followed by a summary judgment motion that's based on a lack of evidence.

Two years later, in *Kumho Tire Co., Ltd. v. Carmichael*, the Supreme Court held that "*Daubert's* general holding—setting forth the trial judge's general 'gatekeeping' obligation—applies not only to testimony based on 'scientific' knowledge, but also to testimony based on 'technical' and 'other specialized' knowledge," and also concluded:

> [A] trial court may consider one or more of the more specific factors that *Daubert* mentioned when doing so will help determine that testimony's reliability. But, as the Court stated in *Daubert*, the test of reliability is "flexible," and *Daubert's* list of specific factors neither necessarily nor exclusively applies to all experts or in every case. Rather, the law grants a district court the same broad latitude when it decides how to determine reliability as it enjoys in respect to its ultimate reliability determination.[12]

Furthermore, the Supreme Court further expanded the considerable latitude granted to district courts by *Joiner's* relaxed abuse of discretion standard of appellate review when, in *Kumho*, the Court concluded that the "trial judge must have considerable leeway in deciding in a particular case how to go about determining whether particular expert testimony is reliable."[13] While "a trial court should consider the specific factors identified in *Daubert* where they are reasonable measures of the reliability of expert testimony,"[14] "[t]hose factors may or may not be pertinent in assessing reliability, depending on the nature of the issue, the expert's particular expertise, and the subject of his testimony."[15] Importantly, *Joiner's* abuse of discretion standard applies not merely to the decision of whether to admit expert testimony, but also "as much to the trial court's decisions about how to determine reliability as to its ultimate conclusion."[16]

As a result of *Daubert*, *Joiner*, and *Kumho*, the text of Rule 702 was revised in 2000:

> Rule 702. Testimony by Expert Witnesses
>
> A witness who is qualified as an expert by knowledge, skill, experience, training, or education may testify in the form of an opinion or otherwise if:
>
> (a) the expert's scientific, technical, or other specialized knowledge will help the trier of fact to understand the evidence or to determine a fact in issue;
>
> (b) the testimony is based on sufficient facts or data;

---

11. *Id.*
12. 526 U.S. 137, 141–42 (1999).
13. *Id.* at 152.
14. *Id.* at 138.
15. *Id.*
16. *Id.* at 139.

(c) the testimony is the product of reliable principles and methods; and
(d) the expert has reliably applied the principles and methods to the facts of the case.[17]

The Advisory Committee notes to the 2000 revisions to Rule 702 merit some mention here. First, "the rejection of expert testimony is the exception rather than the rule" because "*Daubert* did not work a 'seachange over federal evidence law'" and "the trial court's role as gatekeeper is not intended to serve as a replacement for the adversary system." Second, "[w]hen a trial court, applying this amendment, rules that an expert's testimony is reliable, this does not necessarily mean that contradictory expert testimony is unreliable" because "[t]he amendment is broad enough to permit testimony that is the product of competing principles or methods in the same field of expertise." Third, "[n]othing in this amendment is intended to suggest that experience alone—or experience in conjunction with other knowledge, skill, training or education—may not provide a sufficient foundation for expert testimony"; to the contrary, "the text of Rule 702 expressly contemplates that an expert may be qualified on the basis of experience" because "[i]n certain fields, experience is the predominant, if not sole, basis for a great deal of reliable expert testimony." Fourth, "[t]he amendment makes no attempt to set forth procedural requirements for exercising the trial court's gatekeeping function over expert testimony"; instead, because "[c]ourts have shown considerable ingenuity and flexibility in considering challenges to expert testimony under *Daubert*, . . . it is contemplated that this will continue under the amended Rule."[18]

While the states are allowed to adopt their own evidence rules, most have adopted or modified the federal rules, including rules that cover expert testimony. Consequently, since the 2000 revisions to Rule 702, the *Frye* "general acceptance" standard has been superseded by *Daubert* not only in the federal courts, but also in most state courts. Only California, Illinois, Maryland, Minnesota, New York, Pennsylvania, and Washington continue to use the *Frye* standard. Florida and New Jersey more recently migrated to using the *Daubert* standard.

In *Whole Woman's Health v. Hellerstedt*,[19] the Supreme Court reversed the Fifth Circuit's finding that a trial court's decision to admit expert testimony was "clearly erroneous" because it rested upon the ipse dixit of one expert, Dr. Grossman. The Supreme Court observed that Rule 702 states that "an expert may testify in the 'form of an opinion' as long as that opinion rests upon 'sufficient facts or data' and 'reliable principles and methods,' and because 'Dr. Grossman's opinion rested upon his participation, along with other university researchers, in research that tracked 'the number of open facilities providing abortion care in the state by . . . requesting information from the Texas Department of State Health Services . . . [t]hrough interviews with clinic staff[,] and review of publicly

17. Fed. R. Evid. 702 (2000).
18. Fed. R. Evid. 702 Advisory Committee's note to 2000 amendment.
19. 136 S. Ct. 2292 (2016).

available information,'" the district court "acted within its legal authority in determining that Dr. Grossman's testimony was admissible."[20]

In sum, *Daubert* now is a fact of life in all stages of litigation,[21] and the plaintiff's lawyer must carefully traverse this minefield, which otherwise can blow up a good case.

The Prophylactic Use of Daubert *to "Preserve the Record" for Appeal*

Most state and federal appellate courts require that complaints on appeal must first have been brought before the lower court for its consideration. This generally means that to complain on appeal about the relevance and reliability of an expert's admitted opinion, a *Daubert* challenge must first have been made to the district court before the expert testified. Consequently, since *Daubert*, an entire generation of defense lawyers has systematically challenged seemingly every expert proffered by a plaintiff as a prophylactic way to preserve the record for a possible appeal.

The systematic use of *Daubert* challenges has introduced massive costs to the pretrial process, both in terms of the time expended by lawyers litigating the admissibility of experts before trial, and in terms of the huge sums of money paid to such experts to participate in the pretrial *Daubert* process. With trial judges having unbridled discretion to decide how to perform the required *Daubert* analysis, some courts have turned *Daubert* into an expensive process of requiring a trial before the trial on the issue of the admissibility of expert testimony. This process of bringing a plaintiff's experts in for live testimony during pretrial *Daubert* hearings effectively doubles the cost of putting on the plaintiff's case-in-chief. Experts must travel twice, be housed in hotels twice, be prepped twice, and testify twice—all because the plaintiff failed to first provide the Court with practical, persuasive arguments about how best to limit the expense of complying with its gatekeeping obligations under *Daubert*. Some basic commonsense considerations should be offered in this regard.

First, the court's gatekeeping obligation pursuant to Rule 702 should be harmonized with Rule 102's admonition that the Federal Rules of Evidence should be construed as to "eliminate unjustifiable expense." Requiring plaintiffs—often injured individuals whose recovery will be reduced by the cost of repaying litigation expenses—to front the cost of having experts come to testify in court before the trial even begins is a requirement that unnecessarily adds expense to the process. When Rule 56 Summary Judgment practice is conducted entirely with submissions of affidavits or declarations and with live testimony not permitted, it makes no sense that a Rule 702 admissibility inquiry somehow requires a credibility assessment requiring an in-person evaluation of a witness's affect and demeanor. Because *Joiner* and *Kumho* make clear that the trial judge has almost absolute discretion about *how* to conduct its *Daubert* process, the court should do so in the most economically

20. *Id.* at 2316–17.

21. *See Wal-Mart Stores, Inc. v. Dukes*, 564 U.S. 338, 354 (2011) (observing that "[t]he District Court concluded *Daubert* did not apply to expert testimony at the certification stage of class-action proceedings," and noting, "[w]e doubt that this is so . . . .").

efficient manner possible. Economic efficiency dictates permitting the plaintiff's expert to meet a *Daubert* challenge via an affidavit or declaration alone, without the considerable expense concomitant with requiring live pretrial testimony.

Second, the court's gatekeeping obligation pursuant to Rule 702 should be harmonized with Rule 102's admonition that the Federal Rules of Evidence should be construed as to "eliminate unjustifiable expense *and delay*." Avoiding expense and delay concerns not only the time of the parties, but of the Court and jury as well. Nothing in Rule 702 or *Daubert* and its progeny requires a live *Daubert* hearing; it is therefore within a trial court's discretion to require that the *Daubert* challenge be decided on the papers alone. Furthermore, there is nothing in Rule 702, nor in *Daubert* and its progeny, that requires the Court to conduct its *Daubert* inquiry before the trial. Just because a defense lawyer is prophylactically challenging every one of a plaintiff's experts does not entitle that lawyer to many hours or days of the Court's time before the trial begins. It is perfectly acceptable for a trial judge to exercise its discretion to defer ruling on a *Daubert* challenge until the witness is called at trial. The Court may instruct a plaintiff's attorney to call his or her expert witness, prove up the witness' qualifications and methodology, and then permit the opposing side to formally lodge its *Daubert* objection before asking the first expert opinion. This can be done with the jury excused, but it's not required. A trial judge who requires a *Daubert* objection to be made in open court is properly exercising his or her discretion on *how* to conduct the *Daubert* inquiry. Likewise, a judge who does not want to cause delay by excusing the jury for a *Daubert* hearing accomplishes two things—first, the objection will be made much more succinctly, and second, the required ruling can be provided in open court without the interruption that comes with excusing the jury, conducting a *Daubert* hearing, ruling on the motion to exclude, then calling the jury back into the courtroom. A middle path is asking the parties to approach the bench while still in open court, so that a quick *Daubert* motion can be presented, and thereby preserved and the requisite ruling obtained, before allowing the expert testimony to proceed. In this way, no delay is introduced into the trial.

Preventing Armageddon—Protecting the Plaintiff's Experts from Exclusion under Daubert

The pretrial adjudication of the admissibility of expert testimony under *Daubert* can, for a plaintiff, become a de facto summary judgment practice. In a complex case, the exclusion of one of the plaintiff's experts means the plaintiff cannot get to the jury because the required expert testimony on an essential element of proof is lacking. In short, a *Daubert* ruling excluding a plaintiff's expert often is a kill shot to the case. As such, using great care far before a *Daubert* hearing is necessary. Such care must be exercised in choosing one's experts, in developing and presenting the foundation for such opinions in written reports and during depositions, and in formally responding to *Daubert* motions themselves.

Choosing Experts

In choosing experts, a plaintiff's lawyer must keep at least five *Daubert* considerations in mind about notions of relevance, fit, and helpfulness.

First, the requested expert opinion itself should be reviewed for its discussion of relevance, fit, and helpfulness. The following portion of the *Daubert* opinion provides a helpful framework to be referenced before choosing experts:

> Rule 702 further requires that the evidence or testimony "assist the trier of fact to understand the evidence or to determine a fact in issue." This condition goes primarily to relevance. "Expert testimony which does not relate to any issue in the case is not relevant and, ergo, non-helpful." The consideration has been aptly described by Judge Becker as one of "fit." "Fit" is not always obvious, and scientific validity for one purpose is not necessarily scientific validity for other, unrelated purposes. The study of the phases of the moon, for example, may provide valid scientific "knowledge" about whether a certain night was dark, and if darkness is a fact in issue, the knowledge will assist the trier of fact. However (absent creditable grounds supporting such a link), evidence that the moon was full on a certain night will not assist the trier of fact in determining whether an individual was unusually likely to have behaved irrationally on that night. Rule 702's "helpfulness" standard requires a valid scientific connection to the pertinent inquiry as a precondition to admissibility.[22]

Second, concerning *relevance*, one must first ask the question, "what is the particular opinion sought from an expert that is helpful to the jury in resolving a pertinent inquiry?" This requires two initial inquiries. First, the jury instructions and verdict form should be prepared in advance so that in selecting experts, one has a predesigned skeleton upon which the flesh of sought-after expert opinions may be attached. In other words, what are the particular elements of a cause of action about which the expert is to opine? Second, the case law in the jurisdiction where the case is filed should be researched thoroughly to ascertain whether expert testimony on the given issue is required, and to confirm that expert testimony on such a subject has been previously permitted.

Third, concerning *fit*, one must examine the appropriateness of both the expert's background and qualifications and the opinions being sought from the expert. In the medical context, myriad cases hold that a medical degree alone does not entitle a doctor to opine about every aspect of medicine.[23] Likewise, a mechanical engineer is just as unqualified to give opinions about chemical engineering as a meteorologist is in opining on how to properly control the avionics of a Boeing 767. Before hiring an expert, one must carefully study the expert's resume and publication list to ensure that the expert's background

---

22. *Daubert*, 508 U.S. at 591–92 (citations omitted).

23. *See e.g.*, *Christophersen v. Allied-Signal Corporation*, 939 F.2d 1106, 1112–13 (5th Cir. 1991), *cert. denied*, 503 U.S. 912 (1992) ("The questions . . . do not stop if the expert has an M.D. degree. That alone is not enough to qualify him to give an opinion on every conceivable medical question. This is because the inquiry must be into actual qualification. . . ."); *O'Conner v. Commonwealth Edison Co.*, 807 F. Supp. 1376, 1390 (C.D. Ill.1992) ("[N]o medical doctor is automatically an expert in every medical issue merely because he or she has graduated from medical school or has achieved certification in a medical specialty."), *aff'd*, 13 F.3d 1090 (7th Cir. 1994), *cert. denied*, 512 U.S. 1222 (1994). *Cf.*, *Whiting v. Boston Edison Co.*, 891 F. Supp. 12, 24 (D. Mass. 1995) ("Just as a lawyer is not by general education and experience qualified to give an expert opinion on every subject of the law, so too a scientist or medical doctor is not presumed to have expert knowledge about every conceivable scientific principle or disease.").

and expertise involves a precise fit with the subject matter of the opinions sought from that expert.

Fourth, concerning *helpfulness*, one must confirm that the opinions sought relate topically to the issues to be resolved by the jury's verdict. In other words, experts with significant pedigrees often believe themselves to be qualified to opine on the sun, the moon, and the stars; but, in most federal courts, their opinions will be culled down to opinions that have some earthly relationship to the matter at issue in the case. The most prevalent unforced error made by lawyers is permitting their expert to opine on unrelated issues, only to later see the defendant use the same kind of overreach to ignite a full-throated *Daubert* challenge. While choosing an expert typically involves the challenge of lining up their qualifications with their opinions, one also must make sure that the expert does not out-punt his coverage of qualifications. Furthermore, when an expert overstays his or her welcome by opining on matters not helpful to the jury's factual inquiry, a *Daubert* challenge predictably will come their way.

Fifth, publications authored by the expert that are being considered should be carefully collected and analyzed. Initially, this is an important vetting exercise to evaluate the qualifications of the potential expert. Moreover, it permits the plaintiff's lawyer who is writing the check for the expert's services to know on first base any potential problems that may exist with past positions taken or statements made by the expert. Finally, prior publications are an important indicator of the true scope of the expert's actual expertise. With the Supreme Court holding in *Hellerstedt*,[24] which requires that an expert's opinion rest on "sufficient facts or data" and "reliable principles and methods" when that "opinion rested upon his participation, along with other university researchers, in research, . . ." prior scientific work conducted and published by an expert provides an important bulwark against *Daubert* challenges.

Sixth, one should collect all prior *Daubert* decisions that are relevant to the field of study. Westlaw searches can yield a treasure trove of prior court rulings that overrule *Daubert* challenges to the expert in question, or to others positing opinions in the same field. All court decisions that hold the methodologies of the expert in question, or employed by others in the same field of inquiry, to be reliable should be collected, carefully studied, and assembled for future presentation to the court. In short, an expert with a history of *Daubert* exclusions is far more likely to be excluded in the case at bar than an expert who has been universally accepted as an expert by prior courts across the land. Therefore, before writing a check to any expert, a thorough examination of that expert's *Daubert* report card should take place.

Developing the Foundation for Opinions to Be Expressed

An evidentiary foundation for each opinion to be rendered by the expert should be developed early in the process. Can the bases of the opinion be independently tested? Has this subject matter been published after being subjected to the peer review process? Does the methodology employed have a known or a potential rate of error? Has the methodology

24. *Hellerstedt*, 136 S. Ct. at 2316–17.

gained general acceptance within the relevant scientific community? Each of these four general observations first posited by Justice Blackmun in his decision for the Supreme Court back in 1993 should be first and foremost on the minds of both the plaintiff's lawyer and his or her potential expert.

Not every opinion involves a subject matter that is tested and published; however, most scientific methodologies do. If the opinion involves accident reconstruction, the use of photogrammetry, vehicular event data recorders, vehicular crush stiffness data, or basic math that involves the conservation of momentum and energy formulas, has each methodology long been the subject of testing, publication, and general acceptance within the scientific community? If the case being opined upon involves a pharmaceutical product, collecting all the data supplied by the company to regulatory authorities, whether the FDA in the United States, the European Medicines Agency in the European Union, or other regulatory authorities elsewhere across the globe, provides valuable clinical data that can be the published source of information that supports the offered medical opinion. Moreover, post-marketing surveillance data is now omnipresent, and a litigation expert can easily convert them into published, peer-reviewed work involving methodologies that have long been accepted in the field of medical practice risk management. Finally, medical data is so plentiful and well organized in European countries that supply socialized medical care, and even among large health maintenance organizations that reimburse costs for such care here in the United States, that retrospective epidemiological studies can be generated with astounding speed and converted into published, peer-reviewed work in short order. If a case involves oilfield drilling practices, every industry publication on the subject should be culled and put into the expert's file, so that when the expert is giving an opinion, he or she can point to the published work of others as the published foundation for such opinion. In sum, the expert's file should become a library filled with publications on the subject of the offered opinion.

While *Kumho* makes clear that an expert's experience and expertise alone can be the foundation of an appropriate Rule 702 opinion, the *Daubert* factors may still be applied to such an area. Therefore, when relying on experience in a nonscientific field, an expert's file should be populated with published work in that particular field. For example, in the field of psychology, one might believe that diagnoses of psychological conditions are subjective, but that they rely on generally accepted testing. One should collect both the publications concerning such tests—which may include the Minnesota Multiphasic Personality Inventory 2, the Beck Depression Inventory, the Beck Anxiety Inventory, and others—to demonstrate that they have been the subject of testing, publication, and peer review, and are widely accepted in the field, and industry standards reference the acceptability of such tests—like the American Psychological Association's (APA's) Standards for Educational and Psychological Testing (2014) or its Testing Governance discussed on the APA's webpage.

Developing the foundation for each expert's opinion involves segregating each core opinion, and then outlining the bases for each opinion. Listing the published testing and the work related to each basis of an opinion is a good technique for locating potential *Daubert* holes in the opinions in advance. Core opinions likely will be the subject of *Daubert* challenges, unless each scientific opinion has solid, published work about each methodology employed, and each nonscientific opinion where an expert is evaluating conduct against a standard of care has published articles about standards, protocols, or best practices.

Writing the Expert Report

Putting pen to paper or fingers to keys, writing out the expert report also is important in planning for the defense of *Daubert* challenges. One should remember in advance that any *Daubert* challenge and the response to it will cite primarily to the expert report, followed closely by the expert's deposition. Therefore, how the report is crafted is critically important to how the *Daubert* response will be crafted.

One should organize all the underlying literature and testing into one of the four *Daubert* factors, and then footnote each piece of literature and testing inside the expert's report. While heavy footnoting is seen by some as a distraction to a reader, one must remember that expert reports generally are not provided to the jury at trial; hence, they really are to be utilized only by the attorneys attacking or defending the expert, and by the judge who is deciding whether to permit that expert to testify. In writing a report, an expert should recall the need to tie underlying data or published references directly to the opinion being offered. As Chief Justice Rehnquist wrote in *Joiner*:

> Trained experts commonly extrapolate from existing data. But nothing in either *Daubert* or the Federal Rules of Evidence requires a district court to admit opinion evidence that is connected to existing data only by the *ipse dixit* of the expert. A court may conclude that there is simply too great an analytical gap between the data and the opinion proffered.[25]

The best way to avoid such a conclusion by a trial court is to tie the opinion and the data together via ample footnoting in the expert report.

Recall that amendments to Rule 26(b)(3) extend work product protection to communications between an attorney and expert about drafts of expert reports.[26] As such, the plaintiff's lawyer can now ensure that each expert report is heavily annotated with underlying reference material, and thereby *Daubert*-proof the expert report from attack. A good expert report will be heavily outlined, with each core opinion stated intelligibly, followed by a discussion of why that opinion relies on methodologies that meet each of the four *Daubert* factors.

First, how the work giving rise to the opinion *can be independently tested* should be explained in detail. In accident reconstruction work, the particularized math and computer programs used should be set forth in detail. The hallmark of the scientific method is repeatability. In scientific work, one should explain *what* work was performed, *how* the work was performed, and *how* such work followed a methodology that has or can be tested (i.e., repeatability). In this regard, *Daubert* does not require the expert to have performed the work himself or herself; an appropriate expert report can and should rely on the published

25. *Joiner*, 522 U.S. at 146.
26. *See* Fed. R. Civ. P. 26(b)(4)(B).

work of others, as well. For instance, if a specific safety component has been tested previously by others, that previous testing should be set forth in detail in an expert report that addresses that safety component.

Second, the requirement that the methodology employed is one *subject to publication and peer review* is easier to meet than once thought. In a scientific world where a few journals controlled the thought in any field, new methodologies were more difficult to get out for general acceptance. In an Internet world, published materials seem instantly available. However, as hard as it may be to believe, just because something appears on the Internet does not make it true. Instead, one must dig deeper and ensure that the work being relied on is the product of some process involving scientific integrity, often ensured through the peer review process. The quality of the peer review is not dispositive (and often not even relevant) in a *Daubert* hearing; rather, that is a subject for cross-examination. However, ensuring that some peer review at all has occurred is the job of a plaintiff's lawyer doing his or her job on the front end. Detailing that such a peer review has occurred is the job of both the expert writing the report and the lawyer who should be editing it. Finally, there is no requirement in *Daubert* that the expert at issue have the work that they have prepared for litigation actually be published and peer reviewed; rather, the methodologies employed therein must merely have been subjected to publication by someone and peer reviewed by others.

Third, the *known or potential rate of error* should be set forth in the report. If a psychologist uses testing protocols, the underlying publications for those protocols will include a litany of statements about their accuracy. These statements should be annotated in the expert report and footnoted under a discussion of the test itself. If crush stiffness data is utilized by an accident reconstructionist, an extensive discussion about the crash testing of the vehicle giving rise to the crush stiffness data itself should be included. The mere repeatability of crash testing gives rise to the conclusion that the crush achieved can and will be replicated. If the crush achieved across different crash tests is different, the difference between the two tests is in effect "the rate of error." However, math is math, and it will yield the same result over and over again. If an expert is applying conservation of momentum or conservation of energy calculations, one should merely supply the underlying publications as the "how to" guide for that methodology. The fact that a methodology has been proven foolproof over decades and the overwhelming quantity of experiential results has shown it to be infallible does not mean it does not meet this *Daubert* factor. Instead, it merely lacks error; that means the rate of error is zero, the most reliable of all methodologies.

Fourth, the requirement of *general acceptance* has been applied since *Frye* in 1923, and nothing in *Daubert* eliminates its importance. Thus, the expert who is writing a report needs to take special care to provide literature that contains statements of how widespread the use of the methodology is. Use of an industry safety standard should include footnoted references to its use by others elsewhere outside of litigation. Nonjudicial uses of the technique or methodology at issue is an important hallmark of general acceptance. Thus, use of the method in the scholastic community is important. Acceptance by industry of such a technique is a call sign for general acceptance, so references to industry standards, best practices, or company policies that employ the technique should be laid forth in detail in the report.

Fifth, an expert report should include all other reasons believed to support the reliability of the methodology employed. In *Daubert*, the Court cautioned that the four "general observations" were not "a definitive checklist or test."[27] In *Kumho*, the Court later observed that the test of reliability is "flexible," that "*Daubert*'s list of specific factors neither necessarily nor exclusively applies to all experts or in every case,"[28] and that "*Daubert* should be applied flexibly, that its four factors were simply illustrative, and that other factors could argue in favor of admissibility."[29] If there are other reasons a methodology is believed to be reliable, the report should set forth those other reasons, with ample documentary support footnoted.

Finally, a contention that a methodology employed is reliable is best buttressed by prior court decisions so holding. As described earlier, all court decisions that hold the methodologies of the expert in question to be reliable, in addition to acceptance of the reliability of the methodologies by others in the same field of inquiry, should be listed and annotated in the expert report.

The Expert's Deposition

The expert's deposition is the most important day in the defense of an inevitable *Daubert* challenge. In that regard, one of the chief reasons that a detailed report with full and complete annotations to source materials is helpful is that it tends to direct the questioner to the very data and source materials that are supportive of the given opinion. As such, the preparation of the expert's file for deposition is critically significant. Seven steps should be taken before the deposition begins, during the deposition itself, and after the testimony concludes.

First, the expert's report should be placed in a notebook, with numbered dividers behind it separating the footnoted source material. For ease of use, each divider should have a highlighted excerpt of the particular reference made in each numbered footnote. This is impressive to a court evaluating the expert's reliability, and it tends to direct the attention of the opposing attorney to references that help the cause. It also serves as a valuable crutch for an expert under the duress of questioning during a deposition—a veritable three-dimensional cheat sheet available to the expert, almost like an open-book exam in college. The task in deposition is not merely what the expert can recite from his or her memory, but also what can be called up by easy reference to a well-designed deposition notebook strategically placed directly in front of the witness.

Second, pre-marking the expert's file is a clever way to direct the flow of the deposition. Whether it be use of numbered dividers, or an ostensible reply to a subpoena duces tecum via prenumbered documents produced at deposition, pre-marking or prenumbering the

27. *Daubert*, 508 U.S. at 593.
28. *Kumho*, 526 U.S. at 141.
29. *Id.* at 137.

produced expert's file inevitably causes the opposing questioner to follow that sequence in their questioning. As such, strategically numbering the exhibits while following the *Daubert* framework often leads to a deposition transcript that tracks the four *Daubert* factors. This makes developing an excellent *Daubert* response much easier.

Third, providing an impressive quantum of source materials in a report and thereafter at deposition in response to a subpoena duces tecum inevitably causes the opposing questioner to focus on materials and issues the plaintiff wants to focus on, rather than merely focusing on defensive issues. With Rule 30(d)(1) of the Federal Rules of Civil Procedure limiting the duration of an expert's deposition to one seven-hour day absent a stipulation or court order, taking the time to collect and present at deposition a wealth of source materials that support the expert's methodologies is strategically advantageous as well.

Fourth, before the deposition begins (indeed, well before the report itself is even written), experts should become well-versed in the law of *Daubert*. I have had scientists, professors, and engineers appear in my office nonplussed about the issue—"We've heard of that case, but that's not really something we've focused on." Such an expert needs to become an expert in *Daubert* before becoming an expert for you. A thorough prep session about why each of the *Daubert* factors has been met by the expert is a must. A 3″ × 5″ index card should be placed in front of the expert during practice sessions so his or her practice answers are so couched in terms of "testing," "publication," "peer review," "rate of error," and "general acceptance," that the expert is now as comfortable referencing those phrases as he or she is reciting the names of their own children or grandchildren. A good lawyer must indoctrinate the expert that all the work, effort, and dollars will have been a complete waste of time and resources if the team is collectively unable to get that expert before the jury without first tripping over the *Daubert* hurdle before getting to run through the tape at the finish line.

Fifth, unless the rule has formally been invoked on the record, coffee, lunch, and bathroom breaks during a seven-hour deposition should be strategically utilized to remind the expert of the *Daubert* factors. Deposition breaks inevitably are followed by the seemingly clever questioning about what happened during the break: "Did you talk to the plaintiff's lawyer? What did she tell you?" Instead of the typical lie, "She told me, 'just tell the truth,'" the expert should be coached to say, "She told me to explain to you in detail the meanings of 'testing,' 'publication,' 'peer review,' 'rate of error,' and 'general acceptance.'" In this vein, a lawyer should take every chance she gets to remind her expert to focus on *Daubert*.

Sixth, when the defense lawyer finishes questioning a plaintiff's expert, the biggest waste of money is for the plaintiff's lawyer to say, "We'll reserve our questions until the time of trial." Every plaintiff's expert deposition should end with the plaintiff's lawyer taking his or her expert on direct examination and obtaining testimony about five issues: "testing," "publication," "peer review," "rate of error," and "general acceptance." This typically can be done in twenty to thirty minutes, it provides sworn testimony that can be provided to the court with a response to the *Daubert* motion, and allows the plaintiff's lawyer to point out to the judge that such testimony concerning *Daubert* was given under oath, while subject to cross-examination. The fact that it is then 6:00 p.m. and the defense lawyer wants to go catch his plane is irrelevant; the defense had the opportunity to question the witness on

Daubert issues. Thus, if the plaintiff's lawyer is thereafter trying to convince a trial judge to not require the needless expenditure of money by forcing a plaintiff to pay to bring her expert to court for pretrial *Daubert* hearings, prior sworn deposition testimony explaining in detail the methodologies employed, and why the *Daubert* factors were met, is far more persuasive than merely citing to a report and providing a subsequent affidavit that is not subject to cross-examination.

Seventh, post-deposition errata sheets are not insignificant in the defense of *Daubert* challenges. Tired lawyers seeking to end their depositions almost inevitably ask wide-open questions like, "Is there anything else you want me to know?" or "If you were me, is there any other information you have that I haven't asked you about?" Such open-ended question provide an important opportunity to buttress the answers thereto, and therefore the *Daubert* record itself, via a statement of changes on errata sheets permitted by Fed. R. Civ. P. 30(e)(1). Rule 30(e) provides the mechanism by which a deponent may review a deposition transcript and make changes to that testimony:

> (1) *Review; Statement of Changes.* On request by the deponent or a party before the deposition is completed, the deponent must be allowed 30 days after being notified by the officer that the transcript or recording is available in which:
>
> (A) to review the transcript or recording; and
>
> (B) if there are changes in form or substance, to sign a statement listing the changes and the reasons for making them.[30]

Source materials that meet the *Daubert* factors can be listed in errata sheets as long as the reasons for supplying them are timely supplied within thirty days after receiving the transcript from the court reporter.

Responding to a *Daubert* Challenge

The rules to be applied in formally responding to a *Daubert* challenge is that "less is more" and that "more is better." By that I mean, the prose of *Daubert* responses themselves should be short and to the point, but heavily annotated with computer hyperlinks to the attachments, which should be both plentiful in number and substantial in size. Before computerized filing systems, such responses and their attachment were bountiful, with their effectiveness measured by the number of inches of such attachments because courts were simply more inclined to believe some modicum of reliability must exist in a vast expanse of paper. Now, with computerized filing systems, a plethora of hyperlinks to attached documents appropriately highlighted has the same effect—the appearance of a highly organized responsive document.

Formal responses to a *Daubert* challenge should be provided directly to the judge by delivering courtesy copies to the chambers well before a hearing date. The first trick is to achieve a preliminary adjudication in your side's favor before appearing in court. The second

30. Fed. R. Civ. P. 30(e)(1) (emphasis added).

trick is to deliver a paper copy of the response, which allows one to visually achieve the perception of mass via a notebook with numerous attachments following the text of the response itself.

Lastly, any prior decisions from other courts should be provided to the court. The most effective security blanket for a judge is the comfort of seeing colleagues' previous rulings that an expert may qualify, and the expert's opinions reflected sufficient reliability to merit consideration by a jury at trial. In this vein, any judge's favorite opinions are appellate opinions that affirm her own rulings, or the prior opinions written by the judge herself. There is no better way to convince the judge why a *Daubert* motion should be denied than to cite prior decisions where the judge denied prior similar motions.

In conclusion, the ability to navigate experts through the labyrinth of risk that the *Daubert* process presents requires great care, much thought, and significant effort. Given the dispositive nature of a *Daubert* defeat, a plaintiff's lawyer must treat *Daubert* every bit as important as the trial itself. After all, when a *Daubert* motion is lost, there is often no trial at all.

14
DAUBERT CHALLENGES: CLOSING THE EXPERT GATE
The Defense Perspective

Few cases go to trial that do not involve some expert testimony. If a plaintiff requires expert testimony to carry the evidentiary burden for its causes of action, a successful challenge to the expert's credentials or the reliability of the expert's methodology may have a dispositive effect on the case. A case literally can turn on a successful expert challenge.

Both federal courts and state courts throughout the nation describe their function as "gatekeepers" when determining admissibility of expert testimony. Acknowledging the persuasive impact of expert testimony on a lay jury, both federal courts and state courts have developed standards by which trial judges, as gatekeepers, assess admissibility. A defense lawyer's primary objective is to make sure the gatekeeper *closes* the gate. Simply put, an effective defense strategy should always consider a challenge of the plaintiff's experts.

Defining Standards for Admissibility

In federal practice, the admissibility of expert testimony falls within the scope of Rule 702 and Rule 703 of the Federal Rules of Evidence. Many states have adopted Rule 702 and Rule 703 carte blanche and, as a result, look to federal courts for guidance. Rule 702 relates to the credentials of the expert and the relevance of the expert testimony. Rule 703 deals with the reliability of the method used by the expert to support the expert opinion.

The most well-known case that addresses admissibility of expert testimony is the U.S. Supreme Court's decision in *Daubert v. Merrill Dow Pharmaceuticals.*[1] The standards enunciated in *Daubert* now serve as the general yardstick for determining admissibility in what are colloquially known as "*Daubert* challenges." Many states have developed permutations of these standards, while other states apply a different standard that is derived

1. 509 U.S. 579 (1993).

from an earlier decision in *Frye v. United States*.[2] Moreover, many state courts and all federal courts have developed evolved guidelines when addressing expert testimony that involves either "soft science" or nonscientific expert testimony. There are numerous instances when an expert may not be a scientist, but is still an expert in a particular field or industry.

Key Elements of the Frye *Standard*

The *Frye* standard derives from a case that dealt with the admissibility of lie detector test results. In *Frye*, the court determined that expert testimony was not admissible because it could not be established that lie detector results were based on a method "sufficiently established and accepted." The court stated:

> While the courts will go a long way in admitting expert testimony deduced from a well-recognized principle or discovery, the deduction made must be sufficiently established to have gained general acceptance in the particular field in which it belongs.[3]

Key Elements of the Daubert *Standard*

The Supreme Court's decision in *Daubert* rejected the one-prong test in *Frye*, and held that the *Frye* standard was incompatible with Fed. R. Evid. 702 and Fed. R. Evid. 402. The holding in *Daubert* requires the trial court to exercise a "gatekeeping" function when reviewing both the reliability *and* the relevance of expert opinions. The concept of relevance is incorporated into Rule 702 to the extent that admissibility is determined, in part, by an examination of whether the expert's testimony will help the trier of fact understand the evidence or determine a fact in issue.

The factors set forth in *Daubert* include: (1) whether the expert's theory or technique has been tested; (2) whether the theory or technique has been subjected to peer review; (3) the known or potential rate of error governing the theory or technique; and (4) whether there is a scientific community where the theory or technique is accepted.[4] Since the *Daubert* decision in 1993, there have been two subsequent opinions issued by the U.S. Supreme Court that clarify or expand *Daubert*'s reach and application. The first case was *General Electric Co. v. Joiner*.[5] The second case was *Kumho Tire Co. v. Carmichael*.[6]

In *Joiner*, the Supreme Court reinforced the trial court's gatekeeping function, and held that a trial court's decision regarding expert admissibility would be reviewed on appeal under an "abuse of discretion" standard—regardless of whether the court's decision was to admit or exclude the testimony.[7] Thus, the Court made clear that *Daubert* does not create a "redline" standard, but rather, standards that are weighed within the discretion of the trial court. The *Joiner* court also confirmed that Fed. R. Evid. 702 imposes a special obligation

---

2. 293 F. 1013 (D.C. Cir. 1923)
3. *Frye*, 293 F. at 1014 (D.C. Cir. 1923).
4. *Daubert v. Merrill Dow Pharm.*, 509 U.S. 579 (1993).
5. 522 U.S. 136 (1997).
6. 526 U.S. 137 (1999).
7. *Joiner*, 522 U.S. at 142 ("A court of appeals applying 'abuse-of-discretion' review to such rulings may not categorically distinguish between rulings allowing expert testimony and rulings disallowing it.").

upon a trial judge to "ensure that any and all scientific testimony . . . is not only relevant, but reliable."[8]

In *Kumho Tire*, the Supreme Court made clear that the trial court's gatekeeping function extends beyond purely "scientific evidence," and that the standards underlying *Daubert* apply to nonscientists who otherwise have specialized skills or knowledge. This is especially important because many areas that require expertise do not fit cleanly within the multiple factors used as guidelines in *Daubert*. Despite being decided over twenty years ago, *Kumho Tire* is the last and most significant update to what some call the "Daubert trilogy" (along with *Daubert* and *Joiner*) regarding expert testimony.

Prevalence of Daubert

There are forty states that have adopted either the *Daubert* guidelines in their entirety or variations of those guidelines.[9] There are seven states that adhere to the *Frye* standard, including California, Illinois, Maryland, Minnesota, New York, Pennsylvania, and Washington.[10] Four states have adopted unique approaches or hybrids of *Daubert* and *Frye*: Maine, New Jersey, North Dakota, and South Carolina.[11]

Tactical Considerations

Although there are exceptions to this general observation, most plaintiffs' lawyers do not challenge defense experts. There seems to be an underlying concern that what is "good for the goose is good for the gander." That is, challenging defense experts may invite a reciprocal challenge. There also may be a fear that the trial court will "split the baby" and give each side partial relief. This is more dangerous for a plaintiff than a defendant because the plaintiff typically carries the burden of proof.

With that said, defense lawyers should recognize that filing *Daubert* motions frequently does trigger reactionary responses. If defense lawyers believe one or more of the defense experts is essential to the defense of a case, due consideration should be given whether to pick an "expert" fight. This is particularly so if the plaintiff's expert is weak and vulnerable. Sometimes the best strategy is to not challenge, particularly if the plaintiff's expert is vulnerable on cross-examination.

---

8. *Id.* at 141 (quoting *Daubert*, 509 U.S. at 589).

9. *See generally* Christine Funk, *Daubert Versus Frye: A National Look at Expert Evidentiary Standards*, The Expert Institute (Mar. 13, 2018), https://www.theexpertinstitute.com/daubert-versus-frye-a-national-look-at-expert-evidentiary-standards/; *see also*, *In re Amendments to Fla. Evidence Code*, No. SC19-107, 2019 WL 2219714, at *1 (Fla. May 23, 2019) (Florida Supreme Court reversing precedent and approving an amendment to the Florida Evidence Code codifying Florida's new evidentiary standards according to *Daubert* as of May 23, 2019).

10. While all of these states are generally considered "Frye" states, even Frye states appear to be at least *trending* toward the *Daubert* standard, if not outright adopting *Daubert*. *See e.g. In re Amendments to Fla. Evidence Code*, No. SC19-107, 2019 WL 2219714, at *1 (Fla. May 23, 2019) (Florida officially changing standard from Frye to Daubert); *Sargon Enterprises, Inc. v. Univ. of S. Cal.*, 55 Cal. 4th 747, 772 (Cal. 2012) (California Supreme Court reaffirming California's "general acceptance" standard akin to the *Frye* standard while also urging judges to exercise discretion more closely in line with the *Daubert* standard).

11. *See, e.g.*, N.D. R. Evid. 702 (North Dakota Rule of Evidence 702. Testimony by Expert Witnesses), *State v. Hernandez*, 707 N.W.2d 449, 453 (N.D. 2005) (North Dakota Supreme Court rejecting *Frye* while declining to adopt *Daubert*).

There are, no doubt, cases where a defense lawyer is justified in not challenging the plaintiff's expert. This occurs when more strategic benefit is gained by exposing the weakness of the plaintiff's case during cross-examination in the presence of the jury. Sometimes a plaintiff's expert may be particularly vulnerable or weak, either as to theory, method, or qualification, so cross-examination is best used as a vehicle to undercut and embarrass the entirety of the plaintiff's case in the courtroom. These types of strategic decisions involve value judgments that are dictated by the unique circumstances of each case, and these types of tactical decisions should include due consideration of relevant appellate standards.

Allowing a plaintiff's expert to take the stand, even if the proffered testimony is particularly weak, may undercut an appellate point relating to "no evidence" on specific elements of a plaintiff's claim. If a plaintiff's expert testimony is admitted, there may be at least *some* evidence to support an unfavorable verdict. Thus, these types of tactical decisions should be made in the context of appellate review standards in the relevant jurisdiction.

Another tactical decision involves the timing of expert challenges. Although many courts impose scheduling orders with pretrial deadlines, including expert challenge deadlines, there is no reason why expert challenges cannot be prosecuted during the earlier stages of a case. Doing so may facilitate settlement discussions, and also may facilitate summary judgment motions. Filing an aggressive, well-reasoned expert challenge is excellent leverage to promote a favorable settlement. Furthermore, if a plaintiff is dependent upon an expert's opinion to support a particular element of its cause of action, striking or limiting the scope of the expert's opinion on that element may pave the way to an early summary judgment.

On the other hand, by prosecuting expert challenges during the earlier stages of a case, a court may be more willing to grant the plaintiff leave to designate new experts if the initial challenges are successful. If there is substantial time remaining before trial, the trial court may feel inclined to grant this type of relief to the plaintiff, allowing a second bite at the *expert* apple. There is less prejudice to the defendant, who can still undertake relevant expert discovery, and even file renewed challenges. Thus, the timing of any challenge is a factor that should be considered.

Preparing for the Expert's Deposition

The first step to a successful expert challenge is to define the applicable standards. Is the governing standard *Frye*, *Daubert*, or a hybrid? Once defined, the defense lawyer should investigate the opposing expert's background and the method used by the expert *before* proceeding with a deposition. The goal is to explore the expert's background to identify possible ways the expert or the expert opinion fails to satisfy the applicable admissibility standards.

Pre-deposition investigation frequently yields a trove of information that can guide deposition strategy. At a minimum, defense lawyers should consider the following types of inquiries:

- Computer research to identify other expert challenges in other cases that involved the same expert; the opposing expert may have been successfully challenged in other cases on the same or similar issues.

- Internet research of prior publications or articles authored or co-authored by the opposing expert on the same or similar issues. The expert may have provided inconsistent statements in published articles. Equally important, the absence of published articles is evidence that falls squarely within the criteria enumerated in *Daubert*.
- Internet research regarding criticisms of the opposing expert or the expert's method. Members of the scientific community frequently review the published work of other experts and critique the work product or the method of their colleagues. This type of research may lead to the conclusion that the expert's selected method is not generally accepted in the relevant expert community.
- Contacting defense groups, such as the Defense Research Institute (DRI), to determine whether there are any depositions relating to the expert. Many such organizations maintain deposition databases that are available to its members. Again, many well-known experts may have been deposed on several prior occasions about the same or similar issues, and a review of these prior depositions is an important task that can yield valuable information.
- Using defense experts as a resource to prepare for a deposition of the opposing expert. Defense lawyers should consult their retained consulting experts about how and why the plaintiff's expert is vulnerable as to either methodology, qualifications, or both. Strategies should be explored for bringing these vulnerabilities to light.
- Computer research of the trial court and the relevant appellate court regarding successful expert challenges. Prior published opinions should be mined for insights into how the trial court and appellate court view expert challenges, and how expert challenges can be enhanced to improve the likelihood of success.

Taking the Expert's Deposition

Defense lawyers should depose a plaintiff's expert with four essential goals. The first is to limit the witness's options at trial. That is, the defense lawyer should lock in the scope of the expert's opinions so new and different opinions are not offered at trial. The defense lawyer should specifically seek to confirm that there is no additional work the expert intends to undertake, and no additional opinions the expert intends to offer at trial. The goal is to avoid surprise by defining the universe of the opposing expert's possible testimony and the bases for the expert's opinions.

A second goal is to seek common ground and identify concessions or factual admissions the expert may be willing to make that are helpful to the defense case. These concessions may involve factual concessions, concessions on factual assumptions, or concessions on methodology.

A third goal is to create a basis for effective impeachment during cross-examination. Sometimes the best practice is to *not* ask the opposing expert questions that telegraph defense strategy. As a general rule, trial lawyers should not telegraph key cross-examination strategies, but should preserve these strategies so the opposing expert (and opposing counsel) are not fully educated before trial. Otherwise, the opposition will try to correct any infirmities or vulnerabilities before trial. Holding the cards closer to the chest is sometimes a better practice.

A fourth strategy is to generate a foundation for an effective expert challenge. Depending on whether the *Frye* standard, the *Daubert* standard, or some hybrid standard applies, defense lawyers should develop specific questions that are calculated to address each of the elements needed to support an effective challenge in their jurisdiction. Even if an expert challenge is not successful, exploring *Daubert*-like topics at deposition provides an excellent basis for cross-examination at trial. Here are some examples:

- Establish the absence of any publications or articles about the expert's method or theory.
- Establish the absence of any peer-reviewed articles authored by the expert describing the expert's method or theory.
- Establish that the expert has never previously testified about the theory or the method in any prior court of law.
- Establish that the witness does not specialize in a particular field, but is a generalist; for example, the witness has no specific medical disciplines in a medical malpractice case and has no specific legal specialties in a legal malpractice case.
- Establish that the expert has no hands-on, practical experience or expertise in the relevant industry; for example, the witness has never designed products similar to the products at issue; the witness has never been employed by a company that manufactured products similar to the products at issue; the witness does not see patients in a clinical setting.
- Establish that the expert has not performed any prior testing similar to the tests employed and, therefore, is not capable of determining the potential rate of error. Or, you could examine the witness on the high rate of error.
- Seek concessions from the expert that his or her opinions do not require special expertise or skill, but are simply deductions from facts. That is, establish that the expert's testimony relies exclusively on facts that are readily understood or deduced by a jury and, therefore, is not relevant under Fed. R. Evid. 702.
- Establish that the expert's opinions are based on subjective assessments, and not objective, empirical data; therefore, the opinions cannot be tested, which makes the opinions ad hoc and not reliable. The goal here is to establish that the opinions are nothing more than the expert's *ipse dixit*—it is because the experts say it is.
- Establish the expert's failure to review important documents or review important depositions, thereby undercutting the reliability of the opinions.
- Establish the expert's failure to conduct independent research and analysis, and that the witness was provided data at the discretion of and as determined by plaintiff's counsel, thereby rendering the opinions less than objective.
- Establish that the expert was retained at the last minute and did not have sufficient time to conduct a meaningful analysis of important data.
- Establish that the expert was previously excluded by a court; explore the details of the court's decision.

- Identify all cases where the expert previously provided a deposition or trial testimony about similar issues, and specifically identify the cause number, jurisdiction, and the parties' respective counsel. Then, after the deposition, obtain copies of all relevant depositions to mine for impeachment points.

"Daubert-*Proofing*" *Defense Experts*

Defense lawyers should assume they may trigger a reactionary response if they file expert challenges. Thus, the best practice is to assume your experts will be challenged and, accordingly, take steps to "*Daubert*-proof" your expert witnesses.

When retaining an expert, your first inquiry is whether the proposed expert has special skills and expertise relevant to the issue. This should not be limited only to formal education because general experience and training also are important. For example, a shade tree mechanic with a high school education may be more qualified than a doctoral candidate to discuss the mechanisms of the internal combustion engine. The goal here is to determine whether an issue requires expert testimony to help a jury or the trial court better understand the case, and whether the proposed expert has the necessary credentials to do so.

Your second inquiry is whether the proposed expert has been successfully challenged in prior cases. It is critical to always determine whether a potential defense expert was previously excluded or had testimony limited by another court in another case. Computer research should be undertaken as part of this inquiry, and the expert should be asked these questions point-blank. If a proposed expert has been successfully challenged in the past, the expert is vulnerable. This fact certainly will be highlighted in any expert challenge that will be forthcoming.

The third step is to ensure that your expert has been provided all relevant information specific to the case. This means all relevant documents, both good and bad, favorable or unfavorable, must be provided to the expert for review and consideration. Any attempt to withhold relevant, but harmful, information from the expert will come back to haunt you and the witness many times over. It is important to give all relevant information to the expert as soon as possible and not to wait until the last minute. Undertaking a data dump immediately in advance of a disclosure deadline is a red flag because no one will reasonably believe the expert had time to review, digest, and consider voluminous evidence under a compressed schedule. The lesson here: do not wait until the last minute.

Another key point is to avoid overextension. Sometimes expert consultants are eager to please counsel and expand the scope of their involvement. There are a variety of reasons that explain this motivation. Consultants may want to please the trial lawyer because of prior associations or a hope to generate future business. But, if an expert witness is overextended, the witness becomes vulnerable. Expert witnesses should be encouraged to stay within their core expertise and not stretch the limits of their expertise. Defense lawyers should exercise control in this regard and avoid the urge to push an expert into areas where the witness's credentials or data may be lacking.

Another important step is identifying the witness's prior deposition testimony on the same or similar issues. Veteran experts likely have been deposed on multiple occasions by a variety of plaintiffs' lawyers. You should assume the opposing lawyer will do his or her homework and identify key depositions relating to your expert. While defense lawyers have access to databases like DRI, plaintiff's lawyers also have databases, such as the Association of Trial Lawyers of America, and are otherwise networked. You should know about prior depositions and whether there is any inconsistent testimony before you disclose your expert.

You should avoid written budgets that are prepared and submitted by an expert. Although your client may prefer to have a budget that provides expense control, a written budget can lead to significant issues. Expert budgets are likely discoverable in most jurisdictions and can come back to hurt you and the witness. An unfulfilled budget is a ready template for cross-examination as to what the witness did or, equally important, failed to do in connection with the intended scope of work.

Using Consulting Experts to Attack Opposing Experts

Defense lawyers should consider retaining consulting experts to evaluate the opinions and methodology of opposing experts. Appraisers can be retained to comment on the deficiencies of an opposing appraiser and the failure to conform to established appraisal standards. A medical doctor can be retained to demonstrate why the opposing expert has not undertaken a differential diagnosis in a medical malpractice case. An engineer can be retained to identify the deficiencies and flaws in the methodology of the plaintiff's design expert. A forensic accountant can be retained to address the opposing expert's failure to follow Generally Accepted Accounting Principles. The list goes on and on.

Consulting experts are a valuable resource to help frame deposition questions and strategies when deposing the opposing expert. Consulting experts also can be used to develop declarations or sworn affidavits that can accompany an expert challenge, further reinforcing the substance and force of the challenge. Depending on the jurisdiction at issue, consulting experts also can be used as live witnesses at *Daubert* hearings.

What follows is an excellent example of using a consultant to frame an attack on an opposing expert. The case involved a product liability claim arising out of a single vehicle accident that resulted in a rollover and fatal passenger ejection. A well-known college football player was riding in the rear seat of a small SUV when the driver lost control of the vehicle, went off-road and rolled over. The passenger was ejected and killed. The plaintiff's retained expert had developed a computer simulation program that could model dynamic vehicle behavior. He used this program to simulate accident sequences and, by modifying selected vehicle parameters, he allegedly could identify safer alternative designs. He then used this program to claim that if certain adjustments were made to the shock absorbers, the height of the center of gravity, and the stiffness of the front end, the SUV would not have rolled over and the fatal injuries could have been avoided.

After conferring with our consulting expert on computer modeling, and after dozens of hours reviewing data, we identified certain vehicle parameters that had been inputted incorrectly into the program. We were able to obtain concessions from the opposing expert during deposition that, if these vehicle parameters were wrong, then the simulation was wrong. Basically, *garbage in, garbage out*. We subsequently demonstrated multiple errors in the parameters, challenged the reliability of the method that supported the expert's opinions, and filed a companion summary judgment motion. The trial court addressed the expert challenge and, after sustaining our challenge, granted summary judgment. Using our consultant, we established that the plaintiff could not demonstrate a safer alternative design that would have avoided the rollover, ejection, and fatal injuries.

Beware of Failure to Daubert-*Proof Defense Experts*

Daubert-proofing defense experts is crucial. Here is a good example.

The plaintiff filed a wrongful death claim involving a propane explosion. A wife and mother died as a result of injuries suffered from a propane-fueled explosion in an adjoining duplex unit. The principal claim involved an alleged failure to provide propane detectors that would have allegedly alerted tenants on both sides of the duplex to the presence of combustible levels of propane. The defense retained a consulting expert who opined that propane-sensing devices were not always reliable in residential settings because of potential risks of false alarms and malfunction. Propane-sensing devices are typically positioned near the floor because propane is heavier than air and will pool near the floor. Accordingly, household pets may bump into the detectors, causing them to disengage or malfunction.

The defendant's consulting expert had spent years studying a variety of technical issues related to propane and had been deposed on several occasions. He had an impressive background and was well-credentialed. However, he had given a deposition approximately a year before in which the court reporter had made a typographical error, and, unfortunately, he was never provided an opportunity to correct the typo with an errata sheet. The error was substantive and inconsistent with his anticipated testimony. As such, the defense made the tactical decision that it could not use this expert. To do so would expose the witness to significant cross-examination and, in a case already fraught with emotion and potentially significant damages, could lead to a defense loss at trial. Thus, the lesson is do your homework on your own experts before it is too late.

Searching for the Expert's Achilles Heel

Defense lawyers should make it their practice to search for vulnerabilities in the opposing expert's background or methodology. In another example in which I was involved, the plaintiff retained a business valuation expert to opine that the defendant company had shareholder equity of several hundred million dollars. However, the plaintiff's expert had never been involved in valuing a company in this particular industry and admitted, during deposition, she could find no comparable closely held company with published financial statements by which to do any comparison. On the witness stand during a pretrial hearing, she further admitted she did not fully understand how the marketplace for this particular industry operated. She also conceded she did not research how pending federal legislation might impact the viability of this industry segment. Accordingly, her business valuations failed to account for several variables that could directly impact her valuation, rendering her opinion speculative and unreliable. Our expert challenge was sustained, and the expert was excluded from trial.

Keeping the Enemy (Experts) at the Gate

Lay juries frequently are impressed, if not awed, by highly credentialed experts. This becomes a real danger when the expert's "credentials" make an expert's otherwise unreliable testimony more believable. That is why it is important for defense lawyers to close the gates on experts whose methodologies are unreliable, or the data on which they rely is unreliable. A powerful example involves the silicone breast implant litigation that began in the 1990s.

The breast implant litigation was growing in the 1980s, but research was in its infancy.[12] The litigation floodgates burst open after a $7.5 million verdict in the case of *Hopkins v. Dow Corning*—and the appellate decision issued after *Daubert*.[13] Because there was a lack of scientific evidence, the plaintiff heavily relied on its three expert opinions that breast implants caused autoimmune responses.[14] Despite objections to the qualifications and methodology of the plaintiff's experts, the Ninth Circuit upheld the verdict—specifically referring to one expert's "experience as a toxicologist" and "general scientific knowledge."[15]

The effects of the ensuing litigation in the wake of the *Hopkins* verdict, and the following appellate decision, was significant—even forcing one defendant to seek bankruptcy protection. Ultimately, the science evolved and it became increasingly clear that there was insubstantial scientific evidence linking silicone implants with immune deficiencies. Indeed, the opinions of some of the experts who provided crucial testimony in *Hopkins* were excluded only a few years later.[16] But, significant damage already had been done.

This is why defense lawyers should take their expert challenges seriously—because the repercussions can be both immediate and reverberating. The defense needs to do its homework and identify the opposing expert's Achilles heel to prevent unreliable and inconclusive testimony from being admitted. Otherwise, junk science and unreliable opinion testimony may influence jury verdicts, leading to injustices.

---

12. David E. Bernstein, *The Breast Implant Fiasco*, 87 Cal. L. Rev. 457, 471-72 (1999).

13. *Hopkins v. Dow Corning*, 33 F.3d 1116 (9th Cir. 1994); *see also* Bernstein, at 488 ("*Hopkins* was among the first appellate decisions to be issued after *Daubert*.").

14. *Id.*

15. *Hopkins*, 33 F.3d at 1124-25.

16. *See, e.g., Kelley v. American Heyer-Shulte Corp.*, 957 F. Supp. 873 (W.D. Tex. 1997); *Johnson v. Baxter*, No. CV-92-07501 (N.M. Cir. Ct. Feb. 23, 1998); *Bailey v. Dow Corning Corp.*, No. 94-1199-A (Tex. Dallas Cty. Dist. Ct. Sept. 16, 1996); *see generally* David E. Bernstein, *The Breast Implant Fiasco*, 87 Cal. L. Rev. 457, 480-84 (1999) (detailing the history of post-*Hopkins* research that failed to show a connection between breast implants and auto-immune deficiencies).

15

Plaintiff's Case-In-Chief

The Plaintiff's Perspective

The plaintiff's case-in-chief, if done well, is a time when most plaintiff's verdicts are earned. Simply put, if the plaintiff is not well ahead at the end of the plaintiff's case-in-chief, all is most likely lost. Consequently, one must carefully design the plaintiff's case-in-chief while focusing on maximizing impact and momentum, and utilize a witness order that starts and finishes strong, while, for practical and logistical reasons, carefully litter the sequence with deposition excerpts. Witness examinations of the plaintiffs and expert witnesses must be adroitly planned and performed. Finally, common sense must be used by designing the evidence to appeal to the perceptive strengths of all different jurors, and by seeking to limit the need for much of the defense evidence before concluding the plaintiff's evidence.

Maximizing Impact and Momentum

The sequencing of witnesses and changing the manner in which they are called and evidence is introduced is the key to maximizing impact and momentum during the plaintiff's case-in-chief.

Sequencing Witnesses by Topical Area

For sequencing, starting strong and finishing strong is essential, as discussed in the next section of this chapter. More so than just beginning and ending with strong witnesses, however, is the need for topical grouping of witnesses by subject matter. Take one of my typical pharmaceutical defect cases, for example. Six different subject areas of testimony in pharmaceutical cases usually will include: (1) the early laboratory research, animal testing, and human clinical testing performed by the drug company before submission of data to the FDA; (2) the New Drug Application—the final materials actually submitted to the FDA seeking approval to sell the drug; (3) the post-marketing surveillance (or lack thereof) designed to pick up signals of adverse events caused by the drug once it is sold; (4) the consideration of data that shows a signal of damaging side effects occurring to those taking the drug; (5) the internal and external communications that involve the decision of whether and how to warn of such side effects, or to recall the product; and (6) the medical and epidemiological data that demonstrates that the particular drug causes the injury complained of by the plaintiff. In an MDL against a pharmaceutical company, there may be 10 million pages of documents reviewed, thousands of documents selected as deposition exhibits, and more than 100 depositions taken before trial. While the primary job is to deselect from the mass volume of evidence discovered in order to choose only the most valuable trial exhibits and testimony to show to the jury, a second task is to topically organize that evidence so the different topics are addressed in a cognizable fashion at trial. A plaintiff's lawyer trying a complex pharmaceutical case may have six experts, each addressing one of the six topical categories referenced earlier. Related depositions should be played and trial exhibits introduced in the same topical section as the expert for that respective subject. In other words, the case-in-chief must be logically divided up into different topical sections that make sense to the jury as they hear the evidence on each category of information.

Likewise, in an automotive defect case, the automotive engineer should be called after the depositions of employees of the car maker are shown to the jury; the accident reconstruction expert should be called just before or just after all the eyewitnesses to the accident are presented; the injury causation expert should be called around the time video depositions of medical providers are played; and a life care planning expert should be called close to testimony from hospital treaters and rehabilitation specialists about the treatment of the plaintiff's injuries.

This logical division by topic of the entirety of the plaintiff's proof is an important way to maximize the impact of testimony and documentary evidence.

Maintaining Momentum by Changing the Manner in Which Witnesses Are Called and Evidence Is Introduced

Confining citizen jurors to uncomfortable chairs for eight hours a day while they listen to witness testimony they may find boring is quite the challenge; doing so while asking jurors to focus their full attention on the case while they have personal issues at home and professional tasks to complete back at work is almost impossible. Consequently, in order to maintain momentum during the plaintiff's case-in-chief, it is necessary to change up the manner in which different witnesses are called, and change the mode of introduction of documentary evidence.

Within each topical section of the plaintiff's case-in-chief, the evidence should be presented via different modalities—there should be live witnesses mixed in with video-recorded deposition excerpts; you should even read the occasional short deposition excerpt into the record. Moreover, requests for admission, interrogatory answers, and evidentiary stipulations should be read into evidence. This variation of presentation mode makes the total program more diverse and interesting to the jury.

While one could argue that solely calling live witnesses is most interesting to the jury, that approach comes with considerable timing and scheduling risk for the plaintiff's lawyer designing her case-in-chief. Complex civil trials typically involve between four and eight experts on the plaintiff's side. Getting those experts' travel schedules confirmed, their hotel accommodations secured, and their testimony set for a particular date around their other cases is a Herculean logistical task. This task is made all the more difficult if the plaintiff's lawyer has pre-scheduled eight different experts for eight days in a row during the anticipated length of the plaintiff's case-in-chief, only to see the defendant's attorney exhaust a full day and a half of trial time on cross-examination of the first expert witness. With trial judges expecting the lawyers before them to have their witnesses ready with no delay permitted whatsoever, the courthouse halls often can become fully populated with witnesses waiting their turn to testify live. By topically organizing the evidence and scheduling the liberal use of video deposition excerpts on each topic, the plaintiff's lawyer can control the schedule much more effectively than if every witness is presented live. Put another way, the plaintiff's lawyer knows how long video-recorded deposition excerpts are going to take but has no way of knowing how long opposing counsel will take to conduct a cross-examination of a witness called live.

A long litany of depositions should be prepared for presentation via video excerpts. These excerpts should purposefully involve dramatic contrasts in edited lengths, so a plaintiff's lawyer has a wide spectrum of depositions available for use, depending on the time needs of the moment. When a lawyer is out of live witnesses at 4:40 p.m. in the afternoon, having a twenty-minute deposition cut available is a convenient way out of a scheduling jam; it also avoids the potential ire of the court for not having the next witness available to fill out the trial day. However, just because deposition cuts from twenty separate witnesses are available does not mean they all should be used at trial. A key deposition with a bountiful number of exhibits will always be played, but a less important deposition cut down to less than twenty minutes and containing the same useful admissions may be useful in filling out the day in the end-of-the-day timing scenario. With this litany of depositions cut to varying lengths, a plaintiff's lawyer can maintain momentum during the case-in-chief in a subtle manner otherwise unknown to the judge, the jury, and opposing counsel.

Mixing up the way documents are used also is helpful to maintain momentum. Some documents should be foreshadowed during opening statements, with key excerpts called out on PowerPoint slides, while other important documents should be blown up on hardboard demonstratives that are three feet wide and five feet tall. Other documents may be placed before the jury via video presenters known as ELMOs, which project a letter-size document on a large screen. Documents presented by ELMO can be highlighted as discussed, while others presented via computerized presentation can be called out, highlighted, boxed, and grouped together by a professional trial consultant. Documentary concepts also can be summarized in the old-school style by a lawyer writing on a large easel pad during witness examinations.

Physical evidence should be used in a variety of different ways to maintain juror interest. Three-dimensional models of accident scenes with scaled vehicle toys should be used to explain the reconstruction of accidents. Two-dimensional scaled diagrams of accident scenes with the appropriate dimensions of the vehicles drawn into the model at various time intervals before the collision can show the jury concepts of speed, available perception-reaction time, and a failure to reasonably avoid the collision. Vehicle cutaways allow human witnesses to sit in the automobile in question, and they demonstrate injury causation resulting from human interaction with the stiff structural elements of a car. Three-dimensional exhibits that show the widget in a products liability case can be "published" to the jury, so each juror can see and touch the offending product. Computer animations of accident reconstructions, drug efficacy inside the human body, and chemical reactions in petrochemical plants can assist jurors in learning the issues at hand, while three-dimensional models of complex refinery designs can illustrate how an explosion occurred. Full-scale skeletons should be used by medical doctors to explain injuries to the body, while medical equipment used during surgery, debridement, or rehabilitation efforts should be brought into the courtroom to make vivid for the jury the plaintiff's actual hospital treatment experience.

All of these different types of physical evidence should be used with a physically interactive mode of evidence presentation. The good plaintiff's lawyer should ask the court for permission for the witness to step down from the witness stand to show the jury a concept. Interactively moving cars around on scaled accident scene diagrams should occur with the exhibit strategically positioned immediately in front of the jury box. Witnesses should be asked to write concepts down on large notepads positioned on easels adjacent to the jury box. Products that failed should be held by the expert and explained while she is positioned close to the jury. For example, a defective tire that threw its tread and caused a vehicular accident should be placed immediately before the jury box, so the expert can use her own index finger to point out how the tread began to tear off the tire carcass. Members of the questioning lawyer's staff should be summoned to serve as participants and hold five different identically failed tires as part of a presentation on other similar incidents.

Dimensional points being made with expert witnesses require imaginative use of the size of the courtroom, together with a lesson on how a dimension being discussed is "as long as this courtroom" or "as far from the Judge's bench to the back of his courtroom." Lawyers should walk around different parts of the courtroom to make these very dimensional points. One excellent example of this is Joe Pesci's hilarious lawyer character in the legal comedy *My Cousin Vinny*. Pesci's character stretched a fifty-foot measuring tape across the length of an Alabama courtroom before holding up a number of his fingers to demonstrate that an elderly eyewitness couldn't possibly have seen what she testified to moments before. Preplanned movement around the courtroom with purpose is a masterful way to command the attention of the jury and maintain momentum during the plaintiff's case-in-chief.

Courtroom demonstrations in this vein are highly persuasive, but like cross-examinations that should be limited only to those questions to which the answer is known, courtroom demonstrations should be performed only when the lawyer knows exactly what is going to occur. Avoid prosecutor Christopher Darden's snafu when he compelled O.J. Simpson to try to put on a black leather glove only to be excoriated by Johnnie Cochran with the rhyming taunt, "if the glove doesn't fit, you must acquit!"

In designing the case-in-chief, an effective plaintiff's lawyer will carefully assemble a distinct combination of evidentiary presentation. This variety in the mode of documentary or tactile evidence is key to making the plaintiff's case-in-chief interesting for the jury, thereby maintaining momentum in the case.

Witness Order: Start Strong, Finish Strong!

In his article, "The Psychology of Belief: A Study of Its Emotional and Volitional Determinates," published in the *Journal of Abnormal and Social Psychology* in 1925, the New Zealand psychologist Frederick Hansen Lund postulates that matters presented first are more persuasive than matters presented subsequently. Lund's theory became known as the law of primacy, generally accepted as truth until 1954, when Harvey Cromwell published his book, *The Relative Effect on Audience Attitude of the First Versus the Second Argumentative Speech of a Series*. Cromwell put forth the opposite finding—now known as the law of recency—by suggesting that matters presented last were more persuasive than those presented earlier. Scientists have since verified both Lund's law of primacy and Cromwell's law of recency. This science of persuasion should be used in the courtroom; a good trial lawyer designs the plaintiff's case-in-chief with both rules emphasized. In other words, when outlining the case-in-chief—*Start Strong, Finish Strong!*

If there is only one golden nugget available, use it first. This is because the law of primacy is more important in a persuasive exercise that involves many days or weeks. A jury's attention span is at far greater risk of getting lost deep into a case-in-chief than right after opening statements. For this reason, the plaintiff's first witness often is most important. Moreover, in many instances, after a plaintiff's case-in-chief concludes with the pronouncement, "The Plaintiff rests," a short break for the court to hear and rule on directed verdict motions is immediately followed by the defense calling its first witness. Because the defense case often begins on the same day that the plaintiff's case ends, there is no recency effect on persuading the jury. As a result, after the trial is entirely over, most jurors will remember the first plaintiff's witness but not the last one, and this is merely because the last one got lost in the shuffle of the beginning of the defense's case because it took place on the same day. So, what are the considerations of choosing the all-important first witness?

In deciding how to start the case-in-chief, one must decide on an overriding purpose for the first witness. There is no one answer on what the primary purpose of the first witness should be; indeed, that purpose will be different depending on the evidence available in a case. Nonetheless, generally, there are at least six sometimes conflicting purposes to consider in deciding who the first witness should be: First, *start with captivation*. Who is the witness that just blows the defendant out of the water? Is it an eyewitness recounting the bangs of a crash, blood flowing, loud screams, the anguished movement coming with physical pain, and the gory details of what a physical wound looked like? Second, *start with brilliance*. Is it an expert so solid that her mere intelligence will inexorably leave the defense forever behind in this race for justice, never to catch up with the lead the plaintiff has earned? Third, *start with live confrontation*. Is it the defense's own witness, who will be viciously cross-examined by the plaintiff's lawyer and unable to justify the tortious actions of the defendant in front of the jury? Fourth, *start with safety*. Is it merely to set the stage with an innocuous third-party eyewitness who will do no harm to the plaintiff's case if questioned by a skilled defense lawyer? Fifth, *start with a sure thing*. Is it a defense witness called by deposition, with innumerable admissions, and therefore unable to be undone by even the canniest of defense lawyers present at trial? Sixth, *start with emotion*. Is it the plaintiff, with powerful stories of a loving relationship cut short by a death caused by the defendant's tortious conduct? Regardless of the different considerations available, start with a singular goal or purpose. Among others, some primary goals are listed next.

Start with Captivation

Any good movie, book, or story grabs the audience in the first scene. Much like an angler's hook grabbing a fish, a good case-in-chief should immediately captivate the jury, effectively hooking them on the plaintiff's case and rendering them unable to detach themselves from the exercise until the case-in-chief is over. How can you hook the jury immediately with the first witness? Captivate them.

The goal of captivation is met by prosecutors in a criminal case by using the first witness to take the jury through the evidence gathered at the crime scene. In many criminal trials, the gruesome photographs of the autopsy or blood-spattered crime scene do not meaningfully advance the guilt case against the defendant one bit. However, the captivation of the jury that's achieved by doing so makes this a favored technique of criminal prosecutors. Whether in a criminal or a civil case, however, captivation does not wait to set the stage; rather, it barges in rudely and stuns all who are watching with little to no context whatsoever. It can be an eyewitness who did not see the truck hit the back of the car, but she heard it from just off the highway while filling up at a nearby gas station. Then, she ran to the scene and saw the awful anguish of painful screams and cries for help as a dying man who can no longer swallow emits the loud, irregular gurgling of secretions known as "the death rattle" or the agonal respirations that persist for several minutes after his heart stops beating. It can be the firefighter who pulled a six-year-old girl from a burning home, recounting her horrific screams of terror as she wails with arms stretched toward the conflagration, begging for her mother, who expired in the flames. Or the testimony of a rehabilitation specialist detailing how a highly functional lawyer who sustained a brain injury in an accident suffered catastrophic intellectual impairment, unable to talk, unable to feed himself, unable to control his bowel and bladder, unable to groom himself, and unable to even emotionally process life's daily stimuli.

Achieving the goal of captivation with the first witness usually involves painting a picture of the plaintiff before and after they encountered the defendant's tortious actions in the most compelling manner possible. This visual image described by the first witness should be vivid, causing the jury to immediately understand that the case it will evaluate is a highly compelling one, and certainly worthy of their sacrifice of personal time while serving as jurors. The goal of captivation is an especially important one because it transforms most jurors from regular people, highly pissed off that their daily schedule has been interrupted, into highly motivated citizen-servants who are quickly motivated to do their duty well. Experienced trial lawyers can uniformly describe the transformation in the affect and body language of disinterested jurors, who initially lean back in their chair while looking only up at the ceiling of the courtroom with a scowl on their face, into captivated jurors with serious, attentive facial expressions, who lean forward in their seats with attentive eye contact while writing detailed notes about what they are hearing. If securing this transformation of the jurors' attitudes is the goal, the good plaintiff's lawyer must choose that singular compelling witness account that will best achieve the goal of captivating jurors during the very first sworn testimony in the case.

Start with Brilliance

While the Declaration of Independence proclaims that "all men are created equal," in a courtroom, nothing could be further from the truth. Some witnesses are outstanding, while others are train wrecks; some will almost single-handedly win a case, while others are likely to lose it all by themselves. In choosing how to design a case-in-chief, outstanding witnesses should go first and last (complying with the law of primacy and the law of recency), while mediocre witnesses are sprinkled throughout the middle, safely encapsulated between deposition testimonies that can obscure any damage they may cause. With respect to choosing how to begin the case-in-chief, one must consider starting with brilliance.

Good lawyers focus-group the discovery they have secured in order to get a preview of the impact of various witnesses' testimony on juror attitudes. This focus group data should be used to decide how to start and end the case-in-chief. If fact witness evaluations consistently rate one witness above all others in terms of excellence or persuasive impact, the plaintiff's lawyer should seriously consider beginning their case-in-chief with that witness. Likewise, complex cases typically involve multiple experts who need to testify to provide the evidence necessary to get past a directed verdict. Long before the trial begins, the plaintiff's lawyer has watched each expert witness in deposition and has had the chance to evaluate and rank the testifying skill of each expert. Those who ably demonstrated the impressiveness of their background and qualifications and the power of their conclusions by fending off with ease hostile questioning during deposition should be considered as the first witness in the case. The second most impressive expert witness should go last, near the time for the plaintiffs to rest their case. Conversely, an expert who is retained to provide the magic language to establish some scintilla of evidence that supports an element of proof required by law, but who did not perform particularly well in deposition, might find himself lost in the murky middle of other far superior witnesses. Ultimately, experts who are not required to meet an element of proof and who otherwise provide useful but tertiary information may find themselves on the cutting room floor after performing poorly at deposition.

When ranking the skill of one's witnesses, the plaintiff's lawyer should strongly consider starting the case-in-chief with one goal in mind—*start with brilliance*. Who is that one fact witness or expert who no doubt will give the plaintiff the lead? Who is that one person whose brilliance provides the plaintiff's lawyer with the comfort of Linus's security blanket in Charles Schulz's *Peanuts*? That person, together with the brilliance they bring, should be considered for the role of the first witness.

Start with Live Confrontation

Most jurors' preconceived ideas about trials come from watching television shows or movies. Older jurors recall with fondness the powerful gotcha moments secured by Perry Mason. Middle-aged jurors recall my friend F. Lee Bailey's powerful confrontation of the racist Los Angeles police officer Mark Fuhrman during the O.J. Simpson trial. Younger jurors are limited to the forty-second cross-examinations they see in short crime series on streaming TV. Regardless of the length of cross-examinations to which our jurors have been exposed, the fact is that they are exposed to them in the first place because of the power of confrontation. Starting a case-in-chief with confrontation is best achieved with cross-examination. But how do plaintiff's lawyers cross-examine their own witnesses? The answer is, by calling the other side during the plaintiff's case-in-chief.

In "calling the other side," there are a number of choices available to the skilled plaintiff's lawyer. In many jurisdictions, the defense is required to have a corporate representative at trial. In courtrooms where it is not required, many defendants bring a corporate representative anyway, for fear of being taken to task for not showing sufficient interest in the case at hand. With general personal jurisdiction law constricted by the Supreme Court to states where the defendant is "essentially at home," many product liability cases will be tried in a state where the defendant's corporate headquarters are located. With that convenience for the defendant comes the inconvenience of its corporate witnesses being within the subpoena power of a trial court. In many cases, defendants hire local experts from the very jurisdiction where the trial is to take place. Such defense experts are subject to the subpoena power of the court and can be called as the plaintiff's first witness to achieve the benefits of confrontation.

In sum, in most trials, a corporate representative of the defendant or an expert hired by the defendant is available to be cross-examined as the first witness by a lawyer beginning his or her case-in-chief.

The fireworks that come with a plaintiff's lawyer cross-examining a corporate representative of the defendant is truly a sight to behold. No juror has been in court long enough to lose interest in the process yet. The law of primacy tells us that the first witness is the most important one, and the temerity of a lawyer for the plaintiff calling to the stand the defendant's own representative is the height of chutzpah—one that brings both a limitless upside and audacious risk. As to the upside, key admissions can be garnered right out of the box; admiration for the plaintiff's lawyer is earned at the same time disgust with the defendant is achieved. As to downside risk, if the confrontation with the defendant is lost on first base, so is the plaintiff's trial. Richard Nixon said (presumably before Watergate blew up his presidency), "If you take no risks, you will suffer no defeats; but, if you take no risks, you win no victories."[1] Nonetheless, the risks must be measured against the upside of a live cross-examination right out of the box. The risk of cross-examining the corporate representative first comes with massive upsides in a solid case of liability, and with massive risk if the plaintiff's lawyer is trying to make silk out of a sow's ear, which is Texan for trying to make

1. Jim Byron, *The Quotable Richard Nixon*, Richard Nixon Foundation (Apr. 25, 2011), https://www.nixonfoundation.org/2011/04/the-quotable-richard-nixon/.

a good trial case out of a bad lawsuit. As Ralph Waldo Emerson wrote, "When you strike at a king, you must kill him."[2] The same is true with respect to the corporate representative; a plaintiff's lawyer with the guts to call the defendant's corporate representative as the first witness must kill that witness, *or else*. Overall, however, this is a risk I like to take, and most of my trials begin with me calling the defendant's corporate representative as my first witness.

Another advantage of calling the defendant's corporate representative first is that it usually results in a cross-examination of a witness who is not fully prepared for the exercise. Initially, during jury selection, the defense lawyer will almost inexorably introduce their corporate representative to the venire panel, usually with the gratuitous promise that "Witness 'X' will be here with us during the entire trial; that is how important this case is to corporation 'Y.'" Witness "X" is now committed to be present at the trial. Next, in most trials, the parties are required to disclose their witnesses for the following day by 6 p.m., and they allocate no more than half a day for all of the opening statements. As a scheduling matter, this means that the plaintiff's lawyer must disclose his first witness at the same time his opponent is scurrying to prepare his opening statement for the next morning. With an opening statement being finalized, no lawyer has the ability to fully prepare a corporate representative they have only just met before voir dire. The consequence of this scheduling quagmire is that the plaintiff's lawyer gets first crack at the corporate representative, well before the corporation's lawyer can spend days incessantly coaching the witness. This dilutes the potential effectiveness of the witness's testimony in the plaintiff's favor.

Finally, admissions gained from the corporate representative are binding on the corporation itself. Such admissions should be usable in the examinations of future witnesses, including other employees of the defendant, as Rule 705 facts or data to be discussed with plaintiff's own expert, or on the cross-examination of the defendant's experts. By calling the corporate representative first, the domino effect of the admissions become potentially exponential as those admissions are used over and over again with subsequent witnesses.

Start with a Sure Thing

Great defense lawyers have the singular talent of taking the plaintiff's first witness during their case-in-chief and transforming them into a vehicle for communicating the defense's own trial themes. If a plaintiff's lawyer is about to do battle with a defense lawyer with this skill, great care should be exercised to deny a worthy opponent the opportunity to make progress during the plaintiff's case-in-chief. In other words, start with a sure thing, and attempt to deny your opponent the ability to even chip away at that one sure thing.

When I was living and practicing in Corpus Christi, Texas, from 1990 until 2006, my law firms litigated for the plaintiff's side in most of the significant cases in the area. One defense lawyer ended up defending most of them—Darrell Barger. Barger and I both were trained by trying cases with and against Corpus Christi legal giants Guy Allison, Bill Edwards, and David Perry. We both learned from them and others many tricks of the trial lawyer trade, along

2. Goodreads, https://www.goodreads.com/quotes/385864-when-you-strike-at-a-king-you-must-kill-him (last visited Mar. 14, 2020).

with great courtroom techniques to emulate in the future. Unfortunately, Barger became so good that he could defend the indefensible. He could make what was white appear to be black, what was bad appear good, and make it seem like the emperor indeed did have his invisible clothes on. A trial against Barger was, and is still, often an exercise in frustration, with me watching my careful preparation of an excellent lawsuit be corroded by his charm, quickly eroded by his skill, and eventually destroyed by decades of wily experience defending evil corporations in the courtroom.

With this backdrop, I once had an refinery explosion case being defended by Barger's law firm. The one and only advantage of litigating against Barger's firm is that he is always in trial, so I often may enjoy the solitude of conducting discovery without him. I could take depositions defended by the mere humans in his firm while their boss was in a courtroom, trying a case somewhere else. In Texas, such deposition testimony is admissible, regardless of the availability of the witness. Thus, taking a deposition in Texas does not merely involve discovery; it instead involves skillful lawyers conducting their trial direct and cross-examinations in the first instance, so that video recordings of that testimony may be played before the jury. The discovery in my refinery case came together wonderfully, with my depositions of low-level employees convincingly demonstrating their intolerable mistakes, and those of high-level members of corporate management being forced to admit that such mistakes were not the result of mere negligence, but rather the consequence of the gross negligence of the leaders of the corporation starving its refineries of the safety dollars needed for them to operate safely. At the end of the discovery period, thirty-five depositions I had taken yielded around twenty depositions that were pure gold. Even better, the young associate in Barger's firm who had defended these depositions had not asked a single question, ending each deposition merely with "we'll reserve our questions until the time of trial." As a result, with twenty depositions in the can, I had a sure thing in the form of countless admissions by corporate witnesses. Barger had no ability to undo these admissions as long as I chose to play the deposition excerpts rather than call those witnesses live at trial. I had the ability to put on my entire liability case-in-chief with Darrell Barger pinned to his seat. Choosing solely to start with a sure thing, I began my case-in-chief proving liability only with depositions and proving damages with live witnesses. While Barger ultimately won the case on appeal, my trial court victory was the result of my sound choice to start with a sure thing.

Start with Safety

Because the first witness is the one most likely to be remembered by the jury, safety is much more important than the temptation to take risks at that time.

Start with safety. Nelle Harper Lee's Scout Finch in *To Kill a Mockingbird* relayed sage advice she learned from her father: "Never, never, never, on cross-examination ask a witness a question you don't already know the answer to, was a tenet I absorbed with my babyfood."[3] A corollary of Harper Lee's advice with respect to a plaintiff's first witness would be,

3. Goodreads, https://www.goodreads.com/quotes/993974-never-never-never-on-cross-examination-ask-a-witness-a-question (last visited Mar. 14, 2020).

"never, never, never call a person as the first witness if you don't know precisely what they are going to say." Don't guess. A first witness should be one who is thoroughly pinned down in deposition so the version of the facts to be first heard by the jury is a version absolutely known in advance.

Moreover, if there is any risk whatsoever that the first witness may be compromised on cross-examination, that witness should be testifying only about a nonessential issue in the trial, one called solely to set the stage for future witnesses. For example, if the defendant trucking company has admitted the issue of speeding in a truck wreck case because the data from its tractor-trailer's black box revealed its driver was traveling 85 mph in a 65 mph zone, there is little to no risk calling as the first witness an eyewitness who testifies that she saw the truck driving way too fast prior to the collision. Conversely, if the black box shows the driver was traveling at or under the speed limit, there is little be gained by calling the same witness first, because that testimony will be undermined by a cross-examination or subsequent testimony about the conclusive black box data. Similarly, an eyewitness called first to testify that a furniture van failed to brake before hitting a vehicle in an intersection is valuable when the same-day accident scene photographs show no brake marks on the pavement immediately prior to the location of impact. However, if scene photographs document eighty feet of brake marks prior to a gouge in the road evidencing the location of impact, the decision to call an eyewitness who is demonstrably in error would be a poor choice as a first witness.

When the goal is a safe first witness, a good plaintiff's lawyer should remember the medical axiom known as the Hippocratic oath—"First do no harm."

Start with Emotion

In a personal injury case, many lawyers choose to call their injured client first; in a wrongful death case, many choose to call the grieving widow first; in a commercial case, the victim who suffered the loss of a business as a result of financial malfeasance. Regardless of the type of case, the reason for these choices is the same—*emotion*. Ultimately, any lawsuit for money damages is an exercise in attempting to compensate for a loss. Why not, then, begin the evidence by laying out the loss that was sustained, and doing so first up, and with powerful emotion?

The answer to this question depends, in my view, on the strength of the liability case itself. If the liability case is powerful, appealing to left-brain jurors' desire for facts, logic, sequencing, and linear thinking seems the way to go. On the other hand, if the case is stronger on damages than liability, then right-brain jurors' appetite for feelings, imagination, intuition, and holistic thinking may compel a first-witness appeal to *emotion*. In a case where the physically injured plaintiff or the grieving widow is also an eyewitness to a case that has powerfully strong liability facts, calling that person as a first witness becomes a no-brainer because the benefits of *emotion* are coupled with the security of adding, with little risk, to the liability picture. When calling a high-emotion witness first brings with it a risk that the liability case may be compromised early in the case-in-chief, that witness should be deferred until later, when less potential damage on cross-examination is possible.

Lastly, while less important than starting strong, finishing one's case-in-chief with an important witness *is* important. Reserving for the end of the plaintiff's case-in-chief a powerful deposition excerpt or a brilliant expert testifying live is a good way to ensure that the plaintiff rests with a bang, rather than a whimper.

Using Depositions

Many law professors, judges, and jury psychologists teach that playing video recordings of depositions rather than calling the witnesses live is a mistake because of the risk of boring the jurors. However, the practical reality is that many witnesses are either unavailable or simply outside the subpoena power of the trial court, and thus playing their deposition is the only course of action. So, the question becomes not *whether* to use depositions in the plaintiff's case-in-chief, but rather *how* to use depositions in the plaintiff's case-in-chief.

How to use depositions is the secret recipe to a well-baked plaintiff's case-in-chief, and often is the difference between a production that smells like spoiled fish and one that tastes like a delicious coconut cream pie. To achieve the more delectable result, there are at least six "do's" that should be followed in playing deposition videos at trial.

<u>DO #1</u>—*Quality video recordings of depositions should be produced by well-qualified video presentation professionals at the time they are recorded.* Any deposition worth taking is one worthy of being video recorded. However, simply turning on a camera is only the first battle in this technological war of persuasion. Don't hire your cousin to film a deposition; Cousin Eddie is no more qualified to do so than he was to handle human waste in *National Lampoon's Christmas Vacation*. As Clark Griswold said of the character in the movie, "His heart is bigger than his brain." The same is true of a lawyer's least favorite in-law, who is the high school dropout now doubling as a video technician on the side between his AA meetings. In this same vein, be wary of video personnel hired by the local court reporter when taking depositions out of state. If the deposition is important enough to justify traveling across the country to secure the testimony, perhaps a phone call to a well-known local lawyer to first get advice about who does excellent video work in the area is as well. I use the same court reporting and video production company in every case in my office, and we have negotiated down the added expense of their personnel traveling with me. In this way, I can be sure of the qualification of the persons who are ensuring that the testimony I capture is in fact going to be captured on video.

<u>DO #2</u>—*Sound quality must be excellent, or the whole expense of video recording a deposition has been a waste of time.* Every lawyer in the room, and the witness as well, must be wired to their own microphone, which is clipped to their respective tie, shirt, or blouse. If a hired video "professional" shows up with a camera and announces that it will capture the sound from the microphone inside the camera, don't start the deposition, and never hire that person again. Sound quality also should be checked before the deposition begins. Requiring the videographer to have each person in the room introduce themselves and state who they represent is really just a technique to permit the video technician to check the sound quality that is (or is not) being captured. While lawyers and the witness are using the restrooms during the hourly breaks, video technicians should be counseled that such

breaks are an excellent opportunity to double-check that the sound quality captured in the last hour was as good as he advertised.

DO #3—*Integrate the testimony being given with the exhibits or documents being used in the deposition*. Americans are famous across the globe for speaking casually. Our use of pronouns like *him*, *her*, *this*, and *there* is more than frequent—it is pervasive; hence, the transcripts received from depositions that are not video-recorded are full of useless pronoun references that do not properly identify the specifics of the testimony. For this reason, the use of a visual presenter and a video switcher can create a visual record of the exhibit being referenced, the exact language in a document being excerpted, the particular item being pointed to in a photograph, or the specific location on a map as indicated by the witness. Over and above that, moving back and forth between the view of the witness and the documents being referenced results in a more interesting presentation for the jury. Jurors today are exposed to highly edited, visually pleasing montages on television, at the movies, and on Internet-based streaming services. Younger jurors in particular expect a well-produced video presentation instead of a lengthy, single-frame perspective of the testimony of a witness.

DO #4—*Heavily edit depositions so they are short and to the point*. There is a reason that the evening news is only a half-hour long—the news station needs eight minutes of that time for slick and well-produced thirty-second advertisements to pay for its production expenses. Plus, the average viewer will not pay attention to the news for longer than twenty-two minutes. Consequently, most deposition excerpts played to a jury should not last longer than twenty-two minutes. With depositions often taking a full day to complete, it might be tempting for the lawyer who is heroically gathering such vital evidence to edit "their" deposition only slightly, so that none of the good stuff is kept from the jury. This thinking is wrong. First, regardless of how well the deposition was taken, its impact is diminished the longer it takes to play. Second, even if there is a single, critical deposition that cannot be edited to less than one hour because of the many critical admissions therein, which are needed for the appellate record, it must then be accompanied by subsequent video excerpts of other witnesses that are only eight, four, twelve minutes long respectively, as part of an overall effort to achieve forgiveness from the jury for the length of the first deposition.

DO #5—*Editing depositions should be a team effort, and not conducted by a single lawyer who took the deposition*. The first edit of a deposition should be undertaken by the lawyer who takes the deposition. This is so that whatever key admissions that lawyer believes he or she procured are not lost by virtue of allowing someone who knows nothing about the case or the deposition to make the initial edits. Second, a different person should perform the second edit. Ideally, the person who will be tasked to write the appellee's brief in the event of a trial court victory should be involved in making sure key admissions are not lost to the editing process. These admissions should be highlighted if editing is being done via marks on a paper transcript, or bolded or italicized if the process is done digitally by editing a Microsoft Word file. A rough cut of this second edit should be produced for a subsequent visual review. Third, a young associate, paralegal, or staff member should be tasked with watching the video-recorded version of this second edit. Peripheral fluff on issues not critical to the case (and not bolded by the appellate lawyer who did the second edit), sidebars, dead space between the end of a witness's answer and the next question, unimportant dead space between the end of a lawyer's question and the witness's actual answer (usually in the form of reading a document), and other gaps on the video that separate the jury from only substantive answers should be carefully edited out of the video. The third version of the video deposition should contain only the meat of the matter, not the bothersome and time-consuming gristle that initially comes with it. Fourth and finally, depositions should be cross-edited and shortened by the trial lawyer to avoid duplication. A common mistake of young lawyers is hitting the same points over and over again, witness after witness. While the theory of repetition says that jurors will better recall items drummed into them repeatedly, this theory should be applied only to the most significant issues in the case. Otherwise, the trial judge will stop the process to complain that the trial lawyer is wasting the jury's time with repetitious testimony. By editing across different depositions, the trial lawyer can ensure that the critical admissions are in the trial court record at least once, while also considerably shortening the length of the video-recorded excerpts to be played to the jury.

Finally, remember the K-I-S-S principle! This principle teaches that systems work best if they are kept simple, rather than made more complicated. When it comes to playing video-recorded depositions of witness after witness, this acronym can remain the same—K-I-S-S—but the lesson taught is modified only slightly to **K**eep **I**t ***Short***, **S**tupid!

DO #6—*Admissions garnered during depositions should be extracted and topically organized for the purpose of building a trial outline.* The trial outline ensures that before the plaintiff's lawyer rests, he or she has not failed to introduce *some* evidence on each element of proof for the cause of action asserted or the damages being claimed. The primary reason I like to play a significant number of video depositions at trial is that the admissions in them are then in the can for purposes of directed verdict and appellate practice. The admissibility of deposition testimony often is ruled on by the court before trial, which allows for very specific evidentiary promises to safely be made during opening statements. But even if the court postpones ruling until just before testimony is about to be played, the careful plaintiff's lawyer should then topically organize each admission as it makes its way into the evidence so the trial outline may be built in real time. Gaps in proof will become self-evident, permitting the agile trial lawyer to fill in those gaps via subsequent questioning of live witnesses before resting her case-in-chief.

Witness Examinations

All witness examinations during a plaintiff's case-in-chief should have a specific purpose and be succinctly designed to secure particular testimony that can be used in a response to a motion for directed verdict, the closing argument, posttrial argument, or the appellate briefs. No witness should be put on the stand with the lawyer winging it, or ostensibly using merely talent and experience to guide the examination. Each witness important enough to be called at trial is one that's important enough to merit a direct and cross-examination outline, a practice session, and detailed training and instructions about affect and mannerisms before the jury. The need for this level of preparation applies equally to the preparation of plaintiff's witnesses for direct and cross-examination and the actual witness testimony itself.

Preparing Plaintiff's Witnesses for Direct and Cross-Examination

The preparation of witness examinations begins with the process of excerpting key statements from witnesses' reports and key testimony from their depositions, annotating them into a topical outline, deciding which exhibits should be introduced with each witness, sharing the respective draft outline with each witness, practicing the examination with that witness, and then editing and finalizing the planned script of the direct examination. Because the direct examination by a friendly plaintiff's lawyer is only half of the in-court exercise, cross-examination by a hostile opponent should be discussed and practiced as well.

The process of planning a witness's testimony should begin long before the witness appears in the trial war room to be prepped for trial. After the witness's deposition, the plaintiff's lawyer should carefully extract the key points of the testimony and assemble the key evidentiary exhibits for introduction during the witness's direct examination. Together, the testimonial and documentary evidence should be topically outlined before an in-person or telephone meeting to discuss the anticipated trial testimony. Together with the witness, the trial outline should then be edited and finalized, and that screenplay draft should be practiced before the last version of the direct examination script is finalized.

Likewise, a list of possible cross-examination items should be compiled so that preferred answers to each such issue may be collectively crafted. Once all the potential hiccups have been identified, hostile cross-examination on these items should be rehearsed, and the witness's practiced responses evaluated. A technique used with increasing frequency is video-recording these practice sessions so the witnesses can view themselves on video. Nervous ticks and distracting mannerisms can be identified so they may be eliminated before the real exercise in court. Rising tempers, flippant responses, and nonverbal rolls of the eyes or tapping of the legs can be eliminated before the real testimony occurs.

Direct Examination

The actual examination of a witness in the courtroom is directed by the plaintiff's lawyer, but such direction must be stylistic only to avoid objectionable leading of the witness. Once the rule of exclusion is invoked by either party, all witnesses who are not experts cannot view the testimony of prior witnesses, but that does not mean that a lawyer should not allow an upcoming witness to come into the courtroom the night before, or the morning of, in an effort to get the witness comfortable with the physical setting where the sworn exercise will occur. Depending on the dimensions of the courtroom, the location of the witness stand relative to the jury box, and the positioning of the questioning attorney, instructions about when to give eye contact to the jury may differ. Regardless of these dimensional permutations, the witness must be coached that his or her job is not to communicate back and forth solely with the plaintiff's lawyer; rather, primarily it is to look at the plaintiff's lawyer when being questioned, and then to turn and communicate directly to the jurors, while giving them full eye contact during each answer.

The pace of questioning is another important aspect of a good direct examination. It is natural for human beings to talk faster when they are nervous, and the process of testifying before a jury in a court of law is the apex of anxiety-inducing exercises. A good lawyer should sense when his or her witness is nervous or failing to look at the jury and politely instruct the witness, "Now Mr. 'X,' kindly turn to the jury and *slowly* describe to them exactly what you saw out there that day." When a witness is talking too quickly or not loud enough for the court reporter, a gentle reminder to "please *slow down* so the court reporter can get every word down" or to "*speak up* so every one of the jurors can hear what you saw out there that day" is an effective way to steer a witness back on course.

While humor is effective when used by funny people, the general rule during direct examination is to maintain a solemn focus on just delivering needed information to the jury. Likewise, formality in a courtroom often is imposed by the judge, but it is considered polite by jurors, whether required or not. Referring to the witness as "Mr. 'X'" rather than by his first name is appropriate for every witness save the plaintiff when she is being questioned by her own lawyer (who is, of course, now her good friend). Conversely, witnesses should be coached to respond to the lawyer as "Ms. 'Y'" and to the opposing counsel as "Mr. 'Z,'" while the judge is always to be referred to as "Your Honor." Requests to the court or court staff should always begin with a "please," and kindnesses shown to a witness in the form of a tendered cup of water or a tissue upon which to wipe up tears should always be responded to by that witness with a polite, "thank you."

The structure of a direct examination should begin with a foreshadowing of what is to come, a brief statement of why this witness is here—"Mr. 'X,'" you're here because you saw the accident in question, right?" While this admittedly is a leading question, no experienced lawyer will object to this mere framing of the issue at hand as long as it is then followed by direct questions that seek a narrative response. The meat of the direct examination should be divided by the different topics for which the witness was called. The first topic should be precipitated with verbal sign-posting by a skilled lawyer, beginning with, "The first topic I want to cover with you is 'x,'" followed by individual questions that address that topic. When the questioning on the first topic has ended, a helpful lawyerly transition from the first topic to the next should take place: "Mr. 'Y,' we've completed your testimony with respect to 'topic x' and I want to move on with you to discuss 'topic y.'" When approaching the last issue to be discussed, the transition into the last topic should be preceded by an always welcome, "The last topic I want to discuss with you today is . . . ." Finally, when the last question has been posed by the lawyer and answered by the witness, the direct examination should not end with an inside baseball lawyer phrase like "pass the witness"; rather, a more everyman-on-the-street signal to the jury that the questioning has concluded is more appropriate—"Mr. 'X,' those are all my questions for you at this time; I think Mr. 'Opposing Counsel' may have some questions for you now."

Cross-Examination and Impeachment

From the perspective of the plaintiff's lawyer, the opposing lawyer's cross-examination of a witness called during the plaintiff's case-in-chief is perhaps the most nerve-wracking part of a trial. However, impolite and improper nonverbal mannerisms must be avoided. Shaking one's head from side to side when the opposing counsel asks a question that suggests a view contrary to that of the plaintiff is both noticed by and distracting to the jury. Talking loudly to one's co-counsel, or talking out loud with words like "No," "That's not right," "That's just wrong," or "That's bullshit" are always inappropriate, will be considered distracting and impolite by observant jurors, and will run the risk of causing the court to appropriately dress down such conduct in front of the jury.

Another common technique used by plaintiff's lawyers during their opponent's cross-examination of "their" witnesses is to seek to interrupt the examination through objections. This is improper and counterproductive. Frankly, I object very little, if at all, because it seems to me that a jury might view this obstruction as an effort to hide something from them. Furthermore, there is no point that can be made on cross-examination that cannot be responded to during redirect examination. Unless the cross-examination is relegated to an illegitimate hatchet job, professional courtesy demands that opposing counsel be permitted to conduct his own examination without the editorial help of a plaintiff's lawyer seeking only to soften the blow of what is transpiring. Instead, all the energy of obstreperous objections should be preserved and redirected toward . . . well, the *redirect*.

Impeachment of one's witness by opposing counsel often is painful to quietly endure, but unless it is being done improperly and in a manner contrary to the rules, a skilled plaintiff's lawyer should, with stoic facial aplomb, quietly permit the moment to pass. Shooting up from one's chair to shout "OBJECTION!" or making some nonsensical speaking objection only calls more attention to the uncomfortable impeachment taking place. Any impeachment coming from one's opponent should have been planned for well before the witness took the stand, with an even-keeled and confident verbal and nonverbal response from the witness practiced over and over until it looks right. The most effective response to impeachment should come from the witness alone, not the lawyer who called that witness. Instead, a good lawyer should either calmly ignore the moment, or begin writing out a perceived plan of a counterattack on the issue for the redirect examination.

The redirect examination should be carefully planned, especially in jurisdictions or before judges that limit the scope of the cross-examination to the direct, and the scope of the redirect to that of the cross-examination, or in instances where the rules prohibit a recross-examination altogether. If one knows that an erroneous cross-examination is coming up on a particular subject, it would be folly to preempt the upcoming mistake of one's opponent by handling it first during direct examination. Instead, in what might politely be called patience and in what others might impolitely call sandbagging, reserving certain cleanups for the last examination of the witness achieves the persuasive effects of the law of recency, and gives the plaintiff's lawyer the last word on the subject.

Expert Witnesses

The law in many jurisdictions requires expert testimony on specific elements of proof. Therefore, experts are a necessary evil, and an expensive one at that. Excellent experts can make all the difference to a plaintiff's case, while bad ones can most surely sink one.

Expert witnesses should be called only when necessary because expert witness testimony from opposing sides tends to cancel out the other. When required, experts should be called to explain their educational background, their experiential relevant expertise, their past work on the topic at issue before they were ever paid a dollar in this case, and their diligent work completed here to assist the jury to decide complex issues involving the manner before them.

PowerPoint presentations are especially helpful in conducting direct examinations of expert witnesses. PowerPoint presentations prevent lawyers from engaging in tangential nonsense, and they prevent experts from running away from the core issues at hand. Moreover, by building a PowerPoint presentation for each expert, the plaintiff's lawyer can ensure that everything the expert will say has been previously disclosed, either in the required expert report or in the opinions disclosed during the deposition. PowerPoint presentations ultimately are merely a high-tech outline and notepad merged into one, which keeps the lawyer and witness on track, all while impressing the court and the jury with the lawyer's organizational alacrity. Furthermore, with the direct examination PowerPoint prepared, exchanged with the other side, and shared with the court, objections often can be argued and ruled on before the expert takes the stand, thereby minimizing an opponent's opportunity to interrupt the examination through objections. Finally, PowerPoint presentations serve as a reminder to the questioning lawyer of which exhibits are to be offered for introduction into evidence during the expert's direct examination.

Another goal of the direct examination is to pair the plaintiff's expert with the defense expert who was hired on the same subject. The jurors want to know who is testifying on a specific subject from each side. In this vein, a plaintiff's expert politely acknowledging the expertise of his adversary on a topic, but then succinctly setting forth the differences in their respective conclusions, followed by a discrete explanation of why the other expert may be in error, is an exercise that is helpful to the jury. To this end, it is never one expert's job to take potshots at another; that is the job reserved for excellent cross-examinations and persuasive closing arguments by lawyers.

The enemies of expert witness testimony are *hubris*, *verbosity*, and *deception*. Practice sessions with experts often are perceived as unnecessary by these self-professed titans of knowledge and persuasion, but they stand as the most effective bulwark against arrogant paid witnesses conducting themselves in a manner that offends the judge and jury.

If an expert in the courtroom displays the hubris of Donald Trump at a political rally attended only by members of his political base, one can be sure that—just as half of the American electorate would be offended by such arrogance while the other half would love it—at least half of the jurors will become aghast at similar conceit displayed by a paid witness in a court of law. While an election can be won by a simple majority, jury verdicts require either unanimity or at least a super-majority; thus, a pompous expert offending half the jurors is a recipe for failure. By contrast, skilled expert witnesses who humbly acknowledge that their job is only to provide useful information to the jury that is empowered to decide the ultimate factual disputes at issue are very helpful in moving the plaintiff's case far down the track toward justice. A deferential expert who displays humility is far more effective than a domineering one who displays hubris.

Likewise, just because an expert is being paid by the hour does not mean that the lawyer calling that expert at trial must permit him to pretend he is being paid by the word. In the same way Sergeant Joe Friday in *Dragnet* caused his witnesses to get to the point with the admonition, "Just the facts, ma'am," a good plaintiff's lawyer should steer his or her experts away from the trap of loquacity. Once again, the K-I-S-S principle applies: **K**eep **I**t **S**imple, **S**tupid! Especially on cross-examination, an expert who answers questions directly, with merely "yes," "no," or a responsive, yet short, explanation is far more likely to be received well by the jury than one who feels the need to argue the points made by the cross-examining attorney, with minutes of lengthy answers that needlessly fill up pages of trial transcript.

Finally, the notion that the truth from one's expert will sell better than lies from the witness stand should seem self-evident. However, the brilliance and qualifications of some experts leads them into a character defect that causes them to somehow believe that they can bend the arc of truth with just a pinch of deception. Any deception like that will inevitably blow up in their face, while blowing up your case at the same time. Jesus's teaching to his believers in John 8:32, "You will know the truth and the truth will set you free," was most famously invoked by the Reverend Martin Luther King, Jr.'s April 4, 1967, speech at Riverside Church in New York City entitled, "Beyond Vietnam."[4] In trial, the truth will set you free, but a lie will chain you to defeat. The truth, in a court of law, is everything. Once lost, trust is almost impossible to restore. An expert caught lying on the stand is far worse than no expert at all. Sadly, every expert must be reminded of this truism. Practice sessions with experts before they testify must conclude with the instruction that, above all else, "You must tell the truth." During these sessions, I typically remind my expert witnesses, "It's not your job to win the case. Paul Plaintiff will do that himself. Please don't say anything that is not true, because that will lose his case before you ever leave the stand."

Special Considerations

There are at least two other special considerations concerning the plaintiff's case-in-chief that are worthy of special note here. First, a good plaintiff's lawyer should vary the evidence that's presented to appeal to each of the jurors' five senses—sight, hearing, touch, smell, and taste. Second, a good lawyer should deprive the defense lawyer of the usefulness of much of his or her evidence before the conclusion of the plaintiff's case-in-chief.

Appeal to the Jurors' Five Senses

The German philosopher Friedrich Nietzsche accurately concluded that "all credibility, all good conscience, all evidence of truth come only from the senses."[5] Nietzsche was right, so appealing to all five senses is an important key to a persuasive evidentiary case-in-chief.

---

4. "Beyond Vietnam," Stanford – The Martin Luther King, Jr. Research and Education Institute (Apr. 4, 1967), https://kinginstitute.stanford.edu/encyclopedia/beyond-vietnam.

5. Friedrich Nietzsche, Basic Writings of Nietzsche, 278, Modern Library, 2009.

First, the most important evolution of excellent trial lawyers is the transformation from teaching merely through the spoken word from the witness stand to presenting evidence that appeals to jurors who learn by seeing rather than by hearing. Harvard University Psychology Professor Steven Pinker wrote, "We are visual creatures. Visual things stay put, whereas sounds fade."[6] Pinker is correct. Most jurors are visual learners, and they expect to see bells and whistles during modern trials; also, as the old adage goes, "A picture is worth a thousand words." In this vein, I religiously use PowerPoint presentations during opening statements. However, PowerPoint presentations should not be used alone; they should be accompanied by many different modes of visual communication, planned throughout one's selection of exhibits and demonstrative evidence.

Second, some jurors still learn audibly. Yet, audible evidence should not be limited merely to the spoken word from the witness stand. Live courtroom testimony is helpful, but so are 911 recordings and other pieces of evidence that capture or utilize sound that is associated with the event or the case. Animations need sound to make them more impactful; one or more witness should sign off on the accuracy of the presentation to ensure admissibility. YouTube is full of videos that have sound. The use of a video, with testimony that the event that occurred "sounded like that," allows a trial lawyer to introduce sound into his or her evidentiary proof.

Likewise, sounds can fill in the damages story and bring relationships alive. Whether it is a widow tearfully recounting and mimicking her lost husband's snoring noises at night or his belly laughs during the day, sounds bring persons back to life in the courtroom. Laughing testimony about the songs lost spouses sang in the shower, joy-filled stories about that song chosen by a couple for their wedding dance, or tear-filled memories about the song chosen for the funeral service to say goodbye to a loved one are a tangible way to put the jurors in the room with the plaintiff during the most important moments of the life that the plaintiff's lawyer—the courtroom storyteller—is trying to make real for the jury. Similarly, family photos in a death case can be presented together in a video collage with striking accompanying music if testimony has been given about the relevance of a particular song. Wrongful death clients almost inevitably recount mourning their loved ones with repeated episodes of listening to iconic songs about love, death, and loss. Prominent examples of songs testified to by my wrongful death clients include:

- Simon and Garfunkel's 1964 *Sound of Silence*, released three months after the assassination of John Kennedy.
- Elton John's 1973 *Candle in the Wind*, written about Marilyn Monroe's premature passing, then reprised by the artist at Westminster Abbey in 1997 at the funeral of Princess Diana, watched by more than a billion people.
- Pink Floyd's 1975 *Wish You Were Here*, a tribute to founding band member Syd Barrett, who left the band seven years earlier due to mental illness.

---

6. BrainyQuote, https://www.brainyquote.com/quotes/steven_pinker_547621 (last visited Mar. 14, 2020).

- Mike and the Mechanics' 1989 *Until We Die*, about discord in relationships interrupted by death.
- Eric Clapton's 1992 *Tears in Heaven*, written after his four-year-old son fell to his death from an open window in his forty-ninth-floor apartment.
- REM's 1993 *Everybody Hurts*, written about the loss of high school kids to suicide.
- Jeff Buckley's powerful 1994 rendition of Leonard Cohen's *Hallelujah.*
- Mariah Carey and Boyz II Men singing *One Sweet Day* at Princess Diana's memorial service in 1997.
- Johnny Cash's 2002 version of *Hurt* by Nine Inch Nails about heroin addiction often is recalled after losses due to suicide.
- Steven Curtis Chapman's 2007 *Cinderella*, written after the tragic loss of his daughter Maria when his son accidentally backed his vehicle over her in the family driveway.

Plato wrote, "Music is a moral law. It gives a soul to the Universe, wings to the mind, flight to the imagination, a charm to sadness, gaiety and life to everything."[7] Given the billions of dollars spent by Americans each year on music streaming services and the ubiquitous drive-time access to music enjoyed by every juror, reference to a plaintiff's experience with song is an important component of any story involving that person. Sound is not just noise; it's perhaps the easiest way to tell the story the plaintiff's lawyer has been hired to tell.

Third, tactile learners are people who learn by touch. Three-dimensional widgets at issue should be brought into the courtroom. Models of evidence in the case should be used. Medical equipment used in the treatment of a plaintiff should be used. These pieces of evidence should be "published to the jury," with each juror allowed to touch and feel the proof at issue. Testimony about the feel of wounds after amputation, the uncomfortable ridges in scarring and stitches after surgery, and the damaged and uneven skin that follow burn injuries—each invoke the sense of touch. Likewise, narratives about lost relationships in a wrongful death case need to be completed with testimony that recounts the holding of hands, the caressing of each other during romance, and other episodes of affectionate touch. The Canadian writer Margaret Atwood wrote in *The Blind Assassin* that "touch comes before sight, before speech. It is the first language and the last, and it always tells the truth."[8] In this vein, perceived by the index finger of each juror—what their minds can process by virtue of what they either have physically touched themselves, or by virtue of the careful presentation of evidence of what the plaintiff has touched relating to her injury—is key to the plaintiff's story being fully comprehended and appreciated by her jury.

Fourth, smell often is ignored as a mechanism to achieve sensory perception in the courtroom. Regarding liability, the sense of smell can often serve as the warning sign that something bad is about to happen. Propane has a strong, unpleasant smell, like rotten eggs, that is deliberately added to help alert customers of propane leaks. Burning plastic in an air

7. Goodreads, https://www.goodreads.com/quotes/7754855-music-is-a-moral-law-it-gives-a-soul-to (last visited Mar. 14, 2020).

8. Goodreads, https://www.goodreads.com/quotes/112626-touch-comes-before-sight-before-speech-it-is-the-first (last visited Mar. 14, 2020).

conditioning system can warn homeowners of impending fires. Overused brake pads put off the smell of burning rubber, warning drivers of impending doom. Burning smells when the heat is turned on warns of dirty filters, or of broken electrical components in the furnace. Most explosions are predicated on a putrid smell that warns it is coming. Inquiring about smell will assist the effective plaintiff's lawyer in having jurors associate their own experience with the calamity being explained from the witness stand. Likewise, when discussing damages, the use of smell is of great assistance. When describing medical treatment, vivid descriptions of the smell of infection, or of the uncomfortable smell from aging residents of a nursing home, often are effective ways to augment damages. Likewise, in burn cases, the smells associated with the burning of flesh are powerful tools to maximize damages. Inevitably, wrongful death survivors testify about the last mourner leaving the post-funeral reception at one's home, then going into the bedroom, only to be overwhelmed by familiar smells of their lost loved one—in the sheets on the bed where they slept the day before they passed, on the couch they used to sit on when reading, on the clothes they used to wear that are still hanging in the closet. The Russian-born poet and novelist Vladimir Nabokov wrote, "Nothing revives the past so completely as a smell that was once associated with it."[9] The effective plaintiff's lawyer will remember those words, and remember to bring smell into his or her presentation of the evidence. Is there a cup of coffee he used to brew for her first thing each morning before they left for work? Did he barbeque a certain steak or brisket that she can describe the smell of? Did they garden together, or did he bring her a certain flower on special occasions that appealed to her olfactory senses? Smell fills in the gaps of any story, and cements the story together in a most important way.

Fifth, taste is the most difficult sense to communicate to a jury. Our society spends more than $750 billion a year at restaurants and almost $1.5 trillion a year buying food; clearly, the sense of taste is important to us. The New Zealand evangelist Ray Comfort wrote that "even Helen Keller, who was blind and deaf, could see God . . . every taste that touched her tongue told her that there was a God who created all things."[10] The pleasure from taste properly described can be used to give full color and texture to a romantic relationship lost in a wrongful death case. What were the couple's favorite restaurants or favorite foods? Can a widow recite that flavor of ice cream her lost love used to share with her on romantic dates? Is there a special flavor of cake she used to make for him on each of his birthdays? Bringing favorite foods and desserts into testimony about special dates is a key way to bring smiles to the romantics serving on every jury. Conversely, the loss of taste can amplify one's damages. This is most appropriately utilized in cases involving cancer treatment, where the ability to taste often is lost during chemotherapy. Either way, the sense of taste should not be left behind in any presentation of the plaintiff's evidence related to damages.

---

9. GOODREADS, https://www.goodreads.com/quotes/326452-nothing-revives-the-past-so-completely-as-a-smell-that (last visited Mar. 14, 2020).

10. BRAINYQUOTE, https://www.brainyquote.com/quotes/ray_comfort_485364 (last visited Mar. 14, 2020).

Depriving the Defense Lawyer of Evidence before Resting the Case-in-Chief

Before resting the case-in-chief, a plaintiff's lawyer should have thoroughly minimized the evidence with which the defendant's lawyer can wow or surprise the jury during the defense case-in-chief. There are three basic techniques to do this.

First, the depositions of all defense expert witnesses should be conducted with the goal of playing the video of the deposition during the plaintiff's case-in-chief. This initially requires the exchange of detailed expert reports so the depositions of those witnesses can focus solely on securing useful admissions, rather than on taking depositions merely to discover what is to be said from the witness stand at trial. Fortunately, Rule 26(a)(2)(B) of the Federal Rules of Civil Procedure requires the disclosure of detailed expert reports, so open-ended questions that seek the opinions to be testified to or the bases thereof need not be asked. Instead, a useful expert deposition looks for admissions about opinions held by the plaintiff's expert that the defendant's expert in question happens to agree with. If a subject area led both sides to disclose opinions from experts that are very similar but not exactly the same, use the deposition of the defendant's expert to illustrate the narrow gap that separates the two sides' respective expert's opinions.

Second, there are many issues pleaded by a plaintiff with which both sides' experts may agree, and these agreements should be a focus of any expert deposition. I have tried complex automotive product liability cases where both sides' designated experts agreed on their respective opinions about accident reconstruction, injury causation, and the cost of the life care plan to treat the injuries caused. The only experts who disagreed were those testifying on vehicular design. Thus, the parties hired and paid for eight experts—four per side—while only two had any material disagreement. In this scenario, the plaintiff's lawyer during the plaintiff's case-in-chief should make clear to the jury that experts "Dr. A" and "Dr. B" agreed with each other on all accident reconstruction issues, experts "Dr. C" and "Dr. D" agreed with each other about the injuries sustained and how they occurred, and "Dr. E. and Dr. F" largely agreed (within $50,000) on their respective $10 million life care plans, which detail the cost of caring for those injuries for the rest of the plaintiff's life. By doing so during the examinations of each of the plaintiff's experts, the plaintiff's lawyer has eliminated the need for the carmaker's lawyer to call any expert other than his automotive defect witness. Nonetheless, out of habit and largely to justify the exorbitant expense of hiring those experts in the first place, many defense lawyers will call all their experts to testify anyway. When they do, the plaintiff's lawyer can correctly cast the blame for the length of the trial on the defendant's lawyer, who unnecessarily called three experts late in the trial.

Third, the experts disclosed by the defendants should immediately be cross-designated by the plaintiff so the plaintiff may call the defendants' experts via video-recorded deposition excerpts presented during the plaintiff's case-in-chief at trial. After successful depositions of the defendant's experts have yielded broad agreement on most issues, short excerpts of the defendants' experts should be played during the plaintiff's case-in-chief, either directly before or directly after the live testimony of the plaintiff's expert on the same subject. Playing the defendant's expert's deposition excerpts to communicate broad if not almost universal agreement with the plaintiff's expert right before the plaintiff's expert is called live during the plaintiff's case-in-chief is a powerful tonic against a *Daubert* motion prophylactically brought by the defendant's attorney. Moreover, calling the defendant's expert by video-recorded deposition excerpts immediately following the conclusion of the plaintiff's expert's testimony on the same subject provides a persuasive reaffirmation that the plaintiff's expert was correct. Again, defense counsel's refusal to ask an expert for his opinion or the bases thereof during their deposition permits the plaintiff's lawyer to succinctly play only the admissions that were secured from the expert. By doing so, the plaintiff's lawyer has effectively emasculated the ability of the defendant's attorney to effectively present his or her experts during the defendant's case-in-chief.

In conclusion, the plaintiff's case-in-chief is the battleground where trial wars are won and lost. By diligently preparing a plan and then executing it carefully, most trials will be won by the party bringing the lawsuit before their lawyer ever utters the words "The Plaintiff rests."

16
The Plaintiff's Case
The Defense Perspective

The Defense Objectives

For defense lawyers, defining strategic goals during the plaintiff's case is easily done: slow the plaintiff's momentum and maximize defense momentum. Implementing this strategy is more difficult, however—particularly when dealing with skilled lawyers on the opposing side in complex cases. This chapter focuses on practice tips and strategies to make this challenge easier.

An effective attack during the plaintiff's evidence will have lasting effects. The goal is to dig a hole so deep, the plaintiff and plaintiff's counsel cannot dig out. This is done by obviously attacking the credibility of the plaintiff's witnesses and the logic and believability of the plaintiff's claims. Your tools consist of cross-examination, effective impeachment, and examination of your own client when your client is called as an adverse witness. Both scenarios are discussed in this chapter.

Early Planning

Like any stage of any trial, early planning is critical. Success is rarely found in last-minute, rushed preparations. Your cross-examination strategy for each witness will differ depending on the witness's place in the larger factual mosaic. But the foundations are similar because they are derived from the results of discovery and pretrial investigation that begin at the outset of the case. Effective trial themes and cross-examination themes are not identified overnight, but they should be factually supported before trial. Your selection of impeachment exhibits also should be identified well before trial. The bottom line is that you should have a trial plan, which includes a cross-examination plan, *before* your first words are uttered in opening statements.

A successfully planned attack during the plaintiff's case likely will cement the attitudes of defense-leaning jurors. The plaintiff's lawyer needs the first days of the plaintiff's case to generate positive momentum. If this momentum is slowed or stayed, defense-oriented jurors will become more fixed in their viewpoints. They will filter evidence to support their views of the case and look for evidence that supports and justifies their conclusions on who should win and who should lose. Your cross-examinations should keep this in mind.

A successfully implemented attack also relieves pressure on the defense case, making it easier to decide which witnesses should be called. An optimum scenario occurs when a defense lawyer reduces the number of witnesses called in the defense case-in-chief. Slowing or stopping the plaintiff's case frequently translates into reduced needs for defense witnesses to take the stand. This is a good thing because *fewer witnesses means fewer opportunities for mistakes*. Likewise, the plaintiff's lawyer will have fewer opportunities to hurt the defense and reinforce the plaintiff's themes.

By way of example, in a notable case many years ago, a defense lawyer in a major New York firm called no defense witnesses in a high-stakes securities fraud case. He was convinced he had devastated the plaintiff's liability witnesses during cross-examination. Although this was a decision fraught with risk, he was proven right and obtained a complete defense win. Although undoubtedly unique, this example supports the notion that certain defense witnesses need not be called to the witness stand if the objectives of their testimony are already established before the defense case begins. To be sure, the scope and length of the defense case is directly impacted by successes in the plaintiff's case.

Responding to Emotion in the Plaintiff's Case

Skilled plaintiff's lawyers invariably seek to invoke fear, anger, or sympathy during the plaintiff's case. This trial strategy, referred to as the "reptilian" strategy, begins during discovery, is implemented during voir dire, and then reinforced during opening statements. The plaintiff's trial counsel will seek to inject emotion into the evidence at every opportunity, and this strategy will be pursued with each witness in the plaintiff's case.

In a serious personal injury or death case, the skilled opponent will make the jury sympathize or empathize with the plaintiff. The obvious goal is to adjust the equities of the case by inspiring pity. In an appropriate case, the plaintiff's lawyer also may seek to inspire fear that the defendant does not heed appropriate safety standards and thereby threatens the safety of others. This is done to encourage anger by focusing on the defendant's "conscious" indifference or "reckless" conduct toward public safety. Of course, these are the buzz words for punitive damages, and they frequently become the cornerstones of the plaintiff's trial themes.

Even though personal injury cases and death cases present unique sensibilities, these same strategies apply equally to traditional business disputes. From the plaintiff's perspective, there is no such thing as a "mere" breach of contract case or a "traditional" business dispute. Even the most basic disputes can be repackaged with more pejorative characterizations, such as: "broken promises," "lies," "misrepresentations," "intentional interferences," "intentional" breach, fraud, fraudulent inducements, etc. The list goes on and on, but the idea is simple: the plaintiff's lawyers seek to encourage the jury's passion for the plaintiff and the plaintiff's case. There is also the typical, not so subtle suggestion of the *little* guy v. the big guy confrontation, or the not-so-subtle attacks on corporate America. In sum, good plaintiff's lawyers want to light a fire and then stoke that fire at every opportunity with every witness.

So, what is to be done? As defense lawyers, we should understand these tactics and seek to neutralize the *bad* and pejorative evidence. This begins early during the life of the case, when the battle lines are first drawn—*depositions*. Positive evidence should be developed, with every deposed witness showing why our clients, the defendants, are not to blame, and why our clients are good citizens who are concerned about the safety and welfare of society. In business disputes, we should focus on the conduct of the plaintiff—why the plaintiff caused its own damage, or caused the first breach, or failed to exercise due diligence, or why the jury cannot justifiably or reasonably rely on any statements or representations made by the plaintiff. To be clear, the best defense is an offense, and this offense should be in full throttle during your cross-examination of the plaintiff's witnesses.

The challenge is greater in personal injury and death cases. Defense lawyers should *never* demean or minimize damages or loss in a serious injury or death case. To do so will trigger a highly negative reaction with many jurors or even worse, *anger*. By any definition, a serious injury is serious. A death always causes suffering and loss for the survivors and loved ones. Common sense and logic demand that defense lawyers not fight these issues, but respect the sensibilities at issue.

One excellent approach is to concede the seriousness of an injury or acknowledge the loss suffered when a loved one dies in a tragic accident. This can be done when your client is first deposed; your client should exhibit empathy and acknowledge the plaintiff's loss. You also can do this during voir dire, or you can echo this theme during opening statement. In doing so, you minimize the drama the plaintiff's lawyer is trying to create. You also garner immediate respect from many of the jurors. If you fight these issues, you accentuate the emotional drama the plaintiff seeks to create.

Whether or not a serious injury or loss are serious or significant are not fights that defense lawyers should fight. Rather, having earned the jury's respect, focus on the weaknesses of the plaintiff's liability and causation claims. This is done by telling the jury what you intend to do during opening statements, and then systematically delivering on your promises—witness by witness—showing the lack of credibility of the plaintiff's lay witnesses and the lack of reliability of the plaintiff's experts. In essence, you are conceding turf to fight on higher ground.

Preparation Fundamentals

Some states require the parties to identify trial witnesses (excluding rebuttal witnesses) in response to properly propounded interrogatories. Several states also require pretrial disclosures of trial witnesses, similar to joint pretrial orders in federal court. All federal courts require joint pretrial orders, which require identification of key information, such as a short statement of the case, trial exhibits, and trial witnesses that will be called by deposition or as live witnesses. Thus, all lawyers on both sides of the case typically know who will be taking the witness stand and who will testify by deposition. Setting aside purely rebuttal witnesses, there is little surprise over who will testify.

For live witnesses, an actual "witness box" should be created for each witness. For witnesses called by deposition, appropriate designations and counter-designations should be prepared to neutralize the plaintiff's offerings. Video clips should be cut and edited for maximum drama. These video clips should be concise and short. You should always consider the maximum impact in all of your witness choices; the same goes for video testimony. The goal is to capture effective sound bites the jury will remember. Brevity is always recommended because juror attention spans are short. As a general rule, video clips that exceed ten minutes for any specific witness are not recommended.

A witness box for live witnesses is used to promote organization, and should include basic information, such as:

- A witness outline that identifies key cross-examination points and a list of exhibits you intend to use during the cross-examination.
- A page and line summary of key points in the witness's deposition.
- Any witness statements provided by the witness.
- A working copy of the witness's deposition, with flags and highlighting for key impeachment points on key topics.
- A clean copy of the witness's deposition to hand to the witness should it become necessary to impeach the witness on the stand.
- A hard copy of all exhibits you intend to use with the witness, organized in the order of anticipated use.[1]
- Prepared clips of video testimony if you elect to impeach the witness from video testimony; these video clips should be synced with the transcript—the jury can hear the audio on the video and see the text simultaneously on the screen.

For expert witnesses, the file should include depositions the expert gave in other cases on similar topics in case you elect to impeach from prior testimony; this box also should contain any published articles authored by the expert inconsistent with the witness's expected testimony.

Witness Outlines

It is important to have a witness outline for structure. An outline provides control, defines the key topics for the witness, and provides a fallback if you get into trouble. It should include specific goals for each witness; your cross-examination should be focused to achieve these goals. There is great risk in proceeding with an undisciplined cross-examination and attempting to address each point raised during the witness's direct examination. Indeed, some of the best cross-examinations are short—measured in minutes, not hours.

1. As discussed in chapter 6, *supra*, I typically create an exhibit list on a spreadsheet that can be ordered by date, topic category, or witness. If a witness is called to the stand, I can immediately identify which exhibits I may wish to consider using during my examination. I also have key impeachment exhibits at the end this list and can retrieve them quickly.

Every witness outline should identify the relevant deposition testimony or other impeachment evidence you may need if an impeachment opportunity arises. To be clear, you should invite opportunities for impeachment. The more a witness is impeached, the harder and further they fall. There is no doubt that successful, repetitive impeachment translates into loss of credibility for the witness.

It is a mistake to use a witness outline as a script to which you are tied. If you are psychologically tethered to an outline, you risk losing spontaneity and freedom to respond to the witness's answers. That is why I use topical outlines only. I never try to write out questions and then read them verbatim. By using topic categories, I make sure to address key aspects of the witness's testimony I seek to develop, but I still retain the flexibility to move about during the examination. Here is a simple example that shows how an examination could be outlined. The impeachment evidence is identified and ready to go. In this example, the goal is to attack the credibility of a purported eyewitness at an accident scene, and to do so quickly and decisively:

John Doe—An Alleged Eyewitness	
Direct Testimony	**Impeachment**
"I saw the accident happen"	**Dark;** ***Deposition, Page 8, line 3*** **8:00 pm and cloudy;** Ex. 7: ***Weather report*** **No street lights;** Ex. 8: ***Photograph of scene*** **Needs glasses, but did not have glasses;** ***Deposition, Page 20, line 10*** **Standing over 150 yards away** Ex. 5: ***Post-accident measurements***

Every lawyer develops individual techniques at marshaling and presenting impeachment evidence. What works well for one lawyer may not work for others. It is important, however, that you do not become too dependent on your witness outline and become boring or mechanical. Jurors do not like robots. They want to see and hear drama and advocacy. The goal is to be simple and forceful. That is hard to do if you are reading questions.

Principles of Effective Cross-Examination

The key principles of cross-examination involve simplicity, control, and tempo. You want to be in control or, at a minimum, appear to be in control. The messages you send—your key cross-examination points—should be simple. Complex answers to complex questions will be lost on the jury. You want to avoid extended, boring examinations.

Trials involve real-time drama played out on several levels. The jury reacts to what it sees, hears, and *senses*. If a jury senses a hostile witness is controlling the lawyer, the lawyer loses. If the jury senses the lawyer is nervous or lacks confidence in his or her examination, this detracts from the effectiveness of the examination. Thus, a first principle for trial success is that the lawyer must be prepared, in control, and exhibit confidence. Thorough preparation helps achieve this confidence.

Cross-examination points should be limited to points you know you can establish and win. I follow the principles of Irving Younger, a trial practitioner and lecturer on trial advocacy skills. His advice was simple: cross-examinations should be focused, concise, and *never ask a question to which you do not know the answer*. That means each question should be carefully considered. Impeachment evidence should be "in the can" and ready to use should the witness fight. You should try to anticipate what the witness will say and be prepared to handle a quick, and hopefully effective, impeachment response. Moving slowly or being incapable of effective follow-through questions with impeachment will injure your entire cross-examination. The jury will sense that you are losing and the witness is winning.

With that said, there is another school of thought: an effective cross-examination is one where your questions, and the tone of your questions, place the witness in a position of appearing disingenuous. This is done by allowing the witness to talk freely, and then raising questions that suggest that the witness's narrative is unbelievable or exaggerated. This is more difficult to achieve in practice because there are subtleties that must be mastered for an effective examination. Here is an example of providing the rope for the witness to hang himself.

The case involved a product disparagement claim against a publication. A senior editor was personally present at a testing facility where the product was tested. During discovery, we obtained video and audio outtakes from the testing facility. Buried in these outtakes was the unmistakable voice of this editor. He was heard saying—barely audibly—that he was frustrated by the technicians' inability to get a product failure. He then said he would do it *himself*—that is, he would cause a premeditated product failure and would use a new testing protocol to obtain this result. When confronted during cross-examination about what he said, he testified that he could not remember. When he listened to the barely audible recording, he said he still could not remember. The examining lawyer asked him the question again, and again, with the volume slowly ramped up, and he still declined to remember. After one last time, when his words were generally understandable at a loud volume setting, he still refused to concede he made the comments. The examining lawyer had directly implicated the witness's credibility. This was achieved by letting him hang himself with his obstinacy. The lawyer simply provided the rope.

We should recognize that expert witnesses bring to the court an aura of reliability and believability. Jurors typically tend to believe well-credentialed, highly educated experts. That is why *Daubert*[2] and similar cases that involve expert challenges are important. It is important to keep bad experts off the stand so the jury is not confused or duped into believing flawed science or unreliable methodology. The court must be the gatekeeper.[3]

Nevertheless, successful *Daubert* challenges are the exception, and not the norm. It has been my experience that most experts survive pretrial challenges. As a result, you must be ready to mount an effective examination in the presence of the jury. Many of the points in

---

2. *Daubert v. Merrell Dow Pharmaceuticals, Inc.*, 509 U.S. 579 (1993) (articulating the criteria for the admissibility of scientific expert testimony).

3. *See* chapter 14, *supra*, which includes a full discussion of *Daubert*.

your *Daubert* challenge will be included as cross-examination points in your witness outline. In federal court, these principles are set forth in Fed. R. Evid. 702 and 703 and in a wealth of case law that implements these principles. Although *Daubert* originally dealt with "scientific" evidence, its application has been extended to all types of expert testimony.[4] However, different states and jurisdictions have varying procedures to address these issues. Relevant case law for each jurisdiction should be researched and understood before trial.

Your first line of attack on an opposing expert should focus on how the expert either lacks needed qualifications or uses improper or invalid methods under pertinent evidentiary rules. This process is first started in discovery. When you take the expert's deposition, you should explore the witness's credentials (or lack thereof) and the details of his or her opinions. If the method is not recognized within the witness's relevant industry, you should have backup material to support your argument. Frequently, your technical consulting experts guide you on these types of issues. By the time of trial, you should have an arsenal of impeachment evidence at your disposal to demonstrate either a lack of credentials or unreliable methodology.

As a general rule, the plaintiff will call expert witnesses who were timely disclosed; it is likely you had ample opportunity to depose and investigate these witnesses. If deposed, sometimes the best strategy is to not play all your cards. If you exhaust all your cross-examination points during deposition, you will educate the opposing side and witness—and lose the element of surprise. The opposing expert and lawyer will then have time to evaluate your strategy and find a way around your attacks before trial. Therefore, you should consider keeping some of your "powder dry"—holding back key cards and playing them for the first time at trial. It is better to catch the expert off guard and flat-footed because the impact will be far greater in the presence of the jury.

There are many ways to catch an expert by surprise. In lieu of formal discovery, you can mine important information without the opposing side ever knowing the details of your investigation. Here are some examples:

- Locating and using previously undisclosed decisions that have limited or excluded the expert's testimony.
- Locating prior depositions where the expert may have given inconsistent testimony.
- Locating published articles the expert authored or co-authored that may include statements that are inconsistent with the expert's opinions or the methodology used by the expert in this case.
- Locating articles about the topics of the expert's testimony that the expert recognizes as authoritative; the strategy here is to identify publications the expert may agree are authoritative, and then research these publications for information that is inconsistent with the expert's opinions.

The jury will be impressed if you are able to effectively cross-examine the expert with prior inconsistent statements. The witness's credibility will be under fire. If the expert

4. *Kumho Tire*, 526 U.S. at 137 (extending *Daubert's* general holding to include nonscientific expert testimony).

aggressively resists, he will lose credibility. Similarly, if the expert concedes important points on the witness stand, you also win.

Before I retain experts, I ask a potential consultant whether he or she has ever been subject to a *Daubert* challenge either excluding or limiting his or her testimony. This is important information you need to know *before* making the decision to designate. In one case I tried several years ago, I used a forensic accountant who I had known for years. He had consulted on several cases for me in the past and actually testified in trial and evidentiary hearings for me on at least three occasions. I had come to trust our working relationship. Then, at trial, he was cross-examined by opposing counsel who waved an appellate opinion that discussed my expert's testimony in another case. An appellate court had reversed the trial court judgment and held that my expert's testimony was not reliable and could not support the judgment. I heard this for the first time in the courtroom in the presence of the jury. It felt as if time had stopped. I had no prior knowledge of this situation, but later discovered that the expert was well aware of the issue and had never disclosed the prior opinion to me.

I dropped the ball on this occasion by taking things for granted. Fortunately, we won the case and the expert's testimony in my case was not challenged; the expert was just embarrassed. However, the surprise in the courtroom was palpable. As a defense lawyer, I do not like surprises. This lesson taught me to always do my homework and never assume anything. Even when we think we can depend on our expert's credentials, we must conduct our own due diligence. There is no substitute for preparation when it comes to controlling what takes place in the courtroom.

Sometimes you may *not* want to file a *Daubert* challenge before trial. The witness may be so vulnerable you elect to let him testify so you can use the witnesses' vulnerabilities to contaminate the entirety of the plaintiff's case. This strategy carries risk because the failure to file a pretrial motion may be treated as a waiver of the right to assert a later challenge. However, in the right case, it can yield substantial dividends. Here are some examples:

- Perhaps an expert has been excluded on several prior occasions on several similar topics in other cases; instead of seeking to exclude him before trial, you can use the prior court orders to demonstrate the weakness in the entire case. The expert may have been previously designated and excluded in trials dealing with the same theory of design defect. These prior exclusions can contaminate the plaintiff's liability theories in your case. You end up using the expert to advance your trial themes.
- Perhaps an expert was excluded in a case involving the same plaintiff's lawyer. Allowing him to testify, but showing this vulnerability, can impact the credibility of the plaintiff's lawyer and thereby hurt the plaintiff's case in its entirety.

Taking the Opposing Expert on Voir Dire

Some courts may provide limited pretrial procedures for expert challenges. If this is the case, you should consider taking the witness on voir dire. Preferably, this should be done in the presence of the jury for maximum effect.

After the witness has taken the stand, but before the witness offers opinions, you should request the right to examine the witness briefly to test the witness's credentials or lack of reliable methodology. Assuming you have effective impeachment points ready to go, you can draw first blood and take the steam out of the witness's testimony. Even if you are not successful in keeping the witness off the stand, this type of preemptive attack can severely damage the witness's credibility before he ever has a chance to offer opinions. Some jurors may be cynical or skeptical of the witness as a result of your examination. Any witness voir dire should be focused, concise, and brief. Extended voir dire examinations may test the patience of the court.

Presenting Impeachment Evidence

Impeaching any witness—whether lay or expert—should be crisp and to the point. You do not want to get lost in paperwork fumbling around for a page in a deposition or a dog-eared article. You want to have your evidence ready like a loaded gun—*locked and loaded.*

One way to do this is to have your evidence scanned into TrialDirector or a similar program. You can have the impeaching evidence—an article, a witness statement, or a deposition excerpt—ready to go and flash it on the screen. You can have an assistant highlight and enlarge the focused excerpt from the impeachment source. There is much drama here, and the effectiveness of this drama is a direct function of your appearance of control. If you appear ill-prepared, the impeachment will be less effective. Your goal should be the appearance of fluidity and control.

Flip Charts with Experts

An effective technique is to use a prepared flip chart or preprinted demonstrative to establish and record key points made with an opposing expert. The subject matter can range from a lack of credentials to a lack of reliable methodology. Here is an example of a chart that involves a hypothetical automotive product liability case with defective seatbelt allegations:

Topic	Answer
Experience designing seatbelts used in mass production	None
Experience working for a manufacturer	None
# of cases testified for Plaintiffs	34
# of cases testified for Defendants	2
# cases testifying for a manufacturer	0
% of income coming from litigation consulting	85%
# cases consulted with Plaintiff's counsel	7
# of articles published about seatbelts	0

In this example, the initial chart is prepared before trial, and then completed with answers during cross-examination of the expert on the witness stand. The defense lawyer would handwrite the answers to the questions as the testimony unfolds. The jury is therefore viewing real-time preparation of an exhibit that will be used later in final arguments. The jury certainly will recall the chart when it is used later because there is high drama when a chart like this is created in their presence. The importance of the witness's negative answers is reinforced through the ebb and flow of the examination that leads to the quoted answers. The jury will see the lawyer record the answers, and they will infer correctly that the recorded answers are significant because the lawyer is taking time to place the information on the chart.

Adverse Witnesses

You should assume plaintiff's counsel will call one of your defense witnesses adversely. This is a common tactic, and I have done so myself in plaintiff cases I have tried. It can have lasting effects, particularly if the plaintiff's counsel can steal the defendant's thunder and bruise a key defense witness before the defense even has a chance to rebound. This means defense lawyers must be prepared to handle these situations. This also means defense lawyers must prepare key defense witnesses to testify if called adversely. You should prepare your witnesses psychologically for this possibility, and you also should never act surprised if it occurs.

You must consider *who* will serve as the corporate representative at trial when preparing for the possibility that your corporate witness can be called as an adverse witness. If you select someone who knows nothing about the facts of the particular case, the jury will wonder why that person is in the courtroom, and it may appear disingenuous. Likewise, if a senior corporate officer is in attendance, this potentially creates a different landmine if difficult policy or "integrity" questions are asked that reflect on the corporation's likeability or credibility. Again, the plaintiff's lawyer's primary goal is to make the jury dislike your client. Be sensitive to this tactic, and be careful who you bring to trial.

I have been involved in several trials where my client has been called to the stand adversely. In each case, my client representative had familiarity with the case, but did not know all of the detailed facts. There is nothing wrong with this; a corporate witness can certainly defer to those who are more knowledgeable. However, a corporate witness who knows nothing about how the corporation conducts its basic business will likely have little credibility with the jury. The jury will expect that the witness should know something.

If your client or client representative is called adversely, you will be forced to make a decision about whether to conduct your full direct examination in the plaintiff's case. If you are well-prepared, a full direct examination in the middle of the plaintiff's case can cause significant damage and stall or slow the plaintiff's momentum. This strategy, particularly if your witness is strong and has good testimonial skills, can significantly advance your trial themes. You have an opportunity to disrupt the plaintiff's monopoly on jury time in its own case-in-chief. You are basically presenting your case in advance of your case-in-chief. Exhibits should be preplanned and a full direct examination outline should be prepared and in the hopper. This should be finished weeks in advance and ready to go. The goal here is to pre-plan for all eventualities.

Another strategy is to defer your direct examination until your case-in-chief. However, I have never done this. If your witness has been injured by the plaintiff's cross-examination, you may wish to immediately rehabilitate the witness then and there. If you wait, the wounds may deepen, and it may be more difficult to rebound in your case-in-chief.

In one case I tried several years ago, I represented the nominal plaintiff who had filed a declaratory judgment action in a Texas state court. The defendant filed a "bet your company" counter-claim seeking damages in the many millions of dollars. However, because my client was the first to file, I had the right to go first. I therefore called the key witness from the other side as my first witness, and I kept him on the stand for a day and a half. He came across poorly during my cross-examination. After I passed the witness, the defendant (counter-plaintiff) elected to defer direct examination until its case-in-chief. Our case lasted another six trial days and got stronger and stronger, built, in part, on the admissions of the first adverse witness. Then, finally, when the defense case began, the opposing lawyers elected to not recall the battered witness to the stand. In final arguments, I repeatedly focused on this failure. I emphasized that the defendant could offer nothing to fix its case and was merely doing damage control. Our strategy resonated with the jury, who gave the defendant $0 damages on its counterclaim. The case was likely won as a result of this one witness.

Damage Witnesses in Personal Injury and Death Cases

Damage witnesses present differing strategies depending on the sensibilities of the witness. In turn, there will be different strategies in personal injury and death cases which are inherently different from business cases. Typically, more restraint should be displayed in serious personal injury cases or death cases. Where damages are purely economic in nature, a less sympathetic demeanor or tone may be appropriate.

Personal injury cases fall into one of two categories: serious injury and death cases and less serious injury cases where the plaintiff is a suspected malingerer or exaggerating damages. Different strategies may be needed depending on whether you are examining the plaintiff or a third-party witness called to address damages. This may involve a family friend or loved one.

In my experience, nothing but a sympathetic demeanor should be used when it is clear that the injuries are serious, permanent, catastrophic, or where a death has occurred. Genuine compassion is essential when there is no reasonable doubt of loss or harm. If this compassion is absent, or if the jury senses you or your client do not care, your case will take a direct hit. Remember, one of the cornerstones of effective advocacy is *ethos*—credibility and trustworthiness. If you attempt to downplay or diminish a serious injury or loss, you may not only lose credibility—you may inspire resentment.

This does not mean you must concede causation—*you do not*. In fact, you can display significant, appropriate empathy, on the one hand, but clearly fight liability and causation, on the other. This can be done in opening statements where you acknowledge the significance of the injury or loss. This same tone can be echoed in cross-examinations.

If damage *experts* come to the stand, you can be more aggressive. This would include economists who may be testifying to lost wages, life care planners, and medical doctors. You should not feel impeded when examining these witnesses by what they considered or failed to consider. They are paid consultants, and you should approach these types of witnesses as any other expert witness.

If a third-party *lay* witness is called to the stand on damages, you have a more difficult choice. You can elect to not cross-examine these witnesses, and I have seen this done. In doing so, you send a message to the jury that you are reasonable and you are not contesting the seriousness of the loss. However, as a matter of personal experience, I prefer to cross-examine *all* witnesses. Every witness provides another opportunity to control the courtroom and reinforce the integrity of your client's position. If you adopt this strategy, each examination of lay damage witnesses should be short and respectful. I typically thank the witness for his or her time, and then find some positive aspect of the witness's testimony to discuss. I would rather talk to the witness than run the risk the jury may misinterpret my silence if I did not conduct an examination.

Here is an example of an experience I had in a wrongful death case. A young boy, aged ten, lost his father in a tragic accident. The boy had not been deposed before trial. When he was called to the stand, my goal was to keep my examination short and to the point. I discussed his relationship with his father and, through my questions, acknowledged his loss. I slowly developed a rapport with the young boy by showing him deference and respect. I then asked him only a few question on liability matters. I established he was in the front seat of the car when the accident occurred; he could not remember anything about the accident; and he did not see his father after the accident or recall what happened during the accident. My goal was to establish each of these points while acknowledging his loss. I then thanked him for his testimony. The examination lasted less than fifteen minutes. My first goal was to be respectful and compassionate. Then, my goal was to confirm that the child witness could not offer substantive testimony on the merits of the liability claim.

The lesson here is to use good judgment and act reasonably. Defense lawyers should never try to suggest that a seriously hurt individual is not hurt. On the other hand, you can be far more aggressive when dealing with plaintiffs who may not be seriously hurt or who are lawsuit veterans and *professional claimants*. This aggressiveness is needed when dealing with these types of plaintiffs. This is where righteous indignation is appropriate to reinforce the message that the plaintiff's claim is bogus or hyped.

Flip-Chart Summaries

Another helpful technique involves using flip charts with important witnesses, not just experts. During your cross-examination, you can use a flip chart to memorialize key concessions or admission from the witness. I typically write the date at the top of the chart and then identify the witness's full name underneath the date. Then, I write out the admissions or concessions extracted during the examination in longhand. I ask the witness to confirm the substance of the remark. If the witness wants to make a minor edit, I correct the chart and then reconfirm the substance once again. If the remark is then confirmed, I put quotations around the statement. Then, in final argument, I retrieve the chart and direct the jury's attention to the quoted remarks and remind the jury of what was said on what date and by whom. This technique is particularly helpful in long trials when the jury can easily forget how each of the witnesses played a role in the testimony and what they said on the witness stand. The physical activity of writing down and memorializing the witness's testimony underscores the significance of the testimony in the jury's eyes.

Conclusion

The plaintiff's case is a pivotal point in the trial. Either the plaintiff gains momentum or it is stymied by the defense. An effective attack during the plaintiff's case will never occur unless there is a preplanned strategy. You must define the weak points in the plaintiff's case and bring them to light through your cross-examinations. If your client is called adversely, you are given an opportunity to inflict maximum injury on the plaintiff. But, again, you must be prepared to do so.

17
The Directed Verdict Stage

The Plaintiff's Perspective

The plaintiff's counsel should begin evidentiary preparation for the directed verdict stage of the trial at the outset of the case. Counsel should continue preparation for this stage by annotating and topically organizing documents and admissible testimonial evidence collected during discovery. Finally, counsel should complete her preparation for the directed verdict stage by utilizing daily copy of the trial transcript to excerpt key admissions on the elements of proof for each cause of action. The response to the inevitable motion for directed verdict should be prewritten in rough draft format well before the plaintiff's case-in-chief ends with the announcement during trial, "The Plaintiff rests." Finally, the formal response to a motion for directed verdict should be submitted in writing in impressive detail, but argued orally, and with succinct clarity, subliminally messaging the result sought—a summary denial in quick order so that the trial may proceed as it should.

Preparation before Discovery Begins

Well before formal discovery begins, the response to a sure-to-come motion for directed verdict should be outlined. Each of the various causes of action pleaded in the complaint should be dissected into their various elements of proof. The elements of proof for each cause of action should be populated in an app or software that creates outlines, with the documentary and tangible evidence collected before the suit was filed. Key conclusions in the police report, statements included therein that are made admissible by Rule 803(8)(B) of the Rules of Evidence, and photographic proof relevant to various issues to be established should be populated in the proof outline. Likewise, statements made in company emails, drafts of a contract already known to the plaintiff before filing suit, and other documentary proof of the causes of action should each initially be placed in their appropriate section of the proof outline before suit is filed.

Gaps left in the proof outline after inputting preliminary evidence also are important. These evidentiary gaps can help build deposition outlines, revealing the very proof that needs to be collected during the formal discovery process.

Continued Preparation throughout the Discovery Period

Every important interrogatory answer, key requests for admission responded to with "Admitted," significant statements included in admissible documents produced during discovery, and critical testimonial admission gained during depositions should be excerpted, topically organized, and incorporated into the proof outline. Discovery should not end until each element of proof of each cause of action contains some proof that establishes the same. Frankly, a lawyer who ends the discovery period before there is some evidence for each element of proof should be ready to lose the cause of action at issue via a Rule 56 summary judgment. Thus, preparation of a response to an inevitable motion for directed verdict begins with the collection and topical organization of the evidence in preparation for a response to a motion for summary judgment. After all, "th[e] standard [for granting summary judgment] mirrors the standard for a directed verdict under Federal Rule of Civil Procedure 50(a). . . ."[1]

Continued Preparation during the Case-in-Chief

The trial itself offers the best opportunity to augment one's proof outline in an effort to prepare for the response to a motion for directed verdict. Plaintiff's witnesses testify pursuant to direct examination outlines that have been organized to populate evidence for each element of proof with evidence needed to fill the same. Cross-examination of defense witnesses and of the defendants themselves during the plaintiff's case-in-chief offers a singular opportunity to collect admissions. The inquiring eyes of a jury watching every movement and listening to every word spoken in the courtroom is the best barometer of truth ever invented, especially under the guidance of an experienced judge preventing nonresponse and evasiveness from unwilling witnesses. Key admissions gained during live testimony are transcribed by the court reporter. The official transcript should be procured each night by paying the court reporter for daily copy, and the diligent plaintiff's lawyer should excerpt the key admissions contained in the transcript of each witness's trial testimony, topically organize the admissions, and fill them in in the trial proof outline. The evidence contained in this trial proof outline will serve as the evidentiary foundation for the plaintiff's response to the defendant's motion for directed verdict.

Writing the Rough Draft of the Motion for Directed Verdict Response

As the plaintiff's lawyer puts on her case-in-chief, she should begin writing a rough draft of the plaintiff's response to the motion for directed verdict. While many responses can be successfully communicated verbally, undertaking the process of writing out the response

1. *Anderson v. Liberty Lobby, Inc.*, 477 U.S. 242, 250 (1986).

clarifies gaps in the proof and the portions of the argument that require improvement. Moreover, by roughing out a draft of the response, counsel can thereafter procure evidence that is lacking. By writing out the standard that's applicable to a Rule 50(a) motion for directed verdict and reviewing the text of rules 50(a) and 50(b), plaintiff's counsel can fashion a commonsense argument in favor of the efficiency of deferring a ruling on the defendant's motion until after all the evidence ends.

Standard Applicable to a Rule 50(a) Motion for Directed Verdict

Rule 50(a)(1) of the Federal Rules of Civil Procedure provides that "[i]f a party has been fully heard on an issue during a jury trial and the court finds that a reasonable jury would not have a legally sufficient evidentiary basis to find for the party on that issue, the court *may*: (A) resolve the issue against the party; and (B) grant a motion for judgment as a matter of law against the party on a claim or defense that, under the controlling law, can be maintained or defeated only with a favorable finding on that issue."[2]

"[A] directed verdict under Rule 50(a), . . . requires a court to draw all factual inferences in favor of the nonmoving party."[3] "If reasonable minds could differ as to the import of the evidence, . . . a verdict should not be directed."[4]

The Efficiency of Timing Options for Bringing or Ruling On a Motion for Judgment as a Matter of Law

All judges should share a common goal: Never keep the jury waiting. If the plaintiff rests its case in the middle of a Wednesday morning, there is absolutely no justification to allow defense counsel to interrupt the trial evidence schedule with sixty to ninety minutes of legal arguments that have little to no merit made as part of a motion for directed verdict solely to preserve legal issues for appeal. Instead, these points can be submitted in writing; the arguments therein can and should be made at the end of the evidence, with the jury excused.

Rule 50(a)(2) provides that "[a] motion for judgment as a matter of law may be made at any time before the case is submitted to the jury." Consequently, there is no requirement that a motion for judgment as a matter of law be either made or ruled on at the conclusion of the plaintiff's case-in-chief. A trial judge may exercise its discretion to defer ruling on such a motion until the conclusion of all the evidence, thereby avoiding keeping the jury waiting. Moreover, a defense lawyer who wants to merely preserve legal arguments for appeal may likewise choose to merely submit in writing a motion under Rule 50(a), while deferring argument on those points until the motion for judgment as a matter of law is renewed under Rule 50(b) at the conclusion of the defendant's case-in-chief and any rebuttal evidence.

---

2. Fed. R. Civ. P. 50(a) (emphasis added).
3. *Lytle v. Household Mfg., Inc.*, 494 U.S. 545, 546 (1990).
4. *Anderson*, 477 U.S. at 250–51 (citing *Wilkerson v. McCarthy*, 336 U.S. 53, 62 (1949)).

A plaintiff's lawyer who defends against such a motion should first remind the judge of this reality—the defendant can preserve its record and the court can meet its obligation to rule by simply deferring a ruling on a Rule 50(a) motion. Furthermore, there is no rule that requires the court to keep the jury waiting while an appellate specialist for the defense expends an hour of valuable court time by reading arguments into the record. Again, any Rule 50(a) motion can be made in writing and submitted to the court, thereby preserving the legal arguments without wasting everyone's time. Again, the jury is waiting. . . .

Efficiency Gained by Deferring a Ruling

Trial judges should be reminded of the efficiencies that are lost by a decision to grant a directed verdict. First, jurors empaneled by virtue of the parties' rights under the Sixth Amendment to the U.S. Constitution have invested their time to hear the plaintiff's evidence. Jurors should have the right to finish their duty and render a verdict to find facts that the court can use post-verdict to decide whether to issue a judgment. "'Courts should not assume that in determining these questions of negligence juries will fall short of a fair performance of their constitutional function.'"[5]

"[W]hile a district court is permitted to enter judgment as a matter of law when it concludes that the evidence is legally insufficient, it is not required to do so. To the contrary, the district courts are, if anything, encouraged to submit the case to the jury, rather than granting such motions."[6] "Judicial appraisal of the proofs to determine whether a jury question is presented is narrowly limited to the single inquiry whether, with reason, the conclusion may be drawn that negligence . . . played any part at all in the injury or death. Judges are to fix their sights primarily to make that appraisal and, if that test is met, are bound to find that a case for the jury is made out whether or not the evidence allows the jury a choice of other probabilities."[7]

Each response to a motion for directed verdict should cite the teaching of the U.S. Supreme Court in *Bailey v. Central Vermont Ry.*, 319 U.S. 350 (1943). There, Justice Douglas, who delivered the opinion for the Court during World War II, wrote as follows:

> The right to trial by jury is "a basic and fundamental feature of our system of federal jurisprudence." It is part and parcel of the remedy afforded railroad workers under the Employers' Liability Act. Reasonable care and cause and effect are as elusive here as in other fields. But the jury has been chosen as the appropriate tribunal to apply those standards to the facts of these personal injuries. That method of determining the liability of the carriers and of placing on them the cost of these industrial accidents may be crude, archaic, and expensive as compared with the more modern systems of workmen's compensation. But however inefficient and backward it may be, it is the system which Congress has provided. To deprive these workers of the benefit of a

5. *Ferguson v. Moore-McCormack Lines, Inc.*, 352 U.S. 521, 523–24 (1957) (quoting *Wilkerson v. McCarthy*, 336 U.S. 53, 62 (1949)).

6. *Unitherm Food Systems, Inc. v. Swift-Eckrich, Inc.*, 546 U.S. 394, 405 (2006).

7. *Rogers v. Missouri Pac. R.R. Co.*, 352 U.S. 500, 506–07 (1957).

jury trial in close or doubtful cases is to take away a goodly portion of the relief which Congress has afforded them.[8]

As a matter of time invested, permitting the jury to finish its job is more efficient than prohibiting it from doing so, with the consequent risk of appellate reversal. Denial of a motion for directed verdict is "not error," but "merely an exercise of the District Court's discretion, in accordance with the text of the Rule and the accepted practice of permitting the jury to make an initial judgment about the sufficiency of the evidence."[9] By contrast, instances of every federal appellate court reversing trial court orders directing a verdict are legion.[10]

---

8. *Id.* at 354 (citation omitted).

9. *Unitherm*, 546 U.S. at 406.

10. *See, e.g.*, **First Circuit:** *Brennan v. GTE Gov't Systems Corp.*, 150 F.3d 21 (1st Cir. 1997) (reversing directed verdict, holding that whether former employer's proffered reasons for terminating former employee were pretext and whether the true reason was age-based animus were questions for jury); *Santiago v. Fenton*, 891 F.2d 373 (1st Cir. 1989) (reversing directed verdict, holding that a jury question existed as to whether an officer violated an arrestee's Fourth Amendment right to be free from unreasonable seizure of person and his common-law right to be free from false arrest and imprisonment).

Second Circuit: *Taitt v. Chemical Bank*, 849 F.2d 775 (2d Cir. 1988) (reversing directed verdict, holding that issue of whether employee's discharge was in retaliation for his opposition to settlement of a class-action lawsuit brought against the bank was for the jury); *Centronics Financial Corp. v. El Conquistador Hotel Corp.*, 573 F.2d 779 (2d Cir. 1978) (reversing directed verdict, holding fact issue existed as to fraud in inducement).

Third Circuit: *Fletcher v. O'Donnell*, 867 F.2d 791 (3d Cir. 1989) (holding that directed verdict for city had to be reversed, where directed verdict depended on erroneous exclusion of evidence offered of policy or custom tolerating excessive use of force by officers); *Fetsko v. Greyhound Lines, Inc.*, 497 F.2d 399 (3d Cir. 1974) (reversing directed verdict, holding that the evidence presented jury questions with respect to bus driver's negligence on theory that his ability to take evasive action was the result of excessive speed and inattention and as to contributory negligence of decedent driver).

Fourth Circuit: *Satterly v. Raymark Indus., Inc.*, 117 F.3d 776 (4th Cir. 1997) (reversing directed verdict, holding that whether employees' exposure to manufacturer's asbestos products was a substantial factor in employees' asbestos-related injury was for jury); *Teague v. Bakker*, 35 F.3d 978 (4th Cir. 1994) (reversing directed verdict, holding that whether lifetime partnerships could be considered "securities" was a question for the jury).

Fifth Circuit: *Copsey v. Swearingen*, 36 F.3d 1336 (5th Cir. 1994) (reversing directed verdict, holding that evidence was sufficient for the jury on First Amendment claim); *Wilson v. U.T. System Police Dept.*, 973 F.2d 1263 (5th Cir. 1992) (reversing directed verdict, holding that whether officials charged with defamation acted with malice presented question for jury).

Sixth Circuit: *Innotext, Inc. v. Petra'Lex USA, Inc.*, 694 F.3d 581 (6th Cir. 2012) (reversing directed verdict, holding issues existed for jury in determining whether there was a meeting of minds as to the parties to the contract, subject of contract, and representative's unjust enrichment claim); *Osontoski v. Wal-Mart Stores, Inc.*, 143 F.3d 1027 (6th Cir. 1998) (reversing directed verdict, holding that fact issues, including whether spilled liquid on which customer fell was open and obvious, were for the jury to resolve).

Seventh Circuit: *Freeman v. Madison Metro. School Dist.*, 231 F.3d 374 (7th Cir. 2000) (reversing directed verdict, holding that the issue of whether employee rebutted the school district's race-neutral explanation for refusing to return him to work after knee injury was for jury); *Bebout v. Norfolk & Western Ry. Co.*, 982 F.2d 1178 (7th Cir. 1993) (reversing directed verdict, holding that the testimony of a motorist that he did not hear the whistle blow was sufficient to create a triable issue of fact as to whether whistle was blown).

Eighth Circuit: *Steckstor by Santa Cruz v. Hancock*, 984 F.2d 274 (8th Cir. 1993) (reversing directed verdict, holding that evidence was sufficient to create a jury question as to whether the tow truck operator acted negligently); *Carter v. Kurn*, 127 F.2d 415, 420 (8th Cir. 1942) (reversing directed verdict, holding that "it was, we think, for the jury to determine whether the defendants exercised that high degree of care and vigilance required of them in closing and keeping closed the traps and doors on the train in which plaintiff's intestate was a passenger").

Ninth Circuit: *Rattray v. City of Nat'l City*, 36 F.3d 1480 (9th Cir. 1994) (reversing directed verdict, holding that the district court erred in dismissing invasion of privacy claim); *Samarzia v. Clark County*, 859 F.2d 88 (9th Cir. 1989) (reversing directed verdict, holding that evidence of county's discriminatory intent in terminating employee while retaining younger, less senior employees was for the jury).

For this reason, any dispositive ruling sought by a defendant's motion for directed verdict is one that should be ruled on only at the close of all evidence under Rule 50(b), or issued post-verdict on a motion for new trial under Rule 50(c). This is the entire purpose of Rule 50(b), which allows the defendant to renew the motion after the trial, providing that "[i]f the court does not grant a motion for judgment as a matter of law made under Rule 50(a), the court is considered to have submitted the action to the jury subject to the court's later deciding the legal questions raised by the motion." The practical difference between the two is that if the trial judge is wrong at the directed verdict stage, a new trial will be required. By contrast, if the trial judge is wrong at the Rule 50(c) phase, an appellate court can reverse and a corrected judgment can be entered based on the jury's findings, without the necessity of a new trial and the consequent expenditure of further judicial resources.[11]

Submitting the Written Response While Arguing It Orally

The response to a motion for directed verdict should be submitted in writing, setting forth in great quantity and detail all proof that has been introduced before the jury. However, the defendant's motion for directed verdict will have attacked only a few alleged deficiencies in the proof. As such, the oral argument should address only such points, and should be made in the most succinct manner possible so that the trial may quickly proceed. By arguing succinctly, the plaintiff's lawyer suggests to the court that the motion should quickly be denied, or at least deferred, so that the jury may resume its duties when the trial proceeds forward to its next phase—the defendant's case-in-chief.

Tenth Circuit: *Knowlton v. Teltrust Phones, Inc.*, 189 F.3d 1177 (10th Cir. 1999) (reversing directed verdict, holding that evidence that the parent corporation and subsidiary constituted a single employer, and that the parent thus was liable for the subsidiary's discriminatory acts, was for the jury); *Oja v. Howmedica, Inc.*, 111 F.3d 782 (10th Cir. 1997) (reversing directed verdict, holding that the issue of whether a prosthesis contained a manufacturing defect for which the manufacturer could be held strictly liable was for the jury).

Eleventh Circuit: *FDIC v. Marina*, 892 F.2d 1522 (11th Cir. 1990) (reversing directed verdict, holding that whether the rate of interest on a borrower's note referred to the prime rate of interest charged by New York banks was a question for the jury); *Dancey Co., Inc. v. Borg-Warner, Inc.*, 799 F.2d 717 (11th Cir. 1986) (reversing directed verdict, holding that whether manufacturer fraudulently misrepresented testing of carburetor and whether punitive damages were proper were questions for the jury).

D.C. Circuit: *Klein v. District of Columbia*, 409 F.2d 164, 167 (D.C. Cir. 1969) (reversing directed verdict, holding that "unless we can say that, giving appellants all reasonable inferences from the facts, appellants still have not offered any evidence upon which a reasonable man could find that the District failed to keep the sidewalk safe, the directed verdict must be reversed"); *Wabisky v. D.C. Transit System, Inc.*, 309 F.2d 317 (D.C. Cir. 1962) (reversing directed verdict, holding that testimony showing that the decedent was a substantial distance ahead of the streetcar with his back turned toward the streetcar when the defendant's motorman first noticed decedent presented a jury issue as to negligence of the defendant under the last clear chance doctrine).

[Federal Circuit] *In re Burke v. Everest & Jennings, Inc.*, 82 F.3d 435 (Fed. Cir. 1996) (unpublished) (after reversing prior directed verdict, 991 F.2d 812 (Fed. Cir. 1993) (table), reversing district court's summary judgment and holding that the district court's summary finding of nonequivalence was inappropriate in light of the contrary evidence on that issue of fact); *U.S. Philips Corp. v. Windmere Corporation*, 861 F.2d 695 (Fed. Cir. 1989) (reversing directed verdict, holding that there was sufficient evidence to submit antitrust claims to jury); *Rainey v. Union Oil Co. of Cal.*, 732 F.2d 1563 (Temp. Emer. Ct. App. 1984) (reversing directed verdict, holding that questions of whether marketer substantially complied with regulation governing designation of new base period gasoline supplier, and whether supplier tortiously interfered with business advantage were for the jury).

11. Fed. R. Civ. P. 50(e).

18

Directed Verdicts: Crossing the Rubicon

The Defense Perspective

Nothing good happens in trial without planning and preparation. This includes motions for directed verdict.

Typically, there is no turning back for a plaintiff's lawyer once the evidence closes. In many jurisdictions, there is a moment of truth when the plaintiff rests at the close of its case-in-chief. This moment, which is akin to fording the River Rubicon, is a boundary that once crossed, may allow no return. Many trial courts will not allow plaintiffs to reopen and fix significant evidence failures. In federal court, this is particularly true if a motion under Rule 50 is made at the close of all evidence.[1] The directed verdict stage is therefore a pivotal moment in a trial. It is important to note, however, that any realistic hope for a knockout punch through a directed verdict motion starts well before trial. Preparation for this moment realistically starts in the planning of written discovery and witness depositions.

The entirety of the pretrial stages of a case are properly focused on identifying and magnifying the legal and factual weaknesses in the plaintiff's case, while enhancing the strengths of the defense case. Every defense lawyer should understand fully the plaintiff's legal and factual infirmities before the jury is sworn and seated. The skilled defense lawyer then targets these weaknesses. The goal is to reinforce these weaknesses through the cross-examination of a plaintiff's witnesses and through pretrial motions and evidence exclusion. These goals, however, are not achieved without a full understanding of what the plaintiff must prove to carry its burden. With that said, there are several practice tips that, if followed, may enhance the chances for a successful directed verdict.

1. *See* Fed. R. Civ. P. 50.

Know the Relevant Standards

Various state court jurisdictions may have unique standards that govern consideration and appellate review of motions for directed verdict. Every defense lawyer should know and understand these standards and conform directed verdict motions accordingly. Some jurisdictions may require assertion of directed verdict motions at the close of the plaintiff's case to preserve the right to assert posttrial motions, or as a foundation for appellate review to challenge the sufficiency of the evidence issues. All defense lawyers are therefore encouraged to understand these procedural requirements and standards of review for the specific jurisdiction where they practice.

In the federal court system, directed verdicts largely have been replaced by motions for judgment as a matter of law, which are governed by Rule 50 of the Federal Rules of Civil Procedure. These types of motions typically are made *after* the close of all evidence but *before* the case is submitted to the jury.

Evidentiary Standard

Under Rule 50, the substantial evidence test applies—the nonmoving party has failed to adduce "substantial evidence in support of his claim."[2] Appellate review of an order granting judgment as a matter of law is when "all the evidence points one way and is susceptible of no reasonable inferences sustaining the position of the nonmoving party."[3] However, more than merely a scintilla of evidence is required. "In sum, we conclude that the determination of whether a given factual dispute requires submission to a jury must be guided by the substantive evidentiary standards that apply to the case."[4] The federal standard is properly summarized as follows:

> An order granting a motion for judgment as a matter of law under Fed. R. Civ. P. 50 is proper when the court, reviewing the evidence and inferences most favorably to the non-moving party, finds that there is insufficient evidence upon which the jury could properly find for the non-moving party. In ruling on such a motion, the court must apply to substantive evidentiary burden of proof which applies to the non-moving party's claims at trial.[5]

Know the Elements of the Claims You Are Defending

It is rare that a good plaintiff's lawyer inadvertently fails to prove an essential element of his client's claim. Although inadvertence does occur from time to time, the more likely scenario is when a plaintiff *cannot* prove an essential element because the defense lawyer successfully boxed him in or extracted a dispositive admission or concession from one of the

2. *DeMaine v. Bank One, Akron, N.A.*, 904 F.2d 219, 220 (4th Cir. 1990).
3. *Ehrhardt v. Penn. Mut. Life Ins. Co.*, 21 F.3d 266, 269 (8th Cir. 1994).
4. *Anderson v. Liberty Lobby, Inc.*, 477 U.S. 242, 255, 202 (1986); *see Hartnagel v. Norman*, 953 F.2d 394, 396 (8th Cir. 1992) (district court "must bear in mind the actual quantum and quality of the proof applicable to support liability under the applicable law").
5. *Kelley Metal Trading Co. v. Al-Jon/United, Inc.*, 877 F. Supp. 1478, 1482 (D. Kan. 1995) (internal citations omitted).

plaintiff's witnesses. Of course, this does not result from blind luck. It usually results from a carefully implemented strategy.

To avoid inadvertent or careless omissions in proof, many plaintiff's lawyers maintain checklists as backstops to make sure there is sufficient proof to support each element of each alleged claim. Like a pilot and copilot in the cockpit running down a checklist before takeoff, good plaintiff's lawyers do a similar review before resting their case. Otherwise, the case may literally crash and burn.

By keeping a checklist, and annotating this list with testimony and documents actually admitted into evidence, plaintiff's lawyers will marshal important evidence in anticipation of a directed verdict motion. They will be fully armed and ready with a response for the court. Every defense lawyer should do the same.

Defense lawyers must become well-schooled on each of the essential elements of the plaintiff's causes of action. Otherwise, we cannot identify and discern the weakest point in the plaintiff's proof. As defense lawyers, we should monitor the introduction of evidence to determine these weak points. Equally important, we should keep track of potentially dispositive admissions or concessions obtained from the plaintiff's witnesses. Some admissions or concessions will be dispositive and a basis for a successful motion in most jurisdictions. Here are a few examples:

- In a products liability case involving defective design, a concession from the plaintiff's design expert that he or she cannot identify a safer alternative design.
- In a drug liability case, a concession from the plaintiff's medical causation expert that he or she failed to conduct a differential diagnosis.
- In a construction defect case, a concession from the plaintiff's expert that the defect existed when the building was first erected beyond the statute of repose.
- In a tort case, a concession that the harm was discovered or readily discoverable as a basis for asserting a statute of limitations defense.
- In a punitive damage case, a lack of evidence that the defendant acted willfully, intentionally, or recklessly, thereby destroying the scienter requirements for exemplary damages in the particular jurisdiction.

The list goes on and on. The point is to understand the plaintiff's burden of proof for each claim, and to develop testimony or evidence that undercuts the ability to support that burden. Again, this is not something first started on the eve of trial; it begins with the first witness depositions.

To be clear, the deposition record in a case should be developed and molded to support summary judgment motions, motions in limine, and *Daubert*-type challenges of the plaintiff's experts. If you are successful in excluding key evidence or limiting a plaintiff's expert, the plaintiff's ability to carry its burden of proof can be severely restricted and possibly extinguished. Defense lawyers should always attack the weakest link in the plaintiff's claim. These weak links—each a plaintiff's Achilles heel—are rarely discovered after trial begins. Rather, the weakest links in a plaintiff's claim are identified frequently in the early life of the case. The defense lawyer's job is to find these weak links and expose them.

Ultimately, a good defense lawyer is doing the same as the plaintiff's lawyer. Use a checklist and see where the plaintiff's case comes up short—either because of inadvertence or because the defense lawyer was able to undercut the plaintiff's ability to carry its burden.

Avoid Shotgun Motions

Some defense lawyers use a shotgun approach and move for directed verdicts on all of a plaintiff's claims. This typically is not a good strategy. It is a better practice to be selective and focus on discrete, significant weaknesses in the plaintiff's proof. By doing so, the directed verdict argument is not diluted, and the court's attention is better focused.

An unnecessary argument frequently distracts from and confounds key factual and legal issues, making a directed verdict argument less persuasive. Thus, less is best. As the architect Frank Lloyd Wright said, "Less is more only where more is no good."[6] As lawyers, we are the architects of our motions and trial strategies. The wisdom here is to focus our arguments so we can focus the court's attention.

The Plaintiff's Pleadings—Less Is Best

Many plaintiff's lawyers shotgun their pleadings and assert a variety of causes of action that they ultimately do not fully prosecute. The ostensible goal is to make sure no potential claims are omitted. However, by the time of trial, the plaintiff's lawyer may be less interested in pursuing many of these claims, particularly claims that have a higher risk of losing. The directed verdict process is a good way to rid the case of surplus claims without purposefully abandoning these claims. Some plaintiff's lawyers prefer to have the court make these decisions because they perceive better cover with a judge's ruling.

There are distinct reasons underlying these types of tactical decisions: (1) avoiding giving defense lawyers an opportunity to put on harmful evidence concerning weaker claims; (2 avoiding the appearance of losing before the jury; and, (3) simplifying the jury charge. Accordingly, plaintiff's lawyers sometimes "roll over" during the directed verdict stage on weaker claims, while aggressively protecting stronger claims. Having multiple claims can be confusing to a jury. By streamlining the suit, the case is simplified and becomes more focused for the jury.

Obtain a Daily Copy

In complex cases or cases that have significant damage exposure, defense counsel should encourage their clients to underwrite the cost of daily copy from the court reporter. Court reporting technology allows fast turnaround. In fact, turnaround is now a matter of mere hours, or even less. Daily copy is expensive, but both sides can share this cost. Regardless, having access to daily copy provides multiple benefits. Defense lawyers should mine daily copy for significant testimony (admissions and concessions) and use this testimony in closing arguments. This is particularly important in long, extended trials where juror memories are tested.

6. BrainyQuote, https://www.brainyquote.com/quotes/frank_lloyd_wright_100204 (Mar. 14, 2020).

Daily copy also is useful in the charge conference. Thus, ready access to important testimony frequently is helpful in shaping jury questions and instructions. Lastly, daily copy is useful to bolster a directed verdict motion. From the defense perspective, a written record of a startling admission or witness concession will substantially reinforce a directed verdict motion. Otherwise, the court may have a different recollection of the testimony and not recall the drama or significance of specific testimony. If a dispositive admission or concession is in print, the motion will be strengthened. It is hard to ignore admissions recorded in black and white.

Likewise, daily copy is useful to demonstrate that the plaintiff failed to present proof on a discrete element of the claim. Here, *the proof is either in the record or the record becomes the proof there was insufficient evidence.*

Prepare Written Motions

Directed verdicts are more effective if they are reduced to writing. The basis for a directed verdict motion also should be annotated with appropriate case authorities and citations to the record. A well-briefed directed verdict motion is more difficult to deny. Verbal motions are more readily denied.

Verbal directed verdict motions often are rushed, and the court might be forced to rely on its memory recall. However, a court can devote more attention to a written brief, with supporting authorities and record citations. Even if the written motion is denied, the court will have the motion in hand, and it can reconsider its ruling during the post-verdict stages. Essentially, the shelf life of a written motion for directed verdict is longer.

Courts frequently use a directed verdict as an opportunity to "clean up" a case. A written record with a written motion may make the court more comfortable in its rulings. Verbal motions tend to be less focused and more easily defended by the opponent. Sometimes it becomes a test of memories of what the plaintiff did or did not prove or what a plaintiff's witness said or did not say. Daily copy provides a written record, and a written brief can eliminate ambiguity.

Purely Legal Defenses and Prior Summary Judgment Motions

Occasionally, certain types of legal defenses materialize at the close of a plaintiff's case. However, entitlement to a directed verdict on purely legal grounds typically does not arise for the first time during trial. Rather, these types of legal defenses likely existed long before trial and could have been (and *should* have been) a basis for a summary judgment motion. Indeed, summary judgment motions are a useful vehicle for educating the court on purely legal issues. Although a court may deny a summary judgment motion, the same issues can be revisited at trial through directed verdict motions. Courts frequently deny summary judgment motions to see how the case evolves during trial. Accordingly, a well-briefed summary judgment motion is an excellent template for a well-briefed directed verdict motion.

In sum, prepare and plan early; focus on the plaintiff's legal and factual weaknesses; order daily copy; and use daily copy to annotate a written directed verdict motion. Lastly, focus on the weakest elements of the plaintiff's case and avoid a shotgun approach.

19
The Defendant's Case
The Plaintiff's Perspective

A plaintiff's lawyer who expects to enjoy a verdict in his client's favor better be well ahead at the end of the plaintiff's case-in-chief. However, great verdicts are earned during cross-examination of defense witnesses. For this reason, the most important component of any trial for the plaintiff is the exhaustive preparation for the cross-examination of key defense witnesses.

Reminder—Use Key Witness Deposition Cross-Examinations during Plaintiff's Case-in-Chief

A discovery period that involves twenty depositions may yield only three depositions that critically injure the defendant's case. The plaintiff's attorney must make certain to play the videos of those cross-examinations during the plaintiff's case-in-chief.[1] After all, if the deposition cross-examination was as good as the plaintiff's lawyer believes, assume that the defense lawyer noticed as well. A good defense lawyer, knowing he does not have the burden of proof, may deselect witnesses whose testimony was mortally wounded during the discovery process. For this reason, the plaintiff's lawyer must cross-designate defense experts and witnesses, so there is no barrier to calling these witnesses during the plaintiff's case-in-chief.

Sandbagging—Quietly Inducing the Defense Lawyer to Call a Witness Not Known by the Defense to Be Exposed to Annihilation

Preparing for the deposition of a defense expert may yield a golden nugget that was squirreled away by the witness long ago, which clearly, if known by the defense lawyer, would have prevented his designation in the first place. This "witness killer" may be a fake college

1. *See In re Fosamax Prods. Liab. Litig.*, 509 F. App'x 69, 73 (2d Cir. 2013) ("Merck was free to use the testimony of plaintiff's experts to establish its case").

degree on a resume, a statement contrary to the witness's present opinion that was embedded deep in an article published long ago, or an opinion given in another case long ago that is consistent with the plaintiff's position in the present case. Nothing is more powerful than the destruction of a defense expert witness deep into the trial, well within the defendant's case-in-chief. If such a nugget is unearthed before the defense expert's deposition, the good trial lawyer exercises patience and withholds this nugget from the deposition cross-examination, so it may be disclosed only at trial. Often, the decision to withhold such a gem depends on a judgment of whether the case is likely to be settled if such a disclosure is made. In the context of MDLs, where it is known to all that no master settlement will be reached without the data provided by a jury verdict in a bellwether trial, such a prize should be carefully tucked away into one's safe, much like the Hope Diamond itself, to be revealed only when the defendant has placed its reliance on such a flawed witness on the stand.

Constructing the Cross-Examination

Cross-examinations of experts and important substantive witnesses should be thoroughly outlined and scripted. All prior publications authored by a witness, as well as articles cited in such publications, should be collected and thoroughly annotated. Rule 26 testimony lists must be included in the expert disclosure itself. This allows earnest lawyers to collect relevant prior transcripts of such testimonies. Prior testimony should be scoured for key admissions and positions and then topically organized. Online research of Google, Bing, LinkedIn, and the various social media platforms should take place because it often yields important information on positions taken by a witness. Likewise, any financial information about the witness should be collected to learn of previous relationships between the witness and the defendants or their attorneys. With respect to company employees, diligent discovery should have unearthed all relevant communications between the witness and others inside or outside the defendant's corporate organization. These emails must be thoroughly examined, and key admissions therein excerpted and organized either topically or chronologically.

All of these materials should be integrated into a written cross-examination outline. These outlines may be more than 100 pages long, initially. However, if they are prepared far enough in advance, they may be placed on the shelf during the preparation of other outlines, so that there is time to return to them for fine-tuning, editing, and shortening, so only the key points are addressed before the jury. By writing cross-examination outlines well in advance, the opportunity to improve them later is available; additionally, the good lawyer has time to collect the referenced documents, transcripts, and other evidence referenced therein, and to ensure that there is a plan to get those materials into evidence during the actual cross-examination itself.

Preparing a Primer on Cross-Examination for Use with the Court

Because a searing cross-examination raises the temperature in the courtroom by virtue of the considerable heat being brought upon the flawed witness confined to the witness stand, any sane defense lawyer will attempt to mitigate the damage by seeking assistance from the court in the form of rulings meant to restrict the examination itself. Coaching objections must be immediately stopped by the plaintiff's lawyer. Likewise, long sidebars requested by defense counsel should be minimized, with an impatient "Your honor, this is cross-examination" and "He's just trying to interrupt my train of thought." Most importantly, however, is having embedded in the cross-examination outline particular cases at the ready to defend the right to cross-examine on a particular subject, or by using a particular method.

Written cross-examination outlines—with associated case law—are essential here to keep opposing counsel's interruptions from distracting the plaintiff's lawyer from the specific issue being addressed at the time of the objection. Moreover, when the initial objection, or sidebar argument, is swiftly defeated by virtue of a reported opinion—at the ready in triplicate, with the relevant holding flagged and pre-highlighted—it has the prophylactic effect of keeping opposing counsel from interrupting again.

The General Primer on Cross-Examination

The good plaintiff's lawyer should have a generic trial brief on cross-examination ready to be filed immediately after the defendant's motion for directed verdict is overruled. Reminding the judge of the importance of cross-examination and the wide berth traditionally permitted during cross-examination is a key way to convince the court to permit a wide-ranging inspection of the bias and credibility of the defendant's witnesses. General case law on cross-examination, briefly outlined below, should be provided to the court just before the defendant's case-in-chief begins.

The central focus of a trial brief is to remind the court that American jurisprudence has long permitted broad latitude during cross-examination. "For two centuries past, the policy of the Anglo-American system of evidence has been to regard the necessity of testing by cross-examination as a vital feature of the law."[2] America's foremost authority on the law of evidence, Dean John Henry Wigmore of Northwestern Law School, called cross-examination "the age-old tool for ferreting out truth in the trial process" and "beyond any doubt the greatest legal engine ever invented for the discovery of truth."[3]

The Supreme Court has recognized that because "the exposure of a witness' motivation in testifying is a proper and important function of the constitutionally protected right of cross-examination,"[4] confrontation "forces the witness to submit to cross-examination."[5] Therefore, "[t]he partiality of a witness is subject to exploration at trial, and is 'always relevant as discrediting the witness and affecting the weight of his testimony.'"[6] Thus, "cross-examination directed toward revealing possible biases, prejudices, or ulterior motives of the witness as they may relate directly to issues or personalities in the case at hand" is a permitted attack on a witness's credibility.[7] The Supreme Court has therefore long allowed

2. 5 John Henry Wigmore, James H. Chadbourn & Walter A. Reiser, Evidence in Trials at Common Law § 1367 (Rev. 1974).
3. *Id.*
4. *Davis v. Alaska*, 415 U.S. 308, 316–17 (1974) (citing *Green v. McElroy*, 360 U.S. 474, 496 (1959)).
5. *California v. Green*, 399 U.S. 149, 158 (1970).
6. *Davis*, 415 U.S. at 316 (citing 3A Wigmore, Evidence § 940, at 775 (Chadbourn rev. 1970)).
7. *Id.* at 316.

broad latitude to probe credibility by cross-examination,[8] and has held that "it is permissible to impeach a witness by showing his bias under the Federal Rules of Evidence just as it was permissible to do so before their adoption."[9] Even in a post-*Daubert* world, a trial court's "gatekeeping" role is no substitute for "[v]igorous cross-examination."[10] Indeed, "in the Anglo–American legal system cross-examination is the principal means of undermining the credibility of a witness whose testimony is false or inaccurate."[11] For example, a witness testifying while on morphine may be questioned so that the jury may know "whether, at the moment of testifying, she was under its influence, or had recovered from the effects of its last administration, . . ." as this "had a material bearing upon her reliability as a witness."[12]

Finally, while gaps in the credibility of an expert may not result in his opinions being stricken, attacks on the same should be permitted during cross-examination. "As a general rule, the factual basis of an expert opinion goes to the credibility of the testimony, not the admissibility, and it is up to the opposing party to examine the factual basis for the opinion in cross-examination."[13] The strength of an expert's "credentials go to the weight, not the admissibility of his testimony,"[14] and challenges to an expert's methodology is fertile ground for cross examination.[15] Moreover, any inconsistency between trial testimony and prior testimony given is "'the type of inconsistency that the [defendant] should test through cross-examination at trial and allow the jury to weigh in determining the credibility of [the] plaintiff's testimony in support of his . . . claims.'"[16] In this vein, even if an expert witness's "direct and cross-examination are not entirely consistent, the jury ha[s] the ultimate discretion to evaluate his credibility and weigh his presentation."[17] Finally, bias alone will not

---

8. *See Banks v. Dretke*, 540 U.S. 668, 702 (2004) (citing *On Lee v. United States*, 343 U.S. 747, 757 (1952)).

9. *United States v. Abel*, 469 U.S. 45, 51 (1984).

10. *Daubert v. Merrill Dow Pharmaceuticals*, 509 U.S. 579, 596 (1993); *see also McGregor v. Paul Revere Life Ins. Co.*, 92 F. App'x 412, 2004 WL 68692, at *6, n.6 (9th Cir. 2004) (unpublished) ("We also conclude that the trial court did not abuse its discretion by finding that cross-examination was the proper vehicle for addressing Paul Revere's attacks on Dr. Markison's credibility.").

11. *United States v. Salerno*, 505 U.S. 317, 328 (1992) (Stevens, J., dissenting).

12. *Wilson v. United States*, 232 U.S. 563, 567–68 (1914); *see also Russell v. Bryant*, No. 18-7043, 2019 WL 3052758, at *3 (10th Cir. 2019) ("[D]uring the defense's cross-examination of Ms. Good, the jury learned that she was a drug addict, that she had previously pleaded guilty to charges of domestic violence, and that she was mentally ill and had not been taking her medication regularly. It was within the jury's purview alone to assess the credibility of these witnesses, and it is not our place to second-guess the jury's assessment."). *Cf. Flythe v. Dist. of Columbia*, 791 F.3d 13, 22 (D.C. Cir. 2015) ("[W]e agree that the district court erred when it found Eagan's sleep disorder and drug use insufficient to place his ability to perceive or recall facts . . . legitimately at issue and irrelevant to the question . . . whether both officers are lying.") (quotations omitted).

13. *Synergetics, Inc. v. Hurst*, 477 F.3d 949, 955–56 (8th Cir. 2007) (citing *Bonner v. ISP Tech., Inc.*, 259 F.3d 924, 929 (8th Cir. 2001) (quoting *Hose v. Chicago Northwestern Transp. Co.*, 70 F.3d 968, 974 (8th Cir. 1995) (internal citations and quotations omitted)); *Tussey v. ABB, Inc.*, 746 F.3d 327, 337 (8th Cir. 2014) (same); *see also Structural Polymer Group, Ltd. v. Zoltek Corp.*, 543 F.3d 987, 997–98 (8th Cir. 2008).

14. *Williams v. Warren*, 253 F.3d 700, 2001 WL 498501, at *2 (5th Cir. 2001) (per curiam) (citing *Marceaux v. Conoco, Inc.*, 124 F.3d 730, 734 (5th Cir. 1997)).

15. *Miss. Chem. Corp. v. Dresser-Rand Co.*, 287 F.3d 359, 374 (5th Cir. 2002) ("On cross-examination, Dresser had the opportunity to challenge these figures as well as Sterling's credibility and methodology.").

16. *Kuebel v. Black & Decker, Inc.*, 643 F.3d 352, 364 (2d Cir. 2011) (citing *Allen v. Bd. of Pub. Educ. for Bibb Cty.*, 495 F.3d 1306, 1317 (11th Cir. 2007)).

17. *Presidio Components, Inc. v. Amer. Tech. Ceramics Corp.*, 702 F.2d 1351, 1359 (Fed. Cir. 2012); *see also Doan v. United States*, 202 F.2d 674, 680 (9th Cir. 1953) ("It was for the jury who observed him and the manner and emphasis with which he gave his answers on direct and cross-examination to weigh and evaluate his testimony").

disqualify an expert; however, "[t]o the extent bias exists, cross-examination and the testimony of an opposing expert may be used to 'expose' it."[18]

Constrictions on Cross-Examination

The lawyer who is planning a cross-examination must keep certain limitations in mind, although the limitations are not to be put into a trial brief for the court. First, at least in federal court, other than probes into bias and credibility,[19] the scope of cross-examination often is limited to subjects that were inquired about during the direct examination. The Supreme Court held more than a century ago:

> Authorities of the highest character show that the established rule of practice in the Federal courts and in most other jurisdictions in this country is that a party has no right to cross-examine a witness, without leave of the court, as to any facts and circumstances not connected with matters stated in his direct examination, subject to two necessary exceptions. He may ask questions to show bias or prejudice in the witness, or to lay the foundation to admit evidence of prior contradictory statements. Subject to those exceptions, the general rule is that if the party wishes to examine the witness as to other matters, he must in general do so by making him his own witness and calling him as such in the subsequent progress of the cause.[20]

The promulgation of the Federal Rules of Evidence in 1975 led to the same result, because Fed. R. Evid. 611 does provide for limitation of the scope of cross-examination "to the subject matter of the direct examination and matters affecting the credibility of the witness."[21]

Second, the court maintains discretion to limit improper areas of cross-examination,[22] because "'proof of bias' is not a talismanic phrase that extinguishes the trial court's duty to evaluate and possibly exclude evidence otherwise violative of the Rules."[23] "There is a duty to protect [the witness] from questions which go beyond the bounds of proper cross-examination merely to harass, annoy or humiliate him."[24] For example, the marital discord being experienced by a witness has been off limits for almost 125 years, since the Supreme Court held that "the credibility of a witness cannot be impeached by asking her whether she has not had some difficulty with her husband."[25] Appellate courts have properly disapproved of inquiries on cross-examination into whether plaintiffs enjoyed legal resident

18. *Apple, Inc. v. Motorola, Inc.*, 757 F.3d 1286, 1321–22 (Fed. Cir. 2014).

19. *See Davis v. Alaska*, 415 U.S. 308, 316 (1974) ("Subject always to the broad discretion of a trial judge to preclude repetitive and unduly harassing interrogation, the cross-examiner is not only permitted to delve into the witness' story to test the witness' perceptions and memory, but the cross-examiner has traditionally been allowed to impeach, *i.e.*, discredit, the witness").

20. *Wills v. Russell*, 100 U.S. 621, 625–26 (1879).

21. Fed. R. Evid. 611.

22. *United States v. Higgins*, 362 F.2d 462, 464 (7th Cir. 1966) ("[T]he trial court has considerable discretion as to how and when bias may be proved and as to what collateral evidence for purposes of impeachment is material.").

23. *Marcus & Millichap Inv. Servs. of Chicago, Inc. v. Sekulovski*, 639 F.3d 301, 307 (7th Cir. 2011).

24. *Alford v. United States*, 282 U.S. 687, 694 (1931).

25. *Thiede v. Utah*, 159 U.S. 510, 519 (1895).

status.[26] However, "[t]he trial court's discretion is not absolute; it may not foreclose a legitimate inquiry into a witness's credibility."[27]

Third, good taste and the duty of professional decorum confine the scope of cross-examination to matters of relevance, as "[i]t must not be overlooked that abuse of cross-examination to test credibility carries its own corrective. Authorities on practice caution the bar of the imprudence, as well as the unprofessional nature of attacks on witnesses or defendants which are likely to be resented by the jury."[28]

Fourth, while a trial court has discretion to impose time limits on cross-examination, appeals of such decisions are waived if not first objected to below.[29]

Outlining the Goals of Cross-Examinations Well in Advance of Trial

Cross-examinations of witnesses tendered by the defense during its case-in-chief should have specific substantive objectives other than generalized carnage and mayhem directed at the witness/victim. In other words, these cross-examinations should be written with at least six goals: (1) to achieve the important psychological effects of *recency* and *repetition;* (2) to cause the defense witnesses to *state their agreements* with as many facts helpful to the plaintiff's case as possible; (3) to use past and referenced publications to *populate the evidence* with statements helpful to the plaintiff's case; (4) to utilize the defense expert to immunize plaintiff's own experts from *Daubert* exclusions on appeal; (5) to force the defense witness to provide evidence to fill in the plaintiff's required elements of proof; and (6) to introduce into the case the considerable amounts of the *financial remuneration paid by the defendant* to its experts.

Achieving the Psychological Objectives of Recency and Repetition

The goal of *recency* is achieved during the cross-examination of witnesses brought by the defense when a plaintiff's attorney uses such witnesses to reaffirm his or her points brought out during the plaintiff's case-in-chief. In a truck wreck case, both sides inevitably will hire accident reconstructionists, and spend five to six figures on high-end graphics or animations illustrating how the wreck occurred. Depositions of the two sides' experts may reveal no difference in the two opinions—about the point of impact self-evidently revealed by a gouge in the pavement, the principal direction of force often simplistically revealed by the original path of travel on the proverbial clock dial, the distance traveled between the point of impact and the points of rest for purposes of conservation of momentum analyses, or maybe only a difference of 2 mph in the truck's speed at the point of impact. Despite the reality of both sides' reconstructions overlapping each other, telling virtually the same story and fitting each other like a glove, many defense lawyers feel compelled to call their expert

26. *Sifuentes v. Abreo*, 531 F. App'x 481, 497 (5th Cir. 2013).

27. *United States v. Leake*, 642 F.2d 715, 718 (4th Cir. 1981).

28. *Michelson v. United States*, 335 U.S. 469, 487, n.25 (1948) (citing Francis Wellman, The Art of Cross-Examination, 167 *et seq.* (1927)).

29. *See Nichols v. Penn. State Univ.*, 227 F.3d 133, 147 (3d Cir. 2000).

to testify anyway. Perhaps this is caused by feeling a need to justify the bills paid to the defense reconstructionist, believing that the jury will declare the trial's victory based on the superior beauty of the defense trial graphics concerning how the accident occurred, or simply wanting to satisfy the urge to quiet those who might question the trial lawyer's tactical decision to not call such a witness. In any event, the defense calls a reconstructionist whose substantive opinions virtually mirror those of the plaintiff's reconstructionist.

In this scenario, the opportunity to achieve recency exists. Recall that the recency effect is the tendency to remember the information that was most recently presented. While the defendant calls such a reconstructionist to demonstrate that the company's truck was traveling only 79 mph in a 70 mph zone, rather than 81 mph as alleged by the plaintiff, the plaintiff's lawyer now has the opportunity to reaffirm every other good fact about the accident for the plaintiff: (1) the truck driver impacted the plaintiff's vehicle from behind, and thereby failed to make a proper application of the brakes; (2) the point of impact occurred in the plaintiff's lane of travel, thereby eliminating a legitimate claim of contributory negligence; (3) the speed of the defendant's truck at the time of the impact—whether 81 mph as claimed by the plaintiff's expert or merely 79 mph as claimed by the defendant's expert—is nevertheless over the posted speed limit, and therefore, evidence of negligence per se on the part of the defendant driver. These three points—brakes, no contributory negligence, and the existence of negligence per se—were plaintiff's points made long ago during the direct examination of the plaintiff's first witness, her accident reconstructionist brought to begin the plaintiff's case-in-chief. When making those points with the plaintiff's own reconstructionist, the primacy effect was achieved; by reiterating each of them during the cross-examination of the defendant's reconstructionist, the recency effect is achieved as well.

The goal of *repetition* also is achieved by such a cross-examination. Rather than focusing the cross-examination on why the disparate speed conclusions are separated by only 2 mph, a cross-examination designed to reiterate points of agreement between the two competing experts allows the plaintiff's lawyer to repeat themes in the plaintiff's favor. *Repetition* compulsion is the psychological phenomenon in which a person repeats an event or its circumstances over and over again, and includes reenacting the event or putting oneself in situations where the event is likely to happen again. This repetition effectively teaches the points being made.

To achieve *repetition* of points helpful to the plaintiff's case, the cross-examination of the defendant's accident reconstructionist in this scenario should utilize the graphics prepared by both experts. The defendant's graphic should be used first to affirm the lane of traffic where the point of impact occurred, and to extract the admission that the plaintiff was hit in the rear by the defendant's truck while traveling in the plaintiff's own lane of traffic. Once this admission of no contributory negligence is extracted by using the defense expert's own graphic, it should be repeated by taking the defense expert over to the graphic prepared by the plaintiff's accident reconstructionist, for the sole purpose of reiterating the point. Whether the jury is more impressed with the beauty of Defense Exhibit 1 or Plaintiff Exhibit 1, each shows a gouge mark in the plaintiff's lane of traffic, and each demonstrates no contributory negligence by the plaintiff. Likewise, taking the defense reconstructionist through the different photographs selected both by him and his plaintiff counterpart, and repeating the conclusions about the distance traveled by the vehicles between their point of impact and their points of rest achieves *repetition* of the data giving rise to the speed calculations. Finally, using the defendant's graphic, the plaintiff's lawyer should extract the admission that an impact speed of merely 79 mph as opined by the defendant's accident reconstruction expert is in fact above the posted speed limit of 70 mph, and thereby a violation of the law and negligence per se. After this admission is achieved, the plaintiff's lawyer should walk over to his or her expert's accident reconstruction graphics and *repeat* the questioning all over again—on the other hand, if the jury chooses to believe the plaintiff's accident reconstructionist that the speed at impact was 81 mph, not merely 79 mph, that also would constitute a violation of the posted speed limit and therefore of the law, and be negligence per se. The process of these questions and answers seem almost tiresome, and asking the same questions back and forth between the two sets of exhibits can become pedantic, but the goal of *repetition* is achieved, and the jury is educated on the field of the plaintiff's themes.

Achieving Admissions about Helpful Facts

Most complex cases are tried only after conducting considerable jury research. Focus groups and mock trials both offer the plaintiff's lawyer statistically significant proof of which facts tilt the scales in the plaintiff's favor in any given case. Whenever jury research says that a products case is best crystalized in the eyes of a potential jury as a failure-to-warn case, rather than as a design defect case, the plaintiff's lawyer should design each cross-examination of each defense witness with the goal of focusing on the failure-to-warn issues in the case.

In this scenario, the pharmaceutical defendant begins its case-in-chief with the predictable industry witness employed to parrot the defense theme that the product in question contained the warning label approved either by the FDA or by the EPA. On cross-examination, this witness should be converted into a mouthpiece of the facts withheld from the FDA or those not contained in the warning label itself. "*Mr. EPA Labeling Expert*, let me turn your attention to Plaintiff's Exhibit No. 1, an internal Monsanto memo from three decades ago wherein Monsanto scientists concluded that 'glyphosate causes non-Hodgkin's lymphoma.' The information on the label of the jug of Roundup Ready that was sold to my client does not include that information, does it?" "*Mr. EPA Labeling Expert*, let me turn your attention to Plaintiff's Exhibit No. 2, a 1973 letter from *Professor X*, a scientist at Johns Hopkins University, to *Dr. Evil*, Monsanto's lead epidemiologist, wherein *Professor X* informs *Dr. Evil* that his fourteen studies each revealed a doubling of the risk of non-Hodgkin's lymphoma in those exposed to Roundup Ready versus those not exposed; the information on the label of the jug of Roundup Ready that was sold to my client does not include that information, does it?" Over and over and over again, the defense warnings expert can and should be utilized to swallow before the jury each bad fact in the case, to reiterate the concealment of such bad facts from the plaintiff, and to thereby, achieve admissions from the defendant's own witness of facts helpful to the plaintiff's case.

Populating the Evidence with Published Statements That Are Helpful to the Plaintiff

An intentional and specific objective of every cross-examination should be to use past articles written by the testifying expert, as well as the publications referenced by the expert in her expert report, to *populate the evidence* with statements that are helpful to the plaintiff's case.

A trilogy of decisions from the U.S. Supreme Court in the 1990s caused experts to cling to published articles much like Linus clings to his blanket in Charles Schulz's *Peanuts*. First, the Supreme Court observed in *Daubert* that "[t]he fact of publication (or lack thereof) in a peer reviewed journal . . . will be a relevant, but not dispositive, consideration in assessing the scientific validity of a particular technique or methodology in which an opinion is premised."[30] Second, the Court noted in *Joiner* that "nothing in either *Daubert* or the Federal Rules of Evidence requires a district court to admit opinion evidence that is connected to existing data only by the *ipse dixit* of the expert."[31] Third, in *Kumho*, the Court excluded the expert testimony of tire expert Dennis Carlson, noting that the absence of publication and peer review weighed "against the reliability of Carlson's methodology."[32] This language from *Daubert*, *Joiner*, and *Kumho* caused "peer review and publication" to become one of the four reliability factors courts utilize in exercising their "gatekeeping" function in admitting expert opinion testimony.

Subsequent courts have held that "[a]s the gatekeeper, the district court should analyze the proposed expert testimony using several factors, including . . . whether it has been subjected to peer review,"[33] reasoning that "an article's publication by an esteemed periodical which subjects its contents to close scrutiny and peer review, obviously reflects well on the authority of the article itself."[34] Since these Supreme Court rulings, many experts have been excluded for giving opinions without reliance on published, peer-reviewed literature. As one court affirming the exclusion of a plaintiff's expert in a case against Ford Motor Company said, "there is nothing here to submit to peer review . . ."[35] Another court noted in dicta that a methodology may be excluded even after "being successfully employed '1000 times,'" because although that "may sound impressive, the claim is not subject to independent peer review and fails to establish an error rate with which to assess reliability because there was no information about how many times the technique was employed *unsuccessfully*."[36] As a general trend, these kinds of decisions have caused the contents of expert reports to change dramatically. Whereas a report in 1992 recited an expert's robust education,

30. *Daubert*, 509 U.S. at 593–94.

31. *General Elec. Co. v. Joiner*, 522 U.S. 136, 146 (1997).

32. *Kumho*, 526 U.S. at 137.

33. *Anderson v. Westinghouse Savannah River Co.*, 406 F.3d 248, 261 (4th Cir. 2005) (citing *Daubert*, 509 U.S. at 592–94).

34. *Constantino v. David M. Herzog, MD, PC*, 203 F.3d 164, 172 (2d Cir. 2000).

35. *Oddi v. Ford Motor Co.*, 234 F.3d 136, 158 (3d Cir. 2000) (affirming exclusion of expert); *but see Smith v. Ford Motor Co.*, 215 F.3d 713, 721 (7th Cir. 2000) (reversing district court that had treated lack of peer review as dispositive grounds for excluding expert opinion).

36. *United States v. Reynolds*, 626 F. App'x 610, 616 (6th Cir. 2015) (emphasis in original).

credentials, and experience, and then baldly gave the opinion to be offered under Rule 702, today's reports cite to article after article after article as experts grasp at published literature in an effort to prevent their opinion from being stricken under *Daubert*'s "publication and peer review" factor.

Packing expert reports full of published articles leads to opportunity on cross-examination. Summarily put, if an expert cites an article, that expert must now own on cross-examination everything stated in that article. As the U.S. Court of Appeals for the Third Circuit observes, "[p]eer review and publication also provide raw material for the cross-examining attorney to confront the expert with."[37] Thus, every article ever written or cited to by the expert at hand is now fair game for cross-examination. The thorough plaintiff's lawyer should comb through each such article, as well as articles cited therein, and locate statements that are helpful to the cause of the plaintiff's case. Whether or not the expert chooses to adopt the statement itself is of no consequence; the reality is that statements contained in publications cited by expert witnesses stick to them like chewing gum smeared on the bottom of a shoe.

Utilizing the Defense Expert to Immunize Plaintiff's Own Experts from Daubert Exclusions on Appeal

An important component of any outline for the cross-examination of a defense expert is a section designed to protect one's own expert from exclusion by an appellate court. As mentioned earlier, the prophylactic use of *Daubert* motions on every plaintiff expert is now widespread. Just because the trial court has by now permitted the plaintiff's expert to testify does not mean the job is done concerning the *Daubert* record. Indeed, the cross-examination of the defense expert can provide important content for any appellate brief that is defending a verdict on appeal.

By and large, experts competing against each other on a particular subject utilize remarkably similar methodologies. Most accident reconstructionists use the same mathematical formulas, now not even written down, but instead calculated automatically by inputting data into computer programs. Most biomechanicists in an automotive defect case rely on the same published data about the force needed to cause particular injuries. Most epidemiologists cite to the same peer-reviewed studies to reach their conclusions. Most life care planners utilize the same methodology to reach their conclusions on the cost of future care. While their conclusions may differ, their methodologies often do not. *Daubert* reliability exercise relates to methodologies, not to conclusions.

As such, a plaintiff's lawyer who is deposing a defendant's expert should get the expert to sign off on the methodologies employed by his or her counterpart on the plaintiff's side. Experience teaches that these experts often defend each other's methodologies, choosing to politely draw narrow distinctions that give rise to the difference in their respective ultimate conclusions. Admissions gleaned in the deposition of the defendant's expert that the plaintiff's expert's methodologies (1) can and have been tested; (2) have been subjected to

37. *United States v. Mitchell*, 365 F.3d 215, 245 (3d Cir. 2004).

peer review and publication; (3) have a known rate of error; and (4) have attracted widespread acceptance within the relevant scientific community, can be very helpful to the plaintiff. The admission helps first in fighting off a pretrial *Daubert* motion, and again during live cross-examination of the defendant's expert for purposes of creating a record to defend the plaintiff's expert on appeal.

Forcing the Defense Witness to Provide Evidence to Meet the Plaintiff's Required Elements of Proof

The cross-examination of a defense witness should be constructed with the court's charge, or jury instructions, in hand. Corporate representatives testifying at trial ostensibly are speaking on behalf of the defendant itself; consequently, admissions gleaned on cross-examination with respect to *liability* issues are at best binding on the company itself; at worst, they constitute some evidence in support of a verdict rendered for the plaintiff. Thus, the cross-examination of a defense witness should be designed to fill in as many of the required elements of proof as possible for the causes of action pleaded by the plaintiff. While the plaintiff will already have some evidence on each required element (since the case survived a directed verdict motion already), having defense witnesses provide corroborative testimony on the same elements of proof makes the point more powerfully in the eyes of the jury, allows the plaintiff's lawyer in closing arguments to argue that "the parties agree on this point," and creates an evidentiary record that powerfully eliminates that element of proof from the quiver of appellate arrows that will inevitably be aimed at the verdict by the defendant's appellate counsel.

Likewise, *damages* admissions also should be collected from defense witnesses during cross-examinations. In a catastrophic injury case that involves contrasting views of the cost of future care, one can predict that a plaintiff's life care planner will have a higher number than the one offered by the defendant's life care planner. Life care planners have to review medical records in detail. Medical records have pain charts that a good cross-examination will explore in detail with the defense expert to establish the absence of a dispute as to whether the plaintiff suffered past physical pain.

Likewise, life care planners have to review prescription records. Enormous injuries often bring on depression, for which medications have been prescribed. A thorough examination of the antidepressant and antianxiety medications prescribed to the plaintiff during his or her medical treatment will require the defendant's life care planning expert to provide helpful admissions that the plaintiff did indeed suffer from mental anguish in the past.

Life care planners will have familiarized themselves with all surgical records. In burn cases, these surgeries will include painful debridement, where healthy skin is harvested via a medical instrument akin to a cheese grater, then applied to burned areas in an effort to close the wound. These medical procedures typically come with pictures that show the wounds before and after treatment, about which a defendant's life care planner should be questioned to elicit an agreement that the plaintiff has suffered disfigurement. Past and future therapies will have been studied. Cross-examinations of defense life care planners should focus on these therapies to establish the existence of physical impairment in the past.

In sum, whether it be a defendant's expert life care planner or any witness called on the issue of the plaintiff's damages, a properly constructed cross-examination should harvest many admissions that will fill in the record on each element of the plaintiff's damages, both past and future.

Injecting Money into the Case via the Expert Cross-Examination

Corporate defendants that face repetitive allegations of defective products in lawsuits across the country spare no expense in their selection of experts. Accordingly, during the defendant's case-in-chief, plaintiff's lawyers who are preparing to cross-examine defense experts often are faced with the very finest, most pedigreed experts in the world. To secure the services of such experts, the corporate defendant typically turns on the spigot, and a torrent of cash flows from the defendant's corporate coffers into the accounts of the expert witnesses coming to their rescue. Because financial payments to experts involve the experts' bias and credibility, cross-examination on the present and past financial payments made by the defendant to the expert is fair game. This cross-examination permits the plaintiff's lawyer to inject into the evidence amounts of money that would make each of Donald Trump's three wives blush.

When a plaintiff's lawyer asks a jury to return a verdict of $35 million for the nonpecuniary damages her client will suffer over the remaining 35 years of her life, the fact that the defense expert has received compensation from the defendants in the amount of more than one million dollars a year during the litigation helps blunt the enormity of the requested damages. Such evidence relevant to the bias and credibility of the defense expert has a secondary value to the plaintiff—to create a yardstick for the plaintiff's damages ask. Let me offer three examples from cases I have tried.

For a first example, in a pharmaceutical product liability case tried long ago by the two authors of this book, I introduced evidence that the chief executive officer of Warner-Lambert sold $86 million in company stock the day before a new warning was required by the FDA. That $86 million profit—characterized in cross-examinations and during closing arguments as ill-gotten gains—became the basis of an $86 million actual damages ask. During its deliberations, the jury cut that number in half and awarded the plaintiff $43 million in actual damages.

In a second example, I tried multiple cases against the Ford Motor Company during the early 2000s involving allegations of inadequate occupant restraint systems during rollover accidents. In discovery, we collected information that Ford had paid its engineering consultants, Exponent/Failure Analysis, Inc., more than $70 million over the years. Such a dramatic amount was introduced into evidence during the cross-examination of Ford's expert from Exponent, and later recited during closing arguments as a reason why the plaintiff's damages ask must be reasonable. Three of my consecutive verdicts against Ford in 2005—$33 million, $42 million, and $30.6 million—each involved the same defense consulting group and the same evidence concerning the massive amounts Ford had paid Exponent for its services in defending the same defect alleged to have killed or injured my three respective clients. The point is that the cross-examination of experts during the defendant's case-in-chief offers a unique opportunity late in the case to inject large dollar amounts into the evidence, and thereby, to set the stage for a contention in closing argument that plaintiff's damages ask is reasonable by comparison.

In a third example, I tried a burn case decades ago against the Coastal Corporation that resulted in a $122 million verdict. Though reversed on appeal on other grounds, the damages argument is helpful to the point made here. When a defense expert is being compensated at the rate of $500 an hour, a sum that in the eyes of most jurors is an astronomical sum, a plaintiff's lawyer asking for $500 a day for the plaintiff's nonpecuniary elements of damages looks reasonable by comparison. Asking a jury for $500 a day for physical pain and suffering endured by a man burned over 65 percent of his body does not seem excessive when the company that caused those burns defends itself in court by paying an expert mouthpiece $500 an hour. The consequence of this over time is significant—$500 a day is $182,500 a year, which over a forty-year life expectancy yields the total sum of $7.3 million for just one element of damages.

The point of these three examples is the same: use compensation paid to defense experts as a talisman to legitimize for the jury the very large damages you will ask for during closing arguments.

Conclusion

The conclusion of this chapter is merely to succinctly state the following. The plaintiff's singular objective during the defendant's case-in-chief is to stay on the offensive. George Washington wrote in 1799, "Make them believe, that offensive operations, often times, is the surest, if not the only (in some cases) means of defense."[38] Mao Tse-tung wrote that "the only real defense is active defense,"[39] mirroring the writings of Machiavelli and Sun Tzu. As taught by practitioners of Wing Chun, a form of Kung Fu, "The hand which strikes also blocks." These are different ways of saying what football coaches now preach: "The best defense is a good offense."[40] During the entirety of the defendant's case-in-chief, the plaintiff's lawyer should stay on the attack, adding evidentiary points to the scoreboard even as the defense attempts to play out the clock.

---

38. *From George Washington to John Trumbull, 25 June 1799*, Founders Online, https://founders.archives.gov/documents/Washington/06-04-02-0120 (last visited Mar. 14, 2020).

39. Mao Tse-tung, "Problems of Strategy in China's Revolutionary War," *in Selected Works of Mao Tse-tung*, Marxists.org, https://www.marxists.org/reference/archive/mao/selected-works/volume-1/mswv1_12.htm (last visited Mar. 14, 2020).

40. *See The best defense is a good offense*, Wikipedia, https://wikipedia.org/wiki/The_best_defense_is_a_good_offense (last visited Dec. 11, 2019).

20
The Defendant's Case: Focusing the Defense Presentation

The Defense Perspective

The Basic Rules

There are basic guidelines that apply to every defendant's case-in-chief and how we, as defense lawyers, should prepare and order our witnesses and select our exhibits. Each of these guidelines helps win the case.

The first rule is to have a well-considered trial plan, including key trial themes supported by a witness list, order of proof, and key exhibits. This plan should not be ad hoc, but prepared in advance of trial taking into account the applicable legal principles and burdens of proof that govern your case. This plan also should include strategies for attacking the weakest parts of the plaintiff's case. Hopefully, you have successfully damaged the plaintiff's case during your cross-examination of the plaintiff's witnesses, and you have stymied the plaintiff's positive momentum. The defense case-in-chief is then used to reinforce these weaknesses.

Thus, the second rule is to maintain positive momentum by not providing opposing counsel with opportunities to score points and renew adverse momentum. Every skilled plaintiff's lawyer will seize any opportunity to attack the defendant's case. This must be considered when making your final witness selections.

This leads to the third rule: your witness selections and documentary evidence should be used as parts of a strategy to empower defense-oriented jurors with ammunition to argue key points of your case in the jury room. Typically, there will be several jurors who are looking for ways to support you, your client, and your case. Your goal is to equip these jurors with the evidence and the arguments they need to be effective advocates when the jury retires for deliberations. Your evidence may be the last evidence the jury hears, so you want to be as forceful and effective as possible. You want to end with a bang!

Finally, and simply, the fourth rule is "*less is best.*" You should employ time management techniques, which become critical during the later stages of any trial. You should assume the jury is beginning to tire of the case, and you do not want to be blamed for an extended trial. As such, there is no need to shotgun your defenses and address each such defense with particularity. Rather, you should identify key themes that require reinforcement and maintain a sharp focus when selecting your evidence to support these targeted themes. You do not want your case bogged down in tedium. You want to maintain a positive tempo and pace to keep the jury's attention.

The Dual-Focus Plan

All trial plans should be prepared, evaluated, and honed before the trial begins. All winning trial plans, like blueprints, require a thorough understanding of what burdens you and your client must carry for important affirmative defenses. You also should understand how the case will be submitted to the jury. To do this, you must have a strong grasp of what jury instructions and questions will be submitted to the jury. Although every jury charge is revised and modified during the court's charge conference, a draft jury charge is an excellent foundation for developing your outline of needed proof. Again, to derive maximum benefit, this draft charge should be prepared in advance of the trial to help you understand your witness and exhibit needs for the case.

As a beginning lawyer many years ago, one of my mentors counseled me that, as one of the first tasks in every case, lawyers should prepare a draft jury charge. This helps the lawyer organize the case and define discovery objectives. Clearly, as trial lawyers, we need to know the elements of the claims that confront our clients, the elements of our defenses, and who carries the burdens of proof. Because this knowledge provides the cornerstones of any trial plan, we should not assume we understand the law. We should always update this understanding to make sure we are ahead of the learning curve and that we recognize the subtleties of how the jury may be instructed. A failure to understand basic elements will leave you clueless about what proof you need. Unless you are blessed with fortuitus, blind luck, you undoubtedly will lose the case in the absence of this understanding. You likely will miscalculate your proof needs and which witnesses and exhibits satisfy those requirements.

Equally important is the other half of this dual strategy: knowing how to poke holes in the plaintiff's proof. You should have a disciplined understanding of the weaknesses in a plaintiff's case during pretrial discovery. One of your pretrial goals should include identification of these weaknesses during depositions. Admissions and witness concessions obtained during discovery then serve as the foundation for your cross-examinations of the plaintiff's witnesses. The defense case-in-chief presents one more opportunity to do so again.

When devising your trial plan, you should consider which witnesses and documents are available to continue undercutting the merits of the plaintiff's claims. Your goal is to attack the *logos* and *ethos* of the plaintiff's case—the believability and logic of the plaintiff's claims. This could involve eyewitnesses or experts who demonstrate why the plaintiff's claims are illogical or unreasonable. This could involve impeachment of the plaintiff's testimony or the testimony of a key plaintiff's expert. Again, your witness order should be planned ahead of time, and you should be prepared to tell an interesting, logical, believable story through your witnesses. Again, the goal is to keep the jury's attention and interest. You want to have the jury invested in your case, and this requires that you fashion your case to achieve maximum *pathos*, *ethos*, and *logos*.

We should recognize that best laid plans frequently change out of necessity. Trials are dynamic, and they frequently unfold with surprises. Thus, we should be prepared to modify trial plans quickly in response to courtroom developments. For example, you may elect to not call a witness because you no longer need to do so. You may elect to call a witness you had not expected because of something that surfaced during the plaintiff's case. The lesson here is to remain fluid and retain options. This optionality requires that pretrial disclosures of exhibits and trial witnesses be broad and all-inclusive. It is always better to call a witness who is already disclosed on pretrial witness lists than to try to explain to the judge why the witness was not previously identified.

Organizing Exhibits and Using Exhibits

Some defense lawyers think it is necessary to offer every potentially relevant exhibit. This is a mistake because it can be distracting and boring.

I have been involved in cases where we listed several hundred exhibits on our exhibit list. This was a mistake. Even the most complicated cases are not *so complicated* they require hundreds of exhibits to make a point. Most cases, even the most complex, revolve around twenty-five to fifty exhibits. When preparing your exhibit list, you should have an eye on which exhibits are really necessary and which can be discarded.[1]

There are several reasons why you should not offer hundreds of exhibits, one of which involves time management. Laying the predicate and offering exhibits can be time consuming, not to mention tedious. Hopefully, the court will consider exhibit objections before trial and pre-admit exhibits. This reduces the need to ask repeated, foundational questions and allows you to move more freely through your exhibits.

The jury will *never* review hundreds of exhibits when they retire to the jury room. The jury is entitled to all of the admitted evidence. If hundreds of exhibits are accepted into evidence, the jury will enter the jury room surrounded by boxes. It is doubtful that the jury will know where the important exhibits are located in this document "haystack." Fewer exhibits means a smaller haystack when the jury is searching for the "needles" that win the case. This also is why key exhibits should be at the top of your list and bear a low exhibit number. Low numbers are easier to remember when the jury starts to search for specific documents.

The jury also will have a difficult time keeping track of hundreds of exhibits with the various witnesses. Ultimately, jurors can suffer exhibit fatigue. Too many documents cloud or dilute the importance of key documents and confuse the case. Again, the goal is to *simplify*, *simplify*, and *simplify*. The challenge is to hone down the exhibits to critical categories that reflect true priorities. The highest priorities should be marked with lower exhibit numbers.

---

1. *See* chapter 6, *supra*, which includes further discussion and examples for organizing exhibits.

What constitutes a key exhibit will change from case to case. As a general matter, however, critical exhibits include the foundational documents that define the incident, transaction, or occurrence. In a contract case, the key documents are the contract, documents that reflect performance or breach, draft agreements, etc. In a drug liability case, they might include favorable medical records and various administrative records or applications filed with the FDA that show safety and efficacy. In a product liability case, they may include key design documents, failure tree analyses, or product testing documents. Each case is different, and each case will involve a core group of exhibits that the defense will need to offer to explain what happened or, equally important, what did not happen, and why.

You should develop an exhibit list that is cross-referenced with witnesses. Every trial plan should consider how you intend to authenticate key exhibits and sponsor them into evidence. Your trial plan needs to identify which witness is best suited to sponsor particular exhibits and then explain them to the jury. Again, if you wait too long to develop this plan, you may find yourself with an important exhibit and no witness who can lay a proper foundation for admissibility. You also may lose the opportunity to call an important witness who can effectively explain a critical document to the jury.

One practical solution is to create a spreadsheet that identifies each exhibit and prioritizes the exhibits in order of criticality. This spreadsheet can be organized on a witness-by-witness basis so you can make sure each exhibit has a sponsoring witness in the event evidentiary objections are lodged. The following example is for a hypothetical product liability case involving a passenger automobile. The exemplar involves a spreadsheet that can help you organize your case:

Plaintiff v. ABC Car, Inc.				
Ex. #	**Date**	**Description**	**Witness**	**Ranking**
1	1/1/20	Police Accident Report	Investigating Officer	Key
2	1/1/20	Photos of Crash Scene	Investigating Officer	Key
3	2/1/20	Photos of Vehicle		Key
4	2/1/20	Close-up Photos of Seatbelt	Retained expert	Key
5	4/1/20	Design Documents		Background
6	4/1/20	Testing Documents		Background

Here, important evidence related to the occurrence (a vehicle crash) is listed first. Background evidence, which also is important, is coded differently, but follows. By organizing the exhibit list in a spreadsheet format, the list can be reorganized by date, ranking, or witness. You can create immediate chronologies, or you can identify every exhibit you seek to offer through a particular witness. You have organizational options and control at your fingertips.

Time Management

Professional efficiency, if not the *appearance* of efficiency, is important during trial. This translates into a series of simple sub-rules: never belabor unimportant points; do not argue with the plaintiff's witnesses, opposing counsel, or the court; do not waste time with witness examinations that do not advance your case; and always be prepared and crisp in your delivery and witness examinations. Because there always will be jurors who are sensitive to inefficiency, there is great wisdom in getting to the point, and doing so quickly. This will work to your benefit. The jury will know you are serious and will appreciate your obvious efforts to not waste their time.

Efficiency is particularly important in a defendant's case-in-chief. At this point in a trial, the jury has experienced the entirety of the plaintiff's case, including the direct examinations and cross-examinations of the plaintiff's witnesses. Depending on the length or complexity of the case, tedium may be setting into the jury box. You should assume that juror impatience is not far behind. Therefore, you should be sensitive to the potential for evolving attitudes as you plan how to present your defense case, the number of witnesses you intend to call, and the number of exhibits you intend to offer.

Most jurors are excited when they are selected to serve on a jury. But this excitement typically wanes by the time the defense case begins. Some may be looking for closure—a "winding up"—and an exit from the courtroom. Remember that many jurors are wage earners and jury compensation is meager. Many jurors may have a financial need to bring closure to the case. You do not want to be seen as a source of unnecessary delay. The plaintiff has an advantage in this regard. The case is still new and the experience fresh during the plaintiff's case-in-chief. This is not the case by the time the defense case begins.

Equally important is that most jurors have made preliminary, if not final, decisions about who should win and who should lose by the time the defense case begins. These attitudes can change if dramatic evidence surfaces, but it is more likely that juror attitudes are jelled by this point. By now, jurors typically are filtering the evidence they see or hear to support their belief system. It is therefore important to not have a defense case that drags on, covering old territory, or that otherwise bores the jury with cumulative evidence.

As defense lawyers, our goal is to end with a high-energy bang, and not with a tedious whimper. You also want to avoid the risk of alienating jurors who would otherwise support your case or who have not made up their minds. This is why the time-worn adage "*less is best*" remains relevant for all trial lawyers on both sides of the bar.

Applying this principle, we always should avoid cumulative evidence. Otherwise, the jury may believe you are stalling, wasting time, or needlessly prolonging the case. Likewise, you need to avoid calling witnesses who are not needed to support your trial themes. You also should avoid using exhibits that are not needed. Rest assured that the jury will have a good sense of your client and the facts of the case by this point in the trial. Thus, your witness and exhibit selection should focus on strength and excitement. In a perfect world, this means you only should call strong witnesses who have minimal vulnerability on cross-examination, and who will foster good impressions. This is the essence of *pathos* and *ethos*, the principles of advocacy, which we have discussed extensively in this book.

In one notable case I handled, which my client won, it became apparent in post-verdict polling that ours was a Pyrrhic victory. One of the "defense" jurors said he voted for my client because he simply wanted to end the case and avoid further time away from his job. He was actually angry at both sides and all the lawyers, stating he thought that both the plaintiff's case and the defense case lasted too long, and that he was bored. Although I am convinced justice was achieved in this case, it occurred by traveling a rocky road.

A Case on a Stop Watch

Some courts impose time limitations on trial counsel and actually keep score on how much time is used by each lawyer during each stage of the trial. For example, I was involved in a case where the parties each received a total time allocation of twenty-five hours, including all direct and cross-examinations for witnesses in the plaintiff's case and the defendant's case. In such instances, the defense lawyer needs to be careful with how much time is devoted to cross-examinations in the plaintiff's case. If not, valuable time is forfeited during the defense case.

A timed trial forces lawyers to focus their efforts during cross-examinations and direct examinations to better assure they have sufficient time for the entire case. This is particularly important for defense lawyers if they carry a burden of proof on affirmative defenses. If time constraints begin to pressure the case, judicious witness selections and exhibit use become important. At this point, concerns relating to tedium and to jury impatience become secondary to making sure there is sufficient time to present critical evidence. Disciplined time management is paramount.

I have been on the wrong side of the hourglass before. In a hotly contested case with my co-author, Mikal Watts, I was forced to end my examination of an important medical causation witness before I completed direct examination. This case involved allegations of an adverse drug reaction to a recalled prescription drug. Although most of our important defense evidence was successfully introduced, the jury obviously witnessed an abrupt halt to my direct examination, as well as to our entire defense case. It was a messy ending. Although I offered the witness's completed testimony outside the hearing of the jury in a bill of exceptions, it was doubtful that the court's handling of this situation was reversible error.

Time limits typically are respected by appellate courts because it is seen as the proper exercise of a trial court's discretion to manage a trial. Trial courts are entitled to manage their courts, and this is one way of doing so. It is unlikely that these types of decisions will be reversed unless the trial court acts in an abusive or arbitrary manner.

Client Attendance and Corporate Representatives

It is important to have your client present in the courtroom. Because the jury has been asked to invest its time in the jury box, they likely (and reasonably) will expect the defendant to do so as well. This is particularly true during critical parts of the case—voir dire, opening statements, key witnesses in the plaintiff's case, and the defense case. If your client is not in the courtroom during important stages of the trial, there are risks the jury will infer several negatives: your client does not care enough to be in attendance; your client is too self-important to be bothered; or, your client is fearful of taking the stand or hearing the truth in the courtroom. No matter how you look at it, the optics are bad.

If your client is a corporation, you should have a client representative present. You need to personalize your client by presenting flesh and bones. The jury needs to understand that corporations are made of people. Otherwise, the absent entity is criticized more easily. It is easier to return an adverse verdict against a "fictional" person who has not shown up than against a live person in the courtroom. Again, an empty chair sends negative messages to the jury.

Witness Selection

Keep the number of your witnesses to a minimum. Again, efficiency and the appearance of efficiency are major considerations. You should select witnesses from whom you really need testimony to support an affirmative defense or undercut the plaintiff's case. If one or more defense witnesses achieve these same goals, you should select the stronger witness, who is better able to withstand cross-examination. The worst thing that can be done at this point is to expose a weak defense witness to a strong cross-examination. If a defense witness is hurt during cross-examination during the late stages of a trial, there is little time to recover. Again, this consideration underscores the wisdom of following the adage "*less is best*."

You should consider whether the jury expects to hear from particular witnesses whose names have been bandied about in the courtroom. As defense lawyers, we cannot run away from such expectations, so we must make sure these types of "expected" witnesses are available. If the jury's expectations are strong and we fail to deliver, there will be a hole in the defense case.

If "expected" witnesses are not called, some jurors also may wonder why and draw negative inferences. In criminal cases, this occurs when a defendant does not take the stand in his defense. However, in criminal cases, the court typically admonishes the jury against drawing any negative inferences because the criminal defendant is presumed innocent. However, as civil trial lawyers, we do not have these same rights, particularly as it relates to company witnesses, over whom we have control.

One example of an "expected" witness involved a defendant who was called adversely in the plaintiff's case-in-chief but not taken on direct examination. In a business tort case in which I was involved, I actually represented the nominal plaintiff.[2] I called the "defendant" adversely as my first witness and conducted an extensive cross-examination. From my perspective, his case was severely wounded, and my client's case significantly advanced. The defense lawyers then made a strategic decision to defer their direct examination until their case-in-chief. They audibly stated this in the presence of the jury. Then, incredibly, the defense lawyers elected to not call their own client to the stand in their case-in-chief. There can be no doubt the jury was curious. I aggressively argued this failure in my final argument, and told the jury that the defendant was unable to defend or explain his wrongful conduct. I believe the defense lawyer's strategic decision provided a tremendous opportunity and a shot of adrenaline. As noted in chapter 16, we won the case.

2. This case also is discussed in chapter 16, addressing adverse witnesses.

Do Not Be Afraid to Leave Witnesses "On the Bench"

You do not need to call every witness just because you listed an individual on a pretrial witness list. As the dynamics of trial unfold and take effect, your decision about who actually takes the stand will change. This applies equally to fact witnesses and expert witnesses.

In a case I handled several years ago, I designated an expert witness on a professional standard of care. The plaintiff was suing my client for breach of fiduciary duty and negligence. The case had gone well during the plaintiff's case. Then, after consulting with our client, we elected to not call our standard of care expert because we wanted to avoid the risks of cross-examination by our opponent, a highly skilled plaintiff's lawyer. Even though we believed the expert could weather cross-examination, we did not want to give opposing counsel an opportunity to score sound bites with our witness in our case. We did not call the expert witness to the stand. We also won this case.

It is difficult to not call a witness that you have prepared, not to mention explaining to the client that you are not calling an expert who was specially retained and likely paid thousands of dollars. However, it is important to remain adaptable and not be fixated on what you thought was important before trial.

You never want to call a witness who will halt positive momentum or who can actually help the plaintiff carry its burden of proof, particularly in a case where you think the burden has not been carried. In yet another very notable example, a defense lawyer I know made the decision, after consulting with his client, to call *no* defense witnesses in a damage case in the upper nine figures that involved securities fraud allegations. The defense lawyer, a friend of mine, concluded that he had thoroughly destroyed the plaintiff's expert witness on liability, so he elected to not call any witnesses that might allow the plaintiff to score on cross-examination. Although this was a "gutsy" (if not risky) decision, his instinct was correct and he won the case. He also earned well-deserved accolades on the front page of a nationally syndicated legal journal for his tactical decision.

Witness Types

In cases where both liability and damages are contested, many defense lawyers opt to not call damage witnesses whose sole purpose is to rebut plaintiff's damage witnesses. This is particularly true in serious personal injury or death cases. The concern is that you can reinforce the plaintiff's damages if the witness is called. There is a companion concern that the jury may feel uncomfortable if you offer evidence that challenges the extent of damages in a case where a plaintiff was clearly damaged. Placing a damage witness on the stand during the defense case can actually increase exposure because it provides a skilled plaintiff's lawyer with one more bite at the damage apple. This also can have the undesired effect of reinforcing the entirety of the plaintiff's claim, including liability and causation. By challenging "unchallengeable" damages, you run the risk of losing credibility with the jury, and this loss can contaminate how the jury perceives your entire case. You lose *ethos*.

This same sensitivity may not apply in a business case, where juror sensitivities are likely different. In such cases, there actually may be a legitimate need to offset hyperbolic claims of the plaintiff's expert witnesses. There also may be a need to duel with the opposing economists or causation experts, and the jury may need to hear both sides to make informed decisions.

Witness Order

Rules relating to witness order apply equally to the plaintiff's case and the defense case. An effective witness order also requires strategic planning.

A defense case should start strong and end strong. You should never start a defense case with a weak witness who is vulnerable to cross-examination. You should also avoid a highly technical witness as your first witness. Your goal is to capture the jury's attention quickly and to keep the jury's focus. You do not want to start slowly and get bogged down in detail. Ideally, you should consider calling as your first witness a person who is likeable, credible, and capable of introducing the defense case with an overview of interesting background information. The first witness should be an *overview* witness who can connect with the jury and start telling an interesting story.

In a similar vein, you should not end a case with a weak or boring witness. You want to finish strong. Remember that you are seeking to empower defense jurors who may be in your camp. If there are witnesses who are less strong, do not call them at all, if that option is possible. If such witnesses *must* be called for a particular reason, sandwich them into a witness order where they are buffered by stronger witnesses on either side. If they flop, you still have a chance to rebound and end with strength.

Make Your Case Exciting

Plan your defense case to start strong, stay strong, and end strong. This is easier said than done, but it can be accomplished with powerful video clips, effective demonstratives, and charismatic witnesses.

There are basic rules that govern the use of video evidence and demonstratives: video clips should be short, you should use powerful sound bites, and you should avoid extended video testimony. As a general rule, a jury's attention is always short-lived and can be measured in seconds. By the time your case starts, the jury's attention span will be even shorter, particularly for jurors who have made up their minds and started to filter what they see and hear from the witness stand. My rule of thumb is to keep video clips to less than ten minutes in length. Another important consideration is timing.

Do not start the defense case with video, and never end your case with video. This can be anticlimactic. Rather, video depositions should be sandwiched in the middle of your case. You also should consider alternating live testimony and video testimony, thereby avoiding extended stretches of video presentations, which become monotonous.

Also important is what time of day you present video depositions. One practice tip is to present video depositions during the morning session, if possible. If you wait until the end of the day, many jurors will tune out more quickly—they are tired and will lose focus more rapidly. Of course, this can be said of most evidence. Introduction of important evidence is always more effective when presented in the morning, when most jurors are alert and fresh.

Witness Preparations

Effective witness preparations are paramount. An unprepared witness can be disastrous. You should never call an unprepared witness to the stand—this includes emotional preparedness, as well as substantive preparedness. If a witness fails during cross-examination, there may be little chance of recovery and rebound.

Your client may not be accustomed to the drama of the courtroom, so it is important to prepare him or her so they have confidence if they take the stand. They should be prepared for aggressive cross-examinations; they should have good control over the key facts as they know them; and, they should understand their role in advancing defense trial themes.

A witness can either float or sink a case. Thus, your witness preparations should not be ad hoc and done at the last minute. It is always advisable to make your witness selections early in discovery. It is equally important to start your witness preparations well before trial. Witness outlines should be developed before trial and examination rehearsed with your witnesses, particularly with your client representatives. Of course, these outlines can be refined and honed as the trial proceeds. When witness preparations are rushed at the last minute, something will be missed or your witness will have less confidence in how he or she will perform.

A witness cannot be adequately prepared unless you, as the preparing lawyer, are well-prepared. Your preparation should be reflected in your witness outlines, which detail the key exhibits you intend to offer and the key facts you intend to elicit. As a general rule, I prepare trial notebooks—one of which is devoted to motions in limine, exhibit lists, key pleadings, a draft jury charge, and other general trial materials. I then have a separate notebook that contains only witness outlines, organized on a witness-by-witness basis that is consistent with my chosen witness order. These witness outlines correlate with witness boxes—usually one box per witness. Each box will contain an extra copy of the witness outline, pre-marked exhibits I intend to offer or discuss with that witness, and a copy of the deposition the witness may have provided. A page-and-line summary of that deposition also is included. In sum, one notebook and a companion witness box should have everything that is needed in the courtroom.

Rehearsing a direct examination is a good idea. With beginner witnesses, this should be done on several occasions to achieve fluidity. It is like practicing dance steps with a partner. As the examining lawyer, you need to see how the witness "dances" so you can determine how to organize the examination. This includes a valuation of whether the witness's answers are choppy, excessively long, or too short. You want to counsel the witness on how to achieve a fluid, smooth presentation. This is achieved by practice to see how the witness performs. These practice sessions also make the witness more comfortable because the witness knows what to expect from you.

Also important is to practice what the witness can expect from the opposing lawyer. Like preparing witnesses for deposition, you need to teach basic fundamentals to the witness on how to handle difficult questions and how to act when confronted with hard questions. A witness who reacts with terror in his or her eyes will not be effective. A witness who becomes evasive will lose credibility with the jury. A witness who folds under the pressure of cross-examination can undo much of what was gained on direct examination and will leave lasting, negative impressions with the jury. Do not shortchange your witness on time for preparation for cross-examination.

Rehearsing cross-examinations is always helpful, but it is even more helpful to have someone the witness does not know conduct a mock examination. This adds the drama of an unknown personality to the equation, which is useful to get a witness emotionally prepared. The mock examination also should be aggressive, exploring any weaknesses in the witness's testimony. Critical documents—particularly hot documents—should be used in the practice rehearsal. The bottom line is that the witness must be given a sense of what to expect.

The Direct Examination and Leading Questions

The direct examination should follow the pre-prepared witness outline modified by developments during trial. The witness should understand the organization and scope of the examination and should not be presented with surprise questions. Surprise is the enemy of a good direct examination. You do not want to have the witness falter or stumble during the direct because any errors are magnified when the witness is responding to his or her lawyer's questions.

Contrary to popular belief, many courts may permit lawyers to lead their own witnesses, particularly in nonessential areas of testimony. This typically is done to encourage efficiency. As such, most skilled plaintiff's lawyers will not object to leading questions when the questions involve noncritical issues in the case. With that said, it is a better practice to ask as few leading questions as possible. The jury wants to hear the witness talk, and not the lawyer spoon-feeding the witness with the lawyer's words. It is more effective to let the witness provide color and context in the testimony. In this manner, the witness is less of a robot, providing "yes" or "no" answers.

Dressing Well and Behaving Appropriately

Your client and all defense witnesses should dress appropriately for their station and profession. For male witnesses, coats and ties are not always required, but serve as a good default choice. For both men and women, gaudy jewelry and loud clothing should be avoided—*always*. Bling is not good when your witness is being evaluated and judged by a jury. There is always a risk that one or more jurors will be offended by gaudiness. The safer bet is to counsel your witnesses to tone down their appearance and lean toward conservative attire.

All witnesses should take pride in their appearance. A poorly attired witness is a witness who does not inspire empathy. Remember that one of the cornerstones of effective advocacy is *ethos*—likability and credibility. Some jurors will never listen to the substance of testimony if the witness is poorly dressed. We should remain mindful that many people judge books by their covers.

Attitude, Demeanor, and Posture

Defense lawyers should counsel their witnesses to have *some* eye contact with the jury. However, as with anything, a healthy balance should be struck, and exceeding this balance can have negative effects on how the jury sees the witness.

A good middle ground is that defense witnesses should be encouraged to occasionally look at the jury, particularly when trying to emphasize a particular point. However, your witnesses should never stare. This can be discomforting to jurors. Making random eye contact is useful because it displays self-assuredness and self-confidence. At the same time, never looking at the jury also will send different, negative messages—anxiety, fear, or evasiveness. Staring at the jury will send highly negative messages—arrogance or a suggestion that the witness is trying to intimidate. You should remind the witness to find an in-between and not invade a juror's space through excessive, uncomfortable eye contact.

Your witnesses should be instructed to never argue with opposing counsel. When a witness loses his or her temper, bad things happen. In fact, many skilled lawyers actually use cross-examination to find and push a witness's anger button. Juries do not like angry witnesses or witnesses who cannot control their emotions. When a witness loses his or her temper, it suggests that the witness is losing and the opposing lawyer is winning. This is important because some jurors make their decisions on a visceral level—a gut response to what is happening in the courtroom. They may feel that the opposing lawyer is scoring points and winning, and they are attracted to the winning side.

Witness Responsiveness and Dealing with Aggressive Examinations

It is important that you counsel your witnesses to not be evasive. Jurors are quick to spot evasiveness, and they find it alienating. They may even conclude that the evasive witness is avoiding direct responses because they have something to hide. Evasiveness also can trigger the judge's ire and provoke an admonition from the bench, which is never helpful. If that happens, the jury is acutely aware that the witness is doing something wrong. This detracts from the witness's credibility and likeability, and this makes it tougher for the defense lawyer to manage the *ethos* and *pathos* of the defense case. If the jury loses interest in your case or no longer likes your witnesses, you likely will lose its verdict.

A better practice is to counsel your witnesses to yield on cross-examination points that are self-evident or commonsensical. Fighting reasonable propositions is destructive and undermines the likability and credibility of the witness. By putting up a fight, the question and the answer are highlighted and magnified. The resistance to providing an answer to a reasonable question may become more important than the answer itself.

Some of the most effective experts I have seen on the witness stand readily and quietly concede easy points without great fanfare. They know when to pick a fight, and they typically do not pick a fight unless they know they can win. The same should hold true for fact witnesses. There is seldom a question that is asked that cannot be clarified on redirect examination. So, encourage your witnesses to pick their battles, and then clean up any residual problems on redirect. Again, the defense lawyer should already know what fights are needed and what fights are not needed. The witness should be prepared to understand the difference between the two.

If you expect major issues to develop during cross-examination, another good strategy is to elicit testimony in your direct examination that anticipates the issue and blunts the effect of a dramatic cross. Your goal is to take the drama and sting out of any anticipated cross-examination. This can be achieved by asking questions in an almost dismissive nature, to suggest a lack of importance. Then, when opposing counsel uses similar questions, much of the drama has been drained out of the question and the jury is not surprised by the answer.

Conclusion

The defense case-in-chief should be used as an opportunity to reinforce strengths. It should be organized in a manner that is exciting, interesting, and captivating. It should not get bogged down in needless detail and unnecessary exhibits. It should be prepared and organized to minimize opportunities for the opposing counsel to score significant points. Your defense witnesses are advocates for your case. As such, they deserve adequate preparation for how to act in the courtroom and how to weather and fend off an aggressive examination.

21
The Rebuttal Case
The Plaintiff's Perspective

The decision of whether to call rebuttal witnesses is fraught with disclosure issues and the potential for a trial court's discretionary exclusion of rebuttal witnesses. However, the opportunity to persuade the jury by presenting the very last witness in the trial is one that brings much upside via the psychological concept of recency. Therefore, strategic considerations abound with respect to waiting to call witnesses during the rebuttal portion of a trial.

The concept of "rebuttal" arose from the common law, and from two Supreme Court cases, which hold that rebuttal proof that is improperly excluded by the trial courts below merited new trials. In *French v. Hall*, the Supreme Court held in 1886 that the rebuttal witness whose testimony was excluded below "seem[ed] to have been competent in rebuttal as proof of a contradictory statement made by the defendant at another time and place, with a view to discrediting him as a witness."[1] Therefore, the Court ruled that the trial court below erred to the prejudice of the plaintiff and ordered a new trial.[2] Likewise, in *Throckmorton v. Holt*, the proponents of a rebuttal witness had previously introduced evidence that indicated that General Sherman had signed a will as a witness; contestants of the will then produced a witness who testified to the contrary.[3] In rebuttal, the proponents sought to introduce as a witness General Sherman's son, but the trial court sustained an objection to that rebuttal witness.[4] The Supreme Court held that the proponents' rebuttal evidence should have been received.[5]

1. 119 U.S. 152, 155–56 (1886).
2. *Id.* at 172.
3. 180 U.S. 552, 564 (1901).
4. *Id.*
5. *Id.* ("Counsel for the proponents could not anticipate what evidence would be given by their opponents, nor what reasons might be offered by a witness as the ground for an opinion against the genuineness of any signature on the paper . . . We think this evidence was competent in that character, and should have been received. The case in regard to the genuineness of the paper was very closely contested, and was one of the vital points in the trial.").

"Rebuttal is a term of art, denoting evidence introduced by a Plaintiff to meet new facts brought out in his opponent's case in chief."[6] A rebuttal witness for the plaintiff is one who testifies during the rebuttal phase of trial, and who may only "meet new facts brought out in her opponent's case in chief."[7] "'[W]here the proponent has found it necessary or desirable, by reason of the opponent's cross examination, partly to anticipate his case in rebuttal by going to it during his case in chief, for example, on a re-direct examination; here he may take up the same subject again during the rebuttal.'"[8] Although the defendant typically enjoys no rebuttal phase at trial, a "defense witness whose purpose is to contradict an expected and anticipated portion of the plaintiff's case in chief can never be considered a 'rebuttal witness,' or anything close to one."[9]

Disclosure Issues to Watch Out For

In deciding whether to call witnesses during the rebuttal phase of the trial, there are significant disclosure issues to consider with respect to both lay and expert witnesses.

As to *lay* witnesses to be called during rebuttal, percipient witnesses "generally need not be disclosed in advance of trial."[10] As such, trial courts generally require disclosure of prospective witnesses "except 'rebuttal witnesses'" as part of Rule 16 pretrial conference disclosures.[11] However, trial courts also have exercised their discretion to "require offers of proof from all parties regarding witnesses to be called during the rebuttal phase of . . . trial," although "it would be premature to expect parties to make such offers of proof" before the conclusion of defendant's case in chief.[12]

Disclosure Rules about Rebuttal Experts

With respect to expert witnesses to be called in rebuttal, the Federal Rules of Civil Procedure set forth the disclosure requirements. Rule 26(a)(2) specifically governs a party's obligation in disclosing expert testimony. Experts specially engaged to provide expert testimony must furnish written reports that include a "complete statement of all opinions the witness will express and the basis and reasons for them," all "facts or data considered by the witness," and various disclosures related to the expert's qualifications, compensation, and prior expert testimony.[13] Absent a court order to the contrary, the parties must disclose expert testimony "at least 90 days before the date set for trial."[14] A party may also, however,

---

6. *Morgan v. Commercial Union Assurance Co.*, 606 F.2d 554, 555 (5th Cir. 1979) (citing *Mersel v. United States*, 420 F.2d 517, 520 (5th Cir. 1969); *McVey v. Phillips Petroleum Co.*, 288 F.2d 53, 54 (5th Cir. 1961); 6 Wigmore, Evidence § 1873 (Chadbourn rev. ed. 1976)).

7. *Morgan*, 606 F.2d at 556 (citations omitted).

8. *Weiss v. Chrysler Motors Corp.*, 515 F.2d 449, 459 (2d Cir. 1975) (citing 6 Wigmore, Evidence § 1873 at 517 (3d ed. 1940)).

9. *Morgan*, 606 F.2d at 556.

10. *Theoharis v. Rongen*, No. C13-1345RAJ, 2014 WL 3563386, at *3 (W.D. Wash. July 18, 2014).

11. *See Morgan*, 606 F.2d at 555 ("The trial below was preceded by a pre-trial conference, See Fed. R. Civ. P. 16, at which the trial judge ordered disclosure by both parties of all prospective witnesses except 'rebuttal witnesses.'").

12. *Gulino v. Bd. of Educ. of City Sch. Dist. of City of N.Y.*, No. 96 CIV. 8414 (CBM), 2003 WL 1858160, at *2 (S.D.N.Y. Apr. 9, 2003).

13. Fed. R. Civ. P. 26(a)(2)(B).

14. Fed. R. Civ. P. 26(a)(2)(D)(i).

offer rebuttal expert testimony—testimony "intended *solely* to contradict or rebut evidence on the same subject matter" as another party's expert disclosure—within 30 days after the other party's disclosure.[15] Thus, "rebuttal expert disclosures are expected, by default, to come at least 60 days before trial."[16] Rule 26(a)(2) does not otherwise require a rebuttal expert to be disclosed before the deadline for rebuttal disclosures.[17]

What Is a Rebuttal Expert?

Courts interpreting the word "solely" as used in Rule 26(a)(2)(D)(ii) have concluded that "[a]t a bare minimum, a rebuttal expert cannot offer testimony unless the expert whom she rebuts has offered testimony" and "cannot offer evidence that does not contradict or rebut another expert's disclosure merely because she also has also offered some proper rebuttal."[18] Some courts take the loose view that as long as an expert contradicts or rebuts the same "subject matter" as an opposing party's expert, she has offered rebuttal evidence.[19] "A modified version of that viewpoint permits rebuttal testimony that 'question[s] the assumptions and methods' of an opposing expert, without presenting 'new facts' or 'novel argument.'"[20] "Other courts suggest a stricter view—that expert testimony is not rebuttal testimony where it addresses an anticipated (or reasonably anticipatable) portion of the other party's case."[21]

What Is Required in Rebuttal Expert Reports?

Generally, "the party with the burden of proof must disclose any reply reports rebutting specific material in opposition reports," which "must be limited to true rebuttal and should be very brief" and "should not add new material that should have been placed in the opening report. . . ."[22] Moreover, "the reply material will ordinarily be reserved for the rebuttal or sur-rebuttal phase of the trial."[23]

The Consequence of Failing to Disclose

Failures to disclose are governed by Rule 37(c)(1), which states that "[i]f a party fails to provide information or identify a witness as required by Rule 26(a) or (e), the party is not

15. Fed. R. Civ. P. 26(b)(2)(D)(ii) (emphasis added).

16. *Theoharis*, 2014 WL 3563386, at *4.

17. *Id.* (citing *Johnson v. Grays Harbor Comm. Hosp.*, No. C06-5502BHS, 2007 U.S. Dist. LEXIS 95725, at *4, 2007 WL 4510313 (W.D. Wa. Dec. 18, 2007)).

18. *Theoharis*, 2014 WL 3563386, at *3. *See also In re Red Rock Services Co., LLC*, 522 B.R. 551, 571–72 (E.D. Pa. 2014).

19. *Lindner v. Meadow Gold Dairies, Inc.*, 249 F.R.D. 625, 637 (D. Haw. 2008).

20. *Theoharis*, 2014 WL 3563386, at *3 (citing *LaFlamme v. Safeway, Inc.*, No. 3:09-CV-00514, 2010 U.S. Dist. LEXIS 98815, at *8, 2010 WL 3522378 (D. Nev. Sept. 2, 2010)).

21. *Theoharis*, 2014 WL 3563386, at *3 (citing *Downs v. River City Group, LLC*, No. 3:11-CV-00885, 2014 U.S. Dist. LEXIS 26056, at *6–7, 2014 WL 814303 (D. Nev. Feb. 28, 2014); *Gerawan Farming, Inc. v. Prima Bella Produce, Inc.*, No. 1:10-CV-148 LJO JLT, 2011 U.S. Dist. LEXIS 52792, at *12–13, 2011 WL 2670335 (E.D. Cal. May 17, 2011)).

22. *Fields v. Wise Media, LLC*, C 12-05160 WHA, 2013 WL 12174296, at *5 (N.D. Cal. Jan. 25, 2013). *See also Life Tech. Corp. v. Biosearch Tech., Inc.*, NO. C 12-00852 WHA, 2012 WL 4097740, at *4 (N.D. Cal. Sept. 17, 2012).

23. *Oracle America, Inc. v. Google, Inc.*, No. C 10-03561 WHA, 2011 WL 5572835, at *1 (N.D. Cal. Nov. 15, 2011).

allowed to use that information or witness to supply evidence on a motion, at a hearing, or at trial, unless the failure was substantially justified or is harmless."[24]

The Trial Court's Discretion to Refuse Rebuttal Witnesses

If truth and fairness are not to be sacrificed, the judge must exert substantial control over the proceedings,[25] and therefore, the trial judge may exercise discretion in permitting or in refusing rebuttal testimony.[26] "The trial court may potentially be required to admit rebuttal evidence 'where the probative value of proffered evidence is potentially high and where such evidence, though admissible on the case in chief, was unnecessary for the plaintiff to establish in its prima facie case.'"[27] Within limits, however, the judge may control the scope of rebuttal testimony;[28] may refuse to allow cumulative, repetitive, or irrelevant testimony;[29] and may control the scope of examination of rebuttal witnesses.[30] "The primary rule is to exclude all evidence which has not been made necessary by the opponent's case, though this rule may be relaxed at the discretion of the trial court."[31] Accordingly, "the district judge has the discretion to 'limit the scope of rebuttal testimony to that which is directed to rebut new evidence or new theories proffered in the defendant's case-in-chief.'"[32] Moreover, "it is within the trial court's discretion to limit rebuttal testimony to only that which rebuts new matters or opinions presented by the defendant's case-in-chief."[33] In this regard, "[i]t is well settled that evidence which properly belongs in the case-in-chief but is first introduced in rebuttal may be rejected so as to avoid prejudice to the defendant and to ensure the orderly presentation of proof,"[34] although, "the fact that it might have been offered in chief d[oes] not preclude its admission in rebuttal."[35] However, there is "unanimous agreement" that it is properly within the discretion of the trial judge to limit testimony on rebuttal "to that which is precisely directed to rebutting new matter or new theories presented by the defendant's case-in-chief."[36]

---

24. Fed. R. Civ. P. 37(c)(1). *See also In re Asbestos Prod. Liab. Litig. (No. IV)*, Civil Action No. 09-CV-74351x, 2012 WL 661673, at *2 (E.D. Pa. Feb. 8, 2012).

25. *Glasser v. United States*, 315 U.S. 60, 83 (1942).

26. *See generally Geders v. United States*, 425 U.S. 80, 86–87 (1976).

27. *In re Red Rock*, 522 B.R. at 574 (citing *Weiss*, 515 F.2d at 458).

28. *Geders v. United* States, 425 U.S. 80, 86-87 (1976) ("Within limits, the judge may control the scope of rebuttal testimony."). *See also* United *States v. Chrzanowski*, 502 F.2d 573, 575 (3d Cir. 1974); *United States v. Perez*, 491 F.2d 167, 173 (9th Cir.), *cert denied sub. nom., Lombera v. United States*, 419 U.S. 858 (1974).

29. *Hamling v. United States*, 418 U.S. 87, 127 (1974).

30. *United States v. Nobles*, 422 U.S. 225, 231 (1975).

31. *Friend v. Comm'r of Internal Revenue*, 102 F.2d 153, 155 (7th Cir. 1939).

32. *Toth v. Grand Trunk R.R.*, 306 F.3d 335, 345 (6th Cir. 2002) (citing *Martin v. Weaver*, 666 F.2d 1013, 1020 (6th Cir. 1981) (citations omitted), *cert. denied*, 456 U.S. 962 (1982)).

33. *In re Asbestos Prod. Liab. Litig. (No. VI)*, 2012 WL 661673, at *1 (citing *Upshur v. Shepherd*, 538 F. Supp. 1176, 1180 (E.D. Pa. 1982), *aff'd*, 707 F.2d 1396 (Table) (3d Cir. 1983) (citation omitted)).

34. *Emerick v. U.S. Suzuki Motor Corp.*, 750 F.2d 19, 22 (3d Cir. 1984).

35. *Friend*, 102 F.2d at 155 (citing *St. Paul Plow-Works v. Starling*, 140 U.S. 184, 198 (1891)).

36. *Bowman v. General Motors Corp.*, 427 F. Supp. 234, 240 (E.D. Penn. 1977).

In *Toth v. Grand Trunk Railroad*, the Sixth Circuit Court of Appeals appropriately distinguished evidence improperly saved for rebuttal from "real" rebuttal evidence as follows:

> Evidence or theories offered by the defendant are new for rebuttal purposes if, under all the facts and circumstances, the evidence was not fairly and adequately presented to the trier of fact before the defendant's case-in-chief. Where the evidence is real rebuttal evidence, the fact that it might have been offered in chief does not preclude its admission in rebuttal. Furthermore, with respect to real rebuttal evidence, the plaintiff has no duty to anticipate or to negate a defense theory in plaintiff's case-in-chief.[37]

In *Toth*, that court held that "[t]he district court's stated reason for excluding the rebuttal testimony was that it could have been offered in the case-in-chief[,] [but its prior jurisprudence] establishe[d] that this factor is irrelevant, as long as the rebuttal is offered to refute new evidence offered in defendant's case-in-chief,"[38] and that therefore, "Toth had no duty to anticipate GTW's defense."[39] Even if "a plaintiff knew a defendant would present certain evidence, or would have known if the plaintiff had conducted more thorough discovery, is not a proper ground for excluding 'real rebuttal evidence.'"[40]

Strategic Considerations in Saving Witnesses for Rebuttal

"Waiting until the rebuttal deadline carries risk. If an opposing party offers no expert disclosures, or only narrow disclosures, there will be little or nothing to rebut."[41] A plaintiff must weigh the risk of forgoing testimony from a witness during the case-in-chief with the risks and benefits of saving that witness for rebuttal. Clearly, some courts have ruled that "because [the witness] was a rebuttal witness, he could not go over again the areas covered by [another witness] in plaintiff's case in chief."[42] This is because had a court "permitted cumulative rebuttal," it "would have had to allow [the defendant] 'equal time' in rejoinder, thus needlessly prolonging an already long trial."[43] Furthermore, other courts have refused to allow a witness who is available during one's case-in-chief to be reserved for the rebuttal phase of the trial.[44] Finally, by delaying the introduction of one's evidence from the

37. *Toth*, 306 F.3d at 345 (internal quotations omitted).

38. *Id.* at 346–47; *see also In re Red Rock*, 522 B.R. at 574.

39. *Id.* at 347.

40. *Id.* at 346. *See also Theoharis*, 2014 WL 3563386, at *4 ("For that reason, the court declines to adopt the rule that expert testimony on an anticipated portion of an opposing party's case cannot be rebuttal expert testimony."). *See also Pakootas v. Teck Cominco Metals, Ltd.*, No. CV-04-256-LRS, 2012 U.S. Dist. LEXIS 72137, at *6, 2012 WL 183390 (E.D. Wa. Apr. 4, 2012) (explaining that Rule 26 "does not automatically exclude anything an expert could have included in his or her original report") (quoting *Crowley v. Chait*, 322 F. Supp. 2d 530, 551 (D.N.J. 2004)).

41. *Theoharis*, 2014 WL 3563386, at *4.

42. *Bowman*, 427 F. Supp. at 236.

43. *Id.* at 240.

44. Because "in civil litigation generally, courts have recognized that a trial court 'has the discretion to limit the scope of rebuttal testimony to that which is directed to rebut new evidence or new theories proffered in the defendant's case-in-chief," *Settling Devotional Claimants v. Copyright Royalty Board*, 797 F.3d 1106, 1118 (D.C. Cir. 2015) (quoting *Toth*, 306 F.3d at 345 (internal quotations omitted)), when "the proposed rebuttal testimony 'could have been included in the same witness' direct examination," it may be excluded. *Settling Devotional*,

case-in-chief to the rebuttal phase of the trial, the plaintiff's lawyer increases the risk that a motion for directed verdict is granted at the end of the plaintiff's case-in-chief.[45]

If one successfully reserves a rebuttal witness in a manner permitting that witness to testify, the plaintiff's attorney has hit the jackpot—a key witness closing the door on the defendant's theory via the last witness in the case. It is for this reason that the rebuttal phase should be extensively planned well in advance of the trial.

797 F.3d at 1118 (quoting *Waterview Mgmt. Co. v. FDIC*, 203 F.3d 54, 1999 WL 503921, at *2 (D.C. Cir. May 20, 1999) (unpublished) (citation omitted)).

45. *Zamlen v. City of Cleveland*, 906 F.2d 209, 214–15 (6th Cir. 1990) ("Although plaintiffs contended that they had additional evidence in support of their section 1983 claim, they declined the court's suggestion that it might be prudent to present more evidence at this stage, and elected to wait until the rebuttal phase of their Title VII action to proffer additional expert testimony regarding the construction, administration, and scoring of the test." Therefore, "[n]one of this additional evidence was before the district court when it ruled on the motion for a directed verdict," and "[h]aving concluded that the evidence presented was, at best, amorphous, the district court was correct in granting defendants' motion for a directed verdict on the claim of intentional discrimination.").

22

The Plaintiff's Rebuttal: Having the Last Word

The Defense Perspective

Some cases end without a rebuttal case. However, as defense lawyers, we should be keenly aware of the plaintiff's right to get the last word if a proper foundation is laid. Most skilled plaintiff's lawyers seek rebuttal opportunities because they know rebuttal provides a last chance to have the last say. Some even lie in wait for rebuttal opportunities, springing surprise witnesses after the defense closes. As such, there are several practice tips and strategic recommendations to consider.

First and foremost, you should make sure that any rebuttal witness is a "genuine" rebuttal witness, and not a thinly veiled effort by plaintiff's counsel to manipulate the order of witnesses to get a last substantive bite at the apple. This means there must be a legitimate basis for calling the rebuttal witness; this applies both to expert witnesses and to fact witnesses.

Rebuttal typically is justified when the plaintiff is genuinely responding to evidence in the defense case. However, you should oppose any effort to offer rebuttal testimony if the testimony should have been reasonably anticipated in the plaintiff's case-in-chief or if it does not truly respond to something in the defense case. The procedural rules of your jurisdiction should be researched to ensure you assert timely and appropriate objections to stop any subterfuge disguised as "rebuttal."

There are significant differences between rebuttal fact witnesses and expert witnesses. Ordinarily, in federal court, a plaintiff must timely disclose a rebuttal expert before trial.[1] The defendant also should be given the opportunity to depose the rebuttal expert.[2] This

1. *See* Fed. R. Civ. P. 26(a)(2)(D)(ii) (stating rebuttal expert testimony must be disclosed within thirty days of other party's disclosure "if the evidence is intended solely to contradict or rebut evidence on the same subject matter identified by another party").

2. *See* Fed. R. Civ. P. 26(b)(4) ("A party may depose any person who has been identified as an expert whose opinions may be presented at trial.").

occurs after the defendant has disclosed its experts, and the plaintiff has been given an opportunity to respond. Clearly, a plaintiff in federal court will have a hard time justifying late disclosure of a rebuttal expert for the first time at trial if the plaintiff was on notice of the need to disclose during pretrial discovery. The federal rules actually contemplate this.[3]

On the other hand, a plaintiff may have a better chance of disclosing a true rebuttal fact witness whose relevance was not previously known. Again, there may be procedural differences between jurisdictions, so advance research is necessary to define the parties' respective rights. In Texas, a properly phrased interrogatory requires the opposing party to designate all anticipated trial witnesses *except* rebuttal witnesses whose need could not be reasonably anticipated.[4] The rule specifically states:

> **Trial witnesses.** A party may obtain discovery of the name, address, and telephone number of any person who is expected to be called to testify at trial. This paragraph does not apply to rebuttal or impeaching witnesses the necessity of whose testimony cannot reasonably be anticipated before trial.[5]

With that said, all parties in Texas are required to identify persons with knowledge of relevant facts during pretrial discovery as part of the written disclosure process. A plaintiff in Texas may have a difficult time calling a previously undisclosed fact witness as a rebuttal witness if the plaintiff should have timely disclosed the witness's identity during pretrial discovery. Although the plaintiff might not have planned to call a rebuttal fact witness, the plaintiff may have a procedural problem if the witness's identity was previously known but not disclosed. The procedural rules for each jurisdiction should be consulted in this regard.

Objections and Voir Dire

If a rebuttal fact witness is called and the witness was not previously disclosed in response to the court's scheduling orders or proper discovery request, appropriate objections for the relevant jurisdiction must be lodged. First, you should make a record to preserve your objection for appeal. Second, you should seek leave to take the witness on voir dire outside the hearing of the jury to establish when the witness was first contacted by plaintiff's counsel. If you establish that the witness was first contacted before trial ever started, you have a home run. The plaintiff's lawyer will be challenged to show that the witness is responding solely to evidence raised in the defense case-in-chief if the witness was first contacted before the defense case started.

3. *See* Fed. R. Civ. P. 26.

4. *See* Tex. R. Civ. P. 192.3 (d) (stating that disclosure of "trial witnesses" is within the "scope of discovery"); *see also* Tex. R. Civ. P. 197.1 (stating that written interrogatories may "inquire about any matter within the scope of discovery . . . ").

5. *Id.*

Proceedings When Objections Are Overruled

If your objections are overruled and the witness is a potentially impactful witness, you should ask for a brief adjournment of the trial to take a short deposition. This is particularly justified if the witness was not previously disclosed and a deposition is necessary to avoid surprise.

Most courts will allow a brief intermission for a deposition or interview. I have done this on several occasions with leave of court. In one instance, I was allowed to take a witness's deposition the night before the witness took the stand. The court granted two hours to do so. In another case, I was allowed to take a doctor's deposition in the courtroom while the jury took an extended lunchbreak. The topic focused on brain function scores of a victim at the accident scene recorded by first responders. The doctor was being called as an expert to discuss conscious pain and suffering. The trial judge actually listened to the deposition. Fortunately, I was able to develop several cross-examination points before the doctor ultimately took the stand.

I also have been granted leave to interview fact witnesses before they took the stand to discuss the plaintiff's losses and damages. These were lay damage witnesses. The plaintiff's counsel also attended these interviews. I was able to establish the framework for short, concise cross-examinations for each witness. My goal was to gather sufficient information about the witness and the witness's testimony to develop an effective cross-examination without having to scramble in the courtroom in a purely reactive mode.

Many of the same principles hold true for rebuttal experts. In federal court, you likely will have the opportunity to undertake formal discovery.[6] In state court jurisdictions, you should ask leave of court to examine the witness outside the hearing of the jury. Once again, as part of your preliminary cross-examination, your examination should include questions to develop information demonstrating that the witness was known to plaintiff's counsel well in advance of trial, and that there was a failure to timely disclose. With experts, it also is important to lay a foundation for a *Daubert*[7] or similar expert challenge. You should ask leave of court to examine the witness to establish the witness's credentials and the reliability of the expert's methodology. You need to preserve the option to challenge the expert even during the expedited pace surrounding the rebuttal.

Strategic Issues for Defendants

Good plaintiffs' lawyers typically seek a chance at calling a rebuttal witness. You should prepare for this in advance. You also can make strategic choices to not call certain witnesses, to undercut the plaintiff's right to present a rebuttal. An excellent example of this occurs in federal court where the plaintiff will be required to designate rebuttal experts in advance of trial. If you believe the rebuttal expert is particularly dangerous and impactful, you can make a calculated decision to not call the defense expert to whom the rebuttal expert is

6. *See generally* Fed. R. Civ. P. 26.
7. *Daubert v. Merrell Dow Pharms., Inc.*, 509 U.S. 579 (1993).

intended to respond. This may be a prudent decision if your defense expert is not essential to an otherwise successful defense.

This occurred in a case discussed earlier in this book—albeit with a slightly different posturing of the parties. In that case, I represented a nominal plaintiff in a declaratory judgment action. We had designated an economist as one of my experts. In response, the defendant (counter-claimant) designated a well-known, highly credentialed witness to respond to certain portions of our expert's opinions. We elected to not call our witness in our case-in-chief, with the specific intention of closing the door on the opposing witness. When the opposing counsel opened his client's case, he called this witness as one of his first witnesses, who was in the courtroom and ready to take the stand. I had previously taken his deposition, so there were no genuine surprises. However, we argued that the witness was designated *solely* as a rebuttal to my expert who never testified. Because my expert never took the stand, we argued that the opposing expert should not be allowed to testify. The court agreed and sustained our objection.

Timing Considerations

If a rebuttal witness is admitted over your objection, your cross-examination should be short and to the point. The jury is no doubt tired and fatigued at this point, and typically it does not want to hear more "lawyer talk." If you stretch the rebuttal by long-winded examinations, you may inadvertently make the rebuttal *appear* more important than it is. The jury may sense that an extensive cross-examination suggests you are concerned. Also, if your cross-examination is long-winded, you create more opportunities for the witness to hurt your case and more opportunities for the plaintiff to reinforce its trial themes.

Thus, a short, crisp cross-examination is likely more effective. Again, keep in mind that most jurors have already made up their minds by this point. It is doubtful that the rebuttal, or your cross-examination, will win the case for you—so make sure it does not damage you, either.

23
THE MULTIPARTY CASE
The Plaintiff's Perspective

Bringing a case involving multiple parties on one or both sides of a lawsuit leads to motion practice of consolidation under Rule 20(a), severance under Rule 21, whether multiple plaintiffs may go to trial together under Rule 42(a), and additional special strategies for both the plaintiffs and defendants, often involving shifting alliances and concerns of informal understandings akin to now-barred *Mary Carter* agreements. In essence, a multiparty case raises the stakes, presenting greater opportunities and dangers for all involved.

Consolidation and Severance of Multi-Plaintiff and Multi-Defendant Petitions

Whether it be through a class action lawsuit or a multi-plaintiff petition, the Federal Rules of Civil Procedure expressly permit the filing of related claims brought by more than one plaintiff in a single suit. The Supreme Court has observed that "class actions constitute but one of several methods for bringing about aggregation of claims, *i.e.*, they are but one of several methods by which multiple similarly situated parties get similar claims resolved at one time and in one federal forum."[1]

Joinder of Multiple Plaintiffs in a Single Suit

Rule 20(a) has substantially expanded party joinder beyond that allowed under the common law rules and the state codes.[2] Rule 20(a)(1) provides that "[p]ersons may join in one

1. *Spirit Commc'ns Co., LP v. APCC Servs., Inc.*, 554 U.S. 269, 291 (2008) (citing Rule 20(a) (permitting joinder of multiple plaintiffs); Rule 42 (permitting consolidation of related cases filed in the same district court); 28 U.S.C. § 1407 (authorizing consolidation of pretrial proceedings for related cases filed in multiple federal districts); § 1404 (making it possible for related cases pending in different federal courts to be transferred and consolidated in one district court); D. HERR, ANNOTATED MANUAL FOR COMPLEX LITIGATION § 20.12, p. 279 (4th ed. 2007) (noting that "[r]elated cases pending in different federal courts may be consolidated in a single district" by transfer under 28 U.S.C. § 1404(a)); JAY TIDMARSH & ROGER H. TRANGSRUD, COMPLEX LITIGATION AND THE ADVERSARY SYSTEM 473–524 (1998) (section on "Transfer Devices that Aggregate Cases in a Single Venue")).

2. 7 CHARLES A. WRIGHT, ARTHUR R. MILLER & MARY KAY KANE, FEDERAL PRACTICE AND PROCEDURE § 1654 (3d ed. 2011).

action as plaintiffs if: (A) they assert any right to relief jointly, severally, or in the alternative with respect to or arising out of the same transaction, occurrence, or series of transactions or occurrences; and (B) any question of law or fact common to all plaintiffs will arise in the action." Both elements are required for a proper joinder of plaintiffs.[3] In construing Rule 20, the Eighth Circuit Court of Appeals has provided a very broad definition for the term "transaction":

> "Transaction" is a word of flexible meaning. It may comprehend a series of many occurrences, depending not so much upon the immediateness of their connection as upon their logical relationship. Accordingly, all "logically related" events entitling a person to institute a legal action against another generally are regarded as comprising a transaction or occurrence. The analogous interpretation of the terms as used in Rule 20 would permit all reasonably related claims for relief by or against different parties to be tried in a single proceeding. Absolute identity of all events is unnecessary.[4]

"Multiple plaintiffs are free to join their claims in a single suit when '*any* question of law or fact common to all plaintiffs will arise in the action. . . .'"[5] "Not *all* questions of law or fact need be common; rather, only *some* questions must be common."[6] Moreover, the "common question need not predominate; that's a requirement for class actions, not for permissive joinder."[7]

"The purpose of Rule 20(a) is 'to promote trial convenience and expedite the final determination of disputes, thereby preventing multiple lawsuits.'"[8] The Supreme Court has explained that joinder should be used to allow the "broadest possible scope of action consistent with fairness to the parties; joinder of claims, parties, and remedies is strongly encouraged."[9] Likewise, the Eleventh Circuit Court of Appeals emphasized that the Supreme Court has thereby "instructed the lower courts to employ a liberal approach to permissive joinder of claims *and* parties in the interest of judicial economy. . . ."[10] Likewise, the Seventh Circuit Court of Appeals has taught that "[t]he spirit underlying the permissive joinder doctrine is to promote efficiency, convenience, consistency, and fundamental fairness."[11] Accordingly,

---

3. *Deskovic v. City of Peekskill*, 673 F. Supp. 2d 154, 159 (S.D.N.Y. 2009); James W. Moore, Moore's Federal Practice § 21.02[1] (3d ed. 2009) ("Failure to satisfy either prerequisite for permissive joinder constitutes misjoinder of parties.").

4. *Mosley v. General Motors Corp.*, 497 F.2d 1330, 1333 (8th Cir. 1974). *See also* Wright, *supra* (explaining that the transaction/occurrence requirement prescribed by Rule 20(a) is not a rigid test and is meant to be "read as broadly as possible whenever doing so is likely to promote judicial economy.").

5. *Lee v. Cook County, Ill.*, 635 F.3d 969, 971 (7th Cir. 2011) (emphasis in original) (quoting Fed. R. Civ. P. 20(a)(1)(B)).

6. *Wagoner v. Pfizer, Inc.*, No. 07-1229-JTM, 2008 WL 2937249, at *2 (D. Kan. July 24, 2008) (emphasis in original).

7. *Lee*, 635 F.3d at 971.

8. *Biglow v. Boeing Co.*, 201 F.R.D. 519, 520 (D. Kan. 2001).

9. *United Mine Workers of Am. v. Gibbs*, 383 U.S. 715, 724 (1966).

10. *Alexander v. Fulton Cty.*, 207 F.3d 1303 (11th Cir. 2000) (citing *Gibbs*, 383 U.S. at 724 ("Under the Rules, the impulse is towards entertaining the broadest possible scope of action consistent with fairness to the parties; joinder of claims, parties and remedies is strongly encouraged.")).

11. *Nelson v. AIM Advisors, Inc.*, No. 01-CV-0282-MJR, 2002 WL 442189, at *2 (S.D. Ill. Mar. 8, 2002) (citing *Intercon Research Assoc., Ltd. v. Dresser Indus., Inc.*, 696 F.2d 53, 57–58 (7th Cir. 1994)).

"[t]he requirements of Fed. R. Civ. P. 20(a) are to be interpreted liberally 'to enable the court to promote judicial economy, . . .'"[12] while observing "the strong preference in favor of joinder by the courts. . . ."[13]

In determining whether to grant or deny joinder, the court may consider principles of fundamental fairness, prejudice, expense, or delay.[14] Rule 21 gives the court broad discretion to determine when severance is appropriate.[15] Thus, in addition to the preconditions set forth in Rule 20(a), in deciding whether to sever a claim under Rule 21, courts should generally consider, "[1] whether settlement of the claims or judicial economy would be facilitated; [2] whether prejudice would be avoided if severance were granted; and [3] whether different witnesses and documentary proof are required for the separate claims."[16] A severance is not appropriate merely to achieve separate filing fees for each plaintiff.[17] Consequently, a court properly denies severance of multiple plaintiff's claims brought together because fracturing a case into separate lawsuits "would be inefficient, and would not advance the objectives of convenience, judicial economy, expediting resolution of disputes and eliminating unnecessary litigation."[18]

The Eighth Circuit Court of Appeals held in *In re Prempro Products Liability Litigation* that egregious misjoinder was not shown when the different plaintiffs' claims each arose from a series of transactions between HRT pharmaceutical manufacturers and individuals who have used HRT drugs.[19] Since then, courts in Missouri repeatedly have permitted similar claims involving product liability to be brought together by plaintiffs in a single complaint. In *Gracey v. Janssen Pharmaceuticals, Inc.*, the court ruled that sixty-four plaintiffs properly filed suit together in one complaint alleging product liability, reasoning:

> Plaintiffs' claims satisfy Rule 20(a)'s standard. First, plaintiffs' complaint raises common questions of law or fact regarding injuries alleged from use of the same product and arising from the same design, testing, development, labeling, packaging, distribution, marketing, and sales practices for that product. Also, because plaintiffs' allegations relate to defendants' design, manufacture, testing, and promotion of Risperidone—occurrences common as to all plaintiffs—their claims also arise out of the same transaction or occurrence, or series thereof. That is so even if the end-of-the-line exposures

12. *Viada v. Osaka Health Spa, Inc.*, 235 F.R.D. 55, 61 (S.D.N.Y. 2006) (internal citation and quotation marks omitted).

13. *Battison v. City of Electra*, No. 7:01-CV-037-R, 2001 WL 497769, at *3 (N.D. Tex. May 8, 2001) (denying severance due to similar allegations and "the strong preference in favor of joinder by the courts").

14. *Chavez v. Illinois State Police*, 251 F.3d 612, 632 (7th Cir. 2001).

15. *Aregood v. Int'l Flavors & Fragrances, Inc.*, Case No. 1:14-CV-0274-SEB-TAB, 2015 WL 13631742, at *2 (S.D. Ind. Jan. 13, 2015).

16. *Crown Cork & Seal Co., Inc. Master Retirement Trust v. Credit Suisse First Boston Corp.*, 288 F.R.D. 331, 333 (S.D.N.Y. 2013) (quoting *Erausquin v. Notz, Stucki Mgmt. (Bermuda) Ltd.*, 806 F. Supp. 2d 712, 720 (S.D.N.Y. 2011)).

17. *See State ex rel. J.C. v. Mazzone*, 233 W. Va. 457, 759 S.E.2d 200 (2014) (granting writ of prohibition against local rule requiring twenty-five Zoloft cases joined under Rule 20(a) to be treated as separate cases in order to collect individual filing fees). *See also Eddington v. Bureau of Prisons*, Civ. A. No. 19-11232-RGS, 2019 WL 2503163, at *1 (D. Mass. June 17, 2019) ("Where there are multiple plaintiffs in a civil action, it has been the practice of this court to apportion equally the filing fee between or among all plaintiffs.").

18. *Nettles v. Daphne Utils.*, Civ. A. No. 13-0605-WS-C, 2014 WL 1668535, at *2 (S.D. Ala. Apr. 28, 2014).

19. *In re Prempro*, 591 F.3d 613, 623 (8th Cir. 2010).

occurred in different states and under the supervision of different medical professionals. Thus, joinder of all sixty-four plaintiffs' claims under Rule 20(a) is proper.[20]

Likewise, the court in *Fahnestock v. Boehringer Ingelheim Pharmaceuticals, Inc.*, ruled that sixty-eight plaintiffs properly filed suit in a single product liability complaint, with identical reasoning.[21] Furthermore, in *Simmons v. Skechers USA, Inc.*, the court ruled that sixty-five plaintiffs properly filed suit in a single product liability complaint, noting that "[b]ecause plaintiffs' allegations relate to defendants' design, manufacture, and marketing of Shape-ups—occurrences common to all plaintiffs—the court concludes that their claims arise out of the same transaction or occurrence or series thereof . . . even if plaintiffs were injured in different states and their injuries range in severity and type, as their claims are all reasonably related."[22] Other courts there have ruled in the same manner.[23]

Courts elsewhere have denied severance as well, recognizing the efficiency of permitting similar product liability claims brought by different plaintiffs to be filed together in one product liability complaint. In *Abraham v. Volkswagen of America, Inc.*, the Second Circuit Court of Appeals found that multiple plaintiffs injured due to a defect in a particular Volkswagen model were properly joined under Rule 20 when the filed case involved joinder of claims related to an identical product defect.[24] Likewise, the court in *Kehr ex rel. Kehr. v. Yamaha Motor Corp., USA*, denied severance over the defendant's objection that "because the case involves two separate, unrelated accidents, with distinct factual patterns, that they cannot be joined under Rule 20(a)," observing that "[t]here is no requirement, . . . that all questions of law and fact be *identical* in order for there to be permissive joinder under Rule 20(a)" because "the Rule provides for joinder as long as there is *any* question or fact common to all."[25] Similarly, multiple plaintiffs bringing similar claims for injuries manifested

20. *Gracey v. Janssen Pharm., Inc.*, No. 4:15-CV-407 (CDJ), 2015 WL 2066242, at *4 (E.D. Mo. May 4, 2015).

21. *Fahnestock v. Boehringer Ingelheim Pharm., Inc.*, Case No. 4:16-CV-1013 (CEJ), 2016 WL 4397971, at *3 (E.D. Mo. Aug. 1, 2016).

22. *Simmons v. Skechers USA, Inc.*, No. 4:15-CV-340-CEJ, 2015 WL 1604859, at *2 (E.D. Mo. Apr. 9, 2015).

23. *See Matthews v. Fresenius Medical Care North America, Inc.*, No. 4:14-CV-979-JAR, 2014 WL 3579941, at *3 (E.D. Mo. July 21, 2014) (denying severance of claims of multiple plaintiffs brought in a single complaint, reasoning "[t]hat patients treated with GranuFlo had different prescribing physicians and some differences in injuries, or that treatment occurred in different states, fails to undermine the relatedness of these claims and the common issues of law and fact that will arise in all of the claims."); *Townsend v. Hoffman-La Roche, Inc.*, Case No. 4:11-CV-01420-AGF, 2011 WL 13248368, at *2 (E.D. Mo. Sept. 1, 2011) (denying severance, because "[t]he claims of all Plaintiffs are against the same Defendants, related to the same drug, and there is no dispute that the litigation is likely to contain common questions of law and fact."); *Coleman v. Bayer Corp.*, 4:10-CV-01639-SNLJ, 2010 WL 10806572, at *2 (E.D. Mo. Dec. 9, 2010) (denying severance because "all plaintiffs allege that they suffered renal and cardiovascular system injuries resulting from defendants' defective medication, and that defendants knew of the dangers presented but did not warn the plaintiffs.").

24. *Abraham v. Volkswagen of America, Inc.*, 795 F.2d 238, 251 (2d Cir. 1986).

25. *Kehr ex rel. Kehr. v. Yamaha Motor Corp., USA*, 596 F. Supp. 2d 821, 827 (S.D.N.Y. Dec. 5, 2008). *See also Westfield Ins. Co. v. Interline Brands, Inc.*, No. CIV. 12-6775 JBS/JS, 2013 WL 6816173, at *10–11 (D.N.J. Dec. 20, 2013) (severance denied over argument that plaintiffs' claims "are in fact four individual matters involving four separate occurrences and four separate water supply lines," because the complaint alleges "property damage was caused by the same defect in water supply lines 'designed, manufactured, marketed, sold, and/or distributed' by the named defendants.").

as a result of a failure to train may be brought together in a single lawsuit under Rule 20(a).[26] Claims by multiple plaintiffs alleging an employer's pattern and practice of discrimination may be brought as a single lawsuit as well.[27] And cases brought by multiple plaintiffs alleging their injuries each were caused by the same mode of substandard medical care may be brought together.[28]

Joinder of Multiple Defendants in a Single Complaint

"Rule 18 permits very broad joinder of claims, counterclaims, cross-claims, and third-party claims."[29] Rule 18(a) of the Federal Rules of Civil Procedure provides that "[a] party asserting a claim, counterclaim, crossclaim, or third-party claim may join, as independent or alternative claims, as many claims as it has against an opposing party." There is no requirement that the aggregated claims (between parties) be factually related; claims joined under Rule 18 need not be part of the same case or controversy as claims over which the court would have independent original jurisdiction.[30]

Rules 18 and 20 "can work together to allow joinder of multiple claims by multiple plaintiffs against multiple defendants," giving district courts "considerable flexibility in managing

---

26. *Harter v. Carondelet Health Network*, No. CV-15-00343-TUC-RM, 2017 WL 10505261, at *3 (D. Ariz. Jan. 27, 2017) (joinder of multiple claims proper because they "share common factual questions, *e.g.*, whether Defendant failed to maintain VRI equipment and properly train staff to use such equipment" and because they each sought relief under similar laws). *See also Dixon v. Scott Fetzer Co.*, 317 F.R.D. 329, 332 (D. Conn. 2016) (joinder of plaintiffs proper when each allege tortious "hiring and training of independent dealers selling Kirby vacuum cleaners.").

27. *Wagoneka v. KT&G USA Corp.*, Case No. 4:18-CV-859-ALM-KPJ, 2019 WL 4052484, at *4 (E.D. Tex. Aug. 8, 2019) (Johnson, M.J.) (recommending denial of motion to sever under Rule 21 and noting that "[t]hough Plaintiffs' claims arise from 'separate, discrete incidents,' Defendant's conduct toward Plaintiffs, if true, 'forms part of a logically related series of transactions or occurrences under Rule 20.'"); *Mann v. Con-Way Freight, Inc.*, Case No. 16-2196-CM, 2016 WL 6476548, at *3 (D. Kan. Nov. 2, 2016) ("whether Con-Way engaged in a pattern and practice of racial discrimination is a question common to the claims of all the proposed plaintiffs, and satisfies Rule 20(a)(1)(B)."); *Baker v. Hafez Corp.*, No. 13-00641-KD-N, 2014 WL 1760976, at *10 (S.D. Ala. May 2, 2014) (multiple plaintiffs' allegation that their employer pays them less than those of a different nationality, "although asserted by multiple plaintiffs, is properly understood as asserting that it is the defendant's pattern or practice to unlawfully favor employees of the same nationality as Mr. Maghsoud" is an "allegation may therefore be presented in a single lawsuit pursuant to Rule 20(a)(1)."); *Brantley v. Cinergy Corp.*, No. 1:01-CV-378, 2007 WL 2462652, at *10 (S.D. Ohio Aug. 27, 2007) (denying severance because "[w]hile each Plaintiff alleges some unique facts in support of his claims, Plaintiffs also make some parallel or overlapping allegations relating to Cinergy's general work environment and employment practices" and "[t]hese legal and factual parallels suggest both that Plaintiffs' claims are appropriately joined under Rule 20(a) and that severing them under Rule 21 would seriously undermine judicial economy.").

28. *Howes v. Yankton Med. Clinic, PC*, 4:15-CV-04177-KES, 2016 WL 4385898, at *2 (D.S.D. Aug. 17, 2016) (allowing addition of additional plaintiffs to a complaint because both the existing Plaintiff's injuries "and the new plaintiffs' injuries arise out of the same transaction and share common questions of law and fact" when both allege a denial of care by the same defendant). *Cf., Steed v. Doe*, 14-CV-747-JDP, 2016 WL 1179230, at *3 (W.D. Wis. Mar. 23, 2016) (allowing plaintiffs' respective claims for separate incidents to remain joined in one complaint because each relates to the defendant's "policy of granting correctional officers responsibility to distribute and track medications.").

29. *Ashe v. Swenson*, 397 U.S. 436, 455 (1970) (Brennan, J., concurring). *See also American Fire & Cas. Co. v. Finn*, 341 U.S. 6, 10 & n.3 (1951) ("Rules 18, 20, and 23 of the Federal Rules of Civil Procedure permit the most liberal joinder of parties, claims, and remedies in civil actions.") (citations omitted).

30. *Wolde-Meskel v. Vocational Instruction Project Cmty. Servs., Inc.*, 166 F.3d 59, 62 (2d Cir. 1999) (citing 14B Charles A. Wright, Arthur R. Miller, Mary Kay Kane, Richard L. Marcus & Adam N. Steinman, Federal Practice and Procedure § 3704 at 130 (3d ed. 1998)).

and structuring civil litigation for fair and efficient resolution of complex disputes."[31] But, "in actions involving multiple defendants, Rule 20 operates independently of Rule 18" and "joinder of claims under Rule 18 becomes relevant only after the requirements of Rule 20 relating to joinder of parties has been met with respect to the party against whom the claim is sought to be asserted."[32]

The Federal Rules of Civil Procedure "strike a delicate balance between (1) a plaintiff's interest in structuring litigation, (2) a defendant's 'wish to avoid multiple litigation, or inconsistent relief,' (3) an outsider's interest in joining the litigation, and (4) the interest of the courts and the public in complete, consistent, and efficient settlement of controversies."[33] While "[u]nrelated claims against different defendants belong in different suits, . . ."[34] the "rules generally allow for a plaintiff to decide who to join in an action."[35] Accordingly, joinder of all potential claims against a defendant is not required by Rule 18(a), as the rule refers "only to *permissive* joinder, at the party's option."[36]

"While Rule 18 liberally permits joinder of claims, moreover, it, in fact, 'deals only with [the] pleadings.'"[37] Thus, while Rule 18(a) allows joinder of multiple claims, it "did not eliminate the obligation to comply with Rule 8"[38] concerning the general rules of pleading. "[E]ach joined claim, potentially the basis of separate litigation, must have the same foundation it would have needed if the claims had been pursued separately."[39]

Rule 18(b) provides that "[a] party may join two claims even though one of them is contingent on the disposition of the other; but the court may grant relief only in accordance with the parties' relative substantive rights. In particular, a plaintiff may state a claim for money and a claim to set aside a conveyance that is fraudulent as to that plaintiff, without first obtaining a judgment for the money." In *Scott v. Neely*, the Supreme Court held that a court of equity could not even take jurisdiction of a suit "in which a claim properly cognizable only

---

31. *UWM Student Assoc. v. Lovell*, 888 F.3d 854, 863 (7th Cir. 2018).

32. *Pace v. Timmerman's Ranch and Saddle Shop, Inc.*, 795 F.3d 748, 755 n.10 (7th Cir. 2015) (citing *Intercon Research Assocs., Ltd. v. Dresser Indus., Inc.*, 696 F.2d 53, 57 (7th Cir. 1982)). *See also Vermillion v. Levenhagen*, 604 F. App'x 508, 512 (7th Cir. 2015) ("Once Vermillion properly joined parties under Federal Rule of Civil Procedure 20, Rule 18 allows him to join all claims he has against each defendant.").

33. *Pace*, 795 F.3d at 755–56 (citing *Provident Tradesmens Bank & Tr. Co. v. Patterson*, 390 U.S. 102, 109–11 (1968)).

34. *George v. Smith*, 507 F.3d 605, 607 (7th Cir. 2007).

35. *Pace*, 795 F.3d at 756 (citing *Applewhite v. Reichhold Chems., Inc.*, 67 F.3d 571, 574 (5th Cir. 1995)).

36. *Headley v. Bacon*, 828 F.2d 1272, 1275 (8th Cir. 1987). *See also Dore v. Kleppe*, 522 F.2d 1369, 1374–75 (5th Cir. 1975) ("Rule 18 merely permits the joinder of other claims against the same party, but, faced with a very real controversy, the pleader, to flee from res judicata, need not dream up all the imaginable disputes with the adversary dependent on the outcome of the then controversy and as to which predictions on consequential impact would involve theorizing on hypotheticals.").

37. *In re Nintendo Co., Ltd.*, 544 F. App'x 934, 938 (Fed. Cir. 2013) (citing Advisory Committee's 1966 Amendment Notes) ("As the Advisory Committee's 1966 Note explains, 'a claim properly joined as a matter of pleading need not be proceeded with together with the other claims if fairness or convenience justifies separate treatment.'") *See also Mackensworth v. S.S. American Merchant*, 28 F.3d 246, 251 (2d Cir. 1994) ("Rule 18 . . . deals only with pleading requirements.").

38. *Fletcher v. Inmate Bank*, 752 F. App'x 683, 684–85 (10th Cir. 2019), *cert. denied*, 140 S. Ct. 69 (2019).

39. *Chapman v. U.S. Steel, Div. of U.S.X.*, 12 F.3d 1100, 1993 WL 483112, at *1 (7th Cir. 1993) (unpublished) (citing *Frantz v. U.S. Powerlifting Fed'n*, 836 F.2d 1063, 1067 (7th Cir. 1987)).

at law is united in the same pleadings with a claim for equitable relief."[40] That holding, which "was based upon both the historical separation between law and equity and the duty of the Court to insure 'that the right to a trial by a jury in the legal action may be preserved intact,' created considerable inconvenience in that it necessitated two separate trials in the same case whenever that case contained both legal and equitable claims."[41] "Consequently, when the procedure in the federal courts was modernized by the adoption of the Federal Rules of Civil Procedure in 1938, . . . it was deemed advisable to abandon that part of the holding of *Scott v. Neely* which rested upon the separation of law and equity and to permit the joinder of legal and equitable claims in a single action."[42] However, "Rule 18(b) deals only with joinder of remedies at the pleading stage of the litigation and does not govern the question of when and under what circumstances parties may supplement their complaints."[43]

Joining the Claims of Multiple Plaintiffs Together in a Single Suit

Rule 42(a) of the Federal Rules of Civil Procedure provides that "[i]f actions before the court involve a common question of law or fact, the court may: (1) join for hearing or trial any or all matters at issue in the actions; (2) consolidate the actions; or (3) issue any other orders to avoid unnecessary cost or delay." In mass tort litigations, data points are gathered from bellwether trials, which are representative cases tried first and intended to provide the parties with the likely reactions of future juries if similar cases are tried.

As the United States Court of Appeals for the Second Circuit observed in affirming a District Court's decision to hold a single trial for asbestos workers:

> Consolidation is a valuable and important tool of judicial administration. This is especially true when the courts are overwhelmed with huge numbers of cases which involve substantially the same questions of fact, as happens when large numbers of plaintiffs allege that they have developed similar illnesses in reaction to a particular toxic substance. See Fed. R. Civ. P. 42(a). In such circumstances, consolidation permits the federal court to furnish trials in hundreds, even thousands of cases it might otherwise not reach for many years. If carefully and properly administered, as it was by Judge Sweet below, consolidation is also capable of producing, with efficiency and greatly reduced expense for all parties, a fairer, more rational and evenhanded delivery of justice.[44]

The court of appeals discussed another benefit of consolidated trials: the ability for jurors to compare the relative injuries of the plaintiffs and more fairly award compensation:

> One of the most persistent and troublesome problems in the administration of justice in our civil jury system is the unpredictable relationship between different juries'

---

40. *Scott v. Neely*, 140 U.S. 106, 117 (1891).
41. *Dairy Queen, Inc. v. Wood*, 369 U.S. 469, 471 (1962) (citations omitted).
42. *Id.*
43. *Otis Clapp & Son, Inc. v. Filmore Vitamin Co.*, 754 F.2d 738, 743 (7th Cir. 1985).
44. *Consorti v. Armstrong World Indus. Inc.*, 72 F.3d. 1003, 1006 (2nd Cir. 1995) *vacated on other grounds*, 518 U.S. 1031 (1996).

awards, particularly for intangibles such as pain and suffering. It of course should be the goal of the overall administration of such litigation that more seriously injured plaintiffs receive higher compensation than those less seriously injured. However, when each case is tried before a different jury, the relationship between the size of one judgment for intangibles and another will be largely happenstance. *See generally* James F. Blumstein et al., *Beyond Tort Reform: Developing Better Tools for Assessing Damages for Personal Injury*, 8 Yale J. on Reg. 171, 177 (1991). When numerous claims are tried before a single jury, that jury will recognize that an important part of its chore is to scale the relative seriousness of the various plaintiffs' injuries and to see to it that their respective awards are consistent with that scaling.[45]

The court of appeals specifically rejected the argument that jurors would not be able to comprehend the issues in a multi-plaintiff case, and reaffirmed the effectiveness of instructions and other management devices to minimize any risk of confusion or prejudice:

> [N]o logic supports the proposition that the incremental addition of similar cases will reduce the jury's ability to understand and resolve the issues placed before it. Without doubt, consideration of a single toxic tort case is challenging, requiring jurors to grapple with complicated issues of chemistry and medicine. But it does not follow that the jury will be less able to deal with those issues if the same questions are repeatedly put to it over a substantially longer period of time. Quite to the contrary, if a jury spends many weeks, or many months, considering numerous cases of asbestos disease, and repetitively hears the disputes of experts and the arguments of counsel on case after case, that jury is likely to develop a far deeper understanding of the issues than a jury whose exposure to those complicated questions is brief, and requires answering only a single set of questions. . . .
>
> Furthermore, we have noted repeatedly that a district court can greatly assist a jury in comprehending complex evidence through the use of intelligent management devices. *See, e.g., Johnson*, 899 F.2d at 1285; *Malcolm*, 995 F.2d at 349, 352–53. Such management devices include organizing evidence by topic, using charts and visual aids, allowing note-taking by jurors, furnishing the jury with notebooks and albums of pertinent exhibits structured in a manner to help it master complex materials, interim explanations by the judge on issues of law and fact and on the limited use of evidence, interim addresses to the jury by counsel, and questionnaires and special verdict forms to help the jury approach deliberations in a well-organized fashion. . . .
>
> By implementing such measures, [the trial court] insured that plaintiffs and defendants received a trial by jury that fairly addressed the individual claims while effectively managing the resources of the court and giving the parties the benefit of an efficient and economical trial. We have no reason to believe that the consolidation

45. *Id.* at 1007.

> prevented the jury from rendering verdicts based on the evidence as it related to each independent claim. OCF's [Owens Corning Fiberglas] contention of improper consolidation is without merit.[46]

Other Courts of Appeals have reached similar conclusions.[47] Consequently, trial courts across the nation have recognized the efficiencies gained by trying the claims of multiple

---

46. *Id.* at 1007-08. The Second Circuit likewise affirmed a district court's decision, 04-CV-875, 2010 WL 3709278, at *26-30 (E.D. Pa. 1982), to hold a single trial of eight plaintiffs' cases, *Barkley v. Olympia Mortgage Co.*, 557 Fed. Appx. 22, 25 (2d Cir. 2014), finding no abuse of discretion when the district court found "significant benefits" of consolidation—common questions of law and fact, efficiency, and the avoidance of possibly inconsistent verdicts—and only minimal potential prejudice."

47. *Eghnayem v. Boston Scientific*, 873 F.3d 1304, 1321 (11th Cir. 2017) (four persons before a single jury affirmed) ("The long and the short of it is that the district court properly exercised its broad discretion in consolidating these actions and refusing to admit FDA evidence, and the contested fact questions were properly presented to the jury."); *In re DePuy Orthopaedics, Inc.*, 870 F.3d 345, 350 (5th Cir. 2017) (ten plaintiffs before a single jury) (noting fourth bellwether case to be tried with ten New York plaintiffs; mandamus seeking to stop the trial denied); *Id.* (six plaintiffs before a single jury) (noting with no concern expressed that the case was tried with six California plaintiffs to a $1.04 billion verdict); *Acevedo-Garcia v. Monroig*, 351 F.3d 547, 558 (1st Cir. 2003) (twenty-one plaintiffs before a single jury) (the district court's decision to sever an eighty-two-plaintiff case into four separate trials, noting that the solution was "within the discretion of the trial court" and "a legitimate and feasible means of effectively conducting this unwieldy litigation."); *Consorti v. Armstrong World Indus. Inc.*, 72 F.3d. 1003 (2nd Cir. 1995) *vacated on other grounds*, 518 U.S. 1031 (1996) (four asbestos workers tried as one, affirmed); *In re Brooklyn Navy Yard Asbestos Litig.*, 971 F.2d 831, 840 (2d Cir. 1992) (affirming in part, reversing in part a judgment rendered after a consolidated trial of 79 asbestos-related personal injury and wrongful death actions, noting that it was "mindful, moreover, of the difficulties faced by a trial court in managing a complex, multi-plaintiff, multi-defendant mass tort litigation."); *Johnson v. Celotex Corp.*, 899 F.2d. 1281, 1289 (2nd Cir. 1990) (Rejecting defendants' claim that consolidated trial violated due process: "Owens–Illinois specifically contends that the consolidation of Johnson and Higgins and the failure to erect procedural safeguards during the consolidated trial violated appellants' due process rights. Since we have found the consolidation was not an abuse of discretion, and since the trial judge carefully instructed the jury throughout the trial to consider each plaintiff's claims individually, there was no need to provide other procedural safeguards concerning the consolidation."); *Johnson v. Celotex Corp.*, 899 F.2d 1281, 1285 (2d Cir. 1990) (affirming a judgment following a consolidated trial of the claims brought by multiple plaintiffs, noting that "[i]n the instant case, the court properly exercised its discretion in consolidating these two cases for trial."); *In re Bendectin Litig.*, 857 F.2d 290 (6th Cir. 1988) (affirming in part, vacating in part judgment for defense in consolidated trial of 818 cases involving birth defects caused by Bendectin ingestion); *Hendrix v. Raybestos-Manhattan, Inc.*, 776 F.2d. 1492, 1496 (11th Cir. 1985) (Four asbestos cases were consolidated for trial; the court of appeals affirmed consolidation: "In our view, the court's pretrial ruling to consolidate these cases was entirely reasonable. The four cases presented common issues of law and fact, and the factors we have referred to, *supra*, which inform a court's decision whether to consolidate, were duly considered. The striking similarity of these cases became even more apparent at trial, thus demonstrating the wisdom of the trial court's decision."); *Harcon Barge Co., Inc. v. D&G Boat Rentals, Inc.*, 746 F.2d 278, 287 (5th Cir. 1984), citing 9 Wright & Miller, *Federal Practice and Procedure* § 2382 (1971) (five plaintiffs before a single jury) (" The rule is worded as it is to reflect the prior practice to merge the hearing or trial of separate actions so far as is necessary for their expeditious handling. Thus, one or many or all of the phases of the several actions may be merged."); *Kershaw v. Sterling Drug, Inc.*, 415 F.2d. 1009, 1012 (5th Cir. 1969) (Consolidating two cases one day prior to trial, and noting "in charging the jury, the trial judge sufficiently emphasized the importance of separating the Kershaw [sic] and the companion case for consideration and verdict. It is apparent the jury did this."). *But see Malcolm v. Nat'l Gypsum Co.*, 995 F.2d 346 (2nd Cir. 1993) (48 plaintiffs before one jury the trial court consolidated the claims of 48 plaintiffs against 25 different defendants and many additional third-party and fourth-party defendants, where the plaintiffs' claims involved asbestos exposure at over 250 worksites around the world, and the Second Circuit specifically endorsed the use of consolidation to manage asbestos trials, but held that "the maelstrom of facts, figures, and witnesses, with 48 plaintiffs, 25 direct defendants, numerous third-and-fourth party defendants, and evidence regarding culpable non-parties and over 250 worksites throughout the world was likely to lead to jury confusion." The Second Circuit was also careful to note that its "holding today is narrow and amounts to little more than a caution that it is possible to go too far in the interests of expediency and to sacrifice basic fairness in the process." Likewise, in *In re Fibreboard Corp.*, 893 F.2d

plaintiffs at once in a single bellwether trial, and have conducted single trials involving as many as 296 plaintiffs at once.[48]

706, 712 (5th Cir. 1990), the Fifth Circuit issued mandamus as to the trial procedure for forty-one plaintiffs at once, not attacking the consolidation, but rather the substantive legal standards to be tried therein.

48. *See In re Air Crash Disaster at Sioux City, Iowa, on July 19,* 1989, 1991 WL 152914, at *2 (N.D. Ill., Aug. 1, 1991) ("the court orders that all transferred cases [296 passengers and crew on board] to be consolidated or a single trial on punitive damages and liability"); Wilson *v. Johns-Manville Sales Corp.*, 107 F.R.D. 250, 251-252 (S.D. Tex. 1985) (50 plaintiffs tried before a single jury) ("the extensive number of claims pending and the lengthy nature of an asbestos trial, this Court is currently unable to afford each asbestos plaintiff an individual trial . . . allegedly injured parties are being denied their day in court while their claims grow older and the backlog of asbestos cases grows."); *Ball v. Bayard Pump & Tank*, 609 Pa. 98, 15 A.3d 65, 65 (2011) (forty-one plaintiffs tried before a single jury); *In re Toyota Unintended Acceleration Marketing, Sales Practices and Prods Liab. Litig.*, 838 F. Supp. 2d 967, 972 (C.D. Cal. 2012) (twenty-seven plaintiffs before a single jury) (noting that a bellwether class action trial had been set to involve "twenty-seven named putative class representatives"); *Pallano v. AES Corp.*, C.A. No. N9C-11-021 JRJ, 2016 WL 97496, at *2 (Del. Super. Ct. Jan. 4, 2016) (twenty-five plaintiffs before a single jury) (noting same allegation of unlawful dumping, same evidence and witnesses on liability, same expert testimony on causation and damages); *In re Methyl Butyl Ether (MTBE) Prods. Liab. Litig.*, MDL No. 1358 (SAS), No. 1:00-1898, 2008 WL 3163634, at *2 (S.D.N.Y. Aug. 6, 2008) (eighteen plaintiffs before a single jury) ("eighteen of plaintiffs' numerous contaminated wells were selected for a 'bellwether trial' . . . ."); *Banks v. Fluor Corp.*, 450 S.W.3d 308, 363 (Mo. Ct. App. 2014) (16 plaintiffs each bringing four claims; jury received 214 instructions and completed 32 verdict forms, one for each plaintiff in compensatory stage and punitive damages stage, respectively); *Bayshore Ford Truck v. Ford Motor Co.*, No. 99-741 (JLL), 2010 WL 415329, at *13 (D. N.J., Jan. 29, 2010) (sixteen plaintiffs before a single jury) (recognizing the benefits of trying the claims of sixteen truck dealers in a single trial); *In re New York Asbestos Litig.*, 145 F.R.D. 644, 647 (S.D. N.Y. 1993) (12 asbestos plaintiffs tried at once) (consolidating twelve of thirteen cases for trial, but refusing to include one plaintiff with an unrelated cancer, noting that a "court may order consolidation upon its own motion, and the consent of the parties is not required."); *Neal v. Carey Canadian Mines, Ltd.*, 548 F. Supp. 357, 383 (E.D. Pa. 1982) (15 of 24 plaintiffs' cases consolidated into a single trial) ("Consolidation of all fifteen claims resulted in considerable judicial economy, as well as the avoidance of unnecessary litigation costs and attendant delay. Supplier defendants have not shown any demonstrable prejudice resulting from the consolidation of all fifteen claims."); *Adams v. Marathon Oil Co.*, 688 So.2d 75, 76 (La. App. 5 Cir. 1997) (twelve plaintiffs before a single jury) ("Causation and individual damages were tried for twelve plaintiffs identified as the 'Bellwether Plaintiffs' who were selected by the parties as representative class members."); *Canterbury v. Boston Scientific Corp. (In re: Boston Scientific Corporation Pelvic Repair System Products Liab. Litig.*, MDL 2326), 2:12-cv-08633, Dkt. No. 9 (PTO #78, Order Consolidating above Cases for Trial on All Issues, S.D. W.Va. February 19, 2014) (consolidating eleven pelvic mesh cases for trial, and noting that although the plaintiffs were implanted with the device by four different surgeons); *Bard v. Monsanto Company*, Case No. 18-2-00001-7-SEA (In the Superior Court of King County, Washington, Aug. 27, 2019) (ten plaintiffs before a single jury) ("Trial groups shall consist of no more than two families and no more than 10 Plaintiffs per trial."); *Schexnayder v. Exxon Pipeline Co.*, 815 So.2d 156, 158 (La. App. 5 Cir. 2002) (ten plaintiffs before a single jury) (noting that the bench trial of ten bellwether plaintiff claims began in May 2000); *Munjak v. Signator Investors, Inc.*, 2003 WL 23506989, at *2 (D. Kan., Dec. 10, 2003) (nine plaintiffs before a single jury) (concluding that "the cases before it are sufficiently similar factually and legally such that the benefit of consolidation outweighs any potential prejudice arising from delay."); *In re Joint Eastern & Southern Dist. Asbestos Litig.*, 1990 WL 4772, at *3 (S.D. N.Y., Jan. 16, 1990) (refusing to sever nine of eleven cases previously consolidated for a single trial) ("Consolidation is one of the few judicial devices available for dealing with the asbestos bottleneck. It produces significant time-savings and conserves litigation costs . . ."); *Fraynert v. Delaware & Hudson Railway Co., Inc.*, 2012 WL 6929343, at *1 (Pa. Ct. Common. Pleas, Oct. 1, 2012) (eight FELA plaintiffs tried at once) ("Considerations of judicial economy also militate in favor of consolidation for trial since a joint trial will require one jury and consume eight to ten days of trial while separate trials will necessitate eight juries and twenty-four to thirty-two trial days."); *Cotter Corp. v. Am. Empire Surplus Lines Ins. Co.*, 90 P.3d 814, 819 (Colo. 2004) (en banc) (eight plaintiffs before a single jury) (noting that claims of eight bellwether plaintiffs had been tried together); *In re Stand N' Seal Prods. Liab. Litig.*, MDL No. 1804, No. 1:07-md-1804-TWT, 2009 WL 2224185, at **1, 2 (N.D. Ga. July 21, 2009) (seven plaintiffs before a single jury) ("In this case, the Plaintiffs are seven individuals who purchased and used Stand 'n Seal . . . Because the Plaintiffs' claims rely on the same core allegation that aerosolized Flexipel is hazardous, separate trials would require redundant testimony that is not in the interest of judicial economy."); *Marsha Gray v. Wyeth*, Case No. A488234 (Clark County, Nevada) (Aug. 26, 2007) (six plaintiffs before a single jury) ("By Order dated May 17, 2007, this Court set the following six bellwether cases for trial on July 7, 2008."); *In re DePuy Orthopaedics, Inc. Pinnacle Hip Implant Prod. Liab. Litig.*, 888 F.3d 753, 763 (5th Cir. 2018) (five plaintiffs before a single jury) (noting case tried with five Texas plaintiffs to a

Choosing the Target Defendant

While trials often do involve multiple defendants, the wise plaintiff's lawyer typically should focus her ire on a single target defendant. With few exceptions where multiple defendants

---

$502 million verdict); *In re Norplant Contraceptive Prods. Liab. Litig.*, MDL No. 1038, 1996 WL 571535 at *1 (E.D. Tex., Aug. 12, 1996) (five plaintiffs before a single jury) (providing methodology for selecting bellwether plaintiffs and concluding that after discovery, three groups of five women will be selected from this group by the parties for three bellwether trials.); *In re Norplant Contraceptive Prods. Liab. Litig.*, 955 F. Supp. 700, 702 (E.D. Tex. 1997) ("This action is the first of three bellwether trials in MDL 1038 and involves five plaintiffs."); *In re Joint Eastern & Southern Dist. Asbestos Litig.*, 125 F.R.D. 60, 66 (E.D.N.Y. 1989) (five plaintiffs before a single jury) ("Other courts that have confronted this problem have consolidated personal injury and wrongful death claims for trial. . . . These courts' experiences, as well as the availability of cautionary instructions, convinces this court that consolidation is appropriate, notwithstanding the coexistence of personal injury and wrongful death claims."); *Harris v. Biomet Orthopedics, LLC*, Case No. 1:17-cv-00747-ELH, Doc. No. 29, 2019 WL 6117358, at *10 (D. My., Nov. 18, 2019) (four persons before a single jury) ("I conclude that there are common questions of fact and law in these cases, and consolidation will not prejudice Biomet. Therefore, I shall GRANT plaintiffs' Motion. Accordingly, plaintiffs' cases are consolidated for the purposes of trial."); *In re Mentor Corp Obtape Transobturator Sling Prods. Liab. Litig.*, MDL No. 2004, No. 4:08-MD-2004 (CDL), 2010 WL 797273, at *4 (M.D. Ga. Mar. 3, 2010) (four plaintiffs before a single jury) ("the court concludes that a consolidated bellwether trial would provide the parties with an opportunity to obtain results for multiple claims without burdening the Court or the parties with the substantial cost of multiple separate trials."); *Reyes v. Chevron USA, Inc.*, No. H031843, 2008 WL 2690048, at *1 (Cal. App. 2008) (four plaintiffs before a single jury) (trial court ordered parties to select three plaintiffs for bellwether trial "to get a representative sampling of verdicts," and proceeded to trial as to the claims of four of the selected plaintiffs); *Chapulin v. Nevada*, 2009 WL 10692666, at *3 (D. Nev., July 31, 2009) (four plaintiffs before a single jury) ("While it is true that a joint trial of these claims will require the introduction of evidence pertaining to the particular claims of each plaintiff and the alleged injury and damages suffered by each, the burden that this may cause in extending the trial is outweighed by the judicial economy and efficiency of trying the common issues of law and fact in one proceeding."); *In re Joint Eastern & Southern Dist. Asbestos Litig.*, 1990 U.S. Dist. LEXIS 442 (E.D.N.Y. 1990): The district court denied motions to sever five personal injury and four wrongful death cases for trial: "While it is premature at this point to identify the particular measures that will work best here, the experience of these courts, and this court in *Drago*, is convincing that consolidation of these nine Cluster 11 actions will not result in excessive confusion or prejudice."); *McClellan v. I-Flow Corporation*, Civ. No. 07-1309-AA, 2010 WL 11595942, at *3 (D. Ore. July 23, 2010) (three plaintiffs before a single jury) (observing that "[i]f the court accepted defendants' arguments, consolidation would be precluded in almost any circumstance. Courts and juries routinely distinguish evidence presented by different plaintiffs or against different defendants, and I do not find these cases so complicated as to require separate trials."); *McCleland v. Montgomery Ward & Co., Inc.*, No. 95 C 237, 1995 WL 374185, at *2 (N.D. Ill. June 21, 1995) (three plaintiffs before a single jury) (ordering single trial of three plaintiffs' claims over defendant's objection that "similar testimony by multiple plaintiffs constitutes bad character evidence inadmissible under Fed. R. Evid. 404(a)."); *Loewen, Wright, Aderhold & Eddings v. Wyeth*, Civil Actions 2:03-CV-2166-IPJ; 7:03-CV-3240-IPJ; 6:04-CV-1888-IPJ; 2:04-CV-1419-IPJ (Aug. 27, 2011) (three plaintiffs before a single jury) ("These cases shall be ready for jury trial in January 2012 in Birmingham, Alabama."); *DeShiro v. Branch*, 1996 WL 663973, at *3 (M.D. Fla. Nov. 13, 1996) (three plaintiffs before a single jury) ("In weighing these two concerns, the risk of prejudice to Defendants and the cost of severing Plaintiffs' actions, this Court finds that the risk of prejudice does not outweigh the benefit of conducting one trial."); *Arlene Rowatt, et al. v. Wyeth & Upjohn Co., LLC*, Case No. CV-04-01699 (2d Judicial District Court of Washoe County, Nevada, April 25, 2007) (three plaintiffs before a single jury) ("The parties submit this Third Amendment to Joint Case Conference Report in the above-entitled matter to govern the discovery and pretrial dates applicable to the Sept. 10, 2007 trial of Arlene Rowatt's, Pamela Forrester's, and Jeraldine Scofield's claims."); *Phillips v. G&H Seed Co.*, 10 So.3d 339, 341 (La. App. 3 Cir. 2009) (three plaintiffs before a single jury) (observing that cases of three bellwether plaintiffs proceeded to trial together); *In re Syngenta AG MIR 162 Corn Litig.*, 2017 WL 2876767, at *2 (D. Kan. July 6, 2017) (two plaintiffs before a single jury) (ordering three different bellwether trials with two plaintiffs apiece, noting "that the efficiency achieved in combining multiple classes' claims in a single trial outweighs the potential problems."); *In re Levaquin Litig.*, No. 286 (N.J. Sup. Ct., May 3, 2011) (consolidating four plaintiffs into two trials); *In re Welding Fume Prods. Liab. Litig.*, MDL No. 1535, No. 1:03-CV-17000, 2010 WL 7699456, at *4 (E.D. Ohio June 4, 2010) (two plaintiffs before a single jury) (acknowledging order that did not preclude multiple plaintiffs from seeking consolidated trials and recounting that the court had "conducted a single MDL bellwether trial involving two separate plaintiffs who had worked for the same employer."). *See also Barrera v. Hondo Creek Cattle Co.*, 132 S.W.3d 544, 546 (Tex. App.—Corpus Christi Edinburg 2004) (no pet.) (unknown number of plaintiffs before a single jury) (from a group of sixty plaintiffs, the claims of a small group proceeded to trial as a bellwether group).

are hit with large verdicts in a single trial,[49] the anger of a jury will be focused on a single bad actor. The motivational speaker Zig Ziglar once taught, "I don't care how much power, brilliance or energy you have, if you don't harness it and focus it on a specific target, and hold it there, you're never going to accomplish as much as your ability warrants." Ziglar's wisdom applies in the courtroom as well; the good plaintiff's lawyer inexorably picks his victim and then annihilates that one target.

Picking your target for trial is not much different than the strategies employed by predators high up in the food chain while on a hunt—find the weakest prey and attack. As the hyena with Richard "Cheech" Marin's voice in Disney's *Lion King* comically asked while surveying his field of prey, "I'm so hungry, I've got to have a wildebeest; can't I just pick off one of the little sick ones?" Choosing which defendant is the weakest, sickest one is primarily a function of the quality (or lack of quality) of the lawyer chosen to defend it. However, this choice can also be made by virtue of pretrial jury research in which members of the community reveal which defendant is most likely to lose given the facts in each particular case.

Attacking the Weakest Defense Lawyer

The most important factor in selecting a target is the defense lawyer. Huge verdicts typically, but not always, happen because of good liability facts and poor lawyering on the defense side.

While litigating a case against multiple defendants during discovery, the wise plaintiff's lawyer surveys the defense lawyers in the deposition rooms just like the hyena examining the meal-to-be roaming down below on the Serengeti. Then, he decides whom to attack for lunch. If a defense lawyer is known to be obnoxious in front of a jury, pounce. If a defense lawyer is known to mail it in and not prepare for trial, attack. If a defense lawyer has a client caught lying under oath, devour that defendant.

Fortunately for the plaintiffs' lawyer, the performance during discovery of five or six lawyers representing different defendants is much like a tryout for the real show, known as the trial. Natural selection is alive and well, not merely amongst the differing species inhabiting the Galapagos Islands, but also amongst lawyers participating in litigation here in the United States. Were he alive today, Charles Darwin would witness the survival of the fittest, as plaintiff's lawyers cleverly settle with the very best lawyers for sums much lower than a terrible lawyer might have to pay to extricate himself from the same case. I personally have nonsuited defendants represented by the excellent south Texas trial lawyer Darrell Barger for the sole purpose of getting him out of my way, while leaving the sickly prey of lesser lawyers representing his co-defendants available for my consumption during trial.

All other things being equal, the plaintiff's lawyer should choose his or her target by virtue of the relative strength of the lawyers to be faced in a courtroom.

---

49. *See, e.g.*, *Allen v. Takeda Pharm. & Eli Lilly*, No. 6:12-CV-00064, MDL No. 2299, 2014 WL 1394617 (W.D. La. April 7, 2014) (jury verdict of $1.475 million in compensatory damages and punitive damages against both Takeda ($6 billion) and Eli Lilly & Company ($3 billion)).

Attacking the Defendant at Highest Risk during Jury Research

Pretrial jury research in the form of focus groups invaluably yields data about which themes to utilize, while mock trials reveal which defendants are likely to find trouble at trial, and which of their witnesses are likely to be received poorly by the real jury. In this manner, jury research reveals which defendants to target for settlement, and which to target for trial. As the famed martial artist Bruce Lee once observed, "The successful warrior is the average man, with laser-like focus."[50] Learning which defendant should be the object of that focus at trial merits pretrial jury research.

Avoiding the Defendant Who Has the Strongest Experts—Juan Herrera and Texas BBQ

In choosing a target, a plaintiff's lawyer might also consider the relative strength of the experts that were selected by the various defendants. Experts on either side can powerfully determine which way a case swings. If defendant "A" has employed a star expert who is akin to Tom Brady on a football field, LeBron James on a basketball court, or Mike Trout on a baseball diamond, get rid of that defendant (and that expert)! Numerous pretrial partial settlements have involved not merely the payment of money, but also an agreement that a particular defense expert will not be made available to the non-settling codefendants.

A great war story proves this point. Back in the late 1990s, I bought a warehouse to house wrecked vehicles that served as evidence in my burgeoning automotive defect litigation practice. One afternoon, I happened over to the warehouse and observed an expert for General Motors inspecting a vehicle alone. Trying to be friendly, I asked, "Can I buy you some BBQ for lunch?" Juan Herrera, PhD, one of the most talented defense experts in the United States, happily responded, "Let's do it, Mikal." Over grilled chicken, BBQ ribs, brisket, and beans, Juan and I enjoyed our lunch, realized we shared a mutual respect for each other, and became friends. Several subsequent trials saw me cross-examine Dr. Herrera in the most respectful manner possible, one arising from the friendship and respect we had built over south Texas BBQ. Years later, a case one of my associates prepared out in El Paso, Texas, involved the plaintiff's decedent operating a construction grooving machine—a piece of equipment that carved lateral, 12" lines adjacent to the shoulder of the highway as an audible reminder to drivers who are falling asleep at the wheel that they had driven out of their lane of travel and onto the shoulder. A mysterious defect in the road grooving machine caused it to slip from Park to Reverse, sending the operator back into the lane of highway traffic. An inattentive truck driver, traveling well over the speed limit, neglected to take evasive action and impacted the worker, killing him instantly.

Throughout eighteen months of discovery, my lawyers kept regaling me with stories about how one lawyer in El Paso who represented the road grooving machine manufacturer would be their target, because all the other lawyers in the case hated him and wanted to tag his client with primary responsibility for my client's decedent's death. Deposition

50. Goodreads, https://www.goodreads.com/quotes/461996-the-successful-warrior-is-the-average-man-with-laser-like-focus (last visited Mar. 14, 2020).

after deposition led to reports to me of how this lawyer for the road grooving machine manufacturer had offended all the other lawyers in the case, and thereby earned his position as everyone's intended target at trial.

As I prepared for trial, I suddenly received a phone call from my intended target. "Why does everyone pick on me? You don't want to come after me," he huffed.

"That's not what everyone else is telling me," I wryly retorted. "Why should I go easy on you?"

"Because I have Juan Herrera as my expert," he responded. A chill went up my spine. I responded honestly, "I really like Juan Herrera."

Two weeks later, with a jury picked in El Paso, Texas, I stealthily gave an opening statement that never mentioned Dr. Herrera. When Judge Joe Moody instructed me, "Mr. Watts, call your first witness on behalf of the Plaintiffs," I responded, "Your honor, as their first witness, the Plaintiffs call pursuant to the adverse party rule and by trial subpoena, the Defendant's designated engineering expert, Dr. Juan Herrera." Over the course of the first two hours, Dr. Herrera proceeded to skewer every other defendant in the case. Frankly, his genius caused the case to be over after the first witness. A $12.7 million verdict for my widow can be chalked up solely to BBQ. I knew who the best expert in the case was, and I procured his services solely through friendship and trust. By some case of chance, my closing argument pointed not at Dr. Herrera's client, but rather at his victims. The jury returned not only a large verdict for my client, but also correctly allocated fault on the other defendants, and properly away from Dr. Herrera's client. He had proven his client's innocence by enlightening the jury to the guilt of the other defendants. Thus, in deciding who will be one's target, the clever plaintiff's lawyer should decide which defendant has employed the superior expert who can singularly be of help not merely to his own client, but also to the plaintiff.

Shifting Alliances and Informal Mary Carter *Agreements*

While most multiparty defenses begin with a joint defense agreement in which each defendant initially swears its loyalty to the group, this fidelity often disappears as the heat of an impending trial increases. As the pot begins to boil, some defendants escape the heat via settlement, much like a wise lobster jumping out of the pot of water positioned above the fire in a GEICO commercial. Even if multiple lobsters remain in the boiling trial pot together, loyalty during trial can remain tenuous at best. In thirty years of trying cases, I have received affectionate flirtations before trial from individual defense lawyers, encouraging me to redirect my focus to a codefendant. I am reminded of the cartoon of a clever bear in Gary Larson's *Beyond the Far Side;* as viewed by the hunter through a rifle's sights, he points to another bear and encourages the hunter to move his rifle scope accordingly. These flirtations often come with informal nonmonetary consideration: "Here's what I can do for you during trial."

In a pharmaceutical case tried by the two authors more than fifteen years ago, this occurred. Another lawyer had handled the file through discovery and asked me to join his efforts by taking the case to trial. The attorney had sued both the pharmaceutical company Warner-Lambert and a local physician who was well-liked in our community. The case was less than one year old, and I could not dismiss the good doctor without destroying diversity and causing a removal to federal court by Warner-Lambert. However, I could use common sense. The doctor's lawyer and I spoke on the phone, and he assured me that his client adored his patient, who now was my client. The lawyer stated that if his client had known everything that had been revealed during discovery alone from the file cabinets of Warner-Lambert, he would never have prescribed Rezulin, and that his client was willing to so testify. It seemed to me that if his client would deliver at trial, an informal nonaggression pact was in order. As the plaintiff's first witness, the good doctor was called to the stand. He was shown horrific document after horrific document from Warner-Lambert's file cabinets. He appropriately expressed his shock, dismay, and disgust at the company's actions, and earnestly swore that he did not know about the company's actions, and would never have prescribed the drug had he known. He forcefully delivered his lines to the jury with the same anguish delivered by Meryl Streep's Oscar-winning performance at the train station in the movie *Sophie's Choice*, where she had to choose which of her two children would live and which would die. After questioning of the doctor concluded, for good effect, he managed to hug his patient and my client right in front of the jury as he left the witness stand.

This kind of shifting alliance is a reality of multi-defendant trials in America. While not formal *Mary Carter* agreements, such accommodations are informally secured on a daily basis in courtrooms across this country.

Special Strategies in Multi-Plaintiff and Multi-Defendant Cases

Multiparty cases give rise to special opportunities to employ unusual strategies in multi-plaintiff and/or multi-defendant cases.

Special Strategies for Plaintiffs in Multi-Plaintiff Cases

If different plaintiffs are represented by different lawyers, the lawyer representing the second plaintiff should strongly consider deferring his or her opening statement until the first plaintiff rests, and the second plaintiff's case-in-chief is about to begin. There is little to no benefit achieved by the second plaintiff's lawyer getting up right after the first, and repeating the first plaintiff's lawyer's themes. Instead, by deferring her opening statement, the second plaintiff's lawyer can avoid repetition, and more importantly, create a scenario where after the first plaintiff's case-in-chief concludes, the jury then hears stellar oratory about the unique damages suffered by the second plaintiff. Likewise, the lawyers for the first and second plaintiffs respectively can divide up witnesses, either by topic or by sequence, and thereby, offer a more compelling presentation. Moreover, a second plaintiff's damages story can be much more thoroughly told if evidence presented during this second case-in-chief is deferred until after the first plaintiff has concluded her evidence. Likewise, the lawyers for plaintiffs not going first can focus the jury's attention on their clients' unique damages evidence during a closing argument focused not on the liability story already presented by the first plaintiff's lawyer, but instead one addressing only the special damages story specific to the second.

Special Strategies for Defendants in Multi-Defendant Cases

A single trial against multiple defendants offers the lawyer for each defendant the singular opportunity to shed responsibility for the plaintiff's damages by employing cunning trial strategies meant to avoid attention. First, a lawyer representing a derivative or tertiary defendant should realize that in matters of trial defense, often "silence is golden." Multi-defendant trials present a unique opportunity for one defense lawyer to assume the lead and go for the kill, while other defense lawyers duck in the bushes and avoid much of the plaintiff's fire. In my first trial ever, a product liability case against both Ford and its local dealership defendant ably serving as both an in-state jurisdictional and in-county venue defendant, the dealership correctly saw fit to employ the services of my friend, Darrell Barger. Barger knew silence was his best strategy, and jokingly, he promised me five dollars for every question he asked during the trial. Fifteen witnesses in, Ford's attorney enjoyed a particularly fruitful cross-examination of one of our plaintiff's experts, and Barger could no longer contain himself. Right in front of the jury, Barger placed a $20 bill on my computer, and whispered to me, "I have four questions." Of course, his four questions were both piercing and valuable to the defense of his client. However, his utter silence during the remaining five weeks of the trial caused the jury to forget about him and his client. The jury's verdict reflected this lack of focus, and the answers returned therein made it seem like Barger's client was never even there.

Conclusion

In conclusion, the multiparty case is a regular lawsuit on steroids. The opportunities and risks are significant. Whether multiparty pleadings yield consolidation or severance, and whether resulting trials involve many plaintiffs or just one, yield incredible consequence to the case. Skillful plaintiff's lawyers will wisely choose their target, either by virtue of the weakest defense lawyer or the weakest defendant as revealed during pretrial jury research. Opposing counsel should beware of shifting alliances and informal *Mary Carter* agreements, especially in multiparty cases. These strategies dramatically alter the landscape in multiparty trials and can be the difference between victory and defeat in the courtroom.

24

Managing the Benefits and Perils of a Multi-Defendant Case

The Defense Perspective

Any trial that involves multiple lawyers representing multiple defendants presents risks and opportunities. This chapter explores unique considerations associated with these types of multi-defendant cases, the hidden dangers they present, and how to approach these cases strategically.

The defense of a case is no longer homogeneous in a multi-defendant case. There is an inherent lack of control when you surrender the courtroom floor to a codefendant's counsel, who may have divergent trial objectives and unique defenses. Skilled plaintiff's lawyers know this, and they routinely exploit this divergence and loss of control to their advantage. Indeed, in some cases, there may be hidden agendas working against you and your client—that is, there may be undisclosed "trial understandings" between a plaintiff and other defense counsel, placing your client at risk. It is therefore important to understand the relationships between all defendants and how the facts of the case and applicable law may either unite or split the defense. All plaintiff's lawyers want a divided defense, and they will seek to foster shoot-outs where defendants actively blame each other. There is great truth in the adage "A house divided cannot stand."

A House Divided

If defendants begin to openly attack each other's witnesses in the presence of the jury, they effectively do the plaintiff's bidding and reinforce the likelihood of a plaintiff's verdict. In fact, the likelihood of a plaintiff's win *skyrockets* when there is open infighting on the defense side of the courtroom. The jury hears more than one voice suggesting that *at least* one defendant is guilty of causing the plaintiff's injuries or damages. This is an ideal scenario for any plaintiff, and every plaintiff's counsel endeavors to foster this division. If codefendants are successfully divided, it is likely that at least one defendant will be on the receiving end of an adverse verdict. Larger damage awards frequently occur when defendants and their counsel start shooting at each other in open court.

Sometimes divisions are easily visible. This occurs when defense lawyers and their witnesses openly attack the theories, defenses, and witnesses of their codefendants. In other instances, however, a house may be divided in more subtle, less obvious ways. There may be shifting alliances where one or more defendants enter into undisclosed "understandings" with plaintiff's counsel about how the evidence *should* unfold at trial, and this could have significant consequences to other defendants. One or more defendants may not even be aware of what is unfolding, and sometimes it is too late when the effects of these understandings are first recognized. This is why every defense lawyer must consider the risks of self-dealing defendants, and that one way to address these risks is through a joint defense agreement at the beginning of the case.

Red Flags

There are certain red flags you should look for when involved in a case with two or more defendants. One of these is how the case is styled and pled. You should specifically evaluate the order in which the named defendants are listed in the style of the case. This is because some courts require that the order in which the defendants are named dictates the order of proof and argument by which the defendants conduct voir dire, opening statements, and witness examinations. If marginal defendants are at the tail end of a case style, this is a clue about the plaintiff's ultimate intentions. Many plaintiff's lawyers strategically order named defendants in the pleadings with a view to which defendant will be a likely target.

The last-named defendant may be nothing more than a marginal defendant, joined in the lawsuit for purely strategic reasons to help target other defendants, or to defeat diversity jurisdiction and removal. This is particularly true if the liability or causation facts against that defendant are weak. Another tell-tale sign includes instances when individuals—not entities—are the last-named defendants in significant damage cases. This should serve as a clear warning because a sizeable judgment probably is not collectible against such individuals. The question logically arises: why are potentially insolvent defendants in the case?

Another warning sign can emerge as trial approaches. If a codefendant's exhibit list is remarkably shorter than reasonably expected, or if the codefendant's witness list omits important witnesses, you should take immediate note. If a defendant has been aggressively defending the case, and this aggressiveness is suddenly absent on the eve of trial, there is likely something afoot.

The plaintiff's goal is to place a target defendant, like a piece of ham, between two slices of bread. A defense lawyer who is representing a fringe defendant is batting cleanup for the plaintiff's lawyer. The opening remarks of the fringe defendant can minimize the opening statement of the target defendant. A fringe defendant's open-ended questions can undo or neuter an otherwise effective cross-examination of key plaintiff's witnesses. Juries typically pay attention to these tactics because a defense lawyer is actually doing the plaintiff's work. The lesson here is clear: *be wary.*

Realigning Parties

If there is obvious conflict between defendants, you should consider a motion to realign the parties and a motion to readjust allotted jury strikes. Many jurisdictions allow reordering the sequence of argument if this is needed to achieve a fair trial. Various considerations include whether cross actions have been filed, the degree and nature of animosity between the defendants, and the burden of proof that may exist between the defendants.

In Texas, where both authors reside, Rules 265, 266, and 269 of the Texas Rules of Civil Procedure generally prescribe that the party with the burden of proof will open and close the trial. However, the court has broad discretion upon a finding of "good cause" to change the order of proceedings.[1] Rule 269 explicitly directs the court to determine the parties' order of argument;[2] however, the court maintains broad discretion when doing so.[3] Like Texas, most jurisdictions give their courts similar discretion in prescribing the order of argument.[4] Thus, you should consider the standards in your jurisdiction to determine whether party realignment would be beneficial and prevent inequities during trial.

Mary Carter *Agreements and Other Alliances*

Many jurisdictions frown upon agreements between defendants and plaintiffs that distort the fair presentation of evidence and undermine the goal of a fair trial. Such agreements fall short of the traditional settlements that dismiss or nonsuit defendants. Instead, the purpose of a trial agreement is not to settle, but to fashion understandings with select defendants and their counsel to manipulate the presentation of evidence against a primary target defendant. The understanding is premised on the notion of "I'll scratch your back if you scratch mine." By cooperating in targeting another defendant, the participating defendant *may* be provided informal assurances or promises of an ultimate nonsuit, a minimal settlement, or an agreement to not seek collection of any adverse judgment. Some of these "understandings" or assurances may be unenforceable as a matter of law in select jurisdictions.

Depending on the jurisdiction, certain types of arrangements may be illegal and against public policy. In Texas, a version of these types of agreements are historically known as *Mary Carter* agreements. The agreements are so-named based on a Florida case known as *Booth v. Mary Carter Paint Company*.[5] The Texas Supreme Court's decision in *Elbaor v. Smith*[6] declared these types of agreements illegal in Texas. The focus of the inquiry is whether the

---

1. Tex. R. Civ. P. 265.
2. *See* Tex. R. Civ. P. 269 ("[W]here there are several parties having separate claims or defenses, the court shall prescribe the order of argument between them.").
3. *See Texas Emp. Ins. Ass'n v. Garza*, 557 S.W.2d 843, 845 (Tex. Civ. App. - Corpus Christi 1977) ("A presiding judge has broad discretion with respect to the manner in which control of a trial is maintained and to the extent of cross-examination allowed and a judgment will not be reversed for error in either of these areas unless probable prejudice is shown.").
4. *See, e.g.*, La. Code Civ. Proc. Ann. art. 1631(A) (in Louisiana, the court determines the order of presentment and argument when there are several parties with separate claims and defenses), Cal. Civ. Proc. Code 607 (in California, the party with the burden of proof goes first "unless court for special reasons otherwise directs").
5. 202 So.2d 8 (Fla. Dist. Ct. App. 1967).
6. 845 S.W.2d 240 (Tex. 1992).

"agreement" is enforceable, and whether it provides the "settling" defendant a financial incentive in maximizing the outcome for the plaintiff.[7]

Mary Carter-type agreements are not illegal in all jurisdictions. Disclosure of such agreements may make such agreements enforceable and valid:

> Many states, however, have determined that the element of disclosure of the *Mary Carter*-type agreement resolves any potential for prejudice on the nonsettling defendant and therefore the settling defendant will not be accountable for joint and several liability or contribution.[8]

For example, in New York, *Mary Carter*-type agreements may be allowed as long as they are disclosed—which prevents them from being true *Mary Carter* agreements.[9] In *Sierra Rutile Ltd. v. Katz*, the New York Court reasoned:

> Secrecy is part of the essence of a *Mary Carter* agreement. Full disclosure of the agreement, as here, avoids prejudice to the non-settling defendants. When an agreement is out in the open, there can be no confusion as to the settling defendant's motives in the action.[10]

However, in jurisdictions that prohibit *Mary Carter* agreements, mere disclosure of the agreement cannot overcome their polluting effects.[11] It is imperative to know the standard in the jurisdiction at issue regarding *Mary Carter* agreements, as many states allow some variation of *Mary Carter*-type agreements, including, but not limited to, Arizona, California, Louisiana, Minnesota, Missouri, Oregon, Arkansas, Maryland, Kansas, Ohio, Nebraska, New York, and Utah. In addition to Texas, at least three other states explicitly prohibit them:[12] Florida,[13] Nevada,[14] and Oklahoma.[15]

Regardless of jurisdiction, resourceful plaintiff's lawyers predictably seek creative ways—some formal, some informal—to circumvent prohibitions against *Mary Carter* agreements. A less formal option is "agreeing to agree" instead of entering binding,

---

7. *Id.* at 252.

8. Dave Y. Loh & William A. Lesser, *What is a "Mary Carter" Agreement?* American Bar Association (Nov. 9, 2018), https://www.americanbar.org/groups/litigation/committees/admiralty/practice/2018/what-is-a-mary-carter-agreement/.

9. *See id.* (citing *Sierra Rutile v. Katz*, No. 90 Civ. 4913, 1994 WL 577888, *3-4 (S.D.N.Y. Oct. 19, 1994), *Quick v. Crane*, 727 P.2d 1187, 1207 (Idaho 1986), and *Ratterree v. Bartlett*, 707 P.2d 1063, 1076 (Kan. 1985)).

10. *Sierra Rutile*, 1994 W.L. 577888 at *4; *see also* Loh, *supra* (discussing *Sierra Rutile*).

11. *Elbaor v. Smith*, 845 S.W.2d 240, 250 (Tex. 1992)("Equalizing peremptory strikes, reordering proceedings, thoroughly disclosing the true alignment of the parties, and revealing the agreement's substance cannot overcome collusion between the plaintiff and settling defendants who retain a financial interest in the plaintiff's success.").

12. *See* Lisa Bernstein & Daniel Klerman, *An Economic Analysis of Mary Carter Settlement Agreements*, 83 Geo. L.J.2215, 2216 n.6 (1995) (citing Florida, Nevada, Oklahoma, and Texas among states that prohibit *Mary Carter* agreements, and recognizing a split of opinion on whether they are prohibited in Wisconsin).

13. *Dosdourian v. Carsten*, 624 So. 2d 241, 247 (Fla. 1993).

14. *Lum v. Stinnett*, 87 Nev. 402, 488 P.2d 347 (1971).

15. *Cox v. Kelsey-Hayes Co.*, 594 P.2d 354, 359 (Okl. 1978).

enforceable agreements. Personally, I have been involved in trials that involved *Mary Carter* or similar types of agreements, and also cases where plaintiffs used more informal arrangements. Both types of scenarios benefit the plaintiff and can swing the outcome of a case. Here are two examples.

Case No. 1. As a young lawyer, I represented a railroad company that loaded a cherry picker on the back of a flatbed rail car. The arm of the cherry picker loosened after several hundred miles in transit, swung open and hit a bridge truss, causing a derailment of spectacular proportions. The plaintiff, also a railroad company, lost multiple rail cars in the derailment and ensuing fiery explosion; it sued my client and the maker of the cherry picker. I was relatively inexperienced at the time and did not fully appreciate the effects of a *Mary Carter* agreement, which at the time were still allowed in Texas. Here, an argument was implemented by two skilled, veteran trial lawyers. We proceeded to trial, and I found myself sandwiched between the plaintiff's case and the cherry picker manufacturer. The result was not good: the jury found my client to be 90 percent liable; the plaintiff 8 percent responsible; and the manufacturer only 2 percent responsible. Needless to say, this was a course in Trial 101 from the school of hard knocks. Because of this, my antennae have been up in every multi-defendant case for the last thirty-seven years.

Case No. 2. The next case involved a skilled plaintiff lawyer who represented a client allegedly injured by a medication. I represented the pharmaceutical company that manufactured the medication. The prescribing doctor also was a named defendant and was represented by a skilled trial lawyer. The doctor's trial attorney was aggressively attacking the labeling on the medicine. Thus, my case was flanked by aligned lawyers. A motion to realign was unsuccessful. Although the prescribing doctor had testified in deposition, his lawyer found subtle ways to undermine my client's defenses. Again, the result was a significant plaintiff's verdict.

The Joint Defense Agreement

One of the first orders of business in any multi-defendant case is to assess the potential for alliances between plaintiff's counsel and the other defendants. That is why it is wise to call a meeting of all defense lawyers during the initial stages of a case *before* discovery begins. This provides an opportunity to better assess the potential risks of a "rogue" defendant, and to gauge whether other defendants—and their counsel—view the facts and legal issues in a way that is consistent with your perspective. If so, a joint defense agreement is recommended. Several immediate benefits flow from assuring alignment of the defendants' interests through such an agreement:

- Enhanced control over the conduct of other defendants and their counsel. Although this control is mutually shared and contractually limited, a joint defense agreement tends to bind defendants together for a common purpose, and this reduces the chances of a maverick, self-dealing defendant.
- Expenses can be shared, including expenses for common tasks, including common interest experts and, where appropriate, experimentation and testing.

- Both pretrial and trial tasks can be assigned and delegated among defense lawyers, allowing more efficient use of time to prepare for each task (of course, this assumes you have confidence in the skills of the other defense lawyers and their commitment to follow-through).
- There are more "bites at the apple"—meaning, added voices in opening statements and final arguments, and an extra voice or voices during critical cross-examinations. Although the trial court may take steps to make sure a plaintiff is not disadvantaged by giving the defendants more time, the defense case still benefits because the jury is listening to the advocacy of two or more lawyers and their attention will be better focused.

Assuming defense lawyers share trust and confidence in each other, in addition to similar trial objectives, responsibilities can be divided on a witness-by-witness basis. This will make the case more interesting for the jury because they hear more than one voice advocating similar themes. It also helps reduce the burden on individual lawyers in terms of detailed preparations for specific witness tasks, and it reduces expenses for your client. However, there are precautions that should be taken.

Most jurisdictions recognize a common interest or joint defense privilege. In many jurisdictions, this is a species of the attorney-client privilege, which imbue joint-defense communications with protection, confidentiality, and nondisclosure. To effectively collaborate, defense lawyers must be able to communicate without the risk of forced disclosure of their communications. That is why a joint defense agreement is recommended. It also is advisable to have a written agreement that binds the defendants and their lawyers to specific commitments to maintain confidentiality. Common interests sometimes change, and a written agreement helps preserve inter-lawyer communications that have occurred before common interests stop being common.

A typical joint defense agreement[16] will include basic undertakings and understandings, such as:

- The identity of the parties to the agreement.
- An express acknowledgment of and definition of the common interest.
- An appropriate disclaimer that participation in the agreement creates an attorney-client relationship between any lawyer and any defendant other than the client who retained the lawyer.
- An agreement that information exchanged between defendants and their lawyers may be confidential and, if so, will be labeled accordingly and maintained in confidence by the parties and their counsel.
- An agreement that the joint defense agreement is confidential and not discoverable.
- A party's right to exit the agreement at any time for any reason upon written notice.
- A right of each participating defendant to settle the case within its discretion without obligation to any other defendant.

---

16. An exemplar joint defense agreement is included at the end of this chapter.

- A tolling agreement between the participating defendants as to all claims between them for contribution or indemnity.
- An obligation on the part of all participating defendants to maintain the confidentiality of information exchanged before a defendant exits the agreement and the continuation of this confidentiality after the exit.
- A requirement that notice be provided to all participating defendants if plaintiff seeks confidential information.

In many jurisdictions, if the defendants have cross-acted against each other, then the right to invoke a common interest or joint defense privilege may be lost. This is because the parties have become antagonistic and are treated as having no shared interest. Thus, it is advisable to review local authority to verify the effects of a cross-action before confidential information is shared. Again, in most jurisdictions, the defendants can agree to toll claims for indemnity and contribution between them, which removes the necessity of filing cross-actions.

Taking the Lead with Experts

Just as "broth is easily spoiled if there are too many cooks in the kitchen," it is ill-advised to have multiple defense lawyers attempting to control or develop one expert or prepare one witness. What follows are some basic observations.

As to experts, there should be one prominent voice communicating with a specific expert during the development stages of the expert's work product. Otherwise, the expert may get confused by mixed messages, and the process will be burdened by inefficiencies. It is advisable to have one lawyer take the lead and then report back to the defense group on the progress of the expert's work. Of course, all defense lawyers will want to have a say in the final work product, and this is made easier today under the federal rules that treat communications with experts in the drafting of their expert reports as privileged.[17]

As an example, I was involved in a multi-defendant case that involved business tort allegations related to the marketing and sale of income producing property. There were six defendants represented by six different law firms. As a group, we conferred on a fairly routine basis, and we specifically allocated responsibilities for briefing and expert development. My firm took the lead on several of these projects and was largely responsible for working with experts in the development of their opinions and finalization of their expert reports. Because the case was pending in state court, not federal court, the experts did not distribute drafts of the expert reports until they were finalized. However, during this process, I served as a liaison between the experts and the defense lawyer group.

Taking the Lead in Depositions

It also is advisable to have only one lawyer take the lead in depositions rather than an uncoordinated free-for-all that can lead to chaos. It is essential before the deposition begins to

17. *See* Fed. R. Civ. P. 26(b)(4)(B) and (C).

arrive at an understanding of who will take the lead. Once selected, the lead examining lawyer should address all common areas of interest and advance the common deposition goals for the other defendants. Each of the other defendants likely will conduct short, follow-up examinations with client-specific questions but, assuming the lead lawyer did a good job, the other lawyers should stay away from the common areas to avoid careless or redundant examination. This is particularly true of an adverse expert or a plaintiff witness.

For example, if a plaintiff's witness tripped, made admissions, or otherwise provided unfavorable answers, plaintiff's counsel likely will coach the witness to look for an opportunity to clean up the record or restate his answers. Thus, the lawyers on the defense side should *not* present golden opportunities to do this through redundant unnecessary examinations.

Taking the Lead at Trial

Another benefit of an enforceable joint defense agreement is the allocation of trial responsibilities. Again, too many voices addressing a single issue can adulterate trial messages and confuse the jury. Similarly, too many lawyers conducting extended cross-examination of the same witness can lead to mistakes. There is always a risk of inconsistency, even though the trial lawyers are well-intentioned. Allocation of trial responsibilities is, therefore, an effective way to manage these issues.

An excellent example of a coordinated defense involved a month-long trial relating to an Environmental Protection Agency (EPA) Superfund site adjacent to a real estate development. The plaintiff was claiming substantial economic damages due to diminution in real estate values following the discovery that adjacent land had been used as a toxic-waste dump for several decades. There were more than a dozen defendants, and each defendant was represented by separate counsel, which, of course, presented unique challenges.

The defense group selected one lawyer to conduct an opening statement for all of the defendants, with the exception of two defendants. I represented one of the two exceptions and carved out a short, separate opening statement to highlight my client's unique posture. Even then, the entire defense group met nightly to discuss key trial themes, the goals of the opening statement, and the goals for the examination of each witness. The process was both efficient and effective. During the course of a four-week trial, no more than four defense lawyers spoke in the presence of the jury, and we won the case. The lead lawyer was highly skilled, trusted, and later appointed to the federal bench.

Riding Coattails That Are Cut

Plaintiff's lawyers are keen to see who takes the lead in depositions, expert work, and the development of the defense. They know who has devoted effort to understanding and working up a case and who has not. Sometimes, in multi-defendant cases, some lawyers and their clients ride the coattails of others and do little to prepare for trial. They take a passive, backseat role and rely on other lawyers who represent other clients to prepare the case. This can be a bad mistake for the lazy lawyer.

Once the weak and strong lawyers are identified, the plaintiff's lawyer may try to separate the wheat from the chaff and cut a deal with the stronger, more prepared lawyer.

This usually occurs with a settlement on the courthouse steps, leaving the less prepared lawyer confronting an immediate trial with no coordinated leadership. The unprepared lawyer may suddenly face a scenario where experts are de-designated as part of a settlement or significant witness testimony is no longer available. Obviously, this can lead to bad results. The lesson here is for all lawyers to assume and appreciate that the plaintiff can selectively settle with any party at any time. This is not an uncommon scenario, and the lesson is to be prepared.

This scenario actually played out in a wrongful death case in which I represented anautomobile manufacturer. The case involved allegations of a defective transmission. A husband and wife, both seniors, had leased a moving van. They had stopped at a convenience store and the wife alleged she had engaged the vehicle in "park" but the transmission slipped into reverse, running over and trapping her husband under the van. He later died of internal injuries.

The plaintiffs sued the moving van company under theories of defective warnings. On the morning of jury selection, we were surprised by a voluntary nonsuit of our client. The plaintiffs' firm made the strategic decision to dismiss our client from the case, believing the codefendant had been riding our coattails and was unprepared. We paid nothing for the dismissal. With our client's consent, the moving van defendant hired one of our lawyers to assist in the case. The result was a defense verdict.

Conclusion

In multi-defendant litigation, the key for defense counsel is to know who your friends are and always keep an eye out for shifting alliances. Joint defense agreements are a useful tool, but you must always stay alert to make sure your codefendants' objectives and allegiances do not shift. Courthouse settlements and unforeseen nonsuits frequently occur. It is always advisable to cross-designate experts, be prepared to pick up the baton if necessary, and be fully informed and invested in the details of your defense. If a surprise occurs, the shock will not be overwhelming.

EXEMPLAR JOINT DEFENSE AGREEMENT PRIVILEGED AND CONFIDENTIAL ATTORNEY WORK PRODUCT

JOINT DEFENSE AND CONFIDENTIALITY AGREEMENT

THIS JOINT DEFENSE AND CONFIDENTIALITY AGREEMENT (the "Agreement") is entered into by, between and among ______________, ____________, ______________, and ____________, from time to time hereinafter referred to individually as "Party" and collectively as the "Parties," and their respective counsel, _______________, ______________, ______________, and _______________, referred to collectively as "Counsel," as of this _____ day of ________, 2020.

WHEREAS, the purpose of this Agreement is to set forth the terms and conditions of a joint defense capable of responding quickly and effectively to the Matter, as defined herein, and to protect against the disclosure of confidential communications or information (whether oral or written) protected by the attorney-client privilege, the common interest privilege, the attorney work product immunity doctrine, the joint defense privilege, or any other applicable privileges, rules or laws governing the protection and nondisclosure of such communications or information;

WHEREAS, the Parties and Counsel believe and anticipate, on the basis of currently available information, that the nature of the Matter and the relationship among the Parties will present various common legal and factual issues and a mutuality of interest in a joint defense in connection with the Matter, and the Parties' common interest is to rebut or defend against any claims made by Plaintiffs, in litigation or otherwise, that are adverse to the continued development of the Facility, such defensive activities to include, but not be limited to, developing common strategies or asserting joint defenses on some or all issues; facilitating fact gathering; and preserving, to the fullest extent permitted by law, protection against disclosure of any confidential or privileged information relating to such activities and the confidentiality or privilege afforded by the attorney work product immunity doctrine, the attorney-client privilege, the common interest privilege, the joint defense privilege, or any other applicable statutes, regulations, rules or principles governing the disclosure of confidential or privileged information;

WHEREAS, the Parties wish to continue to pursue their separate but common interests, and to avoid any suggestion or claim of waiver of the confidentiality or immunity of communications and documents protected by the attorney-client privilege, the common interest privilege, the joint defense privilege, the attorney work product immunity doctrine or any other privilege or immunity vis-a-vis potentially adverse parties;

WHEREAS, it is the intention and understanding of the Parties that past and future communications among and between the Parties and their affiliates (through Counsel), communications among and between the Parties and their affiliates (through Counsel) and consulting experts retained by a Party or one of its affiliates to assist with the Matter (such experts collectively or individually, "Retained Consulting Experts"), joint interviews of prospective witnesses or any interviews obtained by Counsel on behalf of a Party with the knowledge and consent of the other Party, are and shall remain confidential and privileged and are and shall continue to be protected from disclosure to any third party by any and all applicable privileges and immunities, except as set forth herein;

WHEREAS, in order to pursue a joint defense effectively, the Parties also have each concluded that, from time to time, their interests will be best served by sharing certain confidential or privileged documents, factual material, mental impressions, memoranda, interview reports, litigation strategies and other information whether in written or oral form, including the confidences of each Party and its affiliates (collectively, "Defense Materials"); and

WHEREAS, it is the purpose of this Agreement to ensure that any exchange and/or disclosure of Defense Materials contemplated herein does not diminish in any way the confidentiality or privileged nature of the Defense Materials and does not constitute a waiver of any privilege or immunity otherwise available.

IT IS THEREFORE AGREED as follows:

1. Except as expressly stated in writing to the contrary, any and all Defense Materials obtained by any Counsel ("Receiving Counsel") from any other Counsel and/or any Party or any of a Party's affiliates ("Disclosing Person") are being provided solely for internal use of the Parties and their affiliates and Counsel and shall remain confidential and shall be protected from disclosure to any third party by the joint-defense privilege, the Party's attorney client privilege, the common interest privilege, the attorney work product immunity doctrine and any and all other applicable privileges and immunities. All Defense Materials shall be used solely by the Receiving Counsel in connection with the Matter and shall not be used by the Receiving Counsel or the Party such Counsel represents or such Party's affiliates for any other purpose whatsoever.
2. None of the Receiving Counsel nor the Parties such Counsel represent nor any affiliate of the Parties shall disclose Defense Materials provided by a Disclosing Person or the contents thereof to anyone not a Party or Counsel to this Agreement (except the Parties, their affiliates, Counsel, Retained consulting Experts, or their respective employees or agents actually engaged in working on the Matter) without first obtaining the written consent of Counsel Representing the Disclosing Person. It is expressly understood that nothing contained in this Agreement shall limit the right of the Counsel or the Parties to disclose any of their own documents or information, or any documents or information obtained independently and not pursuant to this Agreement, to anyone as they see fit.
3. If any Party or Counsel designates particular Defense Materials it is producing to another Party or Counsel as "Counsel Only," such Defense Materials shall be disclosed by the receiving Party or its Counsel only to Counsel.
4. The Parties and Counsel shall take all steps reasonably necessary to protect the confidentiality and/or applicable privilege of Defense Materials received from another Party or

Counsel, including advising all persons permitted access to the information or Defense Materials of the contents of this Agreement and that the Defense Materials are confidential and privileged and subject to the terms of this Agreement. Each of the Parties and their Counsel shall maintain a detailed record of all information and Defense Materials provided to any Retained Consulting Expert. No Retained Consulting Expert to whom information and Defense Materials have been provided shall be designated as a Testifying Expert without the prior consent of the Party that provided the information and Defense Materials to the Retained Consulting Expert. Furthermore, the mental impressions and opinions of any Retained Consulting Expert who has reviewed any Defense Materials shall not be presented or disclosed to any other expert (whether or not such expert has been designated as a Testifying Expert in the Matter) for review without the prior consent of the Party providing the Defense Materials to the Retained Consulting Expert.

5. No Party or Counsel shall assert any claim of title or ownership over any Defense Materials received from another Party or Counsel, or any portion thereof. If any Defense Materials consist of computer software disclosed in object code form, no Party or Counsel shall reverse engineer, reverse compile, or disassemble such object code, take any steps to derive a source code equivalent thereof, or allow any other person to do so.
6. If any person or entity requests or demands, by subpoena or otherwise, any Defense Materials from any Party or any affiliate of a Party or Counsel, that Party or Counsel will promptly notify any other Party and/or Counsel who may have rights in such Defense Materials and will take all steps reasonably necessary to permit the assertion of all applicable rights, privileges and immunities with respect to such Defense Materials, including, if possible, permitting any other affected Party and Counsel a reasonable opportunity to intervene and be heard, and otherwise cooperating fully with any other affected Party and Counsel in any judicial proceedings relating to the disclosure of such Defense Materials.
7. Nothing contained herein shall be deemed to create an attorney-client relationship between any Counsel and anyone other than the client of that Counsel and that, although each Party's Counsel has a duty to preserve the confidences disclosed pursuant to this Agreement, each Counsel will not be acting as Counsel for any other Party and will owe a duty of loyalty only to its own client. It is herein represented that each Counsel has specifically advised its respective client of this clause. Solely to the extent not otherwise prohibited by this Agreement, each Party waives the right to object to any Counsel for any other Party acting adversely towards such Party in this Matter or any other litigation.
8. Each Party and its Counsel specifically acknowledge that any Party, or employee of a Party, may become a witness, whether voluntarily or otherwise, in connection with the Matter. In the event that any Party or employee of a Party becomes a witness, nothing in this Agreement shall create a conflict of interest so as to require the disqualification of any Counsel from the representation of its client, based on the existence of this Agreement or any sharing of Defense Materials. By entering into this Agreement, each Party and Counsel knowingly and intentionally waives any conflict of interest or other objection that

might otherwise be available based upon the sharing of information pursuant to this Agreement, and waives the right to seek disqualification of any Counsel based on such Counsel's access to Defense Materials shared by another Party.

9. Nothing in this Agreement shall obligate any Party or Counsel to share or communicate any information or Defense Materials or independently obtained or created materials with any other Party or Counsel hereto.
10. Documents that contain privileged information may be stamped or otherwise designated (including verbal designations) as "Privileged and Confidential - Subject to the Joint Defense Agreement" prior to any exchange between the Parties or Counsel. The absence, however, of such label or legend shall not be interpreted as an indication under this Agreement that such material is not subject to this Agreement or as a waiver of rights.
11. Nothing in this Agreement shall obligate any Party or Counsel to any other matter, unless and until such signatories execute a binding written agreement with regard to such other matter.
12. Any Party or Counsel disclosing Defense Materials pursuant to this Agreement represents that it has the right to make such disclosure under this Agreement, but otherwise makes no representations or warranties, express or implied, as to the quality, accuracy, and completeness of any Defense Materials disclosed hereunder, and such Party or Counsel, its affiliates and representatives shall have no liability whatsoever with respect to the use of or reliance upon the disclosed Defense Materials.
13. Any Party may withdraw from this Agreement, provided, however, that such withdrawing Party shall provide ten (10) days' prior written notice to the other Parties, in which case this Agreement shall no longer be operative as to the withdrawing Party and its Counsel, but shall continue to protect all Defense Materials disclosed by any other Parties and such other Parties' Counsel who have not theretofore withdrawn to the withdrawing Party and its Counsel prior to such withdrawal. The withdrawing Party and its Counsel shall promptly return all Defense Materials received from any other Party or such other Party's Counsel, including copies thereof, and shall continue to be bound by its obligations with respect to such Defense Materials furnished prior to its withdrawal pursuant to this Agreement.
14. Within 30 days after withdrawal pursuant to Paragraph 14 above, each withdrawing Party and its Counsel shall return all Defense Materials furnished to it by the other Parties or Counsel pursuant to this Agreement and the other Parties and their Counsel shall return all Defense Materials furnished by the withdrawing Party or Counsel pursuant to this Agreement; provided that, each Party and its Counsel shall continue to be bound by the obligations of confidentiality and/or applicable privilege with respect to Defense Materials previously furnished pursuant to this Agreement except insofar as permitted under the terms of this Agreement or required by law. Withdrawal of a Party pursuant to Paragraph 14 shall not affect the Agreement as between the other non-withdrawing Parties and Counsel.

15. This Agreement, its terms, and the activities conducted pursuant to this Agreement, constitute confidential Defense Materials. Each Party and Counsel agrees not to disclose this Agreement or its terms to anyone except insofar as permitted under the terms of this Agreement, as necessary to enforce the terms of this Agreement or required by law.
16. This Agreement and all discussions in pursuance thereof shall not constitute an admission of liability by any Party or its Counsel or an admission by any Party or its Counsel of the propriety or validity of any claims assessed in the Matter and shall not be offered or received in evidence in any litigation among the Parties except as necessary to enforce the terms of this Agreement. Nothing in this Agreement shall be construed as a waiver of any defense or immunity which may be available to any Party, and any counterclaim or defense asserted by one Party shall not be construed, through this Agreement, to be applicable to or asserted by any other Party.
17. This Agreement shall be binding upon each Party's and Counsel's respective successors, legal representatives and permitted assigns. This Agreement is solely for the benefit of the signatories hereto.
18. This Agreement constitutes the entire and complete agreement among the Parties and Counsel concerning the Defense Materials and, to the extent inconsistent with any confidentiality and nondisclosure agreement signed by the Parties, supersedes any earlier agreements, whether written or oral, between or among any of the Parties pursuant to which Defense Materials have been exchanged in connection with the Matter.
19. Whenever possible, each provision of this Agreement will be interpreted in such a manner as to be effective and valid under applicable law. If any provision of this Agreement is held to be prohibited by or invalid under applicable law, such provision will be ineffective only to the extent of such prohibitions or invalidity, without invalidating the remainder of such provision or the remaining provisions of this Agreement.
20. The Parties and Counsel acknowledge and agree that a breach of this Agreement by any Party or Counsel may cause continuing and irreparable injury to the business of a Party or its Counsel as a direct result of such violation, for which remedies at law may be inadequate, and that any Party or its Counsel shall therefore be entitled, in the event of any actual or threatened violation of this Agreement by any other Party or Counsel, and in addition to any other remedies available to it, to a temporary restraining order and to injunctive relief against such Party or Counsel to prevent any violations of this Agreement, and to any other appropriate equitable relief, without being required to post bond or other security.
21. No failure or delay by any Party or Counsel to this Agreement to exercise any right, power, or privilege hereunder shall operate as a waiver thereof, nor shall any single or partial exercise thereof preclude any other or further exercise thereof or the exercise of any right, power, or privilege hereunder.
22. This Agreement may be executed in one or more counterparts, all of which taken together shall constitute one and the same instrument.

23. This Agreement may not be amended or modified except by a written agreement signed by each Party and Counsel hereto, who has not theretofore withdrawn, and any such amendment shall not affect any Party or Counsel after such withdrawal.
24. The Parties and Counsel agree that this Agreement shall be construed and enforced in accordance with, and the rights of the Parties shall be governed by, the laws of the State of __________ without regard to conflicts of law principals.
25. Each Counsel represents and warrants that it has performed a thorough conflict check and has advised all Parties of any actual or potential conflicts of interest.

IN WITNESS WHEREOF, the Parties and their Counsel have executed this Agreement as of the date first written above.

a) [illegible] Comp Rule [illegible]

2. This Agreement may be amended [illegible] signed by each Party and Counsel [illegible] any amendment that may affect any Party [illegible].
3. The Parties and Counsel agree that this Agreement [illegible] in accordance with the rights of [illegible] of ______ without regard to conflict of [illegible].
4. Each Counsel represents and warrants that [illegible] check and has advised all Parties of any actual or potential [illegible].

IN WITNESS WHEREOF, the Parties and their Counsel have executed this Agreement as of the date first written above.

25

The Jury Charge

The Plaintiff's Perspective

Jurors predictably are told that they are the judges of the facts and the court is the judge of the law. In reality, it's up to the parties to prepare and argue the charge, after the court rules on the disputed issues to preserve error in a manner that enables the appeal of overruled objections and denials of proposed instructions and jury questions. The work before and during the jury charge conference can be the most complex and difficult work of the trial; it also is the most important work because the contents of the charge can define the line between victory and defeat.

Preparing the Charge

The charge should be prepared early, with simplicity, and by following available pattern jury instructions.

Prepare the Charge Early—Before Discovery Begins

Preparing the charge is an activity that should not occur after the close of the evidence during trial, and not even just before the court's deadline for the parties to submit a draft before trial. Rather, the excellent trial lawyer prepares his charge early, before the first interrogatory or request for admission is served, and before the first deposition question is asked. This is true because the jury charge is like the foundation and framing of a commercial building. The rest of the case simply cannot be properly constructed through the collection of evidence unless the foundation of the building—in this case, the causes of action to be pursued—is decided upon; the elements of each cause of action are framed around that foundation. Only after the foundation of the causes of action is laid down and the framing of the elements of proof is erected can one fill in the rooms of the building with the evidence to be admitted during the trial.

Looking at it another way, as referenced earlier, the jury charge should be prepared early because it serves as the skeleton of the case, upon which the meat of the evidence may be placed, in a process akin to "putting meat on the bones" of your case. Answers to interrogatory and request for admission should be incorporated into the proof outline early, as should key deposition testimony. The discovery period should not end without depositing some evidence into each element of proof in the trial outline. Almost as if the appellee's brief in advance, a good trial lawyer should know long before trial begins the evidence that he will present before saying, "The Plaintiff rests." However, this can be achieved only by preparing the jury charge early.

Prepare the Charge with Simplicity

A mistake commonly made when preparing the jury charge is including each and every cause of action that's conjured up during the initial pleading stage. However, just because a set of facts presents the opportunity to achieve a recovery with five distinct causes of action does not mean that the jury charge should include all five of them. Indeed, the opposite is true because of the risk of jury confusion and inconsistent jury answers. Decades of trying complex product liability cases have taught me that a simple charge with fewer causes of action is far superior to one that is overly complex. As the Supreme Court has recognized, "the danger of juror confusion is particularly high where the jury is faced with instructions on alternative theories of liability under which different parties bear the burden of proof."[1]

In preparing the ultimate charge, culling the number of causes of action is advised. Each given set of facts fits available causes of action in different ways. While an automotive products liability case may have four different causes of action available—design defect, marketing defect, breach of implied warranty of fitness, and negligent design—the trial lawyer should decide which of those causes of action has the elements and the wording that best fits the facts of a particular case, and then choose just one of those causes of action with which to ultimately present the court's charge questions to the jury. Because the jury instructions and jury questions track language from past case decisions, they often are couched in legalese that is foreign and strange to a jury. These strange legal words become even more confusing when used in several different questions that seem to be attacking the same set of facts in four different ways. Simplicity is therefore best achieved by presenting fewer questions that involve fewer causes of action, instead of more questions just to check the box of submitting all the originally pleaded causes of action.

In sum, **K**eep **I**t **S**imple, **S**tupid! The K-I-S-S principle may be the most important lesson on preparing the proposed jury charge.

Use Pattern Jury Instructions to Prepare the Charge

Courts in most jurisdictions have tasked conscientious lawyers with preparing pattern jury instructions for the rest of the bar. These pattern instructions are meant to be a guide with which to prepare a jury charge that reflects the elements of proof required for a cause of action, with instructions appropriately reflecting the law as laid out by prior precedent.

1. *Vance v. Ball State Univ.*, 570 U.S. 421, 444–45 (2013).

As pattern jury instructions have matured over the decades, courts have come to rely more heavily on them and to hold with increasing frequency that it generally is not error to submit charge questions and instructions that follow the available pattern jury instructions.

Indeed, each federal appellate court except Washington, D.C., has articulated the concept that reliance on applicable pattern jury instructions is wise and likely to mean that you avoid appellate reversal.

While the First Circuit Court of Appeals has cautioned that "[t]hough pattern instructions may be a useful reference point, they are not binding,"[2] most other federal appellate courts seem to defer to them as a guiding light.

The Second Circuit Court of Appeals has observed that the New York Pattern Jury Instructions include "draft instructions—with extensive citations to cases, statutes and secondary authorities—[that] are kept up-to-date by a distinguished group of New York Supreme Court Justices and law professors" and "are relied upon in New York courts and in federal courts in diversity actions."[3] That court has held that when "a trial court based jury instructions on pattern jury instructions that reflect our current law, there is no plain error."[4]

The Third Circuit Court of Appeals has cautioned that while "[m]odel instructions are designed to help litigants and trial courts, [they are] not to replace their shared obligation to distill the law correctly when drafting proposed jury instructions." However, it has held that "[g]iven the care put into that drafting, we have observed it is unlikely 'that the use of [a] model jury instruction can constitute error.'"[5]

The Fourth Circuit Court of Appeals found "frivolous" an appellate argument claiming it was error to give a pattern jury instruction previously approved by an appellate court in that circuit.[6]

The Fifth Circuit Court of Appeals has repeatedly encouraged parties to utilize pattern jury instructions. In 2019, the court noted that the Fifth Circuit Pattern Jury Instructions "represent an admirable summary, based on Supreme Court and Fifth Circuit precedent, of the elements of a plaintiff's claim that must be proven at trial."[7] In 2018, it held in *Garza v. Caplin* that a jury instruction about the "good-faith, reasonable belief" standard did not amount to an "obviously incorrect statement of law" because "this language is based on the Fifth Circuit Pattern Jury Instructions."[8] Also in 2018, the court held that "any error was not clear

2. *Teixeira v. Town of Coventry by and through Przybyla*, 882 F.3d 13, 18 (1st Cir. 2018) (holding that "declining to follow a pattern instruction in a particular case is not error per se").

3. *Mulholland v. Philip Morris USA, Inc.*, 598 F. App'x 21, 23 (2d Cir. 2015) (finding no error because "the instruction given by the district court is consistent with the suggested instruction in the New York Pattern Jury Instructions.").

4. *Ruocco v. Hemmerdinger Corp.*, 711 F. App'x 659, 663 (2d Cir. 2017) (observing that "[t]he Modern Federal Jury Instructions supplied the very language that Ruocco and Tomicic now object to, and they have not cited any authority that plainly shows the Modern Federal Jury Instructions were incorrect.").

5. *Robinson v. First State Cmty. Action Agency*, 920 F.3d 182, 190 & n.38 (3d Cir. 2019) (quoting *United States v. Petersen*, 622 F.3d 196, 208 (3d Cir. 2010)).

6. *United States v. Russell*, 971 F.2d 1098, 1108 (4th Cir. 1992), *cert. denied*, 506 U.S. 1066 (1993).

7. *Mason v. Faul*, 929 F.3d 762, 764–65 (5th Cir. 2019) (finding no error in the lower court's use of pattern jury instructions).

8. 745 F. App'x 230, 231–32 (5th Cir. 2018) (per curiam) (citation omitted).

or obvious, because, *inter alia*, question one of the verdict form was essentially identical to this circuit's pattern jury instruction. . . ."[9] In 2015, the Fifth Circuit found in *Williams v. Honeycutt* that "[t]he district court's use of the pattern jury instruction does not rise to the level of clear or obvious error," and that because "[t]he instruction parallels the pattern jury instruction, . . . [t]he jury instruction issued by the district court was appropriate."[10] In *Bagby Elevator Co., Inc. v. Schindler Elevator Corp.*, a case interpreting Texas substantive law under *Erie*, the Fifth Circuit "[found] it persuasive that Texas courts have repeatedly approved the Texas Pattern Jury Charges as a correct statement of the law," and held that under the court's highly deferential standard of review, the district court did not commit reversible error in using the pattern jury instruction.[11]

The Sixth Circuit Court of Appeals in *United States v. Daneshvar*[12] referenced the pattern jury instructions favorably, citing to *United States v. Mari* as explaining the rationale for the instruction and circumstances in which, even if the instruction was given mistakenly, "giving the Sixth Circuit Pattern Jury Instruction on deliberate ignorance was harmless as a matter of law."[13]

The Seventh Circuit Court of Appeals found error in an unavoidable accident instruction given below for the simple reason that "Illinois Pattern Jury Instruction No. 12.03 recommends that the 'unavoidable accident' instruction never be given."[14]

The Eighth Circuit Court of Appeals has, on at least three occasions, approved jury instructions given below by virtue of their reliance on the relevant pattern jury instruction. In *Stockmen's Livestock Market, Inc. v. Norwest Bank of Sioux City*, the court approved of the instruction given below because it reflected "a pattern jury instruction taken directly from South Dakota Civil Pattern Jury Instruction No. 35–01."[15] In *Nat'l Auto. Trading Corp. of China v. Pioneer Trading Co., Inc.*, the court held that "[t]he district court did not commit error by relying upon a pattern jury instruction in fashioning Jury Instruction No. 5."[16] Finally, in *Davis v. Merrill Lynch, Pierce, Fenner & Smith, Inc.*, the court held that the jury instruction complained of "was not fundamentally deficient in analysis or otherwise lacking in reasoned authority" because the instruction given below was "based on South Dakota Pattern Jury Instructions No. 50.11 (1968), which indicates that it is a correct statement of the law in South Dakota."[17]

The Ninth Circuit Court of Appeals, in *ACT Group, Inc. v. WaterFurnace Int'l, Inc.*, approved of a jury instruction regarding copyright protection because "[t]he District Court's formulation

9. *Abbott v. Babin*, 744 F. App'x 854, 856 (5th Cir. 2018).
10. 623 F. App'x. 268, 269 (5th Cir. 2015) (per curiam).
11. *Bagby Elevator Co., Inc. v. Schindler Elevator Corp.*, 609 F.3d 768, 772–73 (5th Cir. 2010).
12. 925 F.3d 766, 782 (6th Cir. 2019).
13. *United States v. Mari*, 47 F.3d 782, 785–86 (6th Cir. 1995).
14. *Cook v. Hoppin*, 783 F.2d 684, 693 (7th Cir. 1986).
15. 135 F.3d 1236, 1246 (8th Cir. 1998).
16. 46 F.3d 842, 844 (8th Cir. 1995).
17. 906 F.2d 1206, 1222 (8th Cir. 1990).

of its jury charge on originality . . . tracked the Ninth Circuit Manual of Model Civil Jury Instructions. . . ."[18]

The Tenth Circuit Court of Appeals has found it "not error" to utilize jury instructions "defining willful and wanton misconduct in language from other Wyoming Supreme Court decisions and modeled after the Wyoming Civil Pattern Jury Instructions."[19] The court also observed through an opinion written by now Supreme Court Justice Neil Gorsuch that "we cannot say the district court plainly erred in offering the instruction it did" because "while the pattern jury instruction could perhaps be more punctilious, . . . [t]he district court's jury instruction was almost identical to the Colorado pattern jury instruction."[20]

The Eleventh Circuit Court of Appeals also has expressed deference to the pattern jury instructions. In *Stepanovich v. City of Naples*, the court noted that "the 'search of the home' instruction the district court gave is a verbatim statement of our pattern jury instructions and an accurate statement of the law."[21] In *Green v. U.S. Steel Corp.*, the court held that "the district court did not abuse its discretion in using the pattern jury instructions.[22] In *Lovette v. Paul*, the court held that the lower court's jury instructions were not plainly erroneous because they "were tailored to the facts of the case and were modeled on the Eleventh Circuit's pattern jury instructions."[23]

Arguing the Charge

"The test for the adequacy of a jury instruction 'is not one of technical accuracy in every detail,'"[24] but rather, whether an instruction "misstate[s] the law or mislead[s] the jury."[25] "Splitting hairs" over a "vanishingly small" gap between the court's instruction and the one being proposed is "insufficient to justify a new trial. . . ."[26] Indeed, the Supreme Court has repeatedly "recognized that even the omission of an element from a jury charge is subject to harmless-error analysis."[27]

Thus, in arguing the jury charge, a trial lawyer must remember that a district court has wide discretion to formulate the jury charge, and more importantly, that any jury instruction will be reviewed on appeal only on an abuse of discretion standard, with an appellate review considering the instructions as a whole rather than a specific instruction given. A verdict will be reversed only when the error is likely to have misled the jury.[28]

18. 700 F. App'x 718, 718–19 (9th Cir. 2017).
19. *Lompe v. Sunridge Partners, LLC*, 818 F.3d 1041, 1060 (10th Cir. 2016).
20. *White v. Deere & Co.*, 670 F. App'x 985, 986 (10th Cir. 2016).
21. 728 F. App'x 891, 901 (11th Cir. 2018).
22. 550 F. App'x 773, 775 (11th Cir. 2013).
23. 442 F. App'x 436, 437 (11th Cir. 2011).
24. *Teague v. Bakker*, 139 F.3d 892, 1998 WL 168876, at *3 (4th Cir. Apr. 8, 1998) (unpublished table decision).
25. *Gowski v. Peake*, 682 F.3d 1299, 1310 (11th Cir. 2012) (per curiam).
26. *Continental Cas. Co. v. Boughton*, 695 F. App'x 596, 600 (2d Cir. 2017).
27. *McFadden v. United States*, 576 U.S. 186, 135 S. Ct. 2298, 2307 (2015) (citing *Neder v. United States*, 527 U.S. 1, 15 (1999)).
28. *Ahsan v. Staples the Office Superstore East, Inc.*, 710 F. App'x 31, 32–33 (2d Cir. 2018) (citing *Hathaway v. Coughlin*, 99 F.3d 550, 552 (2d Cir. 1996)) ("A jury charge is erroneous if it misleads the jury as to the correct legal standard, or if it does not adequately inform the jury of the law.").

The District Court's Wide Discretion to Formulate the Jury Charge

Rule 49 of the Federal Rules of Civil Procedure "provides district courts with broad discretion to frame written questions to the jury."[29] "Few jury charges in cases of complexity will not yield 'error' if pored over, long after the fact . . . "[30] But, appellate courts have "noted the 'powerful interests in orderliness and finality' compelling deferential review of unpreserved jury-instruction errors."[31] "It is well settled the admission or exclusion of a particular jury instruction is left to the sound discretion of the trial court."[32] "If the trial judge's instructions accurately reflect the law, he or she is given wide discretion as to the style and wording employed in its instruction."[33]

Making a Plea for Simplicity While Reminding the Court That a Refusal to Give Tendered Jury Instructions from the Defense Will Be Reviewed Only for an Abuse of Discretion

The court's discretion in formulating its jury charge should be invoked in one's arguments concerning the charge, specifically in a plaintiff's lawyer's plea that the jury instructions and questions should be kept as simple as possible. Inevitably, appellate specialists for the defense spend their time trying to embed 1,000 stink bombs into the charge designed only to confuse the jury away from returning a verdict for the plaintiff. The plaintiff's lawyer must keep the stench of complexity out of the court's charge by reminding the court that it may use its wide discretion to instruct the jury with simple, understandable language.

As the plaintiff seeks simplicity likely to be understood by the jury, the defense seeks complex, myriad instructions designed to keep the jury away from answering "yes" to liability questions. For this reason, the plaintiff's lawyer must remind the district court of three things. First, every "tendered instruction must be 'warranted by the evidence.'"[34] Second, a requested instruction is not required if other instructions already "fairly and adequately present the issues in the case to the jury."[35] Third, because appellate courts review jury instructions for abuse of discretion only,[36] which is a "highly deferential"[37] standard of review, a party challenging only a simple jury instruction faces a heavy burden on appeal.[38]

---

29. *Joy Pipe, USA, LP v. ISMT, Ltd.*, 703 F. App'x 253, 261 (5th Cir. 2017).

30. *Highlands Ins. Co. v. Nat'l Union Fire Ins. Co.*, 27 F.3d 1027, 1032 (5th Cir. 1994).

31. *Abbott v. Babin*, 744 F. App'x 854, 856 (5th Cir. 2018).

32. *Coletti v. Cudd Pressure Control*, 165 F.3d 767, 771 (10th Cir. 1999) (citing *Harris Mkt. Research v. Marshall Mktg. & Commc'n, Inc.*, 948 F.2d 1518, 1528 (10th Cir. 1991)).

33. *McCormick v. Aderholt*, 293 F.3d 1254, 1260 (11th Cir. 2002).

34. *Kozlov v. Associated Wholesale Grocers, Inc.*, 818 F.3d 380, 389 (8th Cir. 2016). *See also Wolfe v. USAA Life Ins. Co.*, 208 F.3d 228, 2000 WL 216936, at *2 (10th Cir. Feb. 24, 2000) (unpublished table decision) (citing *King v. Unocal Corp.*, 58 F.3d 586, 57 (10th Cir. 1995)) ("[W]hen reviewing a jury charge to determine its propriety, the court must consider all the jury heard and then view the charge from the jury's perspective.").

35. *McDole v. City of Saginaw*, 471 F. App'x 464, 2012 WL 1003553, at *9 (6th Cir. Mar. 26, 2012) (unpublished) (quoting *United States v. Carr*, 5 F.2d 986, 992 (6th Cir. 1993)); *Pittman v. Frazer*, 129 F.3d 983, 987 (8th Cir. 1997) (citation omitted).

36. *Wurster v. Plastics Grp., Inc.*, 917 F.3d 608, 614 (8th Cir. 2019); *De Asencio v. Tyson Foods, Inc.*, 500 F.3d 361, 366 (3d Cir. 2007).

37. *Westmoreland v. TWC Admin. LLC*, 924 F.3d 718, 731 (4th Cir. 2019).

38. *Fussman v. Novartis Pharm. Corp.*, 509 F. App'x 215, 2013 WL 474330, at *6 (4th Cir. Feb. 8, 2013) (quotations omitted).

Likewise, a decision by the court to refuse to give instructions tendered by the defense that would make the charge more complex will be reviewed only for an abuse of discretion,[39] which requires an appellate court to have "a definite and firm conviction that the trial court committed a clear error of judgment"[40] in refusing to give the defendant's requested instruction. As such, after a plaintiff's verdict is returned and a judgment is rendered thereon, "to the extent [a] motion for new trial [is] based on the court's refusal to give a requested jury instruction, the refusal is reviewed for abuse of discretion,"[41] and only "constitutes reversible error if (1) the omitted instruction is a correct statement of the law, (2) the instruction is not substantially covered by other delivered charges, and (3) the failure to give the instruction impairs the requesting party's theory of the case."[42]

Reminding the Court That the Defendant Is Not Entitled to Have a Jury Instruction about Every Word Ever Spoken in a Prior Opinion

"No litigant has a right to a jury instruction of its choice, or precisely in the manner and words of its own preference;"[43] rather, "the district court has discretion over the 'style and wording' of instructions."[44] There is, moreover, no case holding that every time a prior court—appellate or otherwise—says something about a principle of law that all subsequent courts must include that statement in every jury instruction given thereafter.[45] Rather, an appellate court will review an allegedly erroneous omission of an instruction with an eye toward the adequacy of the instructions actually given,[46] and "whether the instructions construed as a whole, and in light of the whole record, adequately informed the jury of the controlling legal principles without misleading or confusing the jury to the prejudice of

39. *Chapman v. Milford Towing & Serv. Inc.*, 499 F. App'x 437, 442 (6th Cir. 2012); *Coletti v. Cudd Pressure Control*, 165 F.3d 767, 771 (10th Cir. 1999) ("We review the court's refusal to give a particular instruction for abuse of discretion.") (quoting *United States v. Lee*, 54 F.3d 1534, 1536 (10th Cir.), *cert denied*, 516 U.S. 895 (1995)).

40. *Chapman*, 499 F. App'x at 442 (citation omitted).

41. *Decker v. GE Healthcare, Inc.*, 770 F.3d 378, 391 (6th Cir. 2014). *See also United States v. Ebron*, 683 F.3d 105, 151 (5th Cir. 2012) (refusals to give jury instructions are reviewed for abuse of discretion).

42. *Id.* (quoting *Cummins v. BIC USA, Inc.*, 727 F.3d 506, 510 (6th Cir. 2013)). *See also Golan v. FreeEats.com, Inc.*, 930 F.3d 950, 959 (8th Cir. 2019) ("For an appellant to prevail when challenging the denial of a proposed jury instruction, the proposed instruction must (1) correctly state the applicable law; (2) address matters not adequately covered by the charge; and (3) involve a point so important that failure to give the instruction seriously impaired the party's ability to present an effective case.") (citations omitted).

43. *Smith v. Katz*, 696 F. App'x 582, 593 (3d Cir. 2017) (quoting *Douglas v. Owens*, 50 F.3d 1226, 1233 (3d Cir. 1995)).

44. *Belk v. City of Eldon*, 228 F.3d 872, 881 (8th Cir. 2000) (quoting *Beckman v. Mayo Found.*, 804 F.2d 435, 438 (8th Cir. 1986)).

45. *See McDole*, 2012 WL 1003553 at *9 ("The City's proposed instruction is largely quoted from our [prior] decision . . . . This language has been used in some cases in the summary-judgment context, as a standard for determining whether a plaintiff has satisfied the fourth element of a prima facie case or whether the plaintiff has shown pretext. We have never held that it is required as a jury instruction, however."). *See generally Acord v. General Motors*, 669 S.W.2d 111, 116 (Tex. 1984) ("We explicitly approve the Pattern Jury Charges issue and instruction for design defect cases, and disapprove the addition of any other instructions in such cases, however correctly they may state the law under § 402A of the Restatement (Second) of Torts.").

46. *Cansler v. Hanks*, 777 F. App'x 627, 2019 WL 2502230, at *5 (4th Cir. June 17, 2019) ("We are obliged to 'holistically' examine a claim that an instruction was improperly rejected, viewing it in context of the jury charge as given."). *See also Sims v. Mulcahy*, 902 F.2d 524, 533 (7th Cir.), *cert. denied*, 498 U.S. 897 (1990).

the objecting party."[47] "Refusal of instructions on a party's theory is not reversible error if the instruction given adequately presents the party's theory."[48]

The Supreme Court taught us long ago that "a single instruction to a jury may not be judged in artificial isolation, but must be viewed in the context of the overall charge."[49] In reviewing the adequacy of a jury charge, the court "must look to the entire charge and affirm the trial court if the instructions, taken as a whole, fairly and adequately state the pertinent legal principles involved."[50] Instead, because the Supreme Court has long provided the "well-established proposition that a single instruction to a jury may not be judged in artificial isolation, but must be viewed in the context of the overall charge,"[51] a specific erroneous instruction may not be reversible "in light of the instructions taken as a whole,"[52] because only "charging the jury with an incorrect standard of liability supports granting a new trial."[53] A new trial is required only when "the instructions, taken as a whole, are misleading or give an inadequate understanding of the law."[54]

The upshot of this case law means that a plaintiff's lawyer should argue during the charge conference that the multitude of instructions tendered by defense counsel may be denied unless the normal, simplistically phrased pattern jury charge somehow misstates the law without the defendant's additional requested instructions.

Requested Instructions May Be Denied with the Comfort of Knowing That the Court's Charge Will Not Be Reversed Unless the Alleged Error Influences the Jury's Verdict

An appellate court ordering a new trial based on charge error is exceedingly rare, because to "justify a new trial, jury instruction must be both erroneous *and* prejudicial."[55] A trial court judgment is to be "reversed only if the jury charge leads to a substantial and eradicable doubt [about] whether the jury has been properly guided in its deliberations."[56] By contrast,

---

47. *Bailey v. Cty. of Georgetown*, 94 F.3d 152, 156 (4th Cir. 1996).

48. *McDonald v. Sandvik Process Sys., Inc.*, 870 F.2d 389, 395 (7th Cir. 1989).

49. *Cupp v. Naughten*, 414 U.S. 141, 146–47 (1973).

50. *Gibson v. Gill-Lee Towing, Inc.*, 894 F.2d 401, 1990 WL 2199, at *2 (4th Cir. Jan. 5, 1990) (unpublished table decision) (citing *Spartanburg Cty. Sch. Dist. Seven v. Nat'l Gypsum Co.*, 805 F.2d 114, 1150 (4th Cir. 1986); *Hoggs Oyster Co., Inc. v. United States*, 676 F.2d 1015, 1019 (4th Cir. 1982)).

51. *Kansas v. Marsh*, 548 U.S. 163, 179, n.6 (2006) (quoting *Boyde v. California*, 494 U.S. 370, 378 (1990)).

52. *Caldwell v. Wal-Mart Stores, Inc.*, 229 F.3d 1162, 2000 WL 1335564, at *4 (10th Cir. Sept. 15, 2000) (unpublished table decision) ("Even if the instruction was erroneous in allowing imposition of liability solely because Wal-Mart 'permitted' water to accumulate on its aisle floor, such error was not reversible, in light of the instructions taken as a whole.").

53. *Encompass Office Sol.'s Inc. v. Louisiana Health Serv. & Indem. Co.*, 919 F.3d 266, 275 & n.28 (5th Cir. 2019) (citing *Pinkerton v. Spellings*, 529 F.3d 513, 519 (5th Cir. 2008)) (granting new trial because jury instruction wrongly imposed elevated standard for liability).

54. *Arban v. West Publ'g Corp.*, 345 F.3d 390, 404 (6th Cir. 2003).

55. *Millea v. Metro-North R.R. Co.*, 658 F.3d 154, 163 (2d Cir. 2011) (emphasis added).

56. *Arleth v. Freeport-McMoran Oil & Gas Co.*, 2 F.3d 630, 634 (5th Cir. 1993); *see also Adams v. Austal, U.S.A., LLC*, 754 F.3d 1240, 1248 (11th Cir. 2014).

if there is no "reasonable probability" that any error "affected the jury's verdict," the trial court judgment will not be disturbed.[57]

Rule 61 of the Federal Rules of Civil Procedure provides that "[a]t every stage of the proceeding, the court must disregard all errors and defects that do not affect any party's substantial rights." Accordingly, unless charge error "affects the substantial rights of the parties," an appellate court "will not reverse a judgment due to error in jury instructions."[58]

Consequently, requested instructions may be denied with the comfort of knowing that the court's charge will not be reversed unless the alleged errors actually influenced the jury's verdict. When the remainder of the jury charge accurately sets forth the law, a surplus instruction requested by the defendant and denied by the district court can never meet the standard required to achieve reversal. Simply put, "a jury instruction error that is harmless will not furnish a basis for relief."[59]

Preserving Error

Rule 51 of the Federal Rules of Civil Procedure provides that "[n]o party may assign as error the giving or the failure to give an instruction unless that party objects thereto before the jury retires to consider its verdict, stating distinctly the matter objected to and the grounds of the objection." The objection must be made "out of the jury's hearing before the instructions and arguments are delivered."[60] The rule also states that "[a] party may assign as error . . . a failure to give an instruction, if that party properly requested it and—unless the court rejected the request in a definitive ruling on the record—also properly objected."[61]

The Supreme Court stated more than sixty years ago that it ordinarily will not decide questions not raised or litigated in the lower courts.[62] In light of Rule 51, this rule "has special force where the party seeking to argue the issue has failed to object to a jury instruction. . . ."[63] Accordingly, every federal Court of Appeals since then has required that contentions of charge error be preserved by first presenting them to the district court.

The First Circuit held in 2018 that an original objection lodged was withdrawn when the court explained how the subject was covered elsewhere in the charge and the objecting attorney responded, "Okay, fair enough," and made no further objection on the point.[64] In 2017, the First Circuit cited Rule 51(d)(2) in holding that a failure to object to an instruction

---

57. *BMG Rights Mgmt. (US) LLC v. Cox Commc'ns, Inc.*, 881 F.3d 293, 305 (4th Cir. 2018). *See generally Williams v. U.S. Elevator Corp.*, 920 F.2d 1019, 1024 (D.C. Cir. 1990) (erroneous charge on liability could not affect damages and vice versa, so no reversal required).

58. *Grauer v. Marchese*, 920 F.2d 935, 1990 WL 208772, at *2 (7th Cir. Dec. 12, 1990) (unpublished table decision); *see also Perry v. State Farm Fire & Cas. Co.*, 734 F.2d 1441, 1446 (11th Cir. 1984) (explaining that errors in evidentiary rulings are "harmless if it does not affect the substantial rights of the parties").

59. *Bonkowski v. Allstate Ins. Co.*, 544 F. App'x 597, 608 (6th Cir. 2013) (citing *Johnson Controls, Inc. v. Jay Indus., Inc.*, 459 F.3d 717, 727 (6th Cir. 2006)).

60. Fed. R. Civ. P. 51(b)(2).

61. Fed. R. Civ. P. 51(d)(1)(B).

62. *California v. Taylor*, 353 U.S. 553, 556, n.2 (1957).

63. *City of Springfield v. Kibbe*, 480 U.S. 257, 259 (1987).

64. *Xiaoyan Tang v. Citizens Bank*, 741 F. App'x 11, 13 (1st Cir. 2018).

below required a review under the plain error standard.[65] In 2016, the Court held that the failure to preserve objections to the verdict form below meant that "the plaintiffs cannot argue" on appeal that "any phrasing imperfection seriously impaired the fairness, integrity, or public reputation of the judicial proceedings."[66] In 2010, the First Circuit noted in *Diaz v. Jiten Hotel Management, Inc.*, that only obliquely raising an issue during the charge conference and then saying nothing, "dropping the issue without objecting on the record or attempting to explain why the instruction was in fact necessary (despite the court's clear directive during the jury charge conference that any objections to the court's instructions had be 'specific')" caused "serious doubts as to whether [the] request constituted an objection 'stating distinctly the matter objected to and the grounds for the objection,' as required by Federal Rule of Civil Procedure 51(c)(1)."[67] Importantly, the First Circuit also observed in 2010 in *Booker v. Massachusetts Department of Public Health* that "even if a party properly objected to a proposed instruction prior to the jury charge [conference] and the court then gave the challenged instruction, that objection was forfeited unless the party renewed the objection after the jury charge [conference]."[68]

The Second Circuit held in 2018 that Rule 51(c)(2)(B) requires that "[p]arties must make such objections, at the latest, 'promptly after learning that the instruction or request will be, or has been, given or refused.'"[69] A proposed instruction and correlating argument during the charge conference were "sufficient to preserve the issue for appeal" in *Delee v. Hannigan*,[70] but endorsement of a jury charge was "deemed a true waiver, negating even plain error review" in *Ruocco v. Hemmerdinger Corp.*[71] It has therefore long been the rule in the Second Circuit that "[n]ormally, we will not consider a challenge to a jury charge if a party failed to object at trial."[72]

More than fifty years ago, the Third Circuit held that a lawyer who raised no suggestions or objections to the jury charge waived any error on appeal.[73] In 2018, the court explained why this preservation of error requirement has been strictly and consistently applied in the circuit:

> We repeatedly have stressed the important policy objectives served by Rule 51. The rule affords the trial judge an opportunity to correct any error that may have been made in the charge before the jury begins its deliberations. It also lessen[s] the

---

65. *Denault v. Ahern*, 857 F.3d 76, 87 (1st Cir. 2017).
66. *In re Nexium (Esomeprazole) Antitrust Litig.*, 842 F.3d 34, 61 (1st Cir. 2016) (quotation omitted).
67. 671 F.3d 78, 84, n.5 (1st Cir. 2012) (citing *Linn v. Andover Newton Theological Sch., Inc.*, 874 F.2d 1, 5 (1st Cir. 1989)) ("If there is a problem with the instructions, the judge must be told *precisely* what the problem is, and as importantly, what the attorney would consider a satisfactory cure.").
68. *Booker v. Mass. Dept. of Pub. Health*, 612 F.3d 34, 42 (1st Cir. 2010) (citing *McGrath v. Spirito*, 733 F.2d 967, 968–69 (1st Cir. 1984)).
69. *Benson v. Family Dollar Operations. Inc.*, 755 F. App'x 52, 58 (2d Cir. 2018) (quoting Fed. R. Civ. P. 51(c)(2)(B)).
70. 729 F. App'x 25, 29 (2d Cir. 2018).
71. 711 F. App'x 659, 663 (2d Cir. 2017) (citing *United States v. Hertular*, 562 F.3d 433, 444 (2d Cir. 2009)). *See also Kosmynka v. Polaris Indus., Inc.*, 462 F.3d 74, 83 (2d Cir. 2006) ("It is well established that a party waives its objection to any inconsistency in a jury verdict if it fails to object to the verdict prior to the excusing of the jury.").
72. *Latsis v. Chandris, Inc.*, 20 F.3d 45, 49 (2d Cir. 1994).
73. *United States v. 78.40 Acres of Land*, 384 F.3d 666, 674–75 (4th Cir. 2004).

> burden on appellate courts by diminishing the number of rulings at the trial which they may be called upon to review. Thus, Rule 51 is consistent with the general rule that an appellate court will not predicate error on an issue upon which the district court was not provided with an opportunity to rule. We have followed this proposition strictly, and have refused to consider newly developed arguments[s] concerning [a] jury charge deficiency.[74]

The Fourth Circuit has held that when the district court's jury instruction "was precisely the instruction" appellants "had requested," "any error committed by the district court in giving th[at] instruction was invited error and is not subject to review."[75] In 2001, the Court held that "[w]hen the party asserting a legal theory could have requested a jury instruction on an alternate theory but did not, the argument that a jury charge which instructed on such a theory would have been valid becomes unavailable on appeal."[76] In 1992, the Fourth Circuit held in *United States v. Rowell* that when "defendant's counsel noted no objections . . . at the conclusion of the jury charge [conference,]" "[i]f error was made, it did not constitute reversible error under these circumstances."[77]

The Fifth Circuit held in 2019 in *Gil Ramirez Group, LLC v. Marshall* that objections "not made with particularity at the jury charge conference . . . were not preserved."[78] In *Malik & Sons, LLC v. Circle K Stores, Inc.*, the Fifth Circuit set forth the preservation of charge error requirements demanded by the circuit:

> Federal Rule of Civil Procedure 51 requires parties to object to the jury charge before the jury retires, "stating distinctly the matter objected to and the grounds for the objection." Fed. R. Civ. P. 51; see also *Jimenez v. Wood County*, 660 F.3d 841, 845 (5th Cir. 2011) (en banc) (holding that "a specific, formal, on-the-record objection is required" to challenge jury instructions). When objections to the jury charge are "brought forth with specificity for the first time on appeal," they fail on "compelling procedural grounds." *Patton v. S. Bell Tel. & Tel. Co.*, 387 F.2d 360, 361 (5th Cir. 1968). "The objection must have been made on the specific 'ground raised on appeal, rather than a general objection to the instructions as a whole or an objection on a different ground.'" *Jimenez*, 660 F.3d at 845 (quoting *Fiber Sys. Int'l, Inc. v. Roehrs*, 470 F.3d 1150, 1158 (5th Cir. 2006)).[79]

The Sixth Circuit held in *Bonkowski v. Allstate Ins. Co.* that "[t]he failure of a party to object . . ." during the charge conference "is generally viewed as a waiver of the party's

74. *Yarus v. Walgreen Co.*, 738 F. App'x 94, 99 (3d Cir. 2018).

75. *United States v. Quinn*, 359 F.3d 666, 674–75 (4th Cir. 2004).

76. *Jimenez v. DaimlerChrysler Corp.*, 269 F.3d 439, 448 (4th Cir. 2001).

77. *United States v. Rowell*, 953 F.2d 641, 1992 WL 11123, at *3 (4th Cir. Jan. 28, 1992) (unpublished table decision). *See also Bailey v. Turner*, 736 F.2d 963, 972 (4th Cir. 1984) ("[T]he instructions of the magistrate were proper but, even if not proper, the plaintiff, who was represented by able and experienced counsel, waived any objections to such instructions by failure to object at trial.").

78. *Gil Ramirez Group, LLC v. Marshall*, 765 F. App'x 970, 980 (5th Cir. 2019).

79. 738 F. App'x 808, 813 (5th Cir. 2018).

objection to the jury instruction,"[80] though Rule 51 "allows consideration of an unpreserved jury instruction argument under a plain error standard if the "error in a jury instruction is obvious and prejudicial. . . ."[81]

The Seventh Circuit held in *Latino Food Marketers, LLC v. Ole Mexican Foods, Inc.* that once a case was tried on a different liability theory, a party "cannot now complain that the judge did not give adequate attention to an argument that [Defendant] itself virtually ignored."[82]

The Eighth Circuit held in *Genthe v. Lincoln* that without error being preserved during the charge conference below, "[t]he verdict should be reversed only if the error prejudices the substantial rights of a party and would result in a miscarriage of justice if left uncorrected" because "plain error review is narrow and confined to the exceptional case where error has seriously affected the fairness, integrity, or public reputation of the judicial proceedings."[83]

The Ninth Circuit held in *Kaiser Steel Corp. v. Frank Coluccio Const. Co.* that objecting to the omission of a proposed instruction "only minutes before the jury was to be instructed, referring to its failure to raise the matter earlier as an 'oversight'" enabled the district court to "certainly find" that the objecting party "had waived its objection."[84] This followed the longtime rule in the Ninth Circuit that a trial court in a civil case may properly refuse to recall a jury to give an omitted instruction where no instruction was timely requested and adequate instruction had been given on issue.[85]

The Tenth Circuit held in *Herrera v. Bernalillo Cty. Bd. of Cty. Comm'rs* that its "review is limited to plain error in light of plaintiff's failure to preserve an objection to the district court's instructions at trial."[86] A "passing assertion" only questionably "frame[s] and develop[s] an issue sufficient to invoke appellate review."[87]

The Eleventh Circuit held in *Jones v. Triple Z, Inc.* that "[i]n order to preserve an issue on appeal, we also require a party to object to a jury instruction, distinctly explaining the matter and grounds for the objection prior to jury deliberations,"[88] and observed that "[g]enerally, '[a] party who fails to raise an objection to a jury instruction prior to jury deliberations waives its right to raise the issue on appeal.'"[89]

---

80. 544 F. App'x 597, 608 (6th Cir. 2013) (citing *Clarksville-Montgomery Cty. Sch. Sys. v. U.S. Gypsum Co.*, 925 F.2d 993, 1006 (6th Cir. 1991)) ("We first note that Clarksville's failure to object to a specific charge before and after the jury charge is given constitutes waiver of the objection."). *See also Bar's Products, Inc. v. Bars Products Int'l, Inc.*, 662 F. App'x 400, 415 n.1 (6th Cir. 2016) (Siler, J., concurring in part, dissenting in part) ("Bars admitted at oral argument that it did not object to the jury instructions, suggesting that its motion practice preserved its legal theories. Our law is clear that Bar's conduct amounts to waiver.").

81. *Bonkowski*, 544 F. App'x at 609 (citing *Sovereign Order of Saint John of Jerusalem, Inc. v. Grady*, 119 F.3d 1236, 1243 (6th Cir. 1997)).

82. 407 F.3d 876, 879–80 (7th Cir. 2005).

83. 383 F.3d 713, 718 (8th Cir. 2004) (citing *BBSerCo., Inc. v. Metrix Co.*, 324 F.3d 955, 960 (8th Cir. 2003).

84. 785 F.2d 656, 659 (9th Cir. 1986).

85. *Likins-Foster Monterey Corp. v. United States*, 308 F.2d 595, 603 (9th Cir. 1962). This is consistent with Rule 30 of the Federal Rules of Criminal Procedure, which provides that objections to the jury charge are waived unless raised before the jury retires. *See United States v. Spawr Optical Research, Inc.*, 864 F.2d 1467, 1471 (9th Cir. 1988).

86. 106 F. App'x 670, 672 (10th Cir. 2004) (citing *Veile v. Martinson*, 258 F.3d 1180, 1186–887 (10th Cir. 2001)).

87. *Herrera*, 106 F. App'x at 672 (citing *Murrell v. Shalala*, 43 F.3d 1388, 1389 n.2 (10th Cir. 1994)).

88. 679 F. App'x 986, 987 (Mem.) (11th Cir. 2017).

89. *Id.* (citing *Farley v. Nationwide Mut. Ins. Co.*, 197 F.3d 1322, 1329 (11th Cir. 1999)).

The District of Columbia Court of Appeals held that "[b]ecause appellants never again asserted, either in a mid-trial conference about jury instructions or when specifically queried by the district court immediately after the jury charge, any desire to instruct the jury on the definition of intent as an intention 'to disobey or disregard the law,' they waived their earlier request for that particular instruction," and therefore, "the district court's instructions are reviewed only for plain error."[90]

The Federal Circuit Court of Appeals held in *Allen Organ Co. v. Kimball Int'l, Inc.*[91] that an agreement without objection to the jury charge is an agreement to the law that the jury is to apply, and held in *Bio-Rad Laboratories, Inc. v. Nicolet Instrument Corp.* that "[i]f no objection is raised, the instructions cannot be challenged on appeal unless great injustice would result."[92]

In sum, if a party wishes to complain on appeal of a jury question or instruction in the court's charge, a formal and specific objection during the charge conference is necessary. If a party wishes to complain on appeal of a jury question or instruction omitted from the court's charge, he must tender a proposed jury question or instruction to the court in writing and then obtain a specific ruling from the district court that is refusing to include the same in the court's charge. Absent those steps necessary to preserve error, the plain error standard of review will be applied by the appellate courts, one that rarely is met, if at all.

---

90. *United States v. Khan*, 88 F.3d 1279, 1996 WL 311458, at *1 (D.C. Cir. May 21, 1996) (unpublished table decision). *See also United States v. Dale*, 991 F.2d 819, 950 (D.C. Cir.), *cert denied*, 510 U.S. 1030 (1993) (when no objection is made to a court's jury instructions before a jury retires, the instruction is reviewed only for "plain error affecting a substantial right so that a miscarriage of justice would otherwise result").

91. 839 F.2d 1556, 1556 & n.5 (Fed. Cir.), *cert. denied*, 488 U.S. 8850 (1988).

92. 739 F.2d 604, 615 (Fed. Cir. 1984).

26
The Jury Charge
The Defense Perspective

The jury charge consists of the questions, instructions, and definitions that guide the jury's deliberations and decision in the case. The charge defines the law, as well as the burdens of proof, as applied to the evidence. Any winning trial effort requires a complete understanding of the law and the legal burdens each side must carry. If this understanding is lacking, the risks of an improper charge are increased and the client is placed at a severe disadvantage. Indeed, if this understanding is absent, the trial lawyer is committing malpractice. The lawyer's opening statement likely will be ineffective, and the presentation of evidence likely will be deficient. The jury charge provides the structure and framework for a successful trial. The jury charge is the "bones" of the case.

Trial lawyers are expected to seek a charge favorable to their client's factual and legal position. They are expected to lobby the trial court for a charge that makes it easier for the jury to decide in their client's favor. As trial lawyers, we all want clear, understandable questions to facilitate a favorable verdict. Defense lawyers and plaintiff's lawyers are the same in this regard. We are equal-opportunity lobbyists, and efforts to lobby the trial court for a favorable charge are consistent with our duties of zealous advocacy.

The trial court is the legal umpire calling balls and strikes, and hopefully settling on a charge that is fair to both sides. The trial court expects advocacy from the lawyers as it frames the charge. Although zealous argument is encouraged and respected, *be careful what you ask for.* If the charge is improperly slanted to benefit your client by distorting relevant legal principles, you may be inviting reversible error. Thus, the goal is to advocate a substantially correct charge, but one that is favorable to your case and, perhaps, less favorable to the opposing side. The goal is not to win a verdict because of a flawed charge that invites an appeal. Rather, the objective is to convince the court to submit a substantially correct charge that is both fair and favorable to your client.

Like other aspects of trial preparations, the jury charge should not be prepared at the end of the trial. Some lawyers wait until the end of the case to begin serious analysis of what the charge should include. This is a mistake. Nothing good comes from ad hoc, last-minute preparations. To be most effective, you should prepare a draft jury charge far in advance of trial, during the initial stages of the case. This forces you to research relevant legal principles and begin to see how these principles can be molded to the facts and vice versa. Early preparation is an excellent way of framing important issues. You effectively create a template for how the case should be developed and ultimately tried. You must define the plaintiff's burden, your defense burdens, your client's duties, and the applicable causation standards. Otherwise, you cannot move forward with meaningful pretrial depositions; you cannot identify and develop appropriate expert testimony; and you cannot properly identify your witness and evidentiary needs.

As the facts evolve during discovery, draft jury charges undoubtedly undergo modification and enhancement. By the time the trial date arrives, you will have a firm grasp of what the final charge should look like. You know what evidence needs to be presented, what evidence needs to be rebutted, and what evidence should be excluded. Simply stated, you cannot build a house without a plan and good blueprints. You are the architect of your trial, and you cannot try a lawsuit unless you have a blueprint of how the jury will be charged.

Pattern Jury Charges

Every state jurisdiction has some form of a pattern jury charge and/or pattern jury instruction, although different jurisdictions vary under whose authority such charges are prepared, and whether such charges are binding upon the trial court and the litigants.[1] Regardless of the jurisdiction, pattern jury charges should be considered a useful, first reference point. Indeed, trial courts in many state jurisdictions are reluctant to, if not restricted from deviating from pattern charges, so the published versions of these charges likely dictate what your jury will receive at the end of the trial.[2] Other courts in other states are less compelled to adhere blindly to pattern charges. In any event, a first order of business in every jurisdiction requires us to consult pattern charges as an initial guide. These pattern charges frequently are considered a safe harbor approved by appellate courts which, if used, present minimal risks of reversal.

In some jurisdictions, pattern charges are prepared and approved by committees appointed by the relevant state bar associations. In others, committees may be appointed by the high courts in each state. In even others, pattern charges are dictated by the state high courts themselves. However, regardless of the authority or authorship of pattern charges, the goal of such charges is to set forth a consensus definition of the common law for the state at issue.

1. *See, e.g.*, Illinois: Illinois Pattern Jury Instructions–Civil; Minnesota: Minnesota Jury Instruction Guides; New York: New York Pattern Jury Instructions–Civil; Texas: Texas Pattern Jury Charges.

2. *See, e.g.*, *Ryan v. Fleischman*, 64 Ill. App. 3d 75, 78 (1978) (holding judge may deviate from the Illinois Pattern Jury Instruction only when it "does not accurately state the applicable law").

In Texas, where my law firm is located, the State Bar of Texas appoints committees that are responsible for preparing and updating jury charges for different types of cases, such as simple negligence cases, contract cases, etc.[3] There are several committees with delegated responsibility; each committee is comprised of active or retired judges and respected private practitioners.

Texas, like many states, has developed, supplemented, and amended pattern jury charges over the course of several decades. Thus, in theory, pattern jury charges embody an evolution of what is a consensus of relevant legal principles that govern specific types of cases.

There will always be cases that present novel issues or variations of issues that are not squarely addressed in pattern charges. Defense lawyers should be prepared to advocate jury instructions that are not found in the pattern jury charges, but which are grounded in the common law.

Plaintiff Strategy v. Defense Strategy

Plaintiff's counsel typically prefers broad-form submissions that are reader-friendly and more easily answered by a jury. Complex jury charges with multiple moving parts can lead to juror confusion and enhance the risk of an appellate challenge. Broad-form submissions are also easily prepared and answered, providing optionality to the plaintiff's lawyer on how the case is submitted and argued to the jury. In 1984, former Texas Supreme Court Justice Jack Pope recognized the trial court's deference to broad-form submissions: "Judicial history teaches that broad issues and accepted definitions suffice and that a workable jury system demands strict adherence to simplicity in jury charges."[4]

Sometimes, however, broad-form submissions do not do justice. Complex fact patterns sometimes require more detailed submissions. From a defense perspective, it may be important to make sure the jury's attention is focused on certain conduct, behaviors, or defenses. This can be addressed through instructions or questions. A broad-form submission typically gives the plaintiff's lawyer more flexibility on how he or she will argue the case. A more detailed charge limits optionality.

A frequent defense strategy is to provide more detailed instructions and special issues, particularly in more complex litigation matters. The goal is to provide a framework where a jury can find at least one issue in the defense favor and potentially undermine the verdict.

Trading and Swapping

State court jurisdictions frequently require the parties to submit and exchange draft jury charges, either before or during the early stages of the trial. In federal court, this is usually

3. *See* Texas Pattern Jury Charges Committees, State Bar of Texas, https://www.texasbar.com/AM/Template.cfm?Section=Consider_a_State_Bar_Committee&Template=/CM/HTMLDisplay.cfm&ContentID=47329 (last visited Dec. 11, 2019).

4. *Lemos v. Montez*, 680 S.W.2d 798, 801, (Tex. 1984).

done as part of the pretrial order. The lawyers for both sides of the case frequently meet and engage in a series of exchanges and trades. The plaintiff may seek to incorporate certain language in a particular instruction and is willing to trade for the defendant's concession by providing language desired by the defendant in another portion of the charge. Frequently, there is robust bargaining between plaintiff's counsel and defense counsel leading up to the formal charge conference with the court.

The Charge Conference

The charge conference is when the lawyers try to persuade the court that certain items should or should not be included in the charge. This is the official lobbying stage.

I have been involved in charge conferences when the trial court handed the lawyers a proposed charge and told us that this is what the court intended to submit. There was no negotiation and minimal argument.

On the other hand, I have been involved in charge conferences that lasted more than a day. In several cases, the judge rolled up his sleeves and sat at counsel table, and effectively served as a broker seeking to bridge the gap between the parties on controversial submissions. In one instance, we returned to the courthouse on a Saturday morning to get a charge completed for final argument on Monday.

There should be no doubt that trial judges may attempt to broker agreements. All trial courts are incentivized to broker agreements; in doing so, they reduce the risk of an appellate challenge. The parties may be encouraged to waive the right to object to and challenge a "negotiated" charge.

Some trial courts start discussing the charge informally, before a formal charge conference is convened, and will express opinions about how the charge should be crafted. On the other hand, I have been involved in cases where the court convened a charge conference immediately after the conclusion of the evidence and required the lawyers to finalize the charge in a matter of hours. You should be prepared for rushed exercises because such instances can result in rushed decisions and possible mistakes.

Before the evidence closes, it is a good idea to be ready for the charge conference. This means a well-prepared submission supported by case law annotations, with support from the relevant pattern charge. The charge conference is a critical part of every case, and you want to be fully prepared. In many jurisdictions, this means you need to be ready to tender substantially correct instructions or special issues to preserve error on appeal.

Objections to the Charge

After the charge conference and before final argument, the court will allow each side to make formal objections to the charge. These objections are necessary to preserve error and the basis of an appeal. As trial lawyers, we need to be fully prepared for this stage of the trial. In addition to making sure we articulate well-grounded objections, we must be ready to tender substitute language to replace offensive, objectionable language in the charge. In most jurisdictions, this provides the basis for preserving error on appeal.

There are different types of objections that should be considered. What follows are frequently asserted objections:

- The jury charge includes *improper comment on the evidence*. This objection is appropriate when an instruction or jury question suggests an answer to the jury.
- There's *no evidence to support the charge*. This objection is appropriate when there is no evidence to support a particular element of a claim or defense.
- The charge is *not supported by the pleadings*. This objection should be made when the claim or defense has not been pled and has not been tried by consent.
- The charge *fails to accurately state the law or omits an essential element of a claim or defense*.
- The charge *addresses only a question of law* and should not be submitted to the jury.
- The charge *fails to properly define and place the burden of proof*.
- The charge is *duplicative or conflicting instructions or definitions*.
- The charge includes an *improper inferential rebuttal*.
- The charge includes *improper multicomponent issues*.

Remember, this is not an exhaustive list, and you should not hesitate to object to any element of the jury charge that does not conform to the law in your jurisdiction, and which may prevent your client from receiving a fair trial.

Casteel *Error—The Compound Jury Instruction*

Finally, while broad-form jury charges have become the rule and not the exception, defense lawyers must be wary of land mines—specifically, the commingling of valid theories of liability with invalid theories of liability. In Texas, this is known as a *Casteel* Error.[5] In *Casteel*, the court held that it was reversible error when a broad-form jury charge incorporated thirteen separate theories of liability—but five of the theories were legally unavailable.[6] This was reversible error because "when a jury bases a finding of liability on a single question that commingles invalid theories of liability with valid theories, the appellate court often is unable to determine the effect of this error."[7] However, it is imperative that you recognize potential problems presented by compound instructions that might otherwise be innocuous because failure to timely and specifically object waives your appellate point.[8] Thus, any failure to timely and specifically object may expose your client to liability based on incorrect and unsupportable legal theories.

5. *Crown Life Ins. Co. v. Casteel*, 22 S.W.3d 378 (Tex. 2000).
6. *Id.* at 387.
7. *Id.* at 388.
8. *Id.* at 389 ("When a single broad-form liability question erroneously commingles valid and invalid liability theories and the appellant's objection is timely and specific, the error is harmful . . .").

27

Final Arguments

The Plaintiff's Perspective

The final argument is the zenith of a lawyer's trial experience. A final argument can transform jury doubts into a plaintiff's verdict and a mediocre damage award into one large enough for a feature in the *Wall Street Journal*. The maxim "good to great" reflects the opportunity available in final argument. Most jurisdictions permit the plaintiff to sandwich the defense lawyer's argument between a full opening portion of the final argument and a subsequent rebuttal final argument. The opening portion of the final argument should include the trial themes, carefully touching time-honored "do's" and "don'ts" of good argument. The court's jury questions and instructions should serve as a road map, providing directions with which the jurors can appropriately utilize the evidence they have heard, including excerpted record testimony from the trial showing those jurors that the plaintiffs have indeed met their burden as to every element of each cause of action and damage element pleaded. Finally, a wise trial lawyer—though fully opening—will save at least three key points for a rebuttal argument that offers an incredible opportunity to finish strong, utilizing the psychological phenomenon of "recency." Having the last word in final arguments before the jury retires is a singular opportunity to "bring it home" immediately before the jury begins its deliberations. While improper arguments must be objected to for purposes of preserving error for appeal, such appeals are rarely successful absent the plain error brought forth by improper "golden rule" arguments and appeals to race, regional and local bias, and wealth.

Using Trial Themes

Trial themes that are identified before trial should be introduced during voir dire, focused on during opening statements, communicated throughout the plaintiff's case-in-chief, repeatedly referenced during cross-examinations of defense witnesses, and last but not least, reiterated over and over during the final argument.

The first twenty-five words of the opening portion of the final argument should reintroduce the theme of the case. The theme should be the first thing said, even before the jury is thanked for its service and its diligence in performing its constitutional duty. Moreover, as the lawyer moves from topic to topic, from jury question to jury question, from witness to witness, and from exhibit to exhibit, the one-word or two-word synopsis of the theme must be repeated. Use it like an exclamation point at the end of an important sentence:

> Ladies and gentlemen, I told you when we were selecting you as a jury that this case was about greed, about this defendant's conscious decision to choose money over men, wealth over workers, and profits over people. I think the evidence in the case has shown that the Defendant's greed is why each of you are here. Only the twelve of you working together can right this wrong and bring justice to Paul Plaintiff in the form of a verdict communicating what justice is. Paul and I want to thank you for your jury service, for your sacrifice of your time over the past several weeks so that justice can be done in this courtroom on this day. The Court has asked you to answer certain questions. Question No. 1 is whether the Defendant's negligence caused Paul's injuries. But when we ask ourselves why this happened, we learn that the answer is "greed." Question No. 2 asks what amount of money should be paid to Paul for the damage this Defendant caused to him. Their lawyer is going to get up here and accuse me of overstepping by asking for a large sum of money. But the Court didn't ask you to do half of justice or deliver just a piece of what is required. This lawyer is going to ask you to hold the damages they owe down to a number that, if you buy, will make them smile. Why are they doing this? One word—"greed."

In the exercise called trial which ultimately is about the pursuit of one thing—money damages—the plaintiff's lawyer must seize the theme of greed and beat the defendant over the head with it. There are several reasons for "greed" to be the theme. First, money is the root of all evil, and consequently, most poor or deliberate decisions made by a corporate defendant can be couched in terms of motive with just the word "greed." Second, defense lawyers predictably will try to appeal to the notion of "greed" by attacking the plaintiff's lawyers. Thus, if a theme other than "greed" is selected by the plaintiff's lawyer, that same theme will be used by his opponent in order to bludgeon any damages a plaintiff requests.

Do's and Don'ts of Good Argument

There are basic rules of best practices that should be used in every argument, and these rules include things to "do" and mistakes that one should never make. These "do's" and "don'ts" of good argument apply almost universally.

Things to Do in Every Argument

Every argument should begin with a succinct introduction. As just referenced, a skilled lawyer will always choose a theme phrase and use it repetitively. In product liability cases, I spin off the well-known phrase used in the retail industry, "if you break it, you own it," and instead use the phrase, "if you make it, you own it." This choice of theme phrase is somewhat trite, but it is easy to remember and therefore more likely to be utilized during jury deliberations.

In this manner, the use of rhymes to get a point across is highly effective. No one alive in 1994 will ever forget Johnnie Cochran's famed invocation of the phrase, "if the glove doesn't fit, you must acquit." The K-I-S-S principle should always be used to frame the beginning of every final argument—**K**eep **I**t **S**imple, **S**tupid. The 1992 movie *A Few Good Men* is defined by Jack Nicholson's Colonel Nathan R. Jessup shouting at Tom Cruise's Lieutenant Daniel Kaffee, "You can't handle the truth!" But for purposes of argument, Kevin Bacon's Captain Jack Ross's use of the K-I-S-S principle is excellent. In just twenty-two seconds, the entire case is crystalized:

> The facts of the case are these. On midnight of September 6th, the accused entered the barracks room of their platoon mate, they woke him up, tied his arms and legs with tape, and forced a rag into his throat. A few minutes later, a chemical reaction caused his lungs to begin bleeding, and he drowned in his own blood, and was pronounced dead at 37 minutes past midnight.[1]

Likewise, Denzel Washington's Joe Miller, a homophobic lawyer representing his AIDS-stricken client, Tom Hanks' Andrew Beckett, is another excellent example of making points quickly:

> These are the points I must prove to you. Point Number 1—Andrew Beckett was . . . is . . . a brilliant lawyer. Point Number 2—Andrew Beckett, afflicted with a debilitating disease, made the understandable, the personal, the legal choice to keep the fact of his illness to himself. Point Number 3—His employers discovered his illness, and ladies and gentlemen, the illness I'm referring to is AIDS. Point Number 4—they panicked.[2]

These examples of succinct summations of an entire case in twenty-five seconds or less provide valuable clues about how final arguments should begin—with a quick and well-designed synthesis of the entire case.

Next, the burden of proof should be quickly discussed. While setting forth what the burden of proof is, a plaintiff's lawyer should not cling to "by a preponderance of the evidence" as a security blanket with which to be comforted; instead, this lower burden of proof should be referenced for the jury's future use, but in final argument, the skilled trial lawyer will discard it quickly. Instead, he will proclaim that the evidence just presented far surpassed the limited burden-of-proof hurdle set forth by the law.

As with the evidence in the plaintiff's case-in-chief, the final argument should summarize and refer evidence that hits all five senses. Animations and photographs should be shown and referenced by number to fortify their persuasiveness to those who learn best by visual cues. Utilize 911 or news video recordings that capture important sounds contemporaneous to the event in question for audible learners. For tactile learners, enough three-dimensional evidence should have been put into evidence so that a good lawyer can remind jurors to pass those exhibits around amongst them in the deliberation room so that they literally "may touch the truth." Likewise, evidence appealing to the sense of smell and

1. *A Few Good Men* (1992).
2. *Philadelphia* (1993).

the sense of taste need to be embedded within the proof and called out during any effective final argument.

A good final argument will always address potential elephants in the room, most often including the possibility of blaming the plaintiff. Whether contributory negligence is specifically pleaded or not, the plaintiff's actions giving rise to the event in question must be addressed in every single plaintiff's final argument.

Things Not to Do in Final Arguments

Final arguments are often the portion of the trial where poor lawyering is revealed for all to see. Five mistakes are often made during final arguments that should be avoided at all costs. First, lawyer humor is often inappropriate in serious cases. A lawyer who is not funny should not try to be, especially during final arguments of a major trial. Second, final arguments is no time for false modesty. Matthew McConaughey's Jake Brigance walked Samuel L. Jackson's Carl Lee Hailey from a murder charge in John Grisham's *A Time to Kill* with a final argument that began: "I'm here to apologize. I am young and I am inexperienced. But you cannot hold Carl Lee Hailey responsible for my shortcomings." In real life, such appeals to false modesty are received poorly by most juries. Third, use of the Bible is outstanding on Sunday mornings, and helpful to one's faith walk during the other six days of the week, but a trial lawyer invoking the Bible during final arguments better know it cold. Using God, Jesus, the Bible, the Torah, or the Koran is highly dangerous in a multicultural society with many different religious beliefs, and is even more dangerous because it is likely that someone on the jury might know the Good Book more than the lawyer trying to use it to score points in a final argument. Fourth, telling the jury about how what they have just endured "was their duty" is not likely to be received as well as a simple "thank you" and an empathetic recital of the sacrifice they have made. Fifth and finally, telling the jury what they must do is never a good idea; instead, empowering the jury to do what the evidence calls for is more likely to be received well by jurors who are ready to return home to their own lives.

Using the Jury Charge

Most courts write out jury instructions and questions to be answered by the jury in an instrument often referred to as the court's jury charge. Because most jurors respect the judge, as he or she sits above them in height and is dressed in the full regalia of the judicial robe, formal instructions from the judge are likely revered like the gospel. Accordingly, the lawyer who can wrap himself inside the flag of the court's charge will be far along on the road of success.

Use of the court's jury charge during final arguments should be extensive. Rather than merely reading from the charge and suggesting answers, the court's charge should be put up on a large screen, and different instructions should be highlighted or called out for emphasis. In going through a particular jury question, the different elements of the question should be called up and then the evidence should be presented on each element.[3]

3. *A Time to Kill* (1996).

Using Record Testimony

Presenting the evidence on each element of required proof is essential. How to present the evidence is even more critical. While accomplished trial lawyers can call up meaningful moments from the trial off the top of their heads, doing so without reference to notes often comes with folksy asides that become endless rabbit trails. Using the court's charge and the transcript of the record testimony as a guide tends to keep lawyers tied to the evidence rather than to their own rhetorical flourishes.

Jurors are always instructed by the court that "what the lawyers say in argument is not evidence." I like to play off this instruction by reminding the jurors of that instruction, and then telling them "I'm not going to give you my version of what the evidence is; instead, I'm going to show you what the actual evidence was that you heard. I've enlisted the help of the court's reporter, who has been providing me the official transcript of this trial, so let me show you some of what was said here." In this way, the jurors know that the evidence being discussed during final arguments is solid, because they can see the transcript right up on the screen.

To ensure that all important evidentiary moments are appropriately reviewed during final arguments, I prepare a PowerPoint presentation full of excerpts from the court's charge, and I populate it with the evidentiary highlights that demonstrate that the plaintiff's burden has been met. Generally, I play the video recordings of many witnesses during trial because the excerpts are ruled upon by the court in advance, and consequently, I know exactly what testimony will make it into the evidentiary record during the trial. Additionally, I typically call a defense witness or defense expert to the stand during the plaintiff's case-in-chief. There are several reasons for this, one of which is to get key cross-examinations into the record early and in time to excerpt the key admissions for purposes of preparing the final argument PowerPoint.

The damages questions must be addressed just as specifically, with PowerPoint slides detailing the evidence supporting each element of damage. In this regard, much of the damages portion of the final argument PowerPoint can be prepared long before trial. This is true because the medical records are always admissible under Rule 803(6) of the Federal Rules of Evidence; therefore, those records should be synthesized by each element of damage. A plaintiff enduring a long medical treatment and rehabilitation ordeal will see thousands or tens of thousands of pages of medical records. Those records should be synthesized so that all the pain charts and the pain medicines administered are chronologically summarized in a PowerPoint slide. Likewise, the element of past physical impairment may be proven up with a chronological summary of all physical therapy, occupational therapy, and other rehabilitative treatments. The element of past disfigurement may be proven with a careful chronology and a photographic summary of the surgeries endured during medical treatment. Physical injuries also typically come with anxiety and depression, for which medicinal regimens are prescribed. The administration of antianxiety and antidepressant medications can be summarized chronologically, and will alone support as recovery of damages for the element of past mental anguish. In sum, the portion of the final argument concerning the different elements of damages can be fully prepared before trial begins.

The testimony of damages witnesses—in the form of family, friends, and treating doctors and nurses—can often be secured via deposition well before trial. While "unavailability" may not be shown for purposes of Rule 804 admission of hearsay, most courts will pressure the parties to agree that these depositions may be used as if unavailability existed. Alternatively, the court can admit such testimony under Rule 807 as serving "the interests of justice." Even if such witnesses must be called live, the outline of their testimonies can be prescribed with selected family photographs or selected medical record excerpts, which allows a trial lawyer to create PowerPoint slides on distinct elements of damages well before the trial begins. These same slides may eventually be incorporated into the final argument PowerPoint.

What Is a Full "Open"?

It is important that in going first with the opening portion of the final argument that the plaintiff's lawyer "fully open." By this, I mean that each question asked of the jury is addressed by the opening portion of the final argument, such that the defense may then respond. Many courts will not permit a lawyer to refrain from arguing a particular question, or not offer a suggestion on the appropriate level of damages to award, during the opening portion of the final argument, and then later attempt to do so during rebuttal argument. As in the evidentiary portion of trial, rebuttal is limited to directly responding to points brought up in the defense's opening. The plaintiff's lawyer should not assume that it is safe to hold back pending rebuttal argument. If a court is informed that a particular argument in rebuttal addresses a liability question or a damages element not originally addressed in the opening portion of the plaintiff's argument, the ability to do so in rebuttal will be curtailed or eliminated.

The Plaintiff's Rebuttal

The plaintiff's rebuttal is a singular opportunity to sizzle at the end, to bring home the bacon, and to shine a bright light of excellence upon a case just as it ends. Substantively, however, the plaintiff's rebuttal is an opportunity to rebut and to close.

The opportunity to *rebut* is an important one for at least three reasons. First, defense lawyers tend to use the same arguments case after case after case. In any significant case, the plaintiff's lawyer should order past transcripts of closing arguments given by their opponent. That opponent most likely has used the same themes, the same jokes, the same lines of attack in every closing argument given over the past several years. These pre-scripted defense arguments can be responded to well with some forethought. In this manner, the plaintiff's rebuttal can and should be partially scripted well in advance of the trial.

Second, because the defense is responding to what the plaintiff's lawyer has just said, several mistakes are likely to be made on the fly. These mistakes should be vigorously attacked during the plaintiff's rebuttal. While professional courtesies are appropriate and even called for in the rules, the rebuttal argument is designed for rebuttal, and the last argument of the case is no time to hold back and no time to go easy on an opponent. Ultimately, a jury trial in America is a competition between two lead counsel for the trust of their jury. If the defense lawyer makes mistakes in his closing, those mistakes must be vigorously attacked during the plaintiff's rebuttal, which at its core is the chance to corner the credibility market.

Third, most civil jury trials include jury questions related to both liability and damages. During his closing argument, the defense lawyer will make one of two choices. The first option is to ignore suggesting a damages answer because the jury should answer "no" to the liability questions and will not reach the damages question. Defense counsel's second option is to suggest a lower damages figure than the one proposed by the plaintiff's lawyer. In either event, opportunity abounds for the plaintiff's lawyer's rebuttal. If the defense lawyer chooses to not address damages, the plaintiff's rebuttal should include a retort along the lines of "that lawyer has an argument about everything; he can make 'black' seem 'white,' he can make it seem like the emperor has his invisible clothes on, but not even he could come with an argument about why this Plaintiff should not be awarded every dime I proposed that you write down in your verdict." Conversely, if a defense lawyer suggests a lower amount of damages, that lawyer will have either suggested an offensively low number or suggested a methodology to get to a seemingly reasoned low number that must be attacked during rebuttal. However that lower number was reached, the plaintiff's rebuttal must include the response that "he is throwing out that number solely because he is hoping you'll take my number and his number, add them together and cut it in half to get an average; but the judge didn't instruct you to award the Plaintiff one-half of his damages like that; the taste of justice cannot be secured by providing one-half a loaf. Complete justice requires complete damages; don't deliver one-half of justice by cutting the damages in half as he wants you to do."

Moreover, the opportunity to *close* in rebuttal is significant for at least six reasons. First, the closing portion of a plaintiff's rebuttal is the last chance to express thanks. The start of every plaintiff's rebuttal should be used to once again thank the jury. "Ladies and gentlemen, before I respond to what was just said, I want to first take a moment to thank you one last time for your jury service." Honoring the sacrifice made by citizen jurors is not merely courteous, it is strategically smart. A jury that believes its service is being honored is far more likely to do the honorable thing in its verdict than a jury that believes its time has been wasted and not used in a manner that is appreciated. Good manners requires thanks. Good lawyering does, as well. In this vein, thanking the jury is strategically courteous.

Second, the closing portion of a plaintiff's rebuttal is a call to arms. The jury should be reminded that fate brought twelve people together for a reason—each similarly inconvenienced, taken from their home schedules and their families, required to appear at the courthouse each day, all day, for as long as the trial has lasted, and compelled to listen to testimony day after day. The reason for all of this is the opportunity to right a wrong, to cause peer citizens to do justice. During a plaintiff's rebuttal, the jurors should be reminded that they should come together as one for the sole purpose of doing justice.

Third, the closing portion of a plaintiff's rebuttal is a call to duty. In this moment, jurors should be reminded that what they are doing is not an inconvenience, it is a service by citizens, a right fought for in a war and secured by the wisdom of our nation's founding fathers. In today's political debates over free speech and the right to bear arms, pundits throw around the Bill of Rights like they are some exalted paragon of untouchable virtue. Many forget that along with the First Amendment's right to free speech and freedom of religion and the Second Amendment's right to bear arms comes the Sixth Amendment right to a jury trial in criminal cases, and the same right to a jury trial in civil cases contained in the Seventh Amendment:

> In suits at common law, where the value in controversy shall exceed twenty dollars, the right of trial by jury shall be preserved, and no fact tried by a jury, shall be otherwise reexamined in any court of the United States, than according to the rules of the common law.[4]

The importance of this right to our democracy cannot be overstated. Founding father John Adams in 1774 called representative government and the trial by jury the "heart and lungs of liberty," and said that "without them, we have no other fortification against being ridden like horses, fleeced like sheep, worked like cattle and fed and clothed like swine and hounds." Thomas Jefferson wrote in 1789, "I consider trial by jury as the only anchor ever yet imagined by man, by which a government can be held to the principles of its constitution." As our third president in 1801, Jefferson said that "the wisdom of our sages and the blood of our heroes has been devoted to the attainment of trial by jury. It should be the creed of our political faith." Our fourth president, James Madison, proclaimed that the "trial by jury in civil cases is as essential to secure the liberty of the people as any one of the pre-existing rights of nature." Reminding jurors in the plaintiff's rebuttal argument of these constitutional origins of their jury duty today is an effective way to exalt their service into the realm of historic importance. In the closing arguments of the criminal case brought against me, I invoked these constitutional underpinnings of my jury's service that day:

> Ladies and gentlemen, first I want to thank you. We have been at this for a month, and you have been an excellent jury. A lot of 4 a.m. to midnight days over the last month, as you might imagine. As I've sought comfort, because I can't even look back at my family, because it is so emotional. I have found some solace in King David's words in Psalm 109: "Turn to prayer and be delivered from your accusers." Yet in my prayers, what keeps coming back to me is you, the jury of my peers. If this had happened a thousand years ago, we didn't have this right. In England, where we came from, there was no right to a trial by jury. 801 years ago, we had a Magna Carta that established a judiciary that was independent but still no absolute right to a trial by jury. 240 years ago, we fought a war, and yet at the Constitutional Convention in Philadelphia in the summer of 1787, some states didn't want to guarantee this right. And three guys you may have heard of, a guy named Jefferson, a guy named Washington, and a guy named Madison refused to go along with the ratification of our Constitution until it was put in as an amendment to the Constitution, what we

4. U.S. Const. amend. VII.

> now call the Sixth Amendment and the Bill of Rights. So not only are you the answer to my prayers, you are the only check that our system has against throwing people's liberty away based on false evidence.[5]

This call to duty worked. Twelve citizens of the state of Mississippi did their duty as a jury, analyzing the sixty-six remaining charges against me, and wholly rejected them in total by exonerating me with their verdict.

Fourth, the plaintiff's rebuttal is a call to purpose. A jury verdict is a document with a singular purpose, and that purpose is to communicate to others what justice means in this country. Transposing the jury's verdict from a vehicle to achieve a money judgment into a vehicle to communicate what justice means gives the jury's role greater purpose. In rebuttal, I often remind jurors that their answer to the punitive damages question is much like the volume knob on a radio. With a small number, they must know that only the parties in this courtroom will hear their verdict. With a larger number, the message of their verdict may be heard only in this town on the local news or in the local paper. However, with a truly large number, the jury's message will be heard across the entire nation, and certainly in the boardroom of the defendant. Only a true, large punitive damages award will be heard loudly enough to effect change.

Fifth, the plaintiff's rebuttal is a call for change. At their core, punitive damages were designed to punish and to deter. While *punishment* makes us all feel good, *deterrence* seems more noble and more likely to effect change. Most rebuttal arguments I have delivered include a line borrowed from my first boss and professional mentor, David Perry, an excellent trial lawyer from Corpus Christi made famous in the Ford Pinto days:

> I'm reminded of the most famous speech in American history, the one given by President Lincoln at the battlefield of Gettysburg. In that speech lasting less than two minutes, part of what he said was, "let us the living, be here resolved, that these men shall not have died in vain." Similarly, let us in this courtroom be here resolved that what happened to Paul Plaintiff did not happen in vain. In representing his widow, I'd like to think that his death may have had a purpose—that purpose is you. You have the power through your verdict to keep this from ever happening again. Only you have that power. And you must use it.

Sixth, the plaintiff's rebuttal must also be a call for a plaintiff's verdict. In federal courts, that means a call for unanimity. Nothing less than a unanimous, powerful message will do. Encourage jurors to work hard to find the common ground necessary for a cohesive and powerful verdict. By contrast, in most state courts, less than a unanimous verdict will do. In these scenarios, juries should be reminded that the collective will of the required nine or ten of them should not be watered down by only one or two of them otherwise holding up a plaintiff's verdict. Likewise, the full justice that's obtained only by a large damages verdict should not be denied to the plaintiff simply because a small minority on the jury

5. *United States v. Watts*, No. 1:15CR00065-001, (S.D. Miss. Aug. 17, 2016) (closing argument of Mikal Watts).

wants to award less. Invoke jury instructions against quotient verdicts, and instead push the jury to get to the required level of vote and return a verdict of full damages, signed by the number required.

Handling Improper Final Arguments by Your Opponent

"Counsel are provided wide latitude in making closing arguments, latitude that embraces reasonable inferences from the evidence presented at trial."[6] "No doubt, final arguments must be forceful. And, generally, counsel are allowed a 'reasonable latitude' in making them."[7] While aspects of a closing argument may cross the line between acceptable advocacy and imprudent zeal, an appellate court's "disapproval of portions of the closing is not enough to warrant reversal on that ground."[8] Because "[i]t is only the very rare case when the statements of an attorney during a trial will be so prejudicial 'as to impair gravely the calm and dispassionate consideration of the case by the jury,'"[9] appellate courts have long held that "'the power to set aside [a] verdict for misconduct of counsel should be sparingly exercised on appeal.'"[10]

Nonetheless, any complaint made by an opponent about the closing argument must begin with a contemporaneous objection. A timely objection is necessary to bring to the district court's attention errors in counsel's closing argument.[11] Such a timely objection gives the trial court its only opportunity to restrict improper closing argument in real-time, and even if a closing argument is improperly restricted, Supreme Court caselaw says that to merit automatic reversal, such an error must "infect the entire trial process" and "necessarily render [the trial] fundamentally unfair."[12] Without a timely objection, appellate courts "erect a 'high threshold' to claims of improper closing arguments in civil cases raised for the first time after trial,"[13] and in that regard, "[t]here is an even 'high[er] threshold' for granting a new trial where . . . defendants fail[ ] to object to the alleged misconduct during trial."[14] This higher threshold of appellate court review for "gross injustice"[15] when a party has failed to

6. *Fleming v. City of Los Angeles*, 187 F.3d 646, 1999 WL 493269, at *2 (9th Cir. 1999) (unpublished table decision) (citing *United States v. Sayetsitty*, 107 F.3d 1405, 1409 (9th Cir. 1997)).

7. *Whitehead v. Food Max of Miss., Inc.*, 163 F.3d 265, 275–76 (5th Cir. 1998) (citing *Edwards v. Sears, Roebuck & Co.*, 512 F.2d 276, 283 (5th Cir. 1975)).

8. *Dunn v. HOVIC*, 1 F.3d 1371, 1377 (3d Cir. 1993).

9. *Christopher v. Florida*, 449 F.3d 1360 (11th Cir. 2006) (Barkett, J., concurring in part) (citing *Vineyard v. Cty. of Murray, Ga.*, 990 F.2d 1207, 1213 (11th Cir.), *cert. denied*, 510 U.S. 1024 (1993)).

10. *Clemens v. Wheeling & Lake Erie R.R.*, 99 F. App'x 621, 2004 WL 1166549, at *3 (6th Cir. May 18, 2004) (citing *City of Cleveland v. Peter Kiewit Sons' Co.*, 624 F.2d 749, 756 (6th Cir. 1980)).

11. *See Woods v. Burlington Northern R.R. Co.*, 768 F.2d 1287, 1292 (11th Cir. 1985), *rev'd on other grounds*, 480 U.S. 1 (1987). *See also Brown v. Cox*, 286 F.3d 1040, 1046 (8th Cir. 2002) (affirming grant of remittitur and denial of new trial where the defendant failed to object to the challenged comments made by the plaintiff's lawyer in closing).

12. *Glebe v. Frost*, 574 U.S. 21, 23 (2014) (citing *Neder v. United States*, 527 U.S. 1, 8 (1999)).

13. *Hemmings v. Tidyman's, Inc.*, 285 F.3d 1174, 1193 (9th Cir. 2002).

14. *Settlegoode v. Portland Pub. Sch.*, 362 F.3d 1118, 1120 (9th Cir. 2004) (citing *Kaiser Steel Corp. v. Frank Coluccio Constr. Co.*, 785 F.2d 656, 658 (9th Cir. 1986)). *But see Pingatore v. Montgomery Ward & Co.*, 419 F.2d 1138, 1142–44 (9th Cir. 1969) (a new trial on damages was required when, during closing arguments, plaintiff's counsel cursed, shouted, tore papers used by opposing counsel, and placed an empty chair before the jury and asked where the defendant corporation was).

15. *Portis v. Grand Trunk W. R.R. Co.*, 28 F.3d 1214, 1994 WL 362110, at *3 (6th Cir. 1994). *See also Bridgeport Music, Inc. v. Justin Combs Pub.*, 507 F.3d 470, 478 (6th Cir. 2007).

object is necessary for two reasons:[16] "First, raising an objection after the closing argument and before the jury begins deliberations 'permit[s] the judge to examine the alleged prejudice and to admonish . . . counsel or issue a curative instruction, if warranted.'"[17] "Second, 'allowing a party to wait to raise the error until after the negative verdict encourages that party to sit silent in the face of claimed error.'"[18] Thus, when a contemporaneous objection is not made, appellate courts review the record only for "plain error,"[19] one that will "seriously affect the fairness, integrity, or public reputation of the proceeding."[20] However, a finding of plain error "is seldom justified in reviewing argument of counsel in a civil case."[21]

When an objection is timely made, the impact of most improper arguments can be sufficiently neutralized by the district court's curative instructions.[22] "When a closing argument is challenged for impropriety or error, the entire argument should be reviewed [on appeal] within the context of the court's rulings on objection, the jury charge, and any corrective measures applied by the trial court."[23] When a curative instruction is given, appellate courts review whether the statement at issue was "such as to impair gravely the calm and dispassionate consideration of the case by the jury"[24] and will uphold the denial of a mistrial when "the judge took curative measures."[25]

Some arguments are deemed so improper and so prejudicial that appellate courts will order new trials regardless of whether an objection was made at the time. Appeals to racial prejudice[26] and regional or local bias,[27] and improper arguments seeking a verdict based on

16. *Settlegoode*, 362 F.3d at 1129.

17. *Hemmings*, 285 F.3d at 1193 (citations omitted).

18. *Id.*

19. *See Beene v. Ford Motor Co.*, 513 F. App'x 755, at *3 (10th Cir. 2013) (". . . we will not reverse the trial court's denial of the motion for new trial unless plain error is shown.").

20. *Brough v. Imperial Sterling, Ltd.*, 297 F.3d 1172, 1180 (11th Cir. 2002).

21. *Woods v. Burlington N. R.R. Co.*, 768 F.2d 1287, 1292 (11th Cir. 1985) (per curiam), *rev'd on other grounds*, 480 U.S. 1 (1987); *see also Crutcher v. Com. of Ky.*, 961 F.2d 1576, 1992 WL 98020, at *5 (6th Cir. 1992) (reversing district court's grant of a new trial when no objection was made at the time) and *Missho-Iwai Co., Ltd. v. Occidental Crude Sales, Inc.*, 848 F.2d 613, 619 (5th Cir. 1988) (same).

22. *See Hatfield-Bermudez v. Aldanondo-Rivera*, 496 F.3d 51, 64 (1st Cir. 2007).

23. *Whitehead, Inc.*, 163 F.3d 265, 275–76.

24. *Allstate Ins. Co. v. James*, 845 F.2d 315, 318 (11th Cir. 1988). *See also FDIC v. Stahl*, 89 F.3d 1510, 1519 (11th Cir. 1996) (denying new trial, citing *Allstate*).

25. *Gorio v. Block*, 972 F.2d 1339, 1992 WL 185429, at *6 (9th Cir. 1992) (citing *Mateyko v. Felix*, 924 F.2d 824, 827–28 (9th Cir. 1990), *cert denied*, 502 U.S. 814 (1991) (no error to deny mistrial where counsel made improper statements during examination and closing argument; counsel was made to apologize to opponent and the court gave a curative instruction)).

26. *See Rojas v. Richardson*, 703 F.2d 186, 192 (5th Cir. 1992) (referring to a party as an "illegal alien" was plain error because it was "an obvious and blatant appeal in this case to racial and ethnic prejudice," and required a new trial); *see also Bird v. Glacier Elec. Coop., Inc.*, 255 F.3d 1136, 1150–51 (9th Cir. 2001) (comity not given to tribal judgment when counsel's argument "was replete with appeals to bias, including references to Custer, slavery, the cavalry riding into town to kill, 'white man's magic,' the wealth of the Indian people being taken by the 'conquering people,' and assertions 'that there's an institutional bias in the off reservation society,' and 'functional prejudice [against Indians] that's built in'" because "[t]hese statements were an emotionally-charged appeal to Indian collective memory, encouraging the jury to consider historical racial oppression allegedly perpetrated by the white race against Indians.").

27. *Whitehead*, 163 F.3d at 276 (observing "[t]hat this blatant appeal to sectionalism would be made in a federal court in this day and time is nothing short of amazing," and ordering new trial because counsel's argument included "statements that appealed to local bias," referencing numerous such occasions where "he reminded the jury that Kmart is a national, not local, corporation, with its principal place of business in Troy, Michigan," where

prejudice concerning wealth,[28] or those invoking the golden rule,[29] will also almost automatically lead to a new trial.

"he contrasted that with his status as a Mississippi resident and, implicitly, his clients' similar status: 'as a little old lawyer down here in Mississippi, to take on a national corporation, I knew I had to bring in the best experienced person in security that I knew'; and '[n]ow when I, as a lawyer here in Mississippi, bring a legal action against a national corporation—having done this a few years—they are tough cases'," and where references to Kmart being an out-of-state corporation included "The problem is—way up there in Troy, Michigan—way up there in Troy, Michigan, where they decide to write a two or three inch thick loss prevention manual, they don't think about the customers' safety and security in the parking lot. Because they are more concerned about profits and not people."). *But see Bridgeport Music*, 507 F.3d 470, 478–79 (finding error, but not plain error, when "plaintiffs' counsel argued to the jury, 'This is a joke. They think they can come down here to Nashville, Tennessee, and pull a fast one on the six of you'; argued, "If it is okay to be looked down on and if it is okay to do what the defendants did, then I guess you have to tell them that. But if it is not okay, if in Nashville, Tennessee, we're not going to put up with that, then it is up to you. You six people today stand for the community that we live in"; and "[w]ith respect to punitive damages, plaintiffs' counsel repeatedly asked the jury to 'tell the world that [what defendants did] is not going to happen in Nashville, Tennessee.' Further, "Plaintiffs' counsel also, one time, referred to one of the defendants as a 'multi-million dollar company,' and implied that defendants' expert was 'a fancy guy from New York'.").

28. *United States ex rel. Miller v. Bill Harbert Int'l Constr., Inc.*, 608 F.3d 871, 897–98 (D.C. Cir. 2010) (per curiam) ("[A]rguments to the jury about a defendant's wealth are grounds for new trial," because "[t]he only way the information could have affected the jury was to prejudice it."); *Wash. Annapolis Hotel Co. v. Riddle*, 171 F.2d 732, 740 (D.C. Cir. 1948) (jury argument "that justice should be administered unequally as between the rich and the poor" warranted mistrial).

29. A golden rule argument—which asks "jurors to place themselves in the position of a party," *Prudential Ins. Co. v. N. Am. v. U.S. Gypsum Co.*, 870 F.2d 148, 154 (4th Cir. 1989)—is "'universally condemned because it encourages the jury to depart from neutrality and to decide the case on the basis of personal interest and bias rather than on evidence.'" *Granfield v. CSX Transp., Inc.*, 597 F.3d 474, 491 (1st Cir. 2010) (quotation marks omitted). Improper variations of the golden rule include "(1) to ask jurors how much the loss of the use of their legs would mean to them, *Leathers v. General Motors Corp.*, 546 F.2d 1083, 1085–86 (4th Cir. 1976); (2) to tell jurors "do unto others as you would have them do unto you," *Klotz v. Sears, Roebuck & Co.*, 267 F.2d 53, 54 (7th Cir. 1959); or (3) to tell jurors, in a reverse golden rule argument, "I don't want to ask you to place yourself in [the plaintiff's] position." *Loose v. Offshore Navigation, Inc.*, 670 F.2d 493, 496 (5th Cir. 1982). These golden rule arguments are "per se objectionable" because they have "no legal relevance to any of the real issues . . . ." *Arnold v. E. Air Lines, Inc.*, 681 F.2d 186, 199 (4th Cir. 1982).

28
Final Arguments
The Defense Perspective

Few cases are won in final arguments. As discussed in earlier chapters of this book, most cases are either won or lost during the first days of trial. Juror attitudes are largely set during the first stages of trial, and individual jurors begin to filter what they hear and see in the courtroom. Many jurors consider and adopt evidence supporting their position as the case progresses; they also filter out and reject evidence tending to undermine or contradict their position.

From a practical perspective, this means final arguments should be used for what it really is—an opportunity to provide favorable jurors with cogent arguments they can use to persuade other jurors during deliberation. Final arguments provide opportunities to equip favorable jurors—those jurors inclined to support your position—with ammunition to advocate the key points of your case. The delivery and presentation of messages during final arguments are most effective if you keep this in mind.

Your final argument should also reflect Aristotle's three cornerstones of effective advocacy—*pathos*, *ethos*, and *logos*. As defense lawyers, this means presenting a logical, commonsensical, appealing, and believable story line supported by logical and credible evidence. It also means we should focus on our strengths, the plaintiff's weaknesses, and keep it *simple, simple, simple.*

Preparing for Final Arguments—Daily Copy

Lawyers prepare for final arguments in different ways. A best practice, however, is to identify and reinforce your key evidentiary points the jury will remember in the jury room. This is done by excerpting documents or witness testimony on those points that deserve emphasis and reemphasis. Excerpting testimony from daily copy is a highly effective tool for this purpose. Most court reporters are capable of generating daily transcripts for a fee, and arrangements can be negotiated with court reporters in advance of trial so daily copy is delivered on a daily basis. If the court reporter is not capable of providing such copy, alternative arrangements can be made. I have actually hired the services of a second court reporter for this purpose with leave of court.

Daily copy should be reviewed and highlighted for particularly important testimony. In longer trials, you should try to do this on an ongoing basis to prevent last-minute buildup of unread transcripts. Time is of the essence in trial, and you should make sure you properly allocate your time, which, as the trial progresses, is a valuable but diminishing resource. Thus, your final argument should begin to take shape early in the trial.

You also can use daily copy to remind the jury what the plaintiff's lawyer promised in opening statement, and how these promises were never fulfilled. Actual excerpts from the transcript of an opening statement can be presented to the jury on key promises not kept. You can show how these promises were empty and hollow, making a frontal assault on the plaintiff's case. This is even better than a summary, because the record transcript is the most credible source of what happened and what was said.

The jury will understand that daily copy excerpts reflect actual testimony or attorney statements and not a summary of the testimony. Believability is enhanced significantly.

Preparing Final Arguments—Key Exhibits

You should select only the most important exhibits for use in final arguments, and always avoid exhibit fatigue. Too many exhibits can be numbing to the listener—the jury—and distract from the power of your argument.

Key exhibits should be scanned into a PowerPoint presentation or blown up as bigger-than-life enlargements. They also can be placed on overhead projectors. You may wish to elect more simple technology to avoid the impression that your case is slick and your client has lots of money.

Some courts allow binders with key exhibits to be provided to the jury. If this is the case, select only the exhibits you really need. You do not want the jury to get lost in a maze of less significant exhibits. Binders can be very helpful. They can also become cumbersome and distracting.

Like other aspects of effective trial advocacy, messages in final arguments should be simple and understandable. Again, this is accomplished by focusing on fewer documents rather than many documents.

Final Arguments in Lengthy or Complex Trials

In particularly lengthy or complex trials, those lasting more than one week, or trials having more than just a few witnesses, the jury may forget who the witnesses were, how they fit into the evidentiary mosaic, or what they said. An effective practice for final arguments is to use photographs of the witnesses—usually extracted from a clip from video depositions—and create a poster board presentation with pictures of the witnesses' faces. Combining a witness's picture with excerpts from daily copy of their testimony helps drive their testimony point home. This is a quick and easy way to remind the jury of who said what and when.

The Jury Charge

Plaintiff's lawyers *always* argue the jury charge during final arguments. Plaintiff's counsel sometimes use poster boards with jury questions enlarged; some use PowerPoint presentations with slides incorporating jury questions. I also have seen flip charts. They then pencil-in or ink-in suggested answers. They will encourage the jury to answer "yes" to liability questions, causation questions, and then write in damage numbers. As defense lawyers, we should be mindful of this strategy and be prepared to provide our own suggested answers. Again, enlarged copies of the jury charge on poster boards is an excellent, simple device for delivering messages. Overhead projectors also work well. PowerPoint presentations are perhaps the most sophisticated approach and are managed easily. Defense lawyers should be prepared to argue the charge and why the evidence does not support the plaintiff's claims.

An effective technique is to present a jury question on a video screen via PowerPoint, present the suggested defense answer on the same slide, and then identify in a slide that immediately follows specific evidence supporting the defense argument. Direct quotes from excerpted testimony can be presented in this manner. This effectively sends messages to the jury that they will likely remember when they retire to the jury room. You are providing a specific link between the question to specific evidence in the record. You are essentially connecting dots for the jury.

Using Flip Charts

Another effective technique is to use flip charts during final arguments. During cross-examination of the plaintiff's witnesses, as well as during direct examination of defense witnesses, key points of the witness's testimony can be written on a flip chart, dated, and identified by witness name. This should be done on a witness-by-witness basis. The plaintiff's witnesses may make significant concessions or admissions about the defense case. These admissions or concessions are available and should be reflected on flip charts. The jury's attention will be focused on the lawyer's actions when recording the witness's testimony. Wherever possible, exact quotes are preferred, and quotation marks should be used.

Then, during final arguments, defense lawyers can refer back to the flip chart and recall the jury's attention to these significant moments during the trial. Once again, these flip charts help connect the dots of who said what and when. The fact that these testimonial tidbits are recorded on the flip chart also reinforces the message that this particular testimony is important and reinforces the testimony significance with the jury. The jury actually saw the flip chart evolve, which reinforces its significance.

Demonstratives

Demonstratives are frequently used during trial and, as such, should be used during final arguments to reinforce themes. Demonstratives also can be created for purposes of final arguments. Both will be discussed here.

In my experience, preparing effective demonstratives—charts, PowerPoint slides, etc.—is helpful during *opening* statements. If these same charts are used during witness examinations, the defense messages are reinforced with witnesses. Then, using the same demonstratives in *final* arguments closes the evidentiary circle and, once again, reinforces defense themes. It brings closure to the case. The demonstratives are an effective medium of repeatedly driving home a message.

I also have created demonstratives for specific use in final arguments. One very effective demonstrative is to compare the plaintiff's experts with the defense experts. A chart can be created demonstrating what each expert did, and in the appropriate case, what the plaintiff's experts failed to do. If the case is an expert-heavy, technical case, these types of comparative charts can be an effective advocacy tool. An example follows:

Topic	Plaintiff's Expert	Defense Expert
Post-Graduate Degree	No	Yes
Doctoral Degree	No	Yes
Technical Licenses/Certification	No	Yes
Years of Experience	5 Years	14 Years
Specific Design Experience with Manufactured Products	No	Yes
Prior History of Testifying for Same Plaintiff's Lawyer in Other Cases	8 Times	None
Dynamic Testing	No	Yes
When First Retained	30 Days before Designation	4 Months Before Designation

This referenced chart is clearly one-sided for illustrative purposes only.[1] But, it shows how a comparison between a plaintiff's expert and a defense expert can be effectively presented to the jury when technical issues are driving liability or causation issues. Clearly, an illustrated chart can demonstrate that the defense expert had more time to develop his or her opinions, participated in testing, and was not dependent upon the defense lawyer for business. The chart also demonstrates that the plaintiff's expert is less credentialed and is dependent upon the plaintiff's lawyer for business. This translates into a lack of objectivity and bias and raises questions in the jurors' minds. The goal is to advocate your expert's qualifications and methodologies over the plaintiff's expert.

Pathos

Pathos is always important. The jury must *want* to vote for you. In this context, defense lawyers should be prepared to counter the plaintiff's pleas for sympathy.

One of the most effective plaintiff's final arguments I have heard occurred in a trial where I was opposed by my co-author, Mikal Watts. Appealing to the jury's sense of right and wrong, the argument relating to the value of a human life free of pain and injury incorporated the following poignant concepts:

> Ladies and Gentlemen of the jury, please consider the value of a masterpiece of art. This master work of art is appraised at over $20 million, and it is hanging on the wall

1. Using this type of chart was first brought to my attention by Jerry Glas, an experienced trial lawyer and head of the litigation section at the firm of Deutsch Kerrigan, LLP in New Orleans, Louisiana.

in a famous museum. It is protected by security guards at the entryways and exits. There are burglar alarms and fire alarms to protect the painting. Now, please consider the value of an older woman in her 70s or 80s, standing alone in front of this famous piece of art looking upon it with adoration and wonder. Suddenly, without notice, an emergency occurs. A flash fire breaks out in the room housing the master work of art and where the old woman is standing. She is becoming trapped. Smoke is quickly filling the room. The fire doors are beginning to close. You have an opportunity to save either the piece of art or the lady's life. Which do you choose?

The lesson here is simple. The older woman's life, even at an advanced age, is priceless, and certainly worth more than a piece of art—which, again, is worth $20,000,000. Although a jury is instructed to set aside bias and prejudice as part of the legal charge, all trial lawyers appeal to the heartstrings of the jury, as well as to jurors' minds. It is always important to develop empathy; it is also important to have juries emotionally invest in your case. You always should expect skilled plaintiff's lawyers to inspire either fear, anger, or sadness in their arguments. You should be prepared to counter these appeals.

Preparing for Final Arguments—Delivery

As discussed in earlier chapters, the attention span of an average juror is short. Thus, rarely should a final argument last more than 30 to 45 minutes. Prolonged arguments lose focus; they become boring; they may become alienating. Thus, as a general rule of thumb, brevity is preferred.

Again, most jurors have made up their mind by the time final arguments occur. Prolonged arguments focusing on the details of the evidence is not needed at this point. Rather, the argument should focus on key defense themes and key evidence. Accordingly, it is doubtful that an argument lasting more than 45 minutes is necessary. To be clear, there is a diminishing return with extended arguments. The longer the argument, the less effective it will become. The jury may become confused by what is truly significant and what is less significant. Therefore, final arguments should be reserved only for significant sound bites and related advocacy concerning those sound bites.

For many jurors, the trial experience is new. They come into the courtroom with varying expectations of how a trial is conducted, and they typically look forward to hearing lawyers argue. Of course, final arguments—like voir dire and opening statements—is one of the few opportunities we can talk directly to jurors. Thus, this valuable time should not be squandered on needless, less significant detail. Stay out of the weeds. Your final argument should be artfully crafted to include drama, power, self-confidence, and believability. This allows defense jurors to retire to the jury room with ammunition to advocate your case. Echoing similar practice tips as they relate to other stages of the trial, the goal is to keep it simple, succinct, and loaded with certainty and confidence.

29
Posttrial Motions
The Plaintiff's Perspective

A motion for judgment as a matter of law under Rule 50(a) of the Federal Rules of Civil Procedure is filed prior to submitting the case to the jury and alleges that no evidence exists on a necessary element of proof. A Rule 50(b) renewed motion for judgment as a matter of law, also known as a motion for judgment non obstante veredicto (judgment notwithstanding the verdict, or *judgment n.o.v.* (j.n.o.v.)) is filed after the jury's verdict. A motion under Rule 50(b) after the verdict can be filed only if a motion under Rule 50(a) was filed before the case was submitted to the jury. A motion for new trial under Rule 59 likewise can be filed after judgment is entered. Finally, a motion to set aside the judgment is available under Rule 60(b) for up to one year after the judgment. This chapter discusses the details any careful trial lawyer must know in planning for and filing posttrial motions.

Motions for Judgment as a Matter of Law or Judgment Notwithstanding the Verdict

After a party "has been fully heard on an issue" and "at any time before the case is submitted to the jury," a party may move under Rule 50(a) for judgment as a matter of law.[1] Oftentimes, the court denies such motions without prejudice, and thereby is considered under Rule 50(b) "to have submitted the action to the jury subject to the court's later deciding the legal questions raised by the motion."[2] After the jury has rendered its verdict, a party may renew its motion for judgment as a matter of law under Rule 50(b) with a posttrial motion often referred to as a j.n.o.v.

1. Fed. R. Civ. P. 50(a).
2. Fed. R. Civ. P. 50(b).

Preserving Issues for Appeal Normally Requires a Rule 50(a)(2) Motion for Judgment as a Matter of Law before the Case Is Submitted to the Jury

Rule 50(a)(2) requires that a motion for judgment as a matter of law be made "before the case is submitted to the jury" and "must specify the judgment sought and the law and facts that entitle the movant to the judgment."[3] "[A] motion for j.n.o.v. is technically a renewal of a motion for a directed verdict";[4] thus, Rule 50(b) "generally proscribes judgment n.o.v. on any ground not specifically raised in an earlier motion for a directed verdict at the close of all the evidence."[5] Thus, "[a] motion under Rule 50(b) is not allowed unless the movant sought relief on similar grounds under Rule 50(a) before the case was submitted to the jury."[6] "The perfectly defensible rationale for this requirement is to 'prevent[ ] a party who loses at trial from using a j.n.o.v. motion as a 'trap' after it is too late for the winner of the verdict to cure any alleged deficiencies of proof.'"[7] Consequently, "[u]nder normal circumstances, a defendant's failure to raise an issue in a Rule 50(a)(2) motion with sufficient specificity to put the plaintiffs on notice waives the defendant's right to raise the issue in their Rule 50(b) motion."[8] This means that the "plain error" standard of review will apply, in which an appellate court will reverse only if "the judgment complained of results in a 'manifest miscarriage of justice.'"[9]

Receiving the Verdict with Class

The precursor to effective posttrial motions is the ability to absorb the jury's adverse verdict with class. Frankly, the defendant, their counsel, the court, and the court's staff, each deserve unmitigated professionalism. However, whether the verdict of any case cuts against local defendants, the plaintiff's lawyer has the singular opportunity to market his verdicts. Thus, the skilled plaintiff's lawyer should absorb losses with professionalism and show dignity to opponents when victory is achieved. Keep in mind that judges, their clerks, and their staff are watching everything, and inappropriate responses to a jury's verdict can irreparably damage a lawyer's chances of success during the post-verdict motion phase.

As a matter of course, parties losing a jury trial should ask the court to poll the jury to ensure that the verdict is indeed the verdict of each juror. Given the uniformly strict case law prohibiting consideration of internal jury deliberations in deciding posttrial motions, ensuring that each juror in fact agreed with the verdict must be done in the courtroom by having

---

3. Fed. R. Civ. P. 50(a)(2).
4. *Meriwether v. Coughlin*, 879 F.2d 1037, 1044 (2d Cir. 1989).
5. *Doctor's Assoc., Inc. v. Weible*, 92 F.3d 108, 112 (2d Cir. 1996).
6. *Exxon Shipping Co. v. Baker*, 554 U.S. 471, 519, n. 5 (2008).
7. *Id.* (quoting *Meriwether*, 879 F.2d at 1044); *see also Lambert v. Genesee Hosp.*, 10 F.3d 46, 54 (2d Cir. 1993), *cert. denied*, 511 U.S. 1052 (1994) ("the specificity requirement is obligatory and ensures that the other party is made aware of any deficiencies in proof that may have been overlooked").
8. *Williams v. Runyon*, 130 F.3d 568, 571–72 (3d Cir. 1997) (citing 9A Charles Alan Wright & Arthur R. Miller, Federal Practice and Procedure § 2533 (1995) ("The law is crystal clear that a party may not base its motion for a judgment n.o.v. on a ground that was not argued in its motion for directed verdict.") (internal quotations omitted).
9. *Seibert v. Jackson Cty., Miss.*, 851 F.3d 430, 434–35 (5th Cir. 2017) (quoting *U.S. for Use of Wallace v. Flintco, Inc.*, 143 F.3d 955, 963–64 (5th Cir. 1998)).

the judge poll the jurors. When the jury's answers are "consistent with each other but one or more is inconsistent with the general verdict," the court may "direct the jury to further consider its answers and verdict."[10] Further, answers to polling inquiries received in court may give rise to a motion for new trial or inoculate a verdict from a motion for new trial.

Entering the Judgment

Rule 58(a) generally calls for a judgment to be entered after the trial ends. "A party may request that judgment be set out in a separate document as required by Rule 58(a)."[11] However, pursuant to Rule 58(b)(1), "the clerk must, without awaiting the court's direction, promptly prepare, sign, and enter the judgment when: (A) the jury returns a general verdict; (B) the court awards only costs or a sum certain; or (C) the court denies all relief."[12] Pursuant to Rule 58(b)(2), "the court must promptly approve the form of the judgment, which the clerk must promptly enter, when: (A) the jury returns a special verdict or a general verdict with answers to written questions; or (B) the court grants other relief not described in this subdivision (b)."[13]

When the jury's answers are "consistent with each other but one or more is inconsistent with the general verdict," the court may "approve, for entry under Rule 58, an appropriate judgment according to the answers, notwithstanding the general verdict."[14]

Deadline for Filing a Motion for Judgment N.O.V.

After discharge of the jury, and if "the motion addresses a jury issue not decided by a verdict," the Rule 50(a) movant "may file a renewed motion for judgment as a matter of law and may include an alternative or joint request for a new trial under Rule 59."[15] However, if the motion does not address "a jury issue not decided by a verdict," then a renewed motion for entry of judgment as a matter of law is due "[n]o later than 28 days after the entry of judgment."[16]

Reasons for Granting a Motion for Judgment N.O.V.

"The question before the district court regarding a motion for judgment as a matter of law remains whether the evidence is 'legally sufficient to find for the party on that issue.'"[17] Identically, but only after the jury returns its verdict, a motion for "[j]udgment notwithstanding the verdict raises the issue of whether there was a question of fact for the jury to decide."[18]

---

10. Fed. R. Civ. P. 49(b)(3)(B).
11. Fed. R. Civ. P. 58(d).
12. Fed. R. Civ. P. 58(b)(1).
13. Fed. R. Civ. P. 58(b)(2).
14. Fed. R. Civ. P. 49(b)(3)(A).
15. *Lexington Ins. Co. v. Horace Mann Ins. Co.*, 861 F.3d 661, 668 (7th Cir. 2017).
16. *Id.*
17. *Collins v. Marriott Int'l, Inc.*, 749 F.3d 951, 957 (11th Cir. 2014) (quoting *Chaney v. City of Orlando*, 483 F.3d 1221, 1227 (11th Cir. 2007)).
18. *Hawley v. Dresser Industries, Inc.*, 958 F.2d 720, 723 (6th Cir. 1992) (citing *Chappell v. GTE Products Corp.*, 803 F.2d 261, 265 (6th Cir.), *cert. denied*, 480 U.S. 919 (1987)).

If there is no evidence of,[19] or no required finding on,[20] a required element of liability, then the district court should grant a motion for judgment n.o.v. Likewise, if the record "contains insufficient evidence to support an award of damages, then judgment n.o.v. may be granted as to those damages not supported by the evidence."[21] While ruling on a renewed motion for judgment as a matter of law, the district court may, "[o]n a party's motion filed no later than 28 days after the entry of judgment, . . . amend its findings—or make additional findings—and may amend the judgment accordingly."[22]

Appellate Review of Rule 50 Judgment N.O.V. Is De Novo

An appellate court reviews "de novo the district court's disposition of the motion for judgment as a matter of law pursuant to Federal Rule of Civil Procedure 50(b),"[23] applying "the same standard as the district court."[24] Whether reviewing a district court's granting or denial of a Rule 50(b) motion, the appellate court will "review all the evidence in the record and construe that evidence in the light most favorable to the nonmoving party,"[25]

---

19. *Smith v. Cook Cty.*, 74 F.3d 829, 834 (7th Cir. 1996) (finding no evidence of pretext, affirming district court's judgment n.o.v., while noting "the court examined each piece of evidence presented by Smith and concluded, as do we, that none of the evidence provides any support for a finding of pretext," and observing that "[a]dding together a string of nothings still yields nothing.").

20. *See Romero v. Int'l Harvester Co.*, 979 F.2d 1444, 1454 (10th Cir. 1992) ("under Colorado law, Navistar could only be liable for breaching its duty to warn or protect purchasers of its tractors if those tractors were discovered to have been defective as originally manufactured, under standards applicable to tractors at that time. The jury's finding of no defect and no negligence in design relieved Navistar of any liability for breach of that duty. The district court should therefore have granted Navistar's motion for judgment n.o.v."); *see generally King v. General Elect. Co.*, 960 F.2d 617, 627 (7th Cir. 1992) ("'We do . . . weigh the evidence to the extent of determining whether the evidence is *substantial*; a mere scintilla of evidence will not suffice.' As we have discussed, we believe there was not substantial evidence to support the jury's finding that G.E. engaged in a pattern or practice of discrimination from 1982 until 1985.").

21. *Schmueser v. Burkburnett Bank*, 937 F.2d 1025, 1030 (5th Cir. 1991) (citing *Silor v. Romero*, 868 F.2d 1419, 1422 (5th Cir. 1989)).

22. Fed. R. Civ. P. 52(b).

23. *Armstrong ex rel. Armstrong v. Brookdale Univ. Hosp. and Med. Ctr.*, 425 F.3d 126, 133 (2d Cir. 2005) (citing *Cobb v. Pozzi*, 363 F.3d 89, 101 (2d Cir. 2004)); *see also Encana Oil & Gas (USA) Inc. v. Zaremba Family Farms, Inc.*, 736 F. App'x 557, 564 (6th Cir. 2018) (citing *Mich. First Credit Union v. CUMIS Ins. Soc., Inc.*, 641 F.3d 240, 245 (6th Cir. 2011) ("We review the denial of a motion for judgment as a matter of law de novo.")); *Baugh v. Cuprum S.A. de C.V.*, 845 F.3d 838, 848–49 (7th Cir. 2017) (same); *Murray v. Frye*, 178 F.3d 1284, 1999 WL 267424, at *3 (4th Cir. 1999) (unpublished table decision) (citing *DiMeglio v. Haines*, 45 F.3d 790, 794 (4th Cir. 1995) (same)).

24. *Collins*, 749 F.3d at 956–57 (citing *Pickett v. Tyson Fresh Meats, Inc.*, 420 F.3d 1272, 1278 (11th Cir. 2005)); *see also Burke v. Regalado*, 935 F.3d 960, 991 (10th Cir. 2019) (citing *Etherton v. Owners Ins. Co.*, 829 F.3d 1209, 1224 (10th Cir. 2016) (same)); *Cote v. R.J. Reynolds Tobacco Co.*, 909 F.3d 1094, 1103–04 (11th Cir. 2018) (citing *Goldsmith v. Bagby Elevator Co.*, 513 F.3d 1261, 1275 (11th Cir. 2008)).

25. *Iles v. Autozone Stores, Inc.*, 12 F. App'x 627, 630 (10th Cir. 2001) (citing *Tyler v. RE/MAX Mountain States, Inc.*, 232 F.3d 808, 812)); *see also Seibert v. Jackson Cty. Miss.*, 851 F.3d 432, 434–35 (2nd Cir. 1996) (citing *Cowart v. Erwin*, 837 F.3d 444, 450 (5th Cir. 2016) ("In resolving such challenges, we must draw 'all reasonable inferences and resolve all credibility determinations in the light most favorable to the nonmoving party' and uphold the verdict 'unless there is no legally sufficient evidentiary basis for a reasonable jury to find as the jury did.'")); *Baugh v. Cuprum S.A. de C.V.*, 845 F.3d 843, 848–49 (7th Cir. 2017) (citing *Venson v. Altamirano*, 749 F.3d 641, 646 (7th Cir. 2014) (appellate court must "view the evidence in the light most favorable to Baugh as the non-moving party.")); *Doctor's Assoc., Inc. v. Weible*, 92 F.3d 108, 111–12 (2nd Cir. 1996) (quoting *Baskin v. Hawley*, 807 F.2d 1120, 1129 (2d Cir. 1986)) ("Judgment n.o.v. is proper 'only if the evidence viewed in the light most favorable to the non-movants, without considering credibility or weight, reasonably permits only a conclusion in the movant's favor.'")); *King v. General Electric Co.*, 960 F.2d 617, 627 (7th Cir. 1992) (citing *Graefenhain v. Pabst Brewing Co.*, 827 F.2d 13, 15 (7th Cir. 1987) ("A judgment n.o.v. is properly granted where the evidence presented, combined with all reasonable inferences that may be drawn from it, is insufficient . . . when viewed in the light most favorable to the non-moving party."));

and "must not engage in a weighing or evaluation of the evidence or consider questions of credibility."[26] Using that standard of review, a judgment "n.o.v. is 'improper' if, after viewing the evidence and inferences in the light most favorable to the non-moving party, 'reasonable minds could differ over the verdict.'"[27] Conversely, "[j]udgment as a matter of law is only appropriate 'if the evidence points but one way and is susceptible to no reasonable inferences which may support the opposing party's position,'"[28] when there is "either an utter lack of evidence supporting the verdict, so that the jury's findings could only have resulted from pure guess-work, or the evidence must be 'so overwhelming that reasonable and fair-minded persons could only have reached the opposite result,'"[29] or when there is "such a complete absence of evidence supporting the verdict that the jury's findings could only have been the result of sheer surmise and conjecture, or . . . such an overwhelming amount of evidence in favor of the movant that reasonable and fair minded [jurors] could not arrive at a verdict against him."[30]

Motions for a New Trial

Motions for new trial must be filed no later than twenty-eight days after the entry of judgment. The grounds for a new trial may involve inconsistencies in the jury's answers or grounds historically recognized by courts, including but not limited to, that the verdict is against the weight of the evidence, that the damages are excessive, or that, for other reasons, the trial was not fair to the moving party, such as arguments that a party failed to

---

Hawley v. Dresser Indus., Inc., 958 F.2d 720, 723 (6th Cir. 1992) (citing *Toth v. Yoder Co.*, 749 F.2d 1190, 1194 (6th Cir. 1984) ("In determining whether the evidence is insufficient as a matter of law to support a judgment, a court must view the evidence in the light most favorable to the party against whom the motion for j.n.o.v. is made.")).

26. *Douglas Cty. Bank & Trust Co. v. United Fin. Inc.*, 207 F.3d 473, 477 (8th Cir. 2000); *see also Kirschner v. Office of Comptroller of City of N.Y.*, 973 F.2d 88, 92 (2nd Cir. 1992) (conducting review "without weighing the credibility of the witnesses or otherwise considering the weight of the evidence . . . ."); *Iles*, 12 F. App'x at 630 (quoting *United Int'l Holdings, Inc. v. Wharf (Holdings) Ltd.*, 210 F.3d 1207, 1227 (10th Cir.), *cert. granted in part*, 531 U.S. 978 (2000) ("[t] he jury has the exclusive function of appraising credibility, determining the weight to be given to the testimony, drawing inferences from the facts established, resolving conflicts in the evidence, and reaching ultimate conclusions of fact.")); *Collins*, 749 F.3d 951 at 956–57 (citing *Reeves v. Sanderson Plumbing Prods., Inc.*, 530 U.S. 133, 150 (2000) (the court "may not make credibility determinations or weigh the evidence")); *Baty v. Willamette Indus., Inc.*, 172 F.3d 1232, 1241 (10th Cir. 1999) (quoting *Harolds Stores, Inc. v. Dillard Dep't Stores*, 82 F.3d 1533, 1546–47 (10th Cir. 1996) ("We do not weigh the evidence, pass on the credibility of the witnesses, or substitute our conclusions for [those] of the jury.")).

27. *Stranger v. Sears, Roebuck & Co.*, 904 F.2d 41, 1990 WL 71470, at *1 (unpublished table decision) (citing *Peterson v. Kennedy*, 771 F.2d 1244, 1252 (9th Cir. 1985), *cert. denied*, 475 U.S. 1122 (1986)); *see also Burke*, 935 F.3d at 991 (citing *Elm Ridge Exploration Co. v. Engle*, 721 F.3d 1199, 1216 (10th Cir. 2013) ("Judgment as a matter of law is appropriate only if the evidence points but one way and is susceptible to no reasonable inferences which may support the nonmoving party's position.")); *Baugh* 845 F.3d at 848–49 (" . . . will reverse the district judge's decision only if no rational jury could have found in Baugh's favor").

28. *Iles*, 12 F. App'x at 630; *see generally Quoc Viet Foods, Inc. v. VV Foods, LLC*, 761 F. App'x 784, 785 (9th Cir. 2019) (reinstating the jury verdict as to validity and infringement).

29. *Doctor's Assoc.*, 92 F.3d at 112 (citing *Mattivi v. South African Marine Corp., Huguenot*, 618 F.2d 163, 167–68 (2d Cir. 1990)); *see also Cote*, 909 F.3d at 1104 (citing *Bhogaita v. Altamonte Heights Condo Ass'n, Inc.*, 765 F.3d 1277, 1285 (11th Cir. 2014) (" . . . we 'disturb the jury's verdict only when there is no material conflict in the evidence, such that no reasonable person could agree to the verdict reached.'")); *Wisconsin Alumni Research Found. v. Apple Inc.*, 905 F.3d 1341, 1346–47 (2018). ("A jury verdict will be overturned only if no reasonable juror could have found in the non-movant's favor.")

30. *Kirschner*, 973 F.2d at 92; *see also Dunkin' Donuts of America, Inc. v. Minerva, Inc.*, 956 F.2d 1566, 1569 (11th Cir. 1992) ("If the facts and inferences point overwhelmingly in favor of the moving party, such that a reasonable jury could not arrive at a contrary verdict, then the motion should be granted.").

produce materials in discovery, evidence was admitted or excluded in error, or that argument by counsel was improper. Whatever the grounds, the movant must prove that the error alleged was not harmless. Trial courts have broad discretion in deciding the issue, with appellate courts applying the lenient abuse of discretion standard in reviewing orders regarding new trial motions.

Deadline to File a Motion for a New Trial

Rule 50(d) requires that "[a]ny motion for a new trial under Rule 59 by a party against whom judgment as a matter of law is rendered must be filed no later than 28 days after the entry of the judgment." Likewise, Rule 59(b) requires that "[a] motion for a new trial must be filed no later than 28 days after the entry of judgment," and Rule 59(d) says that "[n]o later than 28 days after the entry of judgment, the court, on its own, may order a new trial for any reason that would justify granting one on a party's motion. After giving the parties notice and an opportunity to be heard, the court may grant a timely motion for a new trial for a reason not stated in the motion. In either event, the court must specify the reasons in its order."

Rule 59(c) says that "[w]hen a motion for a new trial is based on affidavits, they must be filed with the motion," that "[t]he opposing party has 14 days after being served to file opposing affidavits," and that "[t]he court may permit reply affidavits."[31] Furthermore, after a nonjury trial, Rule 59(a)(2) says "the court may, on motion for a new trial, open the judgment if one has been entered, take additional testimony, amend findings of fact and conclusions of law or make new ones, and direct the entry of a new judgment."[32]

Rule 50(c)(1) expressly states that "[i]f the renewed motion for judgment as a matter of law is granted, the court shall also rule on the motion for a new trial. . . ."[33] Thus, if a trial court grants judgment as a matter of law, it also is required to rule at that time on any alternative new trial motion[34] and errs if it fails "to rule on [the] motion for a new trial contemporaneously with the motion for judgment as a matter of law. . . ."[35] Rule 50(c)(2) "gives a party whose jury verdict is set aside by a trial court 10 days in which to invoke the trial court's discretion to order a new trial."[36]

Reasons for Granting a Motion for a New Trial

The Federal Rules of Civil Procedure provide numerous mechanisms with which the trial court may grant a motion for a new trial.

31. Fed. R. Civ. P. 59(c).

32. Fed. R. Civ. P. 59(a)(2).

33. Fed. R. Civ. P. 50(c)(1).

34. *Johnstone v. American Oil Co.*, 7 F.3d 1217, 1224 (5th Cir. 1993), *order on reh'g vacated pending bankruptcy proceedings*, 17 F.3d 728 (5th Cir. 1994); *see also* 9 Charles Alan Wright, Arthur R. Miller & Mary Kay Kane, Federal Practice and Procedure § 2539, n.75 (1973) (listing cases).

35. *Arenson v. S. Univ. Law Ctr.*, 43 F.3d 194, 196 (5th Cir. 1995).

36. *Neely v. Martin K. Eby Const. Co.*, 386 U.S. 317, 321 (1967).

The Jury's Answers May Give Rise to a New Trial

Rule 48(c) states that the court "may order a new trial" if the jury polling "reveals a lack of unanimity or lack of assent by the number of jurors that the parties stipulated to."[37] First, Rule 49(b)(3)(C) provides that "[w]hen the answers are consistent with each other but one or more is inconsistent with the general verdict, the court may: . . . (C) order a new trial."[38] Second, "[w]hen the answers are inconsistent with each other and one or more is also inconsistent with the general verdict, judgment must not be entered; instead, the court must direct the jury to further consider its answers and verdict, or must order a new trial."[39]

"When a new trial motion asserts that the jury verdict is not supported by the evidence, the verdict must stand unless it is clearly, decidedly, or overwhelmingly against the weight of the evidence."[40] Thus, "[a] verdict will stand if it is supported by substantial evidence";[41] however, a new trial may be granted "where the verdict is against the clear weight of the evidence or to prevent injustice."[42] In considering a Rule 59 motion for new trial based on the jury's answers, the district court has "the duty . . . to weigh the evidence as [the court] saw it, and to set aside the verdict of the jury, even though supported by substantial evidence, where, in [the court's] conscientious opinion, the verdict is contrary to the clear weight of the evidence."[43] While "[a] district court's discretion in this area is particularly broad,"[44] "[c]ourts cannot reweigh the evidence and set aside a jury verdict because the jury could have drawn different conclusions or inferences or because the court feels that other results are more reasonable."[45] "A motion for a new trial ordinarily should not be granted unless the trial court is convinced that the jury has reached a seriously erroneous result or that the verdict is a miscarriage of justice."[46]

Other Reasons That Justify a New Trial

Rule 59(a)(1) also provides that "[t]he court may, on motion, grant a new trial on all or some of the issues—and to any party—as follows: (A) after a jury trial, for any reason for which a new trial has heretofore been granted in an action at law in federal court; or (B) after a non-jury trial, for any reason for which a rehearing has heretofore been granted in a suit in equity in federal court." "Rule 59 does not specify the grounds on which a motion for a new trial

---

37. Fed. R. Civ. P. 48(c).

38. Fed. R. Civ. P. 49(b)(3)(C).

39. Fed. R. Civ. P. 49(b)(4).

40. *Burke*, 935 F.3d at 991 (citing *Ryan Dev. Co. v. Indiana Lumbermens Mut. Ins. Co.*, 711 F.3d 1165, 1172 (10th Cir. 2013) (quotations omitted)).

41. *Ratliff v. Schiber Truck Co., Inc.*, 150 F.3d 949, 952 (8th Cir. 1998) (citing *Purchal v. Patterson*, 762 F.2d 713, 715 (8th Cir. 1985)).

42. *Ratliff*, 150 F.3d at 952 (citing *Fireman's Fund Ins. Co. v. Aalco Wrecking Co., Inc.*, 466 F.2d 179, 186 (8th Cir. 1972), *cert. denied*, 410 U.S. 930 (1973)).

43. *Molski v. M.J. Cable, Inc.*, 481 F.3d 724, 729 (9th Cir. 2007) (citing *Murphy v. City of Long Beach*, 914 F.2d 183, 187 (9th Cir. 1990) (quotation omitted)).

44. *York v. Amer. Tel. & Tel. Co.*, 95 F.3d 948, 958 (10th Cir. 1996).

45. *Ratliff*, 150 F.3d at 952 (citing *Tennant v. Peoria and Pekin Union Ry.*, 321 U.S. 29, 35 (1944)).

46. *Armstrong*, 425 F.3d 126, 133.

may be granted," rather, the court is "bound by those grounds that have been historically recognized."[47] Historically recognized grounds include but are not limited to claims "that the verdict is against the weight of the evidence, that the damages are excessive, or that, for other reasons, the trial was not fair to the party moving."[48]

Failure to Produce Materials in Discovery

"A new trial may be warranted for discovery misconduct when the movant can: '(1) prove by clear and convincing evidence that the verdict was obtained through . . . misconduct,' and '(2) establish that the conduct complained of prevented the losing party from fully and fairly presenting his case or defense'"; thus, a "[f]ailure to produce materials requested in discovery can constitute 'misconduct' for Rule 59 purposes."[49] Importantly, this may also give rise to a subsequently filed motion for relief for judgment under Rule 60(b)(2) with respect to "newly discovered evidence that, with reasonable diligence, could not have been discovered in time to move for a new trial under Rule 59(b)."[50]

Evidentiary Rulings That Were in Error

"'[N]ew trials should not be granted on evidentiary grounds unless, at a minimum, the verdict is against the great—not merely the greater—weight of the evidence.'"[51] If, however, "'evidence of a critical nature [wa]s [improperly] excluded and there is no reasonable assurance that the jury would have reached the same conclusion had the evidence been admitted,'" then a motion for new trial should be granted.[52]

No New Trial for Harmless Error

In considering a motion for new trial, the district court must be guided first by Rule 103(a) of the Federal Rules of Evidence and by Rule 61 of the Federal Rules of Civil Procedure. Rule 103(a) says that "[a] party may claim error in a ruling to admit or exclude evidence only if the error affects a substantial right of the party."[53] Rule 61 says that "[u]nless justice requires otherwise, no error in admitting or excluding evidence—or any other error by the court or a party—is ground for granting a new trial, . . ." and that "[a]t every stage of the proceeding, the court must disregard all errors and defects that do not affect any party's substantial rights."[54] An error affects a substantial right of the party only if "there is a significant chance

47. *Molski*, 481 F.3d at 729 (citing *Zhang v. Am. Gem Seafoods, Inc.*, 339 F.3d 1020, 1035 (9th Cir. 2003)).

48. *Id.* at 729 (citing *Montgomery Ward & Co. v. Dunn*, 311 U.S. 243, 251 (1940)).

49. *King v. GEICO Indem. Co.*, 712 F. App'x 649, 651–52 (9th Cir. 2017) (citing *Jones v. Aero/Chem Corp.*, 921 F.2d 875, 878–79 (9th Cir. 1990)).

50. Fed. R. Civ. P. 60(b).

51. *Cote*, 909 F.3d at 1103 (citing *Hewitt v. B.F. Goodrich Co.*, 732 F.2d 1554, 1556 (11th Cir. 1984) (quotation omitted)).

52. *Townsend v. Bayer Corp.*, 774 F.3d 446, 460–61 (8th Cir. 2014) (citing *Harris v. Chand*, 506 F.3d 1135, 1140 (8th Cir. 2007)).

53. Fed. R. Evid. 103(a).

54. Fed. R. Civ. P. 61.

that the error affected the jury's verdict."[55] However, where "there are several errors, each of which is harmless in its own right, a new trial may still be granted if the cumulative effect of those otherwise harmless errors deprives a litigant of a fair trial."[56]

Appellate Review of Orders on a New Trial

Appellate court review of district court rulings on motions for new trial may differ slightly, depending on whether a new trial is granted or denied below.

Review of Denials of Motions for a New Trial

A more deferential standard applies when an appellate court reviews "a district court's denial of a motion for a new trial. . . ."[57] A district court's denial of a motion for new trial may be reversed only for an abuse of discretion, "with the key question being whether a new trial is necessary to prevent a miscarriage of justice."[58]

"A district court has broad discretion in deciding whether to grant a new trial on weight-of-the-evidence grounds,"[59] and "[b]ecause determining 'the clear weight of the evidence' is a fact-specific endeavor, appeals courts are reluctant to second-guess district courts' conclusions."[60] Therefore, when a motion claiming a new trial is appropriate because the jury's verdict was against the clear weight of the evidence is denied below, an appellate court will "draw all inferences from the evidence in favor of the non-moving party, and [will] not weigh the evidence or judge witness credibility."[61] A court will only reverse "where there is an absolute absence of evidence to support the jury's verdict"[62] or when "the verdict is clearly, decidedly, or overwhelmingly against the weight of the evidence,"[63] and conversely,

55. *Barber v. City of Chicago*, 725 F.3d 702, 715 (7th Cir. 2013) (citing *Jordan v. Binns*, 712 F.3d 1123, 1137 (7th Cir. 2013); *3M v. Pribyl*, 259 F.3d 587, 599 (7th Cir. 2001); *Kotteakos v. United States*, 328 U.S. 750, 761–65 (1946) ("To make this determination, we examine the error in light of the entire record, and a new trial will be granted only if we are unable to say with fair assurance that the error did not substantially sway the jury.")).

56. *Jordan v. Binns*, 712 F.3d at 1137 (citing *Christmas v. City of Chicago*, 682 F.3d 632, 643 (7th Cir. 2012)).

57. *Douglas Cty. Bank & Trust Co.*, 207 F.3d at 477; *Cf.*, *Z4 Technologies, Inc. v. Microsoft Corp.*, 507 F.3d 1340, 1347 (Fed. Cir. 2007) (citing *Prytania Park Hotel, Ltd. v. Gen. Star Indem. Co.*, 179 F.3d 169, 173 (5th Cir. 1999) ("We also review the denial of a motion for a new trial under regional circuit law, which, in the Fifth Circuit, provides for reversal only upon an 'abuse of discretion or a misapprehension of the law' by the district court.")); *see also Ratliff*, 150 F.3d at 952 ("Great deference is accorded the district court ruling on a motion for new trial . . . .")); *Hidden Oaks Ltd. v. City of Austin*, 138 F.3d 1036, 1049 (5th Cir. 1998) ("With regard to the district court's denial of the City's motion for a new trial on the breach of contract claim, we note that our standard of review here is even more deferential than our review of the denial of a motion for judgment as a matter of law.").

58. *Maxfield v. Cintas Corp., No. 2*, 563 F.3d 691, 694 (8th Cir. 2009) (citing *Harrison v. Purdy Bros. Trucking Co.*, 312 F.3d 346, 351 (8th Cir. 2002)); *see also McMillian/McMillian, Inc. v. Monticello Ins. Co.*, 116 F.3d 319, 320 (8th Cir. 1997) (citing *Lamb Eng'g & Constr. Co. v. Nebraska Pub. Power Dist.*, 103 F.3d 1422, 1430 (8th Cir. 1997)).

59. *Brooks v. Toyotomi Co., Ltd.*, 86 F.3d 582, 588 (6th Cir. 1996).

60. *Molski*, 481 F.3d at 729; *see also Baker v. Canadian Nat'l/Ill. Cent. R.R.*, 536 F.3d 357, 366 (5th Cir. 2008) ("We apply a deferential standard in reviewing a trial court's refusal to grant a motion for new trial.").

61. *Burke*, 935 F.3d at 991 (citing *Henry v. Storey*, 658 F.3d 1235, 1238 (10th Cir. 2011)).

62. *Berndt v. California Dept. of Corr. and Rehab.*, 715 F. App'x 593, 595 (9th Cir. 2017) (citing *Kode v. Carlson*, 596 F.3d 608, 612 (9th Cir. 2010)); *see also TVIIM, LLC v. McAfee, Inc.*, 851 F.3d 1356, 1362 (Fed. Cir. 2017); *Baker*, 536 F.3d at 366 ((citing *Duff v. Werner Enters. Inc.*, 489 F.3d 727, 729 (5th Cir. 2007)).

63. *Dunlop Tire Corp. v. I.M.E. of Miami, Inc.*, 232 F.3d 900, 2000 WL 1480228, at *1 (10th Cir. 2000) (citing *Black v. Hieb's Enter., Inc.*, 805 F.2d 360, 363 (10th Cir. 1986)); *see also Maxfield*, 563 F.2d at 694 (citing *United States v. Rodriguez*, 812 F.2d 414, 417 (8th Cir. 1987)).

"will not reverse the denial of a new trial motion if there was some 'reasonable basis' for the jury's verdict."[64] Thus, "[t]he district court's denial of [a] motion for a new trial is reversible only if the record contains no evidence in support of the verdict,"[65] because "the absolute absence of evidence to support the jury's verdict makes [refusal to grant a new trial] an error in law."[66] "'In a challenge to a jury award, [the appellate court] is limited to examining whether evidence in the record supports the verdict. If the jury award has a rational basis in evidence, an appellate court must affirm it."[67] Accordingly, "[a]ctual cases of reversal for this reason are extremely few."[68]

A denial of a motion for new trial "based on allegedly improper closing argument" is likewise reviewed under "the deferential, abuse-of-discretion standard,"[69] and denial of a "motion for new trial based on rulings regarding admissibility of evidence may be reversed if the district court clearly and prejudicially abused its discretion by excluding evidence that 'is of such a critical nature that there is no reasonable assurance that the jury would have reached the same conclusion had the evidence been admitted.'"[70] Because "the district court is 'in the best position to determine whether the alleged error affected the substantial rights of any party sufficient to warrant a new trial, . . .'" "[e]ven if an abuse of discretion occurs, a trial court's ruling on a motion for new trial will only be reversed if 'an evidentiary ruling was so prejudicial as to require a new trial which would be likely to produce a different result.'"[71]

---

64. *Allen v. Hylands, Inc.*, 773 F. App'x 870, 873 (9th Cir. 2019) (citing *Hung Lam v. City of San Jose*, 669 F.3d 1077, 1084 (9th Cir. 2017)); *see also Mitchell v. Boelcke*, 440 F.3d 300, 305 (6th Cir. 2006); *Collado v. UPS*, 419 F.3d 1143, 1155 (11th Cir. 2005); *Kapelanski v. Johnson*, 390 F.3d 525, 530 (7th Cir. 2004); *Bryant v. Aiken Reg'l Med. Ctrs., Inc.*, 333 F.3d 536, 545 (4th Cir. 2003); *Colasanto v. Life Ins. Co. of N. Am.*, 100 F.3d 203, 212 (1st Cir. 1996).

65. *Molski*, 481 F.3d at 729 (citing *Farley Transp. Co. v. Santa Fe Trail Transp. Co.*, 786 F.2d 1342, 1347 (9th Cir. 1985)).

66. *Molski*, 481 F.3d at 729–30 (citing *Urti v. Transport Commercial Corp.*, 479 F.2d 766, 769 (5th Cir. 1973) (quoting *Indamar Corp. v. Crandon*, 217 F.2d 391, 393 (5th Cir. 1954))); *see also Keys v. Joseph Beth Booksellers, Inc.*, 173 F.3d 429, 1999 WL 97003, at *3 (6th Cir. 1999) (unpublished table decision) (because "[a]fter a thorough review of the trial transcript, it is clear that the jury returned a verdict consistent with the evidence," the district court therefore "did not abuse its discretion by denying the motion for a new trial.").

67. *Air Safety, Inc. v. Roman Catholic Archbishop of Boston*, 94 F.3d 1, 4 (1st Cir. 1996) (citing *Nydam v. Lennerton*, 948 F.2d 808, 810–11 (1st Cir. 1991); *see also York*, 95 F.3d at 958 (citing *Black*, 805 F.2d at 363 ("Where a party moves for a new trial on the ground that the jury verdict is not supported by the evidence, the verdict must stand unless it is 'clearly, decidedly or overwhelmingly against the weight of the evidence.'")).

68. *Powers v. Bayliner Marine Corp.*, 83 F.3d 789, 796 (6th Cir. 1996) (citing 11 Charles Alan Wright, Arthur R. Miller & Mary Kay Kane, Federal Practice and Procedure § 2819 at 123 (1973) (footnote omitted)); *Brooks*, 86 F.3d at 588 (citing same source for the same proposition).

69. *Cote*, 909 F.3d at 1103 (11th Cir. 2018) (citing *Lanham v. Whitfield*, 805 F.2d 970, 972 (11th Cir. 1986)); *see also Martinez v. Food City, Inc.*, 658 F.2d 369, 372 (5th Cir. 1981).

70. *White v. McKinley*, 605 F.3d 525, 533 (8th Cir. 2010) (quoting *Wilson v. City of Des Moines*, 442 F.3d 637, 641 (8th Cir. 2006)); *but see Hankins v. Russell*, 773 F. App'x 339, 339–40 (8th Cir. 2019) (per curiam) ("We further conclude that the exclusion of these doctors' anticipated testimony—including the authentication of medical evidence Hankins sought to present—was highly prejudicial, and that there is no reasonable assurance that the jury would have reached the same conclusion had the evidence in question not been excluded . . . . Accordingly, we reverse the denial of Hankins' motion for a new trial, and remand the case for further proceedings consistent with this opinion.").

71. *Townsend v. Bayer Corp.*, 774 F.3d 446, 460–61 (8th Cir. 2014) (citing *O'Dell v. Hercules, Inc.*, 904 F.2d 1194, 1200 (8th Cir. 1990)).

Review of Orders Granting Motions for a New Trial

While it is true that a federal trial judge has "discretion to grant a new trial if the verdict appears to [the judge] to be against the weight of the evidence," case law indicates:[72]

> When the trial judge sets aside a jury verdict and orders a new trial, however, our deference to him is in opposition to the deference due the jury. Consequently, in this circuit as in several others, we apply a broader review to orders granting new trials than to orders denying them. And where a new trial is granted on the ground that the verdict is against the weight of the evidence, we exercise particularly close scrutiny, to protect the litigants' right to a jury trial. To prevent an inappropriate substitution of the trial court's judgment for that of the jury, new trials granted on evidentiary grounds will not be upheld "unless, at a minimum, the verdict is against the great—not merely the greater—weight of the evidence."[73]

Consequently, a district court may not substitute its judgment concerning the evidence over that of the jury[74] because of the constitutional right to a jury trial in civil cases included within the Seventh Amendment. The Seventh Amendment in part says that "no fact tried by a jury, shall be otherwise re-examined in any Court of the United States, than according to the rules of the common law."[75]

Conditional Rulings on Motions for a New Trial

The Federal Rules of Civil Procedure provide specific instructions to trial courts with respect to motions for new trial and renewed motions for judgment as a matter of law.

Rule 50(c)

Rule 50(c) provides:

> (1) *In General.* If the court grants a renewed motion for judgment as a matter of law, it must also conditionally rule on any motion for a new trial by determining whether a new trial should be granted if the judgment is later vacated or reversed. The court must state the grounds for conditionally granting or denying the motion for a new trial.
>
> (2) *Effect of a Conditional Ruling.* Conditionally granting the motion for a new trial does not affect the judgment's finality; if the judgment is reversed, the new trial must

---

72. *Gasperini v. Ctr. for Humanities, Inc.*, 518 U.S. 415, 433 (1996); *see also Larson v. Farmers Co-op. Elevator of Buffalo Center, Iowa*, 211 F.3d 1089, 1095 (8th Cir. 2000) (authority to grant a new trial is fully within the discretion of the district court); *Douglas Cty. Bank & Trust Co.*, 207 F.3d at 477 (citing 11 Charles Alan Wright, Arthur R. Miller & Mary Kay Kane, Federal Practice and Procedure § 2818 (2d ed. 1987) (stating that a trial court has broad discretion in granting a new trial, and that the appellate court will defer a great deal to its exercise of this discretion)); *Gray v. Bicknell*, 86 F.3d 1472, 1480 (8th Cir. 1996).

73. *Davis v. Dow Chemical*, 119 F.3d 1, 1997 WL 367812, at *3 (5th Cir. 1997) (citations omitted) (reversing new trial order, reasoning "[t]his was a jury call," after observing that "[t]he trial court may set aside a jury verdict which is against the great weight and preponderance of the evidence.").

74. *Williams v. Chevron U.S.A., Inc.*, 875 F.2d 501, 505 (5th Cir. 1989).

75. U.S. Const. amend. VII.

> proceed unless the appellate court orders otherwise. If the motion for a new trial is conditionally denied, the appellee may assert error in that denial; if the judgment is reversed, the case must proceed as the appellate court orders.[76]

The rule provides that "the court shall also rule on the motion for a new trial . . . by determining whether it should be granted if the judgment [n.o.v.] is thereafter vacated or reversed, and shall specify the grounds for granting or denying the motion for the new trial."[77] Denying a motion for new trial as moot when granting a motion for judgment n.o.v. is therefore error[78] because if "the district court denies the motion for a new trial, defendants may on appeal seek to uphold the court's j.n.o.v. ruling in their favor and may also urge 'that the trial court committed error in conditionally denying the new trial,' without taking a cross-appeal."[79]

Rule 50(e)

Rule 50(e) states that "[i]f the court denies the motion for judgment as a matter of law, the prevailing party may, as appellee, assert grounds entitling it to a new trial should the appellate court conclude that the trial court erred in denying the motion," and therefore, if the appellate court reverses the judgment, it may order a new trial, direct the trial court to determine whether a new trial should be granted, or direct the entry of judgment.[80]

Motion for Relief from Judgment

Rule 60, "Relief from a Judgment or Order," provides that "[o]n motion and just terms, the court may relieve a party or its legal representative from a final judgment, order, or proceeding for the following reasons:

> (1) mistake, inadvertence, surprise, or excusable neglect;
> (2) newly discovered evidence that, with reasonable diligence, could not have been discovered in time to move for a new trial under Rule 59(b);
> (3) fraud (whether previously called intrinsic or extrinsic), misrepresentation, or misconduct by an opposing party;
> (4) the judgment is void;

---

76. Fed. R. Civ. P. 50(c).

77. *Larabee v. M M & L Intern. Corp.*, 896 F.2d 1112, 1116–17 (8th Cir. 1990); *see also Motter v. Everest & Jennings, Inc.*, 883 F.2d 1223, 1229 (3d Cir. 1989).

78. *See generally Betts v. United Airlines, Inc.*, 246 F.3d 672, 2000 WL 1728077, at *2 (9th Cir. 2000) (unpublished table decision).

79. *Larabee*, 896 F.2d at 1116–17 (citing Fed. R. Civ. P. 50(c) advisory committee notes & *Clements v. General Accident Ins. Co.*, 821 F.2d 489, 493 (8th Cir. 1987)).

80. *Larabee*, 896 F.2d at 1117 (citing 5A James W. Moore, Moore's Federal Practice, ¶ 50.14 at 50–104 (1989) & *Cargill, Inc. v. Weston*, 520 F.2d 669, 672 (8th Cir. 1975) ("If an appellate court determines the district court's grant of judgment notwithstanding the verdict was improper, it generally has three options: (1) to order entry of judgment on the verdict; (2) to reverse the denial of the motion for new trial and order a new trial; or (3) to remand to the district court for reconsideration of the motion for a new trial.")); *see also Szekeres v. CSX Transp., Inc.*, 731 F.3d 592, 604 (6th Cir. 2013) ("[W]here the judgment n.o.v. is reversed and the trial court has alternatively granted the motion for a new trial, the case will ordinarily be remanded for a new trial, "but the courts of appeals have authority to order 'otherwise.'").

(5) the judgment has been satisfied, released, or discharged; it is based on an earlier judgment that has been reversed or vacated; or applying it prospectively is no longer equitable; or
(6) any other reason that justifies relief."[81]

While the Rule "concludes with a catchall category – subdivision (b)(6) – providing that a court may lift a judgment for 'any other reason that justifies relief.' Relief is available under subdivision (b)(6), however, only in 'extraordinary circumstances.'"[82]

A motion for relief from judgment must be made "within a reasonable time—and for reasons (1), (2), and (3) no more than a year after the entry of the judgment or order or the date of the proceeding."[83] Rule 60(b) is a powerful tool, used to reverse a jury verdict in favor of the defendant when a defendant had failed to produce inculpatory material before trial,[84] and to reverse a jury verdict in favor of the plaintiff when the plaintiff's expert testified he had not been paid, but was in fact paid by counsel for the plaintiff.[85]

Moreover, nothing in Rule 60(b) limits a court's power to "(1) entertain an independent action to relieve a party from a judgment, order, or proceeding; (2) grant relief under 28 U.S.C. § 1655 to a defendant who was not personally notified of the action; or (3) set aside a judgment for fraud on the court."[86]

---

81. Fed. R. Civ. P. 60(b).

82. *Buck v. Davis*, 137 S.Ct. 759, 772 (2017), citing *Gonzalez v. Crosby*, 545 U.S. 524, 535 (2005), citing *Ackermann v. United States*, 340 U.S. 193, 199 (1950).

83. Fed. R. Civ. P. 60(c).

84. *Rozier v. Ford Motor Co.*, 573 F.2d 1332, 1345 (5th Cir. 1978) (reversing defense verdict in an automotive product liability case).

85. *In re DePuy Orthopaedics, Inc.*, 888 F.3d 753, 790–792 (5th Cir. 2018) (reversing $503 million verdict in a hip implant product liability case).

86. Fed. R. Civ. P. 60(d).

30

Posttrial Motions

The Defense Perspective

Following the Rules

This chapter deals with posttrial motions. This is not the easiest topic for trial lawyers because we do not want to think about losing; our DNA is coded to win. However, without doubt, there is likely no experienced trial lawyer who can brag that he or she never lost a case. Losing a verdict comes with the territory of doing what we do as active trial lawyers. The obvious goal is to win. But, at the end of the day, we need to be familiar with and understand posttrial rules and how those rules help guide the way after a verdict.

In the preceding chapter, Mikal Watts addressed many of the procedural requirements, deadlines, and burdens a posttrial movant must satisfy.[1] To avoid redundancy, this chapter focuses on strategies and tips to help maximize the chances for successful posttrial motion practice and which, if an appeal becomes necessary, will improve the prospects for the appeal.

The first rule regarding posttrial motions is simple: slow down, read the rules in the relevant jurisdiction, and make sure all relevant deadlines are calendared for the most appropriate posttrial motions that fit your case. Failure to comply with posttrial deadlines, or failure to select the most appropriate procedural option, may be jurisdictional or otherwise severely impact your chances of a successful appeal. Incorrect procedural choices can inadvertently waive certain appellate challenges.

Posttrial deadlines usually are not triggered by the jury's verdict but begin after a judgment is entered.[2] This is true of the federal rules and the various state court rules with which I am familiar. Thus, if you win your case, you should move quickly for entry of judgment because it starts posttrial timetables and the deadlines for providing a notice of appeal. Prompt action is the best practice to also assure that you take full advantage of the court's

1. *See* discussion, chapter 29, *supra*.
2. Fed. R. App. P. 4(a)(4).

memory of the evidence. Any extended passage of time may impact the freshness of the case in the mind of the trial court, thus making it more difficult to argue subtleties in the evidence. This could have a significant impact on challenges regarding the sufficiency of the evidence.

In a case I tried several years ago, a veteran trial judge retired from the bench shortly after the jury's verdict but before he entered judgment. Unfortunately, we did not have time to file and schedule a hearing for entry of judgment before the trial judge stepped down. The new judge, appointed by the governor, was unfamiliar with the case and demanded that we wait for an extensive transcript covering our one-month trial to be available. He then requested full briefing with annotations to the record. Our final judgment was not entered until almost *eight months* after our winning verdict.

In another case, it took almost eleven months to have judgment entered on a favorable defense verdict. The trial court had limited hearing dates that aligned with the plaintiff's lawyer's availability. When we finally got to the courthouse, the court ordered us to mediation. The lessons here: if you win, move quickly for entry of judgment and take full advantage of positive momentum. If you lose, you may want to slow down to get a handle on your best arguments. This also allows time to arrange for a supersedeas bond if you need to stay execution of monetary award.[3]

In federal court, the deadlines and types of posttrial motions are set forth in Rules 50, 59, and 60 of the Federal Rules of Civil Procedure. These include motions under Rule 50(b), which assumes you timely filed a motion for judgment as a matter of law (a directed verdict under Rule 50(a)) before submission of the case to the jury. Motions under Rule 50(a) and (b) effectively challenge the sufficiency of the evidence. On the other hand, Rule 59 addresses motions for new trial and sets forth circumstances that may warrant a new trial.[4] Although perhaps labeled differently, there will be similar types of motions in every state court jurisdiction. You should take note that the movant's burdens and the timetables may be different depending on the jurisdiction. It is critical to understand your options and the deadlines on a jurisdiction-by-jurisdiction basis.

In Texas, parties may file posttrial motions that extend the plenary jurisdiction of the trial court. A motion for new trial must be filed within 30 days of the judgment.[5] In contrast, a motion for new trial in federal court must be filed on or before 28 days after entry of judgment.[6] In Texas, once filed, a motion for new trial extends the plenary jurisdiction of the court for 75 days from the date of the judgment, by which time the motion must be either heard and resolved or it is overruled as matter of law.[7]

Sometimes, losing parties will file motions for a new trial but never schedule hearings on the motions—thus, securing a delay before moving forward with an appeal. Once the motion for new trial is denied (by operation of law or by ruling), the losing party has another

3. *See* Fed. R. Civ. P. 62(b).
4. *See* Fed. R. Civ. P. 59.
5. Tex. R. Civ. P. 329b.
6. Fed. R. Civ. P. 59.
7. Tex. R. Civ. P. 329b.

30 days from the denial to file a notice of appeal, potentially allowing the losing party up to 105 days to evaluate and determine appellate options.[8] However, not all jurisdictions allow for this kind of extended timeline. It is imperative to understand the requirements and deadlines in your jurisdiction—both to prevent waiver and to use as a strategic tool to evaluate your client's options.

Polling the Jury

Another important step is to request the court to poll the jury *before* the jury is dismissed. This must be done before the jury is excused to preserve error. Once excused, the right to poll the jury is lost.[9]

The purpose of polling is to assure that the verdict is, in fact, the jury's verdict. Some cases require complete juror unanimity before a verdict can be accepted. This is true in federal court and also applies in many jurisdictions relating to any award of punitive damages. The goal is to identify whether there is a failure in the verdict because the verdict is not supported by the required number of jurors. If polling reveals an error, one of the remedies is a new trial.[10]

Interviewing the Jury

After the jury has been dismissed, many (but not all) courts and jurisdictions allow attorneys to interview jurors following the verdict. If allowed, this is a highly recommended practice—whether you win or lose. If you lose a verdict, it is important to interview the jury to make sure you understand why the jury returned the negative verdict. Equally important, posttrial interviews provide an opportunity to identify any jury misconduct that could support a posttrial challenge and a basis to oppose the entry of judgment.

A notable case in point involved a product liability case defended by a product manufacturer. Following what was perceived as a successful trial, the manufacturer's lawyers were hopeful of a winning defense verdict. But, after extended jury deliberations, a note was sent to the court that bode poorly for the defense. The note queried whether there was any limit on how much the jury could award as damages. Understandably, this note sent the defense lawyers scrambling into the hallway to make emergency calls for settlement authority. A multi-million-dollar settlement was then dictated into the record and the jury was excused. The jury never returned a verdict.

The defense lawyers interviewed several members of the jury, but the foreperson refused to talk about the case and hurriedly left the courthouse. Other jurors remained and spoke freely with the lawyers. They disclosed—*incredibly*—that they did not understand why the defendant settled the case because, as it turns out, the defense was winning. These jurors further disclosed they did not authorize any note. Understandably, the only response to these disclosures was disbelief.

---

8. *Cf.* Tex. R. App. P. 26.1 (losing party has only thirty days to file its notice of appeal if no motion for new trial is filed).

9. *See* Fed. R. Civ. P. 48.

10. *Id.*

The defendant manufacturer then tried to undo the settlement, but the court enforced the settlement because it was dictated into the record in open court. The trial court also denied the request to undertake further discovery regarding the jury deliberations. A perfect storm was brewing. Ultimately, the Texas Supreme Court reversed, and the trial court was ordered to allow the defendant's requested discovery. If the first jury had not been interviewed, this entire sequence of remarkable events likely would not have occurred.

Every jurisdiction has procedural rules relating to jury misconduct, and the burdens necessary to show misconduct vary. Thus, it is important to understand the requirements and the avenues your jurisdiction allows to investigate and challenge an adverse verdict due to jury misconduct.

Getting a New Set of Eyes on the Issues

Trial lawyers are advocates. We want to win, and we are invariably shocked when we lose. If we lose, we may be looking at the jury's verdict through a subjective lens that distorts objectivity. We sometimes become emotionally invested in our cases and lose complete objectivity. Thus, it is wise to consult with an appellate lawyer about posttrial motion practice as well as any ensuing appeal. A new set of eyes providing a fresh look at both the evidence and the law is useful to maximize the effectiveness of the posttrial practice and can help identify the most important pathways for challenging an adverse verdict.

In high-exposure cases, it is often advisable to have an appellate lawyer on your trial team working with you during trial. They can provide assistance on significant evidence rulings, as well as crafting and objecting to the jury charge. By engaging appellate counsel early in the case, there is a significant learning curve already in place and established. This will make posttrial practice much easier. In any event, if the budget allows, it is a best practice to get an appellate lawyer on board immediately after an adverse verdict to help chart the best post-verdict course.

Annotated Motions

The most effective posttrial motions are motions annotated with citations to the record. This is easily done when you order daily transcripts from the court reporter. You can attach citations to specific evidence in support of key factual positions in your posttrial motions or responses. You also can attach entire portions of the transcript to demonstrate why the plaintiff failed to carry its burden. You can cite to key admissions of the witnesses that support entry of judgment for you. You are effectively supplying a factually supported brief to the trial court that will serve as a template for the appeal.

Remittitur

Another important consideration involves remittitur.[11] You should consult the procedural rules in your jurisdiction to determine whether this remedy is available and how to

11. In Texas, remittitur can be pursued through motion practice or sua sponte by the trial court or court of appeals. *See, e.g., Landmark Am. Ins. Co. v. Pulse Ambulance Serv., Inc.*, 813 S.W.2d 497, 499 (Tex. 1991) (motion for

implement this post-verdict remedy, if desired. In Texas, a defendant can seek a new trial on the grounds that the damage verdict is excessive or not supported by the evidence.[12] The court can, of course, either grant or deny the motion. However, the court also has a third option, by which it can conditionally deny the motion but "suggests" that the prevailing party accept a reduced award, or *remittitur*.[13] If plaintiff agrees, then the award will be reduced and judgment will be entered for a lesser amount; however, if plaintiff disagrees, the court may order a new trial.[14] If the plaintiff decides to agree to the remittitur, the defendant must determine whether to accept the lower damage remittance or to move forward with an appeal. If the plaintiff's remittitur was at the request of the court and the defendant decides to appeal after the remittance, the plaintiff can argue to the court of appeals that all or part of the remittitur should not have been required.[15] Therefore, while remittitur (versus a total victory or new trial) may be a hard pill to swallow, defense attorneys should consider the benefits of remittitur before moving forward with an appeal and potentially losing the appeal *and* the remittance.

Conclusion

Posttrial practice can be complex, and the stakes are high. You should know the rules of your jurisdiction and make informed choices. Your goal is relief from a bad verdict and judgment. Thus, it is important to make sure you have the best pathway to a winning appeal.

---

remittitur in effect was motion for new trial and extended appellate deadlines), Tex. R. App. P. 46.3 ("The court of appeals may suggest a remittitur.").

12. Tex. R. Civ. P. 324(b)(4).

13. *See generally Pope v. Moore*, 711 S.W.2d 622 (Tex. 1986); *see also Arkoma Basin Exploration Co., Inc. v. FMF Associates 1990-A, Ltd.*, 249 S.W. 3d 380, 390 (Tex. 2008) ("Technically, neither trial nor appellate courts can order remittitur; they can only suggest a remittitur on condition that a new trial will be granted if it is refused.").

14. *See Rose v. Doctors Hosp.*, 801 S.W.2d 841, 847 (Tex. 1990).

15. Tex. R. App. P. 46.2.

CONCLUSION

This book—*Trial: A Guide from Start to Finish – Perspectives from Opposing Counsel*—was an enlightening journey for both authors, and we hope it achieves its intended purpose. Our goal was to provide a useful guide and practice tips to maximize advocacy skills and trial performance for both sides of the bar. These practice tips were not defined overnight or randomly, but were developed and refined over years of trial practice, which included jury successes and losses. Sometimes, the most enduring lessons are those born from defeat, because these lessons are etched deeply in our memories. Although many of the lessons are based on common sense and instinct, others are learned.

The authors have handled jury trials throughout the country and have had the benefit of trying difficult cases against skilled trial lawyers, as well as against each other. This book distills these experiences and provides practical advice from real trial situations. It starts with preliminary jurisdictional and venue issues and moves through each stage of a typical civil trial. It explores both the tangibles and intangibles that influence how a jury and trial court react to the evidence, the lawyers, and the clients. It also offers recommendations on how to efficiently prepare for each stage of trial and maximize advocacy, including suggestions for:

- Packaging evidence.
- Effective cross-examinations.
- Distilling and simplifying trial themes.
- "Striking" or "picking" a winning jury.
- Maximizing effective opening statements and final arguments.
- Improving efficiencies in handling exhibits both in simple and in complex cases.
- Preparing and presenting witnesses.
- Effectively using demonstratives.
- Crafting a correct and simple charge.
- Preserving error.

By writing this book in this collaborative fashion, each author learned from the other. Happy trials.

  # Table of Cases

D

E

F

G

H

I

Index

C

F

R

S

W